THE LETTERS OF S. AMBROSE

TO THE MEMORY

OF THE

MOST REVEREND FATHER IN GOD

WILLIAM

LORD ARCHBISHOP OF CANTERBURY,

PRIMATE OF ALL ENGLAND,

FORMERLY REGIUS PROFESSOR OF DIVINITY IN THE UNIVERSITY OF OXFORD,

THIS LIBRARY

OF

ANCIENT BISHOPS, FATHERS, DOCTORS, MARTYRS, CONFESSORS,

OF CHRIST'S HOLY CATHOLIC CHURCH,

UNDERTAKEN AMID HIS ENCOURAGEMENT,

AND

CARRIED ON FOR TWELVE YEARS UNDER HIS SANCTION,

UNTIL HIS DEPARTURE HENCE IN PEACE,

IS

GRATEFULLY AND REVERENTLY

INSCRIBED.

THE LETTERS

OF

S. AMBROSE,

BISHOP OF MILAN,

TRANSLATED,

WITH NOTES AND INDICES.

WIPF & STOCK · Eugene, Oregon

Wipf and Stock Publishers
199 W 8th Ave, Suite 3
Eugene, OR 97401

The Letters of S. Ambrose, Bishop of Milan
Translated, With Notes and Indices
By Saint Ambrose of Milan and Walford, H.
Softcover ISBN-13: 978-1-6667-3351-8
Hardcover ISBN-13: 978-1-6667-2820-0
eBook ISBN-13: 978-1-6667-2821-7
Publication date 8/5/2021
Previously published by James Parker and Co., 1881

This edition is a scanned facsimile of the original edition published in 1881.

NOTICE.

THE Translation of S. Ambrose's Epistles was made in the early days of the Library of the Fathers by a friend, now with God, before the check which the Series received through various sorrowful losses. It has now been revised by an accomplished scholar, the Rev. H. Walford, M.A., one of the Masters at Hayleybury.

Over-work has prevented the writing of some introductory remarks.

E. B. P.

CHRIST CHURCH,
Lent, 1881.

CONTENTS.

[Letter of Gratian to AMBROSE]   p 1

LETTER I.

AMBROSE Bishop to the Blessed Emperor and most Christian Prince Gratian.
    p. 2

LETTER II

AMBROSE to Constantius.   p. 5

LETTER III

AMBROSE to Felix   p 16

LETTER IV

AMBROSE to Felix, health   p 17

[LETTERS V and VI

These Letters to Syagrius appear in the original Latin at the end of the Book.   pp. 478, 486]

LETTER VII.

AMBROSE to Justus, health   p. 20

LETTER VIII

AMBROSE to Justus   p 27

[The proceedings of the Council of Aquileia against the heretics Palladius and Secundianus]   p. 31

LETTER IX

The Council which is assembled at Aquileia to our most beloved brethren, the Bishops of the Viennese and the first and second Narbonese Provinces in Gaul,   p 61

CONTENTS. ix

LETTER X.

The holy Council which is assembled at Aquileia to the most gracious Christian Emperors, and most blessed Princes, Gratian, Valentinian, and Theodosius. p. 62

LETTER XI

To the most gracious Emperors and Christian Princes, the most glorious and most blessed Gratian, Valentinian, and Theodosius, the Council which is assembled at Aquileia p. 67

LETTER XII

To the most gracious and Christian Emperors, the glorious and most blessed Princes, Gratian, Valentinian, and Theodosius, the holy Council which is assembled at Aquileia p 70

LETTER XIII

To the most blessed Emperor and most gracious Prince Theodosius, AMBROSE and the other Bishops of Italy p. 74

LETTER XIV

To the most blessed Emperor and most gracious Prince Theodosius, AMBROSE and the other Bishops of Italy p 77

LETTER XV

AMBROSE to Anatolius, Numesius, Severus, Philip, Macedonius, Ammianus, Theodosius, Eutropius, Clarus, Eusebius, and Timotheus, Priests of the Lord, and to all the beloved Clergy and people of Thessalonica, health
p. 80

LETTER XVI

Bishop AMBROSE to his brother Anysius p. 85

LETTER XVII.

Bishop AMBROSE to the most blessed Prince and Christian Emperor Valentinian. p. 87

[The Memorial of Symmachus, prefect of the city] p. 94

LETTER XVIII.

Bishop AMBROSE to the most blessed Prince and gracious Emperor, his Majesty Valentinian. p. 100

LETTER XIX

    AMBROSE to Vigilius   p 114

LETTER XX

    To Marcellina   p. 127

LETTER XXI

To the most clement Emperor, his blessed Majesty Valentinian, AMBROSE, Bishop, sends greeting   p 137

SERMON.

    Against Auxentius on the giving up the Basilicas   p. 142

LETTER XXII

To the lady his Sister whom he loves more than his life and eyes AMBROSE her brother sends greeting   p 157

LETTER XXIII

To the lords, his brethren most beloved, the Bishops throughout the Province of Æmilia, AMBROSE, Bishop   p 165

LETTER XXIV

    AMBROSE to the Emperor Valentinian   p 176

LETTER XXV

    AMBROSE to Studius   p. 182

LETTER XXVI.

    AMBROSE to Irenæus [Studius?]   p 184

LETTER XXVII

    AMBROSE to Irenæus, greeting   p 190

LETTER XXVIII

    AMBROSE to Irenæus, greeting   p 196

CONTENTS. xi

LETTER XXIX

AMBROSE to Irenæus, greeting — p 199

LETTER XXX

AMBROSE to Irenæus, greeting — p 207

LETTER XXXI

AMBROSE to Irenæus, greeting — p 213

LETTER XXXII

AMBROSE to Irenæus, greeting — p 217

LETTER XXXIII

AMBROSE to Irenæus, greeting — p 220

LETTER XXXIV

AMBROSE to Horontianus, greeting — p 223

LETTER XXXV

AMBROSE to Horontianus — p 227

LETTER XXXVI

AMBROSE to Horontianus — p 233

LETTER XXXVII

AMBROSE to Simplician, greeting. — p. 235

[Calanus to Alexander] — p. 246

LETTER XXXVIII

AMBROSE to Simplician, greeting. — p 250

LETTER XXXIX

AMBROSE to Faustinus, greeting — p. 254

LETTER XL

To the most gracious Prince and blessed Emperor his Majesty Theodorius, Bishop AMBROSE sends greeting   p. 257

LETTER XLI

The Brother to his Sister   p 269

[The Letter of Pope Siricius to the Church of Milan]   p 280

LETTER XLII

To their lord, their dearly beloved brother, Pope Syricius, AMBROSE, Sabinus, Bassianus, and the rest send greeting   p 282

LETTER XLIII

AMBROSE to Horontianus   p 287

LETTER XLIV

AMBROSE to Horontianus.   p 295

LETTER XLV

AMBROSE to Sabinus   p 302

LETTER XLVI.

AMBROSE to Sabinus   p. 306

LETTER XLVII.

AMBROSE to Sabinus   p 312

LETTER XLVIII.

AMBROSE to Sabinus   p. 314

LETTER XLIX

AMBROSE to Sabinus   p 317

CONTENTS.

LETTER L.
AMBROSE to Chromatius — p 319

LETTER LI.
AMBROSE, Bishop, to his Majesty the Emperor Theodosius. — p. 324

LETTER LII.
AMBROSE to Titianus. — p. 330

LETTER LIII.
AMBROSE to the Emperor Theodosius — p 331

LETTER LIV
AMBROSE to Eusebius. — p 333

LETTER LV.
AMBROSE to Eusebius. — p 334

LETTER LVI.
AMBROSE to Theophilus. — p 336

[Letter on the case of Bonosus] — p. 339

LETTER LVII
To the most gracious Emperor Eugenius, AMBROSE, Bishop, sends greeting. — p. 341

LETTER LVIII.
AMBROSE to Sabinus, Bishop — p. 345

LETTER LIX
AMBROSE to Severus, Bishop — p. 350

LETTER LX
AMBROSE to Paternus. — p. 351

CONTENTS.

LETTER LXI

AMBROSE to the Emperor Theodosius   p 354

LETTER LXII

AMBROSE to the Emperor Theodosius   p 356

LETTER LXIII

AMBROSE, servant of Christ, called to be Bishop, to the Church of Vercellæ, and to them who called on the Name of the Lord Jesus Christ, grace unto you from God the Father and His Only-begotten Son be fulfilled in the Holy Spirit   p. 357

LETTER LXIV.

AMBROSE to Irenæus, greeting.   p. 395

LETTER LXV

AMBROSE to Simplicianus, greeting.   p 398

LETTER LXVI.

AMBROSE to Romulus   p. 401

LETTER LXVII

AMBROSE to Simplicianus, greeting.   p. 404

LETTER LXVIII

AMBROSE to Romulus   p 409

LETTER LXIX

AMBROSE to Irenæus, greeting   p 410

LETTER LXX.

AMBROSE to Horontianus   p 412

LETTER LXXI

AMBROSE to Horontianus   p 420

LETTER LXXII
Ambrose to Constantius — p. 423

LETTER LXXIII
Ambrose to Irenæus. — p. 433

LETTER LXXIV
Ambrose to Irenæus — p. 437

LETTER LXXV.
Ambrose to Clementianus. — p 441

LETTER LXXVI.
Ambrose to Irenæus, greeting. — p. 444

LETTER LXXVII
Ambrose to Horontianus. — p. 449

LETTER LXXVIII
Ambrose to Horontianus — p. 455

LETTER LXXIX
Ambrose to Bellicius, greeting — p 458

LETTER LXXX
Ambrose to Bellicius, greeting — p. 459

LETTER LXXXI.
Ambrose to certain of the Clergy. — p. 462

LETTER LXXXII.
Ambrose to Marcellus. — p 465

CONTENTS.

LETTER LXXXIII

Ambrose to Sisinnius.　　　　p. 470

LETTER LXXXIV.

Ambrose to Cynegius.　　　　p. 473

LETTER LXXXV.

Ambrose to Siricius　　　　ib

LETTER LXXXVI

Ambrose to Siricius　　　　p. 474

LETTER LXXXVII

Ambrose to Bishops Sigatinus and Delphinus.　　　　p. 475

LETTER LXXXVIII.

Ambrose to Allicas　　　　p. 476

LETTER LXXXIX

Ambrose to Alypius.　　　　ib.

LETTER XC.

Ambrose to Antonius.　　　　p 477

LETTER XCI

Ambrose to his brother Candidianus　　　　ib.

ERRATA.

p. 20. heading for '*skekel*' read '*shekel*.'
152. l. 15. for '*Arianism*' read *Ariminum*.'
183. l. 8. for '*unrestored*' read '*unstained*.'
217. At the end of § 12 add the following sentence. '*A good mother of souls in that Jerusalem which is in heaven*.'
ib. l. 18. for '*life*' read '*wife*.'
219. note, for '*a*' read '*f*,' and for '*cic*.' read '*Cic*.'
258. marg. for '*distonxisti*' read '*distinxisti*.'
285. last ref. for ' 1 *Col*.' read ' *Col*.'
298. l. 29 after '*partly full*,' add '*fulness in the Gospel, half-fulness in the Law*,' and for '*thus*' read '*as*.'
368. l. 10. for '*sinless*' read '*senseless*.'
ib. marg. for '*Ezra viii*,' read '*Ezra viii. 2*.'
pp. 370, 374 are printed 270, 274.
429 mag for '*S. John i 86*,' read '*S. John i. 29*.'

THE LETTERS

OF

S. AMBROSE

BISHOP OF MILAN.

LETTER OF GRATIAN TO AMBROSE. A.D.379.

It is in answer to this that Letter 1 was written by S. Ambrose. It was written by the Emperor Gratian in his 20th year, four years after his succession to the Empire in partnership with his Uncle Valens and his younger brother Valentinian the 2nd, on the death of their father Valentinian the first, 375 A. D. Tillemont (Hist. des Emp. vol. v. p. 158.) calls it 'une lettre toute pleine de piété et d'humilité, et d'ailleurs mesme écrite avec beaucoup d'esprit et d'elegance.'

THE EMPEROR GRATIAN TO AMBROSE BISHOP OF ALMIGHTY GOD.

1. Great is my desire that as I remember you though far away, and in spirit am present with you, so I may be with you in bodily presence also. Hasten then, holy Bishop [a] of God; come and teach me, who am already a sincere believer; not that I am eager for controversy, or seek to apprehend God in words rather than with my mind, but that the revelation of His Godhead may sink more deeply into an enlightened breast.

2. For He will teach me, He Whom I deny not, but confess to be my God and my Lord, not cavilling at that created nature in Him, creatu-which I see also in myself. That I can add nothing to Christ I ac-ram. knowledge, but I am desirous by declaring the Son to commend my-

---

[a] The word in the original is Sacerdos. It is constantly used by S. Ambrose and other writers of his time for Bishops, though they sometimes add a qualifying epithet, 'Summus Sacerdos.' But even alone it is used where the writer is clearly speaking of Bishops, and of Bishops quâ Bishops. Thus it occurs frequently in the Proceedings of the Council of Aquileia, which is itself styled 'Sacerdotale Concilium.' See the Article 'Bishop' by Mr. Haddan in Dict. of Chr. Ant. Vol. 1 p. 210 b., who refers also to Bp. Taylor, Episc. Assert. § 27. It has therefore been rendered 'Bishop' throughout this volume, wherever it is plain that the reference is to Bishops, and 'Priest' wherever it is used in a more general way

Lett. 1. self to the Father also; for in God I can fear no jealousy; nor will I suppose myself such an eulogist as that I can exalt His divinity by my words. Weak and frail, I proclaim Him according to my power, not according to His Majesty.

3. I beg you to bestow upon me the Treatise [b] you gave me before, adding to it an orthodox discussion on the Holy Spirit: prove, I beseech you, both by Scripture and reason, that He is God. God keep you for many years, my father, servant of the eternal God, Whom we worship, even Jesus Christ.

A.D 379

LETTER I.

In this letter S Ambrose replies to the preceding. He apologises for not coming at once to Gratian, and, after praising his humility and faith, promises to come before long, and meanwhile sends him the two books (duos libellos) of the Treatise De Fide, which he had before composed at Gratian's request, begging for time to write on the subject of the Holy Spirit.

AMBROSE BISHOP TO THE BLESSED EMPEROR AND MOST CHRISTIAN PRINCE, GRATIAN.

1. It was not lack of affection, most Christian Prince, (for I can give you no title more true or more illustrious than this,) it was not, I repeat, lack of affection, but modesty which put a restraint upon that affection, and hindered my coming to meet your Grace. But if I did not meet you on your return in person, I did so in spirit, and with my prayers, wherein the duties of a priest more especially lie. Meet, did I say? Nay, when was I absent? I who followed you with an entire affection, who clung to you in thought and heart; and surely it is by our souls that we are present to one other most intimately. I studied your route day by day; transported by my solicitude to your camp by night and day, I shielded it with my watchful prayers, prayers, if not of prevailing merit, yet of unremitting affection.

[b] This forms the two first books of the 'De Fide' still extant among the works of S. Ambrose. The other three books were added afterwards, as S. Ambrose explains at the beginning of Bk. iii, to maintain his statements against the attacks of heretical teachers. The Treatise, 'De Spiritu Sancto,' in 3 books, was sent afterwards in 381 A.D.

2. And in offering these for your safety we benefited ourselves. This I say without flattery, which you require not, and I deem unbefitting my office, but with the greatest regard to the favour you have shewn me. Our Judge Himself, Whom you acknowledge and in Whom you devoutly believe, knoweth that my heart is refreshed by your faith, your safety, your glory, and that not only my public duty but my personal affection leads me to offer these prayers. For you have restored to me quiet in the Church, you have stopped the mouths (would that you had stopped the hearts) of the traitors, and this you have done not less by the authority of your faith than of your power.

3. What shall I say of your late letter? the whole is written with your own hand, so that the very characters tell of your faith and devotion. Thus Abraham of old, when ministering entertainment to his guests, slew a calf with his own hand, and had not, in this sacred service, the assistance of others. But he, a private man, ministered to the Lord and His Angels, or to the Lord in His Angels, you, the Emperor, honour with your royal condescension the lowest of Bishops. And yet the Lord is served when His minister is honoured; for He hath said, *Inasmuch as ye have done it unto one of the least of these, ye have done it unto Me.* [S. Matt. xxv. 40.]

4. But is it only this lofty humility which I praise in the Emperor, and not rather that faith, which you have rightly expressed with a mind conscious of your desert, or which He Whom you deny not hath taught you? For who but He could have taught you not to cavil at that created nature in Him which you see in yourself? Nothing could have been said more pious or more accurate; for to call Christ a creature savours of a contemptuous cavil, not of a reverent confession. Again, what could be more unworthy, than to suppose Him to be like as we ourselves are? Thus you have instructed me, from whom you profess your wish to learn, for I never read nor heard anything better.

5. Again, how pious, how admirable that expression, that you fear no jealousy in God! From the Father you anticipate a recompense for your love of the Son, yet you acknowledge that your praise of the Son can add nothing to

LETT 1. Him, only you wish by praising the Son to commend yourself to the Father also. This He alone hath taught you, Who hath said, *He that loveth Me, shall be loved of My Father.*

S. John xiv. 21

6. You go on to say that you, weak and frail as you are, do not suppose yourself such an eulogist as that you can exalt His divinity by your words, but that you preach Him according to your power, not according to His Majesty. This weakness is mighty in Christ, as the Apostle has said, *When I am weak, then I am strong.* This humility excludes frailty.

7. Certainly I will come, and that speedily, as you command, that I may be present with you and hear and read these things, as they are newly spoken by you. But I have sent two small volumes, for which, approved as they have been by your grace, I shall have no fears; I must plead for time to write on the Spirit, knowing as I do what a judge I shall have of my treatise.

8. Meanwhile however your sentiments and belief concerning our Lord and Saviour, transferred from the Son, form an abundant assertion to express our faith in the everlasting Godhead of the Holy Spirit, in that you cavil not at that created nature in Him which you find in yourself, and suppose not that God, the Father of our Lord Jesus Christ, can be jealous of His own Spirit. For that which is separated from communion with the creature is divine.

9. If the Lord will, I will in this also comply with your Majesty's wishes; that as you have received the grace of the Holy Spirit, so also you may know that He, holding so high a place in the Divine glory, has in His own Name a right to our veneration.

10. May Almighty God the Father of our Lord Jesus Christ, vouchsafe, my Lord the Emperor, chosen by Divine providence, most glorious Sovereign, may He vouchsafe to keep your majesty in all happiness and prosperity to an advanced age, and establish your kingdom in perfect glory and in perpetual peace.

LETTER II.   A.D. 379.

WE gather from the letter itself that Constantius, to whom it is addressed was a newly appointed Bishop, but of what see does not appear In § 27 S. Ambrose commends to his care the see of Forum Cornelii, which was vacant at the time, as being in his neighbourhood. The grounds on which the Benedictine Editors fix the date seem rather vague Its interest however is not historical : it is simply hortatory, urging on Constantius the fulfilment of the duties of his new office, and setting before him the chief subjects to which his preaching should be addressed. From S Ambrose calling him ' my son' (§ 27) it would seem that he was either one of his own clergy, or had been in some way under his guidance It is interesting as shewing how a great Bishop of that age dwelt upon the relations of the Episcopate, not merely to the Clergy under him as their superior, but to the laity of his diocese as their chief teacher.

AMBROSE TO CONSTANTIUS.

1. You have undertaken the office of a Bishop, and now, seated in the stern of the Church, you are steering it in the teeth of the waves. Hold fast the rudder of faith, that you may not be shaken by the heavy storms of this world. The sea indeed is vast and deep, but fear not, *for He hath founded it upon the seas, and prepared it upon the floods.* Rightly then the Church of the Lord, amid all the seas of the world, stands immoveable, built as it were, upon the Apostolic rock ; and her foundation remains unshaken by all the force of the raging surge. The waves lash but do not shake it ; and although this world's elements often break against it with a mighty sound, still it offers a secure harbour of safety to receive the distressed. [Ps. xxiv. 2]

2. Yet although it is tossed on the sea, it rides upon the floods ; and perhaps chiefly on those floods of which it is said, *The floods have lift up their voice.* For there are *rivers*, which *shall flow out of his belly*, who has received to drink from Christ, and partaken of the Spirit of God. These rivers then, when they overflow with spiritual grace, lift up their voice. There is a river too, which runs down upon His saints like a torrent. And there are *the rivers of the* [Ps. xciii. 4. S John vii. 38. Isa. lxvi. 12. Ps. xlvi. 4.]

6 *Should be filled with Scripture, that he may teach others.*

LETT. 2. *flood,* which *make glad* the peaceful and tranquil soul. He that receives, as did John the Evangelist, as did Peter and Paul, the fulness of this stream, lifts up his voice; and like as the Apostles loudly heralded forth to the farthest limits of the globe the Evangelic message, so he also begins to preach the Lord Jesus. Receive to drink therefore of Christ, that your sound may also go forth.

3. The Divine Scripture is a sea, containing in it deep meanings, and an abyss of prophetic mysteries; and into this sea enter many rivers. There are sweet and trans- Prov.xvi. parent streams, cool [a] fountains too there are, *springing* 24. *up into life eternal,* and *pleasant words as an honey-comb.* Agreeable sentences too there are, refreshing the minds of the hearers, if I may say so, with spiritual drink, and soothing them with the sweetness of their moral precepts. Various then are the streams of the sacred Scriptures. There is in them a first draught for you, a second, and a last.

Ps. 4. Gather the water of Christ, that which *praises the* cxlviii. 5. *Lord.* Gather from many sources that water which the Eccles. prophetic *clouds pour forth.* He that gathers water from xi. 3. the hills and draws it to himself from the fountains, he also drops down dew like the clouds. Fill then the bosom of your mind, that your ground may be moistened and watered by domestic springs. He who needs and apprehends much is filled, he who hath been filled waters others, Ib. and therefore Scripture saith *If the clouds be full of rain, they empty themselves upon the earth.*

5. Let your discourses then be flowing, let them be clear and lucid; pour the sweetness of your moral arguments into the ears of the people, and sooth them with the charm of your words, that so they may willingly follow your guidance. But if there be any contumacy or transgression in the people or individuals, let your sermons be of such a character as shall move your audience, and prick the evil Ib.xii.11. conscience, for *the words of the wise are as goads.* The Lord Jesus too pricked Saul, when he was a persecutor. And think how salutary the goad was which from a perse-

[a] Nivei This is the reading all MSS. Ed. Rom. has 'vivi,' which would agree better with the text of S. John

cutor made him an Apostle, by simply saying, *It is hard for thee to kick against the pricks.*

<small>TO CONSTANTIUS</small>

6. There are discourses too like milk, such as Paul fed the Corinthians with; for they who cannot digest stronger food, must have their infant minds nourished with the juice of milk.

<small>Acts ix. 5. 1 Cor. iii. 2.</small>

7. Let your addresses be full of understanding. As Solomon says, *The* [b] *lips of the wise are the weapons of the understanding,* and in another place, *Let your lips be bound up with sense,* that is, let your discourses be clear and bright, let them flash with intelligence like lightning: let not your address or arguments stand in need of enforcement from without, but let your discourse defend itself, so to speak, with its own weapons, and let no vain or unmeaning word issue out of your mouth. For there is a bandage to bind up the wounds of the soul, and if any one cast it aside, he shews that his recovery is desperate. Wherefore to those who are afflicted with a grievous ulcer administer the oil of your discourse to soften the hardness of their heart, apply an emollient, bind on the ligature of salutary precepts; beware lest by any means you suffer men who are unstable and vacillating in faith or in the observance of discipline, to perish with minds unbraced and vigour relaxed.

<small>Prov. xv. 7.</small>

8. Wherefore admonish and entreat the people of God that they abound in good works, that they renounce iniquity, that they kindle not the fires of lust, (I say not on the Sabbath only, but never,) lest they set on fire their own bodies; that there be no fornication or uncleanness in the servants of God, for we serve the immaculate Son of God. Let every man know himself, and possess his own vessel, that, having, so to say, broken up the fallow ground of his body, he may expect fruit in due season, and it may not *bring forth thorns and thistles,* but he too may say, *Our land hath given her increase;* and on this once wild thicket of the passions a graft of virtue may flourish.

<small>Eph. v. 3. 1 Thess. iv. 4. Gen. iii. 18. Ps. lxxxv. 13.</small>

9. Teach moreover and train the people to do what is

---

[b] The Benedictine reference for the first of these texts is Prov. xiv. 3. *The lips of the wise shall preserve them,* with which the Sept. and Vulg. agree. In the second the English Vers. has *The lips of the wise disperse knowledge.* Here S. Ambr. agrees with the Sept.

good and that no one fail to perform works which shall be approved, whether he be seen of many, or be without witness, for the conscience is a witness abundantly sufficient unto itself.

10. And let them avoid shameful deeds, even though they believe they cannot be detected. For though a man be shut up within walls, and covered with darkness, without witness and without accomplice, still he has a Judge of his acts, Whom nothing ever deceives, and to Whom all things cry aloud. To Him the voice of *blood cried from the ground*. Every man has in himself and his own conscience a strict judge, an avenger of his wickedness and of his crimes. Cain wandered about in fear and trembling, suffering the punishment of his unnatural deed; so that death was to him a refuge, relieving the wandering outcast from that terror of death which he felt at every moment. Let no man then either alone or in company commit any shameful or wicked act. Though he be alone, let him be abashed before himself more than before others, for to himself is his greatest reverence due.

Gen. iv. 10.

11. Nor let him covet many things, for even few things are to him as many; for poverty and wealth are words implying want and sufficiency. He is not rich who needs any thing, nor he poor who needs not. And let no man despise a widow, circumvent a ward, defraud his neighbour. *Woe unto him, whose substance has been collected by guile,* and *who buildeth a town, that is his own soul, with blood.* For this it is, which *is built as a city;* and this city avarice builds not but destroys, lust builds not but sets on fire and consumes. Wouldest thou build this city well? *Better is little with the fear of the Lord, than great treasure without that fear.* A man's riches ought to avail to the ransom of his soul, not to its destruction. And a treasure is a ransom, if a man use it well; on the other hand it is a snare, if a man know not how to use it. What is a man's money to him but a provision for his journey? Much is a burthen, a little is useful. We are wayfarers in this life; many walk, but it is needful that we walk aright, for then is the Lord Jesus with us, as we read, *When thou passest through the waters I will be with thee, and through*

Hab. ii. 9—12.
Ps. cxxii. 3.
Prov. xv. 16.
Isa. xliii. 2.

the rivers, they shall not overflow thee; when thou walkest through the fire thou shalt not be burned. But if a man take fire in his bosom, the fire of lust, the fire of immoderate desire he *walketh not through*, but burns this clothing of his soul. *A good name is rather to be chosen than great riches, and loving favour than silver and gold!* Faith is sufficient for itself, and in its own possession is rich enough. And to the wise man nothing is foreign, but what is contrary to virtue; wherever he goes, he finds all things to be his own. All the world is his possession, for he uses it all as if it were his own.

<small>TO CONSTANTIUS
Prov. vi. 27.
Ib. xxii. 1.</small>

12. Why then is our brother circumvented, why is our hired servant defrauded? Little it is said, is gained by the wages of an harlot, that is to say, of frailty so delusive. This harlot is not an individual, but something general; not one woman, but every idle lust. All perfidy, all deceit is this harlot; not she alone who offers her body to defilement; but every soul that barters away its hope, and seeks a dishonourable profit, and an unworthy reward. And we are hired servants, in that we labour for hire, and look for the reward of this our work from our Lord and God. If any one would know how we are hired servants, let him listen to the words, *How many hired servants of my father have bread enough and to spare, and I perish with hunger,* and again, *Make me as one of thy hired servants.* All are hired servants, all are labourers; and let him, who looks for the reward of his labour, remember that if he defraud another of the wages due to him, he also will be defrauded of his own. Such conduct offends Him Who has lent to us, and He will repay it hereafter in more abundant measure. He therefore who could not lose what is eternal, let him not deprive others of what is temporal.

<small>Prov. vi. 26 (not quoted ad verbum).
S Luke xv. 17.
v. 19.</small>

13. And let no one speak deceitfully with his neighbour. *There is a snare in our mouths,* and not seldom is it that *a man is entangled* rather than cleared *by his words. The mouth of the evil-minded is a deep pit:* great is the fall of innocence, but greater that of iniquity. The simple, by giving too easy credit, quickly falls, but when fallen he rises again; but the evil-speaker is so cast down by his own acts that he never can recover himself and escape.

<small>Prov. vi. 2.
Ib. xxii. 14 Sept.
Ib. xiv. 15.</small>

2. Therefore let every man weigh his words, not with deceit and guile, for *a false balance is abomination to the Lord.* I do not mean that balance which weighs the wares of others, (though even in lesser matters deceit often costs dear,) but that balance of words is hateful to the Lord, which wears the mask of the weight of sober gravity, and yet practises the artifices of cunning. Great is God's anger, if a man deceive his neighbour by flattering promises, and by treacherous subtlety oppress his debtor, a craft which will not benefit himself. For what is a man profited, if he shall gain the riches of the whole world, and yet defraud his own soul of the wages of eternal life?

Lett. 2.
Prov. xi. 1.

S. Matt. xvi. 26.

14. There is another balance which pious minds ought to consider, wherein the actions of individuals are weighed, and wherein for the most part sin inclines the scale towards judgement, or outweighs good deeds with crimes. Woe unto me, if my offences *go before,* and with a fatal weight incline to the judgement of death! More terrible will it be if they *follow after,* though they all be manifest to God, even before judgement; neither can things good be secret, nor things full of scandal be concealed.

1 Tim. v. 24.

15. How blessed is he who can extirpate avarice, the root of all evil! he truly need not fear this balance. For avarice is wont to deaden man's senses, and pervert his judgement, so that he counts godliness a source of gain, and money the reward of prudence. But great is the reward of piety, and the gain of sobriety to have enough for use. For what do superfluous riches profit in this world, when you find in them neither a succour in birth nor a defence against death? For without a covering are we born into the world, without provision we depart hence, and in the grave we have no inheritance.

Ib. vi. 10.

16. The deserts of each one of us are suspended in the balance, which a little weight either of good works or of degenerate conduct sways this way or that; if the evil preponderate, woe is me! if the good, pardon is at hand. For no man is free from sin; but where good preponderates, the evil flies up, is overshadowed, and covered. Wherefore in the Day of judgement our works will either succour us, or will sink us into the deep, weighed down as

with a millstone. For iniquity is heavy, supported as by a *talent of lead;* avarice is intolerable, and all pride is foul dishonesty. Wherefore exhort the people of God to trust rather in the Lord, to abound in the riches of simplicity, wherein they may walk without snare and without hindrance. _{TO CONSTANTIUS} _{Zech. v. 7.}

17. For the sincerity of a pure speech is good, and rich in the sight of God, although it walk among snares; yet, because it is innocent of laying wait or enthralling others, it escapes itself.

18. A great thing too it is if you can persuade them to know how to be abased, to know the true garb and nature of humility. Many possess the shew of humility, but not its power; many possess it abroad, but oppose it at home; colourably they pretend it, but in truth they renounce it, in regard of grace they deny it. For *there is one that humbleth himself wickedly and his inward parts are full of deceit. And there is one that submitteth himself exceedingly with a great lowliness.* There is no true humility then but such as is without colour and pretence. Such humility is that which hath a pious sincerity of mind. Great is its virtue. Finally *by one man's disobedience death entered,* and by the obedience of our Lord Jesus Christ came the redemption of all. _{Ecclus. xix. 23, 24. Vulg.} _{Rom. v. 19.}

19. Holy Joseph knew how to be abased, who, when he was sold into bondage by his brethren, and purchased by merchants, *whose feet* as the Scripture saith, *' they hurt in the stocks,'* learned the virtue of humility and laid aside all weakness. For when he was bought by the royal servant, officer of the household, the memory of his noble descent as one of the seed of Abraham did not cause him to disdain servile offices or scorn his mean condition. On the contrary he was diligent and faithful in his master's service, knowing in his prudence that it matters not in what station a man renders himself approved, but that the object of good men is to merit approbation in whatever station they are placed; and the point of importance is that their character should dignify their station rather than their station their character. In proportion as the station is low the merit becomes illustrious. And such attention _{Ps cv. 18.}

LETT. 2. did Joseph exhibit that his lord entrusted to him his whole house, and committed to him all that he had.

20. And so his wife cast her eyes upon Joseph, captivated by the beauty of his form. Now we are not in fault, if either our age or our beauty becomes an object of desire to wanton eyes; let it be artless, and no blame attaches to beauty; if enticement be away, seemliness and grace of form is innocent. But this woman, fired with love, addresses the youth, and at the instigation of lust, overpowered by the force of passion confesses her crime. But he rejects the crime, saying that to defile another man's bed was consonant neither with the customs nor the laws of the Hebrews, whose care it was to protect modesty, and to provide chaste spouses for chaste virgins, avoiding all unlawful intercourse, And that it were an impious deed for him, intoxicated by impure passion, and regardless of his master's kindness, to inflict a deadly injury on one to whom he owed obedience.

21. Nor did he disdain to call the despised Egyptian his master, and to confess himself his servant. And when the woman courted him, urging him by the fear of betrayal, or shedding passionate tears to force his compliance, neither was he moved by compassion to consent to iniquity, nor constrained by fear, but he resisted her entreaties and yielded not to her threats, preferring a perilous virtue to rewards, and chastity to a disgraceful recompense. Again she assailed him with greater temptations, yet she found him inflexible, yea for the second time immoveable; yet her furious and shameless passion gave her strength, and she caught the youth by his robe and drew him to her couch, offering to embrace him, nay, she would have done so, had not Joseph put off his robe; he put it off, that he might not put off the robe of humility, the covering of modesty.

22. He then knew how to be abased, for he was degraded even to the dungeon; and thus unjustly treated, he chose rather to bear a false accusation than to bring the true one. He knew how to be abased, I say, for he was abased for virtue's sake. He was abased as a type of Him Who was to abase Himself even to death, the death of the cross,

Who was to come to raise our life from sleep, and to teach that our human life is but a dream: its vicissitudes reel past us as it were, with nothing in them firm or stable, but like men in a trance seeing we see not, hearing we hear not, eating we are not filled, congratulating we joy not, running we attain not. Vain are men's hopes in this world, idly pursuing the things that are not as though they were; and so, as in a dream, the empty forms of things come and go, appear and vanish; they hover around us, and we seem to grasp yet grasp them not. But when a man has heard Him that saith *Awake, thou that sleepest,* and rises up from the sleep of this world, then he perceives that all these things are false; he is now awake, and the dream is fled, and with it is fled ambition, and the care of wealth, and beauty of form, and the pursuit of honours. For these things are dreams which affect not those whose hearts wake, but affect only them that slumber.

To Constantius.

Eph. v. 14.

23. And holy Joseph certifies this my assertion, that the things of this world are not perpetual or lasting, for he, noble by birth and with a rich inheritance, suddenly becomes a despised servant, and (what enhances the bitterness of servitude) a slave bought for a price by an unworthy master. For to serve the free is esteemed less disgraceful, but to be the servant of servants is a double slavery. Thus from being nobly born he became a slave, from having a wealthy father he became poor, from love he fell into hate, from favour into punishment. Again, he is raised from the prison to the court, from the bar to the judgement-seat. But he is neither depressed by adversity nor elated by prosperity.

24. The frequently changing condition of holy David also testifies how fleeting are the vicissitudes of life. He, overlooked by his father, but precious in the sight of God, exalted by his success, thrust down by envy, summoned to the service of the king and chosen to be his son-in-law, then again disguised in face and appearance, banished from the kingdom, flying from death at his own son's hands, weeping for his own offences, atoning for those of others, nobler in winning back the affection of the heir to his throne, than if he had disgraced him. Having thus tried

every condition he says well, *It is good for me that I have been humbled.*

<small>LETT. 2.
Ps. cxix. 71.</small>

25. This sentence however might well also be referred to Him Who *being in the form of God,* and able to bow the heavens, yet came down, and *taking upon Him the form of a servant,* bore our infirmities. He, foreseeing that His saints would not think it a prize to claim the honour that belonged to them, but would give place to their equals and prefer others to themselves, said, *It is good for me that I have been humbled,* it is good for me that I have subjected myself, that all things *may be subject unto me, and God may be all in all.* Instil this humility into the minds of all, and shew yourself an example to all saying, *Be ye followers of me, even as I am also of Christ.*

<small>Phil. ii. 6. 7.</small>

<small>1 Cor. xv. 28</small>

<small>Ib xi. 1.</small>

26. Let them learn to seek the wealth of good wishes, and to be rich in holiness; the beauty of wealth consists not in the possession of money-bags, but in the maintenance of the poor. It is in the sick and needy that riches shine most. Wherefore let the wealthy learn to seek not their own things, but the things of Jesus Christ, that Christ also may seek them, and recompense to them what is their own. He spent for them His blood, He pours forth on them His Spirit, He offers to them His kingdom. What more shall He give, Who gave Himself, or what shall not the Father give, Who delivered up His Only Son to die for our sakes? Admonish them therefore to serve the Lord soberly and with grace, to lift their eyes with all diligence to heaven, to count nothing gain but what appertains to eternal life; for all this worldly gain is the loss of souls. He who desired *to win Christ, suffered the loss of all things,* which saying, marvellous as it is, falls short of what he had received, for he speaks of external things only, whereas Christ hath said, *If any man will come after Me, let him deny himself,* let him lose himself so that Christ be gained. Fleeting are all things here, they bring loss and not gain; that only is gain, where enjoyment is perpetual, where eternal rest is our reward.

<small>Phil. iii. 8.</small>

<small>S. Luke ix. 23.</small>

27. I commend to your care, my son, the Church which is at Forum Cornelii^c; Being nigh thereunto, visit it fre-

---

<small>^c Forum Cornelii was on the Via Æmilia, about 23 miles S E. of Bononia. It was at this time in the Province Æmilia. The modern name is Imola.</small>

quently until a Bishop for it be ordained; I myself, engaged with the approaching season of Lent, cannot go to such a distance.

TO CONSTANTIUS

28. There you will find certain Illyrians imbued with the false doctrines of Arius; take heed of their tares, let them not come near the faithful, nor scatter their spurious seed. Let them remember what their perfidy has brought upon them[d], let them be quiet and follow the true faith. Difficult indeed it is for minds imbued with the poison of unbelief to rid themselves of this impiety, for it cleaves to them; and if the fatal venom has grown inveterate in them, you must not readily give them credence. For the very sinews and strength of wisdom lie in not giving credence too readily, especially in the matter of faith, which in men is seldom perfect.

29. Yet if any one, whose frailty is suspected and inclination dubious, desire nevertheless to clear himself of suspicion; suffer him to believe that he has made satisfaction, show him some indulgence, for if a man be cut off from reconciliation his mind is estranged. Thus skilful physicians, when they observe what they deem to be well-known diseases, do not apply a remedy, but wait their time, attending upon the sick man, and administering to him such soothing appliance as they can, to the intent that the disease may neither be aggravated by neglect or despair, nor may reject the medicine applied too early, for if an inexperienced physician touch it prematurely, it will never come to a head, just as even an apple, if shaken from the tree while yet unripe, soon withers.

30. Enjoin them too (as I have borrowed a figure from agriculture) to preserve inviolate the laws of common boundary, and to guard those paternal landmarks which the law protects. The affection of a neighbour often exceeds the love of a brother, for the one is often afar off, the other nigh at hand; the witness of your whole life, and judge of your conduct. Allow his cattle to stray at large over the neighbouring bounds, and to rest securely on the green herbage.

Deut. xix. 14.

[d] The Benedictine Editors refer this to the ravages of the Goths after Valens' defeat at Hadrianople A.D. 375. It is on this that they found the date of the letter, but the reference is somewhat vague.

LETT. 3. 31. Let the master too temper with moderation his lawful rule over his servants, seeing that in soul they are brethren. For he is called the father of the family, that he may govern them as sons; for he himself also is God's servant, and calls the Lord of heaven, the Source of all power, his Father.

Farewell; continue to love me, as I do you.

A.D. 380.

LETTER III.

This graceful little letter, written in a tone of playful affectionateness, is addressed to Felix, who was, as the next letter shews, Bishop of Comum. It tells its own story.

AMBROSE TO FELIX.

1. I HAVE received your present of mushrooms; they were of an extraordinary size, so large as to excite admiration. I did not like to keep them hidden, as the saying is, in my bosom, but preferred shewing them to others also. Therefore I gave part to my friends, part I reserved for myself.

2. An agreeable present, but not of weight enough to repress my just complaint against you for never visiting one who has so long loved you. And take heed lest you hereafter have to bear yet heavier fungus-growths [1] of sorrow; for such things have a double signification; sent as gifts they are agreeable, in the body or the mind they are irksome. Prevail with yourself to cause me less sorrow by your absence, for my longing for you is the cause of my distress: make yourself, if you can, less necessary to me.

3. I have made my statement, proved my case. I am forced to assail you with that expression; no ordinary weapon, but one which will hit home [a]. You certainly

[1] tubera

---

[a] Amentata illa non manipularis sententia. Ed. Ben. refers to Junius, Adagiorum Centuriae 3, 10, who says 'Amentatam sententiam dixit D. Ambrosius pro validâ et haud vulgari firmisque argumentis roboratâ. Est autem amentum lori genus quo hasta praeligata validius certiusque libratur evibraturque: hinc amentata sententia ea est quæ neutiquam trivialis est et pedanea, cujusmodi manipularis vocatur, velut a gregario milite profecta, sed eximia et artificio vallata.' He quotes two passages from Cicero, De Orat. 1 57, 242. Brut. 78. 271, in both which places he uses 'amentatæ

shewed alarm; but see now that I am not so much grieved but that I can be playful about it. Hereafter however you must not excuse yourself, though your present excuse is to be a profitable one to me. Yet it were an ill judgment of you, and of me no better, to suppose that your absence is to be compensated by presents, or that I am to be bought off by them. Farewell: love me, as I do you.

LETTER IV.   A.D. 380.

FELIX having replied to the preceding letter, S Ambrose responds in the same affectionate style, rejoicing in the prospect of their meeting, asking meanwhile the prayers of Felix, and promising his own. He ends by praising Felix for 'fighting the good fight of faith,' and assures him of help and blessing.

AMBROSE TO FELIX, HEALTH.

1. ALTHOUGH not in a good state of bodily health, I derived no little alleviation from the perusal of words from a heart so congenial to my own, being refreshed by your discourse as by some soothing potion [a]; and also by your announcement that the day memorable for us both was at hand, that whereon you took on yourself the office of the high-priesthood; of which I was just then speaking with my brother Bassianus [b]. For having begun to speak of the dedication of the Church which he had built in the name of the Apostles, we were led to the subject, for he said that he earnestly desired the company of your Holiness.

2. Wherefore I introduced the mention of your birthday [c], as being on the first of November, and that it was (if I mistook not) close at hand, and to be celebrated on the following day, so that after that it would yield you no excuse. So I made a promise on your behalf; for you too have liberty to do the same as regards me; I made a promise to him,

---

hastæ' of arguments, and also Tertull. adv. Marc iv 33 where he says that our Lord amentavit [Phariseis] hanc sententiam, non potestis Deo servire et mammonæ, where it plainly means, 'gave them this home-thrust.'

[a] puleium, lit. the herb penny royal.

[b] Bassianus is mentioned among the Bishops who took part in the Council of Aquileia, as Bishop of Laus Pompeia, now Lodi Vecchio, S E. of Milan. The modern town of Lodi is about 5 miles from the site of the ancient one.

[c] He means the day of his consecration as Bishop. So S. Ambr. speaks of his own consecration day as his birthday, Comm in Luc. vii. 78.

LETT. 4. and exacted one for myself: for I feel assured you will be present, because you ought to be. It will not therefore be so much my promise that will bind you, as your own purpose, having resolved to do that which you ought. You see then it was rather my knowledge of you, than any rash confidence which induced me to give this pledge to my brother. Come then, lest you put two bishops to shame; yourself for not coming, me for having promised unadvisedly.

3. But we will remember your birthday in our prayers, and do you not forget us in yours. Our spirit shall accompany you; do you also, when you enter the second Tabernacle, which is called the Holy of Holies, do as we do, and carry us also in with you.

When in spirit you burn incense on the golden censer, forget us not; for it is the one which is in the second Tabernacle, and from which your prayer, full of wisdom, is directed to heaven as incense.

Heb. ix. 4.   4. There is the *Ark of the Covenant overlaid round about with gold,* that is, the doctrine of Christ, the doctrine of the Wisdom of God. There is *the golden pot that had manna,* the depository, namely, of spiritual nutriment, and the storeplace of divine knowledge. There is *the rod of Aaron,* the symbol of priestly grace. Before, it had withered, but it *budded* again in Christ. There are *the Cherubim* over the tables of the Covenant, that is, the knowledge of the sacred Lessons. There is the *Mercy-seat,* over which on high is God

Col. i. 15. the Word, *the Image of the invisible God,* Who says to thee,
Exod. xxv. 22. *I will commune with thee from above the Mercy-seat, between the two Cherubim,* for He speaks thus with us, that we may
Ps. lxxviii. 2. understand His saying, or because He speaks things not earthly but spiritual, as He saith, *I will open My mouth in a parable.* For where Christ is, there are all things, there is His doctrine, there the remission of sins, there grace, there the separation of the living and the dead.

Numb. xvi. 48.   5. Aaron indeed once stood in the midst, interposing himself to prevent death passing over to the hosts of the living from the carcases of the dead. But He, as the Word, ever stands within each of us, although we see Him not, and separates the faculties of our reason from the carcase of our deadly passions and pestilential thoughts. He standeth as

He Who came into the world to blunt the sting of death, to stop its devouring jaws, to give to the living an eternity of grace, to the dead a resurrection. {TO FELIX}

6. In His service you are warring a good warfare, His deposit you keep, His money you lend out at interest, as it is written, *Thou shalt lend unto many nations;* the good interest of spiritual grace, which the Lord when He comes will exact with usury; and when He finds that you have dispensed it well, He will give you for few things, many things. Then shall I reap most delightful fruit, in that my judgment of you is approved; the ordination which you received by the imposition of my hands and the benediction in the Name of the Lord Jesus will not be blamed. Work therefore a good work, that in that day you may receive a reward, and we may rest together, I in you and you in me. {Deut. xv. 8.}

7. *Plenteous is the harvest* of Christ, *but the labourers few,* and helpers are difficult to be found. So it was of old, but the Lord is powerful, Who will *send labourers into His harvest.* Without doubt among the ranks of the people of Comum [d] very many have already begun to believe by your ministry, and through your teaching have received the word of God. But He Who gave those who believe will also give them that will help: whereby all occasion will be removed for excusing yourself for your postponed visit, and thus also the grace of your presence will be more frequently shed around me. {S. Luke x. 2.}

Farewell: continue to love us, as you do.

LETTER V.

AMBROSE TO SYAGRIUS.

LETTER VI.

AMBROSE TO SYAGRIUS.

[To complete the character of S. Ambrose as shewn in his Letters, these will be printed at the end of the volume, but, on account of their subject, in the original Latin.]

---

[d] Comum is the modern Como, at the southern extremity of the Lake which takes its name from it.

LETTER VII.

THE Justus to whom this letter and the following are addressed is in all probability S. Justus Bishop of Lyons, who is mentioned below as one of the Bishops who took part in the Council of Aquileia: that he was a Bishop is implied by S Ambrose addressing him as 'brother.' The letter contains a mystical interpretation of the half-shekel of redemption, (Exodus xxx. 12. sqq) and of the didrachma and stater of our Lord's miracle of the piece of money in the fish's mouth, and of the penny of the tribute money. The date given in the margin depends on the truth of the hypothesis that Justus is the Bishop of Lyons Of him it is recorded that he did not return to his See after the Council of Aquileia, but became a monk in the deserts of Egypt. See Newman's Fleury vol. 1 p 25.

AMBROSE TO JUSTUS, HEALTH.

YOUR question, my brother, as to the meaning of that shekel, half of which the Hebrew is commanded to offer for the redemption of the soul, is an excellent admonition to us to direct our intercourse by letter and our converse while at a distance to the interpretation of the heavenly oracles. For what can more unite us than to converse concerning the things of God?

2. Now the half of the shekel is a *piece of silver*, and the redemption of the soul is faith; faith therefore is that *piece of silver* which the *woman* in the Gospel, as we read, having *lost, diligently seeks for, lighting a candle and sweeping the house; and when she finds it, she calls together her friends and neighbours,* bidding them *rejoice with her for that she has found the piece of silver which she had lost.* For great is the loss of the soul, if a man lose his faith, or that grace which by means of faith he had obtained to himself. Do thou therefore *light thy candle. Thy light is thine eye;* that is, the inward eye of the mind. Do thou light this candle, which is fed by spiritual oil, and *gives light to thy whole house.* Seek that *piece of silver*, the redemption of thy soul, which he that loses is troubled, he that finds rejoices.

3. Mercy too is the redemption of the soul; for the redemption of a man's soul are his riches, by which he shews mercy, and expending them, relieves the poor. Wherefore

faith, grace, and mercy, are the redemption of the soul, which is purchased by a piece of silver, that is, by the full price of a larger sum. For thus it is written in the words of the Lord to Moses: *When thou takest the sum of the children of Israel after their number, then shall they give every man a ransom for his soul unto the Lord, when thou numberest them; that there be no plague among them when thou numberest them. This they shall give, every one that passeth among them that are numbered, half a shekel after the shekel of the sanctuary: (a shekel is twenty gerahs:) an half shekel shall be the offering of the Lord. Every one that passeth among them that are numbered, from twenty years old and above, shall give an offering unto the Lord. The rich shall not give more, and the poor shall not give less than half a shekel, when they give an offering unto the Lord to make an atonement for your souls. And thou shalt take the atonement money of the children of Israel and thou shalt appoint it for the service of the Tabernacle of the congregation, that it may be a memorial unto the children of Israel before the Lord, to make an atonement for your souls.* [TO JUSTUS] [Exod. xxx. 12—15.]

4. Did then both the rich man who offered more, and the poor who had less, fail so much, if this half shekel consisted in money and had not hidden excellencies? Whence we are to understand that this half shekel is not material but spiritual, having to be paid by all and rated equally.

5. Again as to heavenly food (for the food and delight of heavenly nutriment is wisdom, whereon they feed in Paradise, the unfailing food of the soul, called in the Divine Word manna) the distribution of this was, we read, so made to each soul as to be equally divided. For they who gathered most and they who gathered least, all gathered according to the direction of Moses; and they made an omer the measure, and it did not exceed to him who gathered much nor fall short to him who gathered little. For each man, according to the number of souls who were with him in the tent, gathered for each an omer, that is, being interpreted, a measure of wine. [Ib. xvi. 17, 18.]

6. Now this is the measure of wisdom, which if it be above measure is hurtful, as it is written, *Make not thyself over-wise.* And Paul has taught that the division of grace [Eccles. vii 16.]

LETT 7. is according to measure, saying, *The manifestation of the*
1 Cor. xii *Spirit is given to every man to profit withal, to one is given*
7—9. *the word of wisdom, to another the word of knowledge,* [to
¹ These another the faith of wisdom by the spirit of knowledge] ¹
words are *by the same Spirit, to another faith by the same Spirit,* and
added by
S Am- that this grace is given according to the will of the Spirit.
brose. In that He divides, He shews His equity, in that He divides as He will, His power. Or He may will to bestow
that upon each which He knows will be profitable.

7. An omer then is a measure, and a measure of wine,
Ps civ. *which maketh glad the heart of man.* For what is the joy
15. of the heart but the draughts of wisdom? This is that
Prov. ix. *wine* which *Wisdom* hath *mingled* in a cup, and given us to
2 drink, that we may receive to ourselves temperance and
prudence, that wine which should be so equally transfused
through all the senses and thoughts and all the emotions
which are within this our house, that we may know how to
abound to all and to be wanting to none.

8. More fully also it may be understood of the Blood of
Christ, to Whose grace nothing can be added nor taken
away. Whether you take little or drink much, to all the
measure of Redemption is perfect.

Exod. 9. The Passover too of the Lord, that is, the lamb, the
xii. 4. fathers are ordered so to eat, that it might be according to
the number of their souls, neither more nor less; that
more should not be given to some, and less to others, but
that it should be according to the number of their souls,
lest the stronger should take more and the weaker less.
For the grace, the gift, the redemption is distributed equally to all. And there ought not to be too many, lest any
go away defrauded of his hope and redemption. Now there
are too many, when any are beyond the number, for the
S. Matt. saints are all *numbered, and the hairs of their heads; for*
x. 30. *the Lord knoweth them that are His.* Neither can there
be too few, lest any be too weak to receive the greatness
of the grace.

10. Wherefore He hath commanded all to bring an equal
faith and devotion to the Pasch of the Lord, that is, to the
Passover. For it is the Pasch, when the mind lays down
its senseless passion, and puts on good compassion, that

it may suffer together with Christ, and take His Passover into itself, so as that He may *dwell in* it, *and walk in* it, *and may* become *its God.* Thus grace is equal in all, but virtue is diverse in each. Let each then take that portion which fits his strength, that neither the stronger may lack nor the weaker be burthened. *To Justus* 2 Cor. vi. 16.

11. This you have in the Gospel; for the same wages are paid to all the labourers in the vineyard; but few attain to the prize, to the reward; few say, *There is laid up for me a crown of righteousness.* For the gift of bounty and of grace is one thing; another the wages of virtue, the recompense of labour. S. Matt. xx. 10. 2 Tim iv. 8

12. Therefore a shekel is our ransom, nay half a shekel. He has redeemed us from death, redeemed from slavery, that we may not be subject to the world, which we have renounced. Whence in the Gospel our Lord bids Peter *go to the sea, and cast an hook,* and *take the stater which he will find in the fish's mouth,* and *give it to them* who required of the Lord and of himself a shekel. This then is that shekel which was exacted by the Law, nevertheless it was not due from the King's Son, but from strangers. For why should Christ ransom Himself from this world, when He came *to take away the sin of the world?* Why should He redeem Himself from sin, Who came down that He might remit to all their sins? Why should He redeem Himself from servitude, Who *emptied Himself* that He might give liberty to all? Why should He redeem Himself from death, Who took flesh, that by His Death He might obtain for all a resurrection? S. Matt. xvii. 27. S. John i. 29. Phil. ii. 7.

13. Truly the Redeemer of all had no need of a redemption; but as He received circumcision that He might fulfil the Law, and came to be baptized that He *might fulfil righteousness,* so also did He not refuse to pay those who required of Him the shekel, but straightway commanded the stater to be given as the tribute for Himself and Peter. For He chose rather to give beyond the Law than to deny the Law's due. At the same time He shews that the Jews acted contrary to the Law, in exacting a shekel from one person, whereas Moses had ordained that half a shekel should be required. On this account He commanded as S. Matt. iii. 15.

it were single pieces to be paid both for Himself and for Peter in the stater. Good is the tribute of Christ, which is paid by the *stater*, for justice is the *balance*¹, and justice is above the Law. Again, *Christ is the end of the law for righteousness to every one that believeth.* This stater is found in the fish's mouth, of that fish which the fishers of men take, of that fish who weighs his words that they may be tried by the fire before they are uttered.

14. This stater the Jews knew not, giving Him up to the betrayer. But the Law exacts half a shekel for the redemption of a soul, and devotes it to God, for she cannot claim the whole. For in the Jew scarcely a portion of devotion could be found. But he who is *free indeed*, a true Hebrew, belongs wholly to God, all that he has savours of liberty. He has nothing in common with him who refuses liberty, saying, *I love my master, my wife, and my children, I will not go out free!* Which refers not only to his lord, but to the weakness of that man who shall have subjected himself to the world, in that he loves the world as his own soul, that is, his intelligence, the author of his will. Nor does it refer only to *his wife,* but also to that delight which cares for household not eternal things. This man's ear therefore his lord nails to his door or threshold, that he may remember these words whereby he chose servitude.

15. This man therefore, O Christian, imitate not; for thou art not commanded to offer half a shekel, but, *if thou wouldest be perfect,* to *sell all thou hast, and give to the poor.* Thou art not to reserve a part of thy service for the world, but to deny thyself altogether, and to *take up thy* Lord's *cross and follow Him.*

16. Now we have learned that the half-shekel was required by the Law, because the other half was reserved for the generation of this world, that is, for secular life, and domestic use, and for posterity, to whom it was necessary that a portion out of the original inheritance should be transmitted. Wherefore our Lord answered the Pharisees, when they tempted Him by the crafty question whether He would advise that tribute should be paid to Cæsar, *Why tempt ye Me, ye hypocrites, shew Me the tribute money.*

And they brought Him a penny on which was Cæsar's image. He saith to them, *Render unto Cæsar the things which are Cæsar's, and unto God the things that are God's;* shewing that they who thought themselves perfect were imperfect in that they paid to Cæsar before God. They with whom the world was their first care would first pay that which appertained to the world; wherefore He says *Render,* that is, render ye, *the things which are Cæsar's*— ye, among whom the image and likeness of Cæsar is found.

<small>TO JUSTUS</small>

17. Wherefore those Hebrew youths, Ananias, Azarias, Misael, and that wiser Daniel, who would not worship the image of the king, who received it not, nor any thing from the king's table, were not bound to pay tribute. For they possessed nothing that was under the power of an earthly king. And so their followers, they whose portion is God, pay no tribute. And so the Lord says, *Render,* that is, Do ye render, who have brought forth the image of Cæsar, with whom it is found, but I owe nothing to Cæsar, because I have nothing in this world. *The prince of this world cometh, and hath nothing in Me.* Peter owes nothing, nor the Apostles, because *they are not of this world* though *they are in this world. I have sent them into this world,* but now *they are not of this world,* because with Me they are above the world.

<small>Dan. iii. 18. and i. 8.</small>

<small>S. John xiv. 30.</small>

<small>S. John xvii. 11, 14, 18.</small>

18. So that which belongs to the Divine Law, not to Cæsar, is that which is commanded to be paid. Yet even this He that was perfect, that is, the preacher of the Gospel, no longer owed, for He had preached more. The Son of God owed it not, nor did Peter who was by grace an adopted son of the Father. *Notwithstanding,* says He, *lest we should offend them, go thou to the sea, and cast a hook, and take up the fish that first cometh up, and when thou hast opened his mouth, thou shalt find a piece of money, that take, and give unto them for Me and thee.* O great mystery! He gives that half-shekel which the Law commanded, He refuses not what is of the Law, for He was *made of a woman, made under the Law.* 'Made,' I say, as regards His incarnation; 'of a woman,' as regards the sex; woman is the sex, virgin the species; the sex relates to her nature, the virgin to her integrity. For wherein He came *under the*

<small>S. Matt. xvii. 27.</small>

<small>Gal. iv. 4.</small>

LETT. 7. *Law*, therein He was *made of a woman*, that is, in the body. On this account He commands a shekel to be paid for Him and Peter, for both were born *under the Law*. He commands it to be paid then according to the Law, that *He might redeem those who are under the Law*.

19. And yet He commands a stater to be paid that they might have their mouths closed, and so not commit sin by excess of talking. And He bids that to be given which was found in the mouth of the fish, that they might acknowledge the Word. For why was it that they who exacted what was of the Law, knew not what was the Law ? For they ought not to have been ignorant of the Word of God; for it is written, *The Word is very nigh unto thee, in thy mouth, and in thy heart*. He therefore paid the whole shekel to God, who reserved no part for the world. For it is to God that righteousness, which is the moderation of the mind, is paid; to God is paid the keeping of the tongue, which is the moderation in speech. *For with the heart man believeth unto righteousness, and with the mouth confession is made unto salvation.*

<small>Deut. xxx. 14.</small>

<small>Rom. x. 10.</small>

20. The half-shekel may also be understood of the Old Testament, the whole shekel for the price of both Testaments, for according to the Law every one was redeemed by the Law, but he who is redeemed according to the Gospel, pays the half-shekel according to the Law, he is redeemed by the Blood of Christ according to grace, having a double redemption both of devotion and of Blood. For not even faith alone is sufficient for perfection, unless the redeemed also obtain the grace of Baptism, and receive the Blood of Christ. Good then is that half-shekel which is paid to God.

21. The half-shekel is not a penny[1], but is different. Again, in the penny is the image of Cæsar, in the half-shekel the image of God, for it is of one God, and formed after God Himself. Beginning from One it is infinitely diffused, and again, from the Infinite all things come back to one, as their end, for God is both the beginning and the end of all things. Wherefore arithmeticians have not called 'one' a number, but an element of number. And this we have said because it is written, *I am Alpha and*

<small>[1] denarius.</small>

<small>Rev. i. 8.</small>

Omega, the beginning and the ending; and, *Hear, O Israel. the Lord our God is One Lord.*

TO JUSTUS
Deut. vi. 4.

22. Be thou then, after the likeness of God, one and the same; not sober to-day, drunken to-morrow; to-day pacific, to-morrow quarrelsome; to-day frugal, to-morrow immoderate; for each person is changed by diversity of manners and becomes another man, in whom that which he was is not recognized, while he begins to be that which he was not, degenerate from himself. It is a grievous thing to be changed for the worse. Be then as the image on the half-shekel, immutable, keeping daily the same deportment. Seeing the half-shekel, observe the image, that is, seeing the Law, observe in the Law Christ the Image of God; for He *is the Image of the invisible* and incorruptible *God*, let Him be displayed before thee as in the mirror of the Law. Confess Him in the Law, that thou mayest know Him again in the Gospel. If thou hast known Him in His precepts, acknowledge Him in works. Farewell, and if you do not think that this shekel has been committed to me unprofitably, doubt not to commit to me a second time whatever you may have to communicate.

LETTER VIII. A.D. 381.

S. AMBROSE in this letter answers the objections raised against the Scriptures, that they were not written according to the rules of art, and illustrates his argument with various passages

AMBROSE TO JUSTUS.

1. VERY many deny that the Sacred writers wrote according to the rules of art. Nor do we contend for the contrary; for they wrote not according to art, but according to grace, which is above all art; for they wrote that which the Spirit gave them to speak. And yet they who wrote on art made use of their writings from which to frame their art, and to compose its comments and rules.

Acts ii. 4.

2. Again, in art there are principally required, a cause,

LETT. 8. a subject, and an end. When then we read that holy
αἴτιον, Isaac said to his father, *Behold the fire and the wood, but*
ὕλη, *where is the lamb for a burnt offering,* which of these is
ἀποτέ- wanting? For he who asks, doubts, he who answers the
λεσμα. query pronounces and solves the doubt. *Behold the fire,*
Gen.
xxii. 7. that is the cause, *and the wood,* that is ὕλη, which in Latin
is 'materia,' what third thing remains but the end, which
the son asked for, saying, *Where is the lamb for a burnt-*
Ib. 8. *offering,* and the father replied, *My son, God will provide*
Himself a lamb for a burnt offering?

3. Let us discuss for a little while the mystery. *God*
shewed a ram hanging by his horns. Now the ram is the
Word, full of tranquillity, moderation, and patience; whereby is shewn that Wisdom is a good sacrifice, and that He
was well skilled in the mode of meritorious propitiation.
Ps. iv. 5. Wherefore the Prophet also says, *Offer the sacrifice of*
righteousness. And so it is a sacrifice both of righteousness and of wisdom.

4. Here then is a mind fervent and glowing as fire which
worketh; here is the thing to be understood, that is the
subject-matter, where is the third, the understanding? Behold the colour, where is the seeing? behold the object of
sense, where is the sense itself? For matter is not seen
by all, and therefore God gives the gift of understanding,
and feeling, and seeing.

5. The Word of God then is the end or completion;
that is, the determination and completion of the discussion,
which is communicated to the more prudent, and confirms
things doubtful. Well do even they who believed not in
the Coming of Christ refute themselves, so that they confess what they think to deny. For they say that the ram
is the Word of God, and yet believe not the mystery of
the Passion, whereas in that mystery is the Word of God,
in Whom the Sacrifice was fulfilled.

6. Wherefore let us first kindle within us the fire of the
mind, that it may work within us. Let us seek for the
subject-matter, what it is that nourishes the mind, as if we
were looking for it in darkness. For neither did the Fathers
Exod. know what manna was: they found manna, it is said, declar-
xvi. 15, ing it to be the Discourse and word of God, from Whom
16.

all instruction as from a perennial fountain flows and is derived. TO JUSTUS

7. This is that heavenly food. And it is signified by the Person of the Speaker, *Behold I will rain bread from heaven for you.* The 'cause' then we have in the operation of God, Who waters our minds with the dew of wisdom; the 'subject-matter' we have in that the minds which see and taste it are delighted, and inquire whence comes this which is brighter than light, sweeter than honey. They have their answer from the text of Scripture: *This is the bread which the Lord hath given you to eat,* and this is the Word of God, Which God appointed and ordained, whereby the minds of the prudent are fed and comforted, which is white and sweet, enlightening the minds of the hearers with the splendour of truth, and soothing them with the sweetness of virtue. Exod. xvi. 4. Ib. 15.

8. The Prophet had learned in himself what was the 'cause' of the thing to be completed. For when he was sent to the king of Egypt to deliver the people of God, he says, *Who am I, that I should go unto Pharaoh,* and deliver my people from the king's power? the Lord answers, *I will be with thee.* Moses asked again, *What shall I say unto them, if they ask, Who is the Lord that hath sent thee, and what is His Name?* The Lord said, *I am that I am, thou shalt say,* I AM *hath sent me unto you.* This is the true Name of God—Eternity. Wherefore the Apostle also says of Christ, *For the Son of God, Jesus Christ, Who was preached among you by us, by me and Silvanus and Timotheus, was not Yea and Nay, but in Him was Yea.* Moses answered, *But behold they will not believe me, nor hearken unto my voice, for they will say, The Lord hath not appeared unto thee.* Then He gave him power to work miracles, that it might be believed that he was sent by God. A third time Moses says, *I am not eloquent, but I am slow of speech, and of a slow tongue; how shall Pharaoh hear me?* the Lord answers, *Go, and I will be with thy mouth, and teach thee what thou shalt say.* Ib. iii. 11—14. 2 Cor. i. 19. Exod. iv. 1. Ib. 10. Ib. 12.

9. These intermingled questions and answers contain the seeds and science of wisdom. The 'end' or 'completion' too is good, for He says, *I will be with thee!* And although

LETT. 8. He had given him power to work miracles, yet as he was still doubtful, that we might know that signs are for them that believe not, but the promise for believers, the weakness of his deserts or of his purpose receives this answer, *I will be with thy mouth, and teach thee what thou shalt say!* Thus a perfect 'end' is preserved.

<small>Exod. iii. 12.</small>

<small>S. Matt. vii. 7.</small>
10. This you have also in the Gospel, *Ask, and it shall be given you, seek, and ye shall find; knock, and it shall be opened unto you.* Ask from the 'cause,' that is, from the Author. You have as your subject-matter things spiritual which cause you to seek; *knock, and* God the Word *opens to you.* That which asks is the mind, which works like fire; it is in things spiritual that the glow of the mind works, as fire on wood; God the Word opens unto you, this is the 'end.' We have also in another part of the Gospel these words of our Lord, *But when they deliver you up, take no thought how or what ye shall speak, for it shall be given you in that same hour what ye shall speak. For it is not ye that speak, but the Spirit of your Father which speaketh in you.*

<small>Ib. x. 19, 20.</small>

<small>Gen. xxvii. 20.</small>
11. These words too of Isaac you have in Genesis, *How is it that thou hast found it so quickly, my son? And he said, Because the Lord thy God brought it to me.* The Lord is the end. He who seeks in the Lord finds. And thus Laban who sought not in the Lord, for he sought idols, found not.

<small>Ib. xxxi. 33.</small>

<small>¹ ὅροι. Ib. xxvii 4.</small>
12. And he has well observed the rules¹ and distinctions as they are called. The first is *Go and take me some venison, that I may eat.* He excites and inflames his mind with the fire, as it were, of his exhortation, that he may labour and seek. The second is, *How is it that thou hast found it so quickly?* This is in the form of a question; the third is an answer, *Because the Lord thy God brought it to me.* The 'end' is God, Who concludes and perfects all things, of Whom we are not to doubt.

13. And there is a 'distinction' too as to spontaneous things; *If you sow not, you shall not reap*ᵃ; for although culture calls forth seeds, yet nature by a certain spontaneous impulse, worketh in them that they spring up.

ᵃ There is no text in Holy Scripture exactly corresponding to this. Lev. xxv. 11 which is referred to by Ed. Ben. is hardly to the point.

14. Wherefore the Apostle says, *I have planted, Apollos watered, but God gave the increase. So then neither is he that planteth any thing, neither he that watereth, but God That giveth the increase!* God gives to you in the spirit, and the Lord sows in your heart. Take care then that He breathe life and sow in you, that you may reap; for if you sow not, neither shall you reap. This is a sort of admonition to you to sow. If you sow not you shall not reap, is a proverb. The end agrees with the beginning; the seed is the beginning, the harvest the end.

TO JUSTUS 1 Cor. iii. 6, 7.

15. Learn, he says, of me; nature aids the learner, and God is the Author of nature. It is of God too that we learn well, for it is a natural gift to learn well; the hard of heart learn not. Nature, which is preserved by the Divine bounty, gives the increase. The final consummation God giveth, that is, the most excellent and Divine Nature and Essence of the Trinity.

Farewell: love us, as you do, for we love you.

THE PROCEEDINGS OF THE COUNCIL OF AQUILEIA A.D. 381. AGAINST THE HERETICS PALLADIUS AND SECUNDIANUS.

The official Record of the Proceedings of this Council seems to be inserted among S. Ambrose's Letters, partly because S. Ambrose took the leading part in them, and partly because they form the subject of the next series of letters, directly of the four first, and more indirectly of the two next, all of which, though written in the name of the Bishops of Italy, we may presume to have been S Ambrose's composition. The Council was held in the year 381 A.D, the same year in which the Second General Council was held at Constantinople. It will be remembered that that Council, being summoned by Theodosius, then Emperor of the East, consisted of Eastern Bishops only. At this time Arianism, though rife in the East, seems not to have been prevalent in the West. S. Ambrose says, (Letter xi. 1) 'as regards the West, two individuals only have been found to dare to oppose the Council with profane and impious words, men who had previously disturbed a mere corner of Dacia Ripensis.' These two men were Palladius and Secundianus. Palladius appears to have applied to Gratian to call a General Council, on the plea that he was falsely accused of Arianism, in 379 A D. Gratian granted his request, but afterwards, as we learn from his letter read at the Council, on the representation of S. Ambrose that such a question as the soundness or heresy of two Bishops might be settled by a Council of the Bishops of the Diocese of Italy, he so far altered his original order as to summon only these, giving permission for others to attend if they pleased. This reconsideration, and perhaps also the troubles that prevailed in the Empire at the time, (Tillemont Vie de S. Ambr. ch. xxiii) caused such delay that it was not till towards the end of 381 A.D that the Council assembled under the presidency of S. Valerian Bishop of Aquileia. The Bishops of Italy, with deputies from Gaul, Africa, and Illyria, to the number of thirty two or thirty three (see note r) met at Aquileia at the beginning of September The discussion recorded in the 'Gesta' took place probably on Septr. 3rd (see note a) but S Ambrose's words in § 2 imply that previous discussions had been held of which no Record had been taken, (diu citra acta tractavimus)

The proceedings commence by the reading of the Emperor's Mandate. Palladius then raises objections on the ground of the absence of the Bishops from the East, and charges S Ambrose with having tricked the Emperor into summoning only a small Council, and declines to take part in a Council which is not General. After some discussion on this point S. Ambrose proposes that Arius' letter from Nicomedia to S Alexander should be read in detail, and Palladius called upon to condemn each heretical proposition. Palladius argues upon each, but eventually returns to his refusal to answer except in a General Council. In the end all the Bishops pronounce their decisions one by one, all agreeing that Palladius' doctrine was heretical and that he should be deposed Secundianus is then more briefly dealt with in the same way. It would seem that the Record is incomplete, as the number of Bishops who give their decision is only 25, and the account of Secundianus' case ends abruptly without recording any decision It may be from the same cause that the Record itself is in one or two places seemingly defective, and the sense confused

Secundianus is not mentioned again in History. Of Palladius it is said by Vigilius, Bishop of Thapsus in Africa, who lived in the latter part of the 5th Century, that after S. Ambrose's death he wrote a reply to his writings against Arianism, which Vigilius himself answered (Tillemont Vie de S. Ambr. xxvi).

The genuineness of the Gesta has been disputed by Père Chifflet, who maintained that they were a forgery of the Vigilius mentioned above: his arguments however are satisfactorily refuted by Tillemont in an elaborate note. (Vol. x. p. 738. note 15. on S Ambr. Life)

1. IN the consulship of the illustrious SYAGRIUS and EUCHERIUS, on the 3rd day of September [a], the undermentioned Bishops [b], sitting in council in the church at

[a] There can be little doubt that the true date is iii Non. Sept. i e. the 3rd of Sept, and not Nonis, the 5th For in 381 A. D. the 5th of Sept was on a Sunday, and it is hardly likely that a Council would have sat from daybreak till one o' clock (Ep. 10. 5) in the Church on such a day, and moreover it would not have been natural for Palladius to say, as he does in § 47. Non respondebo nisi auditores veniant post Dominicam diem, if he were speaking on a Sunday.

[b] The reading of Ed. Rom. has been adopted, which omits the preposition 'cum.' If this were correct, it would imply that the consuls were themselves taking a leading part in the Council; whereas it is clear that they are mentioned solely as the ordinary way of fixing the year; nor had the consuls at this time any other

Aquileia, namely, VALERIAN, Bishop of Aquileia, AM- OF
BROSE, EUSEBIUS, LIMENIUS, ANEMIUS, SABINUS, ABUN- AQUILEIA.
DANTIUS, ARTEMIUS, CONSTANTIUS, JUSTUS, PHILASTER,
CONSTANTIUS, THEODORUS, ALMACHIUS, DOMNINUS,
AMANTIUS, MAXIMUS, FELIX, BASSIANUS, NUMIDIUS,
JANUARIUS, PROCULUS, HELIODORUS, JOVINUS, FELIX,
EXUPERANTIUS, DIOGENES, MAXIMUS, MACEDONIUS,
CASSIANUS, MARCELLUS, and EUSTATHIUS, Bishops:

Ambrose, Bishop, said;

2. 'We have long been dealing with the matter without any Records[c], and now, since our ears are assailed with such sacrilegious words on the part of Palladius and Secundianus, that one can scarce believe that they could have so openly blasphemed, and that they may not attempt hereafter by any subtlety to deny their own words, though the testimony of such eminent Bishops does not admit of doubt, still as it is the pleasure of all the Bishops, let Records be made, that no one may be able to deny his own profession. Do you therefore, holy men, declare what is your pleasure.'

All the Bishops said, 'It is our pleasure.'

Ambrose, Bishop, said, 'Our discussions must be confirmed by the Emperor's Letter, as the subject requires, so that they may be quoted.'

3. The Letter is read by Sabinianus a Deacon;

"Desirous to make our earliest efforts to prevent dissension among Bishops from uncertainty what doctrines they should reverence, we had ordered the Bishops to come together into the city of Aquileia, out of the diocese[d] which

than such ornamental functions. See Gibbon's description, ch. xvii. vol ii ed. Smith p. 206—208.

[c] By 'acta' here are meant formal and official records taken down and published by authority. Thus Jul. Cæsar ordered the 'Acta' of the Senate to be regularly published. Suet. Cæs 20.

[d] It is to be remembered that 'diocese' was then a civil and not an Ecclesiastical term. A 'diœcesis' was an aggregate of provinces, under the charge of a Vicarius, who was subordinate to one of the four Præfecti Praetorio, each Præfectus having under him a number of dioceses. Thus the Vicarius Italiæ, who was subordinate to the Præfectus Prætorio Italiae, had in his diocese fourteen provinces, including both Liguria of which Milan was the capital, and Venetia in which Aquileia was situated. It is to be remembered also that Italia at this time meant only the north of Italy, the rest of Italy being now included in the Diocese of Rome, and under the Vicarius Urbis Romae. See the table given in Smith's Gibbon, vol. ii. p. 315. taken from Marquardt. When the word diocese came into Ecclesiastical use, it was applied, first to "an aggregate not merely of several districts, governed each by its own bishop, but of several provinces (ἐπαρχίαι) each presided over by a

COUNCIL has been confided to the merits of your Excellency. For controversies of dubious import could not be better disentangled than by our constituting the Bishops themselves expounders of the dispute that has arisen, so that the same persons from whom come forth the instructions of doctrine may solve the contradictions of discordant teaching.

4. "Nor is our present order different from our last: we do not alter the tenour of our command, but we correct the superfluous numbers that would have assembled. For as Ambrose, Bishop of Milan, eminent both for the merits of his life and the favour of God, suggests that there is no occasion for numbers in a case in which the truth, though in the hands of a few supporters, would not suffer from many antagonists, and that he and the Bishops of the adjoining cities of Italy would be more than sufficient to meet the assertions of the opposite party, we have judged it right to refrain from troubling venerable men by bringing into strange lands any one who was either loaded with years, or disabled with bodily weakness, or in the slender circumstances of honourable poverty; [e] etc."

5. AMBROSE, Bishop, said; 'This is what a Christian Emperor has ordained. He has not thought fit to do an injury to the Bishops: he has constituted the Bishops themselves Judges. And therefore since we sit together in a Council of Bishops, answer to what is proposed to you. Arius's letter has been read: it shall be recited now again, if you think proper. It contains blasphemies from the beginning; it says that the Father alone is eternal. If you think that the Son of God is not everlasting, support this doctrine in what manner you please: if you think it is a doctrine to be condemned, condemn it. Here is the Gospel, and the Apostle [f]: all the Scriptures are at hand. Support it from what quarter you please, if you think that the Son of God is not everlasting.'

metropolitan. The diocese itself was under an Exarch or Patriarch " Dict. of Chr. Ant. sub voc. 'Creditâ' is here read for 'creditam,' as required by the order of the words.

[e] It is not certain to whom the Emperor's letter was addressed. Some have thought that it was addressed to the Pretorian Prefect of Italy. Tillemont maintained that it was addressed to Valerian, Bishop of Aquileia, in whose see the Council was held. The language, though not decisive, seems in favour of the former supposition In § 7. the Prefect of Italy is spoken of as issuing letters in pursuance of it.

[f] i e. a copy of S. Paul's Epistles.

6. PALLADIUS said: 'You have contrived, as appears by the sacred document[g] which you have brought forward, that this should not be a full and General Council: in the absence of our Colleagues we cannot answer.'

Ambrose, Bishop, said; 'Who are your colleagues?'

Palladius said; 'The Eastern Bishops.'

7. AMBROSE, Bishop, said; 'Inasmuch as in former times the usage of Councils has been that the Eastern Bishops should be appointed to hold them in the East, and the Western Bishops in the West, we, having our place in the West, are come together to the city of Aquileia according to the Emperor's command. Moreover, the Prefect of Italy has issued letters, that if the Eastern Bishops chose to meet, they should be allowed to do so; but inasmuch as they know that the custom is that the Council of the Eastern Bishops should be in the East and of the Western in the West, they have therefore thought fit not to come.'

8. PALLADIUS said; 'Our Emperor Gratian commanded the Eastern Bishops to come: do you deny that he did so? the Emperor himself told us that he had commanded the Eastern Bishops to come.'

Ambrose, Bishop, said; 'He certainly commanded them, in that he did not forbid them to come hither.'

Palladius said; 'But your prayer has prevented their coming: under a pretence of benevolence you have obtained this, and so put the Council off.'

9. AMBROSE, Bishop, said; 'There is no occasion to wander any longer from the subject: answer now. Did Arius say rightly that the Father alone is eternal? and did he say this in agreement with the Scriptures or not?'

Palladius said; 'I do not answer you.'

Constantius, Bishop, said; 'Do not you answer when you have so long blasphemed?'

Eusebius, Bishop, said; 'But you are under an obligation to express frankly the faith you claim the right to hold. If a heathen were to ask of you in what way you believe in Christ, you would be bound not to be ashamed to confess.'

10. SABINUS, Bishop, said; 'It was your own request that we would answer: we are come together this day ac-

[g] i.e. the Emperor's letter.

cording to your wish, and upon your own solicitation, and we have not waited for our other brethren, who might have come. It is therefore not open to you to wander from the subject. Do you say that Christ was created? or do you say that the Son of God is everlasting?'

Palladius said; 'I have told you already: we said we would come and prove that you have not done well to take advantage of the Emperor.'

Ambrose, Bishop, said; 'Let Palladius's letter be read to shew whether he sent us this message, and it will appear that even now he is deceiving.'

Palladius said; 'Let it be read by all means.'

The Bishops said: 'When you saw the Emperor at Sirmium, did you address him, or was it he that pressed you?' And they added: 'What do you answer to this?'

Palladius answered; 'He said to me, "Go." We said: "Are the Eastern Bishops summoned to attend?" He said, "They are." Should we have come if the Eastern Bishops had not been summoned?'

11. AMBROSE, Bishop, said; 'Let the matter of the Eastern Bishops stand over. I enquire at present into your sentiments. Arius's letter has been read to you: you are in the habit of denying that you are an Arian. Either condemn Arius now, or defend him.'

Palladius said; 'It is not within the compass of your authority to ask this of me.'

Eusebius, Bishop, said; 'We do not believe that the religious Emperor said other than he wrote. He has ordered the Bishops to meet: it is impossible that he said to you and no one else contrary to his own letter, that the case was not to be discussed without the presence of the Eastern Bishops.'

Palladius said; 'He did, if the Italian Bishops alone were ordered to assemble.'

Evagrius, Presbyter and deputy, said; [h] [It is plain] 'that he promised to appear within four and even within two days. What then were you waiting for? was it, as you say, that you considered the opinion of your colleagues, the

---

[h] The text here seems defective, nor is there any thing to guide us to supply the lacuna. What is given in the translation is no more than a guess at the meaning of the sentence. The general connection is however clear enough even if it be omitted.

Eastern Bishops was to be waited for? Then you ought to have said so in your message, and not to have pledged yourself to discussion.'

OF AQUILEIA

Palladius said; 'I had come, believing it to be a General Council, but I saw that my colleagues had not assembled. I decided however[1] to come, in accordance with the summons, to bid you to do nothing to the prejudice of a future Council.'

12. AMBROSE, Bishop, said; 'You yourself required that we should sit to-day, moreover, even this very day you have said yourself "we come as Christians to Christians." You have therefore acknowledged us for Christians. You promised that you would engage in discussion: you promised that you would either assign your own reasons or accept ours. We therefore willingly accepted your opening, we wished that you should come as a Christian. I offered you the letter of Arius, which that Arius wrote, from whose name you say that you often suffer wrong. You say that you do not follow Arius. To-day your sentiments must be made clear; either condemn him, or support him by whatever passage you will.'

He went on; 'Then according to Arius's letter Christ the Son of God is not everlasting?'

Palladius said; 'We said that we would prove ourselves Christians, but in a full Council. We do not answer you at all to the prejudice of a future Council.'

Eusebius, Bishop, said; 'You ought to state your profession of faith straightforwardly.'

Palladius said; 'And what do we reserve for the Council?'

13. AMBROSE, Bishop, said; 'He has been unanimously condemned who denies the Eternity of the Son of God. Arius denied it, Palladius, who will not condemn Arius, follows him. Consider then, whether his opinion is approved of; it is easy to perceive whether he speaks according to the Scriptures, or against the Scriptures. For we read: *God's eternal Power and Godhead.* Christ is the Power of God. If then the Power of God is everlasting, Christ surely is everlasting; for *Christ is the Power of God.*'

Rom. i. 20.

1 Cor. i. 8.

---
[1] The reading of Ed. Rom. is here adopted, as alone furnishing a reasonable sense. The Benedictine text is unintelligible.

Eusebius, Bishop, said; 'This is our faith: this is the Catholic doctrine; who says not this, let him be anathema.'

All the Bishops said; 'Anathema.'

14. EUSEBIUS, Bishop, said; 'He says specifically that the Father alone is everlasting, and that the Son at some time began to be.'

Palladius said; 'I have neither seen Arius, nor do I know who he is.'

Eusebius, Bishop, said; 'The blasphemy of Arius has been produced, in which he denies that the Son of God is everlasting. Do you condemn this wickedness and its author, or do you support it?'

Palladius said; 'When there is not the authority of a full Council, I do not speak.'

15. AMBROSE, Bishop, said; 'Do you hesitate after the divine judgements to condemn Arius, when he has *burst asunder in the midst?*' and he added; 'Let the holy men too, the deputies of the Gauls, speak.'

Constantius, Bishop and deputy of the Gauls, said; 'This impiety of that man we always have condemned, and we now condemn not only Arius, but also whoever does not say that the Son of God is everlasting.'

Ambrose, Bishop, said; 'What says also my Lord Justus?'

Justus, Bishop and deputy of the Gauls, said; 'He who does not confess that the Son of God is co-eternal with the Father, let him be accounted Anathema.'

All the Bishops said; 'Anathema.'

16. AMBROSE, Bishop, said; 'Let the deputies of the Africans speak too, who have brought hither the sentiments of all their countrymen.'

Felix, Bishop and deputy, said; 'If any man denies that the Son of God is everlasting, and that He is co-eternal with the Father, not only do I the deputy of the whole province of Africa condemn him, but also the whole priestly company, which sent me to this most holy assembly, has itself also already condemned him.'

Anemius, Bishop, said; 'There is no capital of Illyricum[1]

---

[1] By Illyricum is here meant Illyricum Occidentale, which at this time was under the jurisdiction of the Vicarius Italiæ. (See the Table in Smith's Gibbon, referred to in note d. p. 33) Sirmium, which in the following Century was entirely destroyed by the Goths under Attila, was at this time

but Sirmium: I am its Bishop. The person who does not confess the Son of God to be eternal and co-eternal with the Father, that is, everlasting, I call anathema; and I also say anathema to those who do not make the same confession.'

17. AMBROSE, Bishop, said; 'Hear what follows.' Then it was read; "Alone eternal, alone without beginning, alone true, Who alone has immortality."

Ambrose, Bishop, said; 'In this also condemn him who denies that the Son is very God. For since He Himself is the Truth, how is He not very God?' And he added; 'What say you to this?'

Palladius said; 'Who denies that He is very Son?'

Ambrose, Bishop, said; 'Arius denied it.'

Palladius said; 'When the Apostle says that Christ is God over all, can any one deny that He is the very Son of God?'

18. Ambrose, Bishop, said; 'That you may see with how much simplicity we seek the truth, lo, I say as you say: but I have then only half the truth. For by speaking thus, you appear to deny that He is very God; if however you confess simply that the Son of God is very God, state it in the order in which I propose it to you.'

Palladius said; 'I speak to you according to the Scriptures: I call the Lord the very Son of God.'

Ambrose, Bishop, said; 'Do you call the Son of God very Lord?'

Palladius said; 'When I call Him very Son, what more is wanted?'

Ambrose, Bishop, said; 'I do not ask only that you

---

a place of great importance both civil and ecclesiastical. It is spoken of by Justinian as capital of Illyricum both in civil and episcopal matters (Tillemont, note xv on the Life of S. Ambrose vol. x. p 739). Its ecclesiastical importance is shewn by the contest in which S Ambrose engaged with Justina, two years before the Council, 379 A D. to bring about the election of Anemius as Bishop, when the Empress was using all her influence to cause an Arian Bishop to be appointed. Arianism had been rife there for some time, and Germinus a previous Bishop had been one of the leaders of that party. (Tillemont, S. Ambr ch. xx.) Illyricum had been finally separated into two divisions, Orientale and Occidentale, by Gratian, in 379 A.D, who transferred the Eastern Division to Theodosius when he made him Emperor of the East, from which time it formed part of the Eastern Empire. (Tillemont, Hist. des Emp vol. v. p. 716.)

COUNCIL should call Him very Son, but that you should call the Son of God very Lord.'

19. EUSEBIUS, Bishop, said; 'Is Christ very God, according to the faith of all and to the Catholic profession?'

Palladius said; 'He is the very Son of God.'

Eusebius, Bishop, said; 'We also are by adoption sons; He is Son according to the property of His Divine Generation.' And he added; 'Do you confess that the very Son of God is very Lord by His Birth and essentially?'

Palladius said; 'I call Him the very Son of God, only-begotten.'

Eusebius, Bishop, said; 'Do you then think it is against the Scriptures, for Christ to be called very God?'

20. PALLADIUS being silent, Ambrose, Bishop, said; 'He who says only that He is the very Son of God, and will not say that He is very Lord, appears to deny it. Let Palladius then, if he does confess it, confess it in this order, and let him say whether he calls the Son of God very Lord.'

S. John xvii. 3.

Palladius said; 'When the Son says, *That they might know Thee the only true God and Jesus Christ Whom Thou hast sent,* is it by way of feeling only, or in truth?'

1 S. John v. 20.

Ambrose, Bishop, said; 'John said in his epistle; *This is the true God.* Deny this.'

Palladius said; 'When I tell you that He is true Son, I acknowledge also a true Godhead.'

Ambrose, Bishop, said; 'In this also there is evasion; for you art wont to speak of one only and true Godhead in such manner as to say that it is the divinity of the Father only, and not that of the Son also, which is one only and true. If then you wish to speak plainly, as you refer me to the Scriptures, say what the Evangelist John said; *This is the true God,* or deny that he hath said it.'

Palladius said; 'Besides the Son there is none other that is begotten.'

21. EUSEBIUS, Bishop, said; 'Is Christ very God, according to the faith of all and to the Catholic profession, or in your opinion is He not very God?'

Palladius said; 'He is the Power of our God.'

Ambrose, Bishop said; 'You do not speak frankly; and

so anathema to him who does not confess that the Son of God is very Lord.'

OF AQUILEIA

All the Bishops said; 'Let him be accounted anathema, who will not call Christ, the Son of God, very Lord.'

22. The reader continued; "Alone true, Who alone hath immortality."

Ambrose, Bishop, said; 'Has the Son of God immortality, or has He it not, in respect of His Godhead?'

Palladius said; 'Do you accept or no the words of the Apostle, *The King of kings Who alone hath immortality?*'   1 Tim. vi. 16.

Ambrose, Bishop, said; 'What say you of Christ the Son of God?'

Palladius said; 'Is Christ a divine Name or a human?'

23. EUSEBIUS, Bishop, said; 'He is called Christ indeed according to the mystery of His Incarnation, but He is both God and Man.'

Palladius said; 'Christ is a name of the flesh: Christ is a man's name: do you answer me.'

Eusebius, Bishop, said; 'Why do you dwell upon useless topics? When Arius' impious words were read, who says of the Father that He alone hath immortality, you cited a testimony in confirmation of Arius' impiety, quoting from the Apostle, *Who only hath immortality, dwelling in the light which no man can approach unto.* But if you understand it, he has expressed by the Name of God the dignity of the whole Nature, inasmuch as in the Name of God, both Father and Son are signified.'

Palladius said; 'You also have not chosen to answer what I have asked.'

24. AMBROSE, Bishop, said; 'I ask you to give your opinion plainly, has the Son of God immortality according to His divine generation, or has He not?'

Palladius said; 'In respect of His divine generation He is incorruptible; and by means of His Incarnation He died.'

Ambrose, Bishop, said; 'His divinity died not, but His flesh died.'

Palladius said; 'Do you answer me first.'

Ambrose, Bishop, said; 'Has the Son of God immortality in respect of His Godhead or has He it not? But have you not even now betrayed your fraudulent and insidious

COUNCIL meaning according to Arius' profession?' and he added; 'He who denies that the Son of God has immortality, what think you of him?' All the Bishops said; 'Let him be accounted anathema.'

25. PALLADIUS said; 'A divine offspring is immortal.'

Ambrose, Bishop, said; 'This also have you said evasively, to avoid expressing anything clearly about the Son of God. I say to you, the Son hath immortality in respect of His Godhead, or do you deny it and say that He has not.'

Palladius said; 'Did Christ die or not?'

Ambrose, Bishop, said; 'In respect of the flesh He did: our soul does not die: for it is written, *Fear not them who kill the body, but are not able to kill the soul;* seeing then that our soul cannot die, do you think Christ died in respect of His Godhead?'

S. Matt. x. 28.

Palladius said; 'Why do you shrink from the name of death?'

Ambrose, Bishop, said; 'Nay, I do not shrink from it, but I confess it in respect of my flesh: for there is One by Whom I am released from the chains of death.'

Palladius said; 'Death is caused by separation of the spirit (from the flesh), for Christ the Son of God took upon Him flesh, and by means of flesh he died.'

Ambrose, Bishop, said; 'It is written that Christ suffered: He suffered then in respect of His flesh: in respect of His Godhead He has immortality. He who denies this, is a devil.'

Palladius said; 'I know not Arius.'

26. AMBROSE, Bishop, said; 'Then Arius said ill, since the Son of God also has immortality in respect of his Godhead.' And he added, 'Did he then say well or ill?'

Palladius said; 'I do not agree.'

Ambrose, Bishop, said; 'With whom do not you agree? Anathema to him, who does not frankly unfold his faith.'

All the Bishops said; 'Anathema.'

Palladius said; 'Say what you please; His Godhead is immortal.'

Ambrose, Bishop, said; 'Whose? the Father's or the Son's?' And he added: 'Arius heaped together many impieties. But let us pass to other points.'

27. Then was recited; "Alone wise."

Palladius said; 'The Father is wise of himself, but the Son is not wise.'

Ambrose, Bishop said; 'Is then the Son not wise, when He Himself is Wisdom? For we also say that the Son is begotten of the Father.'

Eusebius, Bishop, said; 'Is there anything as impious and profane as this which he said, that the Son of God is not wise?'

Palladius said; 'He is called Wisdom, who can deny that he is Wisdom?'

Ambrose, Bishop said; 'Is He wise or not?'

Palladius said; 'He is Wisdom.'

Ambrose, Bishop, said; 'Then He is wise, if He is Wisdom.'

Palladius said; 'We answer you according to the Scriptures.'

Ambrose, Bishop, said; 'Palladius, as far as I can see, has attempted to deny also that the Son of God is wise.'

Eusebius, Bishop, said; 'He who denies that the Son of God is wise, let him be anathema.'

All the Bishops said; 'Anathema.'

28. EUSEBIUS, Bishop, said; 'Let Secundianus also answer to this.'

Secundianus being silent,

Ambrose, Bishop, said; 'He who is silent wishes to reserve his judgement.' And he added, 'When he says that the Father alone is good, did he confess the Son or deny Him?'

Palladius said; 'We read, *I am the good Shepherd*, and do we deny it? Who would not say that the Son of God is good?' S. John x. 11.

Ambrose, Bishop, said; 'Then is Christ good?'

Palladius said; 'He is good.'

Ambrose, Bishop, said; 'Arius then was wrong in asserting it of the Father alone, since the Son of God also is a good [k] God.'

---

[k] The context requires the reading 'bonus' for 'omnibus,' which is that of one MS. The same MS. also inserts 'Deum' in Eusebius' next speech, which is required by the argument.

Palladius said; 'He who says that Christ is not good, says ill.'

29. EUSEBIUS, Bishop, said; 'Do you confess that Christ is a good God? For I also am good. He has said to me; *Well done, thou good servant;* and, *A good man out of the good treasure of his heart bringeth forth that which is good.*'

Palladius said; 'I have already said, I do not answer you until there is a full Council.'

Ambrose, Bishop, said; 'The Jews said *He is a good man;* and Arius denies that the Son of God is good.'

Palladius said; 'Who can deny it?'

Eusebius, Bishop, said; 'Then the Son of God is a good God.'

Palladius said; 'The good Father begat a good Son.'

30. AMBROSE, Bishop said; 'We also are begotten of Him and are good, but not in respect of Godhead. Do you call the Son of God a good God?'

Palladius said; 'The Son of God is good.'

Ambrose, Bishop, said; 'You see then that you call him a good Christ, a good Son, not a good God; which is what is asked of you.' And he added; 'He who does not confess that the Son of God is a good God, Anathema to him.'

All the Bishops said; 'Anathema.'

31. The reader likewise continued; "Alone mighty."

Ambrose, Bishop, said; 'Is the Son of God mighty or not?'

Palladius said; 'He Who made all things, is He not mighty? He Who made all things, is He deficient in might?'

Ambrose, Bishop, said: 'Then Arius said ill.' And he added; 'Do you even in this condemn Arius?'

Palladius said; 'How do I know who he is? I answer you for myself.'

Ambrose, Bishop, said; 'Is the Son of God the mighty God?'

Palladius said; 'He is mighty.'

Ambrose, Bishop, said; 'Is the Son of God the mighty God?'

Palladius said; 'I have already said that the only-begotten Son of God is mighty.'

Ambrose, Bishop, said; 'The mighty Lord.'

Palladius said; 'The mighty Son of God.'

32. AMBROSE, Bishop, said; 'Men also are mighty; for it is written, *Why boastest thou thyself in mischief, thou mighty man?* and in another place, *When I am weak, then am I strong.* I ask you to confess that Christ the Son of God is the mighty Lord; or if you deny it, support your denial. For I speak of one Power of the Father and of the Son, and I call the Son of God mighty in the same way as the Father. Do you hesitate then to confess that the Son of God is the mighty Lord?'

Palladius said; 'I have already said, we answer you in discussion as we can; for you wish to be sole judges, and at the same time parties to the case. We do not answer you now, but we will answer you in a General and full Council.'

Ambrose, Bishop, said; 'Anathema to him who denies that Christ is the mighty Lord.'

All the Bishops said; 'Anathema.'

33. It was likewise recited; "Alone mighty, Judge of all."

Palladius said; 'the Son of God, the Judge of all. There is Who gives, there is who receives.'

Ambrose, Bishop, said; 'Did He give by grace or nature? Men also have judgement given them.'

Palladius said; 'Do you call the Father greater or not?'

Ambrose, Bishop, said; 'I will answer you afterwards.'

Palladius said; 'I do not answer you, if you do not answer me.'

Eusebius, Bishop, said; 'Unless you condemn in order the impiety of Arius, we will give you no power of asking questions.'

Palladius said; 'I do not answer you.'

Ambrose, Bishop, said; 'Is the Son of God, as has been read, Judge or not?'

Palladius said; 'If you do not answer me, I do not answer you, as being an impious person.'

34. AMBROSE, Bishop said; 'You have my profession, whereby I will answer you. In the mean time, let Arius' letter be read through.' And he added: 'In that letter you will find that sacrilegious argument also which you are endeavouring at.'

Palladius said; 'When I ask, do you not answer?'

COUNCIL   Eusebius, Bishop, said; 'We call the Son of God equal God.'

Palladius said: 'You are Judge: your note-takers are here.'

Ambrose, Bishop, said; 'Let any of yours write, who please.'

35. PALLADIUS said; 'Is the Father greater or not?'

Eusebius, Bishop, said; 'In respect of His Godhead the Son is equal to the Father. You have it in the Gospel that S. John v. 18. the Jews persecuted Him *because He not only broke the sabbath, but also called God His Father, making Himself equal with God*, what then impious men confessed while they persecuted, we who believe cannot deny.'

Ambrose, Bishop, said; 'And in another place you have:
Phil. ii. 6—8. *Who being in the form of God thought it not robbery to be equal with God, but emptied himself*[1] *and took upon him the form of a servant, and was made in the likeness of men;* ¹ made Himself of no reputation E.T. *and became obedient unto death*. You see that in the form of God He is equal to God. And *he took*, S. Paul says, *the form of a servant*. In what then is He less? In respect surely of His form of a servant, not of the form of God?'

Eusebius, Bishop, said; 'Just as, being established in the form of a servant, He was not less than a servant; so being established in the form of God, He could not be less than God.'

36. AMBROSE, Bishop, said; 'Or say that in respect of Godhead the Son of God is less.'

Palladius said; 'The Father is greater.'

Ambrose, Bishop, said; 'In respect of the flesh.'

S. John xiv. 28.   Palladius said; '*He who sent me, is greater than I*. Was the flesh sent by God or was the Son of God sent?'

Ambrose, Bishop, said; 'We prove this day that the holy Scriptures are falsely cited by you, for thus it is writ-
Ib. 27, 28. ten: *Peace I leave unto you, my peace I give unto you: not as the world giveth, give I unto you. Let not your heart be troubled, neither let it be afraid: If ye loved me, ye would rejoice, because I said, I go unto the Father, for my Father is greater than I.* He did not say, He Who sent me is greater than I.'

Palladius said; 'The Father is greater.'

Ambrose, Bishop, said; 'Anathema to him, who adds to or takes from the holy Scriptures.'

All the Bishops said; 'Anathema.'

37. PALLADIUS said; 'The Father is greater than the Son.'

Ambrose, Bishop, said; 'In respect of the flesh the Son is less than the Father: in respect of Godhead He is equal to the Father: I read therefore that the Son of God is equal to the Father, as also the instances that have been adduced testify. But why should you wonder that He is less in respect of the flesh, when He has called Himself a servant, a stone, a worm, when He has said that He is less than the angels, for it is written: *Thou madest him a little lower than the angels.*' Heb. ii. 7.

Palladius said; 'I see that you make impious assertions. We do not answer you without arbiters.'

Sabinus, Bishop, said; 'Let no one ask for an opinion from him who has blasphemed in such countless opinions.'

Palladius said; 'We do not answer you.'

38. SABINUS Bishop, said; 'Palladius has now been condemned by all. The blasphemies of Arius are much lighter than those of Palladius.'

And when Palladius rose, as if he wished to go out, he said; 'Palladius has risen, because he sees that he is to be convicted by manifest testimonies of the Scriptures, as indeed he has been already convicted: for thus it has been read, that in respect of Godhead the Son is equal to the Father. Let him admit that in respect of His Godhead the Son of God has no greater: it is written: *When God made promise to Abraham, because He could swear by no greater, he swear by himself.* You see therefore the Scripture, that He could swear by no greater. But it is the Son of Whom this is said, since it was He Who appeared to Abraham, whence also He says, *He saw my day and was glad.*' Ib. vi. 13.

S. John viii. 56.

Palladius said; 'The Father is greater.'

Eusebius, Bishop, said; 'When He spake as God, He had no greater; when He spake as man, He had one greater.'

39. PALLADIUS said; 'The Father begat the Son; the Father sent the Son.'

Ambrose, Bishop, said; 'Anathema to him, who denies

council that in respect of His Godhead the Son is equal to the Father.'

All the Bishops said; 'Anathema.'

Palladius said; 'The Son is subject to the Father; the Son keeps the commands of the Father.'

Ambrose, Bishop, said; 'He is subject in respect of His Incarnation. But even you yourself remember that you have read; *No man can come unto me, except the Father draw him.*'

<small>S. John vi 44.</small>

Sabinus, Bishop, said; 'Let him say whether the Son is subject to the Father in respect of His Godhead, or in respect of His Incarnation.'

40. Palladius said; 'Then the Father is greater.'

Ambrose, Bishop, said; 'In another place also it is written; *God is faithful, by Whom ye were called unto the fellowship of His Son.* I say that the Father is greater in respect of the assumption of the flesh, which the Son of God took upon Him, not in respect of the Son's Godhead.

<small>1 Cor. i. 8.</small>

Palladius said; 'What then is the comparison of the Son of God? And can flesh say, God is greater than I? Did the flesh speak or the Godhead because the flesh was there?'

Ambrose, Bishop, said; 'The flesh does not speak without the soul.'

Eusebius, Bishop, said; 'God in the flesh spoke according to the flesh, when He said, *Why do ye persecute² me, a man?* Who said this?'

<small>S John viii. 40. ² But now ye seek to kill me, a man &c. E.V.</small>

Palladius said; 'The Son of God.'

Ambrose, Bishop, said; 'Then the Son of God is God in respect of His Godhead and is man in respect of His flesh.'

Palladius said; 'He took flesh upon Him.'

Eusebius, Bishop, said; 'Accordingly He made use of human words.'

Palladius said; 'He took man's flesh upon Him.'

41. Ambrose, Bishop, said; 'Let him say that the Apostle did not call Him subject in respect of His Godhead, but in respect of His flesh; for it is written, *He humbled himself and became obedient unto death.* In what then did He taste death?'

Palladius said; 'In that He humbled Himself.'

Ambrose, Bishop, said; 'Not His Godhead but His flesh

was humbled and subject.' And he added; 'Did Arius well or ill in calling him a perfect creature?'

Palladius said; 'I do not answer you, for you have no authority.'

Ambrose, Bishop, said; 'Profess what you please.'

Palladius said; 'I do not answer you.'

42. SABINUS, Bishop, said; 'Do you not answer on behalf of Arius? do you not answer to what has been asked?'

Palladius said; 'I have not answered on behalf of Arius.'

Sabinus, Bishop, said; 'You have answered so far as to deny that the Son of God is mighty, to deny that He is true God.'

Palladius said; 'I do not allow you to be my judge, whom I convict of impiety.'

Sabinus, Bishop, said; 'You yourself forced us to sit.'

Palladius said; 'I gave in a request that you might sit, in order that I might convict you. Why have you practised upon the Emperor? You have gained by intrigue that the Council should not be a plenary one.'

Ambrose, Bishop, said; 'When Arius' impieties were read, your impiety also, which harmonized with his, was condemned equally. You have thought fit while the letter was in the midst of being read, to bring forward whatever passages you would: you were told in answer in what way the Son has said that the Father is greater, because in respect of His taking flesh upon Him, the Father is greater than He. You have urged also that the Son of God is subject; and on this head you were answered that the Son of God is subject in respect of His flesh, not in respect of His divinity. You have our profession. Now hear the rest. Since you have been answered, do you answer to what is read.'

43. PALLADIUS said; 'I do not answer you, because what I have said has not been recorded; only your words are recorded. I do not answer you.'

Ambrose, Bishop, said; 'You see that every thing is recorded. Moreover, what has been written is abundant for the proof of your impiety.' And he added; 'Do you say that Christ is a creature or do you deny it?'

Palladius said; 'I do not answer you.'

COUNCIL   Ambrose, Bishop, said; 'An hour ago, when it was read that Arius called Christ a creature, you denied it: you had an opportunity offered you of condemning his perfidy; you would not. Say now at last whether Christ was begotten of the Father or created.'

Palladius said; 'If you please, let my reporters come and so let the whole be taken down.'

Sabinus, Bishop, said; 'Let him send for his reporters.'

Palladius said; 'We will answer you in a full Council.'

44. AMBROSE, Bishop, said; 'Attalus subscribed the formula[1] of the Council of Nicæa. Let him deny it, as he has come to our Council. Let him say to-day, whether he subscribed the formula of the Council of Nicæa or no?'

Attalus remaining silent,

Ambrose, Bishop, said; 'Though the presbyter Attalus is an Arian, yet we give him permission to speak: let him frankly state whether he subscribed the formula of the Council of Nicæa under his Bishop Agrippinus, or no.'

Attalus said; 'You have already said that I have been several times condemned. I do not answer you.'

Ambrose, Bishop, said; 'Did you subscribe the formula of the Council of Nicæa or no?'

Attalus said; 'I do not answer you.'

45. PALLADIUS said; 'Do you now wish the formula to be regarded as general or no?'

Chromatius, presbyter, said; 'You have not denied that He is a creature, you have denied that He is mighty. You have denied every thing which the Catholic Faith professes.'

Sabinus, Bishop, said; 'We are witnesses that Attalus subscribed the Council of Nicæa, and that he now refuses to answer. What is the opinion of all?'

As Attalus did not speak,

Ambrose, Bishop, said; 'Let him say whether he subscribed the formula of the Council of Nicæa or no.'

46. PALLADIUS said; 'Let your reporter and ours stand forward and write down every thing.'

---

[1] By 'tractatus concilii Nicæni' is meant simply the Nicene Creed. This is established by S. Ambr. De Fide iii. 15. 125 (518 Ed. Ben.) where, speaking of the letter of Eusebius of Nicomedia read at the Council, in reference to the word ὁμοούσιος, he says, Hæc cum lecta esset epistola in Concilio Nicæno, hoc verbum *in tractatu fidei* posuerunt Patres, etc.

Valerian, Bishop, said; 'What you have said and what you have denied is already all written.'

Palladius said; 'Say what you please.'

Ambrose, Bishop, said; 'Since Palladius who has been already many times condemned, wishes to be condemned still oftener, I am reading the letter of Arius which he has not chosen to condemn: do you state whether you approve of my doing so.'

All the Bishops said; 'Let it be read.'

Then the words were read. "But begotten not putatively," &c.

Ambrose, Bishop, said; 'I have answered you on the Father's being greater: I have answered you also on the Son's being subject: do you yourself answer now.'

47. PALLADIUS said; 'I will not answer unless arbiters come after the Lord's day.'

Ambrose, Bishop, said; 'You were come with a view to discussion, but since I have charged you with its doctrines, you have seen the letter of Arius which you have not chosen to condemn and which you cannot support: you now therefore shrink back and cavil. I read it to you fully point by point. Tell me whether you believe Christ to have been created; whether there was a time when he was not; or whether the only begotten Son of God has always existed. When you have heard Arius' letter, either condemn it or approve of it.'

48. PALLADIUS said; 'Since I convict you of impiety, I will not have you for judge. You are a transgressor.'

Sabinus, Bishop, said; 'Say, what impieties you object to our brother and fellow-bishop Ambrose.'

Palladius said; 'I have already told you, I will answer in a full Council, and with arbiters present.'

Ambrose, Bishop, said; 'I desire to be confuted and convicted in the assembly of my brethren. Say then what I have said impiously; but I appear impious to you because I support piety.'

Sabinus, Bishop, said; 'Does then he seem impious to you, who censures the blasphemies of Arius?'

49. PALLADIUS said; 'I have not denied that the Son of God is good.'

Ambrose, Bishop, said; 'Do you say that Christ is a good God?'

Palladius said; 'I do not answer you.'

Valerian, Bishop, said; 'Do not press Palladius so much: he cannot confess our truths with simplicity. For his conscience is confused with a twofold blasphemy: he was ordained by the Photinians and was condemned with them, and now he shall be condemned more fully.'

Palladius said; 'Prove it.'

Sabinus, Bishop, said; 'He would not have denied that Christ is true if he were not following his own teachers.'

50. AMBROSE, Bishop, said; 'You have objected to me that I am impious: prove it.'

Palladius said; 'We will bring forward our statement, and when we have brought it, then the discussion shall be held.'

Ambrose, Bishop, said; 'Condemn the impiety of Arius.'

Palladius being silent,

Eusebius, Bishop, said; 'He dwells upon useless subjects. There are so many impieties of Arius, which Palladius has not chosen to condemn, nay rather has confessed by supporting. He who does not condemn Arius is like him, and is rightly to be called a heretic.'

All the Bishops said; 'On the part of us all let Palladius be anathema.'

51. AMBROSE, Bishop, said; 'Do you consent, Palladius, that the other statements of Arius be read?'

Palladius said; 'Give us arbiters: let reporters come on both sides. You cannot be judges unless we have arbitrators and unless persons come on both sides to arbitrate, we do not answer you.'

Ambrose, Bishop, said; 'What arbitrators do you wish for?'

Palladius said; 'There are here many men of high rank.'

Sabinus, Bishop, said; 'After such a number of blasphemies do you wish for arbitrators?'

Ambrose, Bishop, said; 'Bishops ought to judge of laymen: not laymen of Bishops. But tell me what judges you wish for.'

Palladius said; 'Let arbitrators attend.'

Chromatius, the Presbyter, said; 'Without prejudice to condemnation by the Bishops, let those also who are of Palladius' party be heard at full length.'

52. PALLADIUS said; 'They are not allowed to speak. Let arbitrators attend and reporters on both sides, and then they will answer you in a General Council.'

Ambrose, Bishop, said; 'Though he has been convicted of many impieties, yet we should blush that a person who claims the priesthood for himself should seem to have been condemned by laymen, and on this very ground and in this very point he deserves condemnation because he looks to the sentence of laymen, when priests ought rather to be the judges of laymen. Looking to what we have this day heard Palladius professing and to what he has refused to condemn, I pronounce him unworthy of the priesthood, and I judge that he should be deprived [m] thereof in order that a Catholic may be ordained in his place.'

All the Bishops said; 'Anathema to Palladius.'

53. AMBROSE, Bishop, said; 'The most gracious and Christian Emperor has committed the cause to the judgement of the Bishops and has constituted them arbitrators of the dispute [n]. Since therefore the decision appears to have been made over to us, so that we are the interpreters of the Scriptures, let us condemn Palladius, who has not chosen to condemn the sentiments of the impious Arius, and because he has himself denied the Son of God to be everlasting, and made the other statements which appear in our proceedings. Let him therefore be accounted Anathema.'

All the Bishops said; 'We all condemn him; let him be accounted anathema.'

54. AMBROSE, Bishop, said; 'Since all who are met here

---

[m] The reading in Ed. Ben. is 'carendum.' If it is genuine, the word must have acquired a sort of transitive sense and have come to mean 'to be deprived.' No traces of such an use is to be found in Facciolati or in Ducange. Ed. Ben. quotes a parallel use of 'abstinendus' but without any instances. Rom. reads 'privandum,' Chifflet 'curandum,' either of which give the required sense, but seem corrections without MS. authority.

[n] The text in this passage is defective and confused: but the general sense, as given here, may fairly be made out of it as it stands.

are Christian men, brethren approved of God, and our fellow-bishops, let each individual say, what he thinks.'

Valerian, Bishop, said; 'My sentence is that he who defends Arius is an Arian; that he who does not condemn his blasphemies is himself a blasphemer; and therefore I judge that such a man is alien from the fellowship of Bishops.'

Palladius said; 'You have begun to play; play on. Without an Eastern Council we answer you not.'

55. ANEMIUS, Bishop of Sirmium said; 'Whoever does not condemn the heresies of Arius must of necessity be an Arian. Him therefore I judge to be alien from our communion, and to be without place in the assembly of Bishops.'

Constantius, Bishop of Orange, said; 'As Palladius is a disciple of Arius, whose impieties have been long since condemned by our Fathers in the Council of Nice, but have this day severally, when recited, been approved of by Palladius, inasmuch as he was not disturbed at his acknowledging that the Son of God was not of the same Nature with God the Father, and at his calling Him a creature, and saying that He began to be in time, and denying Him to be true Lord, on these grounds, I judge that he should be condemned for ever.'

56. JUSTUS, Bishop, said; 'Palladius who has refused to condemn the blasphemies of Arius, and who seems rather to acknowledge them, can in my judgement no longer be called a Priest or be reckoned among Bishops.'

Eventius, Bishop of Ticinum, said; 'I think that Palladius who has refused to condemn the impieties of Arius, is removed for ever from the fellowship of Bishops.'

57. ABUNDANTIUS, Bishop of Trent, said; 'Since Palladius maintains evident blasphemies, let him know that he is condemned by the Council of Aquileia.'

Eusebius, Bishop of Bologna, said; 'Inasmuch as Palladius has not only refused to condemn the impieties of Arius, impieties written with the pen of the devil, and which it is not lawful so much as to listen to, but has also appeared as the maintainer of them by denying that the Son of God is true Lord, is good Lord, is wise Lord, is everlasting Lord; both by my sentence, and by the judgement of all Catholics I think that he is rightly condemned and excluded from the assembly of Bishops.'

58. SABINUS, Bishop of Placentia, said; 'Since it has been proved to all that Palladius supports the Arian perfidy and maintains its impiety that was counter to the Evangelical and apostolical institutions, a just sentence of the whole Council has been passed upon him, and humble individual as I am, let him by my judgement be deprived once more of the priesthood and banished justly from this most holy assembly.'

Felix and Numidius, deputies of Africa said; 'Anathema to the Sect of the Arian heresy to which by the Synod of Aquileia Palladius is pronounced to belong. But we condemn also those, who contradict the truth of the Nicene Synod.'

59. LIMENIUS, Bishop of Vercellæ, said; 'It is manifest that the Arian doctrine has been often condemned: and therefore, inasmuch as Palladius having been appealed to in this holy Synod of Aquileia has refused to correct and amend himself, and has rather proved himself worthy of blame and defiled himself with the perfidy which he has publicly professed himself to hold, I too by my judgement declare that he is to be deprived of the fellowship of the Bishops.'

Maximus, Bishop of Emona, said; 'That Palladius, who would not condemn, but has rather himself acknowledged, the blasphemies of Arius, is justly and deservedly condemned God knows, and the conscience of the faithful has condemned him.'

60. EXUPERANTIUS, Bishop of Dertona, said; 'As the rest of my Colleagues have condemned Palladius who has refused to condemn the sect and doctrine of Arius, and on the contrary has defended them, I also likewise condemn him.'

Bassianus, Bishop of Lodi, said; 'I have heard along with the rest of my Colleagues the impieties of Arius, which Palladius not only has not condemned but has confirmed. Let him be anathema and be deprived of the priesthood.'

61. PHILASTER, Bishop of Brescia, said; 'The blasphemies and iniquity of Palladius, who follows and defends the Arian doctrine I in company with all have condemned.'

56 *and sentence him to be deprived of his orders.*

COUNCIL Constantius, Bishop of Sciscia, said; 'As the rest of my brother Bishops, I also think that Palladius is to be condemned, who has refused to condemn the blasphemies and impieties of Arius.'

Heliodorus, Bishop of Altinum, said; 'The man who maintains the perfidy of Arius, and of all the heretics with whom Palladius is partner, whose heart is foolish, and who has not confessed the truth, together with the rest of my brother Bishops I condemn.'

62. FELIX, Bishop of Jadera, said; 'I also in like manner unite with all in condemning Palladius, who speaks blasphemies against the Son of God as Arius did.'

Theodorus, Bishop of Octodorum, said; 'We judge Palladius, who has denied Christ to be true God, co-eternal with the Father, to be in no wise either a Christian or a priest.'

Domninus, Bishop of Grenoble, said; 'As Palladius adheres to the perfidy of Arius, I also judge that he is to be condemned for ever, as my brethren also have condemned him.'

63. PROCULUS, Bishop of Marseilles, said; 'Palladius, who by a kind of impious succession to the blasphemies of Arius has defended them in that he does not condemn them, as he has been already designated a blasphemer by the sentence of many venerable Bishops, and pronounced alien from the priesthood, so by my sentence also is marked out in the same manner as condemned for ever.'

Diogenes, Bishop of Genoa, said; 'Palladius who while he does not confess has even denied Christ to be true Lord and God, like and equal to the Father, I together with the rest of my brethren and fellow Bishops adjudge to have the lot of condemnation.'

64. AMANTIUS, Bishop of Nice, said; 'Palladius, who has refused to pull down the sect of Arius, according to the judgement of my brother Bishops, I also condemn.'

Januarius, Bishop, said; 'As all my brother Bishops have condemned Palladius so also do I think that he ought to be condemned by a similar judgement º.'

º It is to be noticed that the sentence of only twenty-five Bishops are here given out of thirty two or thirty three. It is probable therefore that the Record is defective, and that the sentences of the rest have been lost.

65. SECUNDIANUS having withdrawn for a while, and then returned to the Council P,

Ambrose, Bishop, said.; 'You have heard, Secundianus, what sort of sentence the impious Palladius has received, having been condemned by the Council of Bishops: and though we have been displeased that you have not shrunk from his madness, I nevertheless make some special enquiries of you. Do you say that our Lord Jesus Christ, the Son of God, is or is not very God?'

Secundianus said; 'He who denies the Father of our Lord and God Jesus Christ to be true God is not a Christian, nor is he who denies that the Lord is the very Son of God.'

Ambrose, Bishop, said; 'Do you confess that the Son of God is very God?'

Secundianus said; 'I say that He is the very Son of God, the very only begotten Son of God.'

66. AMBROSE, Bishop, said; 'Do you call Him very Lord?'

Secundianus said; 'I call Him the very only-begotten Son of God. Who denies that He is the very Son of God?'

Eusebius, Bishop, said; It is not enough that you confess Him to be the only-begotten Son of God, for all confess this. But what influences us is that Arius said that the Father alone is Lord, alone is true, and denied that the Son of God is very Lord. Do you confess simply that the Son of God is very God?'

Secundianus said; 'Who Arius was, I know not; what he said, I know not. You speak with me, living man with living man. I say what Christ said: *The only begotten Son Which is in the bosom of the Father.* Therefore He asserts Himself to be the only-begotten Son of the Father: the only-begotten Son is then the very Son of God.' S. John i. 18.

67. AMBROSE, Bishop, said; 'Is the very Son of God also very God? It is written in the divine books: *he that sweareth on the earth, shall swear by the true God,* and that this applies to Christ there is no doubt. We there- Isa. lxv. 16.

P Ed. Ben here reads, Et cum Secundianus subripuisset. As subripuisset by itself could have no sense, the reading of Ed. Rom has been adopted, Et cum Secundianus se paullulum subripuisset et postea convenisset. This is adopted in Tillemont's narrative, Il sortit mesme de l'assemblée, mais il revint quelque temps après.

fore profess the true God, and this is our faith and profession, that the only-begotten Son of the Father is very God. Do you then say 'of very God,' and then that the Son is very God.'

Secundianus said; 'Of very God.'

68. AMBROSE, Bishop, said; 'Is the Son of God very God?'

Secundianus said; 'Then would he be a liar.'

Ambrose, Bishop, said; 'In this you practise an evasion to avoid saying very God, but instead thereof, God, very only-begotten, and therefore say simply, The only-begotten Son of God is very God.'

Secundianus said; 'I called Him the only-begotten Son of God.'

69. EUSEBIUS, Bishop, said; 'This Photinus does not deny, this Sabellus confesses.'

Ambrose, Bishop, said; 'And he who does not confess this is justly condemned, and on this point I appeal to you many times though by cavilling you have denied the truth. I do not ask you to call Him merely the very only-begotten Son of God, but to call Him also very God.'

Secundianus said; 'I profess myself the servant of truth. What I say is not taken down and what you say is taken down. I say that Christ is the true Son of God. Who denies that He is the true Son of God?'

70. AMBROSE, Bishop, said; 'He who denies that the only-begotten Son of God is very God, let him be anathema.'

Secundianus said; 'The only-begotten Son of God, very God! why do you state to me what is not written?'

Ambrose, Bishop, said: 'It is plain sacrilege, that Arius denied Christ the Son of God to be very God.'

Secundianus said; 'Forasmuch as Christ is called the Son of God, I call the Son of God very Son [q]; but that He is very God is not written.'

71. AMBROSE, Bishop, said; 'Have you not yet recovered your senses?' And he added; 'Lest it should appear that he has been unfairly treated, let him state his opinion. Let him then say that Christ the only-begotten Son of God is very God.'

[q] This is according to the text of Ed. Rom.

Secundianus said; 'I have already said. What more would you wring from me?' OF AQUILEIA

Ambrose, Bishop, said; 'What have you said? certainly if you had said so great truths, what is said gloriously, may well be often repeated.'

Secundianus said; 'It is written, *Let your conversation be yea, yea, nay, nay.*' S. Matt. v. 37.

72. AMBROSE, Bishop, said; 'He who says that the Father Himself is the Son, is sacrilegious. This I ask of you that you would say that the Son of God is begotten very God of very God.'

Secundianus said; 'I say that the Son is begotten of God, as He says Himself *I have begotten Thee,* and that He confesses Himself to be begotten.' Heb. i. 5.

73. AMBROSE, Bishop, said; 'Is He very God of very God?'

Secundianus said; 'When you add to the Name and call Him very [God], do you understand what the character of your own faith is, and are you a Christian?'

Eusebius, Bishop, said; 'Who has denied that He is very God? Arius and Palladius have denied it. If you believe Him to be very God, you should simply express it.'

74. AMBROSE, Bishop, said; 'If you will not say that He is very God begotten of very God, you have denied Christ.'

Secundianus said; 'When asked about the Son, I answered you: I have answered as to the manner in which I ought to make my profession. We have your statement: we will bring it forward; let it be read.'

Ambrose, Bishop, said; 'You should have brought it forward to-day, but you are attempting a subterfuge. You demand a profession of me and I demand a profession of you. Is the Son of God very God?'

Secundianus said; 'The Son of God is God only-begotten. I also ask him: Is He only-begotten?'

75. AMBROSE, Bishop, said; 'Let reason move us: let us be moved too by your impiety and folly. When you speak of God very only-begotten, you do not apply the 'very' to 'God,' but to 'only-begotten.' And therefore

COUNCIL to remove this question answer me this: Is He very God of very God?'

Secundianus said; 'Did then God not beget God? He Who is very God begat What He is; He begat one true only-begotten Son.'

Ambrose, Bishop, said; 'You do not confess Him very God but you would call Him very only-begotten. I too call Him only-begotten, but also very God.'

Secundianus said; 'I say that he was begotten of the Father, I say to all that he was very begotten [r].'

The Names of the Bishops and Presbyters who were present at the Council.

VALERIAN, Bishop of Aquileia [s].
AMBROSE, Bishop of Milan.
EUSEBIUS, Bishop of Bologna.
LIMENIUS, Bishop of Vercellæ.
ANEMIUS, Bishop of Sirmium in Illyricum.
SABINUS, Bishop of Placentia.
ABUNDANTIUS, Bishop of Brescia.
CONSTANTIUS, Bishop of Orange, Deputy of the Gauls.
THEODORUS, Bishop of Octodurus.
DOMNINUS, Bishop of Grenoble.
AMANTIUS, Bishop of Nice.
MAXIMUS, Bishop of Emona.
BASSIANUS, Bishop of Lodi.
PROCULUS, Bishop of Marseilles, Deputy of the Gauls.
HELIODORUS, Bishop of Altinum.
FELIX, Bishop of Jadera.
EVENTIUS, Bishop of Ticinum [t].

[r] The abrupt termination of the discussion with Secundianus, without any account of a decision in his case, seems to point to the same conclusion as the incomplete list of Bishops who give sentence on Palladius, that the Record is defective. Moreover the unusual number of various readings is generally a sign of a defective text. The force and cleverness of the evasions of Secundianus seem sometimes to be lost thereby.

[s] With regard to the names of the sees, those of which the modern name is as familiar or more familiar than the ancient have been rendered by the modern name, those of which the modern name would be unfamiliar to general readers have been left in their ancient form. It would be affectation to call S. Ambrose Bishop of Mediolanum: on the other hand nothing would be gained by calling Felix Bishop of Jadera, Bishop of Zara.

[t] This name is omitted in the list at the beginning, so that there are thirty three in this list, only thirty two in the other. The two presbyters were probably representatives of Bishops, but it is not stated of whom.

EXSUPERANTIUS, Bishop of Dertona.
DIOGENES, Bishop of Genoa.
CONSTANTIUS, Bishop of Sciscia.
JUSTUS, Bishop of Lyons, also Deputy of the Gauls.
FELIX, Deputy of Africa.
NUMIDIUS, Deputy of Africa.
EVAGRIUS, Presbyter and Deputy.
ARTEMIUS, ALMACHIUS, JANUARIUS, JOVINUS, MACEDONIUS, CASSIANUS, MARCELLUS, EUSTATHIUS, MAXIMUS, CHROMATIUS a Presbyter.

LETTER IX.

A.D.381.

A FORMAL letter from the Italian Bishops assembled at Aquileia, thanking the Bishops of the three Provinces for the presence of their deputies, and announcing officially the condemnation of Palladius and Secundianus.

THE COUNCIL WHICH IS ASSEMBLED AT AQUILEIA TO OUR MOST BELOVED BRETHREN, THE BISHOPS OF THE VIENNESE AND THE FIRST AND SECOND NARBONESE PROVINCES [a] IN GAUL.

1. WE return thanks to your holy unanimity that in the persons of our Lords and brethren Constantius and Proculus you have given us the presence of you all, and at the same time following the directions of former times, have added not a little weight to our judgement, with which the profession of your holinesses also is in agreement, Lords and brethren most beloved. Therefore, as we received with gladness the above mentioned holy men of your order and ours, so do we also dismiss them with an abundant offering of thanks.

2. But how necessary the meeting was will be plain from the mere facts, since the adversaries and enemies of God, the defenders of the Arian sect and heresy, Palladius and

[a] It is probable that similar letters were addressed to the Bishops of the other Provinces of Gaul, who had sent Justus as their deputy, and to Africa and Illyricum, though no record of them remains. Possibly they were identical, except the address. Gaul had at this time been so subdivided, that the Vicariate or civil Diocese consisted of no less than seventeen provinces. See Marquardt's Table, as quoted above.

Lett. 10. Secundianus, the only two who dared to come to the meeting of the Council, received in person their due sentence, being convicted of impiety. Farewell. May our Almighty God keep you safe and prosperous, Lords and brethren most beloved. Amen.

A.D. 381.

LETTER X.

IN this letter, addressed formally to the three Emperors, but really to Gratian, the Council offer their thanks for the summoning of the Council, and announce its results, requesting that they may be enforced by the imperial authority. They also request the removal of Julius Valens from Italy, and that the Photinians may be forbidden to hold assemblies, which they were doing at Sirmium.

THE HOLY COUNCIL WHICH IS ASSEMBLED AT AQUILEIA TO THE MOST GRACIOUS AND CHRISTIAN EMPERORS, AND MOST BLESSED PRINCES, GRATIAN, VALENTINIAN, AND THEODOSIUS.

1. BLESSED be God the Father of our Lord Jesus Christ, Who has given you the Roman empire, and blessed be our Lord Jesus Christ, the only-begotten Son of God, Who guards your reign with His loving-kindness, before Whom we return you thanks, most gracious Princes, that you have both proved the earnestness of your own faith in that you were zealous to assemble the Council of Bishops for the removal of disputes, and that in your condescension you reserved for the Bishops the honourable privilege that no one should be absent who wished to attend, and none should be constrained to attend against his will.

2. Therefore according to the directions of your Graces we have met together without the odium of large numbers and with zeal for discussion, nor were any of the Bishops found to be heretics, except Palladius and Secundianus, names of ancient perfidy, on whose account people from the farthest portions of the Roman world demanded that a Council should be summoned. None however, loaded with the years of a long life, whose gray hairs alone would be entitled to reverence, was compelled to come from the

most distant recesses of the Ocean: and yet nothing was lacking to the Council: no one dragging a feeble frame, weighed down by his campaigns of fasting, was forced by the hardships of his journey to lament the inconvenience of his loss of strength; no one finally, being without the means of coming, had to mourn over a poverty honourable to a Bishop. So that what the divine Scripture has praised was fulfilled in you, most merciful of Princes, Gratian, *Blessed is he that considereth the poor and needy.* TO THE EMPERORS
Ps. xli. 1.
C.P.T.

3. But what a hardship would it have been that on account of two Bishops only, who are rotten in perfidy, the Churches over the whole world should be left destitute of their Bishops. But though owing to the distance of the journey they could not come personally, nearly all from all the western provinces were present by the sending of deputies, and proved by manifest attestations that they hold what we assert and that they agree in the formula of the Council of Nicæa, as the documents hereto attached declare. Therefore the prayers of the nations are now in concert every where on behalf of your Empire, and yet assertors of the Faith have not been wanting to your decision. For though the directions of our predecessors, from which it is impious and sacrilegious to deviate, were plain enough, still we gave them the opportunity of discussion.

4. And in the first instance we examined the very beginning of the question which had arisen, and we thought fit to hear recited the letter of Arius, who is found to be the author of the Arian heresy, from whom also the heresy received its name, the arrangement being thus far even favourable to them, that since they had been in the habit of denying that they were Arians they might either by censure condemn the blasphemies of Arius, or by argument maintain them, or at least not refuse the name of the person, whose impiety and perfidy they followed. But inasmuch as they could not condemn and were unwilling to support their Founder, after they had themselves, three days before, challenged us to a discussion, fixing place and time, and gone forth to it without waiting to be summoned, on a sudden the very individuals, who had said that they would easily prove that they were Christians, (which we

heard with pleasure, and hoped that they would prove,) began to shrink from the engagement on the spot and to decline the discussion.

5. Yet had we much discourse with them: the divine Scriptures were set forth in the midst; and they had the offer made to them of a patient discussion from sun-rise to the seventh hour of the day. And would that they had said little, or that we could cancel what we heard. For when Arius by saying in sacrilegious words that the Father was alone eternal, alone good, alone true God, alone possessing immortality, alone wise and alone powerful, had intended that the Son by an impious inference should be understood to be without these attributes, these men have preferred following Arius to confessing that the Son of God is everlasting God and very God, and good God and wise and powerful and possessing immortality. We spent several hours to no purpose. Their impiety waxed greater and could in no wise be corrected.

6. At last when they saw that they were pressed by the sacrileges of Arius' letter, (which we have appended in order that even your Graces might shrink from it) they started away in the middle of the reading of the letter, and asked us to answer what they proposed. Though it lay not within either order or reason that we should interrupt the plan laid down, and though we had already answered that they were to condemn the impieties of Arius and then we would answer about whatever proposals of theirs they pleased, preserving order and plan, we notwithstanding acceded to their unreasonable wish: on which, falsifying the scriptures of the Gospel, they stated to us that our Lord said, *He that sent Me is greater than I:* whereas the course of the Scriptures teaches us that it is written otherwise.

7. They were convicted of the falsehood even to confession: they were not however corrected by reason. For when we said that the Son is called less than the Father in respect to his taking flesh upon Him, but is proved according to the testimonies of the Scriptures to be like and equal to the Father in respect of His Godhead, and that there could not be degrees of any distinction or greatness,

when there was unity of power; they not only would not correct their error; but began to carry their madness further, so as even to say that the Son is subject in respect of His divinity, as if there could be any subjection of God in respect of His Divinity and Majesty. In short they refer His death not to the mystery of our salvation, but to some infirmity of His Godhead.

TO THE EMPERORS

8. We shudder, most gracious Princes, at such dire sacrileges, and such wicked teachers, and that they might not any longer deceive the people of whom they had a hold, we judged that they should be degraded from the Priesthood, since they agreed with the impieties of the book put before them. For it is not reasonable that they should claim to themselves the Priesthood of Him Whom they have denied. We appeal to your faith and your glory that you would shew the respect of your government to Him Who is the author of it, and judge that the assertors of impiety and debauchers of the truth be kept away from the threshold of the Church, by an order of your Graces issued to the competent authorities, and that Holy Bishops be put into the place of the condemned ones by deputies of our humble appointment.

9. The Presbyter Attalus [b] too who avows his error and adheres to the sacrilegious doctrines of Palladius is included under a similar sentence. For why should we speak of his master Julianus Valens [c]? who although he was close at hand shunned coming to the Council of Bishops for fear he should be compelled to account to the Bishops for the ruin of his country, and his treason to his countrymen: a man, who, polluted with the impiety of the Goths, presumed, as is asserted, to go forth in the sight of a Roman army, wearing like a Pagan a collar and bracelet: which is unquestionably a sacrilege not only in a Bishop, but also

---

[b] There is no mention of the condemnation of Attalus in the Records, another proof that they are not complete.

[c] Julianus Valens was Bishop of Petavio or Pettau on the Drave, into which See he had apparently been introduced in the place of the orthodox Bishop Marcus. for this is, according to Tillemont, the meaning of the word 'superpositus' When Pannonia and Illyricum were overrun by the Goths after Valens' defeat at Hadrianople, (378 A.D.) he deserted his charge. The ravages of the Barbarians are described by S Jerome ad cap i. Zephan vol iii. p. 1645. See Gibbon ch. 26. (from a note in Newman's Fleury, vol. 1 p 38.)

LETT. 10. in any Christian whatever: for it is alien to the Roman customs. It may be that the idolatrous priests of the Goths commonly go forth in such guise.

10. Let your piety be moved by the title of Bishop, which that sacrilegious person dishonours, convicted as he is of atrocious crime even by the voice of his own people, if indeed any of his own people can still survive. Let him at least return to his own home, and cease to contaminate the most flourishing cities of Italy; at present by unlawful ordinations he is associating with himself persons like himself, and he endeavours by help of all abandoned individuals to leave behind him a seed-plot of his own impiety and perfidy: whereas he has not so much as begun to be a Bishop. For, to begin with, at Petavio he was put in the place of the holy Marcus, a Bishop whose memory is highly esteemed: but, having been disgracefully degraded by the people, unable to remain at Petavio, he has been riding in state at Milan, after the overthrow, say rather the betrayal, of his country.

11. Deign then, most pious princes, to deal with all these matters, lest we should appear to have met to no purpose, when we obeyed your Graces' injunctions: for care must be taken that not only our decisions but yours also be saved from dishonour. We must request therefore that your Graces would be pleased to listen indulgently to the deputies of the Council, Holy men, and bid them to return speedily with accomplishment of what we ask for, that you may receive a reward from Christ our Lord and God, Whose Church you have cleansed from all stain of sacrilegious persons.

12. With respect to the Photinians also, whom by a former law you forbad forming assemblies, revoking at the same time the law which had been passed for the assembling of a Council of Bishops [d], we request of your Graces, that as we have ascertained that they are attempting to hold assemblies in the town of Sirmium, you would by now again interdicting their meetings, cause respect to be paid,

---

[d] The reading here is uncertain. Ed. Rom. has 'prout jam et sacerdotum concilio sententia in eos lata est' Nor is it certain to what laws allusion is made. A long note in Ed. Ben does not seem to clear up the matter.

in the first place to the Catholic Church, and next to your own laws, that with God for your Patron you may be triumphant, while you provide for the peace and tranquillity of the Church.

TO THE EMPERORS

LETTER XI. A.D. 381.

THIS letter, which, like the previous one, is really addressed to Gratian, though in accordance with custom formally superscribed with the names of all the three Emperors, urges him to support Damasus as the orthodox and duly elected Bishop of Rome, and to condemn his rival Ursinus, whose interference with their Council, and intrigues with the Arian party they also inform him of.

TO THE MOST GRACIOUS EMPERORS AND CHRISTIAN PRINCES, THE MOST GLORIOUS AND MOST BLESSED, GRATIAN, VALENTINIAN, AND THEODOSIUS, THE COUNCIL WHICH IS ASSEMBLED AT AQUILEIA.

1. YOUR enactments have indeed already provided, most gracious Princes, that the perfidy of the Arians may not any further either be concealed or diffused: for we do not conceive that the decrees of the Council will be without effect; for as regards the West, two individuals only have been found to dare to oppose the Council with profane and impious words, men who had previously disturbed a mere corner of Dacia Ripensis [a].

2. There is another subject which distresses us more, which, as we were assembled, it was our business to discuss duly, lest it should spread through the whole body of the Church diffused over the whole world, and so trouble all things. For though we were generally agreed that

---

[a] Dacia Ripensis. The original Province of Dacia was beyond the Danube. It was conquered and included in the Empire by Trajan. In the time of Aurelian it was abandoned again, and the Danube re-established as the frontier. Then the Roman colonists were removed to the South of the Danube, into the central district of Mœsia, which was then called Dacia Aureliani. This was afterwards divided into two Provinces, called Dacia Ripensis and Dacia Mediterranea, Ripensis being the northern part, extending along the bank of the Danube, whence the name.

LETT. 11. Ursinus [b] could not have overreached your piety (though he allows nothing to be quiet, and amid the many urgencies of war would press upon you with his importunity) still lest your holy tranquillity of mind, which delights in having all persons in its care, should be swayed by the false adulation of that unreasonable person, we think it right, if you condescendingly allow it, to offer you our prayers and entreaties, not only to guard against what may be, but shuddering at past things also which have been brought about by his temerity. For if he found any vent for his audacity, where would he not spread confusion?

3. But if pity for a single person can sway you, much more let the prayer of all the Bishops move you. For which of us will be united to him in fellowship and communion when he has attempted to usurp a place not due to him, and one he could not lawfully have arrived at, and endeavours to regain in a manner most unreasonable what he was most unreasonable in aiming at? Often as he has been found guilty of turbulence, he still goes on, as if his past conduct should inspire no horror. He was often, as we ascertained and saw in the present Council, in union and combination with the Arians at the time when he endeavoured in company with Valens [c] to disturb the Church of Milan with their detestable assembly: holding private meetings sometimes before the doors of the synagogue and sometimes in the houses of the Arians, and uniting his friends to them; and, as he could not go openly himself to their congregations, teaching and informing them in what way the Church's peace might be disturbed. Their madness gave him fresh courage, so as well to earn the favour of their supporters and allies.

[b] "Damasus was made Pope on the death of Liberius A D 366. Ursinus, called by some Ursicinus, was, as Damasus had been, Deacon at Rome, and could not endure the exaltation of his former colleague who is suspected of having taken part with Felix, the successor to the power of Liberius, when exiled by the Arians. Ursinus was factiously consecrated by one Bishop, and a contest ensued in which even much blood was shed Ursinus was banished, and being recalled the next year, was banished again after two months In 371 he was allowed to leave his place of exile, and only excluded from Rome and the suburbicarian provinces. In 378 he held the factious meetings mentioned in the letter, and was exiled to Cologne. He continued to petition Gratian to restore him, and hence the request of the Bishops at Aquileia." Note in Newman's Fleury vol. 1 p. 38.

[c] i.e. Julianus Valens, Bp. of Petavio, mentioned in the preceding letter.

4. When therefore it is written; *a man that is an heretic after*[1] *one admonition reject*, and when another man who spoke by the Holy Spirit has said that beasts such as these should be spurned and not received with greeting or welcome, how is it possible that we should not judge the person whom we have seen united to their society to be also a maintainer of their perfidy? What even if he were not there? We might still have besought your Graces not to allow the Roman Church, the Head of the whole Roman world, and the sacred faith of the Apostles to be disturbed; for from thence flow all the rights of venerable Communion to all persons. And therefore we pray and beseech you that you would condescend to take from him the means of stealing advantage from you.

TO THE EMPERORS Titus iii. 10.
[1] after the first and second admonition E.V. 2 S John 10.

5. We know your Graces' holy modesty: let him not press upon you words unbecoming your ears, or give his noisy utterance to what is alien from the office and name of a Bishop, or say to you what is unseemly. When he ought to have *a good report* even *from those who are without*, let your Graces condescend to recollect what was the testimony with which the men of his own city have followed him. For it is a shame to say and against modesty to repeat how disgraceful is the rumour, with the reproach of which he is wounded. The shame of this ought to have constrained him to silence, and if he partook in any degree of the feelings and conscience of a Bishop, he would prefer the Church's peace and concord to his own ambition and inclination. But, lost to all shame, he sends letters by Paschasius an excommunicated person, the standard bearer of his madness, and so sows confusion, and attempts to excite even Gentiles and abandoned characters.

1 Tim. iii. 3-7.

6. We therefore entreat you to restore by the degradation of that most troublesome person the security which has been interrupted both to us Bishops and to the Roman people, which is at present in uncertainty and suspense since the memorial of the Prefect of the city. And on obtaining this let us in continuous and unbroken course offer thanksgivings to God the Almighty Father and to Christ our Lord God.

A.D.381.   LETTER XII.

> This letter, referring to the settlement of affairs in the East, is really addressed to Theodosius, the Emperor of the East. After expressing the thanks due to the Emperors for the success which has attended their efforts to establish the true faith throughout the Empire, the Bishops beg that Theodosius will use his influence to settle the questions of disputed succession, which were vexing the Churches of Alexandria and Antioch, and endangering the maintenance of Communion between the East and West. They ask therefore that a general Council may be summoned to Alexandria to settle both questions.

TO THE MOST GRACIOUS AND CHRISTIAN EMPERORS, THE GLORIOUS AND MOST BLESSED PRINCES, GRATIAN, VALENTINIAN, AND THEODOSIUS, THE HOLY COUNCIL WHICH IS ASSEMBLED AT AQUILEIA.

1. Most gracious Emperors and most blessed and most glorious princes, Gratian, Valentinian, and Theodosius, beloved of God the Father and of His Son our Lord Jesus Christ, we are unable to match the benefits which your piety has conferred upon us, even with the most overflowing return of thanks. For now that, after many times of trial and various persecutions, which the Arians, especially Lucius[a], who marked his course by the impious murder of monks and virgins, and Demophilus[b] too, an evil source of perfidy, brought on the Catholics, all the Churches of

---

[a] This Lucius was the person who, after the death of S. Athanasius, was forced upon the Church of Alexandria as Bishop, in the place of Peter who had been duly elected, by the Governor of the Province. His crimes and cruelties are recorded at length by Theodoret. Eccl. Hist. iv 21, 22. He was eventually expelled from the see he had usurped, and is mentioned by Socrates, Hist. Eccl. v. 7, as afterwards dwelling at Constantinople and sharing the fate of Demophilus.

[b] Demophilus was originally Bishop of Beroea, (probably Beroea in Thrace,) and was deposed from his office for Arianism. In A.D. 370, on the death of Eudoxius, he was elected by the Arian party Bishop of Constantinople, in opposition to Evagrius. He was supported by Valens who was then Emperor, and Evagrius banished. In 380 A.D. after the accession of Theodosius, matters were changed. Theodosius offered to maintain him in his see, if he subscribed the Nicene Confession, but he refused, and withdrew, and maintained, in conjunction with Lucius and others, Arian worship outside the walls of Constantinople. He died A.D. 386. He is mentioned by S. Ambrose (De Fide 1. 6. 45.) as a leader of one of the various forms of Arianism.

God, in the East especially, have been restored to the Catholics; while in the West scarce two heretics have been found to oppose the decrees of the Holy Council, who can conceive himself able to make an adequate acknowledgement of your goodness?

2. But though we cannot give full expression to your favours in words, we still desire to recompense them by the prayers of the Council; and though in all the several Churches we celebrate our daily vigils for your Empire before our God, still when assembled in one body, than which service we conceive nothing can be more glorious, we offer thanksgivings to our Almighty God both on behalf of the Empire, and of your own peace and safety, because peace and concord have been so shed over us through you.

3. In the West indeed only in two corners, on the borders of Dacia Ripensis and of Moesia did murmurs appear to have been raised against the faith: and these places after the sentence of the Council should, we conceive, be immediately provided for with your Graces' indulgence. But over all tracts and countries and village departments as far as the Ocean, the communion of the faithful remains one and unpolluted. And in the East we have had the greatest joy and delight in learning that the Arians, who had violently invaded the Churches, have been ejected, and that the sacred temples of God are frequented by Catholics alone.

4. But still since the envy of the Devil is never wont to rest, we hear that there are among the Catholics themselves frequent dissensions and implacable discord; and all our feelings are disturbed at ascertaining that many things have been innovated upon, and that persons are molested now who should have been relieved, men who continued always in our Communion. In short Timotheus Bishop of the Church of Alexandria, and Paulinus Bishop of the Church of Antioch [c], who always maintained the concord

---

[c] This refers to the long schism which had existed in the Church at Antioch, ever since 331 A D when Eustathius was deposed by the Arian party: in 361 A D. Meletius was elected as successor to Eudoxius, having previously subscribed the Creed of Acacius (Socr. ii. 44); but on his accepting the Nicene Creed, and acknowledging the Homoousion, he was deposed, and banished by the Emperor Constantius, and Euzoius, an Arian, appointed in his stead, who was afterwards succeeded by Dorotheus, (who

of Communion with us inviolate, are said to be distressed by the variances of other persons, whose faith in former times was scarcely stedfast. These persons, if it be possible, and they are recommended by a sufficient faith, we would wish to have added to our fellowship: but without prejudice to the rights of those who share with us the ancient Communion. And our care for them is not superfluous, first of all because the fellowship of Communion should be clear of all offence, and secondly, because we have long since received letters from both parties, and particularly from those who were divided in the Church of Antioch.

5. Indeed if the irruption of the enemy [d] had not hindered, we had made arrangements to send thither some of our own number, to take the office of umpires and referees for diffusing peace again, should it be possible. But since our desires could not have accomplishment at that time owing to the troubles of the state, we think it right to offer our prayers to your Goodness, asking that by agreement [e] between the factions, on the death of the one, the rights of the Church should remain with the survivor, and that no additional consecration should be forcibly attempted. And therefore we request you, most gracious and Christian Princes, that you would have a Council of all Catholic Bishops held at Alexandria, that they may more fully discuss and define among themselves to

was afterwards transferred to Constantinople, 385 A D.) Meanwhile Meletius had returned from exile, but the extreme orthodox party refused to recognise him, because he had at first been appointed as a Semi-Arian, and elected Paulinus, though the Council of Alexandria had urged them to submit to Meletius, so that, as Socrates says, when recounting the Bishops of the chief sees in the year 379, the the Church at Antioch τριχῇ διῄρητο Paulinus was supported by the Church of Alexandria and by the Bishops of the West, and, as appears from the statements of this letter, a compromise had been proposed, that when either Meletius or Paulinus died, both parties would acknowledge the survivor. The Bishops at Aquileia urge the Emperor to enforce this, not aware that Flavian had already been elected as Meletius' successor at the Council of Constantinople. The schism was thus perpetuated, and continued till 415 A.D

What the difficulty about Timotheus was, is not certain. He had been consecrated Bishop of Alexandria that same year, after the death of Peter, the successor of S. Athanasius. Tillemont (vol x p 139) suggests that it was probably connected with the question of the succession at Antioch.

[d] The enemy are the Goths under Fritigern. See Gibbon ch. 26.

[e] The reading 'pactum' which is suggested by Valerius is here adopted instead of 'factum', which seems to give no satisfactory sense.

whom Communion is to be imparted and with whom it is to be maintained ᶠ. TO THE EMPERORS

6. For though we have always supported the disposition and order of the Church of Alexandria, and according to the manner and custom of our predecessors we retain Communion with it in indissoluble fellowship to these present times, still lest it should be thought that persons have been neglected who have sought our Communion according to the agreement, which we wish should stand, or that the shortest road to that peace and fellowship of the faithful has not been taken, we pray you that when they have discussed these matters in a full assembly among themselves, the decrees of the Bishops may be furthered by the assistance ministered by your Goodness. And allow us to be made acquainted with this, that our minds may not waver in uncertainty, but that, full of joy and relieved from anxiety, we may return thanks to your goodness before Almighty God, not only that heresy is shut out, but also that faith and concord are restored to the Catholics. The prayer which the African and Gallic Churches offer you through their deputies is this, that you would make the Bishops over the whole world your debtors, though the debt already due to your excellence is not small.

7. To offer however our entreaties to your clemency and to obtain what we ask for, we have sent as deputies our brethren and fellow-presbyters, whom we pray you that you would condescend graciously to listen to, and allow to return speedily.

ᶠ Fleury remarks on this 'This letter plainly shews that the Bishops who were there present (i.e. at the Council of Aquileia) either did not acknowledge the Council which had been lately held at Constantinople to be an Œcumenical Council, or that they were not yet informed of what had been transacted in it.

LETT 13.

A D 382.   LETTER XIII.

> In the year following the Council of Aquileia, a Council of the Bishops of the civil Diocese of Italy appears to have been held, over which S. Ambrose presided. It appears to have dealt principally with the questions at issue between the East and West. This letter was written by S. Ambrose in the name of the Council, after the end of its session ('in concilio nuper,' § 3), to Theodosius. The Bishops complain of the election of Flavian to succeed Meletius at Antioch, contrary to the compromise which they urged in the last letter, and maintain Maximus' claim to the see of Constantinople against Nectarius, urging again the necessity of a General Council of both East and West, to settle finally all the questions in dispute between them, and suggest that it should be held at Rome.

TO THE MOST BLESSED EMPEROR AND MOST GRACIOUS PRINCE THEODOSIUS, AMBROSE AND THE OTHER BISHOPS OF ITALY.

1. We knew indeed that your holy mind was devoted to God in pure and sincere faith, but your Majesty has loaded us with fresh benefits in restoring the Catholics to the Churches. And I would that you could have restored the Catholics themselves to their ancient reverence, that they would innovate in nothing against the prescription of our ancestors, and not be hasty either to rescind what what they ought to maintain nor to maintain what they ought to rescind. Therefore we sigh, your Majesty, perhaps with too much grief, but not without sufficient reason, that it has proved easier to get the heretics expelled than to establish concord among the Catholics. For the extent of the confusion that has lately taken place is beyond expression.

2. We wrote to you not long ago, that since the city of Antioch had two Bishops, Paulinus and Meletius, both of whom we regarded as true to the faith, they should either agree with each other in peace and concord, preserving Ecclesiastical order, or at least, if one of them died before the other, no one should be put into the place of the deceased while the other lived. But now on the death of Meletius, while Paulinus is still alive, whom fellowship de-

rived from our predecessors uninterruptedly testifies to have remained in our Communion, another person is said to have been not so much supplied, as super-added, into the place of Meletius, contrary to right and to Ecclesiastical order.

3. And this is alleged to have taken place by the consent and advice of Nectarius[a], the regularity of whose ordination we are not clearly convinced of. For in a Council lately, when Maximus the Bishop, having read the letter of Peter a man of holy memory, had shewn that the communion of the Church of Alexandria remained with him, and had proved by the clearest testimony, that he was [b] consecrated by three Bishops ordaining by mandate within his private house, because the Arians were at that time in possession of the Basilicas, we had no cause, most blessed of Princes, to doubt of his episcopacy, when he testified that he resisted and was forcibly constrained by a majority of the laity and clergy.

4. Still that we might not appear to have settled any thing over-hastily in the absence of the parties, we thought it fit to inform your Grace by letter, in order that his case might be provided for so as best to serve the interests of public peace and concord, because in truth we perceived that Gregory claimed to himself the priesthood of the Church of Constantinople, by no means in accordance with the tradition of the Fathers. We therefore in that Synod, attendance at which appeared to have been prescribed to the Bishops of the whole world, were of opinion that nothing ought to be decided rashly. So at that particular time the persons who declined a general Council and who are said to have had one at Constantinople, where they had

---

[a] In the regard of the question between Nectarius and Maximus, the Western Bishops had been deceived by the latter. Maximus, called the Cynic because he retained the outward garb of a Cynic philosopher after he professed to have become a Christian, was irregularly conscrated at Constantinople, but was never recognised, and was formally pronounced by the Council not to be a true Bishop. He then went about trying to stir up other Churches in his favour. See Prof Bright's Hist. of the Church pp. 160—166

Nectarius was elected after the resignation of Gregory Nazianzen, during the Council of Constantinople. He, like S. Ambrose, was unbaptized and held a high civil office at the time of his election.

[b] This is translated from an ingenious and probable conjecture of Valesius.

LETT. 13. ascertained that Maximus had come hither to plead his cause in the Synod (and this, even if a Council had not been proclaimed it was competent for him to do lawfully and according to the customs of our predecessors, as also Athanasius of holy memory, and since that Peter, brother Bishops of the Church of Alexandria, and several of the Eastern Bishops have done, so as to appear to have sought the decision of the Churches of Rome, of Italy, and of all the West) when, as we said, they saw that he wished to bring the question to a trial with those who denied his episcopate, they were surely bound to wait for our opinion upon it [c]. We do not claim any special privilege of examining such matters, but we ought to have had a share in an united decision.

5. Last of all, it ought to have been decided whether he was to lose his See, before deciding whether another should receive it, especially by persons by whom Maximus complained that he was either deserted or injured. Therefore since Maximus the Bishop has been received into Communion by those of our fellowship on the ground that it was certain that he had been ordained by Catholics, we did not see that he ought to have been excluded from his claim to the Bishopric of Constantinople, and we thought that his allegation ought to be weighed in the presence of the parties.

But since we have learned recently that Nectarius has been ordained at Constantinople, we fear that our communion with the Oriental regions is broken, especially since Nectarius is said to have been left immediately without the fellowship of Communion by the very persons by whom he was ordained.

6. There is therefore no slight difficulty here. And it is not any contention about wishes and ambition of our own that makes us anxious, but we are greatly disturbed by the breaking up and interruption of communion. Nor do we see any way in which concord can be established except either by restoring to Constantinople the Bishop who

---

[c] The text through this long sentence is confused and ungrammatical, but it conveys the general sense expressed in the translation with tolerable clearness.

was first ordained, or at least having a Council of ourselves and of the Eastern Bishops at Rome, to consider the ordination of both of them.

7. Nor does it seem unbecoming, your Majesty, that the persons, who thought the judgement of Acholius, a single Bishop, so well worth waiting for, that they called him to Constantinople from the regions of the West, should be obliged to submit to the discussion of the Bishop of the Church of Rome, and of the Bishops of the neighbourhood and of Italy. If a question was reserved for a single individual, how much more should it be reserved for many?

8. We, however, as it has been suggested to us by the most blessed Prince, your Brother [d], that we should write to your Grace's Majesty, request that when the communion is one, you would be pleased that the judgement should be joint and the consent concurrent.

LETTER XIV.

A.D. 382.

This letter is a reply to one addressed to the Bishops of Italy by Theodosius, in answer to the last. He seems in it to have "undeceived them by informing them what Maximus was, and how different his ordination was from that of Nectarius. He represented to them that these affairs, and that of Flavian, ought to be judged in the East, where all the parties were present, and that there was no reason to oblige those of the East to come unto the West" (Fleury xviii, 17, vol. 1. p 41 Newman's Transl). The Bishops in this reply thank the Emperor for his efforts to appease the differences between the East and West, and profess the disinterestedness of their desire for a general Council, and add, as an additional reason for it, the spread of opinions attributed to Apollinaris, which require to be examined into in the presence of the parties concerned.

TO THE MOST BLESSED EMPEROR AND MOST GRACIOUS PRINCE THEODOSIUS, AMBROSE AND THE OTHER BISHOPS OF ITALY.

1. THE knowledge of your faith, which is diffused over the whole world, has soothed the innermost feelings of our minds; and therefore, that your reign might have the additional glory of having restored unity to the Churches

[d] i. e. Gratian.

Lett. 14. both of the West and East, we have thought it right, most serene and faithful Emperor, at once to beseech and inform your Grace on Ecclesiastical subjects by our letter. For we have been grieved that the fellowship of holy Communion between the East and West was interrupted.

2. We say not a word by whose error or by whose fault this was, that we may not be supposed to be spreading fables and idle talk. Nor can we regret having made an attempt, the neglect of which might have turned to our blame. For it was often made matter of blame to us that we appeared to disregard the society of the Eastern brethren, and to reject their kindness.

3. We thought moreover that we ought to take this trouble on ourselves, not for Italy, which now for this long time has been quiet and free from anxiety on the part of the Arians, and which is troubled with no disturbance of the heretics; not for ourselves, for we seek not our own things, but the things of all; not for Gaul and Africa which enjoy the individual fellowship of all their Bishops, but that the circumstances which have disturbed our communion on the side of the East might be enquired into in the Synod, and all scruple be removed from among us.

4. For not only with regard to the persons about whom your Grace condescended to write, but with regard to others who are attempting to bring into the Church some dogma or other, said to be Apollinaris'[a], there were several things that affected us, to which the knife should have been applied in the presence of the parties, that a person convicted of maintaining a new dogma and proved to be in error should not shelter himself under the general name of the Faith, but at once lay down both the office and name of Bishop, which he was not entitled to by authority of doctrine, and that no threads or artifices of delusion should remain for persons hereafter wishing to deceive. For the person who is convicted, not in the presence of the parties, as your Grace has truly decided in your august and princely answer, will always lay hold of a handle for reviving the enquiry.

[a] The sense is here to be elicited probably by repeating the word 'quod,' so that the sentence should run, 'dog- ma nescio quod, quod Apollinaris asseritur'

5. This was why we asked for a Council of Bishops, that no one should be permitted to state what was false against a person in his absence, and that the truth might be cleared up by discussion in the Council. We ought not then to incur any suspicion either of over-zeal or over-leniency, seeing that we made all our observations in the presence of the parties.

6. In truth we drew up what was quoted, not to decide but to give information, and while we asked for a judgement, we offer no prejudgement. Nor ought it to have been regarded as any reproach to them, when Bishops were invited to the Council, who in many cases were more present by their very absence, since it contributed to the common good. For neither did we conceive it to be a reproach to us when a Presbyter of the Church of Constantinople, by name Paulus, demanded that there should be a Synod both of Eastern and Western Bishops in the province of Achaia.

7. Your Grace observes that this demand, which was made by the Greeks also, was not unreasonable. But, because there are disturbances in Illyricum [b], a neighbourhood near the sea and safer was sought. Nor have we indeed made any innovation in the way of precedent, but preserving the decisions of Athanasius of holy memory, who was as it were a pillar of the Faith, and of our holy fathers of old time in their Councils, we do not tear up the boundaries that our Fathers placed, or violate the rights of hereditary Communion, but reserving the honour due to your authority, we shew ourselves studious of peace and quietness [c].

---

[b] There seems to be something corrupt in the text. Perhaps we should read 'moventur,' 'the dangerous parts of Illyricum are in commotion;' or 'suspecta' has taken the place of some word, such as 'superiora,' which would stand in antithesis to 'maritima'

[c] It may complete the subject of this series of letters to remind the reader that about the same time that the Council of the Italian Bishops was held, Theodosius convened a second Council at Constantinople to deal with the questions raised by the Westerns, where most of the Bishops who had formed the previous General Council re-assembled. They replied to the invitation to another General Council at Rome by a Synodical letter, which is given at full length by Theodoret (Eccles Hist v 9). In it they excuse themselves from attending, on the ground of their presence being required in their own Dioceses, especially after the long exile of many of them, and the prevalence of Arian usurpation, wishing that they 'had the wings of a dove,' to fly to their Western brethren. They then give a summary of the doctrinal decisions of the two Councils, and announce that they have sent three Bishops as deputies to ex-

LETT. 15.

A.D. 383.

LETTER XV.

THIS letter is addressed to the Bishops of Macedonia, in reply to their announcement of the death of Acholius[a], Bishop of Thessalonica. S. Ambrose pronounces a warm eulogium on the departed Bishop, whom he compares to Elijah, especially in leaving in Anysius a successor, like Elisha, endowed with a double portion of his spirit. He recounts the pleasure which he had felt in his intercourse with Acholius at Rome, when they had wept together over the evils of the times, and invokes the Blessing of God upon his successor.

AMBROSE TO ANATOLIUS, NUMERIUS, SEVERUS, PHILIP, MACEDONIUS, AMMIANUS, THEODOSIUS, EUTROPIUS, CLARUS, EUSEBIUS, AND TIMOTHEUS, PRIESTS OF THE LORD, AND TO ALL THE BELOVED CLERGY AND PEOPLE OF THESSALONICA, HEALTH.

1. WHILE longing to keep ever imprinted on my mind the holy man, and while I survey all his acts like one set on a watch-tower, my restless anxiety caused me to drink only too swiftly these bitter tidings, and I learned what I had rather still be ignorant of, that the man whom we were seeking on earth was already at rest in heaven.

2. You will ask who announced this to me, seeing that the letter of your Holinesses had not then arrived. I know not who was the bearer of the tidings: it is, you know, plain all things more fully to them, and, with reference to the disputed successions at Constantinople and Antioch, give their assurance to their brethren that both Nectarius and Flavian were canonically elected, and the elections ratified both by the clergy and the faithful of each diocese, and by the Council, reminding them of the ancient Canon re-affirmed at Nicæa, that each province should settle all such questions for themselves.

[a] Acholius, or Ascholius, as he is called by Socrates, was the Bishop who baptised Theodosius, during an illness which seized him on a campaign against the Goths. He was present at the Council of Constantinople, and afterwards at that of Rome, not as one of the deputies from the East, but probably because his see had been so recently transferred to the Eastern Empire, that he might seem to belong to both East and West. (Tillemont Ambr. ch. xxxi.) It was there that he met S Ambrose, who had gone to Rome to attend the Council, and had fallen ill. His death must have occurred in A D. 383, for his successor Anysius was Bishop before the death of Damasus, Bishop of Rome, who died in A.D 384 Theodoret therefore (B. v. ch 18) must be wrong in making him the Bishop who wrote to S Ambrose an account of the massacre at Thessalonica, which occurred in A.D. 390. But the passage of Theodoret occurs in only one MS., and is perhaps not genuine.

men's wont not willingly to remember the bearer of tidings of sorrow: however, though the sea was then closed, and the land blocked by a barbarian invasion, there was no lack of a messenger, though it was impossible for any one to arrive from abroad; so that it appears to me the saint himself announced his own death to us, for now that he enjoyed the eternal recompense of his labours, and freed from the bands of the body, had been carried by the ministry of Angels to the intimate presence of Christ, he was desirous of removing the error of one who loved him, that we might not be asking for him length of mortal life, while he was already receiving eternal rewards.

3. This veteran then of Christ Jesus is not dead, but has departed and left us, he has changed for heaven this earth below, and clapping the pinions and wings of his spirit he exclaims, *Lo, I have got me away far off!* in the spirit of the Apostle he desired long ago to leave the earth, but he was detained by the prayers of all, as we read of the Apostle, because it was needful for the Church that he should abide longer in the flesh. For he lived not for himself but for all, and was to the people the minister of eternal life, so that he gained the fruit thereof in others, before he experienced it in himself.

4. Now therefore he is a citizen of heaven, a possessor of that eternal city Jerusalem, which is in heaven. There he sees the boundless circuit of this city, its pure gold, its precious stones, its perpetual light though without the sun. And seeing all these things whereof he before had knowledge, but which are now manifested to him face to face, he says, *Like as we have heard, so have we seen in the city of the Lord of hosts, in the city of our God.* Standing there he appeals to the people of God saying, *O Israel, how great is the house of God, and how large is the place of His possession!* Great is He, and hath none end.

5. But what is this? While I consider his merits, and follow as it were in spirit his departure, and mingle with the choirs of saints that escort him, not indeed by my desert but by my affection, meanwhile I have almost forgotten myself. Is then this wall of faith and grace and sanctity taken from us, that wall which, though frequently assaulted

by the Goths [b], their barbarian darts could never penetrate, nor the warlike fury of many nations overpower? They who in other places were spoilers there prayed for peace, and while they marvelled what was this unarmed force which opposed them, the wiser hinted that one like Elisha dwelt within, one who was nearly his equal in age, in spirit quite his equal, and bade them beware lest after the manner of the Syrian army, blindness should fall on them also.

6. However the gifts of Christ to His disciples are various. Elisha led captive into Samaria the army of the Syrians, holy Acholius by his prayers caused the victors to retreat from Macedonia. Do we not see in this a proof of supernatural forces, that though no soldiers were at hand, the victors should thus fly without a foe; is not this too a proof of blindness that they should fly when no man pursued? Though in truth holy Acholius pursued and fought them, not with swords but prayers, not with weapons but good works.

7. Do we not know that the saints fight even when they keep holiday? Was not Elisha at rest? Yes, at rest in body, but in spirit he was active, and by his prayers he fought when the noise of horses and the noise of a great host were heard in the camp of the Syrians, so that they thought that the forces of other princes were marching against them, to succour the people of Israel. So they were seized with great panic and fled, and four lepers, who had gone out to seek for death, spoiled their camp. And did not the Lord work like, or, I might almost say, greater wisdom in Macedonia, by the prayers of Acholius? For it was not by an idle panic nor a vague suspicion, but by a raging plague and burning pestilence that the Goths were troubled and alarmed. In short they then fled that they might escape; afterwards they returned and sued for peace to save their lives.

8. Wherefore in the great deeds of this eminent man we

---

[b] The Goths had been settled within the boundaries of the Empire by Valens in A.D. 376, when they implored his protection against the Huns. He established them in Moesia, where they soon revolted, and ravaged Thrace, uniting with their former enemies, the Huns, and other barbarians. Valens was defeated and slain by them in A.D. 378, and then they overran all the neighbouring provinces. There is a graphic account in Gibbon. ch. xxvi.

have seen former ages revived, and have witnessed those works of the prophet which we read of. Like Elisha he was all his life in the midst of arms and battles, and by his good works made wars to cease. And when tranquillity was restored to his countrymen, he breathed out his holy soul, a misfortune heavier than war itself. Like Elijah he was carried up to heaven, not in a chariot of fire, nor by horses of fire, (unless haply it was but that we saw them not) nor in any whirlwind in the sky, but by the will and in the calm of our God, and with the jubilation of the holy Angels who rejoiced that such a man had come among them.

^{TO THE BISHOPS OF MACEDONIA}

^{2 Kings ii. 4.}

9. Surely we cannot doubt this, when all other particulars agree so well. For at the very moment when he was being taken up, he let fall so to speak the vestment which he wore, and invested with it holy Anysius his disciple, and clothed him with the robes of his own priesthood. His merits and graces I do not now hear for the first time, nor have I first learnt them from your letters, but I recognised them in what you wrote. For as if foreknowing that he would be his successor, Acholius designated him as such by tokens, though in open speech he concealed it; saying that he had been aided by his care, labour, and ministry, thus seeming to declare him his coadjutor, one who would not come as a novice to the chief office of the priesthood, but as a tried performer of its duties. Well does that saying in the Gospel befit him, *Well done, thou good and faithful servant, thou hast been faithful over a few things, I will make thee ruler over many things.*

^{S. Matt. xxv. 21.}

10. So far both you and I participate in holy Acholius, but there is this special bond between him and me, that the man of blessed memory suffered me to become his friend. For on his arrival in Italy, when I was prevented by illness from going to meet him, he himself came and visited me. With what ardour, with what affection did we embrace each other! With what groans did we lament the evil of the times, and all that was happening here! Our garments were bedewed with a flood of tears, while in the enjoyment of our meeting long and mutually desired, we remained locked in each others embrace. Thus what

LETT. 15. I had long yearned for he bestowed, the opportunity of seeing him. For although it is in the spirit, the seat of love, that the greater portion and more perfect knowledge lies, yet we desire to behold our friends in bodily form also. Thus formerly the kings of the earth sought to behold the face of Solomon, and to hear his wisdom.

1 Kings x. 24.

11. He is gone then from us, and has left us tossed on this sea; what is a benefit to him is to the many a heavier calamity than even the rage of the barbarians; for this he repelled, and now who shall bring back his presence to us? Nay, the Lord brings it back, and he himself gives himself back in his disciple. Your judgements give him back, by which you say, *Give to Levi his manifest one, and his truths to Thy holy one.* You have given *his manifest one* inasmuch as he is established by his appointment; you have given a follower of that man, *who said unto his father and to his mother I have not seen thee; neither did he acknowledge his brethren, nor knew his own children. He observed the word of the Lord, and kept His covenant. The people will tell of his wisdom.*

Deut. xxxiii. 8.

Ib. 9.

Ecclus. xliv. 15.

12. Such was the man's life, such his heritage, such his conversation, such his succession. While yet a boy he entered a monastery, and though shut up in a narrow cell in Achaia, yet by grace he traversed the spaces of many countries. The people of Macedonia besought that he might be their Bishop, the priesthood elected him to that office, that where the faith had before been maimed^c by the Bishop, there afterwards the solid foundations of the faith might be established by the Bishop.

13. None other did his disciple imitate, who also himself *said unto his father and to his mother I have not seen thee.* He saw them not with affection, he saw them not with desire, and he knew not his brethren, because he desired to know the Lord. He observed also the word of the Lord and kept His covenant, and will ever offer sacri-

Deut. xxxiii. 9.

---

^c The Benedictine text here reads 'claudebatur.' Several MSS, as the editors mention in a note, have 'claudebat.' They themselves suggest 'claudicabat.' But 'claudebat' really gives the same meaning, and there seems little doubt that it is the true reading. It comes from claudeo or claudo, (for both forms are to be found,) meaning 'to be lame,' 'to halt.' It occurs three times in Cicero.

fice upon His altar. Bless, O Lord, his faith, his holiness, his assiduity. Let Thy blessing descend upon his head and upon his neck. Let him be honourable among his brethren, let him be as the leader of the herd. Let him sift the hearts of his enemies, let him soothe the minds of the saints, and let the judgement of Thy priests flourish in him as a lily. Brethren, farewell, and love me, as I love you.

TO THE BISHOPS OF MACEDONIA

Deut xxxiii.16.

LETTER XVI. A.D. 383.

THIS letter is addressed to Anysius, immediately on his election as successor to Acholius, in answer apparently to one from Anysius, which accompanied that from the Bishops of Macedonia, and announced his appointment He speaks of the responsibility of succeeding so zealous a Bishop as Acholius, whom he praises in enthusiastic terms, and prays that God may make him a worthy successor in every way.

BISHOP AMBROSE TO HIS BROTHER ANYSIUS.

1. I HAVE been for some time sure of what I now read for the first time, and I know well by his merits him whom my eyes have not seen. I grieve that the one event should have happened, I rejoice that the other has ensued; I should have wished that the one had not happened in my lifetime, but it was my hope that after the death of that holy man this alone would ensue, as it ought. So now we have you, once the disciple, now the successor of Acholius of blessed memory, the inheritor alike of his rank and of his grace. This is a great merit, my brother. I congratulate you that there was not a moment's doubt who should be the successor of so great a man. It is a great task too, my brother, to have taken upon you the burden of so great a name, a name of such weight, of such a scale. In you we look for Acholius, and as he was in your affections, so in your ministry is required a copy of his virtue, of his holy life, his vigorous mind in that decrepit body.

2. I have seen him, I confess: my seeing him is due to his merits: I saw him in such sort in the body as to believe

him to be out of the body: I saw the image of him who, knowing not whether it was in the body or out of the body, saw himself transported to Paradise. With such rapid speed had he traversed every region, Constantinople, Achaia, Epirus, and Italy, that younger men could not keep pace with him. Men of stronger bodies yielded to him, knowing that he was free from the shackles of the body, so that he used it more as a covering than as an instrument, at all events that it was his slave not his helpmate, for he had so trained his body that he crucified the world in it, and himself to the world.

Lett.16.
2 Cor.
xii. 2.

3. Blessed is the Lord, and blessed was His youth which He passed in the tabernacle of the God of Jacob, abiding in a monastery, in which, when sought after by His parents and relations He said, *Who is My mother, and who are My brethren?* I know not father, nor mother, nor brethren, save those *who hear the Word of God, and do it.* Blessed also were his maturer years, wherein he was elected to the chief priesthood, having given proof of his virtue by a long service. He came like David to restore peace to the people. He came like that ship bringing with him spiritual treasure, and cedar wood, and precious stones, and those *silver wings of a dove,* with which, lying *in the midst of the lots,* she slept the sleep of tranquillity and peace.

S Matt.
xii. 48.

2 Chron.
ix. 21.

Ps. lxviii.
14.

4. For even the sleep of the saints is operative, as it is written, *I sleep, but my heart waketh,* and as holy Jacob saw in sleep divine mysteries, which waking he saw not, even a passage opened for the saints between earth and heaven, and the Lord regarding him and promising to him the possession of that land. Thus by a brief sleep he attained that which his successors afterwards won by great toil. The sleep of the saints is free from all bodily pleasures, from all perturbation of mind, it brings tranquillity to the mind and peace to the soul, so that, freed from the fetters of the body, it raises itself aloft, and is united to Christ.

Cant. v. 2.
Gen. xxviii.13.

5. This sleep is the life of the saints, the life which holy Acholius lived, whose old age was also blest. That old age is truly venerable which is hoary not with gray hairs

but in good deeds; for those hoar hairs are reverent which belong to the soul, whose works and thoughts are, as it were, white and shining. For what is true old age, but that unspotted life, which lasts not for days or months but for ages, whose continuance is without end, whose length of years is without weakness? For the longer it lives the stronger it waxes; the longer its life lasts the more vigorously does it grow unto a perfect man.   *To Anysius. Wisd. iv. 9.*

6. May God then approve you his successor not only in honor but also in conversation, and may He deign to establish you in His highest grace, that the people may flock to you also, and you may say often, *Who are these that fly as a cloud, and as the doves with their young?* Let them come also as the ships of Tarshish, and take in corn which the true Solomon gives, even twenty measures of wheat. Let them receive the oil and wisdom of Solomon, and let there be peace between thee and thy people, and keep thou the covenant of peace. Brother, farewell: love me, for I too love you.   *Isa. lx. 8. 2 Chron. ix. 21.*

LETTER XVII.   A.D. 384.

This letter was addressed to the Emperor Valentinian the 2nd at the time when a deputation from the Senate at Rome, headed by Symmachus, were seeking to obtain from him the restoration of the statue and altar of Victory. The facts relating to this statue form so important a page in the history of the gradual suppression of paganism in the Empire, that it may be well to give a brief outline of them, especially as this and the following letter, and the 'Memorial of Symmachus' which accompanies them, contain several allusions to them. Constantius 2nd, son of Constantine, when at Rome in 356 A.D , ordered the statue of Victory which stood in the senate-house, 'a majestic female standing on a globe, with flowing garments, expanded wings, and a crown of laurel in her outstretched hand' (Gibbon, ch. xxviii.) and the altar which stood before it, at which the senators were sworn, to be removed, as an offence to the Christians. The altar was restored by Julian, along with the other disused symbols and rites of paganism. It was tolerated by Valentinian 1st, who probably did not venture at once to overthrow Julian's work, (see Memorial of Symmachus § 7, 8) though S. Ambrose (Lett. xvii. § 16) rhetorically represents him as pleading that he was not aware of its being there, and that no one had complained to him of its presence. It was once more removed by Gratian, (see Lett.

LETT. 17.   xvii. § 16.) The pagan party in the Senate then made great efforts to procure its restoration. Gibbon (ch. xxviii. note 13) enumerates four successive deputations sent by them with this object, ' the first, A D 382, to Gratian, who refused them audience, the second, A. D. 384, to Valentinian, the third, A.D. 388, to Theodosius, the fourth, A D 392, to Valentinian ' The two letters of S. Ambrose and the Memorial of Symmachus refer to the second of these deputations In this first one he presses on the Emperor his duty and responsibility as a Christian Emperor, urges that the heathens have deprived themselves of any equitable claim by their persecution of the Christians in former times; asserts that the petition is only that of a minority of the Senate, just as had been the case years before, when they applied to Gratian. He then asks for a copy of the Memorial, in order to answer it in full, and warns Valentinian that he will find no Bishop to admit him to any share in Christian worship if he inflicts this insult on their faith, and reminds him of his brother and father, who would rise from the grave to reproach him.

Though called Letters, these two documents are rather state-papers. S. Ambrose himself in the latter speaks of the former as a ' libellus,' the term usually applied to petitions or memorials.

BISHOP AMBROSE TO THE MOST BLESSED PRINCE AND CHRISTIAN EMPEROR VALENTINIAN.

1. As all who are under the dominion of Rome are enlisted to serve you, the emperors and kings of the earth, so you yourselves are enlisted to serve Almighty God and our holy Faith. For safety cannot be unperilled, save when every man is a sincere worshipper of the true God, the God of the Christians, who governs all things; for He is the only true God, and is to be worshipped by the inmost spirit. *As for all the gods of the heathen, they are but idols,* as the Scripture saith.

Ps. xcvi. 5.

2. Now he that is the soldier of this, the true God, and worships Him in his inmost spirit, offers to Him no insincere or lukewarm service, but a zealous faith and devotion. At any rate no one ought to give his consent to the worship of idols and the observance of profane ceremonies. For no man can deceive God, before Whom all the secrets of the heart are manifest.

3. Seeing then, most Christian Emperor, that not only faith, but the very zeal and care and devotion of faith, is due from you to God, I wonder how some men can have conceived the thought that it was your duty to command the restoration of altars to the gods of the Gentiles, and to

bestow money for the purposes of profane sacrifices. For if you give what has long been appropriated to the emperor's privy purse or the city treasury [a], you will seem to be giving out of what is your own rather than refunding to others what belongs to them.

4. The men who now complain of their losses are those who never spared our blood, and have even laid in ruins the very structures of our Churches. The men who ask for privileges are they who denied to us by the late law of Julian [b] the common right of speaking and teaching, privileges too whereby even Christians have often been deceived, for by these means they sought to entrap some persons, either unawares or else by the desire to avoid the burthen of public duties. And since all men have not courage, many even under Christian Emperors have lapsed.

5. Even had these things never been repeated, I could have proved that your authority ought to have abolished them, but now that they have been severally forbidden by many previous Emperors and abolished at Rome in the interests of the true Faith by your Majesty's brother Gratian of illustrious memory, and abolished by a formal rescript, do not, I beseech you, pluck up again these Christian ordinances, nor rescind your brother's injunctions. In civil matters, if ought is decreed, no man considers that it should be overthrown, and shall a religious precept be trampled on?

6. Let no man beguile your youth; if he be a heathen who asks this of you, let him not ensnare your mind in the bonds of his own superstition, rather his very zeal ought to admonish you with what ardour you ought to defend the true Faith, when he with all the warmth of truth defends falsehood. I myself urge you to shew deference to the merits of illustrious men; but it is certain that God ought to be obeyed above all.

---

[a] 'fisco vel arcæ.' The 'fiscus,' or imperial treasury, received whatever was assigned to the Emperor individually, as distinguished from the 'aerarium,' which received what belonged to the senate, as representing the old respublica: 'arca' is sometimes used in late writers as equivalent to 'fiscus,' sometimes, when distinguished from it, as here, it signifies the city funds, which were distinct from both.

[b] Julian's edict, forbidding the Christians to teach in the schools of grammar and rhetoric, is mentioned with disapproval by Gibbon ch. xxiii.

7. When we have to consult on military matters we should look for the opinion of one who is versed in war, and follow his counsel; when we treat of religion God is to be considered. No man is injured by Almighty God being preferred before him. He may keep his own opinion, you do not constrain any man to worship against his will, and your Majesty ought to have the same liberty, and every one should be content to be unable to extort from the Emperor, what it would be a hardship for the Emperor to desire to extort from him. The very heathen are wont to be displeased by a double-minded man, for every man ought boldly to defend the faith of his own heart, and to maintain his purpose.

8. But if any who call themselves Christians conceive that you should make such a decree, let not bare words affect your mind, let not idle names deceive you. Whoever persuades to this, or decrees it, offers sacrifice to the gods. Yet it is more tolerable that one should sacrifice than that all should fall. Here the whole Senate of Christians is in danger.

9. If at the present day, (which God forbid) an heathen Emperor were to erect an altar to false gods, and compel the Christians to assemble there, in order for them to be present at the sacrifice, so that the breath and mouth of the faithful might be tainted with ashes from the altar, with sparks from the sacrilege, with smoke from the pile, and should force them to vote in a house in which the members were sworn at the altar of an idol, (for on this account it is that they maintain that an altar should be set up, namely, that every one should consult for the public weal, under the obligation of what they consider its sanctity, although the majority of the Senate now consists of Christians,) if this, I say, were the case, Christians would consider themselves persecuted, if they were compelled by such an alternative to come to the assembly, and indeed it is often by violence that they are compelled to come: shall Christians then in *your* reign be compelled to swear on the altar? What is an oath, but an acknowledgement of the divine power of him whom you call upon to attest your truthfulness? Is it in *your* reign that the request and demand is

to force Christians to take part in heathen rites. 91

made, that you bid an altar to be erected, and money expended on profane sacrifices?

10. But this cannot be decreed without sacrilege, and so I beg you not to decree or order it, nor to subscribe any such decree. I appeal to your faith as a minister of Christ; all the Bishops would have appealed with me, had not this report which has reached men's ears that such a thing was either propounded in your Council or petitioned for by the Senate, been so sudden and incredible. But let it not be said that the Senate have petitioned for this; a few heathen have usurped the name of all. For nearly two years ago on an attempt of this kind, holy Damasus the Bishop of the Roman Church, chosen by the judgment of God, sent me a document which the Christian senators in large numbers had presented, declaring that they gave no commission of the sort, that they did not agree or consent to such petitions of the heathen, and they threatened that they would not come either publicly or privately to the Senate if such a decree was made. Is it worthy of your reign, that is of a Christian reign, that Christian senators should be deprived of their dignity, that the profane wishes of the heathen may be carried into effect? This document I sent to your Majesty's brother [c], and it proves that the Senate gave no commission to the deputies about the expenses of superstition.

11. But perhaps it may be said, Why then were they not present in the Senate, when these things were brought forward? They say plainly enough what they wish, by not being present; they have said enough in addressing your Majesty. And yet we need not wonder if they who will not concede to your Majesty the liberty of refusing to command that which you do not approve, or of maintaining your own opinion, should deprive private men at Rome of the right of resistance.

12. Remembering then the commission so lately laid upon me, I again appeal your own faith, I appeal to your own sentiments, not to give your answer in accordance with this heathen petition, or sign your name to such an answer, for it would be sacrilegious. Consult him who

---

[c] i. e. his half brother Gratian.

LETT. 17. is your Excellency's father, the Emperor Theodosius, to whom you have been wont to refer in all causes of importance; and nothing can be graver than religion, more exalted than faith.

13. Were this a civil matter, the right of reply would be reserved for the opposing party: it is a matter of religion, and I, as Bishop, appeal to you, I request to be furnished with a copy of the Memorial which has been sent, that I may answer more at large; and so let your Majesty's father be consulted on the whole matter and vouchsafe a gracious answer. Assuredly should the decree be different, we as Bishops cannot quietly permit and connive at it; it will indeed be in your power to come to the Church, but there you will either not find a priest, or you will find one purposed to resist.

14. What answer will you give to the priest when he says to you, 'the Church seeks not your gifts, because you have adorned the heathen temples with gifts; the Altar of Christ rejects your gifts, because you have erected altars to idols, for it was your word, your hand, your signature, your act: the Lord Jesus refuses and repels your service, because you have served idols, for He has said to you, *Ye cannot serve two masters?* The Virgins dedicated to God enjoy no privileges from you, and do the vestal Virgins claim them? What do you want of the priests of God, when you have preferred to them the profane petitions of the heathen? We cannot enter into fellowship with the errors of others.'

S. Luke xvi. 13.

15. What will you answer to this charge? That it is a boyish error? Every age is perfect in Christ, and fulfilled with God. No childhood in faith can be admitted; for children confronted with their persecutors have boldly confessed Christ.

16. What answer will you make to your brother? Will he not say to you, 'I would not believe myself conquered, for I left you Emperor, I regretted not to die, because you were my successor, I grieved not that I was withdrawn from power, because I believed that my edicts, specially those concerning religion, would continue for ever. These were the memorials of piety and virtue which I had erected,

these trophies of victory over the world, these the spoils of the devil, of the adversary of all, which I had offered up, and in which lies eternal victory. What more could an enemy have deprived me of? You have abrogated my decrees; an act which even he who took up arms against me [d] has not yet committed. Now am I pierced with a more deadly weapon, in that my brother has annulled my ordinances. Your acts tend to the injury of my better part, for while the one destroys my body the other destroys my good name. Now are my laws repealed, repealed too (which makes it more painful) by your adherents and by mine; that very thing which even my enemies had praised in me is repealed. If you have willingly acquiesced, you have condemned the Faith which I held, if you have yielded reluctantly, you have betrayed your own. And so, what is a still heavier calamity, I incur danger in your person also.'

17. What answer will you make to your father [e], who with still greater grief will address you, saying: 'You have judged very wrongly of me, my son, in supposing that I could have winked at the heathen. No man ever informed me that there was an altar in the Roman Senate house [f]; never could I have believed such a crime as that heathen sacrifices should be performed in that common council of Christians and heathens, that is to say, that the heathen should triumph in the presence of Christians, and Christians should be compelled against their wills to be present at sacrifices. Many and various were the crimes committed during my reign, those that were discovered I punished, and if any man escaped unnoticed, is it just to say that I approved that which no one informed me of? You have judged most wrongly of me, if you suppose that a foreign superstition and not my own faith preserved to me the empire.'

18. Wherefore, your Majesty, seeing that if you make

---

[d] i. e Maximus.
[e] Valentinian the 1st.
[f] This is sometimes represented as an exaggerated piece of rhetoric on S. Ambrose's part, not to be regarded as representing a real truth: but it may very well do so, for Valentinian was almost constantly occupied with wars on the frontiers of the empire, and it does not appear from his life that he was ever at Rome during his reign. Milan, not Rome, was the chief seat of the Western Emperors at this time, when they were not with their armies.

MEMORIAL any such decree, you will injure, first God, and next your father and brother, I beseech you to do that which you know will be profitable to your salvation in the sight of God.

THE MEMORIAL OF SYMMACHUS, PREFECT OF THE CITY.

THE occasion on which this Memorial was presented is stated in the introduction to the last letter. It is addressed formally to the three Emperors Valentinian, Theodosius, and Arcadius, but really to Valentinian only, who was at that time sole Emperor of the West. Symmachus was the leading orator and scholar of his day, and his plea is composed with much skill and vigour. Gibbon (ch xxviii.) expresses hearty admiration of the caution with which he 'avoids every topic which might appear to reflect on the religion of his sovereign, and artfully draws his arguments from the schools of rhetoric rather than from those of philosophy,' and gives a summary of its contents in a tone of keen appreciation, as might be expected. We may allow, with Cave (Life of S. Ambrose 3, 3.) that 'it was the best plea the cause would bear.'

1. As soon as the honourable Senate, ever faithful to your Majesty, learnt that offences were made amenable to law, and that the character of past times was being redeemed by pious governors, it hastened to follow the precedent of better times, and give utterance to its long repressed grief, and commissioned me once more to be the spokesman of its complaints, for I was before refused access to the deceased Emperor by evil men, because otherwise justice could never have failed me, most noble Emperors Valentinian, Theodosius and Arcadius, victorious and triumphant, ever illustrious.

2. Filling then a twofold office, as your Prefect I report the proceedings of the Senate [a], as the envoy of the citizens I offer to your favourable notice their requests. Here is no opposition of wills. Men have ceased to believe that disagreement proves their superiority in courtly zeal. To be loved, to be the object of respect and affection is more than sovereignty. Who could suffer private contests to injure the commonwealth? Justly does the

---

[a] The Præfectus Urbi at this time 'was regarded as the direct representative of the Emperor,' and, among other duties, 'he had every month to make a report to the Emperor of the transactions of the Senate,' and also was 'the medium through which the Emperors received the petitions and presents from their capital.' Dict. of Ant sub voc.

Senate assail those who prefer their own power to the honour of the prince.

OF SYMMA-CHUS

3. It is our duty to be watchful for your Majesties. The very glory of this present time makes it the more fitting that we should maintain the customs of our ancestors, the laws and destinies of our country; for it conduces to this glory that you should know it is not in your power to do anything contrary to the practice of your parents. We ask the restoration of that state of religion under which the Republic has so long prospered. Let the Emperors of either sect and either opinion be counted up; a late Emperor observed the rites of his ancestors, his successor did not abolish them. If the religion of older times is no precedent, let the connivance of the last Emperors [b] be so.

4. Who is so friendly with the barbarians as not to require an altar of Victory? Hereafter we must be cautious, and avoid a display of such things. But let at least that honour be paid to the name which is denied to the Divinity[c]. Your fame owes much, and will owe still more, to Victory. Let those detest this power, who were never aided by it, but do you not desert a patronage which favours your triumphs. Vows are due to this power from every man, let no one deny that a power is to be venerated which he owns is to be desired.

5. But even if it were wrong to avoid this omen, at least the ornaments of the Senate-house ought to have been spared. Permit us, I beseech you, to transmit in our old age to our posterity what we ourselves received when boys. Great is the love of custom. And deservedly was the act of the deified Constantius of short duration. You ought to avoid all precedents which you know to have thus been reversed. We are solicitous for the endurance of your name and glory, and that a future age may find nothing to amend.

6. Where shall we swear to observe your laws and statutes? by what sanction shall the deceitful mind be deterred from bearing false witness? All places indeed are full of God, nor is there any spot where the perjured can

---

[b] By the 'late emperor' is meant Julian; 'his successor' is Valentinian the 1st, and the 'last Emperors' are Valentinian the 1st and Valens
[c] There is a play here on the words 'nomen' and 'numen'

be safe, but it is of great efficacy in restraining crime to feel that we are in the presence of sacred things. That altar binds together the concord of all, that altar appeals to the faith of each man, nor does any thing give more weight to our decrees than that all our decisions are sanctioned, so to speak, by an oath. A door will thus be opened to perjury, and this is to be approved of by the illustrious Emperors, allegiance to whom is guarded by a public oath!

7. But Constantius, of sacred memory, is said to have done the same thing. Be it so, let us then imitate his other actions, feeling sure that had any one committed this error before his time, he would never have fallen into it. For the fall of one is a warning to his successor, and the censure of a previous example causes amendment. It was allowable for this predecessor of your Majesties to incur offence in a novel matter, but how can the same excuse avail us, if we imitate that which we know was disapproved?

8. Will your Majesties listen to other acts of this same Emperor more worthy of your imitation? He left uncurtailed the privileges of the sacred virgins, he filled the priestly office with men of noble birth, he allowed the cost of the Roman ceremonies, and following the joyful Senate through all the streets of the eternal city, he beheld with serene countenance the temples, reading the names of the gods inscribed on their pediments, he enquired after the origin of the sacred edifices, and admired their founders. Although he himself professed another religion he maintained the ancient one for the Empire; for every man has his own customs, his own rites. The Divine mind has distributed to cities various guardians and various ceremonies. As each man that is born receives a soul, so do nations receive a genius who guards their destiny. Here the proof from utility comes in, which is our best voucher with regard to the Deity. For since our reason is in the dark, what better knowledge of the gods can we have than from the record and evidence of prosperity? And if a long course of years give their sanction to a religion, we ought to keep faith with so many centuries, and to follow our

parents, as they followed with success those who founded them.

9. Let us suppose Rome herself to approach, and address you in these terms: 'Excellent Emperors, Fathers of your country, respect these years to which pious rites have conducted me. Let me use the ancient ceremonies, for I do not repent of them. Let me live in my own way, for I am free. This worship reduced the world under my laws; these sacred rites repulsed Hannibal from the walls, and the Gauls from the Capitol. Am I reserved for this, to be censured in my old age? I am not unwilling to consider the proposed decree, and yet late and ignominious is the reformation of old age.'

10. We pray therefore for a respite for the gods of our fathers and our native gods [d]. That which all venerate should in fairness be accounted as one. We look on the same stars, the heaven is common to us all, the same world surrounds us. What matters it by what arts each of us seeks for truth? We cannot arrive by one and the same path at so great a secret; but this discussion belongs rather to persons at their ease, it is prayers not arguments which we now offer.

11. What advantage accrues to your treasury from the abolition of the privilege of the Vestal virgins? Shall that be denied under princes the most munificent which the most parsimonious have granted? Their sole honour consists in their wages, so to speak, of chastity. As their fillets adorn their heads, so is it esteemed by them an honour to be free to devote themselves to the ministry of sacrifices. It is but the bare name of exemption which they ask, for their poverty exonerates them from any payment. So that he who reduces their means, contributes to their praise, for virginity dedicated to the public welfare is meritorious in proportion as it is without reward.

12. Far be such gains from the purity of your treasury. The exchequer of good princes should be replenished by

---

[d] Symmachus is thinking of Virgil's invocation,
Di patrii, Indigetes, et Romule, Vestaque Mater, &c.
Georg. i. 498.

The Di patrii are explained as being those brought by Æneas into Italy, Indigetes those native to the soil of Italy.

MEMORIAL the spoils of enemies, not by the losses of ministers of religion. And is the gain any compensation for the odium? Those whose ancient resources are cut off only feel it the more acutely in that you are free from the charge of avarice. For under Emperors who keep their hands from other men's goods and check desire what does not excite the cupidity of the spoiler must be taken solely with a view of injuring the person robbed.

13. The Imperial Exchequer retains also lands bequeathed by the will of dying persons to the sacred virgins and priests. I implore you, as Priests of justice, to restore to the sacred functionaries of your city the right of inheritance. Let men dictate their wills in peace, knowing that under equitable princes their bequests will be undisturbed. Men are wont to take pleasure in this security, and I would have you sympathise with them, for the precedent lately set has begun to harass them on their death-beds. Shall it be said that the religion of Rome appertains not to Roman laws? What name shall we give to the taking away of legacies which no law no casualty has made void? Freedmen may take legacies, slaves are allowed [e] a due latitude of bequeathing by will, only the noble virgins and ministers of sacred rites are excluded from inheriting lands devised to them. What advantage is it to dedicate one's virginity to the public safety, and to support the immortality of the empire with heavenly protection, to conciliate friendly powers to your arms and eagles, to take upon oneself vows salutary for all, and to refrain from commerce with mankind in general? Slavery then is a happier condition, whose service is given to men. It is the state which is wronged, whose interest it never is to be ungrateful.

14. Let me not be supposed to be defending the cause of the ancient religions only; from acts of this kind all the calamities of the Roman nation have arisen. The laws of our ancestors provided for the Vestal virgins and the ministers of the gods a moderate maintenance and just privileges. This gift was preserved inviolate till the time of the degenerate moneychangers, who diverted the mainten-

---

[e] In strict law a slave's peculium was the property of his owner, but custom had allowed it to be regarded as his own property.

ance of sacred chastity into a fund for the payment of base porters. A public famine ensued on this act, and a bad harvest disappointed the hopes of all the provinces. The soil was not here in fault, we ascribe no influence to the stars, no mildew blighted the crops, nor did tares choke the corn, it was sacrilege which rendered the year barren, for it was necessary that all should lose that which they had denied to religion.

15. By all means, if there is any instance of such an evil, let us attribute this famine to the effect of the seasons. An unhealthy wind has caused this blight, and so life is supported by means of shrubs and leaves, and the peasants in their want have had resource once more to the oaks of Dodona [f]. When did the provinces suffer such a calamity, so long as the ministers of religion were supported by the public bounty? When were oaks shaken for the food of man, when were roots dug up, when were opposite regions of the earth cursed with sterility, so long as provisions were furnished in common to the people and to the sacred virgins? The produce of the earth was blessed by its support of the priests, and thus the gift was rather in the nature of a safeguard than of a largess. Can it be doubted that the gift was for the common benefit, now that a general scarcity has attended its discontinuance?

16. But it may be said that public aid is rightly refused to the cost of an alien religion. Far be it from good rulers to suppose that what has been bestowed from the common stock on certain individuals is within the disposal of the Imperial treasury. For as the commonwealth consists of individuals, so that which comes from it becomes again the property of individuals. You govern all, but you preserve for each his own, and justice has more power with you than arbitrary will. Consult your own generous feelings, whether that ought still to be deemed public property which has been conferred on others. Gifts once devoted to the honour of the city are placed out of the power of the donors, and that which originally was a free-gift becomes by usage and length of time a debt. Vain therefore is the fear which

---

[f] Another trace of Virgil: Cum jam glandes atque arbuta sacræ
    Deficerent silvæ et victum Dodona negaret. Georg. i. 158.

LETT. 18. they would impress upon your minds who assert that unless you incur the odium of withdrawing the gift you share the responsibility of the donors of it.

17. May the unseen patrons of all sects be propitious to your Majesties, and may those in particular who of old assisted your ancestors, aid you and be worshipped by us. We ask for that religious condition which preserved the empire to your Majesties' father [g], and blessed him with lawful heirs. That venerable sire beholds from his starry seat the tears of the priests, and feels himself censured by the infraction of that custom which he readily observed.

18. I beg you also to amend for your departed brother what he did by the advice of others, to cover the act by which he unknowingly offended the Senate. For it is certain that the reason why the embassage was refused admittance was, to prevent the decision of the state from reaching him. It is due to the credit of past times to abolish without hesitation that which has been found not to have been the doing of the Emperor.

A.D. 384.

LETTER XVIII.

THIS is S. Ambrose's answer to the Memorial of Symmachus which precedes it. In it he replies in detail to the arguments which Symmachus had advanced, and meets him on his own ground. It is to be remembered in forming an estimate of it, that it is simply a state paper, adopting both the style and method natural to such a document. That it is over rhetorical for our taste may at once be allowed, for that is the character of the literature of the time generally; that it is not so perfect a specimen of the style, regarded merely as a piece of argument, as the document to which it replies, may be granted without disparagement to S. Ambrose, for Symmachus "stood foremost among his contemporaries as a scholar, a statesman, and an orator." (Dict. of Biog. sub voc.) But he fairly meets and refutes Symmachus' arguments, and his retort of his adversary's personification of Rome is happy and telling. The earlier portion is more vigorous than the latter, which is overwrought, especially in the argument against maintaining things as they were. The abundance of allusions to, and quotations of, Virgil are characteristic of the age, and evidences of S. Ambrose's early training in the education of a Roman of high birth and rank.

[g] Valentinian the 1st, as Symmachus mentions above, had tolerated the heathen rites, and this he here represents as having availed to win the special favour of the gods.

BISHOP AMBROSE TO THE MOST BLESSED PRINCE AND GRACIOUS EMPEROR, HIS MAJESTY VALENTINIAN.

THE honourable [a] Symmachus, Prefect of the city, having memorialised your Majesty that the altar, which had been removed from the Senate-house at Rome, ought to be restored to its place, and your Majesty, whose years of nonage and inexperience are yet unfulfilled, though a veteran in the power of faith, not having sanctioned the prayer of the heathen, I also as soon as I heard of it presented a petition, in which, though it embraced all that seemed necessary to be said, I requested that a copy of the Memorial might be furnished to me.

2. Now therefore, not as doubting your faith, but as providing for the future, and assured of a righteous judgement, I will reply to the allegations of the Memorial, making this one request, that you will not look for elegance of phrases but force of facts. For as Holy Scripture teaches us, the tongue of learned and wise men is golden, and endowed with highly-decked words, and glittering with splendid elegance as with the brightness of some rich colour, and so captivates and dazzles the eyes of the mind with a shew of beauty. But this gold, if closely handled, may pass current outwardly, but within is base metal. Consider well, I beseech you, and sift the sect of the Heathens; their professions are grand and lofty, but what they espouse is degenerate and effete, they talk of God but worship idols.

3. The propositions of the honourable Prefect of the city, to which he attaches weight, are these, that Rome (as he asserts) seeks the restoration of her ancient rites, and that stipends are to be assigned to her priests and Vestal virgins, and that it was owing to these being withheld that a general famine has ensued.

4. According to his first proposition, Rome utters a mournful complaint, wanting back (as he asserts) her ancient ceremonies. These sacred rites, he says, repelled

---

[a] This is an official title of honour. There were three ranks among those who held office under the Emperors, 1 Illustres. 2 Spectabiles, 3 Clarissimi, which is the one here applied to Symmachus. The latter was applied to all senators. the other two were reserved for the higher offices of state. See Gibbon, ch. xvii.

Hannibal from the walls, the Gauls from the Capitol. But even here, in blazoning the efficacy of these rites, he betrays their weakness. According to this, Hannibal long insulted the Roman religion, and pushed his conquest to the very walls of the city, though the gods fought against him. Why did they for whom their gods fought, allow themselves to be besieged?

5. For why speak of the Gauls, whom the remnant of the Romans could not have prevented from entering the sanctuary of the Capitol, if the timid cackling of a goose had not betrayed them. These are the guardians of the Roman temples! Where was Jupiter then? Did he speak in a goose?

6. But why should I deny that their sacred rites fought for the Romans? Yet Hannibal also worshipped the same gods. Let them choose therefore which they will. If these rites conquered in the Romans, they were vanquished in the Carthaginians, but if they were thus overcome in the case of the Carthaginians, neither did they profit the Romans.

7. Away then with this invidious complaint of the Roman people; Rome never dictated it. It is with other words that she addresses them: 'Why do you daily deluge me with the useless gore of the innocent flocks? The trophies of victory depend not on the limbs of cattle, but on the strength of warriors. It was by other powers that I subdued the world. Camillus was my soldier, who recovered the standards which had been taken from the Capitol, and slew those who had captured the Tarpeian rock; valour overthrew those against whom religion had not prevailed. Why should I name Regulus, who gave me even the services of his death? Africanus gained his triumph not among the altars of the Capitol, but among Hannibal's ranks. Why do you produce to me the rites of our ancestors? I abhor the rites of the Neros. What shall I say of the two-month Emperors [b], and the ends of princes knit on to their accession? Or is it a thing unheard of, that

---

[b] He is referring apparently to Galba, Otho, and Vitellius, but somewhat exaggerates the brevity of their reigns. Galba reigned nearly seven months, Otho three months, Vitellius nearly eight months.

the barbarians should cross their frontiers? Were those men Christians, in whose miserable and unprecedented fate, in the one case a captive Emperor, in the other a captive world [c] proved the falsehood of the rites which promised victory? Was there then no altar of Victory? I am ashamed of my downfall, the pale cheeks of age gather redness from that disgraceful bloodshed. I do not blush to be converted in my old age along with the whole world. It is surely true that no age is too late to learn. Let that old age blush which cannot improve itself. It is not the hoary head of years but of virtue which is venerable. It is no disgrace to pass to better things. This alone had I in common with the barbarians that of old I knew not God. Your sacrifice is a rite of sprinkling yourselves with the blood of beasts. Why do you look for the voice of God in dead beasts? Come and learn here on earth a heavenly warfare; we live here, but our warfare is above. Let God Himself, the Creator, teach me the mystery of heaven, not man who knew not himself. Whom should I believe about God, sooner than God Himself? How can I believe you, who confess that you know not what you worship?'

TO VALENTINIAN

Wisd. iv. 9.

8. By a single path, he says, we cannot arrive at so great a secret. What you are ignorant of, that we have learnt by the voice of God; what you seek after by faint surmises, that we are assured of by the very Wisdom and Truth of God. Our customs therefore and yours do not agree. You ask the Emperors to grant peace to your gods, we pray for peace for the Emperors themselves from Christ. You worship the works of your own hands, we think it sacrilege that any thing which can be made should be called God. God wills not to be worshipped under the form of stones. Nay, your very philosophers have ridiculed this.

9. But if you are led to deny that Christ is God, because you cannot believe that He died, (for you are ignorant how that this was the death not of His Godhead but of His

---

[c] The captive Emperor is Valerian, who, A.D. 260, was taken prisoner by Sapor king of Persia, and treated with the utmost indignity. The other is his son Gallienus, and S. Ambrose's expression with regard to him may be explained by a sentence of Gibbon, (ch. xi. init.) 'Under the deplorable reigns of Valerian and Gallienus, the empire was oppressed and almost destroyed by the soldiers, the tyrants, and the barbarians.'

flesh, whereby it comes to pass that none of the faithful shall die,) how inconsistent are you, who insult by way of worship, and disparage by way of honour. You consider your god to be a block of wood; what an insulting kind of reverence! You believe not that Christ could die; what a respectful kind of unbelief!

10. But, he says, the ancient altars and images ought to be restored, and the temples adorned as of old. This request ought to be made to one who shares the superstition; a Christian Emperor has learned to honour the altar of Christ alone. Why do they compel pious hands and faithful lips to minister to their sacrilege? Let the voice of our Emperor speak of Christ alone, let him declare Him only Whom in heart he believes, for *the king's heart is in the Hand of God.* Did ever heathen Emperor raise an altar to God? In demanding a restoration of ancient things they remind us what reverence Christian Emperors ought to pay to the Religion which they profess, since heathen ones paid the utmost to their own superstitions.

11. Long since was our beginning, and now they follow us whom they shut out. *We* glory in shedding our blood, a trifling expense disturbs *them.* We consider such things a victory, they esteem them an injury. Never did they confer a greater favour on us than when they commanded Christians to be scourged, and proscribed and slain. Religion made into a reward what unbelief intended for a punishment. Behold their magnanimity! *We* have grown by wrongs, by want, by punishment; *they* find that without money their ceremonies cannot be maintained.

12. Let the Vestal virgins, he says, enjoy their privileges. It is for those to say this, who cannot believe in gratuitous virginity, it is for them to allure by profit who distrust virtue. But how many virgins have their promised rewards obtained them? They have barely seven Vestals. Such is the whole number whom the veiled and filleted head, the dye of the purple vest, the pompous litter surrounded by attendants, high privileges, great gains, and a prescribed period of virginity, have collected.

13. Let them turn their mental and bodily eye to us, let them behold a people of chastity, an undefiled multitude, a

virgin assembly. No fillets to adorn their heads, but a veil of common use though dignified by chastity; the blandishments of beauty not curiously sought out, but cast aside; no purple trappings, no luxurious delicacies, but frequent fastings; no privileges, no gains; all things in short so ordered as to repress any affection in the very exercise of their functions. But in fact by this very exercise their affection to it is conciliated. Chastity is perfected by its own sacrifices. That is not virginity which is bought for money, not preserved for love of holiness; that is not integrity which is bid for at an auction by a pecuniary equivalent, to last but for a time. The first triumph of chastity is to overcome the desire of wealth, for this desire is a temptation to modesty. But let us suppose that virginity ought to be supported by pecuniary bounty. In this case, what an abundance of gifts will overflow upon the Christians; what treasury will contain riches so great? Or do they consider that it ought to be bestowed exclusively on the Vestal virgins? Do not they, who claimed the whole under heathen Emperors, feel some shame in denying that under Christian Princes we ought to participate in the bounty?

14. They complain also that public support is not given to their priests and ministers. What a storm of words is here! To us on the other hand the privileges of inheriting private property [d] is denied by recent laws, and no one complains; we do not feel it to be an injury, for we grieve not at the loss. If a priest would claim the privilege of being exempt from the municipal [e] burthens, he must re-

[d] S Ambrose refers here to a law of Valentinian's, forbidding the Clergy from receiving bequests from widows and unmarried females. It was addressed to Damasus, Bishop of Rome. S. Ambrose's caution in de Off. Min. 1, 20, 87, shews that control was needed S. Jerome, speaking of this law says, 'I do not complain of the law, but grieve that we have deserved it.'

[e] In the provincial towns the political power in the times of the Emperors had passed into the hands of the curia or provincial Senate, and, with the power, many burdensome and extensive duties, were laid upon the curiales or decurions, as they were called. (See § 15) Exemption from these had been granted first by Constantine, afterwards, as it was found that persons sought Holy Orders in order to evade civil duties, the privilege was restrained: and various changes were introduced by different Emperors. A full outline of the various laws is given in a learned note in Newman's Fleury, vol. i. p. 162. where the text is speaking of S. Ambrose's Letter to Theodosius, (infr. Lett. xl.) where he

LETT. 18. linquish his paternal estate and all other property. How would the heathens press this ground of complaint, if they had it, that a priest must purchase the liberty of performing his functions by the loss of his whole patrimony, and at the expense of all his private advantages must buy the right of ministering to the public, and while he claims to hold vigils for the public safety must console himself with the wages of domestic poverty; for he does not sell service but purchase a favour.

15. Compare[f] the two cases. You wish to exempt a Decurio, when the Church may not exempt a priest. Wills are made in favour of ministers of temples; not even profane persons, even of the lowest rank, nor of abandoned character, are excepted; the clergy alone are excluded from the common privilege, by whom alone the general prayer for all men is offered, and the common office performed; no legacy, even of grave widows, no donation is allowed. When no blame can attach to character, a fine is imposed on the office. The legacy which a Christian widow bequeaths to the minister of a temple is valid, that which she bequeaths to the ministers of God is invalid. This I have stated not by way of complaint, but that they may know how much I abstain from complaining of, for I would rather we were losers in money than in grace.

16. But they report that gifts or legacies to the Church have not been taken away. Let them state who has snatched gifts from the temples, a loss which Christians have[g] suffered. Had this been done to the Gentiles, it would rather have been the requital than the infliction of a wrong. Is it now only that they make a plea of justice, put in a claim for equity? Where was this sentiment, when, having despoiled all Christians of their goods, they grudged them the very breath of life, and debarred them from that last burial-rite which was never before denied to any of the dead? Those whom the heathen flung into it, the sea restored. This is a victory of faith, that they them-

again complains of the same hardship The subject is also more fully dealt with by Bingham Antiq B.V. ch iii. § 14—16.

[f] 'Conferte' is here adopted as a manifest emendation of 'conferet.' The transfer of two letters is a common mistake of copyists.

[g] This was the case in Julian's reign, as may be seen in Theod. iii. 12.

selves impugn the acts of their ancestors, in that they condemn their proceedings. But what consistency is there in condemning the acts of those whose gifts they solicit?

17. Yet no man has forbidden gifts to the temples, or legacies to the soothsayers; their lands alone are taken away, because they did not use that religiously which they claimed on the plea of religion. If they avail themselves of our example why did they not copy our practice? The Church possesses nothing but her faith. There are her rents, her revenues. The wealth of the Church is the support of the poor. Let them count up how many prisoners the temples have ransomed, what support they have afforded to the poor, to how many exiles they have ministered the means of life. Hence it is that they have been deprived of their lands, but not of their rights.

18. This is what has been done, and a public famine, as they assert, has avenged this grave impiety, that the private emoluments of the priests have been converted to the public service. For this cause they say it was that men stripped branches of their bark, and moistened their fainting life with this wretched juice. For this cause they were obliged to substitute for corn the Chaonian acorn, and thrust back again to this wretched fare, the food of beasts, they shook the oaks and thus appeased their sore hunger in the woods. As if forsooth these were new prodigies on earth, which never occurred so long as heathen superstition prevailed over the world! But in truth how often before this were the hopes of the greedy husbandmen frustrated by empty oat-stalks, while the blade of corn sought for in the furrows disappointed the race of peasants.

19. Why did the Greeks attribute oracles to their oaks, but that they fancied their sylvan fare was the gift of their heavenly religion? Such are the gifts which they suppose to come from their gods. Who but heathen ever worshipped the trees of Dodona, bestowing honour on the sorry sustenance of the sacred grove [h]? It is not probable that their gods in their anger gave them for a punishment what they were wont when appeased to confer as a gift.

---

[h] The reading of all the other Edd. 'sacri nemoris' for 'agri nemorum' is here adopted, as yielding a clearer sense.

LETT. 18.   20. But what equity were it, that because they are annoyed at the refusal of sustenance to a few priests they should themselves refuse it to every one? in that case their vengeance is more severe than was the fault. But in truth the cause they assign is not adequate to produce so great infirmity of a failing world, as that, when the crops were green, the full grown hopes of the season should all at once perish.

21. Certain it is that many years ago the rights of the temples were abolished throughout the world, is it only now that it has occurred to the gods of the Gentiles to avenge their injuries? Can it be said that the Nile failed to overflow his banks as usual, to avenge the losses of the priests of the City, when he did not do so to avenge his own priests?

22. But supposing that in the past year it was the wrongs of their gods that were avenged, why are the same wrongs neglected in the present year? Now the country people do not pluck up and eat the roots of herbs, nor seek solace from the sylvan berry, nor gather their food from thorns; but rejoicing in their successful labours they wonder at their own harvest, and their hopes fulfilled compensate for their fast, the earth having yielded us her produce with interest.

23. Who then is so inexperienced on human affairs as to be amazed at the vicissitudes of the seasons? And yet even last year we know that most provinces had an abundant harvest. What shall I say of Gaul which was more fertile than usual? The Pannonias [1] sold corn which they had not sown, and the second [k] Rhaetia learnt the danger of her own fertility, for being used to security from her sterility, she drew down an enemy on herself by her abundance. Liguria and Venice are replenished by the fruits of autumn. So then the former year was not withered by sacrilege, while the present has overflowed with the fruits of faith. Nor can they deny that the vineyards pro-

---

[1] Pannonia was at this time divided into three provinces, viz. Pannonia Prima and Secunda, and Valeria Ripensis.

[k] Rhaetia Secunda was the name given to Vindelicia when separated again from Rhaetia proper, shortly before the time of Constantine. it had been united to it about the end of the first century.

duced an overflowing crop. Thus our harvest yielded its produce with interest, and we enjoyed the benefits of a more abundant vintage.

24. The last and most weighty topic remains; as to whether your Majesties should restore those aids which have been profitable to yourselves, for he says, 'Let them defend you, and be worshipped by us.' This, most faithful Princes, we cannot endure; that they should make it a taunt to us that they supplicate their gods in your name, and without your command commit an atrocious sacrilege, taking your connivance as consent. Let them keep their guardians to themselves, let these guardians, if they can, protect their own. But if they cannot protect those who worship them, how can they protect you who worship them not?

25. Our ancestral rites, he says, should be preserved. But what if all things have become better? The world itself, which at first was compacted by the gathering together of the elemental seeds through the vast void, an unconsolidated sphere, or was obscured by the thick darkness of the yet unordered work, was it not afterwards endowed with the forms of things which constitute its beauty, and were not the heaven sea and earth distinguished from each other? The earth rescued from dripping darkness was amazed at its new sun. In the beginning too the day shines not, but as time goes on it is bright and warm with the increase of light and heat.

26. The moon herself, which in the prophetic oracles represents the Church, when first she rises again, and repairs her monthly wanings, is hidden from us by darkness, but gradually she fills her horns, or completes them as she comes opposite to the sun, and gleams with a bright and glorious splendour.

27. In former days, the earth knew not how to be wrought into fruitfulness; but afterwards when the careful husbandman began to till the fields, and to clothe the bare soil with vineyards, it was softened by this domestic culture, and put off its rugged nature.

28. So too the first season of the year itself, which has imparted a like habit to ourselves, is bare of produce, then,

LETT. 18. as time goes on, it blossoms out in flowers soon to fade, and in the end finds its maturity in fruits[1].

29. So we, while young in age, experience an infancy of understanding, but as we grow in years lay aside the rudeness of our faculties.

30. Let them say then that all things ought to have continued as at first; that the world once covered with darkness is now displeasing because it shines with the beams of the sun. And how much better is it to have dispelled the darkness of the mind than that of the body, and that the beam of faith has shone forth than that of the sun. So then the early stages of the world as of all else have been unsettled, that the venerable age of hoary faith might follow. Let those who are affected by this find fault with the harvest too, because it ripens late; or with the vintage, because it is in the fall of the year; or with the olive, because it is the latest of fruits.

31. So then our harvest too is the faith of the soul; the grace of the Church is the vintage of good works, which from the beginning of the world flourished in the saints, but in these last days is spread over the people; to the intent that all might perceive that it is not into rude minds that the faith of Christ has insinuated itself, but these opinions which before prevailed being shaken off (for without a contest there is no crown of victory) the truth was preferred according as is just.

32. If the old rites pleased, why did Rome adopt alien ones? I pass over the covering of the ground with costly buildings, and shepherds' huts glittering with the gold of a degenerate age [m]. Why, to speak of the very subject of their complaint, have they admitted in their rivalry the images of captured cities, and of conquered gods, and the foreign rites of an alien superstition? Whence do they derive their precedent for Cybele washing her chariot in a

---

[1] The Reading 'nuda gignentium' is adopted from Ed. Rom. The phrase occurs in Sallust Jug. 79, 6. 'Gignentia' is used for plants, trees &c. The clause 'quae nos' &c. is strange, but probably refers to the torpidity of winter, which is felt by man as well as by the lower creation.

[m] This passage seems suggested by reminiscences of Virgil, the phrase 'absconditam pretio humum' possibly from Aen. iv, 211 urbem Exiguam pretio posuit, while in the latter part S. Ambrose perhaps had in his mind the description of Evander's town in Aen. viii. See especially ll. 347—366.

stream to counterfeit the Almo[n]? Whence came the Phrygian seers, and the deities of faithless Carthage ever hateful to Rome, her for instance, whom the Africans worship as Cælestis[o], and the Persians as Mitra, the greater part of the world as Venus, the same deity under different names. So also they have believed Victory to be a goddess, which is in truth a gift not a power, is bestowed and does not rule, comes by the aid of legions not by the power of religion. Great forsooth is the goddess whom the number of soldiers claims, or the issue of the battle confers!

33. And her altar they now ask to have set up in the Senate-house at Rome, that is to say, where a majority[p] of Christians assemble. There are altars in all temples, an altar also in the temple of victories. Being pleased with numbers, they celebrate their sacrifices every where. But to insist on a sacrifice on this one altar, what is it but to insult over the Faith? Is it to be borne that while a Gentile sacrifices Christians must attend? Let their eyes, he says, drink in the smoke whether they will or no; their ears the music; their mouth the ashes; their nostrils the incense; and though they loathe it, let the embers of our

[n] The story of Cybele being brought to Rome, and landing outside the city, where the little stream of the Almo joins the Tiber, is told at length by Ovid, Fast iv 250—348. In commemoration of the washing of the Statue and sacred implements at the landing, an annual ceremony was maintained, which seems to have been popular, from the numerous allusions to it in later writers. See Lucan 1. 600, Martial iii 47. 2, Stat. Silv. v. l. 222, Sil. Ital. viii. 365, all quoted in Dict. of Geogr. When the rites were performed away from Rome, the nearest river was conventionally made' the Almo for the time. It is remarkable that Ammianus Marcellinus xxiii, 3, 7. mentions as one of the Emperor Julian's last acts, his keeping the day of this rite, when on his last campaign against the Persians, and performing all the ceremonies at Callinicum or Nicephorium on the Euphrates.

[o] Venus Cælestis is a Latin equivalent of Ἀφροδίτη οὐρανία, and this name was transferred, according to Herodotus (Bk. 1. ch. 105) to the Phœnician goddess Astarte, or Ashtaroth. The same author also (B i. ch 131.) identifies Aphrodite with the Persian goddess Mitra, which however is shewn by Prof. Rawlinson, ad loc., to be an error, as Mithias is the sungod of the Persians. The Temple of Venus Caelestis, or Astarte, at Carthage was very shortly after this time converted into a Christian Church, as recorded by Gibbon on the authority of Prosper Aquitan. (ch. xxviii).

[p] S Ambrose's repeated assertions, that the Christians formed a majority in the Senate, are characterised by writers unfavourable to Christianity as unfounded, but they produce no proof. Gibbon (ch. xxviii. note 12.) simply says that it is an assertion 'in contradiction to common sense.' But as a large majority of the Senate voted for the abolition of the worship of Jupiter about the same time, as Gibbon himself records, common sense would seem rather to agree with S. Ambrose.

Lett. 18. hearths besprinkle their faces. Is it not enough for him that the baths, the colonnades, the streets are filled with images? Even in that general assembly, are we not to meet upon equal terms? The believing portion of the Senate will be bound by the voices of them that call the gods to witness, by the oaths of them that swear by them. If they refuse, they will seem to prove their falsehood, if they acquiesce, to acquiesce in a sacrilege.

34. Where, he asks, shall we swear allegiance to your Majesties' laws and commands? Your minds then, of which your laws are the outward expression, gather support and secure fidelity by heathen rites. Moreover your Majesties' faith is assailed not only when you are present, but also, which is more, when you are absent, for you constrain when you command. Constantius, of illustrious memory, though not yet initiated into the sacred Mysteries, thought himself polluted by the sight of that altar; he commanded it to be removed, he did not command it to be replaced. His order bears all the authority of an Act, his silence does not bear the authority of a precept.

35. And let no one rest satisfied because he is absent. He is more to be considered present who unites himself to the minds of others than he who gives the testimony of his visible presence. It is a greater matter to be united in mind than to be joined in body. The Senate regards you as its presidents who summon its meetings; at your bidding it assembles; to you, not to the gods of the heathen, does she resign her conscience; you she prefers to her children though not to her faith. This is the affection worth seeking, an affection more powerful than dominion, if faith, which preserves dominion, be secured..

36. But perhaps some one may be influenced by the thought that if so, a most orthodox Emperor[q] has been left without his reward; as if the reward of good actions was to be estimated by the frail tenure of things present. And what wise man is there who knows not that human affairs move in a certain cycle and order, and meet not always

---

[q] Referring to the unhappy end of Gratian who in the previous year (A D. 383) had been overpowered by Maximus, who revolted in Britain, and attacked him in Gaul. His troops deserted him and he was put to death by Maximus' orders.

Life uncertain to heathens as well as Christians. 113

with the same success, but their state is subject to vicissitudes?

37. Who more fortunate than Cneius Pompeius was ever sent forth by the temples of Rome? But he, after compassing the circuit of the globe in three triumphs, vanquished in battle, and driven into exile beyond the bounds of the empire he had saved, perished by the hand of an Eunuch[r] of Canopus.

38. What nobler king than Cyrus king of the Persians has the whole Eastern world produced? He too, after he had conquered the most powerful princes in battle, and detained them as his prisoners, was worsted and slain by the arms of a woman[s]. That king who had conferred on the vanquished the honour of sitting at meat with him, had his head cut off and enclosed in a vessel full of blood, and so was bid to satiate himself, exposed to the mockery of a woman. So in the course of his life like is not matched with like, but things most unlike.

39. Again who was more assiduous in sacrificing than Hamilcar[t] general of the Carthaginians? During the whole time of the battle he took his station between the ranks of the combatants, and there offered sacrifice: then, when he found himself vanquished, he threw himself upon the fire on which he was burning his victims, that he might extinguish even with his own body those flames which he had learnt availed him nothing.

40. And what shall I say of Julian? who blindly believing the answers of the diviners, deprived himself of the means of retreat[u]. Thus even when the circumstances are

[r] Pompeius was murdered, as he landed in Egypt, after escaping from Pharsalia, by Achillas an Eunuch and one of the guardians of king Ptolemy
[s] Tomyris queen of the Massagetæ. See the story in Herod i. 214.
[t] This is the first of the famous Hamilcars, the one who led the great invasion of Sicily in B.C 480, and was totally defeated by Gelon. Herodotus, B vii ch 167, tells the story to which S. Ambrose alludes as the account given by the Carthaginians of his end
[u] S. Ambrose is alluding to the famous story of Julian burning his fleet, after crossing the Tigris to attack Sapor, king of Persia, in his own dominions. This was regarded afterwards by the Christians as an act of judicial blindness. See Augustine de Civ Dei iv. 29, v. 21 Ammianus, xxiv. 7. asserts that he repented of the order as soon as it was issued, but was too late to stop the flames. Gibbon endeavours to justify the act, and says, 'had he been victorious we should now admire his conduct.' See his narrative in ch. xxiv. The author of his life in the Dict. of Ant. styles it 'the best thing he could have done, if his march into the interior of Persia, had been dictated by absolute necessity.' Setting these hypotheses aside,

common there is not a common cause of offence, for our promises have deluded no one.

41. I have replied to those who harass me as though I had not been harassed: for my object has been to refute their Memorial, not to expose their superstitions. But let this very Memorial make your Majesty more cautious. For by pointing out that of a series of former Emperors, those who reigned first followed the rites of their ancestors, and their successors did not remove them, and by observing upon this, that if the religion of older ones was not an example, the connivance of the more recent ones was, they have plainly shewn that you owe it to the faith which you profess not to follow the precedent of heathen rites, and to brotherly love not to violate your brothers' ordinances. For if they for the sake of their own cause have praised the connivance of those Emperors, who being Christians, have not abrogated heathen decrees, how much more are you bound to shew deference to brotherly affection, and, whereas you would be bound to wink at what perhaps you did not approve, for fear of detracting from your brothers' decrees, now to maintain what you judge to be in accordance both with your own faith and the tie of brotherhood.

A.D. 385.

LETTER XIX.

VIGILIUS, to whom this letter is addressed, is supposed by the Benedictine Editors to have been the Bishop of Trent, (Tridentum,) who is commemorated in the Roman Martyrology. He had written to S. Ambrose, on his consecration as Bishop, to ask his guidance and instruction, and S Ambrose replies, first with brief general directions, somewhat resembling those of Letter 11, and then dwells at length on the duty of preventing intermarriage between Christians and heathens, and recounts at full length, in support of this, the history of Samson. At the time when heathenism was rapidly dying out, it is clear how important a point this would seem, and we do not wonder at the stress which S. Ambrose lays on it.

AMBROSE TO VIGILIUS.

1. BEING newly consecrated to the sacred office, you and looking only at the actual result, we may fairly think that the Christian interpretation of the facts, even if over-strongly expressed, is the truer.

have requested me to furnish you with the outlines of your teaching. Having built up yourself as was fitting, seeing you have been thought worthy of so high an office, you have now to be informed how to build up others also. *TO VIGILIUS*

2. And in the first place remember that it is the Church of God that is committed to you, and be therefore always on your guard against the intrusion of any scandal, lest the body thereof become as it were common by any admixture of heathen. It is on this account that Scripture says to you *Thou shalt not take a wife of the daughters of Canaan, but go to Mesopotamia, to the house of Bethuel* (that is the house of Wisdom) *and take thee a wife from thence.* Mesopotamia is a country in the East, surrounded by the two greatest rivers in those parts, the Tigris and Euphrates, which take their rise in Armenia, falling, each by a different channel, into the Red sea; and so the Church is signified under the name of Mesopotamia, for she fertilizes the minds of the faithful by the mighty streams of wisdom and justice, pouring into them the grace of Baptism, the type of which was foreshewn in the Red sea, and washing away sin. Wherefore you must instruct the people that they should contract marriage not with strange-born but with Christian families. Gen. xxviii. 1, 2.

3. Let no man defraud his hired servant of his due wages, for we too are the servants of our God, and look for the reward of our labour from Him. You then, (you must say) O merchant, whoever you be, refuse your servant his wages of money, that is, of what is vile and worthless, but to you will be denied the reward of heavenly promises: therefore *thou shalt not defraud thy hired servant of his reward,* as the Law saith. Deut. xxiv. 14.

4. Thou shalt not give thy money upon usury, for it is written that *he who hath not given his money upon usury shall dwell in the tabernacle of God,* for he is *cast down,* who seeks for usurious gains. Therefore let the Christian, if he have it, give money as though he were not to receive it again, or at all events only the principal which he has given. By so doing he receives no small increase of grace. Otherwise to lend would be to deceive not to succour. For what can be more cruel than to give money to one Ps. xv. 1. 6. Ps. xvii. 13.

that hath not, and then to exact double? He that can not pay the simple sum how can he pay double the amount?

<small>Tobit iv. 21.</small>

5. Let Tobit be an example to us, who never required again the money he had lent, till the end of his life; and that rather that he might not defraud his heir, than in order to levy and recover the money he had lent out. Nations have often been ruined by usury, and this has been the cause of public destruction. Wherefore it must be the principal care of us Bishops, to extirpate those vices which we find to prevail most extensively.

6. Teach them that they ought to exercise hospitality willingly rather than of necessity, so that in shewing this favour they may not betray a churlish disposition of mind, and thus in the very reception of their guest the kindness be spoilt by wrong, but rather let it be fostered by the practice of social duties, and by the offices of kindness. It is not rich gifts that are required of thee, but willing

<small>Prov. xv. 17.</small>

services, full of peace and accordant harmony. *Better is a dinner of herbs* with grace and friendship than that the banquet should be adorned with exquisite viands, while the sentiment of kindness is lacking. We read of a people

<small>Judges xx. 44. Gen. xxxiv. 25.</small>

perishing by a grievous destruction on account of the violation of the laws of hospitality. Through lust also fierce wars have been kindled.

7. But there is scarce any thing more pernicious than marriage with a foreigner; already the passions both of lust and disorder, and the evils of sacrilege are inflamed. For seeing that the marriage ceremony itself ought to be sanctified by the priestly veil and benediction, how can that be called a marriage when there is not agreement in faith? Since their prayers ought to be in common, how can there be the love of a common wedlock between those whose religion is different. Often have men ensnared by the love of women betrayed their faith, as did the Jews at Baal-

<small>Num. xxv. 8.</small>

phegor. For which cause Phineas took a sword, and slew the Hebrew and the Midianitish woman, and appeased the Divine vengeance, that the whole people might not be destroyed.

8. And why should I bring forward more examples? I will produce one out of many, from the mention of which

will appear what an evil thing it is to marry a strange woman. Who ever was mightier or more richly endowed from his very cradle with God's Spirit than Samson the Nazarite? Yet was he betrayed by a woman, and by her means failed to retain God's favour. We will now narrate his birth and the course of his whole life arranged in the style of history, following the contents of the sacred Book, which in substance not in form is as follows.

9. The Philistines for many years kept the Hebrew people in subjection; for they had lost the prerogative of faith, whereby their fathers had gained victories. Yet had not their Maker wholly blotted out the mark of their election nor the lot of their inheritance; but as they were often puffed up by success, He for-the most part delivered them into the hand of their enemies, that thus, after the manner of men, they might be led to seek for themselves the remedy of their evils from heaven. For it is when any adversity oppresses us, that we submit ourselves to God; good fortune is wont to puff up the mind. This is proved by experience, as in other instances, so particularly in that change of fortune whereby success returned again from the Philistines to the Hebrews.

10. After the spirit of the Hebrews had been so subdued by the pressure of a long subjection that no one dared with a manly spirit to rouse them to liberty, Samson, fore-ordained by the Divine oracle, was raised up to them. A great man he was, not one of the multitude, but first among the few, and beyond controversy far excelling all in bodily strength. And he is to be regarded by us with great admiration from the beginning, not because in his early abstinence from vice he gave signal proofs of temperance and sobriety, nor on account of his long preserving as a Nazarite his locks unshorn, but because from his very youth, which in others is an age of softness, he achieved illustrious deeds of virtue, perfect beyond the measure of human nature. By these he gained credence to the Divine prophecy, that it was not for nothing that such grace had gone before upon him, that an Angel came down by whom his birth beyond their hopes was announced to his parents, to be the leader and protector of his countrymen,

LETT. 19. now for a length of years harassed by the tyranny of the Philistines.

11. His father was of the tribe of Dan, a man fearing God, born of no mean rank, and eminent above others, his mother was barren of body, but in virtues of the mind not unfruitful; seeing that in the sanctuary of her soul she was counted worthy to receive the visit of an Angel, obeyed his command and fulfilled his prophecy. Not enduring however to know the secrets even of God apart from her husband she mentioned to him that she had seen a man of God, of beautiful form, bringing her the Divine promise of future offspring, and that she, confiding in this promise, was led to share with her husband her faith in the heavenly promises. But he, informed of this, devoutly offered his prayers to God, that the grace of this vision might be conferred on him also, saying, *To me, Lord, let Thine Angel come.*

Judges xiii. 8.

12. I am of opinion therefore that it was not from jealousy of his wife, because she was remarkable for her beauty that he acted thus, as one writer[1] has supposed, but rather that he was filled with desire of the Divine grace, and sought to participate in the benefit of the heavenly vision. For one whose mind was depraved could not have found such favour with the Lord, as that an Angel should return to his house, who, having given those monitions which the Divine announcement made requisite, was suddenly carried away in the form of a smoking flame. This sight, which terrified the man, the woman interpreted more auspiciously, and so removed his solicitude, in that to see God is a sign of good not evil.

[1] He here refers to Josephus Antiq. v. ch. iv.

13. Now Samson, approved by such signal tokens from above, turned his thoughts as soon as he grew up, to marriage; whether this was that he abhorred those vague and licentious desires in which young men are wont to indulge, or that he was seeking an occasion of releasing the necks of his countrymen from the power of the hard yoke of the Philistines. Wherefore going down to Timnath, (this is the name of a city situated in those parts where the Philistines then dwelt,) he beheld a maiden of a pleasing form and beautiful countenance, and he besought his parents, by whose company he was supported in his journey, to ask

her for him in marriage. But they, not knowing that his intention, either, if the Philistine refused her to him, to be more fierce against them, or, if they assented, to remove their disposition to injure their subjects; and since from such a connexion a certain equality and kindliness of intercourse would naturally grow, or, on the other hand, if any offence were given, this desire of revenge would be more vehement, deemed that this maiden ought to be avoided as a foreigner. But after they had vainly attempted to change the purpose of their son by urging upon him these lawful objections, they of their own accord acquiesced in his desire.

14. This request was granted; and Samson on his return to visit his promised bride, turned a little way out of the road, and straightway there met him a lion from the wood, fierce in its savage freedom. Samson had no companion, nor any weapon in his hand; but he felt ashamed to fly, and conscious power gave him courage. He caught the lion as it rushed upon him in his arms, and strangled it by the tightness of his embrace, leaving it near the wayside lying upon the underwood, for the spot was clothed with luxuriant herbage, and planted with vineyards. The skin of the beast he thought would be little esteemed by his beloved bride, for seasons such as these derive their grace not from savage trophies, but rather from gentle joys and festal garlands. On his returning by the same road he found an honeycomb in the belly of the lion, and carried it off as a gift to the maiden and her parents; for such gifts befit a bride. And having first tasted the honey, he gave them the comb to eat, but was silent as to whence it came.

15. But it happened on a certain day that a nuptial feast was held, and that the young men inspirited by the banquet provoked each other to sport by question and answer, and as they assailed each other with wanton jests, as is the wont on such occasions, the contest of pleasure waxed hot. And then Samson put forth this riddle to his comrades, *Out of the eater came forth meat, and out of the strong came forth sweetness,* promising them as a reward of their sagacity if they guessed it, thirty sheets and as many changes

LETT 19. of garments according to the number of the company, while they on their part, if they could not solve the riddle, were to pay a like penalty.

16. But they, unable to untie the knot and to expound the riddle, induced his wife, partly by intimidation, partly by importunate entreaties, to require from her husband the solution of the riddle to be a token of conjugal affection in return for her love. And she, either terrified, and won over as women are wont to be, as if complaining tenderly of her husband's aversion, began to profess grief that she, the consort and intimate of his whole life, had not learnt this, but that she was treated like the others as one to whom her own husband's secret should not be confided.

Judg.xiv. 16. *Thou dost but hate me,* she said, *and lovest me not, thou hast put forth a riddle unto the children of my people and hast not told it me.*

17. Samson's mind, otherwise inflexible, was softened by these and the like blandishments of his wife, and discovered to her his riddle, and she told it to her countrymen. And they, having thus but just learned it on the seventh day, which was the term prescribed for its solution, an-

ib. 18. swered after this manner, *What is sweeter than honey, or what is stronger than a lion?* To which he replied, Nor is ought more treacherous than a woman; *If ye had not ploughed with my heifer, ye had not found out my riddle,* and he straightway went down to Ascalon, and slew thirty men, and taking their spoils, bestowed on the men who had expounded the riddle their promised reward.

18. But the perfidy of the maiden being thus discovered, he abstained from intercourse with her, and returned to his father's house. The damsel, disturbed in mind, and justly dreading that the wrath of this mighty man would be kindled into fury by this wrong, gave her hand to another man, one whom Samson, relying on his fidelity, had brought with him as his bridesman to his marriage. But neither by this expedient of a marriage did she avoid offence. For when the affair was disclosed, and he was forbidden to return to his wife, and her father said that she was married to another man, but that he might, if he chose, marry her sister, he was exasperated by the affront, and determined to take a

public revenge for his domestic injury. Wherefore he took three hundred foxes, and in the heat of summer, when the corn was now ripe in the fields, he tied them together two and two by the tails, and fastened a burning firebrand between them, binding it with a firm knot, and by way of avenging his wrong turned them loose among the sheaves which the Philistines had cut. But the foxes, terrified by the fire, scattered flames whichever way they turned, and burnt the harvest. And the Philistines, incensed by the loss of all their corn in that region, told it to the princes of their land. And they sent men to Timnath, and burnt in the fire the woman who had been faithless to her husband, and her parents and all her house; saying that she had been the cause of this injury and devastation, and ought not to have provoked a man who could avenge himself by a public calamity.

TO VIGILIUS

19. But Samson did not forgive the Philistines their wrong, nor rest content with this measure of vengeance, but he slew them with a great slaughter, and many of them fell by the sword. And he retired to Etam, a torrent in the wilderness, where was a rock, a stronghold of the tribe of Judah. Now the Philistines, not daring to attack him, nor scale the steep heights on which this fortress stood, began to assail with threats of war the tribe of Judah: but when they saw that the plea of the men of Judah was a good one, that it was neither just nor fair nor expedient for them to destroy their own subjects and tributaries, especially for another man's fault, they took counsel, and required that the author of the outrage should be delivered up to them, in order that his countrymen might be exonerated from the consequences of it.

20. These terms being imposed upon them, the men of Judah gathered together three thousand of their tribe and went up to him, and premising that they were subject to the Philistines, and obliged to obey them, not willingly but by terror, they thus sought to turn away from themselves the odium of their act, throwing it upon those by whom they were constrained. Wherefore he thus replied, What kind of Justice is it, O children of Abraham, that the satisfaction I have taken for my bride first over-reached and

LETT. 19. then torn from me should be injurious to me, and that I may not safely avenge this private injury? Have ye so turned your minds to the low offices of slaves, as to become the ministers of the insolence of others, and to turn your arms against yourselves? If I must perish, because I gave free vent to my grief, I had rather perish by the hand of the Philistines. My home has been attempted, my wife tampered with, if I have not been allowed to live without harm from them, at least let my own countrymen be free from the guilt of my death. I did but requite the injury I had received, I did not inflict one. Judge ye whether it was an equal return. They complain of the loss of their home, I of the loss of my wife; compare the sheaves of corn, with a companion of the marriage bed. They have sanctioned my grief by avenging my injuries. Consider to what an office they have appointed you. They desire you to put to death that man, whom they themselves have judged worthy to be avenged on those who wronged him, and to whose vengeance they ministered. But if your necks are thus bowed down to these proud men, deliver me into the hand of the enemy, slay me not yourselves; I refuse not to die, but I shrink from implicating you in my death. If from fear ye comply with their insolence, bind my hands with chains: though unarmed they will break their bonds and find a weapon for themselves. They will assuredly consider that you have satisfied the imposed condition, if you deliver me alive into their hands.

21. When they heard this, though three thousand men had come up, they swore to him that they would make no attempt on his life, only he must submit to be bound, in order that they might formally surrender him, and so keep clear of the crime of which they were accused.

22. Their word being pledged he came out of the cave, and left his fastness on the rock, and was bound with two ropes. When he saw the mighty men of the Philistines drawing near to seize him, his spirit rose within him, and he brake all his bands, and taking up a jaw bone of an ass that lay near he slew a thousand men, and put to flight the rest by this exploit of valour, whole hosts of armed soldiers giving way to one unarmed man. Thus those who

ventured to close with him hand to hand he slew without effort; the others saved themselves by flight. Wherefore to this day the place is called Agon [a], because there Samson by his great valour achieved a glorious contest.

23. And I would that his moderation in victory had been equal to his courage against the enemy. But as is frequently the case, with mind unused to prosperity, he ascribed to himself the issue of the battle, which was due to the Divine favour and protection, saying, *With the jaw bone of an ass have I slain a thousand men.* Nor did he build an altar to God, nor offer a victim, but neglecting sacrifice and assuming to himself the glory, to immortalize his triumph by a memorial name he called the place, The slaying of the jaw bone.

24. And now he began to burn with thirst, and there was no water, and yet he had great need of it. Wherefore perceiving that there is nothing so easy for human strength, as not to be rendered difficult by the absence of Divine aid, he besought God not to lay to his charge that he had ascribed ought to himself, giving Him all the glory of the victory, by the words, *Thou hast given this great deliverance into the hand of Thy servant,* and now help me, for lo, *I die of thirst,* and thirst gives me over into the hand of those over whom Thou hast given me so great a triumph. Wherefore God in His mercy clave a hollow place in the jaw bone which Samson had cast aside, and a stream of water flowed from it, and Samson drank, and his spirit revived, and he called the place 'the invoking of the spring,' because by his suppliant prayers he made amends for his boast of victory, and thus two judgements were opportunely declared, the one that arrogance soon incurs offence, the other that without any offence humility gains reconciliation.

25. Having, in the course of events closed his war with the Philistines, and shunning the sloth of his countrymen, Samson now betook himself to Gaza, which was in the

---

[a] The name given in the Hebrew is Ramath Lehi, which means, 'the hill or lifting up of the jaw-bone' S Ambrose interprets it below 'maxillae interfectionem.' He would seem to be here suggesting a Greek etymology The Benedictine note suggests that the name Agon is a confusion on his part from the word σιαγών in Josephus.

LETT. 19. region of the Philistines, and lodged there. When the men of Gaza knew this they did not dissemble or pass it over, but beset his lodging in haste, and guarded all the doors of the house that he might not escape by night. But Samson knowing their design, in the middle of the night forestalling the snare which had been laid for him, took the pillars of the house in his arms, and carried the whole structure and the weight of the roof on his back, up to a high hill above Hebron, a city inhabited by the Hebrews.

26. But now his licence transgressed the limits not only of his paternal territory, but of good morals, such as ancient discipline had prescribed, and this brought upon him destruction in the end. For although he had experienced in his first marriage the treachery of a foreign wife, and ought to have avoided it in future, he did not shun connecting himself with the harlot Delilah, and by his passionate love of her opened a way for the craft of his enemies to assail him. For the Philistines came up to her, and promised each of them to give·her eleven hundred pieces of silver if she would disclose to them wherein his assurance of strength lay, that by means of this knowledge they might entrap and take him.

27. But she having once prostituted herself for money, began during the banquet and the blandishments of love, cunningly and craftily to inquire of him in what respect his strength excelled that of others, and at the same time, as if solicitous and fearful for his safety, to entreat him to confide to his beloved by what means he could be bound and subdued into the power of others. But he, still self-possessed and unshaken, opposed craft to the allurements of the harlot, and told her that if he were bound with withs yet green and not dried, his strength would be like that of other men. When the Philistines learnt this from Delilah, they bound him while asleep with green withs, and then awoke him as though on a sudden, but found that he had not fallen off from his accustomed fortitude, but bursting its bonds his freed strength was able to resist and drive back a host of assailants.

28. This having failed, Delilah, as if she had been

mocked began with complaints to renew her arts and to require a pledge of his love. Samson, still firm of purpose, intimated to her that, if he were bound by seven ropes which had never been used, he would fall into the hands of the enemy, but this also was in vain. The third time he disclosed part of the secret, and now drawing nearer to his fall, told her that, if the seven locks of his head were unfastened and woven[b] to about a cubit's length, his strength would depart from him. But herein also he deluded those who were plotting against his life.

TO VIGILIUS

29. But last of all the wanton woman complaining that she had been so often deceived, and grieving that her lover deemed her unworthy to be entrusted with his secret, and that under her pretext of succour her treacherous purpose was suspected, won his confidence by her tears. By this means, and because also it was ordained that this man of hitherto unshaken fortitude should fall into calamity, Samson was touched and opened to her his heart. He told her that he possessed within him the power of God, that he was sanctified to the Lord, and that by His command he let his hair grow, and that if it were shorn, he would cease to be a Nazarite, and lose the use of his strength. The Philistines having discoverd through her means the man's weakness, bring her the reward of her perfidy, thus binding her to the commission of the crime.

30. And she, having wearied him by the wanton blandishments of love, threw him into slumber, and then caused the seven locks of his hair to be cut by a razor, whereupon by his transgression of the commandment his strength was immediately lost. When he woke out of sleep, he said, *I will go out as at other times, and shake myself* against mine adversaries, but he was no longer sensible of activity and strength, his vigour was gone, his grace was departed. Wherefore, considering within himself that he had incautiously trusted to women, and that, convicted of infirmity, it would be sheer folly for him to contend any longer, he

Judges xvi. 20.

---

[b] The words 'quasi in cubitum intexti' are probably from the Old Latin Version of the Bible Field, on Origen's Hexapla in loc. (Judg xvi. 13.) mentions that some MSS of LXX read ἐὰν ὑφάνῃς ὡσεὶ πῆχυν or ὡς ἐπὶ πῆχυν which may very well have been translated by some such words as the above in the Old Latin Version which S. Ambrose used.

LETT. 19. gave up his eyes to blindness, and his hands to the fetters, and being bound with chains he entered the confinement from which he had been for a long season free.

31. But in process of time his hair began to grow again; and on the occasion of a great feast Samson is brought out of prison to the assembly of the Philistines, and set in sight of the people. There were nearly three thousand in number, men and women; and they insulted him with bitter reproaches, and carried him about in mockery, a trial harder to be borne than the very reality of captivity by a man conscious of innate power. For to live and die is natural, to be a laughing stock is counted a disgrace. Desirous therefore either of consoling himself by avenging so great an indignity, or of forestalling it for the future by death, he pretended that from the weakness of his limbs and the weight of his fetters he could not support himself, and desired the boy who guided his steps to bring him to the nearest pillars by which the whole house was supported. Being brought near, he grasped with both hands the props of the building, and while the Philistines were intent on the sacrificial feast which they were offering to Dagon their god, by whose help they deemed their adversary had been delivered into their power, reckoning a woman's perfidy as a gift from above, he called unto the Lord, and said, '*O Lord God, remember me I pray Thee this once, that I may be avenged of the heathen for my two eyes,* and that they give not glory to their gods as if by their help they had gotten me into their power. Let me die with the Philistines, that they may find my weakness to have been no less fatal to them than my strength.'

Judges xvi. 28.

32. Then he shook the columns with great force, and broke them in pieces, whereon followed the downfall of the upper roof, crushing Samson himself and casting down all those who were looking on from above. Thus were a great number of men and women slain together, and by an end not unworthy or disgraceful, but excelling all his former victories, the dying Samson obtained a triumph. For although to that point and thenceforward he was invincible, and incomparable during life among men versed in war, yet in death he conquered himself, and shewed an un-

conquerable soul, so as to despise and count for nothing that end of life which all men fear.

33. Thus it was through his valour that the last day of his life was also the sum of his victories, and that he met not a captive but a triumphant end. But to have been entrapped by a woman is to be ascribed to nature rather than to the man, because it was by the condition of his humanity more than through his own fault that he fell; for this is wont to be overcome, and yield to the allurements of wickedness. Wherefore, since Scripture bears witness that he slew more in his death than while in the light of life, it would seem that his captivity happened rather for the destruction of his adversaries than for his own fall and humiliation. For he whose burial was more efficacious than his living strength cannot be said to have found himself inferior. Lastly, he was overwhelmed and buried not by the weapons but by the bodies of his enemies, and thus, covered by his own triumph, he left a glorious memorial to posterity. For he judged his countrymen, whom he found enslaved, twenty years, and buried in his native soil, left them inheritors of liberty.

34. By this example then it is plain that alliances with strangers should be avoided, lest through love for our wife the snares of treachery should be successful.

Farewell and love us, as we love you.

LETTER XX.

A.D. 385.

AFTER the death of Gratian the empire of the West was nominally in the hands of Valentinian the 2nd, but, as he was a mere boy, the real power was exercised by his mother Justina, who was an Arian. S. Ambrose had already resisted her successfully in the question of the election of a Bishop at Sirmium (see note in p. 39), and although he had performed a difficult and dangerous service for them two years before this, in going on an embassy to Maximus after the death of Gratian, Justina and Valentinian were bitterly hostile to him, and supported the Arian faction against him. In March, A.D. 385, S. Ambrose was summoned to the Palace, as he himself relates in the Sermon of which he gives an account in this letter (§ 15 sqq) and called upon to give up one of the Churches, the Portian Basilica, outside the walls, for the use of the Arians. This he refused, and was so energetically supported by the people of Milan, that the demand was for the time withdrawn. Various other efforts were then made either to induce him to yield or to get him out of the way, (one of the latter is recounted in a note on the Sermon against Auxentius § 15) but they all failed At last on the Friday before Palm Sunday a fresh demand is made, not for the Portian Basilica, as a promise had been given that no further claim should be made upon it, but for the New Basilica which was within the walls. It is at this point that the narrative which S Ambrose gives in this letter to his sister Marcellina begins. It recounts the occurrences from the Friday to the Wednesday in Holy Week, when the persecution was again for the time abandoned.

TO MARCELLINA.

1. In nearly all your letters you inquire anxiously about the Church; hear then what is going on. The day after I received the letter in which you told me how you had been troubled in your dreams, a heavy weight of troubles began to assail me. It was not now the Portian Basilica, that is the one without the walls, which was demanded, but the new Basilica, that is, one within the walls, which is larger in size.

2. In the first place some chief men [a], counsellors of state, appealed to me to give up the Basilica, and restrain the people from raising any commotion. I replied as a matter of course, that a Bishop could not give up God's house.

3. On the following day the people expressed their approval in the Church, and the Præfect [b] also came thither, and began to urge us to yield up at least the Portian Basilica. The people were clamorous against this, whereupon he departed, saying, that he would report matters to the Emperor.

4. On the following day, which was the Lord's day,

---

[a] The expression 'principes virtutum' seems to be a phrase from the Old Testament. In the Vulgate we find 'rex virtutum' Ps lxvii, (lxviii E.V) 13, where the E V. has 'kings of armies,' and in Judith xiv. 17 (19 E.V) 'Quod quum audissent principes virtutis Assyriorum,' and in 1 Macc. v 56. 'Azarias princeps virtutis' The 'comites consistoriani' formed a sort of cabinet (consistorium) or privy council to the Emperor. The Benedictine Editors take 'principes virtutum' as meaning the Magistri militum, but the absence of any conjunction is against this.

[b] This must mean the Præfectus prætorio Italiæ, one of the four great Viceroys, under whom the Dioceses of the Empire were placed He was supreme over all Italy, and the countries north of it to the Danube, and the western part of the north of Africa. He had under him three Dioceses, containing thirty Provinces.

having dismissed the catechumens after the lessons and sermon, I was explaining the Creed to some candidates for Baptism in the Baptistery of the Church. There the news was reported to me that, on learning that officials [c] had been sent from the palace to the Portian Basilica, and were putting up the Imperial hangings [d], many of the people were proceeding thither. I however continued my ministrations, and began to celebrate the Eucharist [e].

TO MARCELLINA

5. While I was offering, tidings were brought me that the populace had seized upon one Castulus, whom the Arians called a priest. While making the oblation I began to weep bitterly and to beseech God's aid that no blood might be shed in the Church's quarrel; or if so, that it might be my own, and that not for my people only, but even for the ungodly themselves. But, to be brief, I sent some presbyters and deacons, and rescued the man

6. The severest penalties were immediately decreed; first upon the whole body of merchants. And thus, during the sacred period of the last Week, wherein the debtor was wont to be loosed from his bonds, chains are placed on innocent men's necks, and two hundred pounds' weight of gold is demanded within three days. They reply they will willingly give as much, or twice as much again, so that they may not violate their faith. The prisons too were filled with tradesmen.

7. All the Officials of the palace, the Recorders, the Proctors, the Apparitors of the several Courts, on the pretext of its being unlawful for them to be present at seditious assemblies, were commanded to keep at home, severe threats were held out against men of high rank in case the Basilica was not delivered up. The persecution

---

[c] The title given them is 'Decani.' They seem to have been something like the lictors of the great officers of state under the republic

[d] These 'vela' or hangings were a token that the building was claimed for the 'fiscus,' or private property of the Emperor. Gibbon in his grand way says, 'the splendid canopy and hangings of the royal seat were arranged in the customary manner,'

but, as is noticed by the writer of the Life of S Ambrose in Dict of Christian Biog. it is clear from the sequel of the narrative (see § 20) that they were outside, not inside the Church.

[e] The words in the original are 'missam facere' Prof. Bright in his History notes that this is 'the earliest instance, apparently, of this term being used for the Eucharistic service.'

raged, and had an opening been afforded, they seemed likely to break out into every kind of outrage.

8. I myself had an interview with the Counts and Tribunes, who urged me to give up the Basilica without delay, declaring that the Emperor was acting on his rights, inasmuch as he had supreme power over all things. I replied that if he required of me what was my own, my estate, my money, or the like, I would not refuse it, although all my property really belonged to the poor, but that sacred things were not subject to the power of the Emperor. 'If my patrimony be required,' I said, 'take it; if my person, here it is. Will you drag me away to prison, or to death? I will go with pleasure. I will not entrench myself by gathering a multitude round me, I will not lay hold of the Altar and beg for my life; rather will I offer myself to death for the Altar.'

9. In fact my mind was shaken with fear when I found that armed men had been sent to occupy the Basilica, I was seized with dread lest in protecting the Church, blood might be shed which would tend to bring destruction on the whole city. I prayed that if so great a city or even all Italy were to perish I might not survive. I shrank from the odium of shedding blood, and I offered my own throat to the knife. Some officers of the Goths [f] were present; I addressed them, saying, 'Is it for this that you have become citizens of Rome, to shew yourselves disturbers of the public peace? Whither will you go, if everything here is destroyed?'

10. I was called upon to calm the people. I replied that it was in my power not to excite them, that it was in God's Hand to pacify them. That if I was considered the instigator, I ought to be punished, that I ought to be banished into whatever desert places of the earth they chose. Having said this, they departed, and I spent the

---

[f] 'The introduction of barbarians into the Roman armies became every day more universal, more necessary, and more fatal. The most daring of the Scythians, of the Goths, and of the Germans, were enrolled not only in the auxiliaries of their respective nations, but in the legions themselves, and among the most distinguished of the Palatine troops.' (Gibbon, ch xvii) The Goths were Arians. It was much about this time that Ulfilas, the apostle of the Goths, made his famous translation of the Bible into Gothic See Bright's Hist. of the Church p 157.

whole day in the old Church. Thence I returned home to sleep; that if any man wished to arrest me, he might find me prepared.

11. When, before dawn, I passed out over the threshold, I found the Basilica surrounded and occupied by soldiers. And it was said that they had intimated to the Emperor that he was at liberty to go to Church if he wished it, that they would be ready to attend him if he were going to the assembly of the Catholics; otherwise that they would go to the assembly which Ambrose had convened.

12. Not a single Arian dared come out, for there were none among the citizens, only a few of the royal household, and some of the Goths, who, as of old they made their waggon their home, so now make the Church their waggon. Wherever that woman goes, she carries with her all those of her own communion. The groans of the people gave me notice that the Basilica was surrounded; but while the lessons are being read word is brought me that the New Basilica also is full of people, that the crowd seemed greater than when all were at liberty, that they were calling for a Reader. To be brief, the soldiers themselves, who were found to have occupied the Basilica, being informed of my directions that the people should abstain from communion with them, began to come to our assembly. At the sight of them the minds of the women are agitated, one of them rushes forth. But the soldiers themselves exclaimed that they had come to pray not to fight. The people raised a cry. In the most modest, most resolute, most faithful manner they entreated that I would go to that Basilica. In that Basilica also the people were reported to desire my presence.

14. Then I began the following discourse: Ye have heard, my sons, the lesson from the book of Job, which according to the usual service of the season, is now in course. By use the devil knew that this book was to be declared, already all the power of his temptations is laid open and betrayed, and therefore he exerted himself to-day with greater violence. But thanks be to our God Who hath so confirmed you in faith and patience. I went up into the pulpit to admire Job, I found I had all of you to admire

as Jobs. Job lives again in each of you, in each the patience and virtue of that saint is reflected. For what more opportune could be said by Christian men than that which the Holy Spirit hath spoken in you this day? 'We petition your Majesty, we use no force, we feel no fear, but we petition.' This is what becomes Christians, to desire peace and quiet fear, and still not to let the steadfastness of faith and truth be shaken even by peril of death. For the Lord is our Guide, *Who will save those who hope in Him.*

15. But let us come to the lessons set before us. Ye see that power of temptation is given to the devil to prove the good. The wicked one envies our progress in good, he tempts us in various ways. He tempted holy Job in his patrimony, he tempted him in his sons, he tempted him by bodily pains. The stronger is tempted in his own person, the weaker in that of others. Me too he would fain have despoiled of the riches which I possess in you, and he desired to waste this patrimony of your tranquillity. Yourselves also he desired to snatch from me, my good children for whom I daily offer sacrifice; you he endeavoured to involve in the ruins of the public confusion. Already then I have incurred two kinds of temptation. And perhaps the Lord, knowing my weakness, hath not yet given him power over my body: though I myself desire it, though I offer it, He perhaps still judges me unequal to this contest, and exercises me by diverse labours. Even Job himself did not begin with this contest, but was perfected by it.

16. But Job was tempted by the accumulated tidings of evil, he was tempted by his wife who said, *Curse God, and die.* Ye behold how many things are suddenly stirred up against us, the Goths, the troops, the heathen, the fine of the tradesmen, the punishment of the saints. Ye observe what is commanded, when it is said 'Deliver up the Basilica;' *Curse God, and die.* But here it is not only 'Speak against God,' but also 'Act against God.' The command is, 'Betray the altars of God.'

17. So then we are pressed by the Imperial mandates, but we are strengthened by the words of Scripture, which answered, *Thou speakest as one of the foolish women speak-*

eth. Not slight therefore is that temptation, for temptations which come through the agency of women we know to be more severe. Lastly, Adam also was betrayed by Eve, and thereby it came to pass that he betrayed the Divine commandments. Becoming aware of this error, and his guilty conscience accusing him, he desired to hide himself, but could not; wherefore God says to him, *Adam where art thou?* that is, what wert thou before? where hast thou now begun to be? where did I place thee? whither hast thou fallen? thou ownest thyself naked, because thou hast lost the garments of a good faith. The things wherewith thou desirest to clothe thyself are leaves. Thou hast cast aside the fruit, thou desirest to lie hid under the leaves of the tree, but thou art betrayed. For one woman's sake thou hast chosen to depart from thy God, therefore thou fliest from Him when thou soughtest to see. Thou hast chosen to hide thyself with one woman, to leave the mirror of the world, the abode of Paradise, the Grace of Christ.

[margin: TO MARCELLINA]

[margin: Gen. iii. 9.]

18. Why need I add that Elijah also was cruelly persecuted by Jezebel? that Herodias caused John the Baptist to be put to death? Each man seems to suffer from this or that woman; for me, in proportion as my merits are less, my trials are heavier. My strength is weaker, but I have more danger. Women succeed each other, their hatreds are interchanged, their falsehoods are varied, the elders are gathered together, the plea of wrong to the Emperor is put forward. What explanation is there then of such grievous temptation to such a worm as I am, but that it is not me but the Church that they persecute.

19. At length came the command, 'Deliver up the Basilica;' I reply, 'It is not lawful for us to deliver it up, nor for your Majesty to receive it. By no law can you violate the house of a private man, and do you think that the house of God may be taken away? It is asserted that all things are lawful to the Emperor, that all things are his. But do not burden your conscience with the thought that you have any right as Emperor over sacred things. Exalt not yourself, but if you would reign the longer, be subject to God. It is written, *God's to God and Cæsar's to Cæsar.* The palace is the Emperor's, the Churches are the Bishop's.

[margin: S. Matt. xxii. 21.]

LETT. 20. To you is committed jurisdiction over public not over sacred buildings.' Again the Emperor is said to have issued his command, 'I also ought to have one Basilica;' I answered '*It is not lawful for thee to have her.* What hast thou to do with an adultress who is not bound with Christ in lawful wedlock?'

S. Matt. xiv. 4.

20. While I was engaged with this subject, it was reported to me that the Imperial hangings were taken down, the Church filled with people, and that my presence was required; straightway I turned my discourse to this, saying, How deep and profound are the oracles of the Holy Spirit! Remember, brethren, what was read at matins and how we responded with deep grief of mind, *O God the heathen are come into Thine inheritance.* And truly the heathen came, nay, even more than the heathen, for the Goths came and men of divers nations, they came armed with weapons, and surrounded and seized the Basilica. Ignorant of Thy Greatness we grieved for this, but our ignorance was mistaken.

Ps. lxxix. 1.

21. The heathen came, but truly *into Thine inheritance* they came, for they who came as heathen were made Christians. They who came to invade Thine inheritance, were made coheirs of God; those whom I accounted enemies are become my defenders; I have as comrades those whom I esteemed adversaries. Thus has that been fulfilled which the prophet David spake of the Lord Jesus, that *His Dwelling is in peace*^g, *there brake He the horns of the bow, the shield, the sword, and the battle.* For whose office, whose work is this but Thine, Lord Jesus? Thou sawest armed men coming to Thy temple, on the one hand the people groaning and collecting in a crowd that they might not seem to give up the Basilica, on the other hand the soldiers commanded to use force. Death was before my eyes, lest in the midst of all this madness should break out into licence. But Thou, O Lord plantedst Thyself in the midst, and madest the twain one. Thou restrainedst the soldiers, saying, If ye run to arms, if they who are within My temple are disturbed, *What profit is there in My blood?* All thanks therefore be to Thee, O Christ. It

Ps lxxvi. 2, 3.

Ps xxx. 9.

^g This is the Vulgate rendering of '*At Salem is His Tabernacle.*'

was not an enemy, not a messenger but *Thou O Lord hast delivered Thy people, Thou hast put off my sackcloth and girded me with gladness.*

TO MARCELLINA

Ps. xxx. 11, 12.

22. Thus I spoke, wondering that the Emperor's mind could be softened by the zeal of the soldiers, by the entreaties of the Counts, by the prayers of the people. Meanwhile I am informed that a Secretary was come with the mandate. I retired a little, and he notified to me the mandate. 'What has been your design,' says he, 'in acting against the Emperor's orders?' I replied, 'What has been ordered I know not, nor am I aware what is alleged to have been wrongly done.' He says, 'Why have you sent presbyters to the Basilica? If you are a tyrant I would fain know it, that I may know how to arm myself against you.' I replied by saying that I had done nothing which assumed too much for the Church, but when I heard it was filled with soldiers, I only uttered deeper groans, and though many exhorted me to proceed thither, I replied, 'I cannot give up the Basilica, yet I must not fight.' That afterwards, when I was told that the Imperial hangings were removed, and that the people required me to go thither, I had directed the presbyters to do so, but that I was unwilling to go myself, saying, 'I trust in Christ that the Emperor himself will espouse our cause.'

23. If this seems like domineering, I grant indeed that I have arms, but only in the name of Christ; I have the power of offering up my body. Why, I asked, did he delay to strike if he considered my power unlawful? By ancient right Priests have conferred sovereignty, never assumed it, and it is a common saying that Emperors have coveted the Priesthood more often than Priests sovereignty. Christ fled that He might not be made a king. We have a power of our own. The power of a Priest is his weakness; *When I am weak,* it is said, *then am I strong.* But let him against whom God has raised up no adversary beware lest he raise up a tyrant for himself. Maximus did not say that I domineered over Valentinian, though he complains that my embassage prevented his passing over into Italy. I added, that priests were never usurpers, but that they had often suffered from usurpers.

2 Cor. xii. 10.

24. The whole of that day was past in this affliction; meanwhile the boys tore in derision the Imperial hangings. I could not return home, because the Church was surrounded by a guard of soldiers. We recited the Psalms with our brethren in the little Basilica belonging to the Church.

25. On the following day, the book of Jonah was read in due course, after which, I began this discourse; We have read a book, my brethren, wherein it is foretold that sinners shall return again to repentance. They are accepted on this footing, that their present state is considered an earnest of the future. I added that this just man was even willing to incur blame, rather than behold or denounce destruction on the city; and, since that prophecy was mournful, that he was also grieved because the gourd had withered; that God had said to the prophet, *Art thou greatly angry for the gourd?* and Jonah had answered, *I am greatly angry.* Then the Lord said, if the withering of the gourd was a grief to him, how much more ought he to care for the salvation of so many souls; and therefore that He had suspended the destruction which had been prepared for the whole city.

26. Immediate tidings are brought to me that the Emperor had commanded the soldiers to retire from the Church; and that the fine which had been imposed on the merchants on their condemnation should be restored. What joy then prevailed among the whole people, what applause, what congratulations! Now it was the day whereon the Lord delivered Himself up for us, the day whereon there is a relaxation of penance in the Church. The soldiers eagerly brought the tidings, running in to the altars, and giving the kiss, the emblem of peace. Then I perceived that God had smitten *the worm which came when the morning rose,* that the whole city might be preserved.

27. These are the past events, and would that they were terminated, but the excited words of the Emperor show that heavier trials are awaiting us. I am called a tyrant, and even more than tyrant. For when the Counts besought the Emperor to go to the Church, and said that they did so at the request of the soldiers, he replied, 'You would

deliver me up to chains, if Ambrose bade you.' I leave you to judge what awaits us after these words; all shuddered at hearing them, but there are those about him who exasperate him.

28. Lastly Calligonus the Grand Chamberlain [h] ventured to address himself specially to me. 'Do you, while I live, despise Valentinian? I will have your head.' I replied, 'May God grant you to fulfil your threat: I shall suffer as becomes a Bishop, you will act as befits an enunch.' May God indeed turn them aside from the Church; may all their weapons be directed against me, may they satiate their thirst in my blood!

LETTER XXI. A.D. 386.

S. AMBROSE ends his letter to his sister with forebodings of more troubles. Nor was he wrong. One of the next steps taken was a challenge to dispute publicly before the Emperor with Auxentius the Arian (so-called) Bishop, with regular umpires (judices) appointed on both sides. This letter is his reply to the Emperor, setting forth his ground for refusing, as he had before done at the time of the Council of Aquileia, to allow laymen to be judges of questions of Faith. (See above, Council of Aquil. § 51, 52, 53.)

TO THE MOST CLEMENT EMPEROR, HIS BLESSED MAJESTY VALENTINIAN, AMBROSE, BISHOP, SENDS GREETING.

1. DALMATIUS the tribune and notary cited me at your Clemency's bidding, as he alleged, requiring that I also should choose umpires as Auxentius had done. He did not mention the names of those who had been called for, but he added that the trial would take place in the Consistory, and that your pious judgment would decide between us.

2. To this I make, as I consider, a sufficient answer.

---

[h] On the high rank and great influence of the Præpositus cubiculi, or Grand Chamberlain, see Gibbon ch. xvii. They ranked with the Præfecti prætorio and other highest officers of state as Illustres See note on Lett. xvii. § 1.

Lett. 21. No one ought to deem me contumacious for asserting what your father of illustrious memory not only declared by word of mouth [a] but sanctioned by his laws; that in a matter of the Faith or of any ecclesiastical ordinance, the judges ought to be qualified for it, both competent by office and qualified by profession: (these are the words of the Rescript), that is to say, he would have Bishops judge Bishops. Moreover if a bishop were accused elsewhere also, and a charge of a moral nature to be examined, this too he willed should be referred to the judgment of Bishops.

3. Who then is it who makes a contumacious answer to your Clemency? He who would have you like your Father, or he who would have you unlike? Unless perhaps some persons count cheaply the opinion of that great Emperor, whose faith has been approved by the constancy of his confession [b], and his wisdom proclaimed by the improved condition of the State.

4. When have you ever heard, most gracious Emperor, that laymen had judged a Bishop in a matter pertaining to the Faith? Does their flattery make us cringe so low as to forget the rights of the priesthood, and suppose that what God has committed to me I should entrust to others? If a layman may teach a Bishop, what will follow? a layman will dispute, and a Bishop listen, a Bishop learn of a lay-

---

[a] A reply of Valentinian the 1st to some Bishops of the Hellespont and Bithynia, who demanded permission to meet 'to amend the doctrine of the faith,' is given by Sozomen (vi. 7.) His words are, 'It is not lawful for me, as a layman, to busy myself about such matters as these: let the Bishops, whose business it is, meet by themselves wherever they will.' To the same effect are the words of his which Theodoret reports, (iv 6) when bidding the Bishops of the province elect a successor to Auxentius He bids them choose a fit person, 'that we also, who rule the empire, may sincerely bow our heads to him, and welcome his reproofs, (for, being men, we cannot but stumble,) as a remedial discipline.' What law is referred to is uncertain. The Benedictine Editors, after mentioning some which had been suggested 'think it more probable that the law referred to is not extant'

[b] Gibbon (ch. xxv) in his character of Valentinian says, 'In the time of Julian he provoked the danger of disgrace by the contempt which he publicly expressed for the reigning religion' The story is told by Theod. Eccles. Hist iii. 16. Valentian was in official attendance on the Emperor Julian on one occasion when he went to the temple of Fortune to perform rites. 'On either side of the door were stationed attendants, who sprinkled all who came in with lustral water to purify them, as they believed. When some of the drops fell on his cloak, Valentinian struck the attendants with his fist, saying that he was defiled not purified by them' For this he was dismissed from the court, and sent to a solitary garrison. The same story is told with slight variations by Sozomen. Hist vi. 6

man. Assuredly, if we revert to the volume of Holy Scripture or to the time of old, who is there who will deny that in a cause of the Faith, in a cause, I say, of the Faith, Bishops are wont to judge Christian Emperors, not Emperors to judge Bishops.

5. Hereafter, you will, by God's favour, reach a more mature age, and then you will judge what kind of Bishop he must be who submits the rights of the priesthood to laymen. Your father, who by God's favour attained a riper age, used to say: 'It is not for me to judge between Bishops:' your Majesty now says, 'I ought to judge.' He, although baptized into Christ, considered himself unequal to the weight of so important a judgment; does your Majesty, who have yet to earn for yourself the Sacrament of Baptism, claim to decide concerning the Faith, although still ignorant of the Sacrament of this Faith ?

6. But what sort of judges he will have selected we may leave to be guessed, seeing that he fears to disclose their names. Let them come openly, if indeed there be any, to the Church; let them attend together with the people, not to sit as judges, but for every one to prove his own feelings and choose whom he will follow. The cause is concerning the Bishop of that Church; if the people hear him and suppose he has the better of the argument, let them follow his Faith; I shall not be jealous.

7. I forbear to mention that the people themselves have already decided; I do not urge that the Bishop[c] whom they have they demanded from your Majesty's father; I urge not that your father promised tranquillity for the future if he, having been elected, took upon him the Bishopric. It was in reliance on these promises that I acted.

8. But if he prides himself on the support of any foreigners let him be Bishop in the place whence those come who hold that he should be invested with the name of a Bishop. For I neither acknowledge him as Bishop, nor know whence he comes.

9. How, your Majesty, can we be said to settle a matter in which you have already declared your judgment; nay, have yourself published laws precluding others from de-

[c] He is alluding to his own election.

Lett. 21. ciding otherwise. And when you laid down this rule for others you laid it down also for yourself; for the laws which the Emperor makes he ought to be the first to keep. Would you then have me make trial whether those who are chosen judges will meet, contrary to your decree, or whether they will allege that they have not been able to contravene so rigid and peremptory a command of the Emperor?

10. But this is the part of a contumacious not of a respectful Bishop. See, your Majesty, how you yourself partially rescind your own law; but I would that you would do so not partially but universally, for I would not wish your law to be above the law of God. The law of God has taught us what we should follow, human laws cannot teach us this. They can compel a change in the timid, but they cannot inspire faith.

11. Who therefore when he learns that in one moment it has been published through so many provinces that whoever shall resist the Emperor shall be put to death, whoever shall not give up the temple of God shall immediately be slain; who is there, I say, who either alone or with a few others can say to the Emperor; 'I do not approve your law?' The priesthood are not allowed to say this; are then the laity allowed? And shall he judge concerning the faith, who either hopes for favour or fears giving offence?

12. Lastly, shall I venture to nominate laymen for umpires, who if they keep true to their Faith must be proscribed or put to death, as that law passed concerning the Faith prescribes. Shall I then expose them to the hazard either of prevarication or of punishment?

13. Ambrose is not of such importance as to degrade the priesthood on his account. One man's life is not of as much value as the dignity of the whole priesthood, by whose advice I gave my direction when they suggested that there might be some heathen or Jew, chosen by Auxentius, to whom we might give a triumph over Christ if we committed to him judgment concerning Christ. What else pleases them but to hear of wrong done to Christ? What else can please them but the denial (which God for-

bid) of the Divinity of Christ? Clearly they agree entirely with the Arian, who calls Christ a creature, which heathens and Jews too are willing enough to confess.

14. This was decreed at the synod of Ariminum, and with good reason do I abhor that Council; following as I do the doctrine of the Nicene Council, from which neither death nor the sword can ever separate me. This Faith your Majesty's father, the blessed Emperor Theodosius, both followed and approved. This Faith the provinces of Gaul and of Spain hold, and this they keep with the pious confession of the Divine Spirit.

15. If I have to preach, I have learnt to preach in the Church, as my predecessors did. If a conference is to be held on a matter of Faith, it ought to be a conference of Bishops, as was the case under Constantine of august memory, who laid down no laws beforehand, but left to the Bishops the liberty of judging. The same was the case also under Constantius of illustrious memory, who inherited his father's dignity, but what began well ended badly. For the Bishops had at first subscribed an orthodox confession, but, through the wish of certain persons to judge of the Faith in agreement with the palace, the result was that these judgments of the Bishops were fraudulently changed; they however immediately recalled this perverted decision. And there is no doubt that the majority at Ariminum approved the creed of the Nicene Council[d] and condemned the Arian decrees.

16. If Auxentius appeals to a Synod to discuss questions concerning the Faith, though it would be needless to disturb so many Bishops on one person's account, who, were he an Angel from heaven, ought not to be preferred to the Church's peace, I too will not be absent when I hear that the Synod is assembled. Let the law then be repealed, if you would have the contest entered upon.

17. I would have come to your Majesty's Consistory, to offer this plea in your presence, could I have obtained leave from the Bishops or the people; but they said that

---

[d] This is true of the first decision of the Council, but as S. Ambrose says, 'it ended badly,' for the Bishops were inveigled into accepting a less orthodox formula. See Prof Bright's Hist. p. 94, 98.

an argument concerning the Faith ought to be held in the Church in the presence of the people.

18. I could have wished that your Majesty had not declared that I might go into exile, whither I chose. I went abroad daily, no man guarded me. You should then have sent me wherever you thought fit, for I was ready to submit to any thing; now the Bishops say to me, 'There is little difference between voluntarily leaving Christ's altar and betraying it, for if you leave you will betray it.'

19. And I would I were certain that the Church would not be given up to the Arians, I would then willingly surrender myself to your Majesty's disposal. But if it is I only who am an intruder, why has the command been given to invade all other Churches also? I would it were certain, that no one would disturb the Churches, I would gladly then have any sentence which seems good passed concerning myself.

20. Let your Majesty then be pleased graciously to accept my reasons for not coming to the Church. I have not learned how to stand up in the Consistory except in your behalf[e]; and within the palace I cannot contend, for I neither seek after nor know the secrets of the palace.

21. I, Bishop Ambrose, offer this remonstrance to the most clement Emperor, his blessed Majesty Valentinian.

A.D. 386.

SERMON

AGAINST AUXENTIUS ON THE GIVING UP THE BASILICAS.

THE persecution against S Ambrose still continued. The Court party endeavoured to induce him to leave Milan, in order, they said, to prevent more serious troubles. This he refused to do, and at last he remained for several days and nights continuously within the Basilica[a], attended by a

[e] S. Ambrose here delicately alludes to the service he had rendered to Valentinian in going on his behalf to the court of the usurper Maximus after the death of Gratian, which is referred to in Letter xxiv

[a] 'This was not so great an inconvenience to them as might appear at first sight, for the early Basilicas were not unlike the heathen temples, or our own collegiate chapels, that is, part of a range of buildings, which contained the lodgings of the ecclesiastics, and formed a fortress in themselves, which could easily be blockaded either from within or without' Newman. Ch. of the Fathers. p. 22.

S. Ambrose will not desert his flock,

AGAINST AUXENTIUS

crowded congregation, all determined to protect him from the violence of the court, while a guard of soldiers was at the same time blockading the Church, and preventing any from leaving it. It was during this time that this Sermon was preached. In it S Ambrose first calms the fears of the people lest he should be induced to leave them, assuring them that he will only yield to force, and proceeds to apply the Lessons of the day, the story of Naboth and the Entry into Jerusalem, to the circumstances of the time, giving incidentally several interesting details of the contest between himself and the Court, and alluding to the hymns which he then taught the people to sing.

1. I SEE that you are in an unusual state of excitement, and that your eyes are fixed upon me. I am at a loss to know the cause of this. Is it that you saw or heard that an Imperial message has been brought to me by the Tribunes, commanding me to depart hence whither I would, and that all who would were permitted to follow me. Were you then alarmed lest I should desert the Church, and in fear for my own life abandon you? But you heard my answer. I said that the thought of deserting the Church could not for an instant enter my mind, for I feared the Lord of the Universe more than the Ruler of the Empire; that if I were to be forcibly removed from the Church, it would be my body not my mind which would be driven by violence from thence, that if the Emperor were to act as royal power is wont, I was prepared for that which is the part of a priest to suffer.

2. Why then are you thus disturbed? I will never desert you of my own will, but I may not repel force by force. I shall still be able to mourn, to weep, and to groan; when weapons, soldiers, Goths assail me, my tears are my weapons, for these are the defence of a priest. By any other means I neither can nor ought to resist; but to fly and desert the Church is not my wont, lest any one should impute it to fear of heavier punishment. You yourselves know that I am wont to pay deference to our Rulers, but not to give way to them, and willingly to offer myself to punishment, not fearing what is prepared for me.

3. Would that I could be satisfied that the Church would not be delivered to heretics! I would willingly go to the Emperor's palace, were this accordant with the priest's office, so as to hold our contest rather in the palace

than in the Church. But in the Consistory Christ is not wont to be the accused, but the Judge. Who will deny that a matter of faith should be pleaded in the Church? If any one has confidence in his cause let him come hither; let him not look for the judgment of the Emperor, which already shews its leaning, which has declared plainly by the law he has enacted that he is adverse to the Faith, nor for the expected support of certain intriguers. I will not give occasion to any one to barter for gain a wrong to Christ.

4. The guard of soldiers and the din of the arms which beset the Church, alarm not my faith, but they make me fear that in keeping me here you may incur danger to yourselves. For I have learned ere this not to fear for myself, but I begin now to fear more for you. Permit, I beg, your Bishop to enter the lists; we have an adversary who challenges us; for our *adversary the devil, as a roaring lion, walketh about seeking whom he may devour,* as the Apostle saith. Doubtless he has obtained, he has obtained (not to deceive us, but to warn us, is it recorded) this power of temptation, lest haply I should be removed from the stedfastness of my faith by the wounds of my body. You also have read that the devil thus tempted holy Job in many ways; and last of all he begged and obtained the power of afflicting his body which he covered with sores.

1 S. Pet. v. 8.

5. When it was proposed to me to give up at once the Church plate, I made this reply; That if my own property was required of me, farm or house, gold or silver, anything that lies in my power, I would willingly give it; but that I would withdraw nothing from God's temple, nor surrender what had been committed to me to keep, not to surrender. And further, that I was studying also for the Emperor's good, for it was expedient neither for me to surrender nor for him to receive these things; let him then listen to the words of an independent Bishop: if he regard his own interest, let him abstain from doing wrong to Christ.

6. These are words full of humility, and, I believe, of that affection which a Bishop owes to his Emperor. But since *our contest is not only against flesh and blood, but* also

Eph vi. 12

(which is more trouble) *against spiritual wickedness in high places*, that tempter, the Devil, sharpens the contest by his ministers, and deems that by the wounds of my body the trial must be made. I know, brethren, that these wounds which we receive for Christ, are no wounds : life is not lost by them, but its seed propagated. Permit, I beseech you, the contest to take place, it is for you to be spectators only. Consider that if there is in a city an athlete or one skilled in some other science, it wishes to present him for the combat. Why do ye reject in greater things what ye are wont to wish for even in smaller ones? He fears neither arms nor barbarians, who dreads not death, who is entangled in no fleshly pleasure.

7. Without doubt if the Lord hath appointed me to this combat, it is in vain that you have kept sleepless watch and ward through so many nights and days; the will of Christ will be performed. For our Lord Jesus Christ is Almighty, this is our Faith; and therefore what He bids to be done will be fulfilled, nor does it become us to run counter to the Divine Will.

8. Ye have heard what has been read to-day: the Saviour commanded an ass's colt to be brought to Him by the Apostles and commanded that if any one sought to hinder them they should say, *The Lord hath need of him.* What if now also He hath commanded this ass's colt, that is the colt of that animal which is wont to bear a heavy burthen, such as is the condition of man, to whom it is said, *Come unto Me all ye that labour and are heavy laden, and I will give you rest · take My yoke upon you, for My yoke is easy:* what, I say, if He hath now commanded this colt to be brought to Him, sending forth those Apostles who now having put off the body, wear, invisibly to our eyes, the guise of Angels? Will they not say, should any one seek to hinder them, *The Lord hath need of him*, if either the desire of this life, or flesh and blood, or the conversation of the world, for perhaps we are acceptable to some persons, should seek to hinder them? But he who loves me here, cannot give a better testimony of his affection than by suffering me to become a sacrifice for Christ; because *to be dissolved and to be with Christ is much better; how-*

S Luke xix. 35.

S. Matt. xi. 28. etc.

Phil. i. 23.

beit, to remain in the flesh is more needful for your sakes. Ye have therefore, my beloved brethren, no cause for fear, for I know that whatever I shall suffer, I shall suffer for Christ. And I have read that I ought not to fear those who can kill the flesh, and I have heard One say, *He who loses his life for My sake, shall find it.*

9. Wherefore, if the Lord wills it, I am sure that no resistance will be made. But if He still delay our contest, why should we fear? It is not bodily protection but the Lord's providence which is wont to protect the servant of Christ.

10. You are disturbed at finding some folding doors unclosed which a blind man in returning home is said to have opened. Acknowledge then that human guards are no support. Lo! one who had lost the gift of sight has broken through all your barriers and baffled your guards: but the Lord hath not lost [b] the guard of His mercy. Do you not remember that two days ago there was found open an entrance on the left side of the Basilica which you thought to be closed and guarded? The Basilica was surrounded by armed men who inspected every entrance, but their eyes were blinded so that they could not discover the one which was open; and so it remained open, as you know, for many nights. Cease then all anxiety, for what Christ commands, and what is expedient, shall come to pass.

11. In the next place I will produce to you instances from the Old Testament. Elisha was sought after by the king of Syria, an army was sent to take him, he was surrounded on every side, his servant began to fear, because he was a servant, that is, his mind was not free, nor had he freedom of action. The holy prophet prayed that his eyes might be opened, and said, *Look and see how many more are on our side than against us.* And he looked up and saw thousands of Angels. You see then that the servants of Christ are protected rather by invisible than by visible beings. But when they keep guard around you, they have been called to do so by your prayers; for you have

---

[b] The words 'custodiam' and 'amisit,' are repeated by S. Ambrose from the former part of the sentence. 'Amisit' as applied here recalls the Psalmist's expression, 'Hath God forgotten to be gracious?' Ps. lxxvii. 9.

read that those very men who sought for Elisha on entering Samaria came upon the very man whom they wished to capture, yet they were not able to injure him, but were saved by the intercession of the very man against whom they came.

AGAINST AUXENTIUS

12. Take the Apostle Peter too as an example of both these things. When Herod sought after and took him, he was put in prison; for the servant of God had not fled but stood firm and without fear. The Church prayed for him, but the Apostle was asleep in the prison, a proof that he feared not. An Angel was sent to rouse him from his sleep, and by him Peter was brought out of prison and for the time escaped death.

13. The same Peter, afterwards, after overcoming Simon, by spreading the precepts of God among the people and preaching chastity, stirred up the minds of the heathen against him: and when they sought to put him to death the Christians besought him to retire for a little while. And although he was desirous of suffering, yet he was moved by the sight of the people praying, for they besought him to reserve himself for the instruction and confirmation of the people. To be brief: as he set out from the walls by night, he saw Christ meeting him in the gate and entering the city, whereupon he said, 'Lord, whither goest Thou?' Christ answered, 'I am coming to be crucified again.' This Divine response Peter understood to refer to his own cross, for Christ, Who had put off the flesh by undergoing the suffering of death could not again be crucified, *For in that He died, He died unto sin once, but in that He liveth, He liveth unto God.* Wherefore Peter understood that Christ was again to be crucified in His servant; and so he turned back of his own accord, and when the Christians asked him why, he told them what he had seen, and was immediately seized, and honoured the Lord Jesus by his cross.

Rom. vi. 10.

14. Ye see then that Christ wills to suffer in His servants. What if He saith to this servant also, *I will that he tarry, but follow thou Me?* what if He wills to taste of the fruit from this tree? For if it was His meat to do His Father's Will, it is His meat also to feed upon the suffer

S. John xxi. 22.

ings of His servants. To take an example from our Lord Himself, did He not suffer when He willed, and was He not found when they sought for Him? But when the hour of His passion had not arrived, He passed through the midst of them who sought for Him, and they who saw Him could not detain Him. Which evidently shews that when the Lord wills, each man is found and taken, while he whose time is not come although he meet the eyes, is not captured.

15. And did I not go out daily to make visits, or go to the tomb of the Martyrs? Did I not in going and returning pass close by the Royal palace? And yet no man arrested me, though they wished to drive me from the city, as they shewed afterwards by saying, 'Leave this city, and go where thou wilt.' I expected, I confess, something great, to be burned or slain with the sword for the name of Christ, but they offered me delights in the place of sufferings; and yet the soldiers of Christ seeks not for delights but for sufferings. Wherefore let no man trouble you by the intelligence that they have prepared a carriage [c], or that Auxentius, who calls himself Bishop, has uttered what he thinks terrible words.

16. Many said that executioners had been sent, that the punishment of death had been decreed; I fear them not, nor will I desert my post. For whither should I go to find a place that is not full of nothing but tears and groans? For in every Church the Catholic clergy are ordered to be cast forth; if they resist, to be put to death; all the senators [d] who do not obey this mandate, to be proscribed.

[c] This refers to a story thus recounted in Paulinus' Life of S. Ambrose ch. 12, 'Among many who tried to force S. Ambrose into exile, but through God's protection failed of their purpose, one Euthymius more hapless than the rest, was stirred to such a pitch of frenzy that he hired a house close to the Church, and there kept a carriage, that he might the more readily carry off Ambrose into exile, by seizing him and putting him in the carriage. But *his wickedness fell upon his own pate,* (Ps vii 7) for that very day year, he was himself put into the carriage and from the same house was carried into exile, confessing that it was by the just judgment of God that his wickedness had recoiled on himself, and he was carried into exile in the very chariot which he had prepared for the Bishop. And the Bishop did much to comfort him, by giving him money, and other necessaries'

[d] The word is 'curiales.' see note e on Lett. xviii. To the authorities there referred to add Bingh. Antiq. iv, 4, 4, where Gothofred's enumeration of their duties is given in full in the notes.

And it is a Bishop who writes these orders with his own hand and dictates them with his own mouth, who to prove his learning omitted not an ancient precedent; for we read in the prophet that he saw a flying sickle[1], and in imitation of this Auxentius sent a winged sword through all the cities. And thus *Satan transforms himself into an Angel of light,* and imitates his power for evil purposes.

AGAINST AUXENTIUS

[1] Zech v. 1 [E.V. a flying roll. Vulg. volumen volans.]

17. Thou, Lord Jesus, hast in one moment redeemed the world; shall Auxentius in one moment, so far as in him lies, slay so many people, some with the sword, others by sacrilege[2]? My Basilica he sought with a mouth and hands of blood, and to him our present Lesson may be well applied, *Unto the ungodly, saith God, why dost thou preach my laws?* that is, There is no concord between peace and wrath, *between Christ and Belial.* You remember also how in the Lesson of to-day that holy man Naboth, the owner of a vineyard, was requested by the king to surrender it to him, that he might root up the vines and plant it with common herbs, and that he answered, *God forbid that I should give thee the inheritance of my fathers;* and that king was grieved that what belonged of right to another was refused him when he claimed it as his right, and only gained by the deceit of a woman's artifice. Naboth then defended his vineyard even with his own blood; if he would not surrender his vineyard, shall we surrender the Church of Christ?

2 Cor. xi. 14.

[2] i.e. by causing them to commit sacrilege. Ps 1. 16. 2 Cor. vi. 15

1 Kings xxi. 3.

18. How then did I reply contumaciously? When summoned, I said, 'God forbid that I should surrender Christ's heritage. If Naboth would not surrender the heritage of his fathers, shall I surrender Christ's heritage?' I added moreover, 'God forbid that I should surrender the heritage of my fathers, the heritage of Dionysius, who died in exile for the Faith, of the Confessor Eustorgius, of Myrocles, and of all the faithful Bishops of old time.' I answered as becomes a Bishop, let the Emperor act as becomes an Emperor. He shall deprive me of my life sooner than my Faith.

19. But to whom am I to surrender it? The Lesson just read from the Gospel ought to teach us what it is that is demanded, and by whom. Ye heard it read that, when

SERMON   Christ was sitting on the ass's colt, the children cried out, and the Jews were indignant, appealing to the Lord Jesus, and saying that He should bid them hold their peace, but
S. Luke xix. 40.   He replied, *If these were to hold their peace, the very stones would cry out.* Then He entered the Temple, and cast out the moneychangers, and their tables, and those that sold doves in the Temple of God. This Lesson was read by no direction of ours, but by chance; but it suits well with the present time. For the praises of Christ are always as it were scourges to misbelievers. And now when Christ is praised the heretics say that we are exciting sedition, the heretics say that they were thereby threatened with death; and truly the praises of Christ are death to them. For how can they bear His praises Whose weakness they are proclaiming? Wherefore to this day the praises of Christ are a scourge to the madness of the Arians.

20. The Gerasenes could not bear the presence of Christ, these men, worse than the Gerasenes, cannot even bear the praises of Christ. They see children singing the glory of Christ; for it is written, *Out of the mouth of babes and sucklings Thou hast perfected praise.* They deride their tender years so full of faith, and ask, Why do they cry out? But Christ answers them, *If these should hold their peace the very stones would cry out,* that is, the stranger will cry out, the young men too will cry out, the more mature will cry out, the old men also: stones built into that Stone of Whom it is written, *The stone which the builders disallowed is become the head-stone of the corner.*

Ps. viii. 2.

Ps cxviii. 22.

21. Christ then, invited by these praises, enters His Temple, and takes His scuorge and drives out the moneychangers. For He will not permit those who are slaves of money to be in His Temple, He will not suffer those to be there who sell seats. What are *seats*, but honours? What are *doves*, but simple minds, or souls which embrace a sincere and pure faith? Shall I then introduce into the Temple him whom Christ excludes? For he is commanded to go forth who sells dignities and honours, he is commanded to go forth who would sell the simple minds of the faithful.

22. Wherefore Auxentius is cast forth, Mercurianus is excluded. This is one portent under two names. That it might not be known who he was, he changed his name, and, as there had been here Auxentius the Arian Bishop, so he, to deceive the people whom the other had influenced, called himself Auxentius. Thus he changed his name, but his perfidy he could not change; he put off wolf, and yet put on wolf. It avails him not to have changed his name, what he really is is known. He was known by one name in the regions of Scythia, he is called by another here, he has names differing according to his country. Now therefore he has two names, and if from hence he goes elsewhere he will have a third also. For how will he endure to keep a name which betrays the greatness of his crime? In Scythia he did less wickedly, and yet he was so ashamed as to change his name; here he has dared to do more heinous things, and will he be willing wherever he goes to be betrayed by his name? After writing with his own hand the death warrant of so many people, will he be able to retain his senses unshaken?

23. The Lord Jesus drove out a few from His temple, Auxentius left no one. Jesus casts men out of His temple with a scourge, Auxentius with a sword; Jesus with a rod, Mercurianus with an axe. Our holy Lord drives out the sacrilegious with a scourge, this wicked man persecutes the godly with the sword. Of him ye have to-day said well; 'let him carry his laws away with him.' He shall carry them though he desire it not, he shall carry with him his conscience, though he carry not the writing, he shall carry his own soul inscribed in blood, although he carry not a letter inscribed with ink. *Thy sin, O Judah, is written with a pen of iron and with the point of a diamond, and it is graven in thy heart,* graven that is in the place from whence it came forth. Jer. xvii. 1.

24. Does he moreover, stained as he is with blood and slaughter, dare to mention discussion to me? Those whom he fails to deceive by his arguments he sentences to be smitten with the sword, and he dictates bloody laws with his mouth, writing them with his hand, and thinking that the law can impose a Creed on men. He has never heard

what was read to-day, *A man is not justified by the works of the law*, or, *I by the law am dead to the law that I might live to God*, that is, by the spiritual law he is dead to the carnal interpretation of the law. Let us too by the law of our Lord Jesus Christ die to this law which sanctions the decrees of perfidy. It is not the law which has gathered together the Church, but the faith of Christ. For the law is not of faith: *But the just shall live by faith.* It is faith then, not the law, which makes a man just, because righteousness is not by the law, but by the faith of Christ. But he who rejects faith, and takes law for his rule, bears witness to his own unrighteousness, for *the just shall live by faith.*

25. Shall any then follow this law confirming the Council of Arianism wherein Christ is called a creature? But they say, *God sent His Son, made of a woman, made under the Law.* So then He is *made* they say, that is, created. Will they not consider this very text which they have produced; that Christ is said to be made, but *made of a woman*, that is, He according to His birth from the Virgin was *made*, Who was according to His Divine generation born of the Father? They read too to-day that Christ *redeemed us from the curse of the Law, being made a curse for us.* Was Christ a curse according to His Divinity? But why He should be called a curse the Apostle teaches thee, alleging the text, *Cursed is every one that hangeth on a tree*, that is, He Who in His flesh took upon Him our flesh, in His body carried our griefs and our curses that He might crucify them, for He is cursed, not in Himself, but in thee. Lastly, you have in another place, *Who knew no sin, but was made sin for us,* for He took upon Him our sins, to do away with them by the Sacrament of His Passion.

26. These points, my brethren, I would have discussed more fully with you in his presence, but he, being aware that you were not ignorant of the Faith, fled from your scrutiny, and chose as his advocates, if indeed he chose any, four or five heathens, whom I would willingly have now present in our general assembly, not for them to judge of Christ, but that they might hear the majesty of Christ. They however have already pronounced concerning Auxen-

tius, for when he daily argued before them they gave him no credit. What can be a greater condemnation of him than that he was defeated without an adversary before his own judges? Thus we now have their own sentence against Auxentius.

27. And justly is he to be condemned for choosing heathen judges, for he disregarded the Apostle's precept who says *Dare any of you, having a matter against another, go to law before the unjust, and not before the saints? Do you not know that the saints shall judge the world?* And below he says, *Is it so that there is not a wise man among you, no not one that shall be able to judge between his brethren? but brother goeth to law with brother, and that before the unbelievers?* Ye see that what he offered is contrary to the Apostle's authority. Choose whether we should follow Auxentius or Paul as our master?

28. But why should I speak of the Apostle, when our Lord Himself cries by the Prophet, *hearken unto Me My people, ye that know righteousness, in whose heart is My law.* God says, *hearken unto Me My people, ye that know righteousness.* Auxentius says, Ye know not righteousness. Do ye not see that he now, who rejects the declaration of the heavenly oracles, despises God in you? *Hearken unto Me My people,* saith the Lord. He says not, Hearken ye Gentiles; He says not, Hearken ye Jews. For now they that were the people of God are become the people of error, and they who were the people of error have become the people of God, because they have believed in Christ. Wherefore that people are judges, in whose heart is the Divine, not human, law; the law *written not with ink, but with the Spirit of the living God,* not inscribed on paper but stampt upon the heart; the law of grace not of blood. Who is it then who wrongs you, he who refuses or he who chooses to be heard by you?

29. Hemmed in on all sides, he has recourse to the wiles of his fathers. He wishes to excite odium against me in regard to the Emperor, saying, that a youth yet a catechumen and ignorant of the sacred Scriptures, ought to judge, and to judge in the Consistory. As if last year, when I was summoned to the palace, when in the presence of the

nobles the matter was argued before the Consistory, when the Emperor wished to take away the Basilica, I was then cowed by the sight of the Imperial court, and had not maintained the constancy of a priest, or had suffered our rights to be infringed there. Do they not remember that when the people knew I had gone to the palace they rushed in with an onset that nothing could withstand; and when a Military Count came forth with some light troops to disperse the multitude they all offered themselves to death for the Faith of Christ? Was I not then requested to make a long speech to soothe the people? Did I not pledge my faith that no one should invade the Church's Basilica? And although my good offices were requested as a kindness, yet the coming of the populace to the palace was made a ground of charge against me; into the same odium then they wish me again to fall.

30. I recalled the people, and yet I did not escape odium, and this odium ought, I conceive, to be controuled rather than feared. For what should we fear for the name of Christ? Unless perhaps this which they say ought to move me; 'And ought not the Emperor then to have one Basilica to go to; and does Ambrose desire to be more powerful than the Emperor, so as to exclude him from the liberty of attending Church?' When they say this, they wish to lay hold of my words, like the Jews who tempted Christ with empty words, saying, *Master, is it lawful to give tribute to Cæsar or not?* Must the servants of God always be exposed to odium on Cæsar's account? And does impiety, with a view to calumny, seek to use the Imperial name as a cloak? And can they protest that they do not partake of the sacrilege of these men, whose guidance they follow?

31. Yet see how much worse the Arians are than the Jews. The latter enquired of Christ whether He thought that the right of tribute should be rendered to Cæsar; the former are willing to surrender to the Emperor the rights of the Church. But like traitors, they follow their master, and so let us answer what our Lord and Master hath taught us. For Jesus perceiving the treachery of the Jews, said unto them, *Why tempt ye Me, shew Me a penny. And when they gave it to Him, He said, Whose image and whose su-*

perscription is this? They answered, Cæsar's. Jesus replied, Render therefore unto Cæsar the things that are Cæsar's, and unto God the things that are God's. Thus I also say to them who find fault with me, *Shew Me a penny.* Jesus saw the penny was Cæsar's, and said, *Render unto Cæsar the the things that are Cæsar's, and unto God the things that are God's.* Can they from the seizure of the Basilicas of the Church offer the penny of Cæsar?

32. But in the Church I know one image, that is, the image of the invisible God, of which God said, *Let us make man in Our image, after Our likeness,* that image of which it is written, that Christ is *the brightness of His glory, the express image of His substance.* In this image I behold the Father, as the Lord Jesus Himself said, *He that hath seen Me hath seen the Father also.* For this Image is not divided from the Father, for He hath taught me the unity of the Trinity, saying, *I and the Father are One,* and below, *All things that the Father hath are Mine.* And of the Holy Spirit, saying, that He is the Spirit of Christ, and hath received from Christ, as it is written, *He shall take of Mine, and shall declare it unto you.*

Gen. i. 26.
Heb. i. 3.
S John xiv. 9.
Ib. x. 30.
Ib xvi. 15.
Ib. 16.

33. In what respect then have we not answered with humility? If he ask for tribute we deny it not. The Church lands pay tribute; if the Emperor desire to possess these lands he has the power to claim them; none of us will interfere. The contributions of the people will more than suffice for the poor; let them excite no ill-will on account of the lands, let them take them if it please the Emperor; I give them not, but I do not refuse them. They ask for gold, but I can say, Silver and gold I seek not. But this disbursement of gold they make a cause of offence: this offence I dread not. I have stipendiaries, it is true: my stipendiaries[e] are the poor of Christ, this is a treasure which I am well used to collect. May this offence of bestowing gold on the poor ever be charged upon me! And if they accuse me of defending myself by their means, I deny not, nay I even court the charge; a defence I have,

[e] There is a play here on the word 'aerarios,' as connected with 'aerarium' the treasury The aerarii were the lowest class of people at Rome, and so S. Ambrose calls the 'pauperes Christi' his aerarii, while at the same time they are the treasures of the Church.

but it is in the prayers of the poor. Blind they are and and lame, weak and old, yet are they stronger than the stoutest warriors. Lastly, gifts to the poor make God our debtor, for it is written, *He that giveth to the poor, lendeth to the Lord.* The guards of warriors often gain not Divine grace.

Prov. xix. 17.

34. Moreover they assert that the people have been beguiled by the strains of my hymns^f. I deny not this either. It is a lofty strain, than which nothing is more powerful. For what can be more powerful than the confession of the Trinity, which is daily celebrated by the mouth of the whole people? All zealously desire to make profession of their faith, they know how to confess in verse the Father and the Son and the Holy Spirit. Thus all are become teachers who were scarcely able to be disciples.

35. But what can be more lowly than for us to follow the example of Christ, Who *being found in fashion as a man humbled himself being made obedient unto death.* And again, by obedience He delivered all: *For as by the disobedience of one man many were made sinners, so by the obedience of one Man shall many be made righteous.* If then He was obedient let them learn from Him the lesson of obedience, to which we adhere, saying to them who raise odium against us, on the Emperor's account, *We render to Cæsar the things that are Cæsar's, and to God the things that are God's.* To Cæsar tribute is due, we deny it not; the Church is God's, and must not be given up to Cæsar, because the Temple of God cannot by right be Cæsar's.

Phil. iii. 7.

Rom. v. 19.

---

^f S Augustine mentions in his Confessions (ix. 7.) S. Ambrose's introduction both of Hymns and chanting during this period of trial ' Then was it first instituted that, after the manner of the Eastern Churches, Hymns and Psalms should be sung, lest the people should wax faint through the tediousness of sorrow ; and from that day to this the custom is retained, divers, yea, almost all Thy Congregations throughout other parts of the world following herein ' Oxf. Transl. He speaks in the same passage of the behaviour of the people : ' The devout people kept watch in the Church, ready to die with their Bishop Thy servant.' He also dwells on the effect produced on himself, these events happening shortly before his conversion. ' How did I weep in Thy Hymns and Canticles, touched to the quick by the voice of Thy sweet-attuned Church ! The voices flowed into mine ears, and the Truth distilled into mine heart, whence the affections of my devotion overflowed, and tears ran down, and happy was I therein ' Ib ix 6. It is quite possible that some of the twelve Hymns, acknowledged by the Benedictine Editors as genuine, were then first sung. Among them are the well-known ' Aeterna Christi munera,' ' Aeterne rerum Conditor,' ' Deus Creator omnium,' and others, whose strains are now familiar in English versions.

36. That this is said with due honour to the Emperor no one can deny. For what can be more honourable for the Emperor than to be styled a son of the Church? In saying this we are loyal to him without sinning against God. For the Emperor is *within* the Church, not *over* the Church; a good Emperor seeks the aid of the Church, he does not reject it, we say this humbly, but we assert it firmly. Some men threaten us with fire, sword and banishment. We, the servants of Christ, have learned not to fear. To them that fear not nothing is a cause of alarm. And it is thus written, *arrows of infants are their blows become.* AGAINST AUXENTIUS

Ps. lxiv. 7. vulg

37. It would seem now that we have made a sufficient answer to what was proposed to us. Now I ask them the same question as did the Saviour, *The baptism of John was it from heaven or of men?* And the Jews could not answer Him. If the Jews did not annul the baptism of John, shall Auxentius annul the Baptism of Christ? For that Baptism is not from men but from Christ which the *Angel of mighty Counsel* brought down to us, that we might be justified before God. Why then does Auxentius hold that the faithful, those baptized in the name of the Trinity are to be re-baptized, when the Apostle says, *One faith, one baptism;* why does he say that he is the adversary of men, not of Christ, seeing that he spurns the counsel of God, and contemns that Baptism which Christ gave us for the redemption of our sins. S. Luke xx. 4.

Is. ix. 6.

Eph. iv. 5.

LETTER XXII. A.D. 386.

S. AMBROSE here recounts to his sister the discovery of the relics of S. S. Gervasius and Protasius, which occurred during the time of trial referred to in the last letter, and seems, by the pitch of excitement to which it raised the people of Milan, to have alarmed the court-party, and so to have caused the persecution to be dropped. The simple narrative needs no further introduction. It is strikingly told, and the question of the miracles discussed, in the 'Church of the Fathers' ch. iii. S. Augustine gives a brief account of the event in his Confessions, (ix 7) fully corroborating S. Ambrose's statements, and also speaks of it in De Civ. Dei xxii. 8, 2, and in Serm. de Divers cclxxvi. 5.

158   *The finding of the Relics.*

LETT. 22. TO THE LADY HIS SISTER WHOM HE LOVES MORE THAN HIS LIFE AND EYES AMBROSE HER BROTHER SENDS GREETING.

As I am wont to keep your holiness informed of all that goes on here in your absence, I would have you know that we have found the bodies of some holy martyrs. After the consecration of a Church [a], many began to interrupt me crying with one voice; Consecrate this as you did the Roman Basilica. 'I will do so,' I replied, 'if I find any relics of Martyrs:' and immediately my heart burned within me as if prophetically.

2. In short the Lord lent us aid [b], though even the very clergy were alarmed. I caused the ground to be opened before the rails of the Church of S.S. Felix and Nabor. I found the suitable tokens; and when some persons were brought for us to lay our hands upon, the power of the holy martyrs became so manifest that before I began to speak, one of them, a woman [c], was seized by an evil spirit and thrown down upon the ground in the place where the martyrs lay. We found two men of stupendous size, such as belonged to ancient days. All their bones were entire, and there was much blood. The people flocked thither in crowds throughout the whole of those two days. We arranged all the bones in order, and carried them when evening set in, to the Basilica of Fausta [1]; where we kept vigils throughout the night, and some possessed persons received imposition of hands. The following day we transferred them to the Basilica which they call Ambrosian. During their transportation a blind man was healed [e]. My dis-

[1] now of S. Vitalis and S Agricola Fleury p 104. Eng. Tr.

[a] This is said to be the Church now called 'S Ambrose the greater.' The Roman Church is the one called in the previous letter the 'New Basilica,' and also the Church of the Apostles It was probably called 'Romana' from being near the Porta Romana.

[b] S. Augustine says that it was revealed to him in a dream

[c] These were ἐνεργούμενοι, or persons possessed by evil spirits. On them see Bingh Antiq ni 4, 6 The laying on of hands was part of the rite of exorcism.

[d] The text stands 'arriperetur urna,' nor is there any variation of MSS. noted. But it seems absolutely necessary to read 'una' An 'urna' could have nothing to do with the matter. It might hold ashes, but surely not the bones of two men of marvellous size. The histories founded on the letter all tacitly adopt the emendation, and speak of 'a woman among the possessed.' See Fleury B. xviii 46. Tillemont in Vit

[e] This is distinctly asserted by S. Augustine in all the three passages referred to in the Introduction

course to the people was as follows. When I considered in what overflowing and unprecedented numbers you were met together, and thought on the gifts of Divine Grace which shone forth in the holy Martyrs, I felt myself, I confess, unequal to this task, and thought it impossible that I could find language to express that which we can hardly conceive in mind or endure with our eyes. But when the reading of the regular Lessons of Holy Scripture began, the Holy Spirit, Who spoke by the Prophets, granted us grace to speak somewhat worthy of this great and expectant concourse, and of the merits of the holy Martyrs.

4. *The heavens*, the Psalmist says, *declare the glory of God*. On reading this Psalm the thought arises that it is not so much the material elements as the heavenly merits that seem to offer praise worthy of God. But by the coincidence of the Lesson being read to-day it is made plain what are the *heavens* which *tell of the glory of God*. Behold on my right hand and on my left the holy relics, behold men of heavenly conversation, behold the trophies of a lofty mind. These are the *heavens* which *declare the glory of God*, these are *the works of His hands* which *are told by the firmament*. For it was not worldly snares, but the favour of the Divine operation, which raised them to the firmament of the most sacred Passion, and long beforehand by the evidence of their conversation and virtues bore this testimony of them, that they remained stedfast against the slippery wiles of this world.

5. Paul was an heaven, when he says, *Our conversation is in heaven*. James and John were heavens; they are called *sons of thunder*; and therefore being as it were, an heaven, John saw *the Word with God*. The Lord Jesus Christ Himself was an heaven of perpetual light, when He told forth the glory of God, that glory which no man had before beheld. And therefore He said, *No man hath seen God at any time, but the Only-Begotten Son, Who is in the bosom of the Father, He hath declared Him*. Moreover, if you look for the handiwork of God, hear what Job says, *The Spirit of God hath made me*. And so, strengthened against the temptations of the devil, he preserved his steps stedfast and without stumbling. But let us proceed to what follows.

Lett. 22.	6. *Day unto day,* the Psalm says, *uttereth speech.* These are the true *days,* which no shades of night obscure; these are the true *days,* full of light and eternal radiance, who have *uttered the word* of God not by any mere transient utterance but from their inmost heart, continuing constant in their confession, persevering in their testimony.
Ps. xix. 2.	
Ps. cxiii. 5, 6.	7. Another Psalm we read saith, *Who is like unto the Lord our God, that hath His dwelling so high, and yet regardeth the lowly things that are in heaven and earth.* Truly God hath *regarded the lowly,* Who hath discovered the relics of the martyrs of His Church as they lay hid under the unnoted sod, of those whose souls are in heaven,
Ps. cxiii. 7, 8.	while their bodies are in the earth, *taking up the simple out of the dust and lifting the poor out of the mire,* even those whom ye see, *to set them with the princes of His people.* For whom but the holy martyrs shall we deem to be *princes of the people?* In their number Protasius and Gervasius heretofore long unknown are enrolled, they who have caused the Church of Milan, once *barren* of martyrs,
Ib. 9.	but now *the mother of many children,* to exult both in the honors and examples of her own sufferings?
	8. Nor let this be considered alien from the true Faith: *Day unto day uttereth speech,* soul to soul, life to life, resurrection to resurrection. *And night unto night uttereth knowledge,* that is, flesh to flesh, the flesh whose sufferings have declared to all the true knowledge of faith.
1 Cor. xv. 41.	Bright and fair nights, full of stars: *For one star differeth from another star in glory, so also is the resurrection of the dead.*

9. But many not improperly call this the resurrection of the martyrs; whether they have risen for themselves is another question, for us beyond a doubt they are risen. Ye have heard, nay, yourselves have seen, many cleansed from evil spirits; many also, after touching with their hands the garments of the saints, delivered from the infirmities under which they suffered: ye have seen the miracles of old time renewed, when through the coming of the Lord Jesus, a fuller Grace descended upon the earth; ye see many healed by the shadow, as it were, of the holy bodies. How many napkins are passed to and fro? How

many garments placed on these holy relics, and endowed by the mere contact with the power of healing are reclaimed by their owners. All think themselves happy in touching even the outer-most thread, and whoever touches them will be made whole.

TO MARCELLINA

10. Thanks be to Thee, Lord Jesus, that at this time, when Thy Church requires greater guardianship, Thou hast raised up for us the spirits of the holy martyrs. Let all be well aware what kind of champions I desire, such as are wont to be protectors not assailants. Such are they, O holy people, whom I have obtained for you, a benefit to all, and a hurt to none. These are the defenders whom I desire, these are my soldiers, not the world's soldiers, but Christ's. I fear no odium on account of these; their patronage is safe in proportion to its power. Nay, I desire their protection for the very men who grudge them to me. Let them come then and see my body-guard: I deny not that I am surrounded by such weapons as these; *Some put their trust in chariots and some in horses, but we will magnify ourselves in the Name of the Lord our God.*

Ps xx. 7.

11. The Lesson from Holy Scripture relates how Elisha, when surrounded by the army of the Syrians, told his trembling servant not to fear, *for they*, said he, *that are for us are more than they which are against us;* and in order to convince Gehazi of this, he prayed that his eyes might be opened, and when this was done he saw a countless host of Angels present with the prophet. And we, though we see them not, yet are conscious of their presence. Our eyes were held, as long as the bodies of the saints lay hid in their graves. Now God has opened our eyes, and we have seen the aids which had so often succoured us. Before, we saw them not, although we possessed them. And so, as though the Lord said to our trembling hearts, 'Behold what great martyrs I have given you;' even so *with opened eyes we behold the glory of the Lord*, which as to the passion of the martyrs is past, as to their operation is present. We have escaped, my brethren, no light load of shame; we had patrons and we knew it not. This one thing we have found, wherein we seem to excel our ances-

2 Kings vi. 16 sqq.

2 Cor. iii. 18.

M

LETT. 22. tors; they lost the knowledge of the holy martyrs, and we have gained it.

12. These noble relics are dug out of an ignoble sepulchre; these trophies are displayed in the face of day. The tomb is moist with blood, the tokens of a triumphant death are displayed, the uninjured relics are found in their proper place and order, the head separated from the body. Old men now relate that they have formerly heard the names of these martyrs, and read their titles. The city which had seized on the martyrs of other places had lost her own. This is the gift of God, and yet the favour which the Lord Jesus has conferred in the time of my episcopate I cannot deny, and since I myself am not counted worthy to be a martyr, I have gained these martyrs for you.

13. Bring these victorious victims to the spot where Christ is the sacrifice. But He, Who suffered for all, upon the Altar, they, who have been redeemed by His passion, under the Altar. This spot I had destined for myself, for it is fitting that the priest should rest where he hath been wont to offer, but I give up the right side to the sacred victims: that spot was due to the martyrs. Wherefore let us bury the hallowed relics, placing them in a worthy home, and let us employ the whole day in faithful devotion.

14. The people loudly requested that the deposition of the martyrs should be deferred until the Lord's Day; but at length I prevailed that it should take place on the following day. On that day I delivered a second sermon to the people to the following effect.

Ps. xix. 2. 15. Yesterday I discoursed upon the verse, *Day unto day uttereth speech,* speaking according to my capacity: to-day Holy Scripture seems to me to have prophecied, not only before, but now. For seeing that this your devout celebration has continued night and day, the oracles of prophetic song have declared that these, even yesterday and to-day, are the days of which it is most opportunely said *day unto day uttereth speech,* and these the nights to which the saying is appropriate that *night unto night uttereth knowledge.* For what else have ye done during these two days but utter the word of God with deep emotion, and prove yourselves to have the knowledge of faith?

16. This your celebration some, as is their wont, are envious of. And since their envious minds cannot endure it, they also hate its cause, and proceed to such a pitch of folly as to deny the merits of the martyrs, whose power the very devils confess. But this is not strange; for such is the faithlessness of unbelievers that the confession of the devil himself is often less intolerable. For the devil said, *Jesus, Thou Son of the living God, art Thou come to torment us before the time?* And yet when the Jews heard this they even then denied the Son of God. And now ye have heard the devils crying out, and owning to the martyrs that they cannot bear their tortures, and saying 'Why are ye come to torment us so grievously?' And the Arians say, 'These are not martyrs, nor can they torment the devil nor dispossess any one:' while yet their own words are evidence of the torments of the evil spirits, and the benefits of the martyrs are shewn by the recovery of the healed, and the manifest proof of those that were dispossessed.

TO MARCELLINA

S. Matt. viii. 29.

17. They deny that the blind man received his sight, but he denies not his own cure. He says, 'I who was blind now see.' He says, 'My blindness has left me;' he evidences it by the fact. They deny the benefit, though they cannot deny the fact. The man is well known: when in health he was employed in public trade, his name is Severus, a butcher by business. When his affliction befell him he laid down his employment. He calls as his witnesses those men by whose charities he was supported; he summons as witnesses of his present visitation the very men who bore testimony to his blindness. He declares that when he touched the border of the garment with which the martyrs' bodies were clothed, his sight was restored to him.

18. Is not this like what we read in the Gospel? For the power which we admire proceeds from one and the same Author; nor does it signify whether it is a work or a gift, seeing that He confers gifts in His works and works by His gifts. For what He has enabled some themselves to perform, this in the work of others His Name effects. Thus we read in the Gospel that the Jews, when they saw that the blind man had received his sight, required the testimony of his parents. They asked, 'How has your son

LETT. 22.
S. John
ix. 25.

received his sight?' That blind man said, *Whereas I was blind now I see,* and so too our blind man says, 'I was blind, and now I see.' Enquire of others, if ye believe me not; question strangers, if you suspect his parents of being in collusion with me. The obstinacy of these men is more detestable than that of the Jews, for the latter inquired of the man's parents to solve their doubts; they secretly inquire but openly deny, no longer refusing credit to the miracle but to its Author.

19 and 20. But I would fain ask, what it is they will not believe; is it that any one can be relieved by the martyrs?

S. John
xiv. 12.

But this is not to believe in Christ, for He hath said, *And greater things than these shall ye do.* Or only by those martyrs, whose merits have long been efficacious, and whose bodies have long been discovered? Here I ask whether it is of myself or of the holy martyrs that they are jealous? If of me, have I wrought any miracles by my own means, in my own name? Why then do they envy me that which is not mine? But if of the martyrs (for if not of me it must be of them they are envious) they show that their Creed is different from that of the martyrs. For they would not envy their works unless they deemed the faith which was in them to be that which they themselves have not. This is that Faith sealed by the tradition of our ancestors, which the devils themselves cannot deny, though the Arians do.

21. We have heard to-day those on whom hands were laid, profess that no man can be saved who does not believe in the Father, Son, and Holy Ghost: that he was dead and buried who denied the Holy Ghost, who believed not the Almighty power of the Trinity. This the devil confesses, but the Arians will not own it. The devil says, Let him who denies the divinity of the Holy Spirit be tormented as he himself was tormented by the Martyrs.

22. What I accept from the devil is not his testimony, but his confession. He spoke unwillingly, compelled and tortured. That which wickedness suppressed, force extorted. The devil yields to blows, but as yet the Arians have not learned to yield. How much have they suffered, and like Pharoah, they are hardened by their calamities!

The devil said, as we find it written, *I know Thee Who Thou art, the Son of the Living God.* The Jews said, *We know not who He is.* Yesterday, and the preceding night and day the devils said, 'We know that ye are martyrs,' while the Arians said, 'We know not, we will not understand nor believe.' The devils say to the martyrs, 'Ye are come to destroy us,' the Arians say, 'These torments of the devil are not true torments but pretended and counterfeit.' I have heard of many counterfeits, but no man could ever feign himself a devil. Again, what is the meaning of the agony we see in them, when the hand is laid on them? What room is here for fraud and what suspicion of imposture?

TO MARCEL-LINA
S. Mark i. 24.
S. John ix. 29.

23. But I will not call the words of devils as a testimony to the martyrs: let the sacred sufferings of the martyrs be established by their own supernatural acts; judges indeed they have, namely, those that have been cleansed, witnesses, namely those that have been dispossessed. Better than that of devils is their voice who came diseased and are now healed, better is that voice which the martyrs blood sends forth, for blood has a loud voice which reaches from earth to heaven. Ye have read those words of God, *Thy brother's blood crieth unto Me!* This blood cries by its purple stains, it cries by its signal efficacy, it cries by its triumphant suffering.

Gen. iv. 10.

We have granted your request and have put off till to-day the burial of the relics which should have taken place yesterday.

LETTER XXIII.

A.D. 386.

THIS letter is addressed to the Bishops of the Province of Æmilia, which, as forming part of the political diocese of Italy, was under the ecclesiastical superintendence of the Bishop of Milan, who exercised the powers, if he had not the title, of Exarch. (See Bingham Antiq. ix. 1, § 6, 8.) The Bishops apply to him for his decision as to the proper day for observing Easter in the following year, A.D. 387, in which the first day of the week fell on the fourteenth day of the moon, or, as it is called here, the 'fourteenth moon.' This was a question which for long troubled the Church, and divided the East and West, and much importance was attached to it. The whole question is fully discussed in Dict. of Christ. Antiq. under 'Easter,' in

LETT. 23. a learned article by the Rev. L Hensley. Some interesting remarks on it, in connection with disputes in England, may be seen in Prof. Bright's Early English Ch. Hist. pp. 76—79, and 193—200.

Mr. Hensley has kindly drawn up the following table, which exhibits at a glance the points on which S. Ambrose enters in this letter.

TABLE OF EASTER FROM A D. 373 TO A.D. 387.

A D.	GOLDEN NUMBER.	SUNDAY LETTER.	EASTER TERM.		EASTER DAY.
*373	13	F	March 24	F	March 31
374	14	E	April 12	D	April 13
375	15	D	April 1	G	April 5
376	16	CB	April 21	C	April 27
*377	17	A	April 9	A	April 16
378	18	G	March 29	D	April 1
379	19	F	April 17	B	April 21
*380	1	ED	April 5	D	April 12
381	2	C	March 25	G	March 28
382	3	B	April 13	E	April 17
*383	4	A	April 2	A	April 9
384	5	GF	March 22	D	March 24
385	6	E	April 10	B	April 13
386	7	D	March 30	E	April 5
*387	8	C	April 18	G	April 25

* The asterisks mark the year in which the full moon falls on the Sunday, and which are referred to in the Letter.

TO THE LORDS, HIS BRETHREN MOST BELOVED, THE BISHOPS ESTABLISHED THROUGHOUT THE PROVINCE OF ÆMILIA, AMBROSE, BISHOP.

1. THAT to settle the day of the celebration of the Passover requires more than ordinary wisdom, we are taught both by the Holy Scripture and by the tradition of the Fathers, who, when assembled at the Nicene Synod, in addition to their true and admirable decrees concerning the Faith, formed also for the above-mentioned celebration a plan for nineteen years with the aid of the most skilful calculators, and constituted a sort of cycle to serve as a pattern for subsequent years. This cycle they called the nineteen years' cycle[a], their aim being that we should not waver in uncertain and ungrounded opinions on such a

[a] The word is 'Enneacaidecateris.' Mr. Hensley remarks in his article on Easter, 'It has been often stated that the Council established a particular cycle, that of nineteen years, but this is a mistake.'

celebration, but ascertain the true method and so ensure such concurrence of the affections of all, that the sacrifice for the Lord's Resurrection should be offered every where on the same night.

TO THE BISHOPS OF ÆMILIA

2. My Lords and brethren most beloved, we ought not so far to deviate from truth, or to be of such varying and wandering minds, as to the obligation of this celebration having been imposed upon all Christians: since our Lord Himself selected the day to celebrate it upon, which agreed with the method of the true observance. For it is written: *Then came the day when the Passover must be killed. And He sent Peter and John, saying, Go and prepare us the Passover that we may eat. And they said unto Him, Where wilt Thou that we prepare? And He said unto them, Behold when ye are entered into the city, there shall a man meet you, bearing a pitcher of water: follow him into the house where he entereth in. And ye shall say unto the goodman of the house, the Master saith unto thee, Where is the guest-chamber, where I shall eat the Passover with My disciples? And he shall shew you a large upper room, there make ready.*

S. Luke xxii. 7—12.

3. We observe then that we ought not to go down to places in the earth, but to seek *a large upper room furnished,* for us to celebrate the Lord's Passover. For we ought to wash our senses, so to speak, with the spiritual water of the everlasting fountain, and maintain the rule of the devout celebration, and not follow common notions and go in quest of days according to the moon, whereas the Apostle says, *Ye observe days, and months, and times, and years. I am afraid of you, lest I have bestowed upon you labour in vain.* For it is sure to be injurious[b].

Gal. iv. 10, 11.

4. But it is one thing to observe them after the heathen fashion, so as to decide on what day of the moon you are to attempt anything, for instance, that you should avoid the fifth[c] and begin no work upon it, and to recommend different points in the moon's course for commencing em-

[b] 'Nam incipit espe contrarium.' According to Ducange 'incipio' is used in late Latin in the sense of the Greek verb μέλλω, and here, as it would seem, with the force with which that verb is so often used as equivalent to 'it is likely' or 'it is sure' that such and such is the case: see Lidd. and Scott. μέλλω, ii. 3, 4.

[c] An allusion to Virg. Georg., 1, 276. Ipsa dies alios alio dedit ordine luna Felices operum; quintam fuge, etc.

ployments, or to avoid certain days, as many are in the habit of avoiding days called 'following [d]' or the Egyptian days: it is another thing to turn the observance of a religious mind to the day of which it is written, *This is the day which the Lord hath made.* For although it is written that the Lord's Passover ought to be celebrated on the fourteenth day of the first month, and we ought to look for what is truly the fourteenth moon [e] for celebrating the course of our Lord's Passion, still we can understand from this that to fix such a solemnity there is required either the perfection of the Church, or the fulness of clear faith, as the Prophet said when he spoke of the Son of God, that *his throne is as the sun before me, and as the perfect moon, it shall remain for ever.*

5. Hence it is that our Lord Himself also, when He had performed His wonderful works upon the earth, as if the faith of human minds were now established, observed that it was the time of His Passion, saying, *Father, the hour is come, glorify Thy Son, that Thy Son also may glorify Thee.* For He teaches elsewhere that He sought this glory of celebrating His Passion, where He says, *Go ye, and tell that fox, Behold, I cast out devils, and I do cures to-day and to-morrow, and the third day I am perfected.* In them indeed is Jesus perfected, who begin to be perfect, that with their faith they may believe on the fulness of His Divinity and His Redemption.

6. Therefore we seek out both the day and the hour, as the Scripture teaches us. The prophet David also says, *It is time for thee, Lord, to work,* when he sought understanding to know the testimonies of the Lord. The Preacher also saith, *To every thing there is a season;* Jeremy exclaims, *The turtle and the swallow and the sparrows of the ground observe the time of their coming.* But what can appear more evident than that it is of the Passion of our Lord that it is said, *The ox knoweth his owner, and the ass his master's crib?* Let us then acknowledge this *crib of our Master,* wherein we are nourished, fed, and refreshed.

---

[d] Days immediately following the Kalends, Nones or Ides, considered unlucky by the Romans. See A Gellius v.17. What the 'Egyptian days' were is not ascertained.

[e] This is the ordinary phrase for the day of the lunar month. See Bright Early Engl Ch. Hist. p. 195.

The type of the Passover fulfilled in the Gospel. 169

7. We ought therefore especially to know this time, at which over the universal world the accordant prayers of the sacred night are to be poured forth; for prayers are commended by season also, as it is written, *In an acceptable time have I heard thee, and in a day of salvation have I helped thee.* This is the time of which the Apostle said, *Behold, now is the accepted time, behold, now is the day of salvation.* TO THE BISHOPS OF ÆMILIA

Isa. xlix. 8.

2 Cor. vi. 2.

8. Accordingly, since, even after the calculations of the Egyptians, and the definitions of the church of Alexandria, and also of the Bishop of the church of Rome, several persons are still waiting my judgement by letter, it is needful that I should write what my opinion is about the day of the Passover. For though the question which has arisen is about the approaching Paschal day, yet we state what we think should be maintained for all subsequent time, in case any question of the kind should come up.

9. But there are two things to be observed in the solemnity of the passover, the fourteenth moon, and the first month, which is called *the month of the new fruits*[f]. Therefore that we may not appear to be departing from the Old Testament, let us recite the words of the section concerning the day of celebrating the Passover. Moses warns the people, saying that they must keep the month of the new fruits, proclaiming that it is the first month, for he says, *This month shall be unto you the beginning of months; it shall be the first month of the year to you,* and *thou shalt offer the Passover of the Lord thy God on the fourteenth day of the first month.* Exod. xiii. 4.

Exod. xii. 2.
Lev. xxiii. 5.

10. *The law was given by Moses, but grace and truth came by Jesus Christ.* He therefore, Who spake the law, afterwards coming by the Virgin in the last times, accomplished the fulness of the Law, for He came *not to destroy the Law but to fulfil it,* and He celebrated the Passover in the week in which the fourteenth moon was the fifth day of the week, and then on that very day, as what is said before teaches us, He ate the Passover with his disciples: but on the following day, on the sixth day of the week, He S. John i. 17.

S. Matt. v. 17.

---

[f] S. Ambrose's Latin is 'mensis novorum.' The LXX has ἐν μηνὶ τῶν νέων. The Vulgate ' in mense novarum frugum.'

was crucified on the fifteenth moon. But the sixteenth moon was the *Sabbath which was an high day*, and so on the seventeenth moon He rose again from the dead.

11. We must then keep this law of Easter, not to keep the fourteenth day as the day of the Resurrection, but rather as the day of the Passion, or at least one of the next preceding days, because the feast of the Resurrection is kept on the Lord's day; and on the Lord's day we cannot fast; for we rightly condemn the Manichæans for their fast upon this day. For it is unbelief in Christ's Resurrection, to appoint a rule of fasting for the day of the Resurrection, since the Law says that the Passion is to be eaten with bitterness [1], that is, with grief, because the Author of Salvation was slain by so great a sacrilege on the part of men; but on the Lord's day the Prophet teaches us that we should rejoice, saying, *This is the day which the Lord hath made. let us rejoice and be glad in it.*

12. Therefore it is fit that not only the day of the Passion, but also that of the Resurrection be observed by us, that we may have a day both of bitterness and of joy; fast on the one, on the other be refreshed. Consequently, if the fourteenth moon of the first month fall, as will be the case next time, on the Lord's day, inasmuch as we ought neither to fast on the Lord's day, nor on the thirteenth moon which falls on the Sabbath-day to break the fast, which must especially be observed on the day of the Passion, the celebration of Easter must be postponed to the next week. For the fifteenth day of the month follows, on which Christ suffered, and it will be the second day of the week. The third day of the week will be the sixteenth moon, on which our Lord's Flesh rested in the tomb; and the fourth day of the week will be the seventeenth moon on which our Lord rose again.

13. When therefore these three sacred days run as they do next time into the further week, within which three days He both suffered and rested and rose again, of which three days He says, *Destroy this temple, and in three days I will raise it up*, what can bring us trouble or doubt? For if it raises a scruple that we do not on the fourteenth moon celebrate the particular day either of His Passion or Re-

surrection, we may remember that our Lord Himself did not suffer on the fourteenth moon, but on the fifteenth, and on the seventeenth He rose again. But if any are troubled at our passing over the fourteenth moon, which falls upon the Lord's day, that is the 18th of April, and recommending its celebration on the following Lord's day, there is this authority for doing so.

14. In times lately past, when the fourteenth moon of the first month fell on the Lord's day, the solemnity was celebrated on the Lord's day next ensuing. But in the eighty-ninth year of the Era of Diocletian [g], when the fourteenth moon was on the 24th of March, Easter was kept by us on the last day of March. The Alexandrians and Egyptians also, as they wrote themselves, when the fourteenth day of the moon fell on the 28th day of the month Phamenoth, kept Easter on the fifth day of the month Pharmuthi, which is the last day of March, and so agreed with us. Again in the ninety-third year of the Era of Diocletian, when the fourteenth moon fell on the fourteenth day of the month Pharmuthi, which is the 9th of April, and was the Lord's day, Easter was kept on the Lord's day, the 21st day of Pharmuthi, or according to us on the 16th of April. Wherefore since we have both reason and precedent, nothing should disturb us upon this head.

15. There is yet this further point that seems to require explanation, that several persons think that we shall be keeping Easter in the second month, whereas it is written, *Keep the first month, the month of new fruits.* The case however cannot occur that any should keep Easter out of the month of the new fruits, except those who keep the fourteenth moon so strictly to the letter, that they will not celebrate their Easter on any day but that. Moreover the Jews are going to celebrate the approaching Passover in

---

[g] The Era of Diocletian was the prevalent one at this time, and till the general adoption of the Christian Era, which did not become established until the 8th Century See Mr Hensley's article 'Era' in Dict. of Christ. Antiq. He gives there the rule for reducing the Era of Diocletian, the epoch of which is Aug 29th A.D 284, to the Christian Era, viz, to add 283 years and 240 days to the given date of Diocletian's Era. According to this the Easter of the 89th year of Diocletian would be A.D. 373, and that of the 93rd would be A D 377. The 'times lately past' would probably refer to A D 383, when, as may be seen by the Table, the 'fourteenth moon' fell on a Sunday.

LETT 23. the twelfth and not in the first month, viz. on the 20th of March according to us, but according to the Egyptians on the twenty-fourth day of the month Phamenoth, which is not the first month but the twelfth, for the first month of the Egyptians is called Pharmuthi, and begins on the 27th of March and ends on the 25th of April. Therefore according to the Egyptians we shall keep Easter Sunday in the first month, that is, on the 25th of April, which is the thirtieth day of the month Pharmuthi.

16. Nor do I consider it unreasonable to borrow a precedent for observing the month from the country in which the first Passover was celebrated. For which reason also our predecessors in the ordinance of the Nicene Council thought fit to decide that their cycle of nineteen years should belong to the same month, if one observes it diligently; and they rightly kept the very month of the new fruits, for in Egypt it is in this the first month that the new corn is cut: and this month is the first in respect of the crops of the Egyptians and first according to the Law, but the eighth according to our custom, for the indiction begins in the month of September. The first of April therefore is in the eighth month. But the month begins not according to vulgar usage, but according to the custom of learned men, from the day of the equinox, which is the 21st of March, and ends on the 21st of April. Therefore the days of Easter have been generally kept as much as possible within these thirty-one [h] days.

17. But after keeping Easter Sunday six years ago [1] on the 21st of April, that is on the thirtieth day of the month according to our reckoning, we have no reason to be distressed if this next time also we are to keep it on the thirtieth day of the month Pharmuthi. If any one think that it is the second month, because Easter Sunday will be on the third day from the completion of the month (but this appears to be completed on the 21st of April) he should

---

[h] There is a slight error here. The interval is 32 days, not 31.

[1] There is some uncertainty about the reading here. The original reading in the text was 'biennium,' and, as this clearly did not agree with the facts the Benedictine Editors adopted a suggestion that 'biennium' was a mistaken rendering of a MS. which had 'vi-ennium.' But the period of 6 years would not be precise, as the year referred to must be A.D 379, (see table,) which would be seven years before.

consider that the fourteenth moon, which is our object, will fall on the 18th of April and thus within the regular counting of the month. But what the law requires is that the day of the Passion should be kept within the first month, the month of new fruits.

18. The method then is satisfactory as far as the complete course of the moon is concerned, inasmuch as three more days remain to complete the month. Easter then does not pass on into another month, since it will be kept within the same month, that is, the first. But that it is not fit that we should be tied to the letter, not only does the customary method of keeping Easter of itself instruct us, but the Apostle too teaches us, when he says, *Christ our Passover is sacrificed.* The passage also which has been cited teaches us that we are not to follow the letter, for thus it runs: *And thou shalt sacrifice the Passover to the Lord thy God on the fourteenth day of the first month* [k]. He uses the word 'day' in the place of 'moon;' and so the most skilful according to the law calculate the month by the moon's course, and since the moon's course, that is the first day, may begin with more than one of the nones, you perceive that the nones of May do still admit of being reckoned in the first month of the new fruits. Therefore even according to the judgement of the law this is the first mouth. To conclude, the Greeks call the moon μήνη, owing to which they call the months in Greek μῆνες, and the ordinary usage of foreign nation employs moon in the sense of day.

19. But even the Lessons of the old Testament shew that different days are to be observed for the Passion and Resurrection: for there it runs, *Your lamb shall be without blemish, a male of the first year: ye shall take it out from the sheep or from the goats; and ye shall keep it up until the fourteenth day of the same month, and the whole assembly of the congregation of Israel shall kill it in the evening. And they shall take of the blood, and strike it on the two side posts, and on the upper door post of the house wherein they shall eat it. And they shall eat the flesh in that night, roast with fire,* and further on, *And ye shall eat*

Margin: TO THE BISHOPS OF ÆMILIA

1 Cor. v. 7.

Exod. xii. 18. Lev. xxiii 5. Num. xxviii. 16.

Exod xii. 5-8.

---

[k] The precise words are not found in either of these passages.

LETT. 23.

[margin: ¹ in haste E.T]
[margin: ² against all the gods of Egypt E.T.]
[margin: Exod. xii. 11-14.]

it with anxiety¹: it is the Lord's Passover. For I will pass through the land of Egypt this night, and will smite all the first-born in the land of Egypt, both man and beast; and in all the land of Egypt² will I execute vengeance: I am the Lord. And the blood shall be to you for a token in the houses where ye are, and I will see the blood and I will protect you and the plague of extermination shall not be on you. And I will smite the land of Egypt, And this day shall be unto you for a memorial; and ye shall keep it a feast to the Lord throughout your generations: ye shall keep it a feast by an ordinance for ever.

20. We observe that the day of the Passion is marked out as a fast, for the lamb is to be slain at the evening: though we might understand by evening the last time, according to John who says, *Children, it is the last time.* But even according to the mystery, it is plain that it was killed in the evening, when darkness immediately took place, and true fasting is to be observed on that day, for *thus shall ye eat it with anxiety:* but anxiety belongs to those who fast. But on the day of the Resurrection there is the exultation of refreshment and joy, on which day the people appears to have gone out of Egypt, when the first-born of the Egyptians had been killed. And this is shewn more evidently by what follows, wherein the Scripture says, that after the Jews kept the Passover as Moses ordered, *It came to pass that at midnight the Lord smote all the first-born in the land of Egypt from the first-born of Pharaoh. And Pharaoh called for Moses and Aaron by night, and said, Rise up, and get you forth from among my people, both ye and the children of Israel, and go serve the Lord. And the Egyptians were urgent upon the people, that they might send them out of the land in haste.* Eventually the Israelites went in such manner, that they had not opportunity to leaven their dough, for the Egyptians thrust them out, and would not wait for them to take the preparation they had made for themselves for the way.

[margin: 1 S. John ii. 18.]
[margin: Exod. xii. 29.]
[margin: Ib. 31.]
[margin: Ib. 33.]

21. We have made it clear then that the day of the Resurrection ought to be observed after the day of the Passion, and that this day of the Resurrection ought not to be on the fourteenth moon, but later, as the Old Testament says,

because the day of the Resurrection is that on which the people going out of Egypt, after being *baptized*, as the Apostle says, *in the sea and in the cloud*, overcame death, receiving spiritual bread, and drinking spiritual drink from the rock: and further that the Lord's Passion cannot be celebrated on the Lord's day, and that if the fourteenth moon should fall upon the Lord's day, that another week ought to be added, as was done in the seventy sixth year[1] of the era of Diocletian. For then without any doubt or hesitation on the part of our fathers we celebrated Easter Sunday on the twenty-eighth day of the month Pharmuthi, which is the 23rd of April. And both the course of the moon and the reason of the case concur in recommending this, for next Easter is to be kept on the twenty first moon, for to that day its range has commonly extended.

<small>TO THE BISHOPS OF ÆMILIA</small>

<small>1 Cor. x. 2.</small>

22. Since therefore so many indications of truth are combined, let us after the example of our fathers celebrate the festival of our general Salvation with joy and exultation, colouring our side posts, between which is the door of the word which the Apostle wishes to be opened unto him, with faith in the Lord's Passion. Of this door David also says, *Set a watch, O Lord, before my mouth; keep the door of my lips*, that we may speak of nothing but the Blood of Christ, whereby we have conquered death, whereby we are redeemed. Let the sweet odour of Christ burn in us. To Him let us listen, on Him let us turn the eyes both of mind and body, admiring His works, proclaiming His blessings; over the threshold of our door let the confession of holy Redemption shine resplendent. Let us with fervent spirit keep the holy Feast, *in the unleavened bread of sincerity and truth*, and singing in pious docrtine with one accord the Glory of the Father and of the Son and the undivided Majesty of the Holy Spirit.

<small>Col. iv 3.</small>

<small>Ps. cxli. 3.</small>

<small>1 Cor. v. 8.</small>

---

[1] This would seem to be not quite correct. Mr. Hensley remarks that in A.D. 360. Easter day was on April 23rd but that the 'fourteenth moon' of that year was a Monday and not on a Sunday. The question is discussed in Ideler Chronol. vol. 11 p. 254—257.

His fidelity on his first embassy.

A.D 387.

LETTER XXIV.

S Ambrose here reports the result of his second mission to Maximus in behalf of Justina and her son Valentinian the 2nd He had before gone, as he mentions in this Letter, immediately after the murder of Gratian, A.D. 383, and had then, at much risk to himself, done them good service, and been mainly instrumental in securing peace, and inducing Maximus to abstain from invading Italy, and to leave Valentinian in possession of a share of the Empire Now it seemed certain that Maximus was preparing to cross the Alps and deprive Valentinian of his dominions and probably of his life, and once more Justina and her son seek the aid of the great Bishop, whom they had so cruelly persecuted during the peace he had procured for them. It is very striking to see the persecutors thus reduced to be suppliants of their victim, and the good Bishop at once rendering them the service which they sought. He writes this report while on his way back, and sends it before him, that Valentinian and his mother might learn the truth at once, and lose no time in making preparation to meet their danger. He was commissioned to induce Maximus to maintain peace, and to restore the body of Gratian for burial at Milan. S. Ambrose was less successful in this embassy than in the former one, and Justina and Valentinian had to escape to the East and put themselves under the protection of Theodosius, who took up arms in their behalf, and marched to the West, defeated and captured Maximus at Aquileia, and had him put to death, and so restored Valentinian to the Empire of all the West, A D 388
S Ambrose cannot have started on his mission till after Easter, as this was the year in which he baptized S Augustine.

AMBROSE TO THE EMPEROR VALENTINIAN.

1. OF my fidelity in my former mission you were so well assured as to require from me no account of it. Indeed the very fact that I was detained some days in Gaul sufficiently proved that I had made no promises acceptable to Maximus, nor agreed to any measures which inclined to what was pleasing to him rather than to the establishment of peace. And again, had you not approved of my first mission you would not have committed to me a second. But since as I was on the point of retiring he laid upon me the necessity of a discussion with him, I have thought it best to address to you in this letter an account of my mission, for fear any one should give you an account which mingled truth with falsehood, before my return could declare to you the truth in its perfect and sincere characters.

2. The day after I reached Trèves I presented myself at the palace; a Gaul came out to receive me, who was the Emperor's Chamberlain, and one of the royal eunuchs. I requested an audience; he enquired whether I had your Majesty's commission: I replied that I had. He said that I could only be heard in the Consistory. I answered that this was not usual for Bishops, and at all events that there were matters whereon I required serious conference with his master. To be brief; he consulted his master, and brought back the same answer, so that it was plain that the former had originated with his will. I said that such a course was inconsistent with the office I bore, but that I would not shrink from the duty I had undertaken, and that more especially in your service, and as it really was to support your brotherly affection, I was glad to humble myself.

3. As soon as he had taken his seat in the Consistory I entered; he rose to give me the kiss of peace. I stood among the members of the Consistory; some of them urged me to go up the steps, and he himself invited me. I replied, 'Why do you offer a kiss to one whom you do not acknowledge [a]? for had you acknowledged me you would not have seen me here.' 'You are excited, Bishop,' said he. 'It is not anger,' I said, 'that I feel, but shame at appearing in a place unsuited to me.' 'Yet on your first mission,' he said, 'you entered the Consistory.' 'True,' I replied, 'but the blame rests on him who summoned, not on me who entered.' 'Why,' said he, 'did you then enter?' 'Because,' I replied, 'I was then suing for peace on behalf of one who was inferior to you, but I now appear for your equal.' 'By whose favour' said he, 'is he my equal?' 'By that of Almighty God, who has maintained Valentinian in the empire He bestowed on him.'

4. At length he broke out, 'It is you who have cajoled me, you and the wretch Bauto, who wished by setting up a boy to acquire sovereignty for himself, who also brought barbarians upon me; as if I also had not those whom I could bring, seeing I have so many barbarians in my service and pay. But had I not been withheld at the time of your arrival, who could have resisted me and my power?'

[a] i.e. as Bishop.

5. I answered mildly, 'You need not be excited, for there is no occasion for excitement; listen rather with patience to the reply which I have to make. My reason for coming is, that you have declared that on my first mission you trusted me and were deceived by me. It is a glory to me to have done this for the safety of an orphan Emperor, for whom rather than orphans ought we bishops to protect? For it is written, *Relieve the oppressed, judge the fatherless, plead for the widow;* and in another place, *father of the fatherless, and a judge of the widows.*

6. But I will not make a boast of my services to Valentinian. To speak the truth, when did I oppose your legions, and resist your descent upon Italy? By what works, by what armies, with what forces? Did I block up against you the passes of the Alps with my body? Would that this were in my power, then I should not fear this allegation, nor your charges. By what promises did I beguile you into a consent to peace? Did not Count Victor, whom you had sent to request peace, meet me within the frontier of the provinces of Gaul, near the city of Mayence? Wherein then did Valentinian deceive you, whom you asked to grant you peace before he himself asked for it? Wherein did Bauto deceive you, who shewed fidelity to his Emperor? Did he do so by not betraying his own master?

7. Wherein have I circumvented you? Was it when, on my first arrival, on your saying that Valentinian ought to have come to you as a son to a father, I answered that it was not reasonable for a boy with his widowed mother to cross the Alps in severe winter weather, or without his mother be exposed under critical circumstances to such a journey? My business was to bring a message concerning peace, not to make any promise of his coming: it is certain that I have given no pledge of that, concerning which I had received no commands, and that I did not make any promise whatever, for you said, 'Let us wait to see what answer Victor will bring back.' But it is well known that he arrived at Milan while I was detained here, and that his request was refused. It was only about peace that we felt a common zeal, not about the Emperor's arrival; whose

coming ought not to have been required. I was present when Victor returned. How then did I meet Valentinian? The emissaries who were sent a second time into Gaul to say that he would not come, found me at Valence in Gaul. The soldiers of either party, sent to guard the mountain passes, I met on my return. What armies of yours did I then recall? what eagles did I turn back from Italy? what barbarians did Count Bauto send against you?

8. And what wonder if Bauto, whose native country lies beyond the Rhine, had done so, when you yourself threaten the Roman Empire with barbarian allies, and with troops from beyond the military frontier, whose commissariat was supplied by the taxes of the provinces? But consider what a difference there is between your threats and the mildness of the young Emperor Valentinian. You insisted on making an incursion into Italy accompanied by armies of barbarians, Valentinian turned back the Huns and Alans on their approach to Italy through the territory of the Germans. What need for displeasure is there if Bauto set the barbarians at variance with each other? While you were employing the Roman forces, while he was presenting himself to oppose you on both sides, the Juthungi [b] in the very heart of the Roman Empire were laying Rhætia waste, and so the Huns were called in against the Juthungi. And yet when he was attacking the country of the Alemanni on your frontier, and was already threatening the provinces of Gaul with the near approach of danger, he was obliged to

[b] The Juthungi were a German tribe settled on the north bank of the Danube, in what is now Austria Proper and Moravia. It is uncertain whether they were, as Ammianus Marcellinus describes them, a sept of the Alemanni, or whether they were Goths. It has been suggested that the name is only another form of Gothi or Gothones, (Dict. of Antiq.) The want of a detailed and accurate history of these times, which are just beyond the range of Ammianus, makes it difficult to make out clearly the allusions which S Ambrose here makes. Tillemont explains them thus, 'Bauton seeing the Juthungan Alemanni ravaging Rhaetia, while the Roman soldiers were engaged in guarding the passes of the Alps against Maximus, summoned the Huns and Alans to make war on them. These tribes accordingly pillaged the territories of the Alemanni up to the frontiers of Gaul But on Maximus complaining that they had been brought against him, Valentinian, to deprive him of any pretext for breaking off the peace, induced them to retire in the midst of their victories by presents of money.' He also considers that the reason why the Juthungi came to pillage Rhaetia that year was the extraordinary fertility, and that it is this invasion to which allusion is made in Letter xxiv, 21, where S. Ambrose says that Rhaetia Secunda 'drew down an enemy on herself by her abundance.'

relinquish his triumphs, lest you should be alarmed. Compare the acts of the two; you caused the invasion of Rhætia, Valentinian by his gold has regained peace for you.

9. Look too at the man [c] who now stands at your right hand, whom Valentinian, when he had the opportunity of avenging his grief, sent back to you loaded with honours. He had him in his own territory, and yet restrained his hand: even when he received the tidings of his brother's death, he restrained his natural feelings, and abstained from retaliation, where the relationship was the same, though the rank was not. Compare therefore, yourself being judge, the two actions. He sent back your brother alive; do you restore to him his brother at least now that he is dead. Why do you refuse to him his relation's remains, when he refused not to you those who would assist you against him?

10. But you allege that you are alarmed lest the grief of the troops should be renewed by the return of these remains. Will they then defend after death one whom they deserted in life? Why do you fear him now he is dead, whom, when you might have saved him, you slew? 'It was my enemy' you say, 'that I have slain.' It was not he that was your enemy, but you that were his. He is no longer conscious of my advocacy, do you consider the case yourself [d]. If any one were to think of setting up a claim to the empire in these parts against you, I ask whether you would deem yourself to be his enemy, or him to be yours? If I mistake not, it is the part of an usurper to excite war, of an Emperor to defend his rights. Will you then withhold even the body of him whom you ought not to have slain? Let Valentinian have at least the remains of his brother as a pledge of your peaceful intentions. How moreover will [e] you assert that you did not command him to be slain, when you forbid him to be buried? Will it be believed that you did not grudge him life, when you even grudge him burial?

11. But to return to myself. I find that you complain

---

[c] S. Ambrose means Maximus' brother.

[d] He seems to mean that pity for the dead should move him to less harsh treatment. But perhaps the word 'tuam' may have dropped out, and we should read 'tu tuam causam considera,' 'do you consider your own case.'

[e] It seems necessary here to read 'allegabis' for 'allegabas,' as the past tense would be unmeaning.

of the followers of Valentinian betaking themselves to the Emperor Theodosius rather than to yourself. But what could you expect, when you called for punishment on the fugitives, and put to death those who were taken, Theodosius on the other hand loaded them with gifts and honours. 'Whom,' said he, 'have I slain?' 'Vallio,' I replied. 'And what a man, what a soldier! Was it then a just cause of death, that he maintained his fidelity to his Emperor?' 'I gave no orders,' said he, 'for his death.' 'We have heard,' I replied, 'that the order was given for him to be put to death.' 'Nay,' said he, 'had he not laid violent hands on himself I had ordered him to be taken to Cabillonum [f] and there burnt alive.' 'Yes,' I replied, 'and that was why it was believed that you had put him to death. And who could suppose that he would himself be spared, when a valiant warrior, a faithful soldier, a valuable comrade was thus slain?' At that time, on taking my leave, he said he was willing to treat.

12. But afterwards on finding that I would not communicate with the Bishops who communicated with him, or who sought the death of any one, even though they were heretics [g], he grew angry and bade me depart without delay. And I, although many thought I should be waylaid, set forth gladly, grieving only that the aged Bishop Hyginus, now almost at his last gasp, was being carried into exile. And when I appealed to his guards against their suffering the old man to be driven out without a curtain or a pillow to rest upon, I was driven forth myself.

13. Such is the account of my mission. Farewell, your Majesty, and be well on your guard against a man who conceals war under the cloak of peace.

---

[f] Cabillonum is the ancient name of Châlons-sur-Saône.

[g] He refers to the Bishops Idacius and Ithacius, who had induced Maximus to put Priscillian and others of his party to death, in spite of the remonstrances of S. Martin, who urged Maximus to be content with their having been condemned by ecclesiastical sentence. Priscillian 'had adopted a strange compound of various errors,' (Prof. Bright Hist. p. 160.) chiefly Manichean. There is a full account of Maximus' dealings with them in Fleury, xviii. 29, 30. Newman's Transl. vol 1 p 66—69. S. Ambrose in Letter xxvi. condemns the conduct of these Bishops, and the appeal to the civil sword in Ecclesiastical cases, in still stronger terms.

LETTER XXV.

That this and the following letter were addressed to the same person is clear from their contents, especially from the commencement of Letter xxvi. Whether Studius and Irenæus were two names of the same person, as the Benedictines suggest, or whether there is any error in either title, cannot be ascertained for certain. Is it not most probable that the name of Irenæus, to whom a long series of letters follows, has been affixed to one immediately preceding them by mistake, and that we should put 'Studio' for 'Irenæo' at the head of xxvi?

The letter deals briefly with the question which Studius, a layman apparently and a judge, puts to S. Ambrose, whether he did violence to his duty as a Christian in sentencing criminals to death. S. Ambrose replies that it is lawful, but recommends merciful dealing wherever possible, in hope of amendment of life.

AMBROSE TO STUDIUS.

I recognize in your application to me a pure intention of mind, zeal for the faith, and fear of our Lord Jesus Christ. And indeed I should fear to reply to it, being checked on the one hand by the obligation of the trust committed to you for the maintenance of the laws, and on the other by claims of mercy and clemency, had you not in this matter the Apostle's authority that he who judgeth *beareth not the sword in vain, for he is the avenger of God, upon him that doeth evil.* [Rom. xiii. 4.]

2. But although you knew this, it was not without reason that you have thought fit to make the enquiry. For some there are, although out of the pale of the Church [a], who will not admit to the divine Mysteries those who have deemed it right to pass sentence of death on any man. Many too abstain of their own accord, and are commended, nor can we ourselves but praise them, although we so far observe the Apostle's rule as not to dare to refuse them Communion.

3. You see therefore both what power your commission gives you, and also whither mercy would lead you; you will be excused if you do it, and praised if you do it not. Should you feel unable to do it, and are unwilling to afflict

[a] The Benedictine Editors consider him to be referring to the Novatians.

the criminal by the horrors of a dungeon, I shall, as a priest, the more commend you. For it may well be that when the cause is heard, the criminal may be reserved for judgment, who afterwards may ask for pardon for himself, or at any rate may suffer what is called mild confinement in prison. Even heathen are, I know, wont to boast that they have borne back their axes from their provincial government unrestored by blood. And if heathen do this what ought Christians to do?

4. But in all these matters let our Saviour's answer suffice for you. The Jews apprehended an adultress and brought her to the Saviour, with the insidious intent that if He were to acquit her He might seem to destroy the law, though He had said, *I am not come to destroy, but to fulfil the law,* and on the other hand, were He to condemn her, He might seem to be acting against the purpose of His coming. Wherefore the Lord Jesus, foreseeing this, stooped down and wrote upon the earth. And what did He write but that word of the prophet, *O Earth, Earth, Write these men deposed*[b], which is spoken of Jeconiah in the prophet Jeremiah.

5. When the Jews interrupt Him, their names are written in the earth, when the Christians draw near, the names of the faithful are written not on the earth but in heaven. For they who tempt their Father, and heap insult on the Author of salvation, are written on the earth as cast off[1] by their Father. When the Jews interrupt Him, Jesus stoops His head, but not having where to lay His head, He raises it again, is about to give sentence, and says, *Let him that is without sin cast the first stone at her.* And again *He stooped down and wrote on the ground.*

6. When they heard this they began to go out one by one beginning at the eldest, and this either because they who had lived longest had committed most sins, or because, as being most sagacious, they were the first to comprehend the force of His sentence, and though they had come as the accusers of another's sins, began rather to lament their own.

---

b S Ambrose's Latin is 'scribe hoc viros abdicatos.' The Vulg. has 'scribe virum istum sterilem.' The LXX. γράψον τὸν ἄνδρα τοῦτον ἐκκήρυκτον.

LETT. 25.
S. John
viii. 10, 11.

7. So when they departed Jesus was left alone, and lifting up His head, He said to the woman, *Woman, where are those thine accusers? hath no man condemned thee? She said, No man, Lord. And Jesus said unto her, Neither do I condemn thee, go, and sin no more.* Being the Redemption, He refuses to condemn her, being the Life He restores her, being the Fountain He washes her. And since Jesus, when He stoops down stoops that He may raise up the fallen, He says, as the Absolver of sins, *Neither do I condemn thee.*

8. Here is an example for you to follow, for it may be that there is hope of amendment for this guilty person; if he be yet unbaptized, that he may receive remission, if baptized that he may do penance [c], and offer up his body for Christ. See how many roads there are to salvation!

9. This is why our ancestors thought it better to be indulgent towards Judges; that by the terror of their sword the madness of crime should be repressed, and no encouragement given to it. For if Communion were denied to Judges, it would seem like a retribution on their punishment of the wicked. Our ancestors wished then that their clemency should proceed from their own free-will and forbearance, rather than from any legal necessity. Farewell, and love us, as we on our part love you.

LETTER XXVI.

THAT this letter is addressed to the same person as the preceding, in spite of the discrepancy in the address, is clear from the first sentence (See Introd. to xxv.). It resumes the subject, and dwells in detail on the example of our Lord's dealing with the woman taken in adultery.

AMBROSE TO IRENÆUS. [STUDIUS?]

1. ALTHOUGH in my previous letter I have resolved the question which you proposed to me, I will not refuse your

---

[c] Fleury remarks on this, 'We must remember that the canonical penances inflicted for great crimes were at that time so very severe, that they were equal to a rigorous punishment.'

request, my son, that I would somewhat more fully state and express my meaning. *TO IRENÆUS*

2. Much agitated has ever been the question, and very famous this acquittal of that woman who in the Gospel according to John was brought to Christ accused of adultery. The stratagem which the equivocating Jews devised was this, that in case of the Lord Jesus acquitting her contrary to the Law, His sentence might be convicted of being at variance with the Law, but if she were to be condemned according to the Law, the Grace of Christ might seem to be made void.

3. And still more warm has the discussion become, since the time that bishops [a] have begun to accuse those guilty of the most heinous crimes before the public tribunals, and some even to urge them to the use of the sword and of capital punishment, while others again approve of such kind of accusations and of blood-stained triumphs of the priesthood. For those men say just the same as did the Jews, that the guilty ought to be punished by the public laws, and therefore that they ought also to be accused by the priests before the public tribunals, who, they assert, ought to be punished according to the laws. The case is the same, though the number is less, that is to say, the question as to judgment is similar, the odium of the punishment is dissimilar. Christ would not permit one woman to be punished according to the Law; they assert that too small a number has been punished.

4. But in what place does Christ give this decision? For He generally vouchsafed to adapt His discourses to the character of the place wherein He was teaching His disciples [b]. For instance while walking in the porch of Solomon, that is, of the Wise man, He said, *I and My Father are One;* and in God's Temple He said, *My doctrine is not Mine, but His that sent Me.* It was in the Temple also that He gave the sentence of which we now speak, for in the verse following it is thus written, *These words spake Jesus in the treasury, as He taught in the* S. John x. 30. ib. vii. 16. Ib. viii. 20.

---

[a] See note g on Letter xxiv.
[b] S Ambrose makes the same statement again, De Spirit. iii. 17 'It is important then to notice *where* the Lord maintained this argument, for oft-times His oracles derive their value from the quality of the place where He was.'

LETT. 26. *Temple, and no man laid hands on Him.* What is the Treasury? It is the place of offering for the faithful, the bank of the poor, the refuge of the needy, near which Christ sat, when, according to Luke, He declared that the widow's two mites were to be preferred to the gifts of the rich, thus bearing Divine testimony to a zealous and cordial charity as preferable to the offerings of an affluent munificence.

S. Luke xxi. 2.

5. Now let us consider what He Who passed such a judgment as this contributed when sitting near the Treasury, for not without a purpose did He prefer the woman who threw in two mites. Precious was her poverty, and rich in the mystery of faith. These are the same two pieces of money which the Samaritan in the Gospel left with the host in order to cure the wounds of the man who had fallen among thieves. So too this woman, outwardly a widow, but mystically representing the Church, thought it right to cast into the sacred Treasury this gift whereby the wounds of the poor might be healed and the hunger of the strangers satisfied.

ib. x. 35.

6. Now then it behoves you spiritually to consider what Christ bestows; for He distributed among the people silver tried by the fire of the heavenly oracles, and to the desires of the people He told out money stamped with the Royal image. No one could give more than He Who gave all. He satisfied the hungry, He replenished the needy, He enlightened the blind, He redeemed the captives, He raised the palsied, He restored the dead, nay, what is more, He gave absolution to the guilty and forgave their sins. These are the two pence which the Church cast in, after having received them from Christ. And what are the two pence but the price of the New and Old Testament? The price of the Scripture is our faith, for it is according to the intelligence and will of each that what we read therein is valued. So then the remission of sins is the price of both Testaments, and is announced in type by the Lamb, and accomplished in verity by Christ.

Ps. xi. 7

7. You understand therefore that the purification of seven days brought with it also the purification of three days. The purification of seven days is according to the

Exod xii 3.
Lev. xii. 2.

Law, which, under the semblance of the sabbath that now is, announced a spiritual sabbath; the purification of three days is according to Grace, and is sealed by the witness of the Gospel, for the Lord rose on the third day. Where a penalty for sin is prescribed there also must penitence be, where remission of sins is accorded there follows Grace. Penitence precedes, Grace follows. So that there can neither be penitence without Grace, nor Grace without penitence, for penitence must first condemn sin, that Grace may abolish it. Wherefore John, fulfilling the type of the Law, baptized unto repentance, Christ unto Grace.

_{TO IRENÆUS}

_{S Luke xxiv. 7.}

_{S. Matt. iii 11.}

8. Now the seventh day denotes the mystery of the Law, the eighth that of the Resurrection, as you have in Ecclesiastes, *Give a portion to seven and also to eight.* In the prophet Hosea also you have read that it was said to him, *Go, take unto thee a wife of whoredoms for fifteen pieces of silver*, seeing that by the double price of the Old and New Testament, that is, by the full price of faith, that woman is hired who was attended by a vagrant and licentious train of sojouners.

_{Eccles. xi 2.}

_{Hosea i. 2}

9. *And I bought her to me*, saith the prophet, *for fifteen pieces of silver, and for an homer of barley, and an half homer of barley and a measure*[1] *of wine* ^c. By barley is signified that the imperfect are called to the Faith that they may be made perfect, by the homer is understood a full measure, by the half homer a half measure. The full measure is the Gospel, the half measure is the Law, the fulfilment of which is the New Testament. Thus the Lord Himself saith, *I am not come to destroy the Law, but to fulfil.*

_{Ib. iii. 2.}

_{[1] nevel.}

_{S. Matt v. 17.}

10. Nor is it without meaning that we read in the Psalms of David of fifteen degrees, and that the sun had risen fifteen degrees, when Hezekiah the righteous king received a new supply of life. Hereby was signified the coming of the Sun of Righteousness, Who was about to enlighten by His presence these fifteen steps of the Old and New Testament whereby our faith mounts up to life eternal. And

_{Isa. xxxviii. 8.}

_{Mal. iv. 2.}

---

^c These words are not in the Heb. νέβελ οἴνου. S Ambrose combines In LXX they take the place of the both. half-homer of barley, γομὸρ κριθῶν καὶ

LETT. 26. this leads me to believe that what was read this day from
Gal i. 18. the Apostle of his remaining fifteen days with Peter has a
mystical meaning; for it appears that while the holy Apostles held various discourses among themselves upon the interpretation of the Divine Scriptures a full and bright light fell upon them, and the shades of ignorance were dispersed. But now let us come to the absolution of the woman taken in adultery.

11. A woman accused of adultery was brought by the Scribes and Pharisees to the Lord Jesus with the malicious intent, that, if He was to acquit her, He might seem to annul the Law, if He condemned her, that He might seem to have changed the purpose of His coming, since He came to remit the sins of all men. To the same purport He
S. John said above [d], *I judge no man.* So when they brought her
viii. 15.
Ib. 4, 5. they said, *This woman was taken in adultery, in the very*
Lev. xx. *act; now Moses in the Law commanded us that such should*
8. *be stoned, but what sayest Thou?*

12. While they were saying this, Jesus stooped down and wrote with His finger on the ground. And as they waited for His answer, He lifted up His head and said,
v. 7. *He that is without sin among you, let him first cast a stone at her.* What can be more Divine than this sentence, that he should punish sins who is himself free from sin? For how can we endure one who takes vengeance on guilt in another and excuses it in himself? When a man condems in another what he commits himself, does he not rather pronounce his own condemnation?

13. Thus He spake, and wrote upon the ground. What
S. Matt. then did He write? This, *Thou beholdest the mote that is*
vii. 3. *in thy brother's eye, but considerest not the beam that is in thine own eye.* For lust is like a mote, it is quickly kindled, quickly consumed; the sacrilegious perfidy which led the Jews to deny the Author of their salvation declared the magnitude of their crime.

14. He wrote upon the ground with the finger with
Jer. xvii. which He had written the Law. Sinners' names are writ-
13. ten in the earth, those of the just in heaven, as He said to

---

[d] It was said just afterwards, if the story of the woman taken in adultery be in its right place, which is doubtful

His disciples, *Rejoice, because your names are written in heaven.* And He wrote a second time, that you may know that the Jews were condemned by both Testaments.

TO IRENÆUS
S. Luke x. 20.

15. When they heard these words they went out one after another, beginning at the eldest, and sat down thinking upon themselves. *And Jesus was left alone, and the woman standing in the midst.* It is well said that they went out who chose not to be with Christ. Without is the letter, within are the mysteries. For in the Divine lessons they sought, as it were, after the leaves of trees, and not after the fruit; they lived in the shadow of the Law, and could not discern the Sun of Righteousness.

16. Finally, when they departed Jesus was left alone, and the woman standing in the midst. Jesus about to remit sin remains alone, as He says Himself, *Behold the hour cometh, yea is now come, that ye shall be scattered, every man to his own, and shall leave Me alone;* for it was no messenger, no herald, but the Lord Himself Who saved His people. He remains alone, because in the remission of sins no man can participate with Christ. This is the gift of Christ alone, Who *took away the sins of the world.* The woman too was counted worthy to be absolved, seeing that, on the departure of the Jews, she remained alone with Jesus.

S. John xvi. 32.

Ib. i. 29.

17. Then Jesus lifted up His head, and said to the woman, *Where are those thine accusers, hath no man condemned thee? She said, No man, Lord. And Jesus said unto her, Neither do I condemn thee, go, and sin no more.* See, O reader, these Divine mysteries, and the mercy of Christ. When the woman is accused, Christ stoops His head, but when the accusers retire He lifts it up again; thus we see that He would have no man condemned, but all absolved.

Ib viii. 10.

18. By the words, *Hath no man condemned thee?* He briefly overthrows all the quibbles of heretics, who say that Christ knows not the day of judgment. He Who says, *But to sit on My right hand and on My left is not Mine to give,* says also in this place, *Hath no man condemned thee?* How is it that He asks concerning that which He saw? It is for our sakes that He asks, that we might know the

S. Matt. xx. 23.

woman was not condemned. And such is the wont of the human mind, often to enquire concerning that which we know. The woman too answered, *No man, Lord,* that is to say, Who can condemn when Thou dost not condemn? Who can punish another under such a condition as Thou hast attached to his sentence?

19. The Lord answered her, *Neither do I condemn thee.* Observe how He has modified His own sentence; that the Jews might have no ground of allegation against Him for the absolution of the woman, but by complaining only draw down a charge upon themselves; for the woman is dismissed not absolved; and this because there was no accuser, not because her innocence was established. How then could they complain, who were the first to abandon the prosecution of the crime, and the execution of the punishment?

20. Then He said to her who had gone astray, *Go, and sin no more.* He reformed the criminal, He did not absolve the sin. Faults are condemned by a severer sentence, whenever a man hates his own sin, and begins the condemnation of it in himself. When the criminal is put to death, it is the person rather than the transgression which is punished, but when the transgression is forsaken, the absolution of the person becomes the punishment of the sin. What is the meaning then of, *Go, and sin no more?* It is this; Since Christ hath redeemed thee, suffer thyself to be corrected by Grace; punishment would not reform but only afflict thee. Farewell, my son, and love me as a son, for I on my part love you as a parent.

LETTER XXVII.

A.D. 387.

WHO Irenæus was to whom the series of letters from xxvii to xxxii are addressed is not ascertained. From the affectionate and parental way in which S. Ambrose addresses him, and from Irenæus' applying to him for elucidation of his difficulties in the study of Holy Scripture, it is probable that he was one who had been trained, perhaps converted by him. The Benedictine Editors think that he must have been one of his Milan Clergy. All the letters are occupied in expounding passages of the Old Testament, or in solving questions connected with it; they are specimens of his method of mystical interpretation, in which he took great delight. In this Letter he begins a reply to a question on Exodus viii. 26 and then goes off into a mystical interpretation of Rachel and Leah, making them an allegory, as S Paul does Hagar and Sarah.

TO IRENÆUS

AMBROSE TO IRENÆUS, GREETING.

1. You tell me that you have felt a difficulty in the text *We shall sacrifice the abomination of the Egyptians to the Lord our God.* But you had the means of solving it, for it is written in the book of Genesis, that *a shepherd is an abomination to the Egyptians*, and this not on account of the shepherd himself, but of his flocks. For the Egyptians were tillers of the ground, but Abraham and Jacob, and afterwards Moses and David, were shepherds, and in this function exercised a certain kingly discipline. Exod. viii. 26. Gen. xlvi. 34.

2. The Egyptians then hated sacrifices which were duly offered; the pursuit of virtue, that is, which is perfect and replete with discipline. But that which these evil men hated is in the sight of the good sincere and pious. The licentious man hates the works of virtue, the glutton shrinks from them. And so the Egyptian's body, loving the charms of pleasure, has an aversion to the virtues of the soul, hates its rule, and shrinks from the discipline of virtue, and all such like works.

3. But what the Egyptian shrinks from—he who is an Egyptian rather than a man,—that do thou, who hast the knowledge of what befits man, embrace and follow: and shun those things which they pursue and choose; for these two things cannot agree together, wisdom and folly. Thus as wisdom and continence remove themselves from those who are, as it were, in the ranks of unwisdom and intemperance, so no foolish and incontient man has any part in what belongs to the goods and heritage of the wise and continent man.

4. Again, those women who were sanctified by their marriage, Leah and Rachel, (the one meaning 'wearied,' the other 'strong breath [a]') from aversion not to the ties of

---

[a] Leah means 'wearied,' and the name is supposed to refer to her 'tenderness' or weakness of eyes. (Gen. xxix 16) S Ambrose gives a mistaken meaning to the name Rachel, which really means 'ewe.'

LETT. 27. kindred but to their differing manners, and informed by the much tried Jacob, that he desired to depart in order to shun the envy and sloth of Laban and his sons, made
Gen. xxxi. 14, 15. answer thus: *Is there yet any portion or inheritance for us in our father's house? Are we not counted of him strangers? for he hath sold us, and hath quite devoured also all our money?* Observe first that the slothful and envious man alienates from himself one who labours and keeps strict discipline; he flies from her and seeks to separate himself. Finding that they will be burthensome to him he thinks he has gained by their removal, and esteems this to be his reward, and this the point of his pleasure.

5. Now let us hear how what virtue has, sloth has not:
Ib. v. 16. for they say, *For all the riches which God hath taken from our father, that is ours, and our children's.* Rightly do they say that they were taken away by God's appointment, for it is He Who created the good, for whose sake the slothful are despoiled; for weak and evil men cannot apprehend the beauty of the Divine inheritance; and thus the resolute, and he who hath in him the spirit of a brave man, succeeds to it. But who is strong but God alone Who regulates and governs all things?

6. To these therefore the heritage of God is justly due.
Isa. liv. 17. Wherefore Isaiah also says, *There is an heritage for them that believe in the Lord.* Well saith he, *There is an heritage,* for this is the sole heritage, there is no other. For neither is blind treasure an heritage, nor have any transitory things the advantage of an heritage; that alone is an heritage wherein God is the portion. Wherefore the Saint
Ps. cxix. 57. Ib. 111. of the Lord saith, *Thou art my portion, O Lord,* and again, *Thy testimonies have I claimed as mine heritage for ever.* You see what are the possessions of the just, the commandments of God, His oracles, His precepts, hereby he is enriched, hereby he is fed, hereby he is delighted as by all manner of riches.

7. Now Leah and Rachel, possessing these, required not their father's riches, for therein there was base coin, a senseless outward show, destitute of spiritual vigour. Again, being rich and liberal themselves they accounted their father rather indigent than rich. For no one who partici-

pates in good and liberal discipline deems any foolish man to be rich, but poor and needy, and even abject; and this although he overflow with royal riches, and in the pride of his gold boasts of his own power.

^{TO} IRENÆUS

8. The society of such we must shun then, even though they be united to us by the ties of kindred: the conversation of the foolish is to be avoided, for it infects and discolors the mind, for as *with the clean thou shalt be clean, so with the froward thou shalt be froward.* For it frequently happens that one who listens to an intemperate man against his own resolution, much as he himself desires to maintain the rule of continence, is yet stained by the hue of folly, and thus discipline and insolence truly prove themselves contrary and repugnant to each other.

Ps. xviii. 26.

9. Hence when much-tried Jacob inquired their opinion, they utter the words of virtue now proved by long exercise, *Is there yet any portion or inheritance for us in our father's house?* that is, 'Do you ask us whether we wish to depart from him? As if you knew not that we have no desire of his society, nor are we possessed with that thirst for riches and delight in luxury which is so sweet to most worldlings. These are the things which we deem miserable and alien to our feelings, these are the things which we deem to be full of poverty and want.'

Gen. xxxi. 14.

10. They add also the cause of their departure, that Laban had lost the true glory and those stores of good treasure in which we are born. Vigour of mind has been given us, and the good coinage of God's image and likeness, which is a spiritual coinage. He lost these because he preferred the splendour of this world to things true and profitable for his true life; for the beauty of these things escapes one who is ignorant of the good things of God, while in his judgment of what is beautiful he deludes and deceives himself. Hear then his words and judge.

11. He pursued holy Jacob and his daughters, thinking haply to find upon them some of his own vices, and thus to have a plea for reclaiming them to himself, censuring the righteous, whereas he himself was refuted by reason, and could give no answer or reply why he had any right

to detain him. *Wherefore,* says he, *didst thou not tell me, that I might have sent thee away?* Wherein he discloses what it was the just man feared, namely, such attendance, such a convoy, lest he should go forth escorted by such a company: in the first place because it behoved him not to submit himself to the service of many masters, so as to be dismissed by Laban as a servant: and next because this man, intent upon good discipline and desirous of following the true path of virtue, sought no man to guide him but the heavenly oracles. These, said he, have commanded me to depart from hence and now accompany me on my journey.

12. But how wouldst thou have dismissed me, he would say? Would it have been with such joy as thine which is full of sadness, with cymbals namely and instruments of ill-modulated harmony, and with the sweet notes of flutes sounding forth unpleasing strains, dissonant sounds, discordant noises, mute voices, cymbals jarring upon the sense? Didst thou believe that I could be delighted, that I could be recalled by such things? It is from them that I fled, nor do I fear thy reproachful words. I fled that such things might not follow me, that I might receive no present from thee on my departure.

13. It is not by such guides as these that we arrive at the Church of Christ, to which Jacob was bending his steps, to carry down thither the wealth of the nations and the riches of the Gentiles, that he might transplant thither his posterity, flying from the shadows of empty things, preferring to senseless images of virtues their breathing beauty, and serious things to outward show. You see how the Gentiles deck out their banquets, and proclaim their feasts; but such things are hateful to pious minds, for by their means many are deceived, they are captivated by pleasant food, by the bands of dancers, while they fly from our fasts, deeming them irksome to them, and noxious and troublesome to the body.

14. Or didst thou think that I should desire thy gold? But thou hast not *gold tried by* that *fire* wherein the just are proved. Or was it silver that I desired? But thou hast not silver, for thou possessest not the brightness of

the heavenly words. But perhaps I hoped that thou wouldst give me some of thy slaves to serve me? Nay, I seek for free men, and not the slaves of sin. But perhaps companions of my journey and guides of my path were necessary? Would that they had power to follow me! for I would have shewn them the ways of the Lord. But ye who know not God, how can ye know His ways? The elect of the Lord walk in His ways, not every one who enters them, and yet no man is excluded.

TO IRENÆUS

15. Let him who is prepared follow, let him enter upon the way which leads to Mesopotamia; so that he who seeks that country may pass through the waters, the waters of Tigris and Euphrates, the waters of courage and righteousness, through the tears of penitence, the baptism of grace. Here is the path of the army of God, for all who are in the Church are God's soldiers. There is that flock marked with divers virtues, which Jacob chose for himself; every soul which is not so marked is unlearned and uninstructed, ignorant of discipline: but that which is marked is rich in works and fertile in grace. Gen.xxx. 32.

16. Let him who comes to it first be reconciled to his angry brother. Let him who comes to it inhabit Shechem, that precious and active laboratory of virtue, where injured chastity is so deeply avenged. Let him who comes to it wrestle with God, that he may inure himself to imitate Him, that he may come in contact with the humility of Christ and His sufferings. Let him take up his cross and follow Christ. Lastly, a good combatant *envieth not, is not puffed up*, nay, he even blesses his antagonist with a like gift. Ib.xxxiv. 25. sqq Ib. xxxii. 24.
1 Cor. xiii. 4.

17. Let us then follow holy Jacob and his ways, that we may reach these sufferings, these combats, that we may reach the shoulder [b], that we may attain to patience, the mother of the faithful, and to their father Isaac, that is, one capable of delight [c], abounding in joy. For where patience is, there also is joy, for after tribulation comes patience, and *patience worketh experience*, wherein is *hope, whereby we are not ashamed*, for whoso is not ashamed Rom. v. 3, 4, 5

[b] S. Ambrose often gives this exposition of the name 'Shechem.'
[c] Isaac means 'laughter.' Gen. xxi. 6

the cross of Christ, neither will Christ be ashamed of him.

Farewell, my son; blush not to ask questions of your father, as you blush not to glory in the sufferings of Christ.

A.D. 387.

LETTER XXVIII.

S. AMBROSE in this Letter maintains that Pythagoras derived much of his wisdom from a knowledge of the Hebrew Scriptures, and dwells on his maxim, 'not to follow the beaten track,' as one specially addressed to the priesthood.

AMBROSE TO IRENÆUS, GREETING.

1. IN the writings of certain authors we find a precept of Pythagoras forbidding his disciples to enter upon the common path trodden by the people. Now the source from whence he drew this is not unknown. For as he derived (according to the general opinion) his descent from the Jews, from their learning he derived also the precepts of his school. This rendered him highly esteemed among philosophers, so that he hardly met, it is said, with his equal. Now he had read in the book of Exodus that by the Divine command Moses was bid *put off his shoes from off his feet*. This command was also given to Joshua the son of Nun, namely that they, when desired to walk along the Lord's path, should shake off the dust of the beaten and vulgar tracks. He had also read the command to Moses to go up to the mount with the priests, while the people stood apart. So God separated the priests from the people, and subsequently commanded Moses himself to enter into the cloud.

Exod. iii. 5.
Josh. v. 15.

Exod. xxiv. 13, 14.

2. You see then the separation. Nothing vulgar, nothing popular, nothing in common with the desires and usages and manners of the rude multitude is looked for in priests. The dignity of the priesthood claims for itself a sober and unruffled calmness, a serious life, an especial gravity. How can he be respected by the people, who is in nothing distinct from the people, or different from the

multitude? And what can a man look up to in you who recognizes himself in you, who sees nothing in you which is beyond himself, and who finds in you, to whom he deems respect to be due, the things which he blushes at in himself?

3. Wherefore let us pass over the opinions of the people, and the resorts of the common herd, and the line of the beaten track, the ground also of that common path along which he runs, whose *days are swifter than a post,* of whom it is said, *they flee away, they see no good.* But let us find for ourselves a path secluded from the conversation of the proud, inaccessible to the works of the unlearned, trodden by no polluted person, polluted that is by the stains of his own sloth, and smeared by the smoke of iniquity, his soul darkened and ruinous, one who has never tasted the sweetness of virtue, or at any rate has thought that she should be looked upon askance rather than met with direct regard and with open arms, who moreover (as is the wont of many who seem to themselves witty and polite, and transform the beauty of wisdom into dishonourable guile,) regards not true Grace, but shrouded as it were in darkness, gives no credence to those who live in the light of day, being of the number of the men of Tema and Sheba, who fall off and turn away from the truth; of whom Job says, *Behold ye the ways of them of Tema, the paths of the Sabæans, for they shall be confounded who put their hopes in cities and in riches. So ye also have risen against me without pity, therefore when ye see my wound, be afraid.*

4. Let us then abandon these devious paths of them that turn aside, and this dust of those who fail, who through their lust fall oftentimes in the desert, and let us be converted and follow the way of wisdom, that way which the children of those who boast and glorify themselves have not trodden, that way which destruction knows not, and death is ignorant of; for God hath marked it out; *the depth saith, It is not in me, and the sea saith, It is not with me.* But if you seek for the way of wisdom and discipline, to worship God, and to be subject to Him is wisdom, and to abstain from sin is discipline.

LETT. 28.   5. What then have we to do with the way of this world, wherein is temptation; yea the life itself of men is temptation, and more empty even than vain fables, living in houses of clay, spending nights and days in quest of gain, with their thoughts ever upon it, seeking like hired servants their daily wages, and as they say grasshoppers do [a], feeding on the empty breath of desires. Truly, like grasshoppers, living from day to day, they burst with their own complainings [b]. For what is the semblance of men without gravity or discipline, but that of grasshoppers, born to a daily death, chirping rather than speaking? These beneath the heat of burning desires soothe themselves with a song hurtful to themselves, and quickly die bearing no fruit, and possessed of no grace. Noxious and crooked are their ways as those of serpents, whose bodies are drawn along in poisoned folds, who gather themselves up into a coil of wickedness [c], and cannot raise themselves to heavenly things.

Ps cxviii. 19.   6. But let us enter the gates of the Lord, *the gates of righteousness*, which the righteous entereth and *giveth praise unto the Lord*. But few enter in here, wherefore

S. Matt. vii. 14.   the Lord saith, *Straight is the gate and narrow is the way which leadeth unto life, and few there be that find it.* But the wide gate and broad way, wherein the many walk, leads to death, and carries thither them that travel on it.

7. Let our way then be narrow, our virtue abundant, our steps more careful, our faith more lofty, our path narrow, our energy of mind overflowing, our paths straight, for the steps of virtue cannot be turned aside; wherefore

Prov. ii. 13.   Solomon saith, *Who leave the paths of uprightness.*

8. Let our steps tend upward, for it is better to ascend.

Is. xxxi. 1.   Lastly, as we read to-day, *Woe to them that go down to Egypt!* Not that to pass over into Egypt is blameable, but to pass into their habits, to pass into their cruel perfidy and hideous lusts. He that passes over thither descends, he that descends falls. Wherefore let us avoid the

---

[a] He is here referring to Virg Ecl. 5, 77. Dumque thymo pascuntur apes, dum rore cicadae

[b] Here again he is thinking of Virg. Georg 3, 328 Et cantu querulae rumpent arbusta cicadae.

[c] Here again S. Ambrose is thinking of Virg Georg. 2, 154. Squameus in spiram tractu se colligit anguis.

Egyptian, who is man, not God. For the king of Egypt himself was given over to the dominion of his vices, and compared with him Moses was accounted a god, ruling over kingdoms and subjecting to himself powers. Hence we read that he was addressed thus, *See I have made thee a god to Pharoah.* Farewell, and love me, as indeed you do, with the affection of a son.

TO IRENÆUS

Exod. vii. 1.

LETTER XXIX.

A.D. 389.

AMBROSE TO IRENÆUS, GREETING.

This letter is in fact a meditation on Christ as the true Chief good of man, the true Source of happiness, and Food of the soul, and Fountain of life, to be sought therefore with eagerness, and clung to with all the affection of the soul, which must therefore scorn all meaner delights.

1. While engaged in reading, after resting my mind for a while and desisting from study, I began to meditate on that versicle which in the evening we had sung at Vigils, *Thou art fairer than the children of men,* and, *How beautiful are the feet of them that bring good tidings* of Him. And truly nothing is more beautiful than that chief good, the very preaching of which is beyond measure lovely, and specially the progress of continuous discourse, and the foot-steps, so to speak, of Apostolic preaching. But who is equal to these things? They to whom God gave not only to preach Christ, but also to suffer for Him.

Ps. xlv. 3.
Rom. x. 15,
Is. lii. 7.

2. Let us, as far as we can, direct our minds to that which is beautiful seemly and good, let us be occupied therein, let us keep it in mind, that by its illumination and brightness our souls may become beautiful and our minds transparent. For if our eyes, when obscured by dimness, are refreshed by the verdure of the fields and are able by the beauty of a grove or grassy hill to remedy every defect of the failing vision, while the very pupils and balls of the eye seem to be coloured with the hue of health: how much more does this eye of the mind, beholding that chief good, and dwelling and feeding thereupon, brighten and shine

forth, so as to fulfil that which is written, *My soul shall be satisfied even as it were with marrow and fatness.* Moreover, he who has a skilful knowledge of the souls of his flock, pays attention to wild grasses, that he may obtain much pasturage: for by the sweeter kind of herbage lambs are made fatter, and the milky juice more healthful. On these pastures those *fat ones* have fed, who *have eaten and worshipped,* for good indeed are those pastures wherein is placed the saint of God.

Lett. 29.
Ps lxiii. 6.
Ib. xxii. 29.

3. There is grass also, whereby the flocks of sheep are nourished, for whence come the fleeces of wisdom, and the clothing of prudence. And perchance this is the *grass of the mountain,* upon which the words of the prophet distil *as the showers upon the grass,* and which the wise man carefully gathers, that he may have a fleece for a covering, that is, for a spiritual garment. And thus proper food and clothing are provided for that soul which cleaves to the chief Good, that Good Which is Divine, and which the Apostle Peter exhorts us to seek for, that by the acquisition of such knowledge we may become *partakers of the Divine nature.*

Prov. xxvii. 25.
Deut. xxxii. 2.
2 S Pet. i. 4.

4. The knowledge hereof the good God opens to His saints, and grants it out of His good treasury, even as the sacred Law testifies, saying, *The Lord sware unto thy fathers to give thee and open unto thee His good treasure.* From this heavenly treasure He gives rain to His lands, to bless all the works of thy hands. By this rain is signified the utterance of the Law, which moistens the soul fruitful and fertile in good works, that it may receive the dew of Grace.

Deut. xxviii. 11, 12.
Ib xxxii. 2.

5. The knowledge of this good David sought; as he himself declares, saying, *One thing have I desired of the Lord, which I will require, even that I may dwell in the house of the Lord all the days of my life to behold the fair beauty of the Lord, and to visit His temple.* And that this is the chief Good he straightway added in the same Psalm, *I believe verily to see the goodness of the Lord in the land of the living.* He must be sought after, there He will be clearly seen face to face. This good is in the house of God, in His secret and hidden place. Wherefore he says again, *He*

Ps. xxvii. 4.
v. 13.
Ps lxv. 4.

shall be satisfied with the pleasures of thy house. In another place too he has shown this to be the highest blessing, saying, *The Lord shall bless thee out of Sion, and thou shalt see the good of Jerusalem.* Wherefore blessed is he who dwells then in the vestibule of faith and in the spiritual abode, the dwelling place of devotion and the life of virtue.

^{TO IRENÆUS}

Ps. cxxviii. 5.

6. In Him therefore let us be and in Him abide, of Whom Isaiah says, *How beautiful upon the mountains are the feet of Him that bringeth good tidings, that publisheth peace.* Who are they that preach but Peter, Paul, and all the Apostles? What do they preach to us but the Lord Jesus? He is our Peace, He is our chief Good, for He is Good from Good, and from a good tree is gathered good fruit. And good also is His Spirit, Who takes of Him and *leads His servants forth into the land of righteousness.* For who that hath the Spirit of God within him will deny that He is good, since He says Himself, *Is thine eye evil because I am good?* May this Good which the merciful God gives to them that seek Him come into our soul, and into our inmost heart. He is our Treasure, He is our Way, He is our Wisdom, He is our Righteousness, our Shepherd, the good Shepherd, He is our Life. Thou seest how many goods are in this one Good! These goods the Evangelists preach to us. David seeking for these goods saith, *Who will shew us any good?* And he shews that the Lord Himself is our Good by adding, *Lord, lift Thou up the light of Thy Countenance upon us.* But Who is the Light of the Father's Countenance, but *the Brightness of His Glory,* and the Image of the invisible God, in Whom the Father is both seen and glorified, as He also glorifies His Son?

Isa. lii. 7.

1 Cor. i. 1.

S. Matt. vii. 17.
Ps. cxliii. 10

S. Matt. xx. 15.

Ps. iv. 6.

Heb. i. 3.

8. Wherefore the Lord Jesus Himself is that chief Good which was announced to us by Prophets, declared by Angels, promised by the Father, preached by Apostles. He hath come to us as ripeness; nor as ripeness only, but as ripeness in the mountains; to the intent that in our counsels there should be nothing sour, or unripe, nothing harsh or bitter in our actions or manners, the first Preacher of good tidings hath come among us. Wherefore also He saith, I, Who spoke, am present with[a] you, that is, I

1 Tim. iii. 16.

---
[a] Perhaps quoted from memory from S John iv. 26.

LETT. 29. Who spoke in the Prophets, am present in that Body which I took of the Virgin; I am present as the inward Likeness

Heb. i. 3.

of God, and the *express Image of His person*, I am present too as Man. But who knows Me? For they saw the Man, but His Works made them believe He was above man.

S. John xi. 35.

Was He not as man when weeping over Lazarus? again, was He not above man, when He raised him to life? Was He not as man when scourged? and again, above man when

Ib. i. 29. *He took away the sin of the world?*

9. To Him therefore let us hasten in Whom is the chief Good: for He is the bounty and patience of Israel, Who calls thee to repentance, that thou come not into condemnation but mayest receive the remission of thy sins. He

S. Matt. iv. 17.
Amos v. 14.

saith, Repent. This is He of Whom the Prophet Amos cries, *Seek good*. He is the chief Good, Who is in need of nothing, but abounds in all things. And well may He a-

Col. ii. 9. bound, *in Whom dwelleth all the fulness of the Godhead*
S John i. 16.

bodily; *of Whose fulness we have all received, and in Whom we are filled*, as saith the Evangelist.

10. If then the mind with its capacities of desire and pleasure hath tasted the chief Good, and by means of these two affections hath drank It in, unalloyed by sorrow and fear, it is wonderfully inflamed. For having embraced the Word of God, she knows no measure and yet feels no sa-

Ps. cxix. 68.

tiety, as it is written, *Thou art good and gracious, O teach me Thy statutes*: having embraced the Word of God, she desires Him above all beauty, she loves Him above all joy, she is delighted with Him above all perfumes, she desires often to see, often to look upon Him, often to be drawn to

Cant. i. 3.

Him that she may follow. *Thy Name*, it is said, *is as ointment poured forth; therefore we maidens love Thee*, therefore we strive but cannot attain to Thee. *Draw us* that we may *run after Thee*, that by the *fragrance of Thy ointments* we may gain power to follow Thee.

11. And the mind presses forward to the sight of internal mysteries, to the place of rest of the Word, to the very dwelling of that chief Good, His light and brightness. In that haven and home-retreat she hastens to hear His words, and having heard, finds them sweeter than all other things.

Ps. cxix. 103.

Learn of the Prophet who had tasted and saith, *O how*

sweet are Thy words unto my throat, yea sweeter than honey unto my mouth. For what can that soul desire which hath once tasted the sweetness of the Word, and seen His brightness? When Moses received the Law he remained forty days on the mount and required no bodily food; Elijah, hastening to this rest, prayed that his life might be taken away; Peter, himself also beholding on the Mount the glory of the Lord's Resurrection, would fain not have come down, saying, *It is good for us to be here.* How great then is the glory of the Divine Essence and the graces of the Word, *which things the Angels desire to look into.*

<small>TO IRENÆUS</small>

<small>Exod. xxxiv. 28. 1 Kings xix. 4. S. Matt. xvii. 4. 1 Pet. i. 12.</small>

12. The soul then which beholds this chief Good, requires not the body, and understands that it ought to have as little connexion with it as possible; it renounces the world, withdraws itself from the chains of the flesh, and extricates itself from all the bonds of earthly pleasures. Thus Stephen beheld Jesus, and feared not being stoned, nay, while he was being stoned, prayed not for himself but for his murderers. Paul also, when *caught up to the third heaven,* knew not *whether he was in the body or out of the body caught up,* I say, *into Paradise,* he became invisible to the presence of his own body, and having heard the words of God he blushed to descend again to the infirmities of the body.

<small>Acts vii. 55. 2 Cor. xii. 2.</small>

13. Thus, knowing what he had seen and heard in Paradise, he cried saying, *Why, as though living in the world, are ye subject to ordinances? Touch not, taste not, handle not, which all are to perish with the using.* For he would have us of this world in figure and semblance, not in use or possession, *using as though we used it not,* as our place of sojourn, not of rest, walking through it as in a vision, not with desire, so as to pass as lightly as possible over the mere shadow of this world. In this way S. Paul, who walked by faith not by sight, was *absent from the body and present with the Lord,* and although upon earth conversed not with earthly but with heavenly things.

<small>Col. ii. 20—22. 2 Cor. v. 8.</small>

14. Wherefore let our soul, wishing to draw near to God, raise herself from the body, and ever adhere to that chief End which is divine, Which is everlasting, *Which was from the beginning,* and *Which was with God,* that is, the Word

<small>S. John i. 1.</small>

of God. This is that Divine Being, *in Whom we live and move and have our being.* This is *That which was in the beginning,* the true *I AM.* For *the Son of God, Jesus Christ, was not yea nor nay but in Him was yea.* He bid Moses say, *I AM hath sent me.*

<small>Lett. 29.
Acts xvii. 28.
2 Cor. i. 19.
Exod. iii. 14.</small>

15. With this Good therefore let our soul be, and if possible, be continually, that each of us may say, *My soul is continually in my hand.* And such will be the case, if it be not in the flesh, but in the spirit, and does not entangle itself in earthly things. For when it turns back to carnal things, then the allurements of the body creep over it, then it swells with rage and anger, then it is pierced with sorrow, then it is lifted up with arrogance, then it is bowed down with grief.

<small>Ps. cxix. 109.</small>

16. These are the heavy griefs of the soul by which it is often brought down to death, while its eyes are blinded so that they see not the light of true glory, and the riches of its eternal heritage. But by keeping them always fixed on God, it will receive from Christ the brightness of wisdom, so as to have its vision enlightened by the knowledge of God, and to behold that hope of our calling, and see that which is good and well-pleasing and perfect. For that which is good is well-pleasing to the Father, and that which is well-pleasing is perfect, as it is written in the Gospel, *Love your enemies, that ye may be the children of your Father Which is in heaven, for, He sendeth rain on the just and on the unjust,* which is surely a proof of goodness. Afterwards He concludes by saying, *Be ye therefore perfect, even as your Father Which is in heaven is perfect.* For charity is perfect; in short it is *the fulfilling of the Law;* for what can be so good as *charity* which *thinketh no evil?*

<small>S. Matt. v. 44, 45.

Ib. 48

Rom. xiii. 10.</small>

17. Fly then those regions where dwell envy, ambition, and contention. Therefore let thy mind open itself to receive this Good, that it may mount above the clouds, that it may be *renewed as the eagle,* and like the eagle spread abroad its wings, that with new vigour in its pinions it may fearlessly soar aloft and leave its earthly dwelling-place behind it, *for the earthly habitation weigheth down the mind.* Let it put off old things, let it cast off wandering desires, let it purge its eyes that it may see that Fountain of true wisdom,

<small>Isa. xl. 31.

Wisd. ix. 15.</small>

that Source of eternal life Which flows and abounds with all things and is in want of nothing. For who hath given to Him, seeing that *of Him and through Him and to Him are all things?* TO IRENÆUS
Rom. xi. 36.

18. The Fountain of life then is that chief Good from Which the means of life are dispensed to all, but It hath life abiding in Itself. It receiveth from none as though It were in need, It confers good on others rather than borrows from others for Itself, for It hath no need of us. Thus in the person of man it is said, *my goods are nothing unto Thee.* What then can be more lovely than to approach to Him, to cleave to Him; what pleasure can be greater? He who has seen and tasted freely of the Fountain of living water, what else can he desire? what kingdoms? what powers? what riches? perceiving how miserable even in this world is the condition of kings, how mutable the state of empires, how short the space of this life, in what bondage sovereigns themselves must live, seeing that their life is according to the will of others, not their own. Ps xvi. 2.

19. But what rich man passes to eternal life unless he be supported by the riches of virtue, that gift which is the portion of all, and declared to be impossible for the rich alone? Happiness then does not consist in using these things but in perceiving that whereby you may despise them, may regard them as void of truth [b], may judge them to be empty and fruitless, and may love the true beauty of naked truth which confesses the cheating vanities of this world. S. Matt. xix. 26.

20. Lift up therefore your eyes, O my soul; those eyes of which the Word of God saith, *Thou hast ravished my heart, my sister, my spouse, thou hast ravished my heart with one of thine eyes. Go up then to the palm tree,* overcome the world, that thou mayest reach the height of the Word. Leave out of doors the vain shows of this world, leave its malice, but bring in with you that goodness of mind which has grace in the tree of life, that is, if she wash her robes and enter into the city which is the true grace of the saints, wherein is the Tabernacle of God, Cant. iv. 9.
Ib. vii. 8.

---

[b] 'Veri vana.' This is simply one of the Virgilian expressions of which S. Ambrose is so full. It is taken from Aen x 630, Nunc manet insontem gravis exitus, aut ego veri Vana feror.

around which the scribes of the Lord encamp, where neither day nor sun nor moon afford light, but *the Lord Himself is the light thereof*, and enlightens all that city. For He is the *Light of the world*, not indeed the visible light, but the intellectual brightness of the souls which are in this world, upon which He pours the bright beams of reason and of prudence, and in the Gospel is said to inspire with the breath of His spiritual influences the inmost soul, and the recesses of the mind.

21. If then any man hath begun to be an inhabitant of that heavenly city, an inhabitant, that is, by his life and manners, let him not depart from it, let him not go out again, or retrace his steps, the steps, that is, not of his body but of his mind; let him not turn back. Behind is luxury, behind is impurity. When Lot went up into the mountain he left behind him the crimes of Sodom, but she who looked back, could not reach the higher ground. It is not your feet but your manners which are never to turn back. Let not your hands hang down, or the knees of your faith and devotion become feeble. Let not the weakness of your will be backsliding, let there be no recurrence of crime. Thou hast entered in, remain therefore; thou hast arrived, stay still; *escape for thy life.*

22. In your ascent your steps must tend directly upwards, no man can safely turn back. Here is the way, there, downfall; here ascent, there a precipice. In ascending there is labour, in descending danger; but the Lord is mighty, Who, when thou art founded there will guard and hedge thee round with prophetic walls and apostolic bulwarks. Therefore the Lord says to thee, *Come, get you down, for the press is full.* Let us be found within, not out of doors. In the Gospel too the Son of God saith, *He which shall be upon the house-top let him not come down to take away his vessels.* And this He says not of this house-top, but of that of which it is said, *He spreadeth out the heavens like a vault.*

23. Remain within therefore, within Jerusalem, within thine own soul, peaceful, meek, and tranquil. Leave her not, nor descend in order to raise up this vessel of thine, either with honour, or wealth, or pride. Remain within,

that aliens may not pass through thee, that sins may not pass through thy mind, vain acts, and idle thoughts: and they will not pass, if thou wilt wage a holy war in the cause of faith and devotion, for the love of truth against the snares of passion, and wilt take up the arms of God against spiritual wickedness and the craft of the devil, who tempts our senses by fraud and stratagem, but who is easily crushed by the gentle warrior, who sees no strife, but, as becomes the servant of God, teaches the faith with modesty, and convinces those who oppose themselves. Of him the Scripture says, *Let the warrior who is gentle arise* [c], and let him that is weak say, *I can do all things through Christ which strengtheneth me.*

^{TO IRENÆUS}

Joel iii. 9.
Phil. iv. 13.

24. Supported by this faith, even he who is weak shall prevail, and his soul will be holy, and the prophetic or apostolic mountains shall *drop down new wine* for him, and *the hills shall flow with milk*, like that hill which gave milk to the Corinthians to drink, and water shall flow for him from their vessels, and from their well-heads. *From his belly shall flow living water*, that spiritual water which the Holy Spirit supplies to His faithful; may He vouchsafe to water thy soul also, that in thee may be *a fountain springing up into life eternal.* Farewell: love me as a son, for I love you as a father.

Joel iii. 18.
1 Cor. iii. 2.
S. John iv. 14.

LETTER XXX.

A.D.389.

S. AMBROSE here continues the subject of the last Letter, dwelling especially on the duty of rising above the level of earthly things, and bringing together various passages of the Old Testament which he interprets spiritually as setting forth this Lesson. The true follower of Christ will build Him a Temple in his heart, which his Lord will fill with the adornment of spiritual graces.

AMBROSE TO IRENÆUS, GREETING.

1. AFTER I had finished my last letter and directed it to be conveyed to you, the words which the Lord spake

[c] The Engl. Vers. is 'Prepare war, wake up the mighty men.' The Vulg. 'Sanctificate bellum, suscitate robustos.'

by the prophet Haggai came into my mind, *Is it time for you, O ye, to dwell in your cieled houses?* What is the meaning of this but that we ought to dwell on high, not in low and subterranean abodes? For they who dwell beneath the earth, cannot build the temple of God, but say, *The time is not come, the time that the Lord's house should be built,* because it is the mark of sensual persons to seek underground dwellings, courting the cool of summer, being enervated by indulgence and requiring shady retreats to enable them to bear the heat, or because the slothful live at ease beneath the earth, or lastly because dark and shady places suit them best, concealing, (as they believe,) their crimes. *I am compassed about with darkness, the walls cover me, what need I to fear?* But in vain do they hope for this, when God beholds the hidden depths of the abyss, and discovers all things before they take place.

2. But neither Elijah nor Elisha dwelt in underground dwellings. Moreover the former carried the dead son of the widow up into the loft where he abode, and there raised him to life; and for the latter, that *great woman,* the Shunamite, prepared a *chamber on the wall,* and there she obtained the privilege of conceiving a son, for she was barren, and there also she saw the miracle of his restoration to life. And what shall I say of Peter who at the sixth hour went up upon the house-top, and there learnt the mystery of the baptism of the Gentiles. But the homicide Absalom had reared for himself a pillar in the King's dale, and then, after his death, he was cast into a great pit. So then the saints ascend unto the Lord, the wicked descend to crime; the saints are on the mountains, the wicked in the valleys; *For God is the God of the hills, not of the plains.*

3. Those therefore who dwelt in the plain, where God dwells not, could not have the house of God in themselves; for this is the house which God required of them, that they should build up themselves, and should erect within them the temple of God with the living stones of faith. For it was not the erection of earthly walls nor of wooden roofs that He required, for these, had they existed, would have been destroyed by the enemies' hand; but He sought for that temple which should be raised in men's minds, to

whom it might be said, *Ye are the Temple of God*, wherein the Lord Jesus was to dwell, and from whence He was to proceed for the redemption of the world. Thus in the womb of a Virgin a sacred chamber was to be prepared, wherein the King of heaven might dwell, and the human Body might become the temple of God, Which also when It was destroyed, was to be raised again in three days.

TO IRENÆUS

4. But such a house as this sensual persons, *they who dwell in cieled houses* and delight in chased silver, do not build. For as they despise pure silver, so also they despise simple dwellings. They enlarge the site of their houses, they add more and more, joining house to house and farm to farm, they dig up the ground; so that the very earth itself gives way to their habitations, and like sons of the earth they are laid up within her womb, and hidden in her bowels. They surely are those of whom Jeremiah says, *Woe unto him that buildeth his house in unrighteousness.* For he who builds in righteousness, builds not on earth but in heaven.

Hag. i. 4.

Jer. xxii. 13.

5. *Thou hast built*, saith the Prophet, *a house, measure the upper chambers of it, even airy chambers, furnished with windows, cieled with cedar, and painted with vermilion.* Now he *measureth the upper chambers*, who, having contemplated the judgment of God, judgeth the judgment of the humble and the judgment of the poor. But he who seeks after gain and the blood of the innocent builds not his chambers with judgment, nor keeps the due measure, because he has not Christ, nor looks for the breath of Divine grace upon him, nor does he desire the brightness of full light, nor has he chambers painted with vermilion, for it cannot be said to him, *Thy lips are like a thread of scarlet.*

Ib. 14.

Cant. iv. 3.

6. *A man of this sort*, it is said, *shall not be buried*, for he who has burrowed in the earth, and buried himself alive, so to speak, in a tomb, has deprived himself when dead of the rest of burial. And thus, laid in the pit of carnal pleasures, he has found no grave from whence to rise. Such a man therefore builds no temple to God, because he hath not known the time of his correction. How then can such men build a temple, who like wild beasts betake themselves

Jer. xxii. 19. He shall be buried with the burial of an ass. Engl. Vers.

P

LETT. 30 to dens and hiding places, who like serpents bury themselves in ditches, and burrow in the earth like crafty foxes?

7. Neither does he build a sepulchre for himself who dies before the time, for *he is dead while he liveth;* and he hears not the voice of Haggai, that is being interpreted, of the Feaster, for he enters not the Tabernacle of God, *in the voice of praise and thanksgiving, the sound of one feasting.* For how can he hear His voice, who sees not His works? If he saw them, he would have heard the Word which has been put in His Hand, rejoicing in His acts, whereby *He knocked and it was opened to Him,* and He descended into his soul that He might feed therein upon the food of sincerity and truth.

1 Tim. v. 6.

Ps. xlii 5.

S. Matt. vii. 7.

8. Now because he has not heard, the word of Haggai comes again to hand, and says, Rise up from your *cieled houses* that are weighed down by wickedness, and *go up to the mountain* of the heavenly Scriptures, and *hew wood,* the wood of wisdom, the wood of life, the wood of knowledge; and make straight your ways, direct your acts that they may keep their due order which is useful and necessary for building the house of God.

Hag. i. 8.

9. For if ye do it not, the *heaven over you shall be stayed of her dew,* that is, the heavenly Word, Which descends *as the dew upon the grass,* shall not temper the fevered motions of your bodily passions, nor extinguish the fiery darts of your various desires; and *the earth,* that is, your soul, *shall be stayed from her fruit,* so that it shall be dried up, unless fully watered by the Word of God, and sprinkled with heavenly dew, even the fulness of spiritual Grace.

Ib. 10.

10. And as He knew how slothful they are who dwelt beneath the earth, and in the dark abodes of pleasure, *I will stir up,* it is said, *the spirit of Jerubbabel the son of Shealtiel, Governor of Judah,* and *the spirit of Joshua the son of Josedech, the high priest,* that they may be stirred up to build the Divine house. For *except the Lord build the house, their labour is lost that build it.* Now Zerubbabel means, 'constant overflowing,' like the Fountain of life, and the Word of God, *by Whom and from Whom are all things and in Whom all things consist.* Thus saith the overflowing Fountain, *If any man thirst, let him come unto*

Hag. i. 14.

Ps. cxxvii 1.

Col. i 16, 17.

S. John vii. 37.

Me, and drink; drink, that is, from the stream of the unfailing flood. We read also of Zabulon, a nocturnal flood, that is to say prophetic, but it also is now brightened by the intermixture of this stream, whereby was swallowed up that flood of vanity typified by Jezabel, which was opposed to truth and to the utterances of prophets, and was so torn in pieces by dogs that not a trace of it remained, but all its frame with every mark of its posterity was destroyed. Zerubbabel therefore of the tribe of Judah, and Jesus the High Priest, thus designated both by tribe and name seem to represent two persons, though one only is meant; for He Who as Almighty is born from the Almighty, as Redeemer is born of the Virgin, being the Same in the diversity of His two divisible natures, hath fulfilled as the Giant of salvation[a] the verity of the one Son of God.

TO IRENÆUS

11. Now being about to raise from the dead holy Zerubbabel He says, *Yet once, it is a little while, I will shake the heavens, and the earth, and the sea, and the dry land.* Once before he had shaken these things when He delivered his people from Egypt, when there was in heaven a pillar of fire, dry land among the waves, a wall in the sea, a path in the waters, when in the desert a daily supply of heavenly food was produced, and the rock was melted into streams of water. But He shook them also afterwards in the Passion of the Lord Jesus, when the heaven was covered with darkness, the sun withdrew his light, the rocks were rent, the tombs opened, the dead raised, the Dragon, vanquished on his own waves, saw the fishers of men not only sailing, but even walking on the sea without danger.

Hag. ii. 6.

Exod.xiii. 21.

Ib. xiv. 22.

S. Luke xxiii. 44.

12. The *dry land was also shaken* when the barren Gentile nations began to ripen with the harvest of devotion and

---

[a] This refers to Ps. xix. 5 where the sun, that *rejoiceth as a giant to run his course*, is usually interpreted by the Fathers of the Messiah. It was a very favourite thought with S Ambrose In his Hymn 'De Adventu Domini' he adapts the language of the Psalm to it in words of beautiful simplicity,

Procedit e thalamo suo,
Pudoris aulâ regiâ
Geminæ Gigas substantiæ
Alacris ut currat viam

Egressus Ejus a Patre,
Regressus Ejus ad Patrem,
Excursus usque ad Inferos,
Recursus ad sedem Dei.

In the De Incarn. ch. v. he gives a fuller explanation 'Him the Prophet Daniel describes as a Giant, because being of a twofold nature, He partaketh in one Person both of the Godhead and of a human Body, and exulted in going forth as a Bridegroom from His chamber, like a Giant, to run His course. He is Bridegroom of the faith, and the desert and the Gentiles were so much shaken, that the preaching of the Apostles, whom He sent to call the Gentiles, was so loud and vehement, that *their sound went out into all lands, and their words unto the ends of the world.* So greatly, indeed, was the desert shaken that *more are the children of the desolate than the children of the married wife,* and *the desert blossomed as a rose,* the elect of the Gentiles entered in to the remnant of the people, that the *remnant might be saved according to the election of grace.*

13. *And I will fill,* it is said, *this house with My silver and gold,* with the heavenly oracles, which are as *silver tried in the fire,* and in the brightness of the true light, glistening like spiritual gold in the secret hearts of the saints. These riches He confers on His Church, riches whereby spiritual treasures are increased, and the glory of the house is exalted above the former glory which the elect people enjoyed.

14. For peace and tranquillity of the soul is above all glory of any house; for *peace passeth all understanding.* This is that peace above all peace which shall be granted after the third shaking of the heaven, the sea, the earth and the dry land, when He shall destroy all Principalities and Powers. For *heaven and earth shall pass away,* and all the fashion of this world; and every man shall rise up against his brother with the sword, that is, with the word *piercing the marrow of the soul,* that whatever opposes itself, the *chariot from Ephraim* and *the horse from Jerusalem may be cut off,* as Zechariah says. And thus there will be peace over all, the passions of the body offering no resistance, and the unbelieving mind no obstacle, that *Christ may be all in all,* offering in subjection to the Father the hearts of all men.

15. Wherefore to Him alone is it mystically said, *I will take thee, O Zerubbabel, and will make thee as a signet, for I have chosen thee.* When our mind shall have become peaceful so that it may be said to her, *Return, return, o Shulamite,* which signifies 'peaceful,' or, to use your own soul as being the Word, He is a Giant of earth because He fulfilled all the duties of our daily life, and, though He was ever the eternal God, took upon Him the Mystery of the Incarnation.

name, Irenice, then shall she receive Christ like a signet on herself, that is, the Image of God, that she may be according to that Image, for *as is the heavenly, such are they also that are heavenly.* And it behoves us *to bear the image of the heavenly,* that is, peace.

<small>TO IRENÆUS
1 Cor. xv. 48.
Ib. 49.</small>

16. And that we may know the truth of this, it is said in the Canticles to the soul now fully perfect, that which may the Lord Jesus say to you also, *Set me as a seal upon thine arm;* that peace may shine in your heart and Christ in your works, and that wisdom and righteousness and redemption may be formed in you. Farewell, my son: love me for I love you.

<small>Cant. viii 6.</small>

LETTER XXXI.

IRENÆUS had asked S. Ambrose whether God had greater love for those who had believed from their early years than for those who had been converted later in life. In answering this question, S. Ambrose enters into the history of the Jewish and Christian Churches, which he considers as set forth under the figures of David's two wives.

AMBROSE TO IRENÆUS, GREETING.

1. You have wisely thought it a subject of inquiry, whether there be any difference in God's love towards those who have believed from their childhood, and those who have believed in the course of their youth or more advanced age; for this also has not been past over nor left unnoticed in the sacred Scriptures. For it is not without meaning that the Lord our God says to the Prophet Joel, *Lament to me for the spouse girded with sackcloth and for the husband of her youth,* expressing his grief for the Synagogue, who, before, in her virginity, had been espoused to the Word of God, or, it may be, for a soul which had fallen from her good deeds, that by the heinousness of her sins she had incurred hatred, and through the defilement of impiety and the stains of unbelief had become miserable and despised, and far removed from the grace of that Spouse which had before been counted worthy to be told, *I will*

<small>Joel i. 8.</small>

<small>Hosea ii. 19.</small>

LETT. 31. *betroth thee unto Me in righteousness and in judgment and in lovingkindness and in mercies.*

2. Not without reason is she considered miserable, who has lost gifts of so great a price, and suffered so grievous a loss of her dowry of virtues as to be deprived of the Spouse of her virginity. For according to our merits the Word of God either lives or dies in us; for if our desires and works are good, the Word of God lives and acts in us: if our thoughts and actions are darksome, the Sun of righteousness sets within us. And therefore He bids lamentation to be made for such a soul. For as they have cause of congratulation and feasting with whom the Bridegroom dwells, so that soul is to be mourned for, from whom the Spouse has been taken, as it is written of the Apostles in the Gospel; for *when the Bridegroom shall be taken away from them, then shall they fast in those days.*

Mal. iv. 2.

S. Matt. ix. 15.

3. Thus too this soul, in former times when she possessed the Virgin Word, had joy and gladness. And therefore she fasted not, because it was the season of feasting and refreshment; the Bridegroom was present bestowing by His presence the riches of plenty, stores of heavenly food, and dropping *wine, whereby the hearts of men are made glad.* But after she lost the Bridegroom by her acts, she is commanded to do penance in sackcloth for her sins, and to bewail herself, because Christ, Who is the Virgin Word, died and was crucified for her.

Ps civ. 15.

4. If this soul was espoused from early age, and never bore any other yoke, but from the beginning dedicated the maiden flower of her faith to Christ and as a virgin was united to Him in early days in the mysteries of piety, received a training in holiness as a heifer does the yoke; she is the very soul of the ancient Jewish stock from the family of the patriarchs, who, had she kept her course of faith without stumbling, would have been counted worthy of great things, the Spouse of the Virginal Word, as she who lays hold of Wisdom, *and as a mother shall she meet him, and receive him as a wife married of a virgin.*

Ecclus. xv. 2.

5. The other likewise is procured from the Gentiles, and both are the Spouse of the One Word, which is a great mystery. And this is set forth to you in the book of

Kings; since David had two wives, Ahinoam the Jezreelitess and Abigail whom he obtained afterwards; the first more severe, the latter full of mercy and grace, an hospitable and liberal soul, who saw the Father with open face, having beheld His glory; she who received the divine dew of paternal Grace, as the interpretation of the name signifies. Now what is the dew of the Father, but the Word of God, Who has filled the hearts of all with the moisture of faith and justice? TO IRENÆUS 1 Sam. xxv. 39.

6. Well therefore does the true David say to this soul what was said to Abigail, *Blessed is the Lord God of Israel which sent thee this day to meet me.* And again he says to her, *Go up in peace to thine house; see, I have hearkened to thy voice, and have accepted thy person.* Lastly in the Song of Solomon these are the words of the Bridegroom to the Bride, *Let me see thy countenance; let me hear thy voice.* Ib. 32. Ib 35. Cant. ii 14.

7. And at the time she was dismissed, for she had another husband who in Hebrew was called Nabal, which in Latin means foolish, a man harsh, inhospitable, uncourteous, ungrateful, who knew not how to repay good offices; but after his death, she was *set free from the law of her husband*, and the prophet David took her to wife. By this marriage the mystery of the Church which was to be called from among the Gentiles is signified, for she, having lost the husband to whom she had been married, became converted to Christ, bringing with her a dowry of piety, of humility and faith, enriched also with the patrimony of mercy.

8. But in this place it is not this wife, but that Ahinoam, who was evilly disposed towards her brother, wherefore her brother was made a trouble to her, and in their person it is said, *thou makest us to be a bye-word among the heathen, and that the people shake their heads at us.* The devil, finding her off her guard, fell upon her as a lion, and deprived her of her charms, rooted up *her vine and fig-tree* under which she used to repose, and caused her fruit to wither. Ps. xliv. 15. Mic. iv. 4.

9. But now God, having compassion on them, thus dried up and withered by drought, saith to the prophet, *Lament* Joel i. 8.

LETT. 31. *to Me for virgin girded with sackcloth and for the husband of her youth,* that is to say, over the dead husband of this soul or of the Synagogue. And with her He expostulates in another place, forasmuch as she had forgotten her resolution, forgotten His grace, had wandered from discipline, and had lost her former affections as a wife. Lastly therefore He reproves her with His words, calling to mind and repeating her tenderness and her expressions of affection : 'Didst Thou not call me one of Thy household, the parent and guide of Thy virginity.'

Hosea iv. 6.

10. Wherefore for this soul, to whom through her infidelity the Word of God is dead, and this Virgin Word is dead also, He appoints grief and brings in an Intercessor, that so she may be called to penitence, and may thereby earn compassion But she who is of prudent understanding and very beautiful to look upon, was gained for him, like Abigail, in battle ; her adversaries were conquered, and her husband, he who, surrounded by spiritual wickedness, struggled and fought not to lose his beautiful wife, being dead. On her her victorious and loving Spouse confers sweetness and grace, cleansing her from all that might obscure her beauty, and taking off from her the garments of her captivity, that so, laying aside all the hairs of her head, that is, the curls of sins, which seem to be superfluous parts of our person (for *if a man have long hair it is a shame unto him),* she may strive to come *in the unity of the faith, unto a perfect man, unto the measure of the stature of the fulness of Christ,* that she may lay aside all trouble of mind, and founded in love may grow up in the Lord Jesus, and make increase of the whole body.

1 Cor. xi. 14.
Eph. iv. 13.

11. This is that soul whom the Law shews to thee under the figure of a beautiful woman, and *if thou seest her among the captives, and hast a desire unto her, that thou wouldest have her to thy wife,* it says to thee, *thou shalt bring her home to thine house,* that thou mayest commit to her the whole interior of thy house, the possession of all thy secrets, that thou mayest take away her superfluities, and cut off her transgressions ; and with a razor not too sharp, lest it come to evil, may cut off the slough of thy passions, and thy idle senses. Wherefore it is said, *she shall shave*

Deut. xxi. 12.

Ib. 12.

her head, that so the *wise man's eyes* that *are in his head may meet with no hindrance.* And *she shall remain,* it is said, *in thine house a full month,* bewailing the sins of her nativity, and the lies of her wicked father the devil, who would fain *gather what he hath not laid,* that so, cleansed by the purification of this mystic number, she may obtain the keys of marriage.

<small>TO IRENÆUS Eccles. ii. 14 Deut. xxi. 13. Jer. xvii. 12. Vulg.</small>

12. And it is well said, *After that thou shalt go in unto her,* bidding thee to enter wholly into thy soul, and collect thyself within her, and so dwell in her that thou mayest be not in the flesh but in the spirit, and purpose to associate her to thyself in the commerce of life, knowing that she will communicate to thee of her goods, and that filled with her grace thou mayest say, *I was a witty child, and had a good spirit,* and she may answer thee, *I will take thee, and bring thee into my mother's house, and unto the chamber of her that conceived me.*

<small>Deut. xxi. 13. Wisd. viii. 19. Cant. iii. 4.</small>

13. She then shall be thy life, she shall find thee and kiss thee. *And it shall be, if thou hast no delight in her,* because she chastiseth her body, and bringeth it into slavery, thou shalt not suffer her to be a slave, that is, to the lusts of the body, nor subject her to the flesh, but suffer her to remain free; thou shalt not alienate her, for this were to sell her, nor shalt thou despise her, but shalt allow her to serve God in the chastity of faith and sobriety of good works. Farewell: love me, for I love you.

<small>Deut. xxi. 14.</small>

LETTER XXXII. A.D. 387.

S. AMBROSE in this Letter applies the words of Jeremiah about the partridge (Jer. xvii. 11) to Satan, and from it sets forth the way in which Jesus Christ has overcome him, and rescued man from his power.

AMBROSE TO IRENÆUS, GREETING.

1. *The partridge hath cried, she hath gathered what she hath not hatched*[a]. From the conclusion of my last letter

<small>Jer. xvii. 11.</small>

---

[a] The English Version has '*The partridge sitteth on eggs and hatcheth them not.*' S Ambrose is referring to § 11 of the preceding Letter, where he applies the text to Satan. He makes the same application of it in Letter xlvi. 14.

LETT. 32. I may borrow the opening of the ensuing. The question has been much mooted: with a view therefore of solving it, let us consider what natural history tells us of the nature of this bird. For it is the part of no little sagacity to consider even this, for Solomon knew the nature *of beasts and of fowl, and of creeping things and of fishes* [1]

1 Kings iv. 33.

2. Now this bird is said to be full of craft, fraud, and guile, skilled in the ways of deceiving the fowler, and experienced in the arts of turning him aside from her young ones; omitting no artful stratagem which may draw off the pursuer from her nest and lurking place. And we know that on observing his approach, she beguiles him until she has given her offspring the signal and opportunity for flight. As soon as she perceives they have escaped, she also withdraws herself, leaving her enemy deluded by her treacherous wiles.

3. It is said also to be a bird which copulates indiscriminately, and that the male bird rushes eagerly on the female, and burns with unrestrained desires. Wherefore it has been thought suitable to compare this impure malicious and deceitful creature with the adversary and circumventor of the human race, with him who is the arch-deceiver and author of impurity.

4. *The partridge then cried,* he that is, who derives his name from destroying [1]: even Satan, which in Latin means the adversary [2]. He cried first in Eve, he cried in Cain, he cried in Pharoah, in Dathan, Abiram, Corah. He cried in the Jews, when they demanded gods to be made for them, while the law was being given to Moses. He cried again, when they said of the Saviour, *Let Him be crucified, let Him be crucified,* and, *His blood be on us and on our children.* He cried, when they required that a king should be given them, that they might revolt from the Lord God their King. He cried in every one who was vain and faithless.

[1] perdendo.
[2] contrarius.
Gen iii. 4, 5.
Exod. v. 2.
Num. xvi. 2.
Exod. xxxii. 1.
S. Matt. xxvii. 23-25.
1 Sam. viii. 5.

5. And by these cries he gathered to himself a people whom he had not created; for God made man after His own likeness and image, and the Devil drew man to himself by the allurements of his voice: He gathered to himself the nations of the Gentiles, *getting riches not by right* [3].

Gen. i. 27.
Jer. xvii. 11.
[3] judicio.

Wherefore it is a common saying concerning the rich and covetous man, that he is a partridge gathering riches not by right. But my Jesus, as a good Judge, does all things with righteousness [1], for He came saying, as it is written, *I speak righteousness and judgement* [2] *of salvation.*

[1] judicio.
[2] judicium

Isa. lxiii.

TO IRENÆUS

6. By that grace then He despoiled that partridge the Devil, took from him the ill-gotten riches, even the multitude that followed Him, recalled from error the souls of the Gentiles, and the minds of the nations that wandered from the way. And since He knew that they were beguiled by the voice of the Devil, and in order that He might Himself loose the bonds and chains of ancient error, He cried first in Abel, the voice of whose blood cried out. He cried in Moses, to whom He said, *Wherefore criest thou unto Me?* He cried in Joshua, He cried in David, who says, *Unto Thee do I call, help me.* He cried too in all the Prophets. Wherefore He says also to Isaiah, *Cry,* and Isaiah answers, *What shall I cry?* He cried in Solomon, calling to all with a very loud voice in the power of of Wisdom, *Come eat of my bread, and drink of the wine which I have mingled.* He cried also in His Body, as the *Beam out of the timber* He cried that He might deceive and circumvent the lurking Enemy, saying, *My God, My God, why hast Thou forsaken Me.* He cried that He might spoil him of his prey, replying to the thief, *Verily I say unto thee, this day shalt thou be with Me in Paradise.* Wherefore when Jesus cried, straightway that partridge was left by those whom he had gathered *in the midst of his days.*

Gen. iv.
10. Exod.
xiv. 15
Josh. i. 1.
Ps cxix. 146.
Isa. xl 6.
Prov. ix. 5.
Hab ii 11.
S. Matt. xxvii. 46.
S Luke xxiii 43.
Jer. xvii. 11.

7. Wherefore some have thought that this also agrees with the nature of the partridge, forasmuch as it steals the eggs of others, and hatches them with its own body, seeking by this treachery to gain for itself the offspring of others. But when she whose eggs have been stolen, or nest invaded, or her young have been tempted by a fraudulent resemblance, and deceived by the appearance of beauty, when she, I say, perceives this, she 'picks out the crow's eyes [b]' as the saying is, and, being inferior in strength, puts

[b] 'Cornici oculum effodere' was a familiar Latin proverb for overcoming craft with craft. See cic pro Mur. 11, pro Flacco, 20.

Lett. 33. on and arms herself with cunning. And when all the labour she has bestowed on their nurture has exhausted her store of food, and her young ones have begun to grow up, she utters her cries, and calls to her offspring with the trumpet (as it were) of affection. And they, roused by this natural sound, recognise their mother, and desert their pretended parent. And thus, seeking to gather what he has not hatched, he loses those whom he thought to bring up.

8. Not without need therefore was it that Jesus also cried; it was in order that the whole universe which had been deceived by the voice, the allurements, the art, the specious beauty of the partridge, and enticed by his treacherous wiles, and had wandered from the true Author of their being, might be recalled by the voice of her true Parent, might abandon this deceiver, and desert him *in the midst of his days*, that is, before the end of this world. From him the Lord Jesus has rescued us, and called us to eternal life. Wherefore now, *being dead to the world we live to God.*

Rom. vi. 8.

9. When then this partridge shall have been completely forsaken by his false children, then that foolish one whom God has chosen and who has confounded the wise man, will be saved. Wherefore *if any man seemeth to be wise in this world let him become a fool, that he may be wise.*

1 Cor. i. 27.
Ib. iii. 18.

Farewell my son, and love me, as indeed you do, for I love you.

LETTER XXXIII.

S. Ambrose in this Letter explains more fully the text of Deut (xxi 15 &c) which he had alluded to in Letter xxi, and makes the *two wives* represent qualities.

AMBROSE TO IRENÆUS, GREETING.

1. In a previous letter I said that the soul ought to be delivered from its adversaries, and a bond of life which shall be inseparable entered into with it. And inasmuch as my discourse took as a proof of its assertion that passage

The variety of the allegories of the old Testament. 221

in the Book of Deuteronomy which speaks of the man who had two wives, one beloved and the other hated, you seem to have felt much concern lest any one should suppose this man had taken to himself two souls, which is impossible.

TO IRENÆUS
Deut. xxi. 15.

2. But you yourself know that sometimes, when Scripture uses allegory, it refers some things to the figure of the Synagogue, some to that of the Church; some things to the soul, others to the mystery of the Word, others to souls of different kinds and qualities, which he who has spiritual discernment can distinguish. And so I conceive that it is not two souls, but different qualities of the same soul, which are treated of in the following chapter of the Law. For there is an amiable kind of soul, which desires pleasure, which shuns labour, shrinks from compunction, slights the judgments of God. It is amiable because it seems gentle and sweet for the time, and one that soothes rather than distresses the mind. But there is another severer kind, which is consumed with zeal for God, which, like a strict wife, will not permit or suffer her consort to commit whoredoms, allows no indulgence to the body, gives no licence to delight or pleasure, renounces the hidden deeds of shame, devotes herself to arduous labours and to severe perils.

3. If therefore both have borne children, *he may not*, it is said, *when he maketh his sons to inherit that which he hath, make the son of the beloved first*[1] *before the son of the hated, which is indeed the first*. The meaning of which I conceive not to be so much a simple preference as between two first ones, but rather a declaration that the son of the hated wife alone has the prerogative of being first. Now the word 'primitivus' means as first-born[2], and the first-born are holy, for *every male that openeth the womb shall be called holy to the Lord*. Nevertheless all first-born are not holy, for Esau who was the first-born was not holy.

Ib. 16.

[1] primitivus.

[2] primogenitus.
Exod. xiii. 2.
S. Luke ii. 23.

4. But the holy are the first-born, for it is written in Numbers; *Behold, I have taken the Levites from among the children of Israel instead of all the first-born that openeth the matrix among the children of Israel. For on the day that I smote all the first-born in the land of Egypt, I hal-*

Numb. iii. 12, 13.

lowed unto Me all the first-born in Israel. Wherefore He took the Levites for the first-born, as being holy, for we know that the holy are first-born from the Epistle to the Hebrews, where it is written, *But ye are come to Mount Sion, and unto the heavenly Jerusalem, and to an innumerable company of Angels and to the Church of the first-born.* Wherefore as the first-born of the Church are holy, so also are the Levites, for they also are the first-born. For it is not by the order of their birth but by the gift of sanctification that they are holy; Levi being the third son of Leah and not the first.

5. But he who is sanctified himself opens the womb. What womb? Hear the words, *As soon as they are born they go astray.* As you have understood the first-born who opens the womb, so understand here the womb of the good mother, from which it is not saints, but sinners who go astray. But the Levites are taken away from the midst of Israel, because they have nothing in common with the people, whose earthly first-born are destroyed. The first-born of the world are of another mother, from whose womb Paul was separated when he was called to the grace of God. He received the Word Who is in the midst of our hearts. Whence it is said also, *There standeth One among you, Whom ye know not.*

6. This digression then of ours from one part of the Law to the other, for the purpose of shewing that the first-born is not the son of the beloved, that is of the more remiss and voluptuous wife, has not been needless, although the words of the chapter before us express the same truth: *He may not make the son of the beloved first-born before the son of the hated, which is indeed the first-born.* He is indeed the first-born who is the holy son of a holy mother; just as she is indeed the mother, from whose womb not her true sons but sinners go astray. Wherefore the former is not the son of the true mother, nor the true first-born, but as though he were so, subsistence is indeed provided for him that he may not want, but he is not honoured, that he may become rich. But the other has received double from all, that he may abound; just as in Genesis each of the patriarchs had two changes of raiment given to them by

their brother Joseph, when they were sent back to their father to tell him that he whom he had believed to be dead was found. [TO IRENÆUS]

7. Thus the first-born has received the prerogative of inheritance, as the Scripture says, *He is the beginning of his strength, the right of the first-born is his.* Thus from the first-born Son of God the first-born are holy, and from that beginning, (for He is the Beginning and the Ending,) the beginning is called holy, the beginning is the son to whom the prerogative of the first-fruits is due, according to that which was said to Abraham, *Cast out this bondwoman and her son, for the son of this bondwoman shall not be heir with my son, even with Isaac.* [Deut. xxi. 17. Rev. i. 8. Gen. xxi. 10.]

8. Now the Divine Oracle teaches us that this relates to the inheritance of virtues rather than that of mercy, for the Lord says, *In all that Sarah hath said unto thee, hearken unto her voice; for in Isaac shall thy seed be called.* What other inheritance was there in Isaac which could ennoble his father, but that of sanctity? The son of the handmaid indeed he set over the Gentiles, as bestowing upon him a simple portion of his patrimony, but to the son of Sarah he gave a double portion, for on him he bestowed not only temporal but also heavenly and eternal things. [Ib xxi. 12]

Farewell: love me, for I love you.

LETTER XXXIV.

HORONTIANUS asks whether the soul is from heaven S. Ambrose first refers him to the Book of Esdras, and then dwells upon S. Paul's statement in Rom viii.

AMBROSE TO HORONTIANUS[a], GREETING.

1. You have enquired of me whether the soul is formed of a heavenly substance; for you are too well instructed

---

[a] Horontianus appears to have been, like Irenæus, a pupil of S Ambrose, and to have been ordained by him, and to have been, as the Benedictine Editors say, 'In clericorum contubernio educatus ab infantia.' Nothing more is known of him. See Letter lxx 25

to suppose that the soul is made of blood or fire or any harmony of nerves, as the common herd of philosophers believe, nor as that patrician sect of them, the descendants of Plato assert, does that which moves of itself and is not moved by others appear to you to be the soul, nor indeed have you approved that fifth kind of element which the keen genius of Aristotle has introduced, namely a kind of [1] perfection of which the essence of the soul might be (as it were) framed and compounded.

[1] ἐντελέ-χεια.

2. On this subject I advise you to read the book of Esdras, who despised these trifles of the philosophers, and with a deeper wisdom which he had gathered from Revelation, pointed out that the soul is of a nobler substance.

3. The Apostle also, though he has not said it in so many words, has yet given us to understand, like a good master and spiritual husbandman calling forth the faculties of his disciples by the hidden seeds of doctrine, that our souls are of a better creation and a more excellent nature. For when he says that *the creature was made subject to vanity, not willingly but by reason of Him Who hath subjected the same in hope, because the creature itself also shall be delivered from the bondage of corruption into the glorious liberty of the sons of God,* he shews that the grace of souls is not small, seeing that by their strength and excellence mankind rises to the adoption of the sons of God, having within itself that which is given to it to make it in the likeness and image of God. For souls are not perceived by truth, nor are they seen by the bodily eye, wherefore they bear upon them the likeness of this incorporeal and invisible nature, and excel in their substance corporeal and sensible qualities. *For the things that are seen are temporal,* they represent and are united to things that are temporal, but the things that are not seen are united to the Eternal and Chief Good, *in Him they live and move and have their being,* and suffer not themselves, if they are wise, to be separated or divided from Him.

Rom. viii. 20, 21.

Acts xvii. 28.

4. Every soul therefore, seeing herself shut up in the prison-house of the body, if it be not debased by her connexion with this earthly habitation, groans under the burthen of the body to which she is joined; *for the corrupti-*

2 Cor. v. 4.
Wisd. ix. 15.

ble body presseth down the soul, and the earthy tabernacle weigheth down the mind that museth upon many things, knowing also that she walks *by faith not by sight*, she is willing *to be absent from the body to be present with the Lord*.

^{TO HORON-TIANUS}
2 Cor v. 7, 8.

5. Let us consider then how *the creature hath been made subject to vanity, not* indeed *willingly*, but by the Divine ordinance, which has appointed that our souls should be united to our bodies on account of their hopes, in order that, hoping for good, they should make themselves worthy of a heavenly recompense. *For we must all appear before the judgment seat of Christ, that every one may receive the things belonging to the body*[1]. Every man's soul must therefore consider that she will be rewarded according to deserts of life. And he says well *the things belonging to the body*, that is to say, the body which was assigned to her to govern, that if she have governed it well she may receive the reward for the sake of which she was subjected in hope, but if ill, she may be punished, forasmuch as she did not trust in God, nor aspire to that adoption of sons, and to the liberty of true glory.

Ib. 10.

[1] propria corporis.

6. So then the Apostle has taught that man is a creature subject to vanity. For what is so truly the man as his soul? of its companions he says, *For we that are in this tabernacle do groan being burthened*. David also says, *Man is like a thing of nought*, and, *Every man living is altogether vanity*. Wherefore the life of man in this world is vanity, to which vanity the soul is subject. And when a holy man doeth the things of the body, he doeth them not willingly but *by reason of Him Who hath subjected the same in hope*, he does them for obedience sake. From this example of the soul then let us proceed to the other creatures.

2 Cor v. 4.
Ps. cxliv. 4.
Ib.xxxix. 6.

7. Consider the sun the moon and the stars; these heavenly luminaries, although they shine with an excellent brightness, are yet but creatures, and rise and set in performance of their daily task, obeying the ordinance of the eternal Creator, dispensing the radiance wherewith they are clothed, and giving light by night and by day. As often as the sun is obscured by clouds, as often as is it hidden

by the interposition of the earth, or when the rays of its light are intercepted, eclipses occur, and, as the Scripture saith, *The moon knoweth her going down*[2]. She knows when she shines with a full, and when with a diminished orb. The stars also are overclouded and disappear, while going through the service of this earthly ministry, not willingly indeed but in hope; for they hope for the reward of this their toil from Him Who subjected them. Wherefore they go through it for His sake, that is, to do His will.

8. Nor is it surprising that they bear it with patience, knowing that their Lord, the Creator of all things in heaven and in earth, took upon Him our frail body and our servile state. Should not they then patiently bear the bondage of their corruption, seeing that the Lord of all humbled Himself even to death for the whole world, took upon Him the form of a servant, and was made the sin of the world, nay even a curse for us? Wherefore the heavenly bodies although they groan in that they are subject to the vanity of this world, yet follow the example of His goodness, and console themselves with the expectation of being *delivered from the bondage of corruption into the liberty of glory*, when the adoption of the sons of God, that is, the redemption of all men, shall have arrived. For when *the fulness of the Gentiles shall be come in*, then *all Israel shall be saved*. For what people will He not pardon when He even pardons that persecuting people, who said, *Crucify Him, crucify Him*, and, *His blood be on us and on our children*. But since even the heavenly creation is subject to vanity, albeit in hope, will not He Who is truly Mercy itself and the Redeemer of the world, suffer even the perfidy and insolence into which these men through the vanity of the world have fallen to obtain pardon?

9. To conclude then, both this great and glorious sun, and this moon which is not obscured by the shades of night, and these stars which are the garniture of the heaven, all these now suffer *the bondage of corruption*, for all creatures are corruptible, and the heavens shall perish and *the heaven and earth pass away*. But hereafter the sun and moon and the stars of heaven shall rest in the glory of

the sons of God, when God shall be *all in all*, He Who now in His immensity and mercy is in thee and in us.

TO HORON-TIANUS

10. And shall we not believe that the Angels themselves, who in the toils of this world fulfil divers ministeries, as we read in the Revelation of S. John, do not also groan when made the ministers of vengeance and destruction? Seeing that their life is blessed, would they not rather pass it in their ancient state of tranquillity than be interrupted by the infliction of vengeance on our sins? They who rejoice in the salvation of one sinner must surely groan over the miseries of so grievous sins.

1 Cor. xv. 28.
Rev. iii. 1 &c.

11. If therefore the creatures and powers of heaven suffer the bondage of corruption, but still in hope, that hereafter they may rejoice on our behalf and together with us, let us also alleviate the sufferings of this present time by the hope and expectation of future glory. Farewell, my son; love me, for I love you.

LETTER XXXV.

In this Letter S. Ambrose continues his comment on the passage of S. Paul, especially on the 'groans of creation.'

AMBROSE TO HORONTIANUS.

1. My former Letter was a reply to your inquiry; this is a part of my answer, supplemental not contradictory to the former. In reviewing the latter part of the passage I was struck, I confess, with his adding, *we know that every creature groaneth*, seeing that previously he had said without any addition, *The creature was made subject to vanity*. For he said not every creature, but, *the creature was made subject*. And again he says, *Because the creature itself also shall be delivered from the bondage of corruption*. But in the third place he adds that *every creature groaneth together*.

Rom. viii. 22.
Ib. 20.
Ib. 21.
Ib. 22.

2. Now what does this addition mean? It means haply

that every creature is not *subject to vanity*, and therefore every creature will not be *delivered from the bondage of corruption*. For why should that be delivered which is free and secure from the subjection of vanity and the bondage of that corruption? But they all groan together not in their own but in our pangs, and haply are in travail together of the Spirit of Salvation, the Spirit of sweetness, waiting for the adoption of the sons of God, that in the redemption of the human race they may attain to a common joy and gladness. So then either because of their charity they all groan for our labour, or for us as a member of their body, whose head is Christ. But you may understand this as you please, either as we have said, or simply that every creature groans and travails together.

3. And now let us consider what follows. *And not only they, but ourselves also, which have the first-fruits of the Spirit, even we ourselves groan within ourselves, waiting for the adoption, to wit the redemption of the body.* We are taught in the previous passage what the adoption of sons is; therefore, in order to explain its meaning, to that passage we must recur.

4. *He who through the Spirit*, says S. Paul, *mortifies the deeds of the body shall live.* Nor is it surprising that he should live, since he who has the Spirit of God, becomes the son of God. Wherefore he is the son of God that he may receive not the spirit of bondage, but the spirit of adoption of sons; to the intent that the Holy *Spirit may bear witness with our spirit that we are the children of God.* But this is the testimony of the Holy Spirit, that He it is Who cries in our hearts, *Abba Father*, as it is written to the Galatians. There is also the great testimony that we are the sons of God; namely that we are *heirs of God and joint heirs with Christ.* Now he is joint heir with Him, who is glorified together with Him, and he is glorified together with Him who by suffering for Him suffers together with Him.

5. And in order to encourage us to suffer, he adds that all things which we suffer fall far below and are not worthy to be compared with the recompense of our labours, the reward of future good, which shall be revealed in us, when

we shall be formed anew after the Image of God, and shall be worthy to behold His Glory face to face.

6. And to exalt the greatness of this future revelation, he adds that the creation also waits for this revelation of the sons of God, which now is made subject to vanity, not willingly, but in hope, because it hopes for the reward of its ministry from Christ, or else because it also will be *delivered from the bondage of corruption*, and received into *the glorious liberty of the sons of God*, that there may be one liberty of the creation and of the sons of God, when their glory shall have been revealed. But now, so long as this revelation is delayed, the whole creation groans together, looking for the glory of our adoption and redemption, already travailing with that Spirit of salvation, and willing to be delivered from the servitude of vanity.

7. And to this the Apostle has conjoined the groans of the saints, who have the first-fruits of the Spirit, for they groan also. Of their own merits they are indeed secure, but since the redemption of the whole body of the Church is still future, they suffer together with it. For seeing that the members of this our body still suffer, shall not the other members, although higher, sympathize with the suffering members of one and the same body?

8. And this, I suppose, is why the Apostle has said that the *Son Himself shall be subject unto Him that put all things under Him*, for they who still labour are not yet subject, and in these perhaps Christ still thirsts, in these is still hungry, in these is still naked, in that they do not fulfil the word of God, nor put on Christ, Who is the Garment of believers, and the Robe of the faithful. They also in whom He is sick still need medicine, and therefore are not yet subdued, for this subjection is of strength not of weakness: again, in those who are strong and obey the commands of God, the Son of God is subject. But now His travail is greater in those who do not succour those who are toiling, than in those who still require aid themselves. And this is the pious and true meaning of the subjection of the Lord Jesus, Who will subject Himself, to the intent *that God might be all in all.*

9. We have received the Apostle's meaning, let us now

TO HORONTIANUS

Rom. viii. 21.

1 Cor. xv. 28.

Ib

consider who are they that *have the first-fruits of the Spirit.* With this view let us inquire what is intended under the name of first-fruits or of beginning, *Thou shalt not delay,* it is said, *to offer the first of thy ripe fruits, and of thy liquors*, further on, *The first of the first-fruits of thy lands thou shalt bring into the house of the Lord thy God.* First-fruits and tenths are different, first-fruits are of greater merit, an act of pious consecration. And on this account Abel pleased God, for he delayed not to offer his gift, but offered of the first-fruits of his flock. Although some suppose that there is a difference between [1] first-fruits and first-born[2], in that on gathering in the crops, the beginning, so to speak, of all kinds in the threshing floor are offered, while the first reaping of the harvest is offered to the Lord; but of this we will speak in another place. But by the offering of the first-fruits, the whole harvest appears to be sanctified, but the first-fruits themselves are the most holy.

10. In like manner the saints are the first-fruits of the Lord, and the chief are the Apostles, *for God hath set in the Church first Apostles,* who have prophesied many things and preached the Lord Jesus, for they first received Him. Simeon too received Him, and the prophet Zacharias, John his son, Nathanael, *in whom there was no guile,* who rested under the fig tree, Joseph also who was called just, who buried Him. These are the first-fruits of our faith, nevertheless the nature of other seeds is the same as that of the first-fruits, although in some there is less grace, for *God is able of these stones to raise up children to Abraham.*

11. You have an example in the Lord Jesus Himself. In the resurrection of the dead He is called *the first-born from the dead.* The Apostle also has called Him the first-fruits; *In Christ shall all be made alive, but every man in his own order, Christ the first-fruits, afterward they that are Christ's, who have believed in His coming.* His body is as truly a body as our own, nevertheless He is called the first-born from the dead, because He rose first; and He is called the first-fruits because He is holier than all the other fruits, and they by union with Him are hallowed also. He also as *the Image of the invisible God* is the

Head of those found after that Image; in Him according to His Divinity there is nothing corporeal, nothing temporary; for *He is the brightness of His Father's glory, and the express Image of His Person.* But in our desire to explain the meaning of first-fruits we have greatly extended the length of our letter.

TO HORONTIANUS

Heb. i. 3.

12. Now the Apostles are our first-fruits, chosen from all the first-fruits of that time; to them it is said, *And greater things than these shall ye do,* for the Grace of God hath poured itself into them. These, I say, groaned, waiting for the redemption of the whole body, and they still groan, because many are still toiling, who are yet tossing on the sea. Just as, if a man is reaching the higher shore, but the waves still dash up to his middle, he groans and is in travail until he be wholly out of danger. Verily he groans, who still says to us, *Who is weak, and I am not weak?*

S. John xiv. 12.

2 Cor. xi. 29.

13. We need not then to be perplexed by the words, *We, which have the first-fruits of the Spirit, groan within ourselves, waiting for the adoption, to wit the redemption of our body,* for the sense is plain, forasmuch as they, having the first-fruits of the Spirit, groan, waiting for the adoption of sons. This adoption of sons is the redemption of the whole body, when he who is to be the son of God by adoption shall see face to face that Divine and Eternal Good; for there is the adoption of sons in the Church of God, when the Spirit cries, *Abba, Father,* as it is written to the Galatians. But this will be perfected when all shall rise again in incorruption power and glory who are counted worthy to see the Face of God, for then the human race will judge itself to be truly redeemed. And so the Apostle boasts, saying, *For we are saved by hope.* For hope saves, as also faith, whereof it is said, *Thy faith hath saved thee.*

Rom viii. 23.

Gal. iv 6

Rom viii. 24.

S. Luke xviii. 42.

14. Therefore the creature which *is made subject to vanity not willingly but in hope,* is saved by hope; just as Paul too, knowing that *to die was gain* to him, that he might be freed from the body and be with Christ, remained in the flesh for their sakes whom he wished to win to Christ. Now what is hope but the expectation of things future? Wherefore he says, *But the hope that is seen is not hope.*

Phil i. 24.

Rom viii. 24.

LETT. 35. For it is not what is seen but what is unseen that is eternal, *for what a man seeth, why doth he yet hope for?* The things that we see we seem to possess, how then can we hope for that which we already possess? Thus none of those things 1 Cor. ii. which we hope for can we see; *eye hath not seen, nor ear heard, the things that God hath prepared for them that love Him.*

15. Wherefore, if that which is seen cannot be hoped for, it is not well to read as some do, ' for ᵃ because any one sees a thing he also hopes for it;' unless it may be understood thus, ' for that which any one sees, why does he also hope for or expect it?' For most true it is that we hope for that which we see not, and therefore, although it seem Ps. xl. 1. to be absent from us, we still look for it in patience; *I waited patiently for the Lord, and He inclined unto me.* Lament. And we wait patiently, because *the Lord is good unto them* iii. 25. *that wait for Him.* And it seems to agree with this, that through patience He has given it back to us. We wait for the things which we hope for, but see not. For he does much who hopes and looks for those things which are not seen, and endures because he directs his mind to that which is.

Rom. viii. 16. Now it is well said that *hope that is seen is not hope,* 24. referring to the power and honour and riches of this world. You may see a man distinguished by his retinue and equipages, but he has not hope in his equipages which are seen. Nor is hope in the firmament of heaven, but in the Lord of heaven. The Chaldæan has not hope in the stars which he watches; nor the rich man in his possessions or the avaricious man in usury; but he hath hope who places his hope in Him Whom he sees not, that is, in the Lord S John Jesus, Who stands in the midst of us, yet is not seen. i 26 Finally, *eye hath not seen, nor ear heard the things which* 1 Cor. ii. *God hath prepared for them that love Him.* 9.

^a The difference in the original is only the punctuation, in the first case, ' Nam quod videt quis quid, et sperat :' in the second, ' Nam quod videt quis, quid et sperat?'

The Spirit teaches us how to pray,

TO HORON-
TIANUS

LETTER XXXVI.

S. AMBROSE continues, in reply to a question of Horontianus, his discussion of the passage of S Paul, and explains what are his 'groanings unutterable.'

AMBROSE TO HORONTIANUS.

1. OUR letters are so linked together that we seem to be holding actual conversation with one another, so well do you with your question and I with my explanations supply subject matter for our correspondence.

2. You have intimated your doubt of what spirit it is said that he *maketh intercession for us with groanings that* Rom. *cannot be uttered.* Let us then refer to what has gone be- viii 26. fore, that the passage may make plain what we are seeking. *Likewise,* it is said, *the Spirit helpeth our infirmities.* Does it not seem to you that this is the Holy Spirit, for He is our Helper, as He to Whom it is said, *Thou hast been my* Ps xxvii. *succour, leave me not neither forsake me, O God of my sal-* 9. *vation?*

3. For what other Spirit could teach Paul how to pray? The Spirit of Christ, like Christ Himself, teaches His dis- S Luke ciples to pray, for who could teach us, after Christ, but xi. 1. His Spirit, Whom He sent to teach us, and to direct our prayers, *for we pray with the Spirit and we pray with the* 1 Cor. *understanding also.* That the understanding may pray xiv. 15. well, the Spirit goes before and *leads it forth into the right* Ps cxliii. *way,* so as to prevent carnal things, or what either falls 10. below or exceeds its strength, from secretly stealing over it. *For the manifestation of the Spirit is given to every man* 1 Cor. *to profit withal.* It is written also, Seek great things, and xii 7 small things shall be added unto you; seek heavenly things, vi. 33. and earthly things shall be added unto you.

4. Wherefore He wishes us to seek greater things, not to linger upon earth. And He knows what to bestow upon us, *dividing unto every man severally as He will.* Some- 1 Cor. times, knowing our capacity, which we are ignorant of, He xii. 11. says to us, *Ye cannot receive it now.* I ask for myself the

sufferings of martyrdom, *the* Holy *Spirit is willing*, but sees the weakness of my flesh, and lest, while I seek for greater things I should lose what is less, says to me, 'Thou canst not bear this.' What opportunities have I not had, and yet when near the goal I have been held back [a]. The good physician knows what food is suitable to each disease, and to each season, for the benefit of health. Sometimes food seasonably taken restores health; but if a man eat food unseasonably or of an improper kind, it is dangerous to him.

5. Therefore since we know not what to pray for, nor how to pray, the Holy Spirit prays for us; for He is the Spirit of Jesus our Advocate, and He prays with groans unutterable, for Christ also mourns for us. And God the Father says, *My bowels, My bowels, I am pained at the very heart.* We often read too of Him as being indignant and grieved. He groans to take away our sins, and to teach us to do penance. For there are pious groans, and of prevailing power with God, whereof the Prophet speaks, *And my groaning is not hid from Thee.* For he did not hide himself, like Adam, but said, Behold I am the shepherd, *but these sheep, what have they done? it is I that have sinned, let Thine hand be on me.*

6. Hence then cometh the groaning of the Spirit of God, and those groans of the Prophet [b], truly unutterable because they are divine. So those words which Paul heard in heaven are *unspeakable, which it is not lawful for a man to utter,* but what is hidden from man is known to God. Now He Who is the Searcher of hearts knows all things, but the things which He searches are those which the Spirit hath cleansed. God therefore knoweth what the Spirit prays for, and what is the wisdom of the Spirit Which intercedes for the saints, as it is written, *For the Spirit maketh intercession for us.* For those for whom Christ suffered, and whom He cleansed by His Blood, for them the Spirit also intercedes.

Farewell: love me as a Son, for I too love you.

---

[a] S. Ambrose is evidently referring to his mission to Maximus, and the persecution of Justina

[b] There is another reading of several MSS, 'et ille profecto gemitus,' which seems to offer a better sense, 'and that groaning is indeed truly unutterable, etc.'

The friendship of Ambrose and Simplician.

LETTER XXXVII. A.D. 387.

SIMPLICIAN, to whom this and the following Letters, and several later ones, are addressed, seems, from what little we know of him, to have been a very learned and yet simple-minded man. He was older than S. Ambrose, who speaks in this Letter of his 'fatherly love' towards himself, and was probably his adviser in the early days of his episcopate, and possibly, as the Benedictine Editors, (note on Letter lxv,) suggest, his 'father in the faith,' as having prepared him for his ordination, or even taught him as a catechumen at Rome in earlier days. Paulinus tells us that when S Ambrose was on his death-bed he overheard some of his Clergy discussing the probabilities as to his successor, and when they mentioned Simplician's name, he said, "as if he were taking part in the conversation, 'An old man, but a good one'" Certainly Simplician was unanimously chosen his successor.

In this Letter he dwells in detail upon the theme that goodness is true freedom and sin slavery, which he illustrates at great length and with much rarity of argument. It is one of the most interesting of his expository Letters

AMBROSE TO SIMPLICIAN, GREETING.

1. WHEN we were lately conversing together, in the intimacy of an old-standing affection, you let me see that you were much pleased by my taking a passage from the writings of the Apostle Paul to preach upon to the people. You said further that this was the case, because the depth of his counsels is difficult to grasp, while the loftiness of his sentiment rouses the audience, and stimulates the preacher; and also because his discourses are so fully, for the most part, the interpreters of his meaning, that the expounder of them finds nothing to add of his own, and, if he would say ought, fills the part of a critic rather than of a preacher.

2. However since I recognize herein the feelings of long friendship, and what is still more precious, the tenderness of your paternal regard, (for in length of attachment many may participate, but in paternal love they cannot;) since moreover you consider that I have already done what you ask satisfactorily, I will comply with what you desire, and that the more, as I am admonished and stimulated by my own example, an example not difficult for me to follow,

LETT. 37. since I shall imitate no great one, but myself only, thus returning to my own humble customs.

3. As to the plan pursued in my discourse, seeing that the image and character of the blessed life is delineated therein, I think I have so arranged the argument of it that it will not be disapproved by others, certainly not by yourself who are so partial to me, although it is more difficult to satisfy your judgment than theirs, only your affection softens its severity and renders it more indulgent to me.

4. Now this Letter, written as it is in your absence, has for its subject the sentence of the Apostle Paul, who calls us from slavery into liberty, saying, *Ye are bought with a price, be not ye the servants of men,* shewing that our liberty lies in the knowledge of wisdom. This opinion has been bandied to and fro by philosophers in energetic discussions, while they assert that every wise man is free and every fool a slave.

1 Cor. vii. 23.

5. But this was said long before by the son of David, *The fool changeth as the moon.* The wise man on the other hand is not dispirited by fear, nor changed by power, nor exalted by prosperity, nor cast down by sadness; for where wisdom is, there also is strength of mind, constancy, and fortitude. Now the wise man remains the same in mind, neither depressed nor exalted by the vicissitudes of things, he is not *tossed to and fro as a child, and carried about with every wind of doctrine,* but continues perfect in Christ, grounded in charity, rooted in faith. Hence he is not conscious of failure, he knows not the various losses which befal the soul, but *shall shine forth as the Sun of righteousness Who shines in the kingdom of His Father.*

Ecclus xxvii. 11

Eph iv. 14.

S Matt. xiii. 43.

6. But let us now consider from what source Philosophy more fully derived this, from what discipline and wisdom of the Patriarchs. Did it not come first from Noah who, perceiving that his son Ham had foolishly derided the nakedness of his father, cursed him in these words, *Cursed be Ham*[1], *a servant of servants shall he be unto his brethren,* and set his brethren as lords over him, seeing that they had wisely deemed their fathers old age worthy of honour?

Gen. ix. 25.
[1] Canaan. E.V.

7. Did not also that source of all good discipline, Jacob,

who on account of his wisdom was preferred to his elder brother, instil into the breasts of all the riches of this copious subject? So also the pious father, whose paternal affection was equally strong towards his two sons, although his judgment varied, (for while the ties of blood sway the affections, our judgments are formed according to desert,) and who therefore dispensed to the one grace, to the other mercy, to the wise grace, to the foolish mercy, seeing that Esau could not raise himself to virtue by his own proper strength nor make progress spontaneously, blessed him in rendering him the subject and servant of his brother, shewing thereby that folly was so much worse than slavery that slavery itself is a remedy for it; because a fool cannot govern himself, and unless he has some director he falls by his own will.

8. His father therefore, loving him and careful for his welfare, made him the servant of his brother that he might be ruled by his counsels. And thus wise rulers are given to an indiscreet nation, that by their vigour they may guide the weakness of the people, ruling them by a show of power, and by this weight of authority constraining them against their wills to obey those wiser than themselves, and to submit to the laws. On the foolish son therefore he laid a yoke as on one untamed, and to him who had said he would live by his sword he denied even freedom; that he might not fall away through presumption he set his brother over him, that being subdued by his authority and governance he might make progress towards conversion. And since there are two kinds of service, (for that which proceeds from necessity is weaker, that from free will stronger, for that good is more transcendent which proceeds not from necessity but from free will,) he therefore first laid upon him the yoke of necessity, and afterwards imparted to him the blessing of voluntary subjection.

9. It is not then nature which makes a person a slave, but folly; not manumission which sets free, but discipline. Esau was born free, and was made a servant, Joseph was sold into slavery, and then elected to power, to rule over those who bought him. He disdained not to be sedulous and obedient, but he maintained the height of virtue, he

preserved the liberty of innocence, the dignity of integrity. The Psalmist therefore says well, *Joseph was sold to be a bond-servant, they humbled his feet in fetters.* He was sold, it is said, *to be a bond-servant,* but they could not make him a bond-servant; *they humbled his feet,* not his soul.

10. For how was that soul humbled of which it is said: *His soul pierced the iron?* For while sin pierces the souls of others, (for *the iron* means sin, which has a penetrating power,) the soul of holy Joseph was so far from being vulnerable by sin that it pierced through sin itself. The blandishments of his mistress' charms moved him not, and with reason was he insensible to the flames of lust, seeing that he was consumed by the brighter fire of Divine grace. It is therefore well said of him also, *The word of the Lord inflamed him;* for thereby *he quenched the fiery darts of the Devil.*

11. How was he a bond-servant who directed the princes of the people to store up the corn, that thus they might forestall and provide for future dearth? Or how was he a bond-servant, who gained the whole land, and reduced all the Egyptians to bondage? And this, not in order to impose upon them the condition of an ignoble bondage, but that he might establish a tribute from all but the lands of the priesthood, which he preserved free from tribute, that among the Egyptians also respect for the priesthood might be held inviolable.

12. His being sold then did not make him a slave; for though of a truth he was sold to merchants, yet, if you regard price merely, you will find many who have bought for themselves maidens of an elegant form, and then, captivated by love, have basely enslaved themselves to them. *Apame the concubine of King Darius was once seen sitting at his right hand, taking his diadem off his head, and placing it on her own, and with the palm of her left hand striking his face, while the King gazed upon her with open mouth, glad if she would only smile upon him, and thinking himself miserable and afflicted if she scorned him, laying aside his authority, and seeking to soothe and persuade her to be reconciled to him.*

13. But why should I quote this at so great a length?

Do we not often see parents who have been made slaves TO SIMPLICIAN
by pirates or cruel barbarians ransomed by their children?
Are then the laws of mercy more powerful than the laws
of nature? Is natural affection produced in slavery? People often buy lions and yet have no mastery over them,
nay are so much their slaves that if they see them becoming enraged and shaking out their manes on their brawny
necks, they run away and hide themselves. Money then
determines nothing, for it often buys masters over itself,
nor do catalogues of auctions, for by them the purchaser
himself is often sold and allotted to another. A contract
of sale does not change a man's nature, nor deprive wisdom
of her liberty. Many free men, as it is written, serve a
wise servant, and *there is a wise slave, who governs foolish* Prov. xvii. 2.
masters. LX.

14. Whom then do you consider as more truly free?
Wisdom alone is free, she sets the poor over the rich, and
makes the servants lend at usury to their own masters;
lend, that is, not money but understanding, lend the talent
of that Divine and eternal Treasure which is never wasted,
the mere loan of which is precious: to lend that mystical
money of the heavenly oracles of which the Law says, *Thou* Deut. xv. 6.
shalt lend unto many nations, but thou shalt not borrow.
This the Jew lent to the Gentiles, for he received not instruction from them but imparted it; to him the Lord
opened His treasures, that He might moisten the Gentiles
with the dew of His Word, and might become the Head of
the nations, while He Himself had no head over Him.

15. He then who is wise is free, bought with the price of
the heavenly oracles, with that gold, that silver of the
Divine Word; bought with the price of blood (for it is no
small thing to acknowledge one's Redeemer;) bought with
the price of Grace: he who heard and understood the
words, *Ho every one that thirsteth, come ye to the waters,* Is. lv 1.
*and he that hath no money, come ye, buy and drink and
eat.*

16. He is free who going forth to war, if he have seen
a beautiful woman, and when he spoils his enemies' goods
has found her among them and *has a desire unto her, takes* Deut. xxi. 11.
her to wife, having first *shaved her head and pared her nails,*

and taken *off from her the raiment of her captivity*, taking her no longer as a slave but free, for he understands that prudence and discipline are not liable to a state of bondage. And therefore the Law says, *Thou shalt not sell her at all for money*, for truly she is above all price. And Job says, *Take*[a] *wisdom into thine inmost parts. The topaz of Ethiopia shall not equal it,* for it is more precious than gold and silver.

17. Freedom therefore is not his alone who has never had the auctioneer for his master, nor seen him raising his finger, but he is more truly free, who is free within himself, who is free by the laws of nature, knowing that this law has a moral not merely an arbitrary sanction, and that the measure of its obligations is in accordance not with the will of man but with the discipline of nature. Does such a person therefore seem to you free merely? Does he not rather appear to you in the light of a censor and director of morals? Hence the Scripture says truly that *the poor shall be set over the rich, and private men over those who administer the state*[b].

18. Think you that he is free who buys votes with money, who courts the applause of the people more than the approbation of the wise? Is he free who is swayed by the popular breath, who dreads the hisses of the populace? That is not liberty which he who is manumitted receives, which he obtains as a gift from the blow of the lictor's palm. For it is not munificence but virtue that I hold to constitute liberty; liberty, which is not bestowed by the suffrages of others, but is won and possessed by a man's own greatness of mind. For a wise man is always free, always honoured, always one who presides over the laws. *For the law is not made for the righteous but for the unrighteous,* for the just man is a law unto himself, having no need to fetch for himself from a distance the form of virtue, seeing that he bears it within his heart, having *the works of the law written on the tablets of his heart,* to whom it is said, *Drink waters out of thine own cistern, and running waters out of thine own well.* For what is so near to

---

[a] The Vulgate has, 'Trahitur autem sapientia de occultis.' The E V is, 'The price of wisdom is above rubies.'

[b] This is referred by the Benedictine Editors to Prov. xxii 7. but it does not agree with either the Sept. or Vulgate.

us as the Word of God? This word is in our hearts, and in our mouth; we see it not, and yet possess it.

19. The wise man therefore is free, for he who does that which he wills is free. But it is not every will that is good, but it is the part of a wise man to will all things which are good, for he hates what is evil, having chosen that which is good. If therefore he has chosen what is good, he whose choice is free and who has chosen what he will do is free, for he does what he wills to do: the wise man therefore is free. All that the wise man does he does well. But he that does all things well does all things rightly, and he that does all things rightly does them all without offence or reproach, without causing disturbance or loss to himself. Whoever then has this power of doing all things without offence or reproach, without loss or disturbance to himself, does nothing foolishly but does all things wisely. For he who acts wisely has nothing to fear, for fear is in sin. But where no fear is, there is liberty, and where liberty is, there is the power of doing what one wishes: the wise man therefore alone is free.

20. He who can neither be compelled nor forbidden is no slave; now it belongs to the wise man to be neither compelled nor forbidden; the wise man, therefore, is not a slave. Now he is forbidden who does not execute what he desires, but what does the wise man desire but the things which belong to virtue and discipline, without which he cannot exist? For they subsist in him, and cannot be separated from him. But if they are separated from him he is no longer wise, seeing that he is without the use and discipline of virtue, of which he would deprive himself if he were not the voluntary interpreter of virtue. But if he be constrained, it is manifest that he acts unwillingly. Now in all actions there are either corrections proceeding from virtue, or falls proceeding from malice, or things between the two and indifferent. The wise man follows virtue not compulsorily but voluntarily, for all things that are pleasing he does, as flying from malice, and admits not so much as a dream of it. So far is he from being moved by things indifferent, that no forces have the power to move him hither and thither as they do the herd of men,

LETT. 37. but his mind hangs as in a balance in equal scales, so that it neither inclines to pleasure, nor in any respect directs its desires however slightly to things which ought to be avoided, but remains unmoved in its affections. Whence it appears that the wise man does nothing unwillingly or by compulsion, because were he a slave he would be so compelled; the wise man therefore is free.

21. The Apostle likewise gives this definition, saying, *Am I not an Apostle, am I not free?* Truly he was so free that when certain persons had *come in privily to spy out his liberty*, he *gave place*, as he himself says, *by subjection, no not for an hour, that the truth of the Gospel might be preached.* He therefore who yielded not preached voluntarily. Where free will is, there is the reward of free will; where obligation is, there is the service of obligation. Free will therefore is better than obligation; to will is the part of the wise man, to obey and to serve is the part of the fool.

1 Cor. ix. 1.
Gal. ii. 4.

22. This is also the Apostle's definition, who says, *For if I do this thing willingly, I have a reward but if against my will a dispensation is committed to me.* On the wise man therefore a reward is conferred, but the wise man acts willingly, according to the Apostle therefore the wise man is free. Wherefore he also exclaims, *Ye have been called unto liberty, only use not liberty for an occasion to the flesh.* He separates the Christian from the Law, that he may not seem to yield to the Law against his will; he calls him to the Gospel, which the willing both preach and practise. The Jew is under the Law, the Christian is by the Gospel; in the Law is bondage, in the Gospel, where is the knowledge of wisdom, is liberty. Every one therefore who receives Christ is wise, and he who is wise is free, every Christian therefore is both wise and free.

1 Cor. ix. 17.

Gal. v. 13.

23. But the Apostle has taught me something even beyond freedom itself, namely that to serve is real freedom, *Though I be free from all*, he says, *yet have I made myself servant unto all, that I might gain the more.* What is that which surpasses liberty but to have the Spirit of grace, to have charity? Liberty renders us free to men, but charity renders us beloved by God. Wherefore Christ also says,

1 Cor. ix. 19.

But I have called you friends. Good indeed is charity; whereof it is said, *By love of the Spirit*[c] *serve one another.* Christ also became a servant that He might make all free. *His hands served in the baskets ·* He Who *thought it not robbery to be equal with God, took upon Him the form of a servant,* and was made all things to all men, that He might bring salvation to all. Following this example, Paul was both, as it were, under the Law, and lived without the Law, for the benefit of those whom he desired to gain: to the weak he voluntarily became weak that he might strengthen them; *he ran so as to obtain, he kept under his body that he might be victorious over heavenly powers in Christ.*

TO SIMPLICIAN

S. John xv. 15.
Gal. v. 13.
Ps lxxxi. 6 LXX.
Phil. ii 6.

1 Cor. ix. 24, 27

24. To the wise man therefore even bondage is freedom; whence we may gather that even to be in power is bondage to the fool, and what is worse, while he rules over a few, he serves more and severer masters. For he serves his own passions, his own lusts, their tyranny he can escape neither by night nor day, for he carries these masters within his own breast, and suffers within himself an intolerable bondage. For there is a double bondage, one of the body, another of the soul; now the lords of the body are men, but the lords of the soul are evil dispositions and passions, from which liberty of the mind alone frees the wise man and enables him to depart from his bondage.

25. Let us seek therefore that truly wise man, that truly free man, who although he live under the dominion of many, says freely, *Who is he that will plead with me? from Whose sight I shall not be able to hide myself, only do Thou withdraw Thy hand far from me, and let not Thy dread make me afraid.*

Job xiii. 19—21.

26. And King David, who followed him, said, *Against Thee only have I sinned.* For being supported by the royal dignity, and being, so to speak, master of the laws, he was not subject to them but was liable to God alone, Who is the Lord of hosts.

Ps. li. 6.

27. Hear another free man; *But with me it is a very small thing that I should be judged of you, or of man's judgment: yea, I judge not mine own self,* for I know nothing *against* myself, ... *but He that judgeth me is the Lord.*

1 Cor. iv. 3, 4.

[c] τοῦ πνεύματος is inserted in a few MSS, and Spiritus is in the Vulgate.

LETT. 37. The freedom of the spiritual man is a true freedom, because *he judgeth all things, yet he himself is judged of no man,* because he knows himself to be subject to nothing which has any participation in the creature, but to God alone, Who only is without sin, of Whom Job also says, *God liveth Who hath taken away my judgment,* for the just man can only be judged by Him *in Whose sight the heavens are not clean, nor the light of the stars pure and clean.*

1 Cor. ii. 15.

Job xxvii. 2.

Ib. xxv. 5.

28. Will any one bring forward those verses of Sophocles which say 'Jupiter, and no mortal man is ruler over me?' How much more ancient is Job, how much older is David? Let them acknowledge then that they have borrowed from us the more excellent of their sayings.

29. Who then is wise but he who has arrived at the very mysteries of the Godhead, and has known the hidden things of wisdom to be manifested to him. He then alone is wise who has taken God as his guide, to conduct him to the secret resting-place of truth, and although but a mortal man has become by grace the heir and successor of the eternal God, and partaker, as it were, of His sweetness, as it is written, *Wherefore God, even thy God hath anointed thee with the oil of gladness above thy fellows.*

Ps. xlv. 8.

30. Now if any man will examine more closely these matters, he will perceive what great assistance the wise man finds and what great obstacles the foolish, in the very same things; that to the one freedom is an aid, to the other bondage is an impediment. For the wise man rises as a conqueror, having vanquished and triumphed over lust, fear, sloth, sadness and other vices. This he does until he casts them out from the possession of his mind, driving and excluding them from all its bounds and limits, for as a cautious general he knows how to guard against the incursions of robbers, and those hostile stratagems which the wicked enemies of our soul are frequently attempting with their fiery darts; for we have both wars in peace and peace in war. Whence also he says, *Without were fightings, within were fears.* But *in all these things we are more than conquerors through Him that loved us.* He says this because he was terrified neither by straits nor persecutions, nor hunger, nor danger, nor death.

2 Cor. vii. 5.
Rom. viii. 37.

31. But he who fears these things, who dreads death, how is he not a slave? Truly he is a slave, and that in a miserable bondage; for nothing so subjects the mind to all kind of bondage as the fear of death. For how can the abject and vile and ignoble sense raise itself up, when it is deeply sunk in the pit of corruption, through the lusts of this life. Behold, how much he is a slave: *I shall be hid,* he says, *and I shall be a fugitive and a vagabond in the earth, and it shall come to pass that every one that findeth me shall slay me.* Therefore as a slave he received a sign, but even thus he could not escape death. Thus the sinner is a slave to fear, to cupidity, to avarice, to lust, to malice, to anger, nay, he is a greater slave than if he were set under tyrants. *(TO SIMPLICIAN. Gen. iv. 14.)*

32. But they are free who live by the laws. Now true law is right reason, true law not sculptured on tablets, nor engraved in brass, but impressed on the mind, and fixed in the senses; for the wise man is not under the law, but is a law unto himself, bearing the work of the Law in his heart, inscribed and formed therein by a kind of pen natural to himself. Are we then so blind as not to see the manifest characters of things, and the images of virtues? And how unworthy is it that whole nations should obey human laws, that they may become thereby partakers of liberty: but that wise men should neglect and abandon the true law of nature formed according to the image of God, and true reason, the sign-bearer of liberty; since there is so much liberty therein, that when children we are unconscious of any bondage to vice, being removed from anger, free from avarice, ignorant of lust. How miserable therefore, that we who are born in liberty should die in bondage!

33. But this arises from the levity of our mind and the infirmity of our character; because we are occupied by idle cares, and superfluous actions: but the heart of the wise man, his works and deeds, ought to be stedfast and immoveable. Moses taught us this, when his hands became heavy, so that Joshua the son of Nun could scarcely hold them up. And therefore the people were victorious when works not of a perfunctory kind, but full of gravity and virtue were being carried on, not the works of a mind un- *(Exod. xvii. 12.)*

steady, and staggering to and fro in its affections, but of one firmly rooted and established. The wise man therefore stretches out his hands, but the fool draws them together, as it is written, *The fool foldeth his hands together, and eateth his own flesh,* meditating on carnal more than spiritual things. But not so did that daughter of Juda, who stretched forth her hands and cried to the Lord, *Thou knowest that they have borne false witness against me.* She thought it better not to sin and to incur the calumnies of her accusers, than to commit sin under the veil of impunity. And by the contempt of death she preserved her innocence. Not so, either, the daughter of Jepthah, who by her own consent confirmed and even encouraged her father's vow concerning her own immolation.

34. For I will not produce the books of philosophers on the contempt of death, or the gymnosophists of the Indians, of whom the answer of Calanus[a] to Alexander, when he commanded him to follow him, is especially commended. 'To what praise' said he 'do you consider me entitled, 'that you require me to travel to Greece, if I can be com-'pelled to do that to which my will consents not?' A reply truly full of dignity, and yet his mind was more full of liberty. He wrote this letter also

CALANUS TO ALEXANDER.

35. "Your friends persuade you to lay hands and even constraint on the Indian philosophers, not even in their dreams beholding our works. Our bodies you may remove from place to place, our souls you cannot compel to do what they do not will, no more than wood or stone to utter sounds. A great fire burns pain into living bodies and begets corruption; on this fire we are, for we are burning alive. There is neither king nor prince who can compel us to do what we have not determined to do Nor are we like the philosophers of Greece, who have conceived words rather than realities, in order to give celebrity to their opinions; in our case realities are associated with words and words with realities; our acts are swift and our discourses short, we enjoy a delightful freedom in the exercise of virtue.

36 and 37. Excellent words, but still words; excellent constancy, but that of a man; excellent letter, but that of

---

[a] The story of Calanus and Alexander is related in Arian vii 2 It is also more briefly alluded to by Plutarch Alex. 65. Neither writer mentions this letter.

a philosopher. But amongst us, even maidens through desire of death have mounted even up to heaven by the lofty steps of virtue. Why should I mention Thecla, Agnes, or Pelagia, who sprouting forth as noble tendrils [1] have hastened to death as if to immortality? The virgin exulted among lions, and dauntlessly beheld the roaring beasts. And to compare our history with that of the Indian philosophers, what Calanus boasted in words holy Laurence proved by his acts, for he was burnt alive, and surviving the flames said, 'Turn me and eat me.' Nor did the youths of the race of Abraham[2] or the sons of the Maccabees strive less boldly; the former sung while in the midst of the flames, and the latter, during their punishment, asked not to be spared, but reproached their persecutor in order to enrage him more. The wise man therefore is free.

TO SIMPLICIAN

[1] vibulamina. Gr. μοσχεύματα.

[2] i. e. the three children in the furnace.

38. But what can be more sublime than holy Pelagia, who was surrounded by persecutors, but before she came into their presence said; 'I die willingly, no man shall touch me, no one with wanton look shall defile my chastity, I will carry away with me my modesty, my honour untainted; these ruffians shall reap no profit from their insolence. Pelagia will follow Christ, no man shall deprive her of her liberty, no man shall see her free faith made captive, her illustrious chastity, her inheritance of wisdom. What is enslaved shall remain here, not amenable to any duty.' Great therefore is the freedom of that pious virgin, who encircled by her persecutors gave way not the least in the midst of these great dangers to her integrity and her life.

39. But he is not free over whom anger reigns, for he is subject to the yoke of sin; for *an angry man diggeth out sin*, and, *Whosoever committeth sin, is the servant of sin*. Neither is he free who is enslaved to avarice, for he cannot possess his vessel. Neither is he free who seeing his desires and pleasures, fluctuates in his devious course. He is not free who is bowed down by ambition, for he obeys the rule of another. But he is free who is able to say, *All things are lawful unto me, but all things are not expedient, all things are lawful for me, but I will not be brought under the power of any. Meats for the belly, and the belly for*

Prov. xxix. 22. stirreth up strife. E.V. S John viii. 34.

1 Cor. vi. 12, 13.

LETT. 37.　*meats.* He is free who says, *For why is my liberty judged*
1 Cor. x. *of another man's conscience?*
29.
　　　　40. Liberty therefore belongs to the wise man not to the
Prov　　fool; for *he who binds a stone in a sling is like him who*
xxvi 8.　*giveth honour to a fool,* for he wounds himself, and while
brandishing his dart chiefly endangers his own body. Certainly as he is stung by the sling, and by the falling of the stone the evil is increased, so the fall of a fool when he is set at liberty is more rapid. Wherefore the power of a fool is rather to be retrenched than any new liberty added, for slavery is suitable for him. And therefore it is added,
Ib 9.　*As a thorn goeth up into the hand of a drunkard, so is a parable in the mouth of fools.* For as he is wounded by his cups, so is the fool by his deeds. The one by drinking involves himself in sin, the other by acting subjects himself to censure, and by his deeds is drawn into bondage.
Rom. vii. Paul saw himself *brought into captivity by the law*
23.　*of sin,* and therefore, in order to be freed, he fled to the grace of liberty.

Ps. xxxii.　41. Fools then are not free, for it is said to them, *Be ye*
10　*not like to horse and mule, which have no understanding, whose mouths must be held with bit and bridle lest they fall upon thee. Great plagues remain for the ungodly;* for they have need of these, in order that their folly may be restrained. It is good discipline which requires this, not
Prov.xiii. severity. Further, *he that spareth his rod hateth his son ·*
24.　for a man's own sins scourge him still more severely. For heavy is the weight of crime, heavy the scourges of sin;
Ps　　they are heavy as a sore burthen, they inflict wounds upon
xxxviii.　the soul, and make the ulcers of the mind to stink.
4, 5.
　　　　42. Wherefore let us lay aside this grievous burthen of slavery, let us renounce sensuality, and the evil delights which bind us with the bonds, as it were, of lusts, and fetter us with chains. For these delights profit not the fool, and whoever has given himself to them from his boyhood will abide in bondage; living he will be as dead. Let sensuality then be cut down, let evil delights be pruned away, and let him who has been wanton bid farewell to his former courses. For the vine which has been cut down bears fruit, that which has been partly pruned puts forth leaves,

that which has been neglected grows too luxuriantly. Therefore it is written, *Like a field is the foolish man, and like a vineyard the man void of understanding*, if you leave him alone, he will become desolate. Let us then tend this body of ours, let us chasten it, let us reduce it to subjection, let us not neglect it. TO SIMPLI-CIAN Prov. xxiv 30.

43. For our members are *instruments of righteousness*, they are also *instruments of sin*. If they are raised upwards, they are instruments of righteousness, that sin should not reign in them: if our body has died to sin, transgression will not reign therein, and our members will be free from sin. Let us not therefore obey its lusts, nor *yield our members instruments of unrighteousness unto sin*. If you have looked upon a woman to lust after her, your members are the instruments of sin. If you have spoken and solicited her, your tongue and your mouth are instruments of sin. If you have removed the landmarks which your fathers set up, your members are instruments of sin. If you have hasted *with swift feet to shed the blood* of the innocent, your members ars instruments of sin. Rom. vi. 13. Ib. Ps. xiv. 6.

44. On the other hand, if you have seen a poor man, and taken him into your house, your members are instruments of righteousness. If you have rescued one who was suffering wrong, or one who was being led to execution; if you have cancelled the bond of the debtor, your members are instruments of righteousness. If you have confessed Christ (for *the lips of knowledge are the instruments of understanding*,) your lips are the members of righteousness. He who can say, *I was eyes to the blind, and feet was I to the lame, I was a father to the poor*, his members are members of righteousness. Prov. xiv. 7. Job xxix. 15.

45. Being therefore set free from sin, and redeemed, as it were, at the price of the Blood of Christ, let us not be made subject to the bondage of men or of passion. Let us not blush to confess our sins. Behold how free he was who could say, *I feared not the multitude of the people; that I should not confess my sin in the sight of all*. For he that confesses his sin is released from servitude, and *the just accuses himself in the beginning of his speech*. Not only the free but the just man also; but justice is in liberty Job xxxi. 33. Prov. xviii. 17

LETT. 38.
Ps. xxxii. 6.

and liberty in confession, for as soon as a man shall confess he is absolved. Lastly, *I said I will confess my sins unto the Lord, and so Thou forgavest the wickedness of my sin.* The delay of absolution depends on confessing, the remission of sins follows closely on confession. He therefore is wise who confesses; he is free whose sin is remitted, for he contracts now no debt of guilt. Farewell: love me as indeed you do, for I also love you.

A.D. 387.

LETTER XXXVIII.

In this Letter S Ambrose continues the subject, maintaining that the truly wise man is not only free but rich also, illustrating his statements with instances from the Old Testament.

AMBROSE TO SIMPLICIAN, GREETING.

1. WHEN we lately pointed out, taking our theme from the epistle of the Apostle Paul, that every wise man is free, we seemed to have fallen into philosophical discussion. But afterwards, in reading the epistle of the Apostle Peter, I perceived that every wise man is also rich: and this he says without distinction of sex, for he writes that all a woman's ornaments consist in a virtuous life, not in costly jewels, *Whose adorning*, he says, *is not that outward adorning of plaiting the hair, and of wearing of gold, or of putting on of apparel, but the hidden man of the heart.*

1 S. Pet. iii. 3, 4.

2. Here then are two things, both that there is a man within the man, and that he is rich who seeks not for himself the enjoyment of any riches. And he has well said, *the man of the heart*, in that the whole man of wisdom is hidden, as is wisdom itself, which is not seen but understood. No one before Peter used such an expression as, *the man of the heart*, for the outward man consists of many members, but the inward man of the heart is entirely full of wisdom, full of grace, full of beauty.

3. *In that*, he says, *which is not corruptible, even the ornament of a meek and quiet spirit, which is in the sight of God of great price.* And he is truly rich, who can appear rich in the sight of God, in whose sight the earth is small, the world itself is narrow, but God considers him only to be rich who is rich for eternity, who lays up the fruit not of riches, but of virtues. And who is rich before God but that meek and quiet spirit which is never corrupted? Does not he appear to you to be rich, who possesses peace of mind and the tranquillity of rest? who desires nothing, is not tossed by the storms of lust, despises not old things, seeks not new, so as by his constant desire to become poor in the midst of riches? TO SIMPLI-CIAN 1 S. Pet. iii. 4.

4. That peace is truly rich, which *passeth all understanding.* Peace is rich, modesty is rich, faith is rich, for *to the faithful the whole world is a possession.* Simplicity is rich, for there are also the riches of simplicity; for she scrutinizes nothing, has no mean, no suspicious, no deceitful thoughts, but pours herself forth with pure affection. Phil. iv. 7. Prov. xxviii. 10.

5. Goodness too is rich, and if a man preserve it he is fed by the riches of the heavenly inheritance. To quote also the more ancient examples of Scripture, *Happy,* it is said, *is the man whom God correcteth* Therefore *despise not thou the chastening of the Almighty . . . . in famine He shall redeem thee from death, and in war from the power of the sword. Thou shalt be hid from the scourge of the tongue; . . . . the beasts of the field shall be at peace with thee, and thou shalt know that thy tabernacle shall be in peace.* For the vices of this flesh being subdued, and those passions which are wont to war against the soul, your tabernacle shall be undisturbed, your house without offence, your seed shall not fail, your posterity shall be as the smell of a fruitful field, your burial as the harvest. For while others are looking for theirs to fail, the heap of your corn will be carried ripe into the heavenly garners. Job v. 17 —24. Gen xxvii 37. Job v. 26.

6. Fit it is that the righteous ever lendeth, while the wicked man is in want. He lendeth justice, he lendeth the commandments of God to the poor and needy; but the fool does not possess even that which he believes himself to possess. Do you suppose that he can be said to possess, Ps. xxxvii 26.

Lett 38 who brooding over his treasure night and day, is troubled by covetous and wretched anxiety? Such a one truly wants; although to others he appears rich, to himself he is poor, because he who is still grasping after more and desiring more uses not that which he possesses. For where there are no bounds to desire, what profit can there be in riches? No man is rich who cannot carry away with him that which he has, for that which is left behind, is not our own but another's.

Gen. v. 24.
Wisd. iv. 11.
2 Kings ii. 11.

7. Enoch was rich who carried away with him that which he had, and laid up all the riches of his goodness in the heavenly treasure-house; he was *taken away lest that wickedness should alter his understanding.* Elias was rich, who riding in a chariot of fire carried the treasures of his virtues up to the heavenly mansions. Not small were the riches he left to his heir, and yet he himself did not lose them. Who would have called him poor even then, when

1 King. xvii 9.

being himself in need of the sustenance of daily food, he was sent to the widow that he might be nourished by her, when at his voice the heaven was shut and opened, when at his word the barrel of meal and the cruse of oil failed not for three years, but overflowed; when it was replenished not diminished by use? Who would call him poor

2 Kings i. 14.
Ib. ii. 8.

at whose word there came fire down from heaven, whom the river impassible by others could not retard, retiring back to its source that the prophet might pass over dry-shod?

8. Ancient history tells us of two neighbours, king Ahab and the poor Naboth; which of these do we believe to be the richer, which the poorer? The one, endowed with the royal support of riches, insatiable and not to be replenished with wealth, coveted the little vineyard of the poor man; the other, despising in his mind the golden fortunes of kings, and imperial treasures, was content with his own vines. Does not he appear richer and more kingly, who was sufficient to himself, and controlled his own desires, coveting nothing that belonged to another? Does not he, on the other hand, appear most needy, in whose eyes his own gold was accounted vile, and another man's vine precious. But learn for what reason he was most needy:

because *riches unjustly gotten are vomited up again*, but *the root of the righteous yieldeth fruit, and flourishes like a palm-tree.* [TO SIMPLICIAN. Job. xx. 15.]

9. Is not he more needy than the poor man, who passeth away like a shadow? To-day the ungodly is in great power, to-morrow he is not, and his place can no more be found. But what is it to be rich, unless it be to abound? But who abounds whose mind is contracted, and therefore straightened, and what abundance can there be in straits? He therefore is not rich who does not abound. Wherefore David says well, *The rich lack and suffer hunger*; for although they possessed the treasures of the Divine Scriptures, they still lacked in that they did not understand, and hungered in that they tasted not the food of spiritual grace. [Prov. xii. 12 Ps. xcii. 11 Ps. xxxvii. 35, 36. Ps. xxxiv 10 LXX, Vulg.]

10. Nothing can therefore be richer than the temper of the wise man, nothing poorer than that of the fool. For since the kingdom of God belongs to the poor, what can be richer? And therefore the Apostle says well, *O the depth of the riches both of the wisdom and knowledge of God!* Well also David, who *had as great delight in the way of the heavenly testimonies as in all manner of riches.* And Moses says expressly, *Naphtali, satisfied with favour.* Now Naphtali means when translated, 'abundance' or 'increase.' So that to be satisfied and to abound go together, but where there is the hunger of desire and insatiable lust, there truly is poverty. But since scarcely any desire of money or of this world can be satisfied, it is added, *full with blessing.* [S. Matt. v. 3. Rom. xi. 33. Ps. cxix. 14. Deut. xxxiii 23. Ib. 23.]

11. It is in accordance with these principles that the Apostle Peter has declared that the ornament of women consists not in gold and silver and apparel, but in the secret and hidden man of the heart. Wherefore let no woman put off the dress of piety, the ornament of grace, the inheritance of eternal life. [1 S. Pet. iii 3.]

Farewell: love me, for I love you.

LETT. 39.

A.D 387.

LETTER XXXIX.

S. AMBROSE in this Letter seeks to rouse Faustinus from excessive grief for his sister's death, first on the ground of duty towards the children left to his care and protection, and then on the higher ground of submission to the Divine will, and realization of Christian hopes.

AMBROSE TO FAUSTINUS, GREETING.

1. I was well aware that you would grieve with bitter grief for the death of your sister: still you should not go into banishment, but rather give yourself back to us, for although mourners are little inclined to receive consolation, it is sometimes necessary for them. But you have fled to the recesses of the mountains, and made your dwelling in the caves of wild beasts, laying aside all customary human converse and, what is worse, the use of your own reason.

2. Is it in accordance with your esteem for your sister, that human nature, which ought to be much regarded by you for producing a woman so excellent, should on her account be of less value in your eyes? In quitting this life it doubtless was a consolation to her to believe that she left you behind her as a parent to your nephews, a guardian of their tender years, a succour to their destitution; but you so utterly withhold yourself both from your nephews and from us, that we do not reap any benefit from what she thus found a ground of consolation. These dear pledges invite you not to grieve, but to comfort them, that in seeing you they may believe their mother to be still alive. In you then let them recognize her, in you let them enjoy her presence, in you think that she still survives to them.

3. But you grieve that she has been lately cut off in the flower of her age. This however is the common fate not only of men, but of states and countries themselves. Coming from Bononia[a] you left behind you Claterna, Bononia

---

[a] S. Ambrose is here imitating the consolation offered by Ser. Sulpicius to Cicero on the death of his daughter See Ep. ad Div. iv, 5, 4

itself, Matina, Rhegium; Brixillum was on your right, in front of you Placentia, by its very name still recalling its ancient lustre, on the left you saw with pity the wastes of the Apennines, you surveyed the fortresses of these once flourishing tribes, and remembered them with sorrowful affection. Do not then the carcases of so many half-ruined cities, and states stretched on their bier beneath your eyes, do not these remind you that the decease of one woman, holy and excellent as she was, is much less deplorable, especially as these are for ever laid prostrate and destroyed, but she though removed from us for a while is passing a more blessed life elsewhere?

TO FAUSTINUS

4. Wherefore I deem that you ought not so much to deplore her, as to offer for her your prayers; make her not sorrowful by your tears, rather commend her soul to God by oblations.

5. Perhaps however you will declare yourself to be secure of her merits and faith, you cannot endure the feeling of regret at seeing her no longer after the flesh, which is to you a better grief. And does not the Apostolic saying move you that *henceforth we know no man after the flesh; yea, though we have known Christ after the flesh, yet now henceforth know we Him no more.* For our flesh cannot be perpetual and lasting, it must needs die that it may rise again, it must be dissolved that it may rest, and sin come to an end. We too have known many according to the flesh, but now we know them no more. *We have known the Lord Jesus,* says the Apostle, *after the flesh, yet now henceforth know we Him no more.* For now He has put off the coil of the body, and is not seen in fashion as a Man, but has died for all and all are dead in Him, to the intent that being renewed by Him and quickened in the Spirit they may no longer live to themselves but to Christ. Wherefore the same Apostle also says elsewhere, *I live, yet not I, but Christ liveth in me.*

2 Cor. v. 16.

Gal. ii. 20.

6. And well indeed was it that he who had before known Christ after the flesh, who had before persecuted and oppressed with bitter hatred the disciples of the Man, and the attendants on His bodily presence, but who now recognized His invisible workings, discerning not His bodily presence

Acts ix. 1. &c.

but His power,—well indeed was it that he became the teacher of the Gentiles, and began to instruct and prepare the worshippers of His Divinity to become preachers of the Gospel. Wherefore he added, *if any man be in Christ, he is a new creature,* that is, he that is perfect in Christ is a new creature, for all flesh is imperfect. And the Lord saith, *My spirit shall not always strive with man, for that he also is flesh.* No carnal man then is in Christ, but *if any man be in Christ he is a new creature,* formed by newness not of nature but of grace. These *old things* which are according to the flesh *have past away, all things are made new.* And what are they but the things which *the scribe instructed unto the kingdom of heaven* knows, *like unto that householder, who brings forth out of his treasure things new and old;* neither old things without new, nor new things without old? Thus too the Church saith, *things new and old have I laid up for Thee.* For old things, that is, the hidden mysteries of the Law are passed away, all things are made new in Christ.

7. This is the new creature of which the Apostle writing to the Galatians saith, *For in Jesus Christ neither circumcision availeth any thing nor uncircumcision, but a new creature,* already our flesh now renewed flourishes, and having before borne the thorns of inveterate sin hath now found the fruit of grace. Why then need we grieve, if we can now say to the soul, *thy youth is renewed like the eagles?* And why should we bewail the dead, now that by our Lord Jesus *the world has been reconciled to the Father?* Since then we hold the benefits which Christ hath given, we are to you as well as to all ambassadors in Christ's stead, that you may know His Gift to be irrevocable, that you may believe what you always have believed, and not bring your opinion into discredit by too much sorrow. For the Lord Jesus was made sin that He might *take away the sin of the world,* and we all might be *made the righteousness of God in Him,* now no longer subject to the penalty of sin, but sure of the reward of righteousness.

Farewell; love me, for I love you.

LETTER XL.

TO THEODOSIUS
A.D. 388.

IN the year 388 A.D. the synagogue of the Jews at Callinicum in Mesopotamia was burnt by the Christians, at the instance, it was asserted, of the Bishop. Some monks also in the same district, having been insulted by some Valentinian heretics, while singing Psalms in processsion on the Festival of the Maccabees, (Aug 1st.) had burnt their conventicle. Theodosius had ordered that the Bishop should re-build the synagogue at his own cost, and that the monks should be punished, and the whole matter carefully sifted, and justice done. This Letter is written by S. Ambrose to remonstrate. He urges his plea with the boldest importunity, and, as he tells his sister in the following letter, Theodosius eventually yielded.

TO THE MOST GRACIOUS PRINCE AND BLESSED EMPEROR HIS MAJESTY THEODOSIUS, BISHOP AMBROSE SENDS GREETING.

1. NEARLY incessant are the cares which harass me, most excellent Emperor, but never was I in such trouble as at present; for I see I must be on my guard against the danger even of a charge of sacrilege. Wherefore I beseech you patiently to hear my address. For if I am unworthy to be heard by you, I am unworthy to offer for you, or to have your vows and prayers intrusted to me. Will you not hear him whom you wish to be heard in your behalf? Will you not hear him pleading for himself whom you have heard when pleading for others? Will you not dread the consequences of your own judgment; and fear to render him unworthy to be heard in your behalf, by treating him as unworthy of a hearing from you.

2. But it is neither the part of an Emperor to deny liberty of speech, nor of a Bishop not to utter what he thinks. There is no quality more amiable and popular in an Emperor than to cherish freedom even in those who owe him military allegiance. For there is this difference between good and bad rulers, that the good love freedom, the bad slavery. And there is nothing in a Bishop so offensive in God's sight, or so base before men, as not freely to declare his opinions. For it is written, *I spake of Thy testimonies also even before kings, and was not ashamed,* Ps. cxix. 46. and in another place, *Son of man, I have made thee a watchman unto the house of Israel; with the intent,* it proceeds, Ezek. iii. 17.

that if the righteous man doth turn from his righteousness and commit iniquity, because thou hast not given him warning[1] *that is,* hast not told him what to beware of, *his righteousness which he hath done shall not be remembered; but his blood will I require at thine hand. Nevertheless, if thou warn the righteous man, that the righteous sin not, and he doth not sin, he shall surely live, because he is warned; also thou shalt deliver thy soul.*

3. I prefer then, to have fellowship with your Majesty in good rather than in evil; and therefore the silence of a Bishop ought to be displeasing to your Clemency, and his freedom pleasing. For you will be implicated in the danger of my silence, you will share in the benefits of my outspokenness. I am not then an officious meddler in matters beyond my province, an intruder in the concerns of others, but I comply with my duty, I obey the commandment of our God. This I do chiefly from love and regard to you, and from a wish to preserve your well-being. But if I am not believed, or am forbidden to act on this motive, then in truth I speak from fear of offending God. For if my own danger could deliver you, I would consent to be offered for you, though not willingly, for I would rather that without danger to myself you should be accepted and glorified by God. But if I am to suffer under the charge of silence and dissimulation without effecting your exculpation I had rather you should deem me too importunate than useless or mercenary. For it is written, in the words of the holy Apostle Paul, whose teaching you cannot gainsay, *Be instant in season, out of season. reprove, rebuke, exhort with all long-suffering and doctrine.*

4. We then also have One Whom it is even more dangerous to displease; especially as even Emperors themselves are not offended with any man for fulfilling his function, but you patiently give ear to every one speaking concerning his own department, nay you reprove him for not acting in accordance with his line of duty. Can that then which you readily accept from your soldiers, seem to you offensive in a Bishop; seeing that we speak not according to our own wills, but as we are commanded? For you know that it is written, *when ye shall be brought before*

governors and kings take no thought how or what ye shall speak, for it shall be given you in that same hour what ye shall speak. For it is not ye that speak, but the Spirit of your Father Which speaketh in you. Were it in civil causes that I had to speak, my not obtaining an audience would not give me such apprehension, although even then justice ought to be observed, but in God's cause whom will you hear, if you hear not the Bishop, at whose great peril it is that sin is committed? Who will dare to tell you the truth, if a Bishop does not?

5. I know that you are pious, merciful, meek and gentle, having at heart the faith and fear of the Lord; but some failings oftentimes escape our notice. Some men *have a zeal of God, but not according to knowledge*, and we ought, I think, to beware lest this steal even over faithful souls. I know your piety towards God, your lenity towards men; I am myself indebted to your courtesy for many benefits. Wherefore I feel greater fear, and deeper solicitude lest even your own judgment should hereafter condemn me for having failed, through cowardice or flattery, in saving you from a fall. If I had seen you sin against myself, I ought not to have kept silence, for it is written, *If thy brother shall trespass against thee, go and tell him his fault; then rebuke him before two or three witnesses, and if he shall neglect to hear them, tell it unto the Church.* Shall I then be silent in the cause of God? Now then let us consider what it is I have to apprehend.

6. The military Count of the East[a] reported that a synagogue had been burnt, and that this had been done at the instigation of the Bishop. You decided that the others should be punished, and that the synagogue should be rebuilt by the Bishop himself. I will not insist on the propriety of calling for the Bishop's own statement; for the clergy are wont to check disturbances and desirous of peace,

---

[a] 'Oriens' or 'the East' was the title of the great civil 'diocese' which included Syria, Palestine, Cilicia, Cyprus, Mesopotamia, and some adjacent districts, and corresponded to the Patriarchate of Antioch in the ecclesiastical division. It was originally under one chief called 'Comes orientis,' but it would appear from this passage, as is asserted by Gothofred, that the civil and military functions had been divided, and there were now two officers, 'Comes orientis militarium partium,' and 'Comes orientis civilium partium.' The subject is somewhat obscure.

Lett. 40. save when they are themselves moved by some offence against God or insult to the Church. But suppose this Bishop to have been too eager in setting fire to this synagogue, and now to grow timid before the judgment-seat, has your Majesty no fear, lest he should acquiesce in your sentence, no apprehension of his becoming apostate?

7. Do you not fear, what will certainly be the case, that he will meet your officer with a refusal; and so he will be obliged to make him either an apostate or a martyr, and both of these are adverse to your interests and savour of persecution, that he should be forced either to become an apostate or undergo martyrdom. You see then whereunto this matter tends; if you think the Bishop firm, avoid driving his firmness to martyrdom; if you think him frail, shun exposing his frailty to a fall. For a heavy responsibility lies on him who has caused one who is weak to fall.

8. Under these circumstances I suppose that the Bishop will say that he himself kindled the fire, gathered the crowd, collected the people; so as not to lose an opportunity of martyrdom, and in place of the weak to offer up a bolder victim. O happy falsehood; obtaining for others acquittal, for himself Grace. This is my request also to your Majesty, that you would turn your vengeance upon me, and, if you consider this a crime, impute it to me. Why do you order the absent to be punished? you have the guilty person before you, you hear his confession, I openly affirm that I myself set the synagogue on fire, or at least, that I ordered others to do so; that there might be no place in which Christ is denied. And if it be objected, why did I not set it on fire in this very city? It began to be burnt, I reply, by the Divine judgment, my work was superseded. And to speak the truth, I was the less zealous because I expected no punishment. Why should I do that which being unavenged would also be unrewarded? These words are a shock to modesty, but they also bring back grace; they provide against the commission of that which may offend Almighty God.

9. But suppose that no one will cite the Bishop to do this; for this is what I have begged of your Clemency, and

though I have not yet read that the edict is revoked, I will nevertheless assume it to be so. But what if other more timid persons, from a fear of death offer to rebuild the synagogue from their own funds, or the Count, finding this previously ordained, should himself command it to be restored at the expense of the Christians? Your Majesty will then have an apostate Count, and you will entrust your victorious banner, your labarum, which is consecrated by the name of Christ, to one who is the restorer of the synagogue which knows not Christ. Command the labarum to be carried into the synagogue, and let us see if they do not resist.

10. Shall then a building be raised for perfidious Jews out of the spoils of the Church, and shall that patrimony, which by Christ's mercy has been assigned to Christians, be transferred to the temples of the unbelieving? We read that temples were in former days erected from the spoils of the Cimbri and other enemies of Rome. Shall the Jews inscribe this title on the front of their synagogue: 'The temples of impiety built from the spoils of Christians?'

11. But the maintenance of discipline is perhaps what influences your Majesty. Is the show of discipline then weightier than the cause of religion? Police should give place to religion.

12. Has your Majesty never heard that when Julian commanded the temple at Jerusalem to be restored, they who cleared away the rubbish were destroyed by fire from heaven? Are you not afraid lest this should now happen? Surely you ought not to have commanded what Julian commanded.

13. But why are you thus moved? Is it generally because a public building has been burnt, or because it is a synagogue? If you are moved by the conflagration of the meanest edifice, (and what else could there have been in so obscure a town,) does not your Majesty remember how many prefects' houses have been burnt at Rome, and yet no man enacted vengeance for them? Nay, if any Emperor had desired to punish such an act severely, he would rather have injured the cause of those who had suffered so great a loss. Which then is the more fitting, that the partial

burning of some houses at Callinicum [b], or the burning of the city of Rome should be punished, if indeed either of them ought to have been so. At Constantinople, a while ago, the Bishop's [c] house was burnt, and your Majesty's son interceded with you, that you would not avenge the wrong done to him, the youthful Emperor, nor the burning of the Bishop's palace. Your Majesty should consider, that, if you should in like manner command this act to be punished, he may again intercede to prevent it. The former boon however was happily obtained from the father by the son, for it was only fitting that he should first remit the injury to himself. A good distribution of favour and well allotted it is, that the son should be petitioned for his own loss, and the father for the offence against his son. In this case there is nothing which you need keep back on your son's account, beware also lest you derogate ought from God.

14. There is then no adequate reason for any such commotion, that the people should be so severely punished for the burning of any building; much less seeing that it is a synagogue that has been burnt, a place of unbelief, a house of impiety, a receptacle of madness, which God Himself hath condemned. For thus we read what the Lord our God spake by the mouth of Jeremiah, *Therefore will I do unto this house, which is called by My Name, wherein ye trust, and unto the place which I gave to you, and to your fathers, as I have done to Shiloh. And I will cast you out of My sight, as I have cast out all your brethren, even the whole seed of Ephraim. Therefore pray not thou for this people, neither lift up cry nor prayer for them, neither make intercession to Me, for I will not hear thee. Seest thou not what they do in the cities of Judah?* God forbids him to intercede for those whom you think worthy of being avenged.

15. Were I pleading according to the law of nations, I should assuredly recount how many Churches the Jews burnt in the time of Julian's reign: two at Damascus, one

---

[b] Callinicum was in Osrhoene, a name given to the north-western part of Mesopotamia.

[c] Socrates, Bv ch. 13, mentions that Nectarius' house was burnt by the Arian party in the same year in which this letter was written.

When Churches were destroyed no vengeance was taken. 263

of which is but just repaired, and that at the expense, not of the synagogue, but of the Church, while the other is still a mass of shapeless ruins. Churches were likewise burnt at Gaza, Ascalon, Berytus, and nearly every town in that region, and yet no man asked for vengeance. At Alexandria too the most beautiful Church of all was burnt down by the Gentiles and Jews. The Church has not been avenged, shall then the synagogue be?

16. And shall the burning of the temple of the Valentinians likewise be punished? For what but a temple is the place where Gentiles assemble? The Gentiles indeed reckon twelve gods, the Valentinians worship thirty two Æons[d], whom they call gods. Concerning these I am informed that they have called for punishment upon some monks. For the Valentinians having endeavoured to stop them as they were going in procession according to ancient custom, chanting psalms, to celebrate the festival of the Maccabees, the monks exasperated by this affront, set fire to one of their rudely constructed temples in some country village.

17. How many have to offer themselves to this choice, remembering that in Julian's time he who threw down the altar and disturbed the sacrifice was condemned by the judge, and suffered martyrdom. And accordingly the judge who tried him was never considered other than a persecutor, no man would associate with him, no man deemed him worthy of a kiss of greeting. Were he not now dead, I should fear your Majesty's taking vengeance upon him. Nevertheless he escaped not the Divine vengeance, but saw his son die before him.

18. But it is reported that the judge was ordered to take cognizance of the matter, and was informed that he ought not to have reported upon it, but to have punished it, that the offerings which had been taken away were to be demanded back. Other particulars I will omit; but when the Jews burnt our Churches, nothing was restored, nothing demanded, nothing sought for. But what could the synagogue possess in that distant place, when everything in it was but of little value, nothing precious or abundant.

[d] See a note in Newman's Fleury, p. 160.

LETT. 40. In short of what could a fire deprive the treacherous Jews? These are devices of the Jews who wish to accuse us falsely, that through their representations an extraordinary military tribunal may be appointed, and an officer sent, who perhaps will say what one said here before your accession, 'How shall Christ help us, when we fight for the Jews against Christ? when we are sent to take vengeance on their behalf? They have lost their own armies, and they wish to destroy ours.'

19. Nay, what are the calumnies into which they will not rush, who by false witnesses have slandered Christ Himself? who are false even in matters relating to God? Whom will they not charge with the guilt of this sedition? whom will they not thirst after, even though they know them not? They desire to see rank after rank of Christians in chains, to see the necks of the faithful placed under the yoke, the servants of God hidden in darkness, smitten with the axe, delivered to the fire, or sent to the mines, that their pains may be slow and lingering.

20. Will your Majesty give this triumph to the Jews over the Church of God? this victory over the people of Christ, this joy to the unbelievers, this felicity to the Synagogue, this grief to the Church? They will place this solemnity among their feast-days; numbering it among those wherein they triumphed over the Ammonites, or Canaanites, or over Pharaoh king of Egypt, or which delivered them from the hands of Nebuchadnezzar king of Babylon. This festival they will add in memory of the triumph they have gained over Christ's people.

21. Although they refuse to be bound by Roman laws, deeming them even criminal, they now pretend to claim vengeance according to those laws. Where were those laws, when they burnt the roofs of the consecrated Basilicas? If Julian avenged not the Church because he was an Apostate, will your Majesty, being a Christian, avenge the injury done to the Synagogue?

22. And what will Christ hereafter say to you? Do you not remember what he said to holy David by the prophet Nathan? 'I have chosen thee the youngest of thy brethren, and from private life have made thee Emperor.

2 Sam. vii 8.

I have placed thy offspring upon the Imperial throne. I have put barbarous nations under thy feet, I have given thee peace, I have delivered thine enemy captive into thy hands. Thou hadst no corn to support thy army, I opened to thee the enemies' gates, the enemies' granaries, by their own hand; they gave thee the very stores which they had provided for themselves. I confounded the counsels of thy enemy, so that he laid bare his own plans. The very usurper of thy empire I so bound, and so fettered his mind, that although he had the means of flying from you he shut himself in with all his followers, as if fearing lest any should escape you. His lieutenant [e] and his forces on the other element, whom I had before dispersed to prevent their combining to make war on thee, I now called together again to render thy victory complete. Thy army, an assemblage of many fierce nations, I caused to keep faith and peace and concord, as if they had been one nation. And when there was imminent danger lest the perfidious plots of the barbarians should penetrate the Alps, I gave thee victory within the very barrier of the Alps, that thy victory might be without loss. Thus I made thee to triumph over thy enemy, and thou art giving my enemies a triumph over my people.'

23. Was it not the very reason why Maximus was abandoned, that before he set out on his expedition, hearing that a synagogue had been burnt at Rome, he sent an edict thither, acting as if he were the guardian of public order. Wherefore the Christians said, No good awaits this man. That king is become a Jew, and we have heard of him as a protector of order, but Christ, who died for sinners, shortly after put him to the proof [f]. And if this was said of words only, what will be said of actual punishment? So he was soon defeated by the Franks and by the Saxons, in Sicily, at Siscia [g], at Petavio, and in every quar-

[e] Andragathius, who commanded a fleet in Maximus' interest expecting Theodosius to come to Italy by sea.
[f] The Benedictine editors say 'tota hæc pericope in uno Cod. Reg desideratur. forte non male.' It is difficult to elicit any sense from it
[g] Siscia, now Sissek, was a large town in upper Pannonia, on the south bank of the Save. Petavio, now Pettau, was on the Drave. It seems likely that 'in Sicilia' should be omitted, as being only a false meaning for 'Siscia' There is no mention of Sicily being in any way connected with the war. But see Tillemont, Theod. art. xlv.

ter of the globe. What has a devout man in common with an unbeliever? The precedents of his impiety ought to be obliterated together with the impious man himself. That which injured the vanquished, that at which he stumbled, the victor ought to condemn, not to imitate.

24. Now I have recounted these things to you not as though you were ungrateful; rather I have spoken of them as being rightly bestowed, that reminded thereby you may love much, as being one on whom much has been bestowed. To Simon's answer our Lord thus replied, *Thou hast rightly judged;* and then, turning straightway to the woman who had anointed His feet with ointment, and was the type of the Church, He said to Simon, *Wherefore I say unto thee, her sins, which are many, are forgiven, for she loved much · but to whom little is forgiven, the same loveth little.* This is that woman who entered the house of the Pharisee, and cast out the Jew, but gained Christ. For the Church shut out the Synagogue, and why is it now attempted, that, with the servant of Christ, that is, from the breast of faith, and abode of Christ, the Synagogue should shut out the Church.

25. It is from affection and regard for your Majesty, that I have introduced these things into my pleading. The beneficence which has led you, at my request, to liberate many persons from exile, from prison, from the extreme penalties of death, obliges me to incur the danger of offending you for the sake of your own good, rather than lose in one moment that privilege of every Bishop which I have for so long possessed. For no man can feel greater confidence than he who zealously loves, no man certainly ought to injure him who is careful for his well-being. And yet it is not the loss of favour I deprecate, but the danger to salvation.

26. Yet how important it is that your Majesty should not think of enquiry or punishment in a matter with regard to which no one up to this time has ever held enquiry or inflicted punishment! It is a grievous thing to hazard your faith for the sake of Jews. When Gideon killed the consecrated calf, the Gentiles [h] said, Let the gods them-

---

[h] S. Ambrose is quoting from memory and slightly varies the facts from the narrative in book of Judges.

selves avenge this affront towards them. Who is to avenge the Synagogue? Christ Whom they slew, Whom they denied? Or will God the Father avenge them, seeing that by rejecting the Son they have rejected the Father also. Who is to avenge the heresy of the Valentinians? how will your Piety be able to avenge them, seeing that you have commanded them to be shut out, and forbidden them to meet together? And should I bring forward to you the example of King Josiah as approved of God, will you condemn in this case that for which he is praised.

27. But if you do not place sufficient confidence in me, let your Majesty command the presence of those bishops whom you do approve, and let the question be discussed, what ought to be done so as not to injure the Faith. If in financial matters you consult your Courts, how much more fitting is it that in the cause of religion you should consult the Bishops of the Lord?

28. Let your Clemency consider what dangerous spies and liers in wait the Church has against her, if they find ever so small an opening they will plant a dart therein. I speak after the manner of men; but God is feared more than men, and is rightly preferred to Emperors themselves. If any man thinks obedience should be paid to a friend, a parent, or a neighbour, am I wrong in deeming that God should be obeyed, and that in preference to all others. Let your Majesty consult for your own well-being, or suffer me to consult for mine.

29. What shall I hereafter answer, if it shall appear that by an edict issued from hence Christians have been slain by the sword, or beaten to death with clubs or thongs loaded with lead? How shall I justify such an act, how shall I excuse it to those Bishops who having discharged the office of the priesthood for thirty years, nay for many more, have now bitterly to bewail, being deprived of their sacred functions and called to undertake municipal offices. If[1] those who fight for you are set free after a certain period of service, how much more ought you to consider those

---

[1] See a learned note in Newman's Fleury vol 1 p. 162, on the exemption of the Clergy from municipal offices, compare also Letter xviii. 14, and the note there.

who fight for God! How I repeat, shall I defend this to the Bishops who complain in behalf of the clergy, and write word that the Churches are overborne by violent oppression.

30. This however I desired should be made known to your Majesty; about this you will deign to deliberate and direct according to your will; but as to that which distresses and rightly distresses myself, exclude and reject it from your consideration. You do yourself whatsoever you have commanded to be done; even if he[k] do it not, I would rather that you should be merciful than that he should refuse to do what he has been commanded.

31. Here are persons in dealing with whom you ought still to invite and earn the Clemency of God towards the Roman empire; here are persons for whom rather than for yourself you have to hope; let their grace, their wellbeing, appeal to you in what I now say. I fear your entrusting your cause to the judgement of others. As yet you are committed to nothing. Herein I will pledge myself for you to our God, fear not your oath. That change cannot be displeasing to God which is made for His honour. You have no need to alter your former letter whether it be yet dispatched or not, but command another to be written which shall be replete with faith and piety. It is open to you to change, it is not open to me to keep back the truth.

32. You have forgiven the people of Antioch[l] their offence against you, you have recalled the daughters of your enemy[m], you have committed them to be nurtured by their relative, you have bestowed money from your treasury on the mother of your enemy. This great piety, this great faith towards God will be obscured by your present act. Having thus spared your armed foes, and preserved your enemies, do not, I beseech you, so eagerly seek for vengeance upon Christians.

---

[k] i. e. the Count of the East
[l] This refers to the famous sedition at Antioch, when the mob, enraged at the imposition of new taxes, overthrew the Emperor's statues, and dragged them through the city. After a period of suspense, during which S Chrysostom preached the Homilies on the Statues, Theodosius, who had at first been violently enraged, sent them a free pardon. This was in the previous year
[m] i. e of Maximus.

33. And now I entreat your Majesty not to disdain to listen to my fears both for yourself and myself; for it is the saying of an holy man, *Woe is me, wherefore was I born to see this misery of my people?* is it that I should incur the risk of offending God? Assuredly I have done what is most respectful to you: I have sought that you should listen to me in the palace, that you might not have to listen to me in the Church.

TO MARCEL-LINA
1 Macc. ii. 7.

LETTER XLI.

A D. 388.

THE BROTHER TO HIS SISTER.

IN this Letter to his sister S. Ambrose relates the sequel of the affair referred to in the preceding one. That Letter failed to produce the effect which he had hoped for, and so he was driven to fulfil the threat with which he had ended it, and 'make the Emperor listen to him in the Church.' He gives his sister a full account of the sermon which he preached before the Emperor, and how he insisted on a promise that the matter should be quashed altogether, before he would celebrate the Eucharist, and how the Emperor at last gave way, and so all ended as he had wished.

1. You have kindly written me word, holy sister, that you are still anxious about me, because I told you of my own anxiety; this makes me wonder that you have not received the letter, in which I told you that tranquillity had been restored to me. Complaints had been made that a synagogue of the Jews had been burnt by the Christians, at the instigation of their Bishop, and also a conventicle of the Valentinians; and while I was at Aquileia a decree was issued that the synagogue should be rebuilt by the Bishop, and that the monks who had set fire to this building of the Valentinians should be punished. Wherefore, when I found that my personal endeavours were of little avail, I wrote and despatched a letter to the Emperor, and on his going to the Church, I delivered this discourse.

2. In the book of the Prophet it is written, *Take to thyself the rod of an almond tree;* and with what intent the Lord said this to the prophet we ought to consider, for it

Jer. i. 11.

was not written without a purpose, and we also read in the Pentateuch that the rod of Aaron the priest, budded after being long laid up. Now the rod seems to signify that prophetic or sacerdotal authority ought to be unswerving, and to exhort rather to what is useful than to what is pleasing.

<small>LETT. 41.
Num.
xvii. 8.</small>

3. And the reason why the prophet is bidden to take the rod of an almond is this, that the fruit of this tree has a bitter rind and hard shell, while its inside is juicy, and so in like manner the prophet should hold out what is hard and bitter, and not shrink from declaring painful things. So too with the priest: his teaching may seem bitter for a time to some, and, like Aaron's rod, may for a long while be laid up in the ears of dissemblers, yet afterwards, when it is thought to have withered, it puts forth buds.

4. Hence the Apostle says, *What will ye, shall I come unto you with a rod, or in love, and in the spirit of meekness.* First he speaks of *a rod*, and as with *the rod of an almond tree* had smitten the wanderers, that he might afterwards comfort them with the spirit of meekness. Just so did meekness restore the man whom the rod had driven from the Divine sacraments. To his disciple too he gave the same injunctions, *Reprove, beseech, rebuke.* Here are two harsh terms and one gentle; but they are only harsh, that they may themselves be softened. For like as bitter food or drink becomes sweet to these bodies which are laden with excess of gall, and on the other hand sweet repasts are bitter to them, so also when the mind is wounded it languishes under the flattering touch of pleasure, but is healed again by the bitterness of correction.

<small>1 Cor. iv. 21.</small>

<small>2 Cor. ii. 10.</small>

<small>2 Tim. iv. 2.</small>

5. Thus much let it suffice to have gathered from the lesson from the Prophets, let us next consider what that from the Gospel would teach us: *And one of the Pharisees desired the Lord Jesus that He would eat with him; and He went into the Pharisee's house and sat down to meat. And behold, a woman in the city, which was a sinner, when she knew that Jesus sat at meat in the Pharisee's house brought an alabaster box of ointment, and stood at His feet behind Him weeping.* And then the passage was recited as far as the words, *Thy faith hath saved thee, go in peace.*

<small>S. Luke vii. 36—38.</small>

How simple, I added, are the words of this Gospel lesson, how profound its counsels! Wherefore, seeing that it is spoken by the *great Counsellor*, let us consider its depth.

TO MARCELLINA

Is. ix. 6

6. Our Lord Jesus Christ believed that kindness has a greater power of constraining and inciting men to do what is right than fear; and that love avails more for correction than terror. And so, when He came on earth by the Virgin's womb, He first sent His free grace, forgiving our sins in baptism to make us more grateful to Him. Then if we will repay Him with such services as befit grateful men, He has declared by this example that He will give fresh gifts of grace to every man. Had He only remitted to us our first debt, He would have seemed cautious rather than merciful, more heedful of our amendment than munificent in His rewards. To allure is merely the cunning of a narrow mind, but it is befitting to God that those whom He has invited by grace He should lead forward by the increase of that grace. And so He first bestows on us His gifts in baptism, and afterwards if we serve him faithfully gives more abundantly. And so the benefits of Christ are both the incentives and the rewards of virtue.

7. Let no man be alarmed at the word *creditor*. We were indeed under an unforgiving creditor, who could not be satisfied by anything less than the death of his debtor; then the Lord Jesus came and found us burthened with a heavy debt. This debt no man could satisfy by his natural innocence; I had nothing of my own wherewith to purchase my freedom, and therefore He bestowed on me a new kind of acquittance; He made me debtor to Himself, seeing I had no means of discharging my debt. Now we became debtors not by nature but by our own fault; by our sins we contracted heavy debts, so that we who were free came under a bond; for he is a debtor who has received of his creditor's money. Now sin is from the devil, this is the money which belongs to the wicked one as his patrimony; for as virtues are the treasure of Christ, so crimes are the riches of the devil. He had brought the human race under the perpetual slavery of an inherited liability by that heavy debt which our improvident ancestor transmitted by inheritance to his posterity. But then the Lord Jesus came,

He gave His life for the life of all, and shed His blood for the blood of all.

8. Thus we have changed our creditor, not discharged our debt, nay we may even say we have discharged it, for although it remains, our bond is cancelled, the Lord Jesus having *said to the prisoners, Go forth; to them that are in darkness, Shew yourselves;* your sins therefore are forgiven. Thus He has forgiven all, nor is there any one to whom He has not shewn mercy. For so it is written, that He has *forgiven all trespasses; blotting out the hand-writing of the ordinances that was against us.* Why then do we hold the bonds of others? why would we exact our claims from others when we have obtained remission of our own? He Who has shewn mercy to all requires of each of us that what he remembers to have been remitted to himself he should himself remit to others.

9. Beware lest you begin to incur heavier blame as a creditor than you did as a debtor; as that servant in the Gospel to whom his Lord forgave all his debt began to exact from his fellow servant what he himself had not paid; wherefore his Lord was wroth, and exacted from him with the greatest severity what he had before remitted to him. Let us beware therefore lest the same evil befal us, lest by not remitting our debts we also be called on to pay what had been forgiven us, for so it is written in the words of the Lord Jesus, *So likewise shall My heavenly Father do also unto you, if ye from your hearts forgive not every one his brother their trespasses.* Let us then forgive small things to whom great have been forgiven, and understand that the more we forgive the more acceptable we shall be to God, for we are so much the more acceptable to God the more we have been forgiven.

10. Further, when the Pharisee was asked by our Lord, *Which of them loved him most,* he answered, *I suppose that he to whom he forgave most.* Whereupon the Lord said, *Thou hast rightly judged.* The Pharisees judgment is praised, but his affection is blamed. Of others he judges correctly, but what he believes of others, he does not believe in his own case. Thus you hear the Jew praising the discipline of the Church, praising its true graces, honour-

ing its priests; but when you exhort him to believe he refuses to do so, and thus follows not himself what he praises in us. His eulogy then is not complete, though Christ has said to him, *Thou hast rightly judged,* for Cain also offered rightly, but did not divide rightly, wherefore God said unto him, *If thou offer rightly, but divide not rightly, thou hast sinned; be still.* And so this man offered rightly, because he judges that Christ, having forgiven Christians many sins, ought to be more earnestly loved by them; but he has not divided rightly, because he believes that He Who remitted the sins of men could possibly be ignorant of them.

TO MARCEL-LINA

Gen. iv. 7.

11. And therefore He says to Simon, *Seest thou this woman? I entered into thine house, thou gavest Me no water for My feet, but she hath washed My feet with tears.* We are all one body of Christ, the Head is God, and we are the members: some perhaps as the Prophets, may be the eyes; others the teeth, as the Apostles, who have filled our hearts with the food of the Evangelical preaching, and of whom it is written, *His eyes shall be red with wine, and his teeth white with milk.* They are His hands who perform good works: His belly are they who bestow the strength of nourishment on the poor: Some too are His feet also, and would that I might be counted worthy to be even His heel. He then who pardons the very lowest their sins, pours water on the feet of Christ, and while he frees only the mean, yet washes the feet of Christ Himself.

S. Luke vii. 44.

Gen. xlix. 12.

12. He also pours water on the feet of Christ who cleanses his conscience from the pollution of sin; for Christ walks in the breast of each of us. Beware then lest your conscience be defiled, or you thus begin to stain the feet of Christ. Beware lest He encounter the thorn of wickedness within you, whereby His heel as He walks in you may be wounded. The reason why the Pharisee did not pour water on the feet of Christ was because his soul was not clean from the stain of wickedness. How could he cleanse his conscience, who had not received that water which Christ gives? But the Church has that water, and the Church has tears, the waters of Baptism and the tears of penitence. For faith, which mourns for former sins, is also wont to

LETT. 41. avoid fresh ones, wherefore Simon the Pharisee as he had no water so neither had he tears. For how could he have them, who did no penance? but as he believed not in Christ so neither had he tears. Had he had them, he would have washed his eyes that he might see Christ, Whom as yet, when he first sat down, he saw not. For had he seen Him, he would not have doubted of His power.

13. Nor had the Pharisee hair, in that he knew not the Nazarite; but the Church had hair, and she sought for the Nazarite. Hairs are considered a superfluous part of the body, but if they are anointed they send forth a good smell, and are an ornament to the head, but if not anointed with oil they grow heavy. So likewise riches are a burthen, if you know not how to use them, if you sprinkle them not with the odours of Christ. But if you feed the poor, if you wash and cleanse their filth, their wounds, you have truly wiped the feet of Christ.

S. Luke vii. 45.

14. *Thou gavest Me no kiss, but this woman, since the time I came in, hath not ceased to kiss My feet.* A kiss is the sign of love. But how could the Jew possess this, who knew not peace, who received not peace from Christ

S. John xiv. 27.

when He said, *Peace I leave with you, My peace I give unto you?* This kiss belongs then not to the Synagogue but to the Church, to her who looked for Him, who loved Him,

Cant. i. 2.

who said, *Let Him kiss me with the kisses of His mouth.* For the ardour of that lingering desire, which had grown with waiting for the Lord's coming, she sought slowly to quench by His kiss, and to satisfy her thirst by this gift.

Ps. li. 17.

Wherefore the holy Prophet says, *Thou shalt open my lips, and my mouth shall shew Thy praise.* He then who praises the Lord Jesus kisses Him; and he who praises surely

Ib. cxvi. 10.
Ib. lxxi. 8.

believes in Him. Thus David Himself says, *I believed, and therefore have I spoken;* and before, *Let my mouth be filled with Thy praise, and let me sing of Thy glory.*

15. Concerning the gift of special grace the same Scripture also teaches thee that he who receives the Spirit kisses

Ib. cxix. 131.
[1] spiritum.
Rom. x. 10.

Christ, for the holy Prophet says, *I opened my mouth, and drew in the spirit*[1]. He then kisses Christ, who confesses Him; *For with the heart man believeth unto righteousness, and with the mouth confession is made unto salvation.* He kisses the feet of Christ, who, reading the Gospel, recognizes the acts of the Lord Jesus, and admires them with pious affection; thus religiously kissing, as it were, the Lord's steps as He walks. We kiss Christ then with the kiss of Communion; *Whoso readeth let him understand.*

^{TO MARCELLINA}

S. Matt. xxiv. 15.

16. But how can the Jew have this kiss? For as he believed not in His Advent, so neither did he believe in His Passion, for how can that man believe that He suffered, who believes not that He came? Hence the Pharisee had no kiss save haply that of the traitor Judas. But neither had Judas this kiss, and therefore when he would have shewn to the Jews that kiss which was the concerted sign of his betrayal, the Lord says to him: *Judas, betrayest thou the Son of man with a kiss?* that is, 'Thou offerest a kiss, though thou hast not the love that the kiss should express, thou offerest a kiss who art ignorant of the mystical meaning² of the kiss.' What is required is not the kiss of the lips, but of the heart and mind.

S. Luke xxii. 48.

² sacramentum.

17. But you will say that he kissed the Lord. True it is he kissed Him with his lips, and this kiss the Jewish people has, wherefore it is said, *This people honoureth Me with their lips, but their heart is far from Me.* Wherefore he has not the kiss who has not faith and charity; for by a kiss is conveyed the force of love. Where love is not, nor faith, nor charity, how can there be any sweetness in kisses?

S. Matt. xv. 8.

19. Now the Church ceases not to kiss the feet of Christ, and therefore in the Song of songs she asks not for one but many kisses; like holy Mary she is attentive to all His discourses, she receives all His words, when the Gospel is read, or the Prophets; she *keeps all His sayings in her heart.* The Church, alone, then, as being the spouse, has kisses, for a kiss is, as it were, the pledge of marriage and the privilege of wedlock. How can the Jew have kisses who believes not in the Spouse, who knows not that He is already come?

Cant. i. 1.

S. Luke ii. 51.

19. Nor is it kisses alone that he lacks, but oil also, wherewith to anoint the feet of Christ, for if he had had oil he would before now have bowed down his neck. For Moses says, *It is a stiff-necked people;* and the Lord says

Exod. xxxiv. 9.

that the priest and levite passed by on the other side, nor did either of these pour oil and wine into the wounds of him who had been wounded by robbers; had they possessed this oil they would have poured it into their own wounds. But Isaiah says, *They cannot apply ointment nor oil nor bandage.*

20. But the Church has oil wherewith she dresses the wounds of her children, that the hardness of the wound may not sink inwards; she has oil, which she has received secretly. With this oil Asher has washed his feet, as it is written, *A blessed son is Asher; and he shall be acceptable to his brethren, dip his foot in oil.* With this oil therefore the Church anoints the necks of her children, that they may receive the yoke of Christ; with this oil she has anointed the martyrs to purify them from the dust of this world; with this oil she has anointed confessors, that so they might not yield to labour, or sink down through weariness, or be overwhelmed by the waves of this world; it is for the purpose of refreshing them with spiritual oil that she has thus anointed them.

21. The Synagogue possesses not this oil, for she hath not the olive, she did not recognize that dove which brought back the olive branch after the deluge. This same dove afterwards descended, when Christ was being baptized, and abode upon Him, as John testifies in the Gospel, saying, *I saw the Spirit descending from heaven like a dove, and it abode upon Him.* But how could he see the dove, who saw Him not upon whom the Spirit descended as a dove?

22. So then the Church both washes the feet of Christ, and wipes them with her hair, and anoints them with oil, and pours ointment upon them, in that she not only tends the wounded and comforts the weary, but also sprinkles over them the sweet odours of grace. Nor is it upon the rich and powerful only that she sheds this grace, but on men of low birth also, she weighs all in an equal balance, she receives all in the same bosom, and cherishes them in the same lap.

23. Christ died once, and was buried once, nevertheless He daily desires that ointment should be poured upon His

feet. Now what are these feet of Christ whereon we pour ointment? The feet of Christ are they of whom He saith Himself, *Inasmuch as ye have done it unto one of the least of these My brethren, ye have done it unto Me.* These feet that woman in the Gospel tends[1], and washes with her tears, when the lowest have their sins remitted, their faults washed away, their pardon granted. These feet he kisses who loves even the lowest of the holy congregation. These feet he anoints with ointment, who imparts even to the weaker brethren the graces of His meekness. In these the martyrs, in these the Apostles, in these the Lord Jesus Himself declares that He is honoured. TO MARCELINA

S. Matt. xxv. 40.

[1] refrigerat.

24. Thou seest what instruction the Lord imparts, how by His example He stimulates thee to devotion; for He instructs by His censure. And He thus accuses the Jews, *O My people, what have I done unto thee, and wherein have I wearied thee? testify against Me. For I brought thee up out of the land of Egypt, and redeemed thee out of the house of servants;* adding, *and I sent before thee Moses, Aaron, and Miriam. Remember what Balak* devised against thee, he, that is, who sought the aid of enchantments, but I suffered him not to hurt thee. Truly thou wert oppressed while sojourning in foreign lands, thou wert laden with heavy burthens: I sent Moses Aaron and Miriam before thy face, and he who had spoiled the strangers was himself despoiled. Thou, who hadst lost thine own goods gainedst others, thou wert delivered from the enemies that surrounded thee, and in the midst of the waters thou sawest in safety the death of thine enemies, for the same wave which had separated and carried thee forward flowed back again and drowned the Egyptians. When thou wert in want of food while journeying through the wilderness, did I not *rain bread from heaven* for thee, and scatter food around thee, whereon thou wentest? Did I not subdue all thy enemies and bring thee into the region of the cluster of grapes? Did I not deliver up to thee Sihon (which means 'proud') king of the Amorites (that is, chief of them that provoked thee); did I not also deliver to thee alive the king of Ai, whom, subject to the sentence of the ancient curse, thou nailedst to the wood and hangedst upon a tree? What shall I say

Micah vi. 3, 4.

Ib 5. and Num. xxiii. 2.

Exod. xiv. 29.

Ib. xvi. 4.

Num. xiii. 24. Ib. xxi. 24.

Joshua viii. 23. Ib. 29.

of the slaughter of the hosts of the five kings, who strove to exclude thee from the promised land? *And what doth the Lord require of thee, o man, for all these things, but to do justly and to love mercy, and to walk humbly with thy God?*

25. And to king David himself, that meek and holy man, what was His expostulation by the prophet Nathan? I chose thee, He says, the youngest among thy brethren; I filled thee with the spirit of meekness; by the hand of Samuel, in whom was My Spirit and My Name, I anointed thee king. And from an exile I made thee a conqueror, taking out of the way that former king whom an evil spirit instigated to persecute the priests of the Lord. Upon thy throne I set one of thy seed not so much as an heir as a colleague. I made even strangers subject to thee, that they who resisted might serve thee, and wilt thou deliver My servants into the hands of My enemies, wilt thou take away that which was My servant's, whereby both thou wilt be branded with sin, and My adversaries will have whereof to glory?

26. Seeing therefore, O Emperor, (for I will now not only discourse of you but address myself to you) how severe the Lord's censures are wont to be, you must take care, in proportion as you become more illustrious, to submit so much the more humbly to your Maker. For it is written: When the Lord thy God shall have brought thee into a foreign land, and thou shalt eat the fruits of others, say not, 'By my own strength and righteousness I obtained these things,' but, 'The Lord God gave them to me, Christ in His mercy conferred them on me,' and therefore by loving His body, that is, the Church, pour water on His feet and kiss His feet; thus shalt thou not only absolve those who have been taken in sin, but in giving to them peace you will bring them into concord and restore to them rest. Pour ointment on His feet, that the whole house wherein Christ sits at meat may be filled with the odour of thy ointment, and let all who sit at meat with Him rejoice in thy fragrance; that is to say, pay such regard even to the lowest, that in their absolution the Angels may rejoice, as they do over one sinner that repenteth, the Apostles may be glad,

The final result of S. Ambrose's appeal. 279

the Prophets may exult. For *the eye cannot say unto the hand, I have no need of thee, nor the head to the feet, I have no need of you.* Since therefore each member is necessary, do thou protect the whole body of the Lord Jesus, that He also of His divine mercy may protect thy kingdom.

TO MARCEL- LINA

1 Cor. xii. 21.

27. On my coming down he says to me, 'You have been preaching at me to-day.' I replied that in my discourse I had his benefit in view. He then said, 'It is true, I did make too harsh a decree concerning the reparation of the synagogue by the Bishop, but this has been rectified. As for the monks, they commit many crimes.' Then Timasius, one of the Generals-in-chief[a], began to be very vehement against the monks. I replied to him, 'With the Emperor I deal as is fitting, because I know that he fears God, but with you, who speak so rudely, I shall deal differently.'

28. After standing for some time, I said to the Emperor, 'Enable me to offer for you with a safe conscience, set my mind at rest.' The Emperor sat still, and nodded, but did not promise in plain words; then, seeing that I still remained standing, he said that he would amend the order. I said at once that he must quash the whole enquiry, for fear the Count[b] should make it an opportunity for inflicting wrong on the Christians. He promised that it should be done. I said to him, 'I act on your promise,' and repeated the words again. 'Do so' said he. Then I went to the altar; but I would not have gone, if he had not given me his distinct promise. And indeed so great was the grace attending the oblation, that I myself was sensible that this favour he had granted was very acceptable to our God, and that the divine Presence had not been withheld. Then all was done as I wished.

---

[a] The Latin title is 'Magister equitum et peditum.' When the Præfecti Prætorio became civil rather than military officers, the chief command of the armies was transferred to two high officers, called, one 'Magister equitum,' and the other 'Magister peditum.' When the empire was divided these became four, and eventually the number was increased to eight, who were all called 'Magistri equitum et peditum.' See Gibbon ch. xvii. 3

[b] i. e. the 'Comes Orientis,' under whose jurisdiction the matter was, and who had sent the report to the Emperor. see Lett. xl. 6.

THE LETTER OF POPE SIRICIUS TO THE CHURCH OF MILAN.

LETTER
A.D. 389.

THE Letter of Siricius was addressed to the Church of Milan to inform them of the sentence of excommunication passed against Jovinian and his followers. Jovinian had been a monk, but had abandoned the ascetic life and rushed into extremes of self-indulgence· there is a good description of him in Tillemont, (Vie de S. Ambr. 63, 64,) who calls him ' cet Epicure des Chrétiens.' The false doctrines with which he ' barked at the true doctrines of the Church' are stated in this Letter and in the reply of the Synod of the Church of Milan which follows Jovinian was answered by S. Jerome, who writes against him with much vehemence.

SIRICIUS TO THE CHURCH OF MILAN.

1. I WOULD fain always, beloved brethren, send you tidings of joys, sincere as you are in love and peace, so that by means of the mutual interchange of letters we might be pleased by the tidings of your welfare[1]. Our ancient Adversary however [a] does not suffer us to be free from his attacks, he who is a liar from the beginning, the enemy of truth, envious of man, in order to deceive whom he first deceived himself, the adversary of chastity, the teacher of sensuality, who is fed by cruelty, punished by abstinence, who hates fasts, asserting, as his followers also give out, that they are superfluous, having no hope of things to come, obnoxious to the censure of the Apostle, *Let us eat and drink for to-morrow we die.*

[1] sospitatis indicio.

1 Cor. xv. 32.

2. O miserable boldness, O craft of a desperate mind! Already was this unknown language of heresy spreading through the Church like a cancer, seeking to fill the breast, and plunge the whole man in destruction: and unless the Lord of Sabaoth had broken through the snare which they had laid, the public exhibition of so much evil and hypocrisy would have led to ruin the hearts of many simple ones, for the human mind is easily drawn aside towards evil, choosing rather to fly through open space, than to travel with pain along the narrow way.

3. Wherefore it was very necessary, most dearly beloved, to commend what has been done here to your notice and consideration, lest through the ignorance of any priest, the Church might be infected by the contagion of these most wicked men who are breaking in upon it under a religious pretext, as it is written and the Lord has said, *Many*

S. Matt. vii.15,16.

[a] This sentence as it stands in the text is incomplete, the ' quia ' having no correlative The 'at vero quia seems like ' at enim' in Classical Latin, or perhaps the ' quia' should be omitted

come to you in sheeps' clothing, but inwardly they are ravening wolves; ye shall know them by their fruits.

These are they who under a mean garb boast themselves as Christians, that walking under the semblance of piety they may enter the house of prayer and utter the words of wily disputation, *that they may privily shoot at them which are true of heart,* and, seducing them from Catholic truth, may draw them over, after the example of Satan, to the madness of their own doctrines, beguiling the simplicity of the flock.

Ps. xi. 2.

4. And indeed from the times of the Apostles up to now we have heard and known by experience of many malignant heresies, but the sacred truth of the Church has never been assailed by the barking of such dogs as those who have now suddenly broken in upon us, with the doctrines of unbelief fully sprouted, enemies of the faith; who by the fruit of their works have betrayed whose disciples they are. For while other heretics misunderstanding single points have proposed to bear away and abstract from the Divine system of teaching, these men, *not having on a wedding garment,* wound the Catholics, perverting, as I have said, the continuity of the New and Old Testament, and interpreting it in a diabolical spirit, have by their alluring and false arguments already begun to ruin some Christians, and to make them associates of their madness, not keeping within themselves the poison of their iniquity: but some of their chosen ones have betrayed their blasphemies by writing a rash discourse, which the rage of a desperate mind has led them openly to publish, favouring, as it does, the cause of the Heathens.

S. Matt. xxii. 12.

5. But of their madness I suddenly received intelligence by means of a shocking writing which certain faithful Christians, men of high rank, and signal piety, caused to be conveyed to me, unworthy as I am, in order that the opposition of these men to the Divine Law might be detected by the discernment of the Clergy and repressed by a spiritual sentence. Assuredly we receive without scorn the vows of those marriages which we assist at with the veil [b], but virgins, for whose existence marriage is necessary, as being devoted to God, we honour more highly.

6. Having therefore held an assembly of my clergy it became clear that their sentiments were contrary to our doctrine, that is, to the Christian law. Therefore, following the Apostolic precept, we, seeing that they were *preaching another Gospel than that which we received,* have excommmnicated them. Know therefore that it was the unanimous sentence of us all, as well of the presbyters and deacons as

Gal. i. 8.

---

[b] See Letter xix, 7. S. Ambrose in De Abraham B 1. c 9, 93 alludes to the use of the veil in Christian marriages.

LETT. 42. of the other clergy, that Jovinian, Auxentius, Genialis, Germinator, Felix, Prontinus[c], Martianus, Januarius, and Ingeniosus, who were discovered to be the promoters of the new heresy and blasphemy, should be condemned by the Divine sentence and our judgment, and remain in perpetual exclusion from the Church.

7. Nothing doubting that your Holinesses will observe the aforesaid decree, I have sent you this Epistle by my brethren and fellow-priests, Crescens, Leopardus and Alexander, that they, with a fervent spirit, may perform a religious and faithful service.

A.D. 389.

LETTER XLII.

IN this, their reply to Siricius, drawn up in all probability by S. Ambrose himself, the Council of Milan thank him for his care, and announce that they have followed his example and condemned Jovinian and his followers in the same way. They dwell upon his errors, particularly on his disparagement of virginity, on his denial of the true virginity of our Lord's Mother, on his contempt of widowhood, and of fasting, and condemn him as a follower of Manes. They argue in especial detail against his argument with regard to the Virgin Mary, which differs from that of Helvidius and other assailants of the ἀεὶ παρθένος.

TO THEIR LORD, THEIR DEARLY BELOVED BROTHER, POPE SIRICIUS, AMBROSE, SABINUS, BASSANIUS, AND THE REST SEND GREETING.

2. IN your Holiness' Letter we recognized the vigilance of a good shepherd, for you faithfully guard the door which has been entrusted to you, and with pious solicitude watch over the fold of Christ, being worthy to be heard and followed by the sheep of the Lord. Knowing therefore the lambs of Christ, you will easily discover the wolves, and meet them as a wary shepherd, so as to keep them from scattering the Lord's flock by their unbelieving life and dismal barking.

2. We praise you for this, our Lord and brother dearly beloved, and join in cordial commendations of it. Nor are we surprised that the Lord's flock was terrified at the rage of wolves in whom they recognized not the voice of

[c] This name appears in the reply of the Milan Synod as Plotinus, which is probably the true form.

Christ. For it is a savage barking to shew no reverence to virginity, observe no rule of chastity, to seek to place every thing on a level, to abolish the different degrees of merit, and to introduce a certain meagreness in heavenly rewards, as if Christ had only one palm to bestow, and there was no copious diversity in His rewards.

3. They pretend that they are giving honour to marriage. But what praise can rightly be given to marriage if no distinction is paid to virginity? We do not deny that marriage was hallowed by Christ, for the Divine words say, *And they twain shall be one flesh,* and one spirit, but our birth precedes our calling, and the mystery of the Divine operation is much more excellent than the remedy of human frailty. A good wife is deservedly praised, but a pious virgin is more properly preferred, for the Apostle says, *He that giveth his virgin in marriage doeth well, but he that giveth her not in marriage doeth better; for the one careth for the things of the Lord, the other for the things of the world.* The one is bound by the chains of marriage, the other is free from chains; the one is under the Law, the other under Grace. Marriage is good, for thereby the means of continuing the human race has been devised, but virginity is better, for thereby the heritage of the heavenly kingdom is regained, and the mode of attaining to heavenly rewards discovered. By a woman care entered the world; by a virgin salvation was brought to pass. Lastly, Christ chose virginity as His own special gift, and displayed the grace of chastity, thus making an exhibition of that in His own person which in His Mother He had made the object of His choice.

4. How great is the madness of their dismal barkings, that the same persons should say that Christ could not be born of a virgin, and yet assert that women, after having given birth to human pledges, remain virgins? Does Christ grant to others what, as they assert, He could not grant to Himself? But He, although He took on Him our flesh, although He was made man that He might redeem man, and recal him from death, still, as being God, came upon earth in an extraordinary way, that as He had said, *Behold I make all things new,* so also He might be

born of an immaculate virgin, and be believed to be, as it is written, *God with us.* But from their perverse ways they are induced to say 'She was a virgin when she conceived, but not a virgin when she brought forth.' Could she then conceive as a virgin, and yet not be able to bring forth as a virgin, when conception always precedes, and birth follows?

LETT 42.
S. Matt. i. 23.

5. But if they will not believe the doctrines of the Clergy, let them believe the oracles of Christ, let them believe the admonitions of Angels who say, *For with God nothing shall be impossible.* Let them give credit to the Creed of the Apostles, which the Roman Church has always kept and preserved undefiled. Mary heard the voice of the Angel, and she who before had said *How shall this be?* not asking from want of faith in the mode of generation, afterwards replied, *Behold the handmaid of the Lord, be it unto me according to thy word.* This is the virgin who conceived, this the virgin who brought forth a Son. For thus it is written, *Behold a Virgin shall conceive and bear a Son;* declaring not only that she should conceive as a virgin, but also that she bring forth as a virgin.

S. Luke i. 37.

Ib. 34.

Ib. 38.

6. But what is that *gate of the sanctuary,* that *outward gate which looketh towards the East, which remains shut, and no man,* it is said, *shall enter in by it but the Lord, the God of Israel.* Is not Mary this gate, by whom the Saviour entered into the world? This is the gate of righteousness, as He Himself said, *Suffer us to fulfil all righteousness.* Blessed Mary is the gate, whereof it is written that *the Lord hath entered in by it, therefore it shall be shut* after birth; for as a virgin she both conceived and brought forth.

Ezek xliv. 1, 2.

S. Matt. iii. 15.

Ezek. xliv. 2.

7. But why should it be incredible that Mary, contrary to the usage of natural birth, should bring forth and yet remain a virgin; when contrary to the usage of nature, the sea saw and fled, and the floods of Jordan retired to their source. It should not exceed our belief that a virgin should bring forth, when we read that a rock poured forth water, and the waves of the sea were gathered up like a wall. Nor need it, again, exceed our belief that a man should be born of a virgin, when a running stream gushed

Ps. cxiv. 3.

Exod. xvii. 6.
Ib. xiv. 22.

Widowhood a good estate.

forth from the rock, when iron swam upon the waters, and a man walked upon them. If therefore the waves carried a man, could not a virgin bring forth a man? But what man? Him of Whom we read, *The Lord shall send them a Man Who shall deliver them; and the Lord shall be known to Egypt.* Wherefore in the old Testament a Hebrew virgin led the people through the sea, in the New Testament a royal virgin was elected to be a heavenly abode for our salvation.

<small>TO SIRICIUS
Numb. xx. 11.
2 Kings vi. 6.
S. Matt. xiv. 26.
Is. xix. 20, 21.
Exod. xv. 20.</small>

8. But what more? let us also subjoin the praises of widowhood, since in the Gospel next after that most illustrious birth from a virgin, comes the widow Anna; she who *had lived with an husband seven years from her virginity; and she was a widow of about fourscore and four years, which departed not from the temple, but served with fastings and prayers night and day.*

<small>S. Luke ii. 36, 37.</small>

9. And fitting it is that these men should despise widowhood, which is wont to keep fasts, for they regret that they should have been mortified by these for any time, and avenge the wrong they inflicted on themselves, and by daily banquets and habits of luxury seek to ward off the pain of abstinence. They do nothing more rightly than in thus condemning themselves out of their own mouth.

10. But they even fear lest their former fasting should be reckoned against them. Let them choose whichever they like: if they ever fasted, let them repent of their good work, if never, let them confess their own intemperance and luxury. And so they assert that Paul was a teacher of excess. But who can be a teacher of temperance if he was a teacher of excess, *who chastised his body and brought it into subjection,* and recorded his performance of the service he owed to Christ by many fastings; and this not for the purpose of praising himself and his doings, but that he might teach us, what example to follow. Did he then teach excess who said, *Why, as though living in the world, are ye subject to ordinances? Touch not, taste not, handle not, which all are to perish with the using;* who also says, *Not in indulgence of the body, not in any honour to the satisfying and love of the flesh, not in the lusts of error, but in the Spirit by Whom we are renewed.*

<small>1 Cor. ix. 27.
2 Cor. vi. 5.
1 Col. ii. 20. sqq.</small>

11. If what the Apostle has said is not enough, let them hear the Prophet saying, *I chastened myself with fasting.* He therefore who fasts not is uncovered and naked and exposed to wounds. And if Adam had clothed himself with fasting he would not have been found to be naked. Nineveh delivered itself from death by fasting. And the Lord Himself says, *This kind goeth not out but by prayer and fasting.*

12. But why need we say more to our master and teacher? seeing that these persons have now paid the worthy price of their perfidy, who have on this account come even hither, that no place might remain where they were not condemned; who have proved themselves to be truly Manichees, by not believing that He came forth from a virgin. What madness is this, almost equal to that of the modern Jews? If He is not believed so to have come, neither is He believed to have taken upon Him our flesh, therefore He was seen only in figure, He was crucified only in figure. But He was crucified for us in truth, He is in truth our Redeemer.

13. He is a Manichee who denies the truth, who denies that Christ came in the flesh; and therefore the remission of sins is not their's; but it is the impiety of the Manichees which both the most merciful Emperor has abhorred [a], and all who saw them have fled from as a plague. Witnesses thereof are our brethren and fellow-presbyters, Crescens, Leopardus, and Alexander, fervent in the Holy Spirit, by whose means they have been exposed to common execration, and driven as fugitives from the city of Milan.

14. Wherefore you are to know that Jovinian, Auxentius, Germinator, Felix, Plotinus, Genialis, Martianus, Januarius and Ingeniosus, whom your Holiness has condemned, have also, in accordance with your judgment, been condemned by ourselves.

May our Almighty God keep you in safety and prosperity, Lord and brother most beloved.

---

[a] There are three laws in the code of Theodosius directed against the Manichees, one of the year 372, A.D. which forbade them to hold assemblies, one of 389, A.D. and one of 391. A.D. ordering their banishment. It is probably the second of these that is referred to, though Gothofred refers it to the third, in which case the date of the Letter must be altered.

Here follows the subscription.

I Eventius [b], Bishop, salute your Holiness in the Lord, and have subscribed this Epistle.

MAXIMUS, Bishop.
FELIX, Bishop.
BASSIANUS, Bishop.
THEODORUS, Bishop.
CONSTANTIUS, Bishop.

By command of my lord Geminianus Bishop, and in his presence, I Aper, Presbyter, have subscribed.

Eustasius, Bishop, and all the Orders have subscribed.

LETTER XLIII.

THIS Letter is a reply to a question from Horontianus, why man, the highest work of God's creation, was made the last. S. Ambrose brings forward various analogies to shew that the last is first, and each with an enthusiastic and poetical description of man's greatness, and of his dominion over the other works of creation.

AMBROSE TO HORONTIANUS.

1 You have intimated to me your surprise at finding in my Treatise on the Six days of Creation, that, while you found both the Sacred Narrative and the tenor of my discourse assigning greater gifts to man than to any other creature in the earth, still that the land and the waters brought forth all flying and creeping things and things in the waters before him for whose sake they were all created: and you ask me the reason of this, which Moses was silent about, and I did not venture to touch upon.

2. And perhaps that spokesman of the Divine Oracles purposely kept silence, lest he should seem to render himself the judge and counsellor of the Divine ordinances; for to give utterance to that with which he was inspired by the Spirit of God is one thing, to interpret the will of God is

Gen. i. 16.

---

[b] All these names except Geminianus occur in the list of Bishops present at the Council of Aquileia. See p. 60.

LETT. 43. another. I am of opinion however that we, not as speaking in God's Name, but as gathering up scattered principles of reason from human usage, may be able, from the way in which God has disposed other things for man's use, to come to the conclusion that it was fitting for man to be the last work of creation.

S. Luke xiv. 16.
3. For he who sets out a banquet, like that rich man in the Gospel, (for we must compare Divine things with each other the better to draw our conclusion,) prepares every thing first, kills his oxen and fatlings, and then bids his friends to supper. The more trivial things therefore are prepared in the first place, and then he who is worthy of honour is invited. Hence the Lord also first provided for the food of man all other animals, and then invited to the feast man himself, as His friend: and truly His friend, seeing that he was partaker of the Divine Charity and heir of His Glory. To man himself it is that He says: *Friend, how camest thou in hither?* So then all things that precede are to minister to the need of the friend, and it is the friend who is invited last.

S. Matt. xxii. 12.

4. Take another instance. What is the world but a sort of arena of continual strife? Wherefore also in the Apocalypse the Lord says, *To him that overcometh will I give a crown of life;* and Paul says, *I have fought a good fight;* and in another place, *No man is crowned except he strive lawfully.* He who institutes this combat is Almighty God. Now he who in this world offers a combat, does he not first provide all things which are necessary thereto, and prepare the chaplets of victory before he summons the athletics to contend for the prize; and all this that the conqueror may not suffer delay, but retire from the contest crowned with his reward? Now the rewards of man are the fruits of the earth and the lights of heaven; the former for the use of this present life, the latter for the hope of life eternal.

Rev. ii. x.
2 Tim. iv. 7.
Ib. ii. 5.

5. As a wrestler therefore he enters the lists last of all; he raises his eyes to heaven, he sees that even the heavenly creation *was made subject to vanity, not willingly, but by reason of him who hath subjected the same in hope.* He sees that *the whole creation groaneth in pain together, waiting*

Rom. viii. 20.

for redemption. He sees that labour awaits us all. He raises his eyes, he sees the circlets of lights, he surveys the orbs of the moon and stars: *For the just, who overcome, shall be as the stars in heaven.* And he chastises his body, that it may not be his enemy in the combat, he anoints it with the oil of mercy, he exercises it with daily trials of virtue, he smears himself with dust, he *runs* to the goal of the course but *not as uncertainly,* he aims his blows, he darts forth his arms, but not into empty space, he strikes the adversary whom he sees not, for he has respect to Him alone to Whom all enemies give way, even those who are invisible, in Whose Name the powers of the air were turned aside. It is he therefore who poises the blow, but it is Christ Who strikes, it is he who lifts up his heel, but Christ Who directs it to the ground. Lastly, although Paul saw not those whom he struck, he was not *as one that beateth the air,* because by the preaching of Christ he wounded those evil spirits which assaulted him. Rightly therefore did man, for whom a race was prepared, enter the course last, that he might be preceded by heaven which was to be, as it were, his reward.

6. But we wrestle not only *against spiritualities of wickedness in high places,* but also *against flesh and blood.* We wrestle with satiety, with the very fruits of the earth, with wine, by which even a righteous man was made drunk, and the whole people of the Jews overthrown; we wrestle with wild animals, with the fowls of the air; for our flesh, if pampered by these, cannot be brought to subjection; we wrestle *with perils of the way, with perils of waters,* as Paul says; we wrestle with rods of the wood, those rods with which the Apostles were beaten. You see how severe are our combats. Thus the earth is man's trial-ground, heaven is his crown; and fitting therefore it was that as a friend, what was to minister to his wants should precede him, as a combatant, his reward.

7. Take another illustration. In all things the beginning and the ending are most excellent. If you look upon a house, it is the foundation and the roof which are more considerable than the other parts, if you look upon a field it is the sowing and the harvest, the planting and the vin-

tage. How sweet are the grafts of trees, how pleasant are the fruits! In the same manner also was the heaven created first, and man last, as a kind of heavenly creature upon earth. For although in body he is compared with the beasts, in mind he is numbered among the inhabitants of heaven; for *as we have borne the image of the earthy; we shall also bear the image of the heavenly.* How should he not be heavenly, who is made after the image and likeness of God?

marginal: 1 Cor. xv. 49. Gen. i. 27.

8. Rightly therefore in the creation of the world the heaven is both first and last, wherein is that which is beyond heaven, even the God of heaven. And of man is rather to be understood the text, *Heaven is my throne*, for God does not sit above the element, but in the heart of man. Wherefore the Lord also says, *We will come unto Him, and make our abode with Him.* Heaven therefore is the first work in the creation of the world, and man the last.

marginal: Is. lxvi. 1. S. John xiv. 23.

9. Heaven is of the world, man above the world; for the former is a portion of the world, the latter is an inhabitant of Paradise, and the possession of Christ. Heaven is thought to be undecaying, yet it passes away; man is deemed to be incorruptible, yet he puts on incorruption; the fashion of the first perishes, the latter rises again as being immortal; yet the hands of the Lord, according to the authority of Scripture, formed them both. For as we read of the heavens, *And the heavens are the work of Thy hands;* so also man says, *Thy hands have made me and fashioned me*, and again, *The heavens declare the glory of God.* And as the heaven is resplendent with stars, so are men bright with the light of good works, for their works shine before their Father Which is in heaven. The former is the firmament of heaven which is on high, and the latter firmament is not unlike to it, whereof it is said, *Upon this rock will I build My Church;* the one is the firmament of the elements, the other of virtues, and the last is more excellent; *they sucked honey out of the firm rock,* for *the Rock is the flesh of Christ,* which redeemed the heaven and the whole world.

marginal: Ps. cii. 25. Ib. cxix. 73. Ps. xix. 1. S. Matt. v. 16. Ib. xvi. 18. Deut. xxxii. 13. 1 Cor. x. 4.

10. Why should I add further, carrying you, as it were,

through the whole course, that God made man *partaker of the Divine nature*, as we read in the Epistle of Peter? Whence one says not improperly, *We also are His offspring*, for He made us akin to Himself, and we are of a rational nature, that we might seek for that Godhead *Which is not far from each one of us, in Whom we live and move and have our being.*

11. Having therefore conferred on man that which is the greatest of graces, He granted to him as to that creature who was dearest and very nearest to Him, all the things which are in this world, that he might want for nothing which is necessary either for life or for a good life, some of which things were to be supplied by the abundance of earthly plenty to minister pleasure, others again by the knowledge of heavenly secrets, to arouse man's mind by the love and desire of that discipline which should enable us to reach the summit of the Divine mysteries. Both these therefore are most excellent gifts, both to have all the riches of the world subject to him, all flying and creeping things and fishes, and, as being lord of the elements, the use of the sea, and without toil or want, after the model and likeness of his adorable Creator, to abound in all things, living in the greatest plenty, and also to open paths for himself, and make progress, so as to ascend to the royal abode of heaven.

12. You will easily discover that the traveller along this arduous path is the man, who has been so fashioned in purpose of heart and will, as to be, as far as possible, estranged from his body, as not to enter into any fellowship with vice, nor suffer himself to be smoothed down by the words of flatterers: one who does not, when riding on the chariot of prosperity, despise the humble, shun sorrow, discard and disparage the praises of the holy, nor, by desire of glory or of wealth, grasped at too prematurely, exhaust all the ardour of hope; one whose mind is not bowed down by sadness nor broken by injury, which is not harrassed by suspicion, nor excited by lust, whom the passions of the body do not overcome, whom no desire of vanities or charms of pleasure disquiet and disturb. Add to all this the virtues of chastity, soberness and temperance; let

LETT. 43. him be able easily to curb the irregular sallies of light passion, set bounds to his pleasures and desires, clear up ambiguity by an equitable judgment, by tranquillity of mind settle what is doubtful, and with all the strifes of the mind and body reconciled, so to speak, preserve in a just balance the concord of the exterior and interior man unimpaired, stilling them as they lie within his own breast, while, should he be called to it, no evil counsellor is able to turn him away from the crown of suffering, such a man surely will be adopted not only as a friend but a son by the Father, that he may obtain the riches of His glory and inheritance.

13. Rightly therefore did he come last, being, as it were, the end of nature, formed to righteousness, and the arbiter of right among other creatures. And, if we may employ the illustration, as among men *Christ is the end of the Law for righteousness to every one that believeth*, so are we as beasts in the sight of the Lord, for thus says the Prophet, *I became as a beast before Thee*. Yet what comparison is there between the two, when He has redeemed those who were ready to perish, and we put them to death, He calls slaves to liberty and we inflict bondage on the free? *But who is like God?*

Rom. x. 4.

Ps. lxxiii. 21.

Ps. lxxxix. 9.

14. Man however came forth the last of all created things, in form comely, in mind lofty, to be admired by all creatures, having in him, after the image of the eternal God, an invisible intelligence [1] clothed in human form. This is that intelligence or power of the soul which claims to itself, as the ruling principle, authority over the soul and body. This it is that all other living creatures dread although they see it not, just as we fear God Whom we see not, and fear Him only the more because we see Him not.

[1] νοῦς.

15. For, if we may presume to speak of ourselves *after His image and likeness*, as Scripture says, in the same way as He is established in the fulness of His Majesty, and sees all things, heaven, air, earth and sea, embracing the universe and penetrating each part, so that nothing escapes Him, and there is nothing which does not consist in Him and depend on Him, and which is not full of Him, as He Himself says, *I fill heaven and earth, saith the Lord*, so

Gen. l. 26.

Jer. xxiii. 24.

likewise the mind of man sees all things and is not seen, but maintains its own essence invisible. By means of discipline forethought and perception she apprehends hidden things, dives into the secret of the deep, and those lurking-places which are spread throughout all lands, scrutinizing the nature of both elements, after the likeness of the great God Whom she imitates and follows, Whose image in minute portions is represented in each individual. She raises herself likewise into the air, and rising above the cloudy region, soars, in zeal for knowledge and thirst for wisdom, to the height of heaven, and resting there awhile, rapt in wonder at the heavenly constellations and charmed with their brightness, looks down upon the things of earth. Then she approaches also to Hesperus and Arcturus and those other stars which although Planets err not, and sees that they keep their course without stumbling, that course along which, in order the better to visit all regions, they seem to circuit and to wander. And thus with greater ardour she raises herself to the very bosom of the Father, wherein is the Only-Begotten Son of God Who declares the secrets of God, which in the time to come are to be revealed face to face. But even now He discloses them partly and in a figure to those whom He deems worthy, and at the same time sheds forth from the Spirit and from His own countenance floods of resplendent light, so that he who is illuminated thereby may say, *But it was as a fire blazing in my bones and I am melted on all sides, and cannot stay.* And David says, *Let my sentence come forth from Thy presence!* [s. John i. 18. Jer. xx. 9. Ps. xvii. 2.]

16. By this vigour of mind, therefore, to return to the point from whence I have digressed, whereby she subjects to herself things external, comprehends in her view things distant and separate from each other, and subdues the more powerful animals, she has inspired the rest with such reverence for herself, that they emulously obey her as their king, and pay ready attention to her voice. Nay, although they are irrational they still acknowledge reason, and fix within themselves that discipline which nature has not given them. Furthermore wild beasts, seeing man's gentleness, grow gentle under his rule. Often have they closed their jaws, re-

called by the sound of the human voice. We see hares caught without injury by the harmless fangs of dogs, and even lions, if they hear man's voice, letting their prey escape: leopards also and bears urged on and recalled by the sound of his voice: the horses stimulated by the applause of man, and slackening their speed at his silence: nay, often, untouched by the lash they outstrip others that are scourged on, so much more powerfully does the scourge of the tongue incite them.

17. But what shall I say of the creatures' services to man? In order to please him the ram nourishes his fleece, and is plunged in the stream to enhance its beauty; sheep also crop the best herbage to distend with sweeter juice of milk their teeming udders; and, that they may offer to man their gifts, suffer the pangs of travail; bulls groan all day under the plough pressed down in the furrows; camels, besides the service of bearing burthens, suffer themselves to be shorn like rams, so that each animal contributes to man, as to a king, its service, and pays its annual tribute. The horse, exulting in such a rider, prances proudly, and curving his neck when his master mounts, gives his back to afford him a seat. And if you are still at a loss why man was made last, let the same animal teach us that this is to be deemed an honour not a slight. For he bears one who came after him, not despising but fearing him, and bearing him with pain to himself from place to place. In a moment of time man reaches far distant places and traverses long distances, transported sometimes on single horses, sometimes in triumphal chariots [a].

18. And since I have mentioned triumphal chariots it is needful that I should add thereto the chariot of Elijah which carried him through the air, and those of elephants, whereon man sits as conqueror, and governs although he be last and they precede him. And thus the steersman of a ship sits in the stern, and yet guides the whole ship. Whence I deem it not without a purpose that we are told in the Gospel that the Lord Jesus was asleep in the stern of the ship; and that when awakened He commanded the wind and the sea, and laid the storm, shewing thereby that

[a] This whole passage is full of expressions borrowed from Virgil.

He came last because He came as the Pilot. Wherefore the Apostle says, *The first man Adam was made a living soul, the last Adam was made a quickening Spirit. Howbeit that was not first which is spiritual, but that which is natural, and afterwards that which is spiritual*, and then he adds, *The first man is of the earth, earthy, the second man is from heaven, heavenly.*

To Horontianus
1 Cor. xv. 45, 46.
Ib 47

19. Rightly therefore is man the last, being as it were the consummation of the whole work, the cause of the world, for whose sake all things were made; the habitant, as it were, of all the elements, he lives among beasts, swims with fishes, soars above birds, converses with Angels, dwells upon the earth, and has his warfare in heaven, ploughs the sea, feeds upon air, tills the soil, is a voyager over the deep, a fisher in the floods, a fowler in the air, in heaven an heir even joint-heir with Christ. These things he does by his diligence.

Rom. viii. 17.

20. Hear also things above man's natural power. Moses walked along the bottom of the sea, the Apostles upon the surface, Habbacuc flew without wings, Elijah conquered upon earth, and triumphed in heaven.

Farewell, my son; love me for I also love you.

Exod. xiv. 29.
S. John xxi. 7.
Bel and the Dragon 36.

LETTER XLIV.

A.D. 389.

S. AMBROSE here first dwells on the distinction between God and the Universe which is His work. He then speaks of the six days of Creation, and of the mystical meaning of the numbers seven and eight, applying various passages of Scripture in which they occur, and bringing forward analogies from nature.

AMBROSE TO HORONTIANUS.

1. You have done well to mark the prophet's distinction between the Creator and His works, or rather, God's own distinction, for Moses wrote not of himself, but by inspiration and revelation, particularly in what relates to the formation of the world. For the One being impassible,

LETT. 44. the other liable to suffering, he has referred that which was impossible to God the Creator, but the passible part, without life or motion of its own, but receiving life and motion and form from its Creator, he has assigned to the world; and as this world, after its creation, ought not to be left without a ruler, or unprotected by any father, he therefore plainly describes the invisible God as the Ruler and Governor of this visible world. *For the things which are seen are temporal, but the things which are not seen are eternal.*

2 Cor. iv. 18.

2. He therefore states the creation of the world to have taken place in six days, not that God required time to form it in, for He can do in a moment what He wills, for *He spake the word, and they were created,* but because things which are made, need some certain order, and order requires both time and number. And especially for the purpose of giving us a model for our works has He observed a certain number of days and certain seasons; for we also require time wherein to do aught perfectly, so as not to be precipitate in our counsels and works; nor to neglect their proper order. For when we read that God, as Scripture tells us, has *made all things in wisdom,* and by a certain counsel disposition and order, it is agreeable to reason that He should first have made the heavens which are the most beautiful; it is fitting slso that we should first raise our eyes thither and conceive that it behoves us to aim at ariving thither, and that we should consider that it is to be preferred to all earthly habitations.

Ps. cxlviii. 5.

Ps. civ. 24.

3. Wherefore in six days He created the world, on the seventh day He rested from His works. The number seven is good, and we treat it not according to the manner of Pythagoras and other philosophers, but according to the form and divisions of spiritual grace, for the prophet Isaiah has set forth the seven principal virtues of the Holy Spirit. This sacred seven, like the venerable Trinity of the Father Son and Holy Ghost, knows neither time nor order, and is the origin of number, not bound by any of its laws. Wherefore as the heaven the earth and the sea were formed in honour of the eternal Trinity, and also the sun moon and stars, so in like manner we observe that it is according to this sevenfold circle of spiritual virtues, and this swiftly

Gen. ii. 2.

Is. xi. 2.

revolving orbit of Divine operation, that a certain sevenfold ministry of planets, whereby this world is illuminated, has been created. And their service is said to agree with the number of these stars, which are fixed, or, as they are called in Greek, ἀπλανεῖς [a]. The North has likewise received its Latin name (Septemtrio) from being irradiated by seven stars, upon the brightness of which as their guide pilots are said specially to fix their gaze.

TO HORON-TIANUS

4. And this peculiar property has come down from heaven to earth; for not to speak of the sevenfold fashion of the head, in the two eyes, the two ears and nostrils, and the mouth whereby we enjoy the taste of great sweetness, how wonderful is it that in the seventh month most men are conceived, and he that is afterwards born receives at that time the commencement of his vital course. But in the eighth month we perceive that by a natural law the season of bringing forth is suspended, and if some fatal compulsion has opened the barriers of the womb, the danger both of the mother and her offspring is nigh at hand.

5. But he who is born on the seventh day, although he be born well, is born to labour, but he who on the eighth day, obtains the mysteries of regeneration, is consecrated by grace, and called to the inheritance of the celestial kingdom. Great in the virtues of the Spirit is the grace of the holy number seven, but the same grace answers to the number seven, and consecrates the number eight. In the first we have the name, but in the latter the fruit, and therefore the grace of the Spirit, conferred on the eighth day, restored to Paradise those whom their own fault had banished.

6. The Old Testament too knew this number eight which in Latin we call the Octave, for the preacher says, *give a portion to seven and also to eight.* The number seven belongs to the Old Testament, the number eight to the New, for then Christ rose, and the day of new salvation shone upon all. This is the day whereof the Prophet says, *This is the day which the Lord hath made, let us rejoice and be glad in it:* for on that day the brightness of full and per-

Eccles. xi. 2.

Ps. cxviii. 24.

---

[a] This title seems here to be applied especially to the constellations of the Pleiades and Hyades, each of which consisted of seven stars.

LETT. 44. fect circumcision was infused into the hearts of men. On this account the Old Testament also gave a part to eight in the solemnity of circumcision. But this still lay in darkness:

Mal. iv. 2. then came *the Sun of righteousness,* and by the consummation of His passion revealed His rays of light; these He unfolded to all, and opened the brightness of eternal life.

7. These then are that seven and eight whereof Hosea says that by that number he purchased to himself, and Hosea iii. 2. acquired the fulness of faith, for thus it is written, *So I bought her to me for fifteen pieces of silver, and for an homer of barley, and an half homer of barley, and a measure of wine* [b]. But in the former verses God had commanded him to hire to himself an harlot, and it is manifest that he did so, in that he has mentioned the price of her hiring. Now the fifteen pieces of silver are made up of the numbers seven and eight, wherefore they represent these numbers. And by the price of the two Testaments, that is, of perfect faith, the prophecy hath received the consummation of its faith and the Church her fulness. For by the first Testament the people of Israel were gained, by the second the heathen and Gentiles. And so by a perfect faith the harlot is hired, seeking herself a consort either among the Gentiles, or from the adulterous people of the Jews, who had deserted their Lord, the Author of their virgin faith, and spread their congregations over the breadth of the whole world.

8. With regard to the words, *an homer of barley, and half an homer of barley,* in the homer we have a full measure, in the half homer the measure is but partly full; thus S. Matt. v. 17. we read in our Lord's own words, *I am not come to destroy the law, but to fulfil the law.* And in another place the Micah v. 5. Lord says by the prophet Micah, *Then shall there be peace in the land of Israel, when the Assyrian shall come into his land; and there arose against him seven shepherds, and* [1] morsus homi- num. E. V. 'principal men.' *eight bites* [1] *of men.* For the faithful people will then enjoy perfect peace and be freed from all temptations and vanities, when peace and grace shall have shut out the vanity of this world from our hearts, the peace, that is, of the Old, the grace of the New Testament.

[b] See note on Letter xxvi. 9

9. The *seven shepherds* are the precepts of the law, whereby the flock not yet endued with reason are led through the wilderness by the rod of Moses, and governed. The *eight bites of man* are the commandments of the Gospel, and the words of the Lord's mouth. *For with the heart man believeth unto righteousness, and with the mouth confession is made unto salvation.* Those *bites* are good whereby we have tasted the gift of eternal life, and in the Body of Christ have received the remission of sins. In the Old Testament the bite of death is bitter, wherefore it is said, *Prevailing death has devoured*ᶜ. In the New Testament sweet is the taste of life, which has swallowed up death, wherefore the Apostle says, *Death is swallowed up in victory. O death, where is thy sting, O grave, where is thy victory?* [margin: TO HORONTIANUS; Rom. x. 10.; Isa. xxv. 8.; 1 Cor xv. 54, 55.]

10. Moreover, to use the testimony of the Apostles, when God made man, *He rested from all His works on the seventh day.* But when the Jews wilfully disobeyed the commands of their God, the Lord said, *If they shall enter into My rest.* And therefore the Lord appointed another day, whereof He says, *To-day if ye will hear My voice.* For in general Scripture speaks of two days, yesterday and to-day, of which it is said, *Jesus Christ the same, yesterday to-day and for ever.* On the first day the promise is made, on the second it is fulfilled. But since on the former day neither Moses nor Joshua brought the people into their rest, Christ, to Whom the Father said, *This day have I begotten Thee,* has brought them in to-day, for by His Resurrection Jesus has obtained peace for His people. The Lord Jesus is our rest; Who says, *To-day shalt thou be with Me in Paradise.* For rest is in heaven, not on earth. [margin: Heb. iv. 4.; Ib. 3; Ps. xcv. 8.; Heb. xiii. 8.; S Luke xxiii. 43.]

11. Why then need I watch the rising and setting of the stars, at whose rising the fallows should be ploughed up and pierced by the hard plough-shares, and at whose setting the fruitful crop should be cut down by the sickle? One star suffices for me in the place of all others, *the bright and morning Star,* at Whose rising was sown the seed not [margin: Rev. xxii. 16.]

ᶜ Devoravit mors praevalens. The E. V. is, 'He will swallow up death in victory' The Vulg. has, 'Praecipitabit mortem in sempiternum.'

LETT. 44. of corn but of martyrs; when Rachel wept for her children, and offered in the stead of Christ her children washed in her own tears. The setting of this Star raised from the tomb not the senseless relics of the funeral pile, but the triumphant bands of the re-animated dead.

12. Let then this number seven be observed by us, seeing that the life of man passes through seven stages to old age, as Hippocrates the teacher of medicine has explained in his writings. The first age is infancy, the second boyhood, the third youth, the fourth adult age, the fifth manhood, the sixth fulness of years, the seventh old age. Thus we have the infant, the boy, the youth, the young man, the man, the elder, the aged.

13. Solon however made ten periods of life, each of seven years; so that the first period, or infancy, should extend to the growth of the teeth, to chew its food, and utter articulate words so as to seem intelligible; boyhood again extends to the time of puberty and of carnal temptation; youth to the growth of the beard; adult age lasts until virtue has attained its perfection; the fifth is the age of manhood, fitted, during its whole course, for marriage; the sixth belongs also to manhood, in that it is adapted to the combat of prudence, and is strenuous in action; the seventh and eighth period also exhibit man ripe in years, vigourous in faculties, and his discourse endowed with a grace of utterance not unpleasing; the ninth period has still some strength remaining, and it speech and wisdom are of a chastened kind; the tenth period fills up the measure, and he who has strength to reach it, will after a full period of years knock late at the gate of death.

14. Thus Hippocrates and Solon recognized either seven ages, or periods of age consisting of seven years. In this then let the number seven prevail; but the octave introduces one uninterrupted period during which we grow up into a perfect man, in the knowledge of God, in the fulness of faith, wherein the measure of a legitimate period of life is completed.

Eph. iv. 13.

15. In our inward parts also the virtue of the seventh number is manifested; for it is said that we have within us seven organs, the stomach, heart, lungs, spleen, liver,

and the two kidneys, and outwardly seven also, the head, the hinder parts, the belly, two hands and two feet.

16. Very excellent are these members, but subject to pain. Who then can doubt that the office of the Octave, which has renewed the whole man, so as not to be susceptible of pain, is more exalted? Wherefore the seventh age of the world being completed, the grace of the Octave has shone upon us, that grace which has made man to be no longer of this world, but above the world. But now we live not according to our own life but to that of Christ. For to us *to live is Christ, and to die is gain, and the life which I now live in the flesh I live by the faith of the Son of God.* So says the Apostle, whence we gather that the 20. day of the world is come to a close. Again, at the last hour the Lord Jesus came, and died for us, *and we are all dead in Him, that we may live to God.* It is not then our former selves that now live, *but Christ liveth in us.*

TO HORONTIANUS

Phil. i. 21. Gal. ii. 20.

1 S John ii. 18. 2 Cor. v 15.

17. The number seven is passed away, the octave is arrived. Yesterday is gone, to-day is come, that promised day wherein we are admonished to hear and follow the word of God. That day of the Old Testament is passed away, that new day is come, wherein the New Testament is perfected, whereof it is said, *Behold, the days come, saith the Lord, when I will make a new covenant with the house of Israel, and with the house of Judah, not according to the covenant that I made with their fathers in the day when I took them by the hand to lead them out of the land of Egypt.* He adds too the reason why the Testament was changed, *Because they continued not in My covenant, and I regarded them not, saith the Lord.*

Jer xxxi. 31, 32; Heb viii. 8, 9.

Ib. 9.

18. The priests of the Law, the tribunals of the Law have passed away; let us draw nigh to *our new High Priest, to the throne of grace,* to the guest of our souls, to the Priest, *Who is not made after the law of the carnal commandment, but* elected *after the power of an endless life* [d]. For *He took not this honour to himself,* but was chosen by the Father, as the Father Himself saith, *Thou art a Priest for ever, after the order of Melchisedech.* Other priests offered for

Heb. iv. 14.

Ib. vii. 16.

Ib. 17. Ps. cx. 4.

---

[d] The word 'vitae' is here inserted as necessary to the sense, and to the accuracy of the quotation.

LETT. 45. themselves and for their people; this Man, not having sin, that He should offer for Himself, offered Himself for the whole world, and by His own blood entered into the Sanctuary.

19. He then is the new Priest and the new Victim, not of the law but above the law, the universal Mediator, the Light of the world, Who said, *Lo I come,* and came. To Him then let us draw near in the fulness of faith, adoring and beseeching and hoping in Him, Whom with our eyes we see not, but Whom we embrace with our hearts, to Whom be glory and honour for ever. Farewell, my son; love me, for I love you.

Heb. x. 7.

A D. 385.

LETTER XLV.

S Ambrose replies to the inquiry of Sabinus whether he had written concerning Paradise, and what was his opinion concerning it. Having first touched on the historical description of the place, he proceeds to the mystical explanation of it. And having shewn that Paradise is situate in the principal region of the soul, he teaches what is signified by the several parts thereof, and what men should imitate in the serpent. Lastly, having declared the greatness of human weakness and what great love God has shewn us from the beginning, he exhorts men to fly the pleasures of the senses.

AMBROSE TO SABINUS.

1. Having read my work on the six days of creation, you have thought good to enquire whether I have added ought concerning Paradise, and to express your strong desire to know what opinion I hold concerning it. I have, in truth, written on this subject, though not yet a veteran priest.

2. The opinions about it I have found to be many and various. Josephus, as an historian, tells us it is a place filled with trees and thick shrubs, and that it is watered by a river which divides itself into four streams. Its waters being thus gathered into one, this region does not entirely empty and deprive itself of its feeders, but up to this day bursts out into fountains and sends forth its winding streams, nourishing by them her offspring as from the full breasts of a pious mother.

3. Others expound it differently, but all agree that in Paradise is the deep rooted Tree of life, and the Tree of Knowledge whereby good and evil are discerned, the other trees also, full of vigor, and life, endued both with breath and reason. Wherefore we conclude that the real Paradise is no earthly one which can be seen; that it is placed in no spot of ground, but in the highest part of our own nature, which receives animation and life from the powers of the soul, and from the communication of the Spirit of God.

4. Moreover, Solomon by inspiration of the Spirit has plainly shown that Paradise is in man himself. And seeing that he declares the mysteries either of the soul and the Word, or of Christ and the Church, he says of the virgin soul, or of the Church which he wished *to present as a chaste virgin to Christ, A garden enclosed is my sister, my spouse, a spring sealed up, a fountain closed.*

5. 'Paradisus' is the Greek, 'hortus' the Latin name. And in the Latin text we read that Susannah was in a paradise. Adam too was in a paradise. Let it not trouble you then that some Latin manuscripts have the word 'hortus,' others 'paradisus.'

6. Where the chaste wife is, there also is the virgin; the chosen virgin has indeed her barriers and enclosures, but both are in a garden, that thus by the shade of virtue they may be shielded from the heats of the body and concupiscence of the flesh.

7. Hence also Paradise is in our highest part, thick set with the growth of many opinions, and wherein chiefly God hath placed the Tree of life, that is, the root of piety, for this is the true substance of our life, that we should offer due service to our Lord and God.

8. He has likewise planted within us a seed-plot of the knowledge of good and evil; for man alone of all creatures of the earth possesses the knowledge of good and evil. Divers other plants are also there, whose fruits are virtues.

9. Now since God knew that man's affections, once endued with knowledge, would more readily incline towards craft than towards perfect prudence, (for how could the qualities of His work be concealed from His discerning

eye, Who had set up certain boundaries in our soul?) He desired to cast out craft from Paradise, and as the provident Author of our salvation, to place therein the desire of life and the discipline of piety. Wherefore He commanded man to eat of every tree which is in Paradise, but that of the tree of knowledge of good and evil he should not eat.

10. But since all creatures are subject to passions, lust, with the stealth of a serpent, has crept over man's affections: well therefore has holy Moses represented lust under the similitude of a serpent; for it creeps upon its belly like a serpent, not walking on foot, nor raised up on legs, gliding along by the sinuous contortions, as it were, of its whole body. Its food, as that of the serpent, is earthly, for it knows not heavenly food, but feeds on carnal things, and changes itself into various kinds of desire, and bends to and fro in tortuous wreaths. It has poison in its fangs, whereby the belly of every luxurious man is ripped up, the glutton is slain, the licker up of dishes perishes. How many have been burst by wine, weakened by drunkenness, distended by gluttony.

11. Now I understand why the Lord God breathed on the face of man; for there is the seat and there are the incitements to lust, the eyes, the ears, the nose and the mouth; it was to fortify our senses against lust. Now it was this lust, which, as a serpent, inspired us with craft, for it is not lust but labour and constant meditation, which, by God's grace, gives perfect wisdom.

12. Now since the posterity of Adam are involved in the snares of the serpent, let us imitate herein the fraud of the serpent, and not run our head into danger, but be careful of its security beyond that of our other members, for *the head of every man is Christ*. Let this remain safe, that the poison of the serpent may not harm us. For *Wisdom is good with an inheritance*, that is, with faith, for there is an inheritance to them that believe in God.

13. But if that first man, who, dwelling in Paradise, conversed with God, could fall so easily, though made of that virgin clay which had lately been formed and created by the word of God, nor as yet clotted with gore and the murder of kindred, nor polluted by iniquity and shame;

nor condemned in our flesh to the curse of a guilty posterity; how much more easily afterwards did the smooth-worn path of sin lead the human race to a greater fall, when, one after another, generations more and more depraved succeeded others less wicked?

14. For if the magnet has such natural power as to attract iron to it, and transfuse itself into the character of iron, so that often when persons, wishing to try the experiment, apply iron rings to the same stone, it retains all equally firmly: whereas, if to that ring to which the stone adheres you add another, and so on in succession, although the natural power of the magnet reaches through all in succession, it binds the first with a firm, the hindermost with a slighter bond: if such be the case, how much more must the condition and nature of the human race have fallen from a pure state into one less pure, seeing that it was always attracted to a generation more wicked than itself?

15. For if the power of nature is diminished even by passing through those substances which are not capable of sin, how much more must its vigour be abated by minds and bodies polluted by the stain of crime? Wherefore, seeing that wickedness had increased, that innocence had decayed, that *there was no one that did good, no, not one;* the Lord came in order to form anew, nay to augment, the grace of nature; *that where sin had abounded, grace might much more abound.* It is plain then both that God is the Creator of man, and that there is one God not many gods; but that there is one God Who made the world, and one world, not many worlds, as the philosophers assert.

Ps. xiv. 3.
Rom. v. 20.
1 Cor. viii. 5, 6.

16. First therefore He created the world, and then its inhabitant, man, that the whole world might be his country. For if, up to this day, wherever the wise man goes, he finds himself a citizen, he understands his own position, he considers himself no where as a stranger or sojourner, how much more was that first man an inhabitant of the whole world, and, as the Greeks say, a cosmopolite, he who was the recent creation of God, conversing continually with Him, the fellow-citizen of the saints, the seed-plot of virtue, set over all creatures in the earth sea and

LETT. 45. air, who considered the whole world to be his dominion; whom the Lord defended as His own work, and as a loving Father and Maker never deserted? In fine He so cherished this His creation, as to redeem him when lost, to receive him when banished, when dead to raise him to life by the passion of His Only-begotten Son. Wherefore God is the Author of man, and, as a good Creator, loves His own work, as a gracious Father, abandons not him, whom, in the character of a rich householder, He has redeemed at the cost of His own possessions.

17. Let us be on our guard therefore that this man, that is, our understanding[1] be not enervated by that woman, that is passion, who was herself deceived and beguiled by the pleasure of our senses; that she do not circumvent and draw him over to her own maxims and opinions. Let us fly pleasure as a serpent; it has many allurements, and especially as regards man. For other animals are captivated by greediness after food; man, in that the powers of his eyes and ears are more varied, is exposed to greater dangers.

Farewell; love me, as you indeed do, for I love you.

[1] νους.

A.D. 389.

LETTER XLVI.

SABINUS, who was Bishop of Placentia, had written to S. Ambrose to tell him of an Apollinarian heretic, who appears, after being condemned at Placentia, to have gone to Milan. S. Ambrose in this reply states how he had answered him from Holy Scripture, and refuted his false interpretations, especially of the passage in the Epistle to the Philippians, and announces that he has baffled him, and that he is 'preparing to flee.'

AMBROSE TO SABINUS.

1. THE man of whom you have written to me as a disseminator of pernicious doctrines is a very light character, and has already received the reward of his poison. For he has been replied to publicly, and what he had sown in private he has reaped openly. I had previously esteemed him vain and envious only, but when this language of his reached

my ears, I immediately answered that he was infected by the venom of Apollinaris, who will not admit that our Lord Jesus became a servant for us when He took upon Him our flesh; and this, although the Apostle declares that *He took on Him the form of a servant.* This is the bulwark, this is the hedge of our faith; he who destroys this shall be destroyed himself, as it is written, *Whoso breaketh an hedge, a serpent shall bite him.*

[marginal: TO SABINUS. Phil. ii. 7. Eccles. x. 8.]

2. At first I gently asked him, Why do you what is in itself good with evil intent? For I esteem it a favour if any one who reads my writings will tell me of any thing which causes him surprise. And this, first, because even in things which I know I may be deceived. Many things pass by the ear unheeded, many things sound differently to others, it is well, if it be possible, to be on one's guard in all matters. Next, because it does not become me to be disturbed, seeing that many questions are mooted concerning the words of the Apostles and those of the Gospel and our Lord Himself, if things are found in my writings also, which people consider subjects of dispute. For many indulge their own humour, like that man who compassed the whole world, that he might find some one to censure, not one whom he might deem worthy of imitation.

3. Now this man discovered a nasty means of cavilling at something in my writings, since in commenting upon the passage in which the Lord Jesus said, *I thank Thee, Father, Lord of heaven and earth,* I stated that it was intended to show that He is the Father of the Son and the Lord of the creature. Nevertheless in the Psalm the Son has plainly called the Father, Lord: *They that looked upon Me shaked their heads: help Me, O Lord My God.* For speaking in the form of a servant He called Him Lord Whom He knew to be His Father; though equal in the form of God, proclaiming Himself to be a servant according to the substance of His flesh; for slavery is of the flesh, lordship of the Godhead.

[marginal: S. Matt. xi. 25. Ps. cix. 25, 26.]

4. First then your great sagacity perceives that what is said in the Gospel has reference to the times of the Gospel, when the Lord Jesus dwelt among men in human form; but now *we know Christ according to the flesh no longer.*

[marginal: 2 Cor v. 16]

LETT 46. Be it that He was so seen and known by them of old, now
2 Cor v. *old things are passed away, all things are become new.* But
17. all things are from God, Who has reconciled us by Christ
unto Himself; for we were dead, and therefore One was
Phil. ii 7. made a servant for all. Why do I say, a servant? He was
made sin, a reproach, a curse. For the Apostle has said
2 Cor. v. that *He was made sin for us,* that the Lord Jesus *was made*
21.
Gal iii. *a curse for us.* He has said, *when all things shall be sub-*
13. *dued unto Him, then shall He also Himself be subject.* Peter
1 Cor. xv.
28. also said in the Acts of the Apostles, *In the name of Jesus*
Acts iii. 6. *Christ of Nazareth, rise up and walk.* Then he said also,
Ib 13. that God had *glorified His Servant Jesus,* and no one brings
any charge against him concerning the time. But in the
Rev. v. Apocalypse He is called *a Lamb* by John, in the Psalm He is
12
Ps xxii. called *a worm and no man.* He was made all these things
6 that He might blunt the sting of our death, that He might
1 Cor. xv. take away our slavery, that He might abolish our curses,
55.
our sins, our reproaches.

5. These things and others and many more you have
written me word that you answered to one who consulted
you; and, seeing that they are contained in Holy Scripture,
how should any one hesitate to utter what has been thus
piously written, tending as they do to the glory of Christ,
[1] dimi- not to His disparagement? For if it is said of His gift, that
nuit
Exod. is, of the manna, that *he that gathered little had no lack*[1], *he*
xvi. 18
[2] ampli- *that gathered much had nothing over* [2], could He Himself
avit. suffer diminution or increase? For in what respect was He
Is. liii. 4. diminished by taking upon Him our bondage, our infirmities?
Phil. ii. 7. He was humbled, He was in the form of a servant, but He
Ib. 11.
Ps. xxii. 7. was also in the glory of God the Father. He was a worm
S. Luke upon the Cross, but He also forgave the sins of His perse-
xxiii. 34. cutors. He was a reproach, but He is also the glory of the
Isa. xl. 5. Lord, as it is written, *The glory of the Lord shall be revealed,*
and all flesh shall see it together. What did He lose Who
Ib. liii. 2. is wanting in nothing? *He had* indeed *no form or comeli-*
ness, but He had the fulness of the Godhead. He was
accounted weak, but He ceased not to be the Power of God.
He was seen in human form, but there shone upon earth
the Divine Majesty and the glory of the Father.

6. Well therefore has the Apostle repeated the same

word, saying of the Lord Jesus, *Who being in the form of God thought it not robbery to be equal with God; but made Himself of no reputation and took upon Him the form of a servant.* What is the meaning of *in the form of God* but in the fulness of the Godhead, in the expression of the Divine perfection? Being therefore in the fulness of the Godhead, He *emptied Himself* of it, and received the fulness of human nature and perfection: as nothing was wanting to Him as God so neither was there any thing wanting to His completeness as Man, that in either *form* He might be perfect. Wherefore David also says, *Thou art fairer than the children of men.*

TO SABINUS Phil. ii 6, 7.

Ps. xlv 2.

7. The Apollinarian is confuted, he has no refuge to turn to, he is caught in his own net. For he himself had said, He took upon him the form of a servant, He was not chosen to be a servant. I ask again therefore, what is the meaning of *in the form of God?* He replies, In the nature of God. For there are those, says the Apostle, *which by nature are no gods.* I enquire, what is the meaning of *took upon Him the form of a servant?* Doubtless, as I have stated, the perfection of the nature and condition of man, that He might be in the likeness of man. And he has said well *the likeness*, not of the flesh, but *of men*, for He is in the same flesh. But since He alone was without sin, but all men are in sin, He was seen *in the form of man.* Wherefore the prophet also says, *He is a man yet who can know him*[a]*?* Man according to the flesh, but beyond man according to the Divine operation. When he touched the leper He was seen as man, but above man when He cleansed him. When He wept over Lazarus dead, He wept as man, but He was above men when He commanded the dead to come forth with bound feet. He was seen as man when He hung upon the cross, but above man when the graves were opened and He raised the dead.

Gal iv. 8.

Phil ii 7.

Ib.

Jer. xvii. 9.

S. Matt. viii. 2, 3. S. John xi. 33, 44.

S. Matt xxvii. 52.

8. Nor has the Apollinarian venom any cause for complaining because it is thus written, *And being found in fashion*[1] *as a man*, for Jesus is not hereby denied to be man, for in another place Paul himself calls Him, *The Mediator between God and man, the man Christ Jesus*, but

Phil. ii. 8. [1] specie 1 Tim. ii. 5.

[a] This agrees with the LXX, καὶ ἄνθρωπός ἐστι καὶ τίς γνώσεται αὐτόν,

rather His manhood is established. For it is the custom and manner of Scripture so to express itself, and we read also in the Gospel, *And we beheld His glory, the glory as of the Only-begotten of the Father.* In the same way therefore that He is called *as* the only-begotten, yet it is not denied that He is truly the only-begotten Son of God, so He is said to be *as* man, yet it is not denied that the perfection of manhood existed in Him.

<small>Lett. 46.</small>
<small>S. John i. 14.</small>

9. While, then, He was in the form of a servant, humbled even unto death, He yet remained in the glory of God. What injury then was His state of subjection to Him? We read that He was made a servant, because we read that He was made of a Virgin and created in the flesh, for every creature is a servant, as the Prophet says; *For all things serve Thee.* Wherefore also God the Father says, *I have found David My servant, with My holy oil have I anointed him. He shall call Me, Thou art my Father, my God, and my strong salvation; and I will make him My first-born;* and in another Psalm, *Preserve Thou my soul for I am holy. save Thy servant,* and afterwards in the same Psalm, *Give Thy strength unto Thy servant, and help the son of Thy handmaid.* Thus I have collected the words of the Father and of the Son, that I may answer not with human arguments but by the Divine oracles.

<small>Phil. ii. 7.</small>
<small>Gal. iv. 4.</small>
<small>Ps. cxix. 91.</small>
<small>Ib.</small>
<small>lxxxix. 20. 26, 27.</small>
<small>Ib.</small>
<small>lxxxvi. 2</small>

10. In another passage He says, *Into Thy hands I commend My spirit,* and, *Thou hast set My feet in a large room,* and, *I became a reproof among all Mine enemies.* And in the same Psalm, *Shew Thy servant the light of Thy countenance.* By the mouth of Isaiah too the Son of God Himself says, *From my mother's womb the Lord hath called My name, and He hath made My mouth like a sharp sword, in the shadow of His hand hath He hid Me, and made Me a polished shaft; in His quiver hath He hid Me; and said unto Me, Thou art My servant, O Israel.* For the Son of God is also called Israel, as in another place, *But thou, Israel, My Servant Jacob, whom I have chosen.* For He alone hath truly not only seen but also declared God the Father.

<small>Ps. xxxi. 5.</small>
<small>Ib. 8.</small>
<small>Ib. 11.</small>
<small>Ib. 16.</small>
<small>Isa. xlix. 1—3.</small>
<small>Ib. xli. 8.</small>
<small>S. John i. 18.</small>

11. And it goes on, *In whom I will be glorified. Then I said, I have laboured in vain, I have spent my strength for*

<small>Isa xlix. 3, 4, 5.</small>

nought, and in vain: yet surely my judgment is with the Lord, and my work with my God. And now saith the Lord that formed me from the womb to be His servant, to bring Jacob again to Him and Israel. Who hath gathered the people of God but Christ? Who is glorified before the Lord? Who is the Power of God? He to Whom the Father hath said, *It is a light thing that Thou shouldest be My servant*[2]*, and He to Whom He says Behold, I will give Thee for a covenant of the people, for a light of the Gentiles, that Thou mightest be My Salvation unto the end of the earth.* Of Him He has also spoken by the mouth of the prophet Ezekiel, saying, *I will set up one Shepherd over them, and He shall feed them, even My Servant David, He shall feed them, and He shall be their Shepherd. And I the Lord will be their God, and My Servant David a Prince among them.* Now king David was already dead, and therefore the true David, the truly humble, the truly meek, the true Son of God, strong of hand, is announced by this name; he also is intended in the book of the prophet Zechariah, where God the Father says, *Behold I will send my servant, the Orient*[b] *is His name.* Did then His being *clothed in filthy garments* deprive the Sun of righteousness of the brightness of His Godhead?

TO SABINUS

[2] puerum. Isa. xlix. 6. Ib. xlii. 6. xlix. 6.

Ezek. xxxiv. 23, 24.

Zech. iii. 8. Ib. iii. 3.

12. And why need I say more? Shall we deem servitude to be a state of greater weakness than that of being made sin, of being a curse, a reproach, than the infirmities which He bore for our sakes that we might be saved from them? For He was made all of these that He might relieve the world from them. But they will not admit that He was made a servant, a reproach, a curse, because they affirm that the Word and the flesh are of one substance, and say, Because He redeemed us He is called a servant, and ought to be called sin. And they do not perceive this to be the glory of Christ, that in His Incarnation He took upon Him the state of a servant that He

---

[b] 'Ecce ego mittam servum meum, Oriens nomen Ejus.' Vulg. has 'Ecce ego adducam servum meum Orientem.' 'Oriens nomen Ejus' comes in v. 12 'Behold I will bring forth my servant the Branch.' The same word in the original is used also in Is. iv. 2 Jerem. xxiii. 5. xxxiii 15. and in all those passages the Vulg renders it by 'Germen.' In the passages of Zech. and Jerem. the LXX. have the word ἀνατολή. The word in the original means 'a sprout' or 'shoot.'

312 *and became a curse that we might be blessed.*

Lett. 46. might restore liberty to all; He bore our sins, that He might take away the sin of the world.

13. He was made a servant, He was made sin and a curse, that thou mightest cease to be a servant of sin, and that He might absolve thee from the curse of the Divine judgment. He therefore took upon Him thy curse, for *Cursed is every one that hangeth on a tree.* He was made a curse upon the cross, that thou mightest be blessed in the kingdom of God. He was disgraced, He was vilified and set at nought. He said, *I have laboured in vain,* through Whom Paul was enabled to say, *I have not laboured in vain.* This He did that He might confer on His servants the fruit of good works and the glory of the preaching of the Gospel, whereby the world might be released from the burthen of its toil.

Gal. iii. 13.
Is xlix. 4.
Phil. ii. 16.

14. On hearing these things *the partridge*[b] *was left in the midst of her days,* she who cried *that she might gather the things which she did not lay,* and was overcome by the voice of the Lord Jesus. And even now is she preparing for flight.

Jer. xvii. 11.

Farewell; love me, for I love you.

A.D. 390.

LETTER XLVII.

This brief letter was sent with a book which Sabinus had asked for. It is a friendly invitation to a regular correspondence, as bringing friends together in spirit who are severed in body.

AMBROSE TO SABINUS.

1. I have transmitted the volume you asked for, written more clearly and neatly than the one which I had previously sent, in order that by the facility of its perusal your judgment of it might be unimpeded. For the original copy was written not for appearance, but for use, for I do not always employ a scribe, especially at night, at which time I am unwilling to be a trouble and a burthen to others, and further, because the words I am then dictating flow on with a kind of impetuosity, and in a rapid stream.

2. But as I am desirous to select with precision the

[b] See Letter xxxii. 1.

words which my old age employs in its familiar intercourse, and to proceed with a slow step, I think the use of my own hands in writing befits me better; that I may seem rather to conceal my words than lustily give vent to them; and may not have to blush at the presence of him who is writing for me, but, having no one in the secret of my words, may weigh what I write with eye as well as with ears. For, in the words of Scripture, the tongue is swifter than the hand; *My tongue is the pen of a ready writer.* TO SABINUS

Ps. xlv. 2.

3. And though you may perhaps say that the swiftness is here attributed to the writer, the meaning will nevertheless not escape you that it is only the swiftness of a ready writer which can take down the words of the prophetic tongue. The Apostle Paul also wrote with his own hand, as he says himself, *I have written unto you with mine own hand.* He did it to show honour, we do it from bashfulness. Gal. vi. 11.

4. But while your judgement of my book is still in suspense, let us entertain each other by letters; the advantage whereof is that although severed from each other by distance of space we may be united in affection; for by this means the absent have the image of each other's presence reflected back upon them, and conversation by writing unites the severed. By this means also we interchange thoughts with our friend, and transpose our mind into his.

5. Now if, according to your admonition, there is any savour of ancient writings in our letters, not only do our minds seem to be united by this progress in true doctrine, but also the form and fashion of a more intimate converse seems to be set forth, in that the discussion which is thus entered upon by mutual inquiry and reply appears to place in presence of each other those friends who in this manner challenge and engage one another.

6. And why need I produce the example of our ancestors, who by their letters have instilled faith into the minds of the people, and have written to whole nations together, and have shewn themselves to be present although writing from a distance, according to the words of the Apostle, that he was *absent in body, but present in spirit,* not only in writing but also in judging. Again, he condemned them 1 Cor. v. 3.

while absent by epistle, and also absolved them by epistle; for the epistle of Paul was a certain image of his presence and form of his work.

7 For the epistles of the Apostles were not, like those of others, *weighty and powerful, but his bodily presence weak, and his speech contemptible,* but his letter was of that kind that such as was the substance of his work such also was the form of his precept; for *such,* says he, *as we are in word by letters when absent, such will we be also in deed when we are present.* He imprinted the image of his presence on his letters, he declared its fruit and testimony in his work.

Farewell; love me, as indeed you do, for I love you.

LETTER XLVIII.

S Ambrose in this letter begs Sabinus to examine the books which he sends to him carefully, and to criticise them freely, as a proof of true friendship, and at the same time adding to the value of the works.

AMBROSE TO SABINUS.

1. You have sent me back my volumes, and I shall hold them in greater esteem owing to your judgment. I have therefore sent you others, not so much because I was delighted at wishing for your favourable judgment, as of that truth which I have asked and you have promised to declare to me; for should any thing strike you I would rather it had the correction of your judgment before it goes abroad beyond the power of recal, than that you should praise what is blamed by others. It is on this account that I have requested to have your opinion of those things which you asked me to write, for I have not so much desired that what I publish from time to time should be read by you, as that they should be submitted to the account which your judgment shall take of them. And this judgment, as one said of old, will not require [a] a long sitting and delay. For surely it is easy for you to judge of my writings.

[a] He is quoting from a letter of Cicero's. Ep. ix. 3. Longi subsellii, ut noster Pompeius appellat, judicatio et mora.

2. Thus far, on your invitation, I have thought it right to proceed; it is now your part to discern clearly and examine carefully what requires correction, that you may thus escape being inculpated in those faults which may have stolen unawares upon myself. For somehow over and above that want of caution which envelops me as with a mist, every one is beguiled in what he himself writes, and its faults escape his ear. And as a man takes pleasure in his children even though deformed, so also is a writer flattered by his own discourses however ungraceful. How frequently are words put forth uncautiously or understood less charitably than one means; or some ambiguity escapes from us; things, moreover, which are to be subjected to the judgment of others we ought to weigh not so much by our own as by another's opinion, and to separate from it every grain of malevolence.

<small>TO SABINUS</small>

3. Be so kind therefore as to lend an ear of keen attention, peruse the whole thoroughly, test my discourses, see whether they contain, not rhetorical charms and persuasive words, but a sound faith and a sober confession. Affix a mark on words of doubtful weight and which are deceitful in the scales, that the adversary may not make out any thing to tell in his favour. Let him meet with defeat if he enters into the contest. That book is in a bad condition, which cannot be defended without a champion; for a book which goes forth without a mediator has to speak for itself; my book however shall not go forth from me, unless it receive authority from you. When then you bid it go forth, and give your word for it, let it be left to its own keeping.

4. But, since *the kingdom of God is not in word but in power*, if a word offend you consider the *power* of its profession. By profession I mean that decision of faith which we hold, as handed down by our fathers, against the Sabellians and Arians, that we worship God the Father and His Only-begotten Son and the Holy Spirit, that this Trinity is of one Substance Majesty and Divinity; that in this *Name of the Father and of the Son and of the Holy Ghost*, we baptize, as it is written; that the Son, co-eternal with the Father, took upon Him our flesh, born of the Holy Spirit and of the Virgin Mary, equal to the Father as touching His

<small>1 Cor. iv. 20.</small>

<small>S. Matt. xxviii. 19.</small>

Lett. 48.
Col. ii 9.
Phil. ii. 7, 8.

Godhead, in the form of God, that is, in all the fulness of the Godhead Which *dwells in Him*, as the Apostle says, *bodily;* Who, in the person of man, *took upon Him the form of a servant, and humbled Himself even unto death*.

5. Wherefore as against Photinus this is our sentence, and as against Apollinaris it is also a proper safeguard; our confession, namely, that as in the form of God He lacked nothing of the Divine nature and fulness, so in that human form there was nothing wanting in Him so as to cause Him to be judged imperfect as Man; for He came in order to save man altogether. Truly it would not have been fitting that He Who had accomplished a perfect work in others should suffer it to be imperfect in Himself; for if aught was wanting to Him as Man, then He did not redeem the whole man, and if He did not redeem the whole man, He deceived us, for He said that He had come in

Heb. vi. 18.

order to save the whole man. But since it is *impossible for God to lie,* He deceived us not; wherefore, seeing that He came to redeem and save the whole man, He took upon Him the whole of that which belonged to human perfection.

6. Such, as you will remember, is my belief. Should my words in any passage raise a doubt, still they will not raise any prejudice as to my faith, for if the mind continue stedfast, it extends its protection over ambiguous language, and preserves it from error.

7. This preface then I send you, and will insert it, if you please, in the books of our letters, and place it among their number; that so it may be recommended by your name, and by our letters to each other our mutual love in the Lord, may be increased: that, finally, you may so read as to give me your judgment, and to communicate to me whatever may strike you, for true love is proved by constancy. For the present we have chosen that which old men find more easy, the writing of letters in ordinary and familiar language: subjoining, should such present itself, any appropriate passage from the sacred Scriptures. Farewell, my brother, and love one who is your lover, for I greatly love you.

LETTER XLIX. A.D 390.

S Ambrose says that he never feels less solitary, than when by himself writing to a friend. He then dwells on the benefit of solitude; especially in that we may then have God present with us, and lay open our souls to Him.

AMBROSE TO SABINUS.

1. Since you also take pleasure in receiving my letters, by means of which, although separated from each other, we discourse together as if present, I will for the future more frequently converse with you by letter when I am alone. For[a] I am never less alone than when I seem to be so, nor ever less at leisure than in the intervals of labour. For then I summon at pleasure whom I will, and associate to myself those whom I love most or find most congenial; no man interrupts or intrudes upon us. Then it is that I more intimately enjoy you, that I confer with you in the Scriptures, that we converse together more at length.

2. Mary was alone when addressed by the Angel, alone when the *Holy Ghost came upon her, and the power of the Highest overshadowed her.* She was alone when she effected the salvation of the world, and conceived the Redemption of the universe. Peter was alone when the mystery of the sanctification of the Gentiles all over the world was made known to him. Adam was alone, and he fell not, because his mind adhered to God. But when the woman was joined to him he lost his power of abiding by the celestial precepts, and therefore he hid himself when God walked in Paradise.

S. Luke i. 35.

Acts x. 10.

Gen. iii. 8.

3. And even now, while I read the sacred Scriptures, God walks in Paradise. The book of Genesis, wherein the virtues of the Patriarchs bud forth, is Paradise; Deuteronomy, wherein grow the precepts of the Law, is also Para-

---

[a] He is here quoting from Cicero De off. iii. 1, where Cicero gives as a saying of Scipio Africanus, on the authority of Cato, 'numquam se minus otiosum esse quam quum otiosus, nec minus solum quam quum solus esset' It is quoted again by S. Ambrose in De off. Min. iii. 1, 107.

dise, wherein the tree of life brings forth good fruit, and diffuses over all nations the precepts of eternal hope.

4. So when I hear, *Love your enemies*, when I hear, *Sell that thou hast, and give to the poor;* when I hear, *unto him that smiteth thee on the one cheek offer also the other;* when I hear these things and do not perform them, nay, when I barely love him who loves me, when I will not part with what I have, when I desire to avenge the injuries I have received, and to recover what has been wrested from me, whereas the Scripture bids me give up more than I have been asked for or deprived of, I perceive that I am acting contrary to the commands of God. Thus opening the eyes of my conscience, I perceive that God is present and walking with me; I desire to hide, I desire to clothe myself; but I am naked in His sight unto Whom *all things are naked and opened!* I am abashed therefore, and desire to conceal the shame of my crimes as though they were the secret members of my body; but since God sees all things, since I am manifest to Him, though covered with leaves and shaded by thickets, I think to conceal myself from Him by the covering of my body. This is that coat of skins, in which Adam was clothed when he was cast out of Paradise, neither shielded from the cold, nor protected from scorn, but exposed to misery as well as guilt.

5. From whence it appears that it is when alone that we offer ourselves to God, that we open to Him our souls, that we put off the cloak of fraud. Adam was alone when placed in Paradise; alone also when made in the image of God: but when cast out of Paradise he was not alone. The Lord Jesus was alone when He redeemed the world; for it was no herald or messenger, but the Lord Himself alone Who redeemed His people, although He, in Whom the Father always dwells, can never be alone. Let us also then be alone, that the Lord may be with us. Farewell: love me, for I also love you.

LETTER L.

TO CHROMATIUS

THIS letter contains an interesting discussion of the question how an evil man like Balaam could be employed by God to utter true prophecies, and deals with other difficulties which arise out of Balaam's history.

AMBROSE TO CHROMATIUS.

1. DOES God lie? Truly He lies not, because it is impossible for God to lie. And further, does this impossibility arise from infirmity? No, truly, for how can He be Almighty if He cannot do all things? What then is impossible to Him? Not that which is difficult to His Power, but what is contrary to His Nature. *It is impossible*, it is said, *for Him to lie*. This impossibility comes not of infirmity, but of Power and Majesty, for truth admits not of falsehood, nor God's Power of the weakness of error. Wherefore *let God be true and every man a liar*. Heb. vi. 18.

Rom. iii. 4.

2. The truth therefore is always in Him; *He remains faithful,* change or *deny Himself He cannot.* But if He deny that He is true, He lies, but to lie belongs not to power but to weakness. Nor can He change, for His nature admits not infirmity. This impossibility therefore comes of His fulness, which cannot be diminished or increased, not of infirmity, which, in that it increases itself, is weak. Whence we gather that this impossibility on the part of God is indeed most powerful. For what can be more powerful than to be ignorant of all infirmity?

3. There is however another *weakness of God* which *is stronger than men*, and a *foolishness of God* which *is wiser than men*, but this has reference to the Cross, the former to His Godhead. If then His weakness is strength, how can that which comes of His power be weak? Let it therefore be an axiom with us that God lies not. 1 Cor. i. 25.

4. But there was no diviner of auguries in Israel according to the law of God. How then was it that Balaam said that he was forbidden by the oracle of God to go and curse the people of Israel, and yet he went, and the Angel of the Lord who had forbidden his going, met him, and stood in the way of the ass that carried him, and nevertheless the Angel himself bid him go, only he must speak that which Deut. xviii. 10.

LETT. 50. should be put into his mouth? If there was to be no deceiver in Israel, how did this oracle of God, declaring things for true, come to him who was a deceiver? If he spoke as the oracle of God, whence did he derive the grace of the Divine inspiration?

5. But you are not to wonder that the Lord should put into the mouth of a diviner what he should speak, when you read in the Gospel that it was put into the mouth even of the prince of the Synagogue, one of the persecutors of Christ, that *it is expedient that one man should die for the people?* Herein then is no merit of prophecy, but an assertion of the truth; that by the testimony even of adversaries the truth might be declared, so that the perfidy of unbelievers might be confuted by the words even of their own diviners. Just so Abraham [a] the Chaldæan is called to belief, that the superstition of the Chaldæans might be put to silence. It is not therefore the merit of him who utters, but rather the oracle of God Who calls, the grace of God Who reveals.

S John xi. 50.

6. Now what was the guilt which Balaam incurred, but that he spoke one thing, and designed another? For God requires a clean vessel, not one defiled by uncleanness and pollution. Balaam therefore was tried, not approved, for he was full of deceit and treachery. Again, when he first enquired whether he should go to that vain people, and was forbidden, he excused himself: afterwards, when more honourable messages were sent, he who ought to have refused consent, seduced by ampler promises and more abundant gifts, was led again to enquire of God, as if many gifts could influence the mind of God.

Numb. xxii. 12.

Ib. 19.

7. Answer was made to him as to a covetous man, not as to one who sought the truth, that so he might rather be deceived than rightly informed. He set out, an Angel met him in a narrow place, and shewed himself to the ass,

Ib. 25.

---

[a] This is the reading of most MSS, according to the Benedictine Editors. And, though the connection of ideas is somewhat abrupt, they explain it to be, that, as the gift of faith was bestowed on Abraham the Chaldean, so the gift of prophecy was bestowed on Balaam. All the other Editions have 'Balaam' instead of 'Abraham.' This makes the connection easier, but then 'adscitur ad fidem' is strangely applied to him, and it could only mean, 'is employed to utter the truth.' He might be called a Chaldean as the common name among the Romans for Eastern diviners generally

but not to the diviner. To the former he revealed himself, the latter he crushed; yet, that he might at length be recognized by him, he opened his eyes also. He saw, but even yet he did not believe the manifest oracle, and though his very eyes ought to have convinced him, he answered confusedly and doubtingly.

TO CHROMATIUS

8. Then the Lord, being angry, said to him by the Angel, *Go with the men, but only the word that I shall speak unto thee, that shalt thou speak.* As an empty instrument you shall give utterance to My words. It is I Who will speak, not you; you will only echo what you hear and do not understand. You will gain no advantage by going, because you will return without either a reward of money or progress in grace. Again, these are his first words, *How shall I curse whom God hath not cursed?* in order to shew that the benediction of the Hebrew people depended not on his will but on the grace of God.

Numb. xxii. 35.

Ib. xxiii. 8.

9. *From the top of the rocks,* he says, *I see him;* for I cannot embrace within my ken this people, which shall dwell alone, marking out their boundaries, not so much by the occupation of space as by the abode of virtue, and extending them into eternal ages by the distinctive peculiarity of their manners. For which of the bordering nations shall be numbered with this one, which is raised above their fellowship by its exalted righteousness? Who shall understand the nature of its generation? Their bodies we indeed perceive to have been compounded and fashioned of human seed, but their minds have sprung from higher and wondrous seed-plots.

10. *Let my soul die with their souls,* die to this bodily life, that with the souls of the just it may attain to the grace of that eternal life. Herein even then was revealed the excellence of our heavenly Sacrament and of holy Baptism, by the operation whereof men die to original sin and to evil works; that being transformed by newness of life into fellowship with the just they may rise again to live as do the just. And what wonder is it that it should be so, when men die to sin in order to live to God?

Ib. 10.

11. Balak hearing this, was wroth and said, 'I brought thee to curse and thou blessest.' He answered, 'I am re-

Ib. 11.

proved for that of which I am not conscious; for I speak nothing of my own, but utter sounds like *a tinkling cymbal.*' Again, being carried to a second and a third place, although he wished to curse, he blessed; *He hath not beheld iniquity in Jacob, neither hath he seen perverseness in Israel; the Lord his God is with him.* And afterwards he commands seven altars and sacrifices to be prepared. He ought, indeed, to have departed, but his weak mind and mutability of purpose led him to believe that he could turn aside the Will of God: he himself, the while, being in a trance, desired one thing but spoke another.

12. *How goodly,* said he, *are thy tents,* O host of the Hebrews! *As the valleys are they spread forth, as gardens by the river's side and as cedar trees beside the waters.* A man shall come out of Jacob, and shall subdue many nations, and his kingdom shall be exalted on high: in the earth also he shall extend his dominion in Egypt. *Blessed is he that blesseth thee, and cursed is he that curseth thee.* Now to whom did he point but to the people of Christ? God blesses him into whose heart the Word of God enters, *even to the dividing asunder of the soul, and of the joints and marrow;* in him Balaam would have found the grace of the Lord if he had acted according to the intent and purpose of his heart. But since an evil mind is confuted by its own counsels, and the secrets of the soul are betrayed by events, his mind was thus discovered by the treachery which followed.

13. Therefore also he met with a worthy reward of his malice. For finding while in his trance that he could not curse, he gives his advice to the king, saying, 'Such is the utterance of what God has commanded, hear now my counsel against the oracles of God. This people is just, it has the protection of God: since it has not given itself to divinations and auguries, but to the eternal God above; and therefore its faith excels that of others. But sometimes even faithful minds fall through corporeal charms and the blandishments of beauty. Numerous are your women, and many of them not uncomely; now the male sex is in no respect more prone to fall than through the frailty with which it is captivated by female beauty, particularly if their

minds are excited by frequent converse, and thus become inflamed as by a torch; if, while they drink in the hope of enjoying, their passions are kept in suspense. Let your women therefore cast their hooks by their converse, let them offer no obstacles to a first access, but roam abroad and spread themselves through the camp, exposed to view and affable of speech. Let them so artfully deal with these men as not to admit them to carnal intercourse until they shall have proved the strength of their love by becoming participators in sacrilege. For they may thus be deprived of the protection of heaven, if they shall themselves depart by sacrilege from the Lord their God.'

14. Unrighteous therefore, as the counsellor of fornication and sacrilege, was Balaam; for thus it is plainly written in the Apocalypse of John the Evangelist, when the Lord Jesus says to the Angel of the Church of Pergamos; *Thou hast there them that hold the doctrine of Balaam, who taught Balak to cast a stumbling-block before the children of Israel, to eat things sacrified unto idols, and to commit fornication; so hast thou also them that hold the doctrine of the Nicolaitans.* Wherefore it appears that from hence has flowed the impiety of the Manichees, like that of Manasseh, who mingle and unite sacrilege with impurity.

15. Neither, then, was God unjust, nor His purpose mutable; for He detected Balaam's mind and the secrets of his heart, and He therefore tried him as a diviner, He did not choose him as a prophet. Surely he ought to have been converted if it were only by the grace of such great oracles and the sublimity of his revelations, but his mind, full of iniquity, brought forth words but did not yield belief, seeking to frustrate by its counsels that event which it had predicted. And since he could not defeat the prophecy, he suggested deceitful counsels whereby the fickle people of the Jews were tempted but not overcome; for by the righteousness of one priest all the counsel of this wicked man was overthrown, and that the host of our fathers could be delivered by one man was much more wonderful than that it could be deceived by one man.

16. This little gift I have sent to your Holiness, because

you wish me to compile somewhat from the interpretations of the ancient authors. But I had undertaken to write letters in a familiar style, savouring of the tone of thought of our fathers; and should you relish their flavour I shall be emboldened to send you of the same kind hereafter. For I prefer conversing garrulously with you like an old man concerning heavenly things, which is called in Greek αδολεσχῆσαι: *Isaac went forth into the field*, αδολεσχῆσαι, seeing in his mind, on the approach of Rebecca, the mysteries of the Church which was to come: this conversing with you with the words of an old man, that I may not seem to have abandoned my art, I prefer, I say, to uttering in a more vehement style things no longer adapted to our studies or strength.

Farewell: love me, for I also love you.

A.D 390

LETTER LI.

> THIS is the famous Letter addressed by S. Ambrose to Theodosius after the massacre at Thessalonica. The details of that occurrence are too familiar to need repeating here. In this Letter S. Ambrose explains to the Emperor why he had avoided meeting him on his return to Milan, and urges him with respectful and most affectionate, but firm remonstrance, to follow David in penitence as he had followed him in crime, and tells him that God Himself had in a vision forbidden him to offer the Sacrifice of the Eucharist in his behalf while he remained impenitent. The Letter, far from deserving Gibbon's scornful title of 'a miserable rhapsody on a noble subject,' may rather be regarded as a model of dignified remonstrance, well befitting an eminent prelate addressing a great earthly Sovereign.

AMBROSE, BISHOP, TO HIS MAJESTY THE EMPEROR THEODOSIUS.

1. VERY pleasant to me is the remembrance of your long friendship, and I also bear a grateful sense of those benefits which at my frequent intreaties you have most graciously extended to others. You may be sure then that it could not be from any ungrateful feeling that on your arrival, which I was wont to long for so ardently, I shunned your presence. The motives of my conduct I will now briefly explain.

2. I found that I alone in all your court was denied the natural right of hearing, in order to deprive me of the power of speaking too: for you were frequently displeased at decisions having reached me which were made in your Consistory. Thus I have been debarred from the common privilege of men, though the Lord Jesus says, *Nothing is secret which shall not be made manifest.* Wherefore I did my utmost to obey with reverence your royal will, and I provided both for you and for myself; for you, that you should have no cause of disturbance, to which end I endeavoured that no intelligence should be brought me of the Imperial decrees; and as to myself, I provided against my not seeming to hear, when present, from fear of others, and thus incurring the charge of connivance, and also against hearing in such manner that while my ears were open my mouth must be closed, and I must not utter what I heard, lest I should injure those who had fallen under suspicion of treachery.

TO THEODOSIUS

S. Luke viii. 17.

3. What then was I to do? was I not to listen? But I could not close my ears with the wax of the old tales. Must I disclose what I heard? But then I had reason to fear that the same result which I apprehended from your commands would ensue from my own words; that they might become the cause of bloodshed. Was I then to be silent? But this would be the most miserable of all, for my conscience would be bound, my liberty of speech taken away. And what then of the text, *if the priest warn not the wicked from his wicked way, the wicked man shall die in his iniquity*, but the priest shall be liable to punishment, because he did not warn him?

Ezek. iii. 18.

4. Suffer me, gracious Emperor. You have a zeal for the faith, I own it, you have the fear of God, I confess it; but you have a vehemence of temper, which if soothed may readily be changed into compassion, but if inflamed becomes so violent that you can scarcely restrain it. If no one will allay it, let no one at least inflame it. To yourself I would willingly trust, for you are wont to exercise self-control, and by your love of mercy to conquer this violence of your nature.

5. This vehemence of yours I have preferred secretly to

commend to your consideration, rather than run the risk of rousing it publicly by my acts. And so I have preferred to be lacking somewhat in duty rather than in humility, and that others should complain of my want of priestly authority, rather than that you should find any want of respect in me, who am so devoted to you; and this in order that you may restrain your emotions, and have full power of choosing what counsel to follow. I alleged as my reason, bodily sickness, which was in fact severe, and not to be mitigated but by more gentle treatment; still I would rather have died than not have waited two or three days for your arrival. But I could not do so.

6. An act has been committed in the city of Thessalonica, the like of which is not recorded, the perpetration of which I could not prevent, which in my frequent petitions before the court I had declared to be most atrocious, and which by your tardy revocation you have yourself pronounced to be very heinous: such an act as this I could not extenuate. Intelligence of it was first brought to a synod held on the arrival of the Gallican Bishops: all present deplored it, no one viewed it leniently; your friendship with Ambrose, so far from excusing your deed, would have even brought a heavier weight of odium on my head, had there been no one found to declare the necessity of your being reconciled to God.

7. Is your Majesty ashamed to do that which the Royal Prophet David did, the forefather of Christ according to the flesh? It was told him that a rich man, who had numerous flocks, on the arrival of a guest took a poor man's lamb and killed it, and recognizing in this act his own condemnation, he said, *I have sinned against the Lord.* Let not your Majesty then be impatient at being told, as David was by the prophet, *Thou art the man.* For if you listen thereto obediently and say, *I have sinned against the Lord,* if you will use those words of the royal Prophet, *O come let us worship and fall down, and kneel before the Lord our Maker,* to you also it shall be said, Because thou repentest, *the Lord hath put away thy sin, thou shalt not die.*

8. Another time, when David had commanded the people to be numbered, his heart smote him, and he said unto the Lord, *I have sinned greatly in that I have done, and now, I*

beseech thee O Lord, take away the iniquity of thy servant, for I have done very foolishly. And Nathan the prophet was sent again to him, to offer him three things, to choose one of them, which he would; seven years famine in the land, or to flee three months before his enemies, or three days pestilence in the land. *And David said, I am in a great strait, let us now fall into the hand of the Lord, for His mercies are great, and let me not fall into the hand of man.* His fault lay in wishing to know the number of all the people which were with him, a knowledge which ought to have been reserved for God.

<small>TO THEODOSIUS</small>

<small>2 Sam xxiv. 12.</small>

<small>Ib. 14</small>

9. And Scripture tells us that when the people were dying, on the very first day and at dinner time, David saw the Angel that smote the people, he said, *Lo, I have sinned and done wickedly; but these sheep, what have they done? let Thine hand, I pray Thee, be against me, and against my father's house.* So the Lord repented, and commanded the Angel to spare the people, and that David should offer sacrifice: for there were then sacrifices for sin, but we have now the sacrifices of penitence. So by that humility he was made more acceptable to God, for it is not wonderful that man should sin, but it is indeed blameable if he do not acknowledge his error, and humble himself before God.

<small>Ib 17.</small>

10. Holy Job, himself also powerful in this world, saith, *I covered not my sin, but declared it before all the people.* And to the cruel king Saul Jonathan his son said, *Let not the king sin against his servant, against David;* and *Wherefore then wilt thou sin against innocent blood to slay David without a cause?* For although he was a king he still would have sinned in slaying the innocent. Again when David was possessed of the kingdom, and heard that innocent Abner had been slain by Joab the Captain of his host, he said, *I and my kingdom are guiltless before the Lord for ever from the blood of Abner the son of Ner,* and he fasted for sorrow.

<small>Job xxxi. 33 (the sense, not the words) 1 Sam. xix. 4. Ib. 5.</small>

<small>2 Sam. iii 28.</small>

11. This I have written, not to confound you, but that these royal examples may induce you to put away this sin from your kingdom; for this you will do by humbling your soul before God. You are a man; temptation has fallen upon you; vanquish it. Sin is not washed away but by

Lett. 51.
S. Matt.
xxviii.20.

tears and penitence. Neither Angel nor Archangel can do it. The Lord Himself, Who alone can say *I am with you*; even He grants no remission of sin save to the penitent.

12. I advise, I entreat, I exhort, I admonish; for I am grieved that you who were an example of singular piety, who stood so high for clemency, who would not suffer even single offenders to be put in jeopardy, should not mourn over the death of so many innocent persons. Successful as you have been in battle, and great in other respects, yet mercy was ever the crown of your actions. The devil has envied you your chief excellence: overcome him, while you still have the means. Add not sin to sin by acting in a manner which has injured so many.

13. For my part, debtor as I am to your clemency in all other things; grateful as I must ever be for this clemency, which I have found superior to that of many Emperors and equalled only by one, though I have no ground for charging you with contumacy, I have still reason for apprehension: if you purpose being present, I dare not offer the Sacrifice. That which may not be done when the blood of one innocent person has been shed, may it be done where many have been slain? I trow not.

14. Lastly, I will write with my own hand what I wish should be read by yourself only. As I hope for deliverance from all tribulation from the Lord, it has not been from man, nor by man's agency that this has been forbidden me, but by His own manifest interposition. For in the midst of my anxiety, on the very night whereon I was about to set out, I saw you in a vision coming into the Church, but I was withheld from offering Sacrifice. Other things I pass over, which I might have avoided, but I bore them for your sake, I believe. May the Lord cause all things to turn out peacefully. Our God gives us divers admonitions, by heavenly signs, by prophetic warnings; and by visions vouchsafed even to sinners, He would have us understand that we ought to beseech Him to remove from us commotions, that He would bestow peace on you, our rulers, that the Church, for whose benefit it is that we should have pious and Christian Emperors, may be kept in faith and tranquillity.

15. Doubtless you wish to be approved by God. *To every thing there is a season,* as it is written; *It is time for Thee Lord,* saith the prophet, *to lay to Thine hand,* and, It is an acceptable time to God. You shall make your oblation when you have received permission to sacrifice, when your offering will be pleasing to God. Would it not be a delight to me to enjoy your Majesty's favour, and act in accordance with your will, if the case permitted it? Prayer by itself is a sacrifice; it obtains pardon while the oblation would be rejected, for the former is evidence of humility, the latter of contempt: for God Himself tells us that He prefers the performance of His commandments to sacrifice. God proclaims this, Moses announces it to the people, Paul preaches it to them. Do that which you understand is for the time better. *I will have mercy,* it is said, *and not sacrifice.* Are not those therefore rather to be called Christians who condemn their own sin than those who think to excuse it? *The just accuses himself in the beginning of his words.* He who, having sinned, accuses himself, not he who praises himself, is just.

To Theodosius. Eccles. iii. 1. Ps cxix. 126. S. Matt. ix. 13. Prov. xviii. 17. Vulg.

16. I would that previously to this I had trusted rather to myself than to your accustomed habits. Remembering that you quickly pardon, and revoke your sentence, as you have often done, you have been anticipated, and I have not shunned that which I had no need to fear. But thanks to the Lord, Who chastises His servants, that they may not be lost. This I share with the prophets, and you shall share it with the saints.

17. Shall not I value the father of Gratian at more than my own eyes? Your other sacred pledges too claim pardon for you. On those whom I regarded with impartial affection I conferred by anticipation a name that is dear to me. You have my love, my affection, my prayers. If you believe my words, I call on you to act according to them; if, I say, you believe, acknowledge it, but if not, excuse my conduct in that I prefer God to my sovereign. May your gracious Majesty, with your holy offspring, enjoy in happiness and prosperity perpetual peace.

LETTER LII.

A.D. 392.

TITIANUS, or Tatianus, for both forms of the name are given, was a person in high position under Theodosius, and filled the office of Prætorian Præfect. He had incurred, as this Letter implies, the enmity of the Emperor's favourite minister Rufinus, who eventually procured his exile. He is here congratulated on Rufinus' removal from the position of 'Master of the offices,' and thereby from exercising an unfavourable influence on some private suit in which Tatianus was engaged.

AMBROSE TO TITIANUS.

1. You have obtained a harmless victory, enjoying the security of victory without the bitterness of entreaty; for Rufinus from being Master of the Offices [a], has been made in his consulate a Prætorian Præfect. By this he has acquired more power for himself, but to you he can be hurtful no longer, for he is become the Præfect of another district. I greatly rejoice both with him, as a friend, in having thus received an increase of honour, and at the same time a relief from odium, and also with you, as a son. And this, because you are delivered from him whom you deemed would be too rigid a judge to you, so that if you shall have arranged your business with your grand-daughter, it will have arisen from your affection, not from fear.

2. Exert yourself, therefore, to obtain an adjustment, both the hope and profit of which are now greater: the hope, because the father of your grand-daughter, who promised himself much from the sentence of Rufinus, has no longer anything to hope from him; for Rufinus is now concerned about other things, and neglects the past, or has laid it aside together with the office which he then held; the father now looks rather to the merits of his cause, than to a patron of his sentiments; the fruit too of an adjustment will be sweeter, for the credit of it must be ascribed to yourself; for you might have scorned it, and have not

---

[a] The Magister officiorum was a sort of Chief Secretary of state, both for home and foreign affairs. A summary of his duties may be seen in Gibbon ch. xvii, iv, 2. It was the influence which this post gave him over Theodosius which enabled Rufinus to stir the Emperor's passionateness to the crime of Thessalonica.

done so, regarding the pious claims of kindred, rather than the angry suggestions of injury.

Farewell: love me as a son, for I love you as a parent.

LETTER LIII.

A.D. 392.

S AMBROSE here writes to Theodosius to express his grief at the death of Valentinian II, and mentions the preparations made for his burial. S. Ambrose spoke his funeral oration, which is extant, and is full of expressions of deep attachment. Valentinian had been slain by Arbogastes, who put Eugenius on the throne.

AMBROSE TO THE EMPEROR THEODOSIUS.

1. YOUR Majesty's letter has broken my silence; for I had persuaded myself that in sorrow so great I could do nothing better than withdraw into retirement. But not being able to conceal myself in any retreat, or abdicate my bishopric, I at least retired within myself by silence.

2. I am filled, I confess, with bitter grief, not only because the death of Valentinian has been premature, but also because, having been trained in the faith and moulded by your teaching, he had conceived such devotion towards our God, and was so tenderly attached to myself, as to love one whom he had before persecuted, and to esteem as his father the man whom he had before repulsed as his enemy. I have mentioned this not for the sake of recalling former wrongs, but as a proof of his conversion. For the one he learnt from others, the other was his own, and retained by him when once received from you, so firmly, as to fortify him against all the arguments of his mother. He professed that he owed his education to me, he longed for me as for a careful parent, and when some pretended to have received tidings of my arrival, he anticipated it with impatience. Moreover, on those very days of public mourning, although he had within the limits of Gaul holy and eminent bishops of the Lord, he thought proper nevertheless to write to me to confer upon him the Sacrament of Baptism. By this request, in an unreasonable but affectionate way, he gave testimony of his love towards me.

3. Shall I not then sigh after him with my inmost spirit, shall I not embrace him in the secret recesses of my heart and soul? Shall I deem him dead to me? Yes, indeed to me he is assuredly dead. How thankful was I to the Lord, that he was so changed towards me, so improved, and had assumed a character so much more mature. How thankful also was I to your Clemency, in that you had not only restored him to his kingdom, but also, what is more, had disciplined him in your own faith and piety. Shall I not weep therefore that he, while fresh in years, and before he had obtained as he desired the grace of the Sacraments, has met with a sudden death? It has been a solace to my mind that you have yourself condescended to testify to my grief. I have your Majesty for judge of my affections and interpreter of my thoughts.

4. But hereafter we shall have time for sorrow; let us now care for his sepulture, which your Clemency has commanded to take place in this city. If he has died without Baptism, I now keep back what I know. We have here a most beautiful porphyry vessel, and well adapted for the purpose; for Maximian the colleague of Diocletian was so buried. There are also very precious tablets of porphyry, to encase the covering in which the royal remains are inclosed.

5. All this was prepared, but we waited for your Majesty's order; and its arrival has comforted your holy daughters, sisters of your son Valentinian, who greatly afflict themselves, and the more in that for a long while they received no answer. This has been no small solace to them, but so long as his remains lie unburied, they do not spare themselves, for they daily imagine that they are celebrating the funeral of their brother. And in truth they never are without many tears and heavy sorrow, and whenever they visit his body they return almost lifeless. It will be for their good therefore, and for that of his beloved remains, that the burial should shortly take place, lest the heat of summer should wholly dissolve them, for its first fervour is scarcely past.

6. I observe your command and commend it to the Lord; may He love you, for you love the Lord's servants.

A friendly letter.

TO
EUSEBIUS

LETTER LIV. A.D. 392.

THE Eusebius to whom this and the following letters are addressed is probably not the Bp. of Bologna who took a leading part in the Council of Aquileia, though he appears to be also connected with Bologna, (Lett. lv. 2.). S. Ambrose does not write to him in the style in which he would address an eminent Ecclesiatic. He was probably a layman, on very intimate terms with S. Ambrose, as the whole tone of the Letters implies. Both are on affairs of private life, both, especially the latter, are written in a tone of playful pleasantry and a not irreverent adaptation of sacred things, such as has often marked the familiar correspondence of a great Bishop.

Eusebius seems to have had a son Faustinus, and this son a large family, of whom another Faustinus an Ambrosius and an Ambrosia are here mentioned. It was to this Eusebius, on the occasion of Ambrosia's dedication as a professed Virgin, that S. Ambrose wrote the treatise 'De Institutione Virginis.' She is the 'sancta soror,' the 'holy sister' of Lett. liv.

AMBROSE TO EUSEBIUS.

1. THE Secretary of the Prefecture, who had got into trouble on account of the works at Portus[a] is now safe in port. He came at the right moment, for as soon as I received your letters I saw the Prefect, and interceded for him; and he immediately pardoned him, and ordered the letter which he had dictated for the sale of his goods to be recalled. Even if his arrival had been less speedy, no man would more readily have admitted the embarrassments attending that work of repairing the port than he who would have made shipwreck therein had he not had you for his pilot; and from whence he could otherwise only have escaped with his bare life.

2. The little Faustinus is suffering from a cough, and has come to his holy sister to be cured, and came willingly, for he found that the complaint of his stomach is better cared for here. He also considers me to be a physican and looks to me for his dinner. So he has his medicine here twice a day, and he had begun to get strong, but while from their too great love they keep him away, his stomach-cough has

[a] The adjective Portuensis generally refers to the town called Portus, which grew up in the times of the Emperors on the harbour of Ostia. It is probable therefore that the reference is to some work of which the person spoken of had the superintendence.

LETT 55 returned, worse than before, and unless he returns to his medicines he will still suffer from it.

Farewell: love me, for I also love you.

A.D.392.

LETTER LV.

AMBROSE TO EUSEBIUS.

1. THE two Faustinuses are herewith restored to you, the two little Ambroses stay with me. You have in the father what is best, in the younger son what is most agreeable; for you have at once the summit of virtue, and shew forth the grace of humility. I have what is intermediate between father and younger son. With you is the head of the whole family, and the continuous succession of a name handed down; with me remains that frugal mean which both depends upon the head, and has a common being with what follows it. You have him who is our common rest, who when he comes to me in my turn, smooths all the cares of my soul. You have him who alike by his life and works, and by his offspring has found favour with our Lord, you

Gen. viii. 11. have him who in the storms of this world nourished a spiritual dove, to bring him the fruit of peace, anointed with the

Ib. 20. oil of chastity. You have him who built an altar to the Lord, he whom God blessed together with his sons, and

Ib. ix. 1. said unto them, *Be fruitful and multiply;* with whom He
Ib 9 established the covenant of His peace, that it might be
Ib. 12. unto *him and his sons for perpetual generations.*

2. You have then one who is an heir of Divine benediction, a partner in grace, a sharer in righteousness. But take care, I beseech you, that this our husbandman Noah,

Ib. 20. the good planter of the fruitful vineyard, does not become inebriated with the cup of your love and favour, as one filled with wine, and so indulge too long in rest, and then if haply he fall asleep the longing for our Shem awake him.

Ib. 23 3. There also is Japhet the youngest of the brethren, who with pious reverence may cover his father's nakedness, whom his father may see even in sleep and never dismiss from his remembrance, but keep him ever in his sight and in his bosom, and when he wakes may know *what his younger son has done unto him.* In Latin his name signifies 'health,' in that grace is spread over his lips and over his life, wherefore God hath blessed him, because he, going backward, one may say, to Bologna, covered his father with the pious garment of charity, and shewed honour to piety; of whom also his father said, *God shall enlarge Japhet, and he shall dwell in the tents of Shem.* Wherefore also in the enumeration of this generation he is preferred to his elder brother, he is substituted for him in the blessing: he is preferred in regard of honour to his name, he is substituted in regard of the prerogative of elder birth and the honour due to nature.

To Eusebius

Gen. ix. 24.

Ps. xlv. 3.

Gen. ix. 27.

Ib. x. 1.

4. Now in Latin Shem signifies a 'name.' And truly is this Ambrose of ours a good name, in whose tents Japhet may be enlarged, *because a good name is rather to be chosen than great riches.* Let him therefore also be blessed, let his name be above gold and silver, let the seed of Abraham be in his portion, let all his blessing rest on his posterity, and on the whole family of the just man. But no one is cursed, all are blessed, for blessed is the fruit of Sarah.

Prov. xxii. 1.

5. The Ambroses salute you, the beloved Parthenius salute you, so does Valentinian, disposed to humility, which is in Hebrew 'Canaan', being as it were the servant of his brother, to whom he has also given place as regards his name. And therefore he is like Nimrod, mighty in his double name, a great hunter upon the earth, of whom it is said; *Even as Nimrod the mighty hunter before the Lord.* For being somewhat rude in intellect, but of great bodily strength, he surpasses in strength those whose genius he cannot equal; so that he would seem to carry with him the Comacine[a] rocks, and to resemble them in his outward appearance, being as he is somewhat like a bull, wrathful at being set aside, at being deprived of his paternal name,

Gen. ix. 26.

Ib. x. 9.

---

[a] As Lake Larius was sometimes called Lacus Comacinus in the times of the Emperors, (Dict of Geogr. voc. Comum,) it is probable that the 'Comacinæ rupes' were some familiar rocks on its margin. The comparison to a bull is simply an adaptation of Virgil's 'Et faciem tauro propior,' Georg iii. 58.

at being subjected, through an inhabitant of the capital, to one from Bologna, for he knows not the blandishments of infancy, and sprung without suffering injury from his nurse's bosom.

Farewell: love me for I love you.

A.D. 392.

LETTER LVI.

A NOTE in p. 71 gives a brief outline of the schism in the Church of Antioch up to the time of the Council of Aquileia, which made some efforts to bring about a settlement. Meletius was then succeeded by Flavian, so that there still remained two rival Bishops, Flavian and Paulinus. Another opportunity for closing the schism came at Paulinus' death, at the end of 388 A.D., but so far from allowing the wound to be so healed Paulinus on his death-bed consecrated Evagrius as his successor in violation of the Canons of Nicæa, (Theod. H.E. v. 23) which 'do not allow a Bishop to appoint his successor, but require all the Bishops of the province to be summoned to elect, and forbid consecration without at least three consecrating Bishops.' The western Bishops therefore continued to press Theodosius to call a Council to deal with the matter, which was accordingly assembled at Capua. Flavian, though ordered by the Emperor, did not appear, and the Council referred the question to the decision of Theophilus of Alexandria and the Bishops of Egypt, who were not committed to either side, and in this letter S Ambrose replies to Theophilus who had written to him that Flavian still refused to submit himself to their decision and again appealed to the Emperor, and urges him to summon Flavian once more, and endeavour to bring the matter to a peaceful issue, advising him to consult also Siricius, the Bishop of Rome. He points out that both parties rely rather on the weakness of their opponent's case than on the soundness of their own, and expresses a hope that an end may be put to the schism, and peace restored to the Church. Tillemont, in note 41 on the Life of S. Ambrose, discusses the date of the Synod of Capua, and fixes it at the end of A.D. 391, chiefly on the ground that Theodosius did not return to Constantinople from Milan till November of that year, while it must have been held before the disturbance in the west occasioned by the revolt of Arbogastes and the death of Valentinian, which took place in the spring of A D. 392.

AMBROSE TO THEOPHILUS.

1. EVAGRIUS has no good ground for preferring his claim, Flavian has cause to fear, and therefore avoids the trial. Let our brethren pardon our just grief, for on account of these men the whole world is agitated, yet they do not sympathize with our grief. Let them at least patiently

suffer themselves to be censured by those whom they perceive to have been for so long a time harassed by their obstinacy. For between these two who would agree upon nothing which appertains to the peace of Christ, a grievous discord has arisen and spread through the whole world.

2. To this shipwreck of pious peace the holy Council of Capua had at length opened an haven of tranquillity; that communion should be given to all throughout the East who profess the Catholic faith, and that the cause of these two men should be referred to the judgment of your Holiness, and to our brethren and fellow-bishops of Egypt, as assessors. For we deemed your judgment likely to be true, in that, having embraced the communion of neither party, it would be inclined by no favour towards either side.

3. But while we were hoping that by these most equitable decrees of the Council a remedy was now provided, and an end put to discord, your Holiness writes word that our brother Flavian has again had recourse to the aid of prayers, and to the support of Imperial Rescripts. And thus the toil of so many Bishops has been spent to no purpose; we must have recourse once more to the civil tribunals, to the Imperial Rescripts, once more must they cross the seas, once more, though weak in body, exchange their own country for a foreign soil, once more must the Holy Altars be deserted that we may travel to distant lands, once more crowds of indigent Bishops, whose poverty was before no burthen to them, but who now need external aid, must suffer want themselves, or at any rate use for their journey what else had fed the poor.

4. Meanwhile Flavian, alone exempt, as he fancies, from the laws, does not come when all others are assembled. The money-lender and debtor meet each other, these men alone cannot meet: Flavian by his own will deprives himself of Episcopal fellowship, and will not appear in person either at the Imperial order, or when cited by his brethren.

5. Nevertheless, even this cause of offence does not induce me to consider our brother Evagrius entirely in the right, although he seems to himself the more defensible

LETT. 56. either because Flavian avoids him, or because he thinks his opponent to be in no better case than himself, each of them relying more on the defects of his opponent's ordination than on the validity [a] of his own. We however would recall them to a better course, wishing them to be aided rather by the goodness of their own cause than by the defects of others.

6. Now since you have stated in your letter that some form may be devised touching this matter, whereby the discord of our brethren may be removed; and as the holy Synod has trusted the right of cognizance to the unanimous judgment of yourself and our other fellow-bishops from Egypt, it is fitting that you should again summon our brother Flavian, so that, if he should persist in not choosing to appear, you may then without prejudice to the decrees of the Council of Nice, and also of the Synod of Capua, take such measures for the preservation of general peace as may not destroy what has been built up: *For if I destroy what I have built, or build again what I destroyed, I make myself a transgressor.* Let the grace of that peace which has been obtained be thus preserved by all, and the refusal of either party to appear will not have the effect of frustrating it.

Gal. ii. 18.

7. Moreover we are of opinion that it will be well for you to refer to our holy brother the Bishop of the Roman Church; for we do not doubt that what you shall determine he also will approve. For the resolution that is come to will be useful, and our peace and quiet will be secure, if such a decree is made by your advice as shall not create discord in our communion. And thus we also, receiving the series of your decrees, and assured that the Roman Church has given its undoubting approbation to what has been done, shall with gladness participate in the result of this trial.

---

[a] The word 'bonis' must certainly here be inserted in the text, 'uterque alienae magis ordinationis vitiis quam suis bonis fretus,' as suggested by the Benedictine Editors. It occurs just below in the corresponding sentence, 'suis potius bonis quam alieno vitio defendi.'

LETTER ON THE CASE OF BONOSUS.

This letter is certainly not written by S. Ambrose, though included among his letters. The writer of it speaks of 'our brother Ambrose' Tillemont discusses the authorship in a note, (45.) and makes it probable that it was written by Siricius.

The case of Bonosus had been brought before the Synod of Capua, and they had decided that it should be referred to the Bishops of Macedonia, under the presidency of Amysius Bishop of Thessalonica, as being his nearest neighbours. These Bishops seem to have written a letter to consult Siricius, the Bishop of Rome, and this is believed to be his reply, in which he declines to interfere with their decision, only adding a few remarks upon one point. Bonosus was Bishop of Sardica[b] in Illyria, and the founder of an obscure sect. They were accused of Photinianism, and Bonosus is called a fore-runner of Nestorius, but the Helvidian doctrines of which this letter speaks are the most clearly ascertained of their errors. The sect survived at least till the vith Century.

A LETTER CONCERNING THE DECIDING OF THE CASE OF BONOSUS, A D. 392 ACCORDING TO THE DECREE OF THE SYNOD OF CAPUA. or 393.

1. You have written to us a Letter concerning Bishop Bonosus in which, either from love of truth or from modesty, you enquire our opinion. But since it has been the judgment of the Council of Capua that those who are neighbours to Bonosus and his accusers should be assigned as his judges, and specially the Macedonian Bishops, who, with the Bishop of Thessalonica, should judge of his acts and writings, we have to remark that the function of judging cannot appertain to ourselves. Otherwise, were the question of the Synod at this day still open, we might well have decided concerning these things which are included in what you have written at length. Having taken upon yourselves this judgment, it is now your part to form your decision on the whole question, to give no power of retreat or escape either to the accusers or the accused; for, being chosen by the Synod to conduct the examination, you have taken upon you its functions.

2. Again, when Bishop Bonosus, after your judgment, sent to our brother Ambrose to enquire his opinion whether he should break into and enter upon the church which was closed to him, he received for reply that he must do nothing rashly, that everything must be carried on modestly, patiently and in order, that nothing contrary to your decision must be attempted, that you, to whom the Synod had committed such authority, would appoint what appeared to you agreeable to jus-

[b] He is sometimes spoken of as Bishop of Nairsus in Dacia Mediterranea (see Note in p 67.) but Tillemont (note 43 in Life of S. Ambrose) has made it probable that there were two Bishops of the name of Bonosus, one of Nairsus, and the other of Sardica, the latter of whom is the one dealt with by the Synod of Capua.

LETT. 56. tice. The first point therefore is that judgment should be given by those to whom the power of judging has been given; for you, as we have said, judge in place of the entire Synod; as to ourselves it does not befit us to judge as though by the authority of the Synod.

3. Assuredly we cannot deny that he is justly blamed concerning the sons of Mary, and that your Holiness deservedly repudiated the opinion that from the same Virgin womb, of which according to the flesh Christ was born, other offspring was produced. For the Lord Jesus would not have chosen to be born of a Virgin, if He had conceived she would be so wanting in continence as to suffer that birthplace of the Lord's Body, that palace of the eternal King, to be polluted by human intercourse. To propound such an opinion as this, what is it but to fortify the unbelief of the Jews who say that it was impossible He could be born of a Virgin, and who, thus confirmed by the authority of Christian Bishops, will strive with greater earnestness to overthrow the true faith?

S. John xix. 26, 27.
4. What else can be the meaning of that text wherein the Lord says to His Mother of John the Evangelist, *Woman, behold thy son*, and again to John of Mary, *Behold thy mother?* With what purpose was it that while the Lord was hanging upon the cross and atoning for the sins of the world, He declared also the integrity of His Mother? Wherefore was it said but that unbelief might close its lips and be silent, nor dare to offer any insult to the Mother of the Lord? He therefore, in pronouncing upon and asserting His Mother's chastity,

S. Matt. i. 18.
likewise bears witness that she was only espoused to her husband Joseph; and that she was ignorant of that carnal commerce which is the accustomed right of the marriage bed; for, had it been that she was to conceive children of Joseph, He would not have chosen to separate her from the company of her husband.

5. But if this is not enough, the Evangelist has added his testimony,

S. John xix. 27.
saying that the *disciple took her unto his own home*. Did he then cause a divorce? Did he carry her off from her husband? How can he who reads this in the Gospel stagger and waver to and fro as one who has been shipwrecked?

6. This then is the testimony of the Son concerning His Mother's chastity, this is the rich heritage of Mary's immaculate Virginity, this

Ib. 30.
is the consummation of the entire work. He spake thus, and *gave up the ghost*, crowning the whole mystery with a good end of filial duty.

7. We have also read and perused the whole of the instructions, as well what relates to Senecio being joined with our brother and fellow-bishop Bassus in the government of his Church, as what relates to other matters, and we now look for the direction of your sentence.

S. Ambrose explains his abssence from Milan.

TO
EUGENIUS

LETTER LVII.

VALENTINIAN II. having been murdered by Arbogastes, one of his Generals, the latter, not venturing to claim the empire for himself, set up Eugenius, who was really his puppet, as Emperor of the West. Theodosius temporised with him, till he should be fully prepared to attack him, and it was whilst he was thus for a time accepted as Emperor that S. Ambrose addressed this letter to him. He excuses himself in it for withdrawing from Milan when Eugenius came there, on the plea that he was bound to fear God rather than man, and reproves him for granting the restoration of their former revenues to the heathen temples, which Gratian and Valentinian had before refused, and exposes the futility of his plea that he was merely granting favour to his friends, reminding him that God sees the heart. He quotes at length the conduct of the Jews in the time of Antiochus, as recorded in the Book of Maccabees, as a precedent which Christians were bound to follow. At the same time he says that he is willing to address Eugenius in matters which do not affect his duty to God.

TO THE MOST GRACIOUS EMPEROR EUGENIUS,
AMBROSE, BISHOP, SENDS GREETING.

1. I withdrew from Milan from fear of God, to Whom I am wont to refer, as far as I am able, all my acts, never turning my mind from Him nor making more account of any man's favour than of the grace of Christ. By preferring God to every one else I wrong no man, and trusting in Him, I dare to tell your Majesties, the Emperors, my poor thoughts. Wherefore I will not refrain from saying to your most gracious Majesty what I never refrained from saying before other Emperors. And that I may preserve the order of events, I will touch one by one the points which relate to this transaction. The illustrious Symmachus, when prefect of the city, memorialised [a] the Emperor Valentinian the younger, of august memory, begging that he would command what had been withdrawn from the temples to be restored. He performed his part in accordance with his own wishes and mode of worship. It became me also, as Bishop, to recognize the duties of my office. I presented two petitions to the Emperors wherein

[a] He is referring to the 'Memorial of Symmachus.' p. 94. The 'two petitions,' libellos duos, are Letters 17 and 18.

LETT. 57. I declared that a Christian man could not contribute to the expenses of the sacrifices; that I had not advised the withdrawal of the payments, but that I did advise that they should not be now decreed, and lastly, that he would seem to be giving rather than restoring these expenses to the images; for what he had not withdrawn, he could not be said to restore, but of his own free-will to give it for the uses of supersition. Lastly, if he had done so, he either must not come to the Church, or if he did, he would either not find a priest, or one who would withstand him. Nor could it be offered as an excuse that he was only a catechumen, for it is not lawful for catechumens to contribute to the expense of idols.

3. My petitions were read in the Consistory; Count Bauto, a man of the highest military rank, and Rumoridus, himself too of the same dignity, and from the first year of his boyhood attached to the Gentile worship, were present. Valentinian then listened to my suggestion, and did nothing but what our faith reasonably required. And they submitted to his officer.

4. Afterwards I openly addressed myself to the most gracious Emperor Theodosius, and hesitated not to speak to him face to face. He having received the intimation of a similar message from the Senate, although it was not the whole Senate who asked it, at length gave his consent to my suggestion, and so for some days I did not come near him, nor was he displeased thereat, for I did not act for my own advantage but for his profit, and that of my own soul also;

Ps cxix. 46. *I was not ashamed to speak in the king's presence.*

5. Once more an Embassy was sent from the senate to the Emperor Valentinian, of blessed memory, when he was in Gaul, but was able to extort nothing from him. At that time I was absent and had not written anything to him.

6. But when your Majesty assumed the reins of government it was found that this boon had been granted to men of eminence in the state but in religion heathens. And perhaps it may be said, your Majesty, that it is not a restitution to the temples on your part, but a boon to men who had deserved well of you. But the fear of God ought,

you know, to lead us to act with constancy, as is done in the cause of liberty not only by priests but by those who serve in your armies or are reckoned among the provincials. Envoys petitioned you, as Emperor, for restitution to the temples, but you consented not; others again required it, but you resisted; yet subsequently you have thought fit to grant it as a boon to the petitioners themselves.

7. The Imperial power is indeed great, but let your Majesty consider the greatness of God; He sees all hearts, He scrutinizes the inmost conscience, He knows all things before they come to pass, He knows the secrets of your breast. You will not suffer yourselves to be deceived, and do you hope to hide anything from God? Has not this suggested itself to your mind? Although they urged their suit with such perseverance, ought not your Majesty from respect for the most high and true and living God, to have resisted still more perseveringly, and to have refused what was derogatory to the Divine law?

8. Who grudges your bestowing upon others whatsoever you chose? We do not pry closely into your munificence, nor are we jealous of the advantages of others; but we are the ministers of the Faith. How will you offer your gifts to Christ? your acts will be estimated by few, your wishes by all; whatever they have done will be ascribed to you, whatever they have not done to themselves. You are indeed Emperor, but you ought all the more to submit yourself to God. Else how shall the priests of Christ dispense your gifts?

9. There was a question of this kind in former times, and then persecution itself yielded to the faith of our fathers, and heathendom gave way. For *when the game that was used every fifth year was kept at Tyre,* and the wicked king of Antioch had come hither to see it, *Jason sent special messengers from Jerusalem, to carry three hundred silver drachms,* and give them *to the sacrifice of Hercules.* But our fathers would not give the money to the heathen, but sent trusty persons to make declaration that such money was not to be devoted to sacrifices to the gods, *for this was not convenient,* but was to be applied to other expenses.

LETT. 57. And it was decreed that, forasmuch as Jason had said that the silver was sent for the sacrifice of Hercules, that which was sent ought to be so applied. And yet seeing that they who brought it pleaded in opposition, in their zeal and devotion, that it should not be employed for sacrifice but for other exigencies, the money was applied to build ships. They sent the money, that is, because they were compelled, but it was not applied to sacrifices, but to other public expenses.

10. Again, they who brought the money might have been silent, but they were led to violate secrecy because they knew whither it was being carried, and so they sent men who feared God, and who were to do their endeavour that the money might be applied to the equipment of ships, and not to the temple. Thus they entrusted the money to men who were to plead the cause of the Divine law, and He who cleanses the conscience was made Judge of the matter. If those who were in the power of others took these precautions, it cannot be doubted what it was your Majesty's duty to do. You, whom no man constrained, who were in no man's power, ought certainly to have referred for advice to the priest.

11. For my own part, although I was alone in the resistance I then made, still others both willed and advised it. Being thus bound by my own words both before God and before all men, I have felt that I had no other choice or duty but to consult for myself, for I could not properly trust to you. For a long time I stifled and concealed my grief, I gave no hint to any one, but now I am no longer at liberty to dissemble, or to be silent. And this was why, at the beginning of your reign, I made no reply to your letters, because I foresaw that what you have done would happen. Afterwards, when you found I did not answer, and sent to demand a reply, I said, 'The reason why I do not write is that I think it will be wrung from him [b].'

12. But when a just occasion for the exercise of my office

---

[b] He means that the reason why he declines all communication with Eugenius, who wished to secure his great political influence on his side, was, that he felt sure that Eugenius, though at present temporising with both parties, would in the end yield to the pressure of the pagan party, and restore the revenues to the heathen temples. 'Extorquendum' is, in accordance with late Latin idiom, a mere future passive.

arose, I both wrote and petitioned for those who were anxious on their own account, with a view of shewing that in the cause of God a due fear of Him affected me, and that I did not set a higher value on flattery than on my own soul; but that in the matters wherein petition is proper to be made to you, I paid just deference to your authority, as indeed it is written, *honour to whom honour, tribute to whom tribute.* For seeing that I cordially deferred to a private person, how should I not defer to the Emperor? But as you desire deference to be shewn to yourselves, suffer us to defer to Him from Whom you would fain prove your authority to be derived.

<small>TO SABINUS</small>

<small>Rom. xiii. 7.</small>

LETTER LVIII.

<small>A.D. 393.</small>

<small>IN this letter S Ambrose informs Sabinus that Paulinus and Therasia had resolved to give up all their wealth to the poor, and retire to Nola, and complains of the objections raised against such self-denial, ending with a mystical interpretation of David dancing before the ark.</small>

<small>AMBROSE TO SABINUS, BISHOP.</small>

1. CREDIBLE information has reached me that Paulinus, the lustre of whose birth was inferior to none in the region of Aquitania, has sold both his own possessions and those of his wife, and entered upon a course of life which enables him to bestow upon the poor the property which has been converted into money; while he himself having become poor instead of rich, as one relieved of a heavy burden, has bid farewell to his home his country and his kindred, in order to serve God more diligently; and he is reported to have chosen a retreat in the city of Nola, to pass the rest of his days in avoiding the turmoil of life.

2. The lady Therasia too approaches closely to his zeal and virtue, and objects not to the resolve he has taken. Having transferred her own property to other owners, she follows her husband, and contented with his little plat of ground will console herself with the riches of religion and

LETT. 58. charity. Offspring they have none, and therefore desire to leave behind them good deeds.

3. When the great of the world hear this, what will they say? That a man of his family, his ancestry, his genius, gifted with such eloquence, should have seceded from the senate, that the succession of a noble family should become extinct, such things, they will say, are not to be borne. And though they, when they perform the rites of Isis, shave their heads and eyebrows, they nevertheless call it an unworthy deed should a Christian man out of zeal for holy religion change his habit.

4. Truly I grieve that, while falsehood is so respected, there should be such negligence as regards the Truth, that many are ashamed of seeming too devoted to our holy religion, not considering His words Who says, *Whosoever shall be ashamed of*[1] *Me before men, of him will I also be ashamed*[2] *before My Father Which is in heaven.* But Moses was not thus ashamed, for though invited into the royal palace he *esteemed the reproach of Christ greater riches than the treasures of Egypt.* David was not thus ashamed when he danced before the Ark of the testimony in the sight of all the people. Isaiah was not thus ashamed, when he walked naked and bare-foot through the people, proclaiming the heavenly oracles.

[1] confusus fuerit.
S Matt. x 33.
S. Mark viii. 38.
[2] confundar
Heb. xi. 26
2 Sam. vi. 20.

Isa. xx. 4.

5. Viewed by the outward eye what can be a more unseemly spectacle than an imitation of the gestures of players, and a wreathing of the limbs after the manner of women? Lascivious dances are the companions of luxury and the pastime of wantonness. What did David himself mean by singing, *O clap your hands together, all ye people?* If we regard the bodily action we must suppose that he clapped his hands as if mingling with female dancers, and shouted with unseemly noise. Of Ezekiel too it is said, *Smite with thine hand, and stamp with thy foot.*

Ps. xlvii. 1.

Ezek. vi. 11.

6. But the things which viewed corporeally are unseemly, when viewed in regard to holy religion become venerable, so that they who blame such things will involve their own souls in the net of blame. Thus Michal reproves David for his dancing and says to him, *How glorious was the king of Israel to day, who uncovered himself to day in the eyes of*

2 Sam. vi. 20.

his handmaids! And David answered her, *It was before the Lord, which chose me before thy father, and before all his house to appoint me ruler over the people of the Lord, over Israel: therefore will I play before the Lord, and I will be yet more vile thus, and will be base in mine own sight, and of the maid-servants which thou hast spoken of, of them shall I be had in honour.*

TO SABINUS Ib 21, 22.

7. David therefore did not shrink from female censure, nor was he ashamed to hear their reproaches for his religious service. For he played before the Lord as being his servant, and was the more pleasing to Him in that he so humbled himself before God, as to lay aside his royal dignity and to offer to God the very lowest ministry, as though he were a servant. She also who censured such dancing was condemned to barrenness and had no children by the king, that she might not bring forth a proud offspring; and so, as it turned out, she obtained no continuance of descendants or of good deeds.

8. If any one is still doubtful, let him hear the testimony of the Gospel, for the Son of God said, *We have piped unto you, and ye have not danced.* Therefore were the Jews abandoned, because they danced not, nor clapped their hands, and the Gentiles were called in, who gave to God spiritual applause. *The fool foldeth his hands together and devoureth his own flesh,* that is, he entangles himself in corporeal matters, and devours his own flesh, like prevailing death,ᵃ and so he shall not find eternal life. But the wise man, who so holds up his works that they may shine before his Father Which is in heaven, has not consumed his flesh but has raised it to the grace of the resurrection. This is that glorious dance of the wise man which David danced, and thus by the loftiness of his spiritual dancing he ascended even to the throne of Christ, that he might see and hear *the Lord saying to his Lord, Sit Thou on My right hand!*

S. Matt. xi. 17.

Eccles. iv. 5.

S. Matt. v. 16.

Ps. cx. 1.

9. Now if you are of opinion that this interpretation of the dancing has not been made unreasonably, do not spare yourself the trouble of reading a little further, in order that we may consider together the case of Isaiah, how, as is well known to you, he was uncovered, not in mockery but glo-

Isa. xx. 4.

ᵃ See Letter xliv 9, and note c there

LETT. 58 riously, in the sight of the assembled people, as one who reported with his own mouth the oracles of God.

10. But perhaps it may be said, Was it not then disgraceful for a man to walk wholly uncovered through the people, seeing that he must be met both by men and women? Must not the sight itself have shocked the eyes of all, especially of women? Do not we ourselves generally shrink from looking upon naked men? And are not men's persons concealed by garments that they may not offend the eyes of beholders by an unseemly spectacle?

11. In this I also acquiesce; but consider what it was this act represented, and what was set forth under this outward show; it was, that the young men and maidens of the Jews should be led away prisoners, and walk naked, *like as My servant Isaiah*, it is said, *hath walked naked and barefoot*. This might also have been impressed in words, but God chose to render it more expressive by example, that the sight itself might thus strike greater terror, and what they shrunk from in the person of the prophet, that they might dread for themselves. In which of the two then does the baseness most shock us; in the person of the prophet, or in the sins of those unbelievers which deserved to fall into this great misery of captivity?

Isa. xx. 3.

12. But what if there was nothing worthy of reproach in the prophet's body? He indeed alluded not to corporeal but to spiritual things; for in his ecstasy of mind he says, not *I will hearken what* I shall say, but, *what the Lord God shall say in me*. Nor does he consider whether he is naked or clothed. Again, Adam before his sin was naked, but knew not he was naked, because he was endued with virtue; after he had committed sin he saw that he was naked, and covered himself. Noah was uncovered, but he blushed not, because he was full of gladness and spiritual joy, while he who derided him for being naked, himself remained subject to the disgrace of perpetual baseness. Joseph too, that he might not be basely uncovered, left his garment, and fled away naked; now which of the two was base in this instance, she who kept another's garment, or he who put off his own?

Ps. lxxxv. 8.
Gen. ii. 25.
Ib. iii. 7.
Ib. xxxix. 12.

13. But that it may be more fully evident that the pro-

phets regard not themselves nor what lies at their feet, but heavenly things, when Stephen was stoned he saw *the heavens opened, and Jesus standing on the right hand of God;* and therefore he felt not the blows of the stones, he regarded not his bodily wounds, but his eyes were fastened on Christ, he clung closely to him. So also Isaiah looked not on his own nakedness, but offered himself to be the organ of the Divine voice, that he might utter what God spake within him.

TO SABINUS

Acts vii. 56.

Isa. xx. 2.

14. But be it supposed that he saw himself, could he not do that which he was commanded? Could he believe that to be base which God enjoined? Sarah, because she laughed, was convicted of unbelief; Abraham was praised, because he doubted not the word of God; yea, he received a very great reward, because he believed that at God's command, even parricide might be piously committed.

Gen. xviii. 12.
Ib. xv. 6.
Ib. xx. 3.

15. What cause for shame then had the prophet here, when one thing was enacted, but that of which it was a figure was quite different? The Jews, being deserted by God for their wickedness, began to be vanquished by their enemies, and were fain to betake themselves to the Egyptians, to be a protection to them against the Assyrians, whereas had they consulted for good, they ought rather to have returned to the faith. The Lord, being angry, shews that their hope was vain in thinking that the offence against Him could be removed by a greater sin, for that very people in whom the Jews were trusting, were themselves to be vanquished. This was the meaning as regards the actual history.

16. But this history itself is a figure, signifying that he trusts in the Egyptians who is given up to impurity, and enslaved to wantonness. For no man abandons himself to excess but he who departs from the precepts of the true God. But as soon as a man waxes wanton, he begins to fall off from the true faith. And then he commits two grievous crimes, lassitude as regards the flesh, and sacrilege as regards the mind. He then who follows not the Lord his God ingulfs himself in impurity and lust, those pestilential passions of the body. But he who has engulfed and plunged himself in such wallowing places, falls

LETT. 59. also into the snare of unbelief; for *the people sat down to*
Exod. *eat and to drink,* and required that gods should be made
xxxii. 6. for them. Hereby the Lord teaches us that he who gives
up his soul to these two kinds of vices, is stript of the
garment, not of a woollen vest, but of living virtue; that
clothing which is not temporal but eternal.

Farewell, love me, for I also love you.

A D.393.

LETTER LIX.

S AMBROSE here writes to Severus, Bishop of Naples, to tell him of one James, a presbyter of Persia, who was seeking a retreat from the world in Campania. This leads him to dwell on the contrast of the many troubles with which he is surrounded at Milan.

AMBROSE TO SEVERUS, BISHOP.

1. JAMES, our brother and fellow-presbyter, has come from the depths of Persia, and chosen the coast of Campania and your pleasant abodes for his resting-place. You see in what spot he has anticipated for himself the enjoyment of a haven sheltered, as it were, from the storms of this world, where, after his long toils, he may spend the remainder of his life.

2. For your coast, removed not only from danger, but from all tumult, fills the senses with tranquillity, and transports the mind from the fearful and raging billows of care to an honourable rest. So that those words of David concerning the holy Church, which belong in common to all, appear to be especially fitting and appropriate to
Ps. xxiv. yourselves; *For He hath founded it upon the seas, and pre-*
2. *pared it upon the floods.* For a mind undisturbed by inroads of barbarians and the evils of war, has leisure for prayer, devotes itself to the service of God, cares for the things of the Lord, cherishes those things which belong to peace and tranquillity.

3. We meanwhile, exposed to the outbreaks of the barbarians and the storms of war, are tossing in the midst of troubles, and from these toils and dangers can only gather

that those of our future life will be still more grievous. Wherefore that saying of the Prophet seems to accord with our condition, *I saw the tents of Cushan in affliction.* _{TO PATERNUS} _{Hab. iii. 7.}

4. For since I have now lived in the body fifty and three years, among the shadows of this world, whereby the truth of future perfection is obscured, and have already endured such heavy afflictions, am I not camping in the tents of Cushan, and having my habitation among the dwellers of Midian? For these, owing to their consciousness of their darksome works, dread being judged even by mortal men, *but he that is spiritual judgeth all things, yet he himself is judged of no man.* _{Ps. cxx. 5.} _{1 Cor. ii. 15.}

Farewell, my brother; love me, as indeed you do, for I also love you.

LETTER LX.   A.D. 393.

IN this Letter S. Ambrose urges Paternus not to break the laws both of God and man by promoting a marriage between his son and his daughter's daughter, who were within the forbidden degrees of relationship, and shews him what confusion would arise from such an union.

AMBROSE TO PATERNUS.

1. I HAVE read your greeting, my like-minded friend Paternus, but the question on which you ask my advice, wishing to marry your son to your grand-daughter by your daughter, is by no means paternal, but unworthy of you both as grand-father and as father. Consider therefore what it is you ask about, for in all that we wish to do, we ought first to investigate the nature of the deed, and then we shall be able to estimate whether it is worthy of praise or blame. For instance, carnal intercourse with women is a pleasure to some, physicians even say it is healthful to the body; but we must consider whether it be with a wife or a stranger, with a married or an unmarried woman. If a man have commerce with one who is espoused and given to him he calls it marriage; he who assails the chastity of

LETT. 60. one who belongs to another commits adultery, by the very name of which the temerity of the attempt is generally repressed. To slay an enemy is accounted a victory, to slay a criminal is justice, to slay an innocent man murder, and if a man is conscious of this he withholds his hand. Wherefore I beg that you also will consider what it is you propose.

2. You wish to arrange a marriage between our children. But I would ask whether you would have equals or those who are unequal joined together? if I mistake not, they are wont to be called 'pairs [1].' He who yokes oxen to the plough, or horses to the chariot, chooses pairs, that both their age and their form may harmonize, that there be no natural difference, nor blemish of diversity. You are proposing to unite your son and your grand-daughter by your daughter, that is, that he should marry his sister's daughter, true though it is that he was born of a different mother from his professed mother in law. Consider what restraint is implied in the very names; he is called her uncle, she is called his niece. Does not the very sound of the names[a] recal you, when the one has in it the sound of grand-father, and the other refers alike to uncle and to grand-father? How great again is the confusion of the other terms? You will be called both grand-father and father in law, she too will receive the different names of niece and daughter in law. The brother and sister also will exchange different names, she will be the mother in law of her brother, he the son in law of his sister. The niece will marry her uncle, and the affection of these your unstained offspring be exchanged for an irregular love.

3. On this point you tell me that the holy man your Bishop is looking for my sentiments. I cannot think or believe this. For if this were so, he would himself have chosen to write, but by not doing so he has intimated that he considers there is no ground for doubt upon the point. For how can there be any such doubt, when the prohibition of marriage between first cousins extends, according to the Divine law, to those who are related in the fourth

[1] compares.

[a] The argument here turns on the Latin words. 'Avunculus,' uncle, is a mere diminutive of 'avus,' grandfather; and the one word 'neptis' is used both for niece and granddaughter without any distinction.

degree. But this is the third degree, which even by the civil law seems to be excepted from the fellowship of marriage.

TO PATERNUS

4. But let us first inquire what are the decrees of the Divine law, for you allege in your letters that an union between such persons must be considered as allowed by that Law, in that it is not forbidden. I however assert that it is actually forbidden; for seeing that first cousins are forbidden slighter familiarities, much more must I deem this forbidden which contains within it the bond of a much closer union. For he who affixes censure to lighter offences does not acquit but rather condemn heavier ones.

5. But if you consider it to be permitted because it is not specially forbidden, neither will you find it forbidden by the words of the Law that the father should take his daughter to wife. But is this lawful, merely because it is not forbidden? By no means; it has been interdicted by the law of nature, by that law which is in the hearts of each of us, by the inviolable rule of piety, on the ground of nearness of kin. How many things of this kind will you find which are not forbidden in the law promulgated by Moses, but which are yet forbidden by the voice of nature.

6. There are many things which are lawful, but which are not expedient, for *all things are lawful, but all things are not expedient, all things are lawful, but all things edify not*. If then the Apostle recalls us even from those things which edify not, how can we imagine that may be done which is not permitted by the oracle of the Law, and which edifies not, because it differs from the rule of piety? Yet those very things in the old Law which were more severe were mitigated by the Gospel of the Lord Jesus. *Old things are passed away, behold, all things are become new.*

1 Cor. x. 23.

2 Cor. v. 17.

7. What is so usual as a kiss between an uncle and a niece, which he owes to her as a daughter, she to him as a parent? Will you therefore cast suspicion on this kiss of unoffending piety by proposing such a union, will you deprive your beloved offspring of a sacrament so venerable?

8. But if the Divine law pass by you unheeded, at least the laws of Emperors, from whom you have received such ample honours, ought not to have been so disregarded. Now the Emperor Theodosius forbad even cousins by

either the fathers' or mothers' side to be united under the name of marriage, and affixed a severe penalty upon any rash union of brothers' children. And yet these are equal as regards each other, but, as they are bound together by the ties of mankind and brotherly union, he would have them owe their birth to piety.

9. But you will say this rule has been relaxed in favour of some. The law however is not prejudiced thereby, for that which is [not] [b] enacted for general use is only profitable to him in whose favour the relaxation takes place, and so the odium is much less. Now although we read in the Old Testament of one calling his wife his sister, it is unheard of that any man should marry his niece and call her his wife.

10. It is indeed a curious plea which leads you to assert that your grand-daughter is not connected with your son, her uncle, by any close bond, merely because they have no relationship by the father's side [1]. As if an uterine brother and sister, born that is, of the same mother but by a different father, would be united together when of a different sex, for as much as they have no relationship by the father's side [2], but are only united to each other by the mother's side [3].

[1] agnatio.
[2] agnatio.
[3] cognatio.

11. You ought therefore to relinquish your intention, which, even were it lawful, would not tend to propagate your family, for your son owes to us grand-children, your dear grand-daughter owes to us great-grand-children.

Farewell to you and all yours.

A.D.394.

LETTER LXI.

This letter was addressed to Theodosius after his victory over Eugenius. S. Ambrose in it explains his absence from Milan, and after expressing his gratitude to God for His blessing on the arms of Theodosius, urges the Emperor to a merciful use of his victory.

AMBROSE TO THE EMPEROR THEODOSIUS.

1. You seem to have supposed, most blessed Emperor,

[b] The 'not' is inserted according to the suggestion of the Benedictine Editors. There seems a contradiction in terms without it.

Ambrose explains his absence from Milan,

as I understood from your Majesty's letters, that I had removed to a distance from Milan because I believed your cause was forsaken by God. But in my absence I was not so foolish, nor so unmindful of your virtues and good deeds, as not to feel sure that the assistance of heaven would aid your piety, and assist you to rescue the Roman Empire from the cruelty of a barbarian robber, and the rule of an unworthy usurper.

2. Wherefore I made immediate haste to return, as soon as ever I was aware that he whom I thought it right to avoid was gone, for I had not deserted the Church of Milan, which the judgment of God had committed to me, but I shunned the presence of one who had involved himself in sacrilege. So I returned about the first of August, and from that day I have been in residence here, and here your Majesty's letter [a] has found me.

3. Thanks be to our Lord God, Who has responded to your faith and piety, and revived among us the pattern of ancient sanctity, giving to us to see in our own times what we marvel at in the Lessons of Holy Scripture, so effectual a presence, I mean, of Divine aid in battle [b], that no mountain tops delayed your passage, no hostile arms presented any impediment.

4. For this you think I ought to give thanks to the Lord our God; and this I will willingly do, conscious of your good deeds. That victim is certainly pleasing to God, which is offered in your name; and how great faith and devotion does this evince! Other Emperors, as soon as ever they gain a victory, order triumphal arches or other badges of triumph to be erected, but your Clemency pro-

---

[a] 'Apices' here and in § 5 undoubtedly means 'a letter.' 'Apex,' in late Latin, is used for a single letter written, and 'apices,' like 'literae,' for a continuous writing. Aulus Gellius (xiii. 30, 10, xvii. 9., 12.,) quoted in White's Dictionary, uses the phrase 'literarum apices,' and in Cod. Just. ii. 8. 6. we find 'Augusti apices' for 'the Emperor's rescripts.'

[b] Theodoret, v. 24. gives a detailed account of the ways in which the special intervention of heaven was displayed in Theodosius' campaign against Eugenius. S. Aug. De Civ. Dei, v, 26. says that Theodosius 'contra robustissimum Eugenii exercitum magis orando quam feriendo pugnavit,' and, after mentioning stories told by eye-witnesses of the manifest intervention of God on his behalf, quotes the well-known lines of Claudian,

O nimium dilecte Deo cui fundit ab antris
Æolus armatas hyemes, cui militat æther,
Et conjurati veniunt ad classica venti.

Lett. 62. vides a victim for God, and desires that oblations and thanksgivings should be offered to the Lord by the priests.

5. I therefore, though unworthy and unequal to such an office, and to the offering of such prayers, will yet tell you how I have acted. I carried with me your Majesty's letter to the altar, and laid it thereon, bearing it in my hand, when I offered the Sacrifice; that so your faith might speak with my voice, and the Imperial letter itself might perform the functions of the priestly oblation.

6. Truly the Lord is merciful to the Roman Empire, seeing that He hath chosen such a prince and parent of princes, whose virtue and power, raised on so great and triumphant an eminence of dominion, is supported by such humility as to vanquish Emperors in valour and priests in humility. What shall I wish for, or what shall I desire? You possess everything; from your stores therefore I will obtain the sum of my wishes; your Majesty is pitiful, and has great clemency.

7. But I desire for you again and again an increase of mercy, than which the Lord hath given nothing more excellent; that by your clemency, the Church of God, as it rejoices in the peace and tranquillity of the innocent, so it may also rejoice in the absolution of the guilty. I would chiefly ask you to pardon those who have sinned for the first time. May the Lord preserve your Clemency. Amen.

A.D. 394.

LETTER LXII.

In this letter also S. Ambrose urges on Theodosius a merciful use of his victory, and appeals to him specially for some of the defeated party who had sought the protection of the Church. He acknowledges the greatness of the request, but pleads for it on the score of the divine favour which had been miraculously displayed in his behalf.

AMBROSE TO THE EMPEROR THEODOSIUS.

1. Although I lately wrote to your Clemency even a second time, still I was not satisfied to fulfil my duty of corresponding with you letter by letter; for your gracious

benefits have so often laid me under obligation that by no services can I pay my debt to your Majesty, most blessed Emperor.

2. The very first occasion ought not therefore to have been omitted, but through your chamberlain I ought to have offered to you my thanks, and laid before you the expression of my duty; and this that my omitting to write previously might not seem to arise from sloth rather than necessity: I had also to inquire for some mode whereby I might offer to your Goodness my proper and dutiful greeting.

3. Rightly then do I send my son Felix the Deacon, to convey to you my letter, and to offer to you in my name both my dutiful respects, and also a memorial in behalf of those who, suing for mercy, have fled to the Church, the Mother of your piety. Their tears have constrained me to anticipate your Clemency's mind by my petition.

4. Our request is indeed a great one, but it is addressed to one on whom the Lord has bestowed unheard-of and wonderful things, to one whose mercifulness we have experienced, and whose piety we have as a hostage. We confess then that we look for even more, for as you have surpassed yourself in valour, so also you must surpass yourself in pity. For your victory is considered to have been bestowed on you in the primitive manner, and miraculously, as it was on Moses, on holy Joshua the son of Nun, on Samuel and on David, not by human respect but by the outpouring of celestial grace. Wherefore we look for a measure of pity corresponding to that by means of which such a victory has been earned.

LETTER LXIII.   A.D.396.

THIS, the longest and latest, and certainly not the least interesting, of S Ambrose's Letters, is addressed to the Church of Vercellæ, which, owing to intestine divisions, had been for some time without a Bishop. S Ambrose first urges them to remember Christ's Presence among them, and to proceed to Election with that thought especially in their minds. He then speaks of two followers of Jovinian, Sarmatio and Barbatianus,

LETT. 63. who had introduced their evil doctrines among them, and so fostered divisions. This leads him to dwell at length on the evils of sensuality and the benefits of self-denial, on the profit of fasting, and the excellence of a virgin life, and bids them 'stand fast,' and not be led astray by false teachers. Then he recurs to the subject of the election of a Bishop, and bids them lay aside all evil feelings, and choose one worthy of so high an office, setting before them the examples of our Lord Himself, of Moses and Aaron. He then speaks of the qualities to be looked for in a true Bishop, and urges them to choose one worthy to succeed to the see of the holy martyr Eusebius, and, recurring to the examples of the old Testament, dwells on the history of Elijah. He ends by a general exhortation to all the Church of Vercellæ to the chief Christian virtues, after the model of S. Paul's Epistles, to which the outline of this letter bears a general resemblance. Some questions as to its genuineness have been alluded to in the notes. There seems no sufficient reason for doubting that it is a genuine letter of S Ambrose. It is thoroughly Ambrosian in style and method, and in its treatment of Scripture, especially of the history of the old Testament and of the lives of the great saints of the old dispensation. It was written not more than a year before S. Ambrose's death.

AMBROSE, SERVANT OF CHRIST, CALLED TO BE BISHOP, TO THE CHURCH OF VERCELLÆ, AND TO THEM WHO CALL ON THE NAME OF THE LORD JESUS CHRIST, GRACE UNTO YOU FROM GOD THE FATHER AND HIS ONLY-BEGOTTEN SON BE FULFILLED IN THE HOLY SPIRIT.

1. I AM overcome by grief that the Church of the Lord, which is among you, has still no Bishop, and alone in all the regions of Liguria and Æmilia, of Venetia [a] and the adjacent parts of Italy, stands in need of those ministrations which other Churches were wont to ask at her hands, [1] Intentio. and, what causes me still more shame, the contention [1] which causes this delay is ascribed to me. For as long as there are dissensions among you, how can either we deter-

[a] The word here used is plural, Venetiarum. From this it has been argued that this letter must be of later date than S. Ambrose's time, as Venetiæ is the usual name for the city, which was not founded till the time of Attila. (Gibbon ch xxxv. vol. iv. p 242 ed. Smith.) But he certainly uses the plural form in Letter xviii. 21, which is undoubtedly his, and therefore, as Tillemont has pointed out, no argument can be founded on this against the present letter It is possible that under the plural form he intends to include Venetia and Histria, which are reckoned together as one consular province in the civil division of the empire, (see Marquardt's Table, in Smith's Gibbon vol ii p. 315.) and also as one ecclesiastical province in the Exarchate of Milan, (see Bingham ix. 1, 6) By 'finitimis Italiæ partibus' he probably means Flaminia and Picenum Annonarium, which were also included in the 'Diocese' of Italy and Exarchate of Milan

mine anything, or you make your election, or any man accept the election, so as to undertake among men who are at variance an office difficult to bear the weight of, even among those that agree?

TO THE CHURCH OF VERCELLÆ

2. Are you the scholars of a confessor, are you the offspring of those righteous fathers, who as soon as they saw holy Eusebius [b], though before he was unknown to them, put aside their own countrymen, and forthwith approved of him; and required no more than the sight of him for their approval? Rightly did he who was chosen unanimously by the Church, turn out so eminent a man, rightly was it believed that he whom all demanded was chosen by the judgment of God. It is fitting therefore that you follow the example of your fathers, especially since it behoves you, who have been trained by so holy a Confessor, to be better than your fathers, forasmuch as you have been trained and taught by a better preceptor; and to show forth a visible sign of your moderation and concord, by unanimously agreeing to the choice of a Bishop.

3. If the Lord has said, *If two of you shall agree as touching any thing that they shall ask, it shall be done for them of My Father which is in heaven For where two or three are gathered together in My name, there am I in the midst of them;* how much less, when many are assembled in the name of the Lord, where all agree together in their petitions, how much less ought we in any wise to doubt that there the Lord Jesus will be present to inspire their will and grant their petition, to preside over the ordination and confer the grace?

S. Matt. xviii 19, 20.

4. Make yourselves therefore worthy that Christ should stand in the midst of you; for wheresoever is peace there is Christ, for Christ is *Peace;* wheresoever is righteousness there is Christ, for Christ is *Righteousness.* Let Him stand in the midst of you, that you may see Him, that it be not said to you also, *There standeth One among you,*

Eph. ii. 14.
1 Cor. i. 30.
S. John i. 26.

---

[b] It is to be noted that Eusebius, who died in A.D. 371, was not the last Bishop of Vercellæ, but Limenius, whose name occurs among the Bishops who took part in the Council of Aquileia. This has also been made an argument against S. Ambrose's authorship, but there does not seem much weight in it. Eusebius was much the more famous man of the two, and his teaching and example and the memory of his labours and martyrdom are naturally appealed to by S. Ambrose.

LETT. 63. *Whom ye know not.* The Jews saw Him not, for they believed not on Him; we behold Him by devotion, and see Him by faith.

5. Let Him therefore stand in the midst of you, that you may have the *heavens* which *declare the glory of God,* opened to you; that you may do His will and work His works. The heavens are opened to him who sees Jesus, as they were opened to Stephen, when he said, *Behold I see the heavens opened, and Jesus standing at the right hand of God.* Jesus stood as an intercessor, He stood, as being eager to assist His soldier Stephen in his combat; He stood as being prepared to crown His martyr.

<small>Ps. xix. 1.</small>

<small>Acts vii. 56.</small>

6. Let Him therefore stand in the midst of you, that you may not fear Him when seated on His throne, for seated thereon He will judge, according to the saying of Daniel, *I beheld till the thrones were cast down, and the books were opened, and the Ancient of days did sit.* And in the 82nd Psalm it is written, *God standeth in the congregation of princes, He decideth among gods.* So then being seated He judges, standing He decides. He judges concerning them that are not perfected, He decides among the gods. Let Him stand for you as a Defender, as the good Shepherd, that cruel wolves may not attack you.

<small>Dan. vii. 9, 10.</small>

<small>Ps. lxxxii. 1.</small>

7. Nor is it without reason that my admonition directs itself to this point; for I hear that Sarmatio and Barbatianus [c] have come among you, vain boasters, who assert that there is no merit in abstinence, no grace in a strict life, none in virginity, that all are to be rated at one price, that they who chastise their flesh, in order to bring it into subjection to the body, are beside themselves. But had the Apostle Paul thought it a madness, he never would have practised it himself, nor written it for the instruction of others. Yet he thus glories, saying, *But I keep under my body, and bring it into subjection, lest that by any means, when I have preached to others, I myself be found a reprobate* [1]. So that they who chastise not their own bodies, yet would fain preach to others, are themselves accounted reprobates.

<small>1 Cor. ix. 27.</small>

<small>[1] reprobus.</small>

---

[c] These were, it appears, followers of Jovinian. See above, Introd. to Letter of Siricius, p. 280.

8. For is there aught so reprobate[1] as that which excites us to impurity, to corruption, to wantonness? as the fuel of lust, the enticer to pleasure, the nurse of incontinence, the incentive of desire? What new school has sent forth these Epicureans? No school of philosophers, as they affirm, but of ignorant men who are setters forth of pleasure, who persuade to luxury, who hold chastity to be useless. *They were with us, but they were not of us,* for we blush not to say what the Apostle John said. It was when placed here that they first fasted, within the monastery they were under restraint; there was no room for licence, all opportunity of jesting and altercation was cut off.

9. This these men of delicacy could not bear. They departed, and when they desired to return were not received, for I had heard many things concerning them against which it behoved me to be on my guard; I admonished them, but in vain. Thus they began to boil over and spread abroad what might prove the miserable incentives of all kinds of vice. Thus they lost the fruits of their fasting, they lost the fruits of having contained themselves a little while. And now with Satanic malice they envy others those good works, the fruits of which they have themselves lost.

10. What virgin can hear without grieving that her chastity will have no reward? Far be it from her readily to give credence to this, still less let her lay aside her earnestness, or change the intention of her mind. What widow, were she to find her widowhood profitless, would choose to preserve inviolate her first marriage-vow, and live in sorrow, instead of allowing herself to be comforted? What wife is there who hearing that no honour is due to chastity, might not be tempted by unwatchful heedlessness of mind or body? And that is why the Church, in her sacred Lessons, in the discourses of her priests, daily sends forth the praises of chastity, the glory of virginity.

11. Vainly then has the Apostle said, *I wrote to you in an Epistle not to company with fornicators:* and lest perhaps they should say, 'We speak not of the fornicators of this world, but we say that he who has been baptized into Christ ought not to be deemed a fornicator, but whatever

TO THE CHURCH OF VERCELLÆ
[1] reprobum.

1 S. John ii. 19.

1 Cor. v. 9.

his life may be, it will be accepted by God,' the Apostle has added; *Yet not altogether with the fornicators of this world,* and below, *If any man that is called a brother be a fornicator, or covetous, or an idolater, or a railer, or a drunkard, or an extortioner; with such an one no not to eat. For what have I to do to judge them also that are without?* And to the Ephesians, *But fornication, and all uncleanness or covetousness, let it not once be named among you, as becometh saints,* adding straightway, *For this ye know, that no whoremonger, nor unclean person, nor covetous man, who is an idolater, hath any inheritance in the kingdom of Christ and of God.* This, it is plain, is said of the baptized, for they receive an inheritance who are baptized into the death of Christ, and are *buried together with Him, that they may rise together with Him.* Wherefore they are *heirs of God,* and *joint-heirs with Christ,* heirs of God because the Grace of God is conveyed to them, and coheirs of Christ because they are renewed according to His life; heirs also of Christ because by His Death He grants to them as Testator His inheritance.

_{LETT 63}
_{1 Cor. v. 10.}
_{Ib. 11, 12.}

_{Eph v. 3.}
_{Ib. 5.}

_{Rom. vi. 3.}
_{Ib viii. 17.}

12. Now such as these, who have somewhat to lose, ought more to take heed to themselves than they who have nothing. These ought to act with greater caution, to avoid the snares of vice and the incentives to sin, which chiefly arise out of meat and drink. *The people sat down to eat and drink, and rose up to play.*

_{1 Cor. x. 7}
_{Exod xxxii. 6}

13. Even Epicurus himself, whose example these men prefer to that of the Apostles, he, the champion of pleasure, while he denies that it produces evil, denies not that certain consequences flow from it, from which evils are generated: he maintains too that not even the life of the licentious, which is filled with pleasures of this kind, can be said to be objectionable, unless it be assailed by the fear of pain or death. How far removed he is from the truth, may be discovered even from this, that he declares pleasure to be the work of God in man as its originator, as his follower Philomarus[d] maintains in his Epitomes, referring this opinion to the Stoics as its authors.

_{Gen. iii. 1—4.}

[d] Nothing is known of this man, nor is even the name certain, as there are many various readings. The Benedictines suggest that it may mean Philodemus, who is mentioned by Diog. Laert x, 3. as a follower of Epicurus, and is also spoken of by Cicero, De fin. 11, 35 and by Horace, Sat 1, 2, 121.

14. But this is refuted by holy Scripture, which teaches us that pleasure was instilled into Adam and Eve by the snares and enticements of the Serpent. For the Serpent itself is pleasure, and, in accordance with this, the passions of pleasure are various and slippery, and infected by the poison, so to speak, of corrupt enticement. Hence it is plain that Adam, deceived by the sensual appetite, fell from his obedience to God, and the reward of grace. How then can pleasure recal us to Paradise, when it alone cast us out of Paradise?

15. Wherefore the Lord Jesus, willing to strengthen us against the temptations of the Devil, fasted before His combat, to teach us that otherwise we cannot conquer the snares of evil. Moreover, the Devil himself employed the force of pleasure in launching the first dart of his temptations, saying, *If Thou be the Son of God, command that these stones be made bread.* To which the Lord replies, *Man shall not live by bread alone, but by every word of God;* nor would He do it, although within His power, that He might teach us by this wholesome precept to attend rather to love of reading, than to pleasure. Now seeing they deny that we ought to fast, let them be prepared with some reason why Christ fasted, unless it were that His fast might be an example to us. Lastly in a subsequent instance He has taught us that except by fasting evil cannot easily be conquered. These are His words, *This kind of evil spirits goeth not out but by prayer and fasting.*

16. Or what can be the meaning of Scripture which teaches that Peter fasted, and that it was while he was fasting and praying that the mystery of the baptism of the Gentiles was revealed to him? what but to convince us that the Saints themselves by fasting are advanced in virtue? It was while fasting that Moses received the Law, and in like manner, Peter, while fasting, was taught the grace of the New Testament. To Daniel also it was vouchsafed through fasting to stop the mouths of the lions, and to behold the events of times to come. Lastly, what hope of salvation can there be for us, unless by fasting we wash away our sins, since Scripture says, *Fasting and alms purge away sin?*

17. Who then are these new teachers who deny the merit of fasting? Are they not heathen words which say, *Let us eat and drink?* And well does the Apostle tell them, saying, *If after the manner of men I have fought with the beasts at Ephesus, what advantageth it me, if the dead rise not? let us eat and drink, for to-morrow we die.* That is to say, What did it profit me to contend even unto death, save that I might redeem my body? For in vain is it redeemed if there is no hope of the resurrection. If therefore all hope of this is to be abandoned, let us eat and drink, let us not lose the fruit of things present, seeing that future things are not within our grasp. It is for those then to indulge in meat and drink, who have nothing to hope for after death.

18. Lastly, the Epicureans, the champions of pleasure, assert that death is nothing to us: what is dissolved, they say, is insensible, and what is insensible is nothing to us. By this they show plainly that they live by the body only and not by the mind, and do not perform the functions of the soul but of the body only, in that by separation of soul and body they deem all their vital functions to be dissolved, the merits of their virtues and all vigor of their souls to perish, that with his bodily senses the whole man fails, and that, though the body itself is not immediately dissolved, the mind leaves not a relic behind it. Then they would have the soul perish sooner than the body, whereas even according to their own opinion they ought to remember that the flesh and bones remain after death; and, would they abide by the truth, they ought not to deny the grace of the resurrection.

19. Well therefore does the Apostle, confuting these persons, admonish us not to be overthrown by such opinions, saying, *Be not deceived, evil communications corrupt good manners. Be sober*[1] *unto righteousness and sin not; for some are ignorant of God.* To be sober then is good, for drunkenness is sin.

20. But as to Epicurus, this advocate of pleasure, him of whom we make such frequent mention, in order to prove that these men are disciples of the heathens, and follow either the sect of the Epicureans or the man himself who

---

Lett. 63.

1 Cor. xv. 32.

Ib. 33, 34.
[1] sobrii estote. Vulg.

was excluded even by philosphers from their company as the pattern of luxury, what if we can prove even him to be more tolerable than these men? Now he asserts, as Demarchus[e] tells us, that it is not drinking-bouts, nor banquettings, nor the birth of sons, nor the embraces of women, nor a large supply of fish and such delicacies provided for sumptuous feasts, it is not these which make life sweet, but sober discourse. He added also that they who are not excessive in seeking the dainties of the table, are moderate in the use of them. The man who cheerfully limits himself to the juices of plants and to bread and water, despises delicate feasts, for from these arise many evils. Elsewhere too they say that it is not excessive banquets and revels which make pleasure sweet, but a temperate life.

21. Seeing then that philosphy has renounced these men, shall not the Church exclude them? They themselves too, as is usual in a bad cause, often attack themselves by their own arguments. For although it be their main opinion, that there is no sweetness of pleasure but that which arises from eating and drinking; yet, perceiving that they cannot lay down so shameful a definition without the utmost disgrace, and that none stand by them, they have sought to disguise it under the gloss of colourable arguments, and thus one of them has said, In seeking pleasure by means of feasting and song, we have lost that which is derived from hearing that Word whereby alone we can be saved.

22. Do we not then perceive in this complicated discussion how inconsistent and variable these men are? Scripture condemns them, for it has not passed over those whom the Apostles confuted, as Luke records in the Acts of the Apostles, which he has written in narrative style, *Then certain philosophers of the Epicureans*[f], *and of the*

---

[e] Nothing is known of Demarchus, whom S. Ambrose here quotes. The Benedictines suggest that it may be a mistake for Hermarchus, who was Epicurus' successor as head of his school, and who wrote books in defence of the Epicurean philosophy He is mentioned several times by Cicero.

[f] Though the so-called Epicureans of later days perverted his theory to what is generally known as Epicureanism, Epicurus himself certainly did not mean by pleasure sensual pleasure. 'Pleasure was not with him a momentary and transitory sensation, but he conceived it as something lasting and imperishable, consisting in pure and noble mental enjoyments. 'He was a man of pure simple and temperate habits.' Dict of Biog. in voc. Vol ii p. 34, 35.

LETT 63. *Stoics encountered him. And some said, What will this babbler say? other some, He seemeth to be a setter forth of strange gods.*

23. Yet not even from this number did the Apostle part devoid of success. For Dionysius the Areopagite, and Damaris his wife, with many others, believed. And thus by their acts this assembly of the learned and eloquent proved themselves vanquished by the simple discourse of the faithful. What then do these men mean by attempting to pervert those whom the Apostle has won, and Christ redeemed with His own blood, insisting that the baptized have no need to apply themselves to the exercise of virtue; that they are not injured by revellings, by excess of pleasure; that they who deprive themselves of such things are foolish; that virgins ought to marry and bear children; widows also ought to renew that carnal commerce which they had better never have known; and that although they might be able to contain themselves they are mistaken in refusing again to enter into the bond of marriage?

24. What then? Shall we put off the man and put on the beast? shall we strip off Christ, and be clothed over and over with the garments of Satan? The very heathen sages held that pleasure was not to be esteemed honourable, lest they should seem to couple men with brutes, and can we instil the habits of animals into the human breast, and engrave on the rational mind the irrational instincts of wild beasts?

25. Yet there are many kinds of animals, who when they have lost their mate, will no longer copulate, but lead, as it were, a solitary life. Many also feed on simple herbs and only quench their thirst in the pure stream; you may also often see dogs refuse food which they have been forbidden, and, if bid to refrain, close up their hungry jaws. [g] Do men then require to be recalled from that in which even mute animals have learnt from man's teaching not to transgress?

26. But what is more excellent than abstinence, which

---

[g] This must be the sense if we retain the interrogation. If it is omitted the passage would mean, 'Men then are recalled from that, in which' &c, i.e., it is plainly unfitting for men to do that, in which &c.

makes even the years of youth to be old, and produces an old age of conduct? For as by excess of food and drunkenness even old age is inflamed, so on the other hand, the insolence of youth is restrained by sparing food and by the flowing stream. Fire without us is quenched by the pouring on of water, no wonder then if even internal heat is allayed by draughts from the brook; for the flame is nourished or fails, according as it is fed or not. As hay, stubble, wood, oil, and the like are the fuel of fire, and feed it, and if you withdraw or do not supply them the fire is quenched, so also the warmth of the body is nourished or diminished by food; by food it is excited and by food allayed. Gluttony therefore is the mother of lust.

27. And shall we not say that temperance is accordant with nature, and with that Divine law, which in the very origin of all things, gave us to drink of the fountains and to eat of the fruit of trees? After the flood the just man found himself tempted by wine. Wherefore let us use the natural drink of temperance, and would that we all could do so. But since we are not all strong, the Apostle says, *Use a little wine for thine often infirmities.* It is to be drunk then because of infirmity not for pleasure, and therefore as a remedy, sparingly, not as a luxury, profusely.

28. Again, Elijah, when the Lord God was training him to the perfection of virtue, found *a cake baken on the coals, and a cruse of water at his head; and in the strength of that meat he fasted forty days.* Our fathers, when they passed over the sea on foot, drank water, not wine. It was when fed on their homely food and drinking water, that Daniel repressed the rage of the lions, and the Hebrew children saw the fiery furnace playing round their limbs with harmless flames.

29. And why should I speak of men only? Judith, in no wise moved by the luxurious banquet of Holofernes, won a triumph which men's arms had found desperate, by the sole merit of her temperance, delivering her country from invasion, and slaying with her own hand the captain of the host: a manifest example both that this warrior dreaded by the people had become enervated by his luxury, and that temperance in food had made this woman stronger

than men. It was not in her sex that she surpassed nature, but by her spare diet she conquered. Esther obtained favour from the proud king by her fasts. Anna, *a widow of about fourscore and four years*, serving in the temple *with fastings and prayers night and day*, came to the knowledge of Christ, and John the Teacher of abstinence, and, as it were, a new Angel upon earth, was His herald.

30. O foolish Elisha! to feed the prophets with wild and bitter gourds; O Ezra[h] unmindful of Scripture though from memory thou dost restore Scripture! O sinless Paul, to glory in fasting, if fasting avails nothing!

31. But how can that not profit whereby our vices are purged? And if you offer it together with humility and mercy, then, as Isaiah has said by the Divine Spirit, *thy bones shall be made fat, and thou shalt be like a watered garden!* Thy soul then is fattened, and its virtues are enriched by the spiritual fat of fasting, and thy fruits are multiplied by the richness of thy mind, that thou mayest be made drunk, as it were, with soberness[1], as is that cup whereof the Prophet speaks, *And my cup which inebriateth me, how goodly is it!*

32. But not only is that temperance praiseworthy which is sparing in food, but that also which restrains desires. For it is written, *Go not after thy lusts, but refrain thyself from thine appetites. If thou givest thy soul the desires that please her, she will make thee a laughing stock to thine enemies!* and again, *Wine and women will make men of understanding to fall away!* Hence Paul teaches temperance even in marriage; for he who commits excess therein is, as it were, an adulterer, and violates the Apostolical law.

33. But how can I express the greatness of the grace of virginity, which was counted worthy to be chosen by Christ, to be the bodily temple of God, wherein dwelt, as we read, *the fulness of the Godhead bodily!* A virgin conceived the Saviour of the world, a virgin brought forth the Life of the universe. Ought not then virginity to be above all other states[1] which was profitable to all in Christ? A virgin

---

[1] Sobrietatis inebrietas.

[1] Sola.

[h] S Ambrose is alluding apparently to Ezra proclaiming and keeping a fast to remove God's anger against his people. Should we not read 'memoriae' for 'memoriâ?' Ezra did restore the Scriptures *to* the memory of the people, but it does not appear that he restored them *from* memory?

bore Him Whom this world cannot contain or support. He, born of the womb of Mary, preserved inviolate her chastity, and the seal of her virginity. Therefore Christ found in the Virgin what He would take for His own, what the Lord of all would assume to Himself. By the woman and the man our flesh was cast out of Paradise, by the Virgin it was re-united to God. *TO THE CHURCH OF VERCELLÆ*

34. And what shall I say of the other Mary[1], the sister of Moses, who, leading the female band, passed on foot over the straights of the sea? By the same grace Thecla was reverenced even by lions, so that the unfed beasts, lying at the feet of their prey, underwent a holy fast, neither with wanton look nor sharp claw venturing to harm the virgin, for even by a look the sanctity of virginity is profaned. *Exod. xv. 20.*

35. Again, with what reverence has the holy Apostle spoken, *Now concerning virgins I have no commandment of the Lord, yet I give my judgement as one that hath obtained mercy of the Lord.* Commandment he has not, but counsel; for that which is above the Law is not commanded, but counselled and advised. Nor is any authority assumed, but grace is shewn, and that not by any chance person, but by him who *hath obtained mercy of the Lord.* Are then the counsels of these men better than those of the Apostles? The Apostle says, *I give my counsel,* but they dissuade all from leading a virgin's life. *1 Cor vii. 25.*

36. And we ought to wonder at the greatness of the commendation of it which the Prophet, or rather Christ in the person of the Prophet, has expressed in one short verse. *A garden inclosed is my sister, my spouse, a spring shut up, a fountain sealed.* Christ says this to the Church, whom He would have *a virgin without spot or wrinkle.* Virginity is a fertile *garden,* which bears many fruits of a good odour; *a garden inclosed* because it is surrounded on all sides with the wall of chastity; *a fountain sealed,* in that virginity is the fountain and source of modesty, and that which keeps unbroken the seal of purity; that fountain wherein is reflected the image of God, since with chastity of body accords likewise holy simplicity. *Cant. iv. 12.* *Eph. v. 27.*

---

[1] Mary and Miriam are really the same name, the former having come through the Greek form Μαρία.

Lett. 63.	37. Nor can any one doubt that the Church herself is a virgin, whom even at Corinth the Apostle Paul espoused,
2 Cor. xi. 2.	that he *might present her a chaste virgin to Christ.* Thus
1 Cor. vii.	in his first Epistle he gives counsel and sets a high value on the gift of virginity, for that it is not disquieted by the needs of this present world, nor defiled by its corruptions, nor agitated by its storms. In the latter he espouses the Corinthians to Christ, that so, in the purity of that people, he may ratify the virginity of the Church.
Ib. 26.	38. Answer me now, O Paul, in what way *for the pre-*
Ib. 32.	*sent distress* dost thou give counsel? *He that is unmarried,* thou sayest, *careth for the things that belong to the Lord,*
Ib. 34.	*how he may please the Lord,* adding further, *the unmarried woman careth for the things of the Lord,* that she may be holy both in body and spirit. She has therefore a bulwark against the storms of this world, and thus shielded and fortified by the Divine protection she is disquieted by none of the blasts of this world. Counsel then is good, because
Ib. 35. [1] laqueus.	therein lies profit, but in commandment is a bond[1]. Counsel leads forward the willing, commandment binds the reluctant. So that if any follow this counsel, and repent not, she hath profited; on the other hand, if she change her purpose, she hath no ground to accuse the Apostle, for she ought to have judged better of her own weakness, and thus she is responsible to herself for her own choice, for she has bound herself by a bond and knot heavier than she can bear.
	39. Wherefore, as a good physician, who desires both to preserve for the strong the stability of their virtue, and to restore health to the weak, he gives to the one counsel,
Rom. xiv. 2.	to the other a remedy; *Whoso is weak, let him eat herbs;* let him take a wife; he that is stronger, let him use the
1 Cor. vii. 37—40.	strong meat of continence. And he well adds; *He that standeth stedfast in his heart, having no necessity, but hath power over his own will, and hath so decreed in his heart that he will keep his virgin, doeth well. So then he that giveth her in marriage doeth well, but he that giveth her not in marriage doeth better. The wife is bound by the law as long as her husband liveth; but if her husband be dead she is at liberty to be married to whom she will; only in the*

Lord. *But she is happier if she so abide, after my judgment, and I think also that I have the Spirit of God.* Now having the counsel of God consists in examining all things diligently, in urging what is best, and pointing out what is safest.

40. A careful guide points out many ways, that each person may walk on which he will, and which he finds suitable for himself: provided only he lights on one which will lead him into the camp. Good is the way of virginity, but, being lofty and steep, it requires the stronger sort. Good too is the way of widowhood, not so difficult as the former, but, being rocky and rough, it requires the more cautious sort. Good too is the way of matrimony, but, being smooth and direct, it arrives by a longer circuit at the camp of the faithful, and this way is trodden by the larger number. We have therefore the rewards of virginity, the merits of widowhood, there is also a place for conjugal chastity. They are the degrees and advances of several virtues.

41. Stand stedfast therefore in your hearts, that no man may unsettle or overthrow you. The Apostle has taught us what 'to stand' signifies, that is, what was said to Moses, *For the place whereon thou standest is holy ground;* for no one stands but he who stands by faith, who stands firm in the resolution of his heart. In another place too we read, *But as for thee, stand thou here by Me.* Both are addressed to Moses by the Lord, both *the place whereon thou standest is holy ground,* and *stand thou here by Me,* that is to say, 'thou standest with Me, if thou standest in the Church. For the place itself is holy, the land itself bears the fruit of holiness, and is rich with the haunts of virtue.'

42. 'Stand therefore in the Church, stand where I appeared to thee, there I am with thee. For where the Church is, there is the most secure resting-place for thy soul; there is the support of thy mind, when I appeared to thee out of the bush. Thou art the bush, I am the fire: the fire in the bush, and I in the flesh. And therefore am I the fire, that I may give thee light, that I may burn up thy thorns, that is, thy sins, and discover to thee My grace.'

LETT. 63.   43. Stand firm therefore in your hearts, and drive away from the Church those wolves which seek to carry off prey. Let there be no sloth in you, nor an evil mouth or bitter tongue. Sit not with vain persons, for it is written, *I have not dwelt with vain persons.* Listen not to those who detract from their neighbours, lest, hearing others, ye be yourselves excited to do likewise, and it be said to each of you, *Thou satest and spakest against thy brother.*

Ps. xxvi. 4.

Ib. l. 20.

44. Sitting we speak against others, but standing up we praise the Lord, as it is said; *Behold now, praise the Lord, all ye servants of the Lord; ye that stand in the house of the Lord.* He who sits, to speak of the habit of the body, is, as it were, dissolved by ease, and relaxes the energy of his mind. But the careful watchman, the unwearied scout, the wakeful sentinel who keeps the outposts of the camp, these stand. The brave warrior also, who would prevent the designs of his enemy, stands[j] ready in his rank ere he is looked for.

Ps. cxxxiv. 1, 2.

45. *Let him that standeth take heed lest he fall.* He who stands is free from detraction, for it is by the talk of the idle that slander is disseminated and rancour displayed. Wherefore the Prophet says, *I have hated the congregation of the wicked, and will not sit among the ungodly.* And in the 37th Psalm, which is full of moral precepts, he has placed in the very outset, *Be not malignant among them that are malignant, neither be thou envious against the evil-doers.* Malignity does more harm than malice, for its property is neither pure simplicity nor open malice; but a hidden malevolence, and it is more difficult to guard against what is concealed than against what is known; and so our Saviour bids us beware of evil spirits, for they captivate us by the outward show of charming pleasures, and the false show of other things, holding forth honour as a lure to ambition, wealth to riches, power to pride.

1 Cor. x. 12.

Ps. xxvi. 5.

Ib. xxxvii. 1.

46. Wherefore in every act, but especially in the search after a Bishop, by whose model the life of all is formed, malignity ought to be absent, that by a composed and peaceful exercise of judgment he may be preferred to all

---

[j] A reminiscence of Virgil's,
Ante expectatum positis stat in agmine castris. Georg. iii, 348.

who is to be chosen from all and who may heal all, For *a gentle-minded man is the physician of the heart*, of that whereof our Lord also in the Gospel has professed Himself a Physician, *They that be whole need not a physician, but they that are sick.*

^{margin:} TO THE CHURCH OF VERCELLÆ Prov. xiv. 30 LXX. S Matt. ix. 12.

47. He is the good Physician, Who has taken upon Him our infirmities, Who has healed our sicknesses, and yet He, as it is written, *glorified not Himself to be made an High Priest*, but *He that said unto Him*, even the Father, *Thou art my Son, this day have I begotten Thee*, as He saith also in another place, *Thou art a Priest for ever after the order of Melchisedeck.* And as He was to be the type of all priests, He took upon Him our flesh, that *in the days of His flesh, He might offer up prayers and supplications with strong crying and tears unto* God the Father, *and though He were the Son* of God, might even *learn obedience from the things He suffered*, in order to teach us, that He might become to us the Author of salvation. Finally, having accomplished His sufferings, and being Himself made perfect, He gave health to all, He bore the sin of all.

^{margin:} Heb. v. 5. Ib. 7.

48. Thus He Himself chose Aaron the High Priest, that human ambition might not sway the choice, but the grace of God; no voluntary offering, nor taking upon himself, but a heavenly call, that he might offer gifts for sins, who could have compassion on sinners *for that he himself also, it is written, is compassed with infirmity.* A man should not *take this honour to himself, but he that is called of God as was Aaron*; so also Christ did not assume but received His priesthood.

^{margin:} Numb. xvii. 8. Heb. v. 2. Ib. 4.

49. And further, since the succession derived by descent from Aaron produced heirs of his race rather than partakers of his righteousness, therefore there came the antitype of that Melchisedeck whom we read of in the Old Testament, the true Melchisedeck, the true King of Peace, the true King of Righteousness, for this is the interpretation of his name; being *without father, without mother, without descent, having neither beginning of days, nor end of life,* which also has reference to the Son of God, for in His Divine generation, He had no mother, and in His birth from the Virgin Mary He knew no father; Who, born of the

^{margin:} Ib. vii. 2, 3.

LETT. 63. Father alone before the world, and from the Virgin alone in the world, could have no beginning of days, for He *was in the beginning.* And how could He have any end to His
Rev. i. 8. life, Who is the Author of life to all? He is *the Beginning and the Ending.* But this is referred to also by way of example, that a Bishop ought to be without father and without mother, in that it is not nobility of birth, but holiness of life and preeminence in virtue that is chosen in him.

50. Let him possess faith and ripeness of conduct, not one without the other, but let both continue in one, with good works and deeds. Wherefore the Apostle Paul wishes
Heb. xi. 9. us to be imitators of those who *by faith and patience possess the promises* of Abraham, of him who by patience was counted worthy to receive and possess the grace of the blessing promised to him. The prophet David has admonished us that we ought to be imitators of holy Aaron, for he has proposed him to us, among the saints of the
Ps. xcix 6. Lord, as an example for our imitation, saying, *Moses and Aaron among his priests, and Samuel among such as call upon His Name.*

51. An example worthy to be followed by all truly was he, seeing that when death, owing to the rebels, was spread-
Numb. xvi. 48 ing among the people, he placed himself between the living and the dead, thereby to arrest death so that no more might perish. Of a priestly mind and temper truly was he, who thus with pious zeal offered himself, as a good Shepherd, for the Lord's flock. Thus he broke the sting of death, checked its violence, refused to let it pass. Thus piety aided his services, because he offered himself for those who resisted.

52. Wherefore let those also who separate themselves learn to fear the anger of the Lord, and to appease His priests.
Ib. 32. What? did not the earth open and swallow up Dathan Korah and Abiram on account of their schism? For when Korah Dathan and Abiram stirred up two hundred and
Ib. 3. fifty men against Moses and Aaron to separate themselves from them, they rose up against them, saying, *Let it suffice for you that all the congregation are holy, every one of them, and the Lord is among them.*

53. Wherefore the Lord was angry and spake to the whole congregation. *The Lord knoweth them that are His, and hath drawn His saints to Himself; and those whom He hath not chosen, He has not so drawn to Himself.* And the Lord commanded that Korah and all those who together with him had rebelled against Moses and Aaron, the priests of the Lord, should take censers, and put incense therein, that he who was chosen of the Lord, might be declared to be holy among the ministers of the Lord.   TO THE CHURCH OF VERCELLÆ
2 Tim. ii. 19.

54. And Moses said unto Korah, *Hear, I pray you, ye sons of Levi, seemeth it but a small thing unto you that the God of Israel hath separated you from the congregation of Israel, to bring you near to Himself to do the service of the tabernacle of the Lord?* and below, *Seek ye the priesthood also? for which cause both thou and all thy company are gathered together against the Lord: and what is Aaron that ye murmur against him?*   Numb. xvi. 8, 9.

Ib.10,11.

55. The whole people therefore, weighing the cause of offence, that these men, though unworthy, wished to fill the office of the priesthood, and therefore separated themselves, murmuring against the Lord, and censuring His judgment in the choice of their priests, were seized with great fear, and oppressed with apprehension of punishment. But at the general entreaty that all may not be involved in destruction through the insolence of a few, the guilty are marked out, and two hundred and fifty men with their leaders are separated from the rest, the earth quakes and is rent asunder in the midst of the people, a deep gulf is opened and swallows up the offenders, and thus they are removed from the pure elements of creation, so as neither to pollute the air by breathing it, nor the heavens by looking on them, nor the sea by their touch, nor the earth by their burial.

56. The punishment ceased, the wickedness ceased not; for owing to this very act a murmuring arose among the people that by means of the priests the people had perished. Indignant at this the Lord would have destroyed all, had He not first been moved by the prayers of Moses and Aaron, and afterwards, at the intercession of Aaron His

Lett. 63. priest, (in order to render their pardon more humiliating,) consented to spare their life at the prayer of those, whose prerogative they had denied.

Numb. xii. 1.

Ib. 10.

57. Miriam the prophetess herself, she who with her brethren had crossed the straights of the sea dryshod, because, being still ignorant of the mystery of the Ethiopian woman, she had murmured against her brother Moses, became leprous white as snow, and even at the prayer of Moses was scarcely healed of this great plague. This her murmuring however is to be considered as a type of the Synagogue, which, uninstructed in the mystery of this Ethiopian woman, that is, of the Gentile Church, utters daily reproaches, and envies that people by whose faith she herself will also be relieved from the leprosy of her un-

Rom. xi. 25.

belief, according as we read, *that blindness in part is happened to Israel, until the fulness of the Gentiles be come in.*

58. And that we may observe that it is Divine rather than human grace which operates in priests, of all those rods which Moses received from the tribes and laid by, the rod of Aaron alone budded, and thus the people perceived that the Divine commission is a gift which is to be looked for in a priest, and though they before thought that a similar prerogative belonged to themselves, they now ceased to claim the same privilege for a merely human election. But this rod, what else does it indicate, but that priestly grace never decays, and in the utmost lowliness has in the exercise of its functions the flower of strength committed to it, or because this also has reference to a mystery? Nor is it without a meaning that we deem this to have taken place near the end of the life of Aaron the priest. It appears to be intimated that the ancient Jewish people, decaying and worn away by the long-continued infidelity of their priesthood, will in the latter times be reclaimed to zealous faith and devotion by the example of the Church, and by the aid of reviving grace will again put forth the blossoms which have so long been dead.

Numb. xx. 26.

59. But what is signified by the fact that on the death of Aaron it was not to all the people, but to Moses alone, who is among the priests of the Lord, that God gave the

command to invest with the garments of Aaron the priest Eleazar his son, what but to teach us that a priest ought to be consecrated by a priest, and clothed with his proper garments, that is, with priestly virtues; and then, when it appears that he lacks no part of his priestly array, but is complete in all things, that he should be brought near to the holy altars. For being about to offer for the people, he ought to be chosen by the Lord, and approved by the people; and this lest some grave cause of offence should be found in him whose duty it is to intercede for the sins of others. No ordinary degree of virtue befits a priest, for he ought sedulously to shun not only more heinous sins, but even the smallest; he ought to be open to compassion, not to revoke his promise, to raise the fallen, to sympathise with sorrow, to preserve meekness, to love piety, to drive away or stifle wrath, to be a trumpet to rouse the people to devotion, or to soothe them into tranquillity.

TO THE CHURCH OF VERCELLÆ

Heb. v. 1.

60. It is an old saying; Accustom yourself to be single-minded that your life may be as a picture, and ever preserve the same stamp which it has received. How can he be one and the same, who at one time is inflamed with anger, at another, boils with bitter indignation, whose countenance burns and then changes to paleness, varying and changing colour every moment. But suppose that it is natural to be angry, or that for the most part there is cause to be so; it also is the part of a man to moderate his wrath, and to resist being carried away by brutal fury, so as not to know how to be appeased; it is his duty not to embitter family discord, for it is written, *A wrathful man diggeth up sin.* He is not one with himself who is double-minded, nor he who cannot restrain his wrath, of whom David says well, *Be ye angry, and sin not.* Such a one does not command his anger, but rather indulges his natural passions, which cannot indeed be prevented but may be moderated. Although then we are angry, let our passion admit only such emotion as is according to nature, not sin which is contrary to nature. For it is intolerable that he who undertakes to govern others should be unable to govern himself.

Prov. xv. 18.

Ps. iv. 4. Vulg. LXX.

LETT 63. 61. And so the Apostle has given us a model, that it
1 Tim.iii. behoves a *Bishop* to be *blameless,* as he also says elsewhere,
2.
Tit. i 7. *For a Bishop must be blameless, as the steward of God, not
self-willed, not soon angry, not given to wine, no striker, not
given to filthy lucre.* For how can the compassion of the
almsgiver and the avarice of the coveter agree together?

62. I have set down those things which I have learnt
are to be avoided; it is the Apostle who teaches what vir-
Ib. 9. tues are needed, and he tells us that the *gainsayers* are to
be *convinced* with patience, and commands a Bishop to be
Ib. 6. *the husband of one wife,* and this not in order to exclude
him from marriage, (for this is beyond the bounds of the
precept,) but that by conjugal chastity he may preserve
the grace of his Washing; nor again, that he may feel
that he has the sanction of Apostolical authority for begetting children after he is a priest, for he speaks of one
having children, not of one begetting them or marrying
again.

63. And I have thought it better to touch upon this, because many persons argue as if the being *husband of one
wife* had reference to a man marrying once after Baptism,
seeing that by Baptism all the sin which would interpose
any obstacle is removed. True indeed it is that in Baptism all sins and offences are washed away, so that even
to one who has polluted his body with many women not
united to him by wedlock, all is remitted. But Baptism
does not dissolve marriage, if a man has married again, for
it is sin, not the Law, which is destroyed by the Bath, and
in marriage there is no sin but a law. Being therefore a
law it is not dissolved as if it were a fault, but retained, in
that it is a law. Now the Apostle has laid down a rule
saying, *If any be blameless, the husband of one wife.* So
that if any man be blameless, the husband of one wife, he
comes under the forms of the rule for undertaking the
priestly office, but he who marries again incurs not indeed
the sin of pollution, but loses the prerogative of a priest.

64. We have declared what the law prescribes, let us
speak also of what is prescribed by reason. But in the
first place we are to understand that the Apostle has not
ordained this with reference to Bishops and Presbyters

only, but that the Fathers of the Nicene Council[k] have also decreed that no man should be a cleric at all who has contracted a second marriage. For how can he give consolation or honour to a widow; how can he exhort her to continue a widow, or to preserve that faith to her husband which he has not preserved to his own first marriage? Or what difference would there be between the people and the priest, if they were bound by the same laws? The life of the priest ought to be pre-eminent as well as his graces, for he who obliges others by his precepts ought himself to observe the precepts of the law.

to the church of vercellæ

65. How vehemently I resisted ordination[l] and when I was at last constrained to consent, how I strove that it might be postponed[l] but the popular impulse[1] prevailed over prescribed[2] rules. And yet it was approved by the judgement of the Bishops of the West, and its example followed by those of the East[1]; and this notwithstanding the prohibition to ordain a *novice, lest he be lifted up with pride.* If my ordination was not postponed, it was owing to a constraining force, and if proper humility be not wanting to the priest, where the fault does not lie with him no blame will be imputed.

[1] impressio. [2] praescriptio. 1 Tim. iii. 6.

66. But if even in other Churches such deliberation is used in ordination, how much care is required in that of Vercellæ, where two duties seem equally required of the Bishop, monastic severity and ecclesiastical discipline. For Eusebius of blessed memory was the first to bring together in the West these two differing requisites, and though living in the city observed the monastic institute, and with the government of his Church united the sobriety of an ascetic life. Great increase accrues to the grace of the priesthood

---

[k] The reading here varies. Ben has 'in Concilio Nicaeni tractatus,' which may mean 'the Council which made the Nicene Creed,' (for the phrase 'Nicaenus tractatus' as applied to the Creed see note l on Acts of Council of Aquileia.) Another reading is 'in Concilii Nicaeni tractatu,' and another 'in Concilio Nicaeno tractatus.'

There is a difficulty about S Ambrose's statement, as there is nothing on the subject in the Canons of Nicaea The Benedictine editors, after discussing other explanations, suggest that S. Ambrose may have had an inaccurate copy of the Canons, with the one he here quotes inserted from some other Council. Some unauthentic documents professing to give Nicene regulations on the subject are quoted in Dict. of Christian Antiq. Art. Digamy

[l] The most conspicuous instance was Nectarius, See note a, on Letter xiii.

63. when young men are thus obliged to practise abstinence and to obey the laws of chastity, and, though living within the city, to renounce its customs and ways.

67. Hence sprung those famous men Elijah, Elisha, and John the son of Elizabeth, who clothed *in sheepskins, being destitute, afflicted, tormented, wandered about in deserts,* in mountains thickets and precipices, among pathless rocks, in horrid caves, through marshy fords, *of whom the world was not worthy.* Hence Daniel, Ananias, Azarias and Misael, who were brought up in the royal palace, were fed sparingly as though they had been in the desert, with coarse food and water to drink. Rightly then did the king's servants prevail over kingdoms, shake off the yoke and set at nought captivity, *subdue kingdoms,* conquer the elements, *quench the violence of fire, escape the edge of the sword, stop the mouths of lions, out of weakness were made strong,* shrank not from the *mockings* of men, seeing that they hoped for heavenly rewards, nor dreaded the darkness of the prison, since on them had shone the brightness of eternal light.

Heb. xi. 37.
Ib. 38.
Dan. i. 16.
Heb. xi. 33, 34.

68. Following their example, holy Eusebius[m] left his country and kindred, and preferred foreign sojourn to the enjoyment of home. For the faith's sake he also chose and desired the hardships of exile, having for his companion Dionysius of blessed memory, who chose a voluntary banishment in preference to the Emperor's friendship. Thus when these illustrious men, beset by arms, hemmed round by soldiers, were being carried off from the greater church, they triumphed over the imperial power. Troops of soldiers and the din of arms could not rob them of their faith, but they subdued the fierceness of the brutal mind, depriving it of power to hurt the Saints. *For,* as it is written in Proverbs, *the king's wrath is as the roaring of a lion.*

Prov. xix. 12.

69. He confessed himself vanquished, by requesting them to relinquish their purpose, but they deemed their pen of reeds more powerful than his iron swords. Thus it was unbelief, not the faith of the Saints, which was wounded

---

[m] Eusebius and Dionysius Bishop of Milan were driven into exile by the Emperor Valens, because they refused at the third Council of Milan, A D. 355, to subscribe the condemnation of Athanasius. There is a brief but graphic account of the circumstances in Bright's History of the Church, pages 70—73.

and fell: they for whom a heavenly abode was prepared needed not a sepulchre in their own country. They wandered through the world *as having nothing, yet possessing all things.* Every place whither they were sent appeared full of delights, nor could they feel any want who always abounded in faith. They were tempted but not overcome, in fastings in labours, in watchings, in prisons; *out of weakness they were made strong.* Fed to the full by fasting they looked not for the charms of pleasure; refreshed by the hope of eternal grace, the burning summer parched them not, nor did the cold of icy regions break them down; for the warm breath of devotion invigorated them; they feared not the bonds of men, for Jesus had loosed them; they desired not to be redeemed from death, for they looked forward to be raised again by Christ.

TO THE CHURCH OF VERCELLÆ

2 Cor. vi. 10.

Heb. xi. 34.

70. Holy Dionysius again prayed that his life might close in exile, fearing that, if he returned, he should find the minds of the clergy or people perplexed by the doctrines and customs of the unbelieving, and he won this grace and carried with him with calm mind the peace of the Lord. Thus as holy Eusebius first lifted up the standard of confession, so blessed Dionysius, dying in his exile, won a higher title even than martyrdom.

71. Now this endurance in holy Eusebius throve under the monastic discipline, and by being accustomed to a stricter rule, he imbibed a power of bearing hardships. For it is certain that in the higher kinds of Christian devotion these two things are the most excellent, the Clerical function and the Monastic rule. The first is trained to be obliging and courteous in its behaviour, the second is accustomed to abstinence and endurance; the one lives as on a theatre, the other in secret; the one is seen, the other hidden. It is the saying of one who was a noble combatant, *We are made a spectacle unto the world, and to Angels.* Worthy truly was he to have Angels as his spectators, when he wrestled that he might attain the prize of Christ, when he contended that he might lead on earth an Angel's life, that he might overcome the wickedness of spirits in heaven, for *he wrestled with spiritual wickedness.* Rightly was the world a spectator of him whom it was called on to imitate.

1 Cor. iv. 9.

Eph. vi. 12.

72. Thus one of these lives is on the stage, the other in the cell; the one contends with the distractions of the world, the other with the lusts of the flesh; the one subdues, the other flees from corporal pleasures; the one regulates, the other refrains itself, for to the perfect it is said, *If any man will come after Me, let him deny himself, and take up his cross, and follow Me.* Now he follows Christ who can say, *Nevertheless I live, yet not I, but Christ liveth in me.*

<small>LETT. 63.</small>

<small>S Matt. xvi. 24.</small>

<small>Gal. ii. 20.</small>

73. Paul denied himself, when, knowing that *chains, bonds and tribulations awaited him* in Jerusalem, he voluntarily exposed himself to these dangers, saying, *Neither count I my life dear unto myself, so that I might finish my course with joy, and the ministry, which I have received of the Lord Jesus.* And though many stood round him, weeping and beseeching, they did not affect his resolution, so strict a censor over itself is a ready faith.

<small>Acts xx. 24.</small>

74. Thus the one kind of life fights, the other retires into seclusion; the world is triumphed over by the one, and placed at a distance by the other; *to the one the world is crucified, and to it the world,* to the other the world is unknown; the one has more temptations and therefore a more signal victory; the other falls less frequently and more easily keeps guard over itself.

<small>Gal. vi. 14.</small>

75. So also Elijah himself, that the word of his mouth might be confirmed, was sent by the Lord to the brook Cherith. Both Ahab and Jezebel threatened him, Elijah feared and rose up, *and went in the strength of that* spiritual *meat forty days and forty nights unto Horeb the mount of God;* and he came thither unto a cave, and lodged there, and afterwards was sent from thence to anoint kings. Thus he was inured to endurance by dwelling in the desert, and as though fed by coarse viands unto the fatness of virtue, went forth increased in strength.

<small>1 Kings xvii. 3.</small>

<small>Ib. xix. 8.</small>

76. John also grew up in the desert, and baptized the Lord, and there first exercised himself in constancy, that afterwards he might reprove kings.

<small>S. Luke iii 2.</small>

<small>Ib. 19.</small>

77. And now, seeing that we have cursorily passed over, in treating of holy Elijah's dwelling in the desert, the names of places which are not without meaning, let us return to

consider this. Elijah was sent to the brook Cherith, there the ravens fed him, in the morning they brought him bread, in the evening flesh. And with reason did they bring him bread in the morning, for *bread strengthens man's heart,* and it was with mystical food that the prophet was fed. In the evening he was supplied with flesh. Understand what thou readest; for Cherith is understanding, Horeb signifies, 'heart' or 'as heart;' of Beersheba the signification is the 'well of the seventh,' or 'of the oath.'

<small>TO THE CHURCH OF VERCELLÆ</small>
<small>1 Kings xvii. 3—6.</small>
<small>Ps. civ. 15.</small>
<small>1 Kings xix. 8.</small>
<small>Ib. 3.</small>

78. Elijah first went to Beersheba, to the mysteries and sacraments of the Divine and holy Law, afterwards he was sent to the Brook, to the stream of that *river* which *makes glad the city of God.* Here you perceive the two Testaments, and their single Author; the ancient Scriptures as a deep and dark well whence you have to draw water with difficulty, for He Who was to fill it full was not yet come, as He said in after times, *I am not come to destroy the Law, but to fulfil it.* Therefore the Saint is commanded by the Lord to pass over the brook, for he who shall drink of the New Testament is not only a river, but *out of his belly shall flow rivers of living water,* rivers of understanding, rivers of meditation, spiritual streams, which yet are dried up in time of unbelief, lest the profane and faithless should drink of them.

<small>Ps. xlvi. 4.</small>
<small>S. Matt. v. 17.</small>
<small>S. John vii. 38.</small>

79. And there the ravens acknowleged the Lord's prophet whom the Jews acknowleged not. They fed him whom that royal and noble nation persecuted. Who is Jezebel who persecuted him, but the Synagogue, vainly flowing, vainly abounding in the Scriptures, which it neither keeps nor understands? Who are the ravens that fed him, but they whose young ones call upon Him, to whose cattle He *giveth fodder,* as we read, *and feedeth the young ravens that call upon Him.* These ravens knew whom they were feeding; for they had a spiritual intelligence, and brought food to that stream of sacred knowledge.

<small>Ps. cxlvii. 9.</small>

80. He too feeds the prophet who understands and keeps what is written. Our faith supports him, our advance gives him nourishment; he feeds on our minds and senses, his discourse is sustained by our understanding of it. We give him bread in the morning, in that, placed in the light of

the Gospel, we bring to him the stablishing of our hearts. By these things is he nourished and strengthened and fills the mouths of them that fast, to whom the unbelief of the Jews administered no food of faith. All prophetic words are fasting diet to them, for they cannot discern its interior richness, to them it is food weak and thin, such as cannot make fat their bones.

81. Perhaps the reason why they brought him flesh in the evening was that it is, as it were, stronger food, such as the Corinthians, who were weak, could not bear, and were therefore fed with milk by the Apostle; and thus in the evening of the world stronger meat was brought, in the morning of the world bread. And so since it was the Lord Who commanded this food to be administered to him, we may suitably address Him in this place with these prophetic words, *Thou makest the outgoings of the morning and evening to praise Thee*, and below, *Thou preparest their corn, for so Thou providest for the earth.*

82. But now I think we have said enough of the teacher, let us now follow up the lives of his disciples, who have given themselves to praise the Divine Name, and celebrate it with hymns night and day. For this is the service of Angels, always to be praising God, and with frequent prayers to propitiate and beseech the Lord. They give themselves to reading, and occupy their minds with continual labours, separated from all female society, they mutually protect each other. What a life this is, wherein there is nothing you need to fear, but much for you to imitate! The pain of fasting is repaid by tranquillity of mind, alleviated by custom, made supportable by rest, or beguiled by occupation; worldly solicitude does not burthen nor outward troubles engross it, nor do the distractions of the city draw down upon it any difficulty.

83. For the maintenance or teaching of this gift an instructor is to be sought: what kind of one he ought to be you perceive, and by your unanimous aid we shall be able to obtain him, if you mutually forgive one another, if any of you consider himself injured by the other. For it is not the sole condition of virtue not to hurt him who has not hurt you, but it consists also in forgiving him who

has injured you. We are generally injured by the fraud of others, by the guile of our neighbour, but we must not deem it to be the part of justice to repay guile with guile, and fraud with fraud. For if justice be a virtue, it must be free from the imputation of crime, and not return evil for evil. For what kind of virtue is it for you to do yourself what you punish in another? This is merely to propagate iniquity, not to punish it; and the character of the person whom you injure, whether he be just or unjust, makes no difference, for you ought not to have done evil. Nor does the mode of your trangression signify, whether it proceed from the desire of avenging yourself, or of injuring others, for in neither kind are you free from blame. There is no difference between being ungodly and unjust, and therefore it is said, *Fret not thyself because of the ungodly, neither be thou envious against the evil-doers,* and above, *I have hated the congregation of the wicked.* Thus he comprehends all, without exception; he points to their wickedness without enquiring for the cause. [Ps. xxxvii. 1.] [Ib xxvi. 5.]

84. And what can be a better model than the Divine justice? For the Son of God says, *Love your enemies.* And again He says, *Pray for them which despitefully use you and persecute you.* So far does He remove the love of revenge from the perfect, that he enjoins upon them charity towards their persecutors. And as in the Old Testament He said, *To Me belongeth vengeance, I will repay,* so in the Gospel He commands us to pray for them that injure us, that He Who has threatened to punish them may not do so. For He desires you to pardon of your own free-will, with which He agrees according to His promise. And if you call for vengeance, you know that the unrighteous is more severely punished by his own thoughts, than by judicial severity. [S. Matt. v. 44.] [Deut. xxxii. 35.]

85. And as no man's life can be free from adversities, let us take care that they do not befal us by our own fault. For no man is condemned more severely by another's judgment than the foolish man, who is the author of his own misery, is by his own. Wherefore let us avoid such occupations as are troublesome and contentious, which bear no fruit, but only bring obstacles. But we ought to

see that we have no cause to be ashamed either of our choice or of our act; for it is the part of a prudent man, to guard against having to feel frequent sorrow for his acts, since it is the prerogative of God alone never to repent. For what is the fruit of justice but calmness of mind, or what does living justly bring with it, but a life of tranquillity? According to the model of the master will be the condition of the whole house. But if this is required in a family, how much more in the Church, where both rich and poor, bond and free, Greek and Scythian, noble and plebeian, are all one in Christ Jesus.

Col. iii. 11.

86. Let no man suppose that because he is rich more deference ought to be shewn him. In the Church he is rich, who is rich in faith, for the faithful have a whole world of riches. What wonder is it that the faithful should possess the world, seeing he possesses the heritage of Christ, which is more precious than the world? *Ye were redeemed with precious blood,* is said to all, and not to the rich only. But if ye would be rich, follow him who says, *Be ye holy in all manner of conversation.* This is said not to the rich only but to all, for He judges without respect of persons, according to the faithful testimony of His Apostle. Wherefore, says he, *pass the time of your sojourning here* not in indulgence, nor pride, nor elation of heart, but *in fear.* Upon this earth ye have received what is temporal, not what is eternal, use therefore those temporal things as knowing that you must shortly depart hence.

1 S. Pet. i. 19.

Ib. 15.

Ib. 17.

87. Trust not therefore in riches, for all these things must be left behind, and faith alone will accompany you; justice indeed, if faith precede, will also be your companion. Why do riches entice you? Not with *silver and gold,* not with silken vests and riches *were ye redeemed from your vain conversation; but with the precious blood of Christ.* He therefore is rich who is an *heir of God, and co-heir of Christ.* Despise not then a poor man, it is He Who hath made thee rich. Scorn not a needy man; lo! *the poor crieth, and the Lord heareth him.* Reject not a needy man; for Christ, when He was *rich became poor,* and this for thy sake, *that by His poverty He might make*

Ib. 18, 19.

Rom. viii. 17.

Ps. xxxiv. 6.

2 Cor. viii. 9.

thee rich. Exalt not thyself therefore, as though thou wert rich, for He sent forth His disciples without money.

88. And the chief of these said, *Silver and gold have I none.* He glories in his poverty as if he shunned contamination. *Silver and gold* he says, *have I none,* he does not say, gold and silver, for he who knows not the use of these things knows not the relative value of them. *Silver and gold have I none,* but faith I have. I am rich enough in the name of the Lord Jesus, which is above every name. Silver I have none, nor do I ask for it, gold I have not, nor do I desire it, but I have that which ye that are rich are without, which even ye esteem of more value, and this I give to the poor, namely, to say in the name of Jesus, *Strengthen ye the weak hands and lift up the feeble knees.*

_{TO THE CHURCH OF VERCELLÆ}

Acts iii. 6.

Phil. ii. 9.

Isa. xxxv. 3.

89. But if ye would be rich, become poor. For ye shall in all things be made rich, if ye become poor in spirit. It is not money but the disposition which makes a man rich.

90. There are those who humble themselves when riches abound, and this is well and prudently done, for the law of nature is enough for all, and what suffices to her is easily found, but where lust is, there, in the abundance of riches, is still poverty. And no man is born poor, but becomes so. Thus poverty lies not in nature but in our notions of it, and therefore to find riches is easy to nature, but difficult for lust. In proportion to man's gains this thirst for gain increases, and he is, as it were, inflamed by the intoxication of his lusts.

91. Why do ye seek to accumulate riches as though they were necessary? Nothing is so necessary as to know what is not necessary. Why do ye cast the blame upon the flesh? it is not the lust of the belly, but the desires of the mind which make a man insatiable. Is it the flesh which blots out the hope of the future; is it the flesh which takes away the sweetness of spiritual grace; is it the flesh which obstructs faith; is it the flesh which in every way defers to the frantic domination of vain opinions? The flesh loves rather that frugal temperance, which relieves it of its burthen, which endues it with health, for so it rids itself of keen anxiety, and obtains for itself tranquillity.

92. But riches in themselves are not blameable. For *the* Prov. xiii. 8.

Lett. 63. *ransom of a man's life are his riches,* for he who gives to the poor, redeems his soul. There is therefore scope for virtue even in these material riches. Ye are as it were pilots, in a great sea. If any man steers well his ship, he quickly passes over the sea, and reaches his haven, but he who cannot manage his property is sunk together with his burthen. Wherefore it is written, *The rich man's strength is his strong city.*

Prov. x. 15.

93. And what is this city but Jerusalem, which is in heaven, in which is the kingdom of God? Good is this possession, which brings perpetual fruit. Good is this possession, which we do not leave behind us, but possess in heaven. He who finds himself in this possession says, *The Lord is my portion.* He says not, My portion stretches and extends itself to such and such limits. He says not, My portion is among such and such neighbours, unless haply with reference to the Apostles, the prophets and the saints of the Lord, for these are the portion of the just. He says not, My portion is in the meadows, or in the woods, or in the fields, unless perchance in the fields of the wood, wherein the Church is found, of which it is written, *We found it in the wood.* He says not, Troops of horses are my portion, for *a horse is counted but a vain thing to save a man.* He says not, Herds of oxen asses or sheep are my portion, except so far as he numbers himself among those herds which *know their owner,* and with that ass which shuns not the *crib* of Christ; that lamb too is his portion which was *brought to the slaughter,* and *that sheep which before her shearers was dumb, which opened not his mouth, by whose humility judgment has been exalted.* And it is rightly said, *before her shearers* because, on that Cross He put off what was but accidental, not part of His essence, for He put off His body, but lost not His Divinity.

Ps. cxix. 94.

Ib. cxxxii. 6.
Ib. xxxiii. 16.
Isa i 3.
Ib. liii. 7.

94. It is not every one therefore who can say *the Lord is my portion.* Not the covetous man, for avarice comes and says; Thou art my portion, I have thee in subjection, thou art my slave, thou hast sold thyself to me with that gold, thou hast adjudged thyself to be mine with these goods. The sensual man says not, Christ is my portion, because luxury comes and says, Thou art my portion, I have brought

thee into subjection to myself by that banquet, I have caught thee by the snare of those feasts, I keep thee in my bondage by the constraints of thy gluttony. Wilt thou not acknowledge that thou didst set a higher value on the indulgence of thy appetite than on thy life? I condemn thee by thine own judgment; deny it if thou canst; but thou canst not. Again, thou hast reserved nothing for thy subsistence, thou hast spent it all on thy table. The adulterer cannot say, *The Lord is my portion,* for lust comes and says, I am thy portion, thou hast enslaved thyself to me by the love of that damsel, by a night spent with that harlot thou hast committed thyself to my dominion. The traitor cannot say, *Christ is my portion,* because his wickedness immediately seizes upon him and says, He is deceiving thee, O Lord Jesus, this man is mine.

95. We have an example of this, for, when Judas had received the sop from Christ, the devil entered into his heart, as claiming him for his own possession, retaining his right to his own portion, and saying, This man is not Thine but mine; my servant, Thy betrayer; to me, then, he manifestly belongs. With Thee he sits at table, but it is I who feed him, from Thee he has received bread, from me money; with Thee he drinks, but to me he has sold Thy Blood. And the event proved how truly he spoke. Then Christ departed from him, and Judas also left Jesus, and followed the devil.

96. How many masters has he, who deserts that one Master! But let us not desert Him. Who would fly from Him Whom Paul and Timothy follow, bound with chains, but voluntary ones, chains which do not bind but loose, chains in which they glory, saying, *Paul, a prisoner of Jesus Christ, and Timothy.* Bondage under Him is more honourable than freedom and release from others. Who then would fly from peace, who would fly from salvation, who would fly from pity, who would fly from redemption?

97. Ye see, my sons, what they have become who have followed this course, how they, though dead, still work. Now as we join in praising their virtue, let us also study to attain to their diligence, and silently recognize in ourselves that which we speak of with approval in others. Nothing effeminate, nothing frail can deserve praise, *The kingdom of*

TO THE CHURCH OF VERCELLÆ

S. John xiii. 2.

Philem. i. 1.

S. Matt. xi 12.

LETT. 63. *heaven suffereth violence, and the violent take it by force.*
Our fathers ate the Paschal lamb in haste. Faith makes
good speed, devotion is lively, hope unwearied; it loves
not perturbations of the soul, but it loves to pass from profitless inactivity to fruitful labour. Why put off till tomorrow? you may still gain to-day; beware lest you fail
to attain the one, and lose the other also. The loss even
of one hour is not unimportant; one hour forms part of
our whole life.

98. There are some young persons who wish straightway
to arrive at old age, that they may no longer be subject to
the will of their elders, and there are old men who would
return if they could to youth. Now I can approve of neither of these desires; the young men, disdaining things
present, desire that their life may be changed, the old
men that it may be prolonged. But it is in the power of
the young to become old by gravity of mind, and of the old
to grow young by vigorous actions. For it is not age so
much as discipline which brings with it correction of life.
How much more therefore ought we to lift up our hopes to
the kingdom of God, where our life will be renewed, and
where there will be a change not of age but of grace.

99. It is not by indolence or sleep that we obtain for
ourselves a reward. The sleeper cannot work, there comes
no fruit from indolence, but rather loss. Esau, being slothful, lost the first-fruits of blessing, choosing to receive rather than to seek for food. The industrious Jacob found
grace at the hands of both his parents.

100. But Jacob, although superior in virtue and grace,
gave way to his brother's anger, who was indignant that his
younger brother should be preferred to him. Wherefore
Rom. xii. it is written, *Give place unto wrath,* to the intent that dis-
19. pleasure against another may not draw you also into sin,
while wishing to resist and to be avenged. If you will consent to yield you may remove the blame both from yourself
and from him. Imitate the patriarch, who by his mother's
Gen. advice went into a far country. And who was this mother?
xxvii. 43. Rebecca, that is, patience. For who could give this counsel but patience? The mother loved her son, and chose
that he should be separated from herself rather than from

God. And thus as a good mother she gave benefits to both her sons, but on her younger son she conferred a blessing which he had power to keep. For she did not prefer one son to the other, but she preferred diligence to sloth, faith to unbelief. And even on her elder son she conferred no little favour, for she sent away the younger, to save him from unworthy fratricide.

101. His piety not his fault having thus banished him from his parents, he conversed with God, he increased in his estate, in his children, in grace. Nor was he elated by these things on meeting with his brother, but he humbled himself and did obeisance, not to his brother, implacable as he was, but to God Whom in his person he honoured. Therefore he bowed down to him seven times, being the number which signifies remission, for it was not a man that he adored, but Him of Whom He foresaw in spirit that He should come in the flesh, *to take away the sins of the world.* And this mystery is unfolded to you in the reply of Peter, who says, *How oft shall my brother sin against me and I forgive him, till seven times?* Thus you see this forgiveness of sins is a type of that great sabbath, of that perpetual rest of grace; and therefore it receives the gift of contemplation.

102. But what is the meaning of his setting in array his wives, and sons, and all his servants, and commanding them to bow themselves to the earth? It was not to the earth, as an element, which is often filled with blood, which is the receptacle of crimes, and which is made hideous by desolate rocks, or by precipices, or by a barren and hungry soil, but as that Flesh Which was to be our salvation. And perhaps this is that mystery which the Lord has taught thee in the words, *I say not unto thee, until seven times, but, until seventy times seven.*

103. Do ye therefore forgive the wrongs done to you, that ye may be the sons of Jacob. Be not provoked as was Esau. Imitate holy David, who as a good teacher, has left us an example in the words, *For the love that I had unto them, lo! they take now the contrary part, but I give myself unto prayer,* and so when men reviled him, he prayed. Prayer is a good shield, a shield which wards off contumely, which repels curses, and throws them back on

the heads of those who utter them, so that they are wounded by their own weapons: *Let them curse,* it is said, *but bless Thou.* That curse of men is to be courted, for it obtains for us a blessing from the Lord.

104. For the rest, my most dearly beloved, remembering that *Jesus suffered without the gate,* do ye go forth from this earthly city, for your city is Jerusalem, which is above. Do ye dwell there that ye may say, *For our conversation is in heaven.* Jesus went forth from the city, that ye, going forth from the world, may be above the world. Moses alone, who saw God, had his tabernacle without the camp when he talked with God; and when sacrifices were offered for sin, the blood indeed was carried to the altar, but the bodies were burned without the camp; for no man living among the temptations of this world can lay aside sin, nor can his blood be accepted by God until he has put off the defilement of this body.

105. Love hospitality, for thereby holy Abraham found favour in God's sight, received Christ as his guest, and Sarah, already worn with age, obtained grace to bear a son; Lot also escaped the flames which destroyed Sodom. And thou also mayest receive Angels, if thou wilt offer hospitality to strangers. And what shall I say of Rahab, who, by performing this office, escaped destruction?

106. Compassionate those who are kept in bondage, as though ye also were bondsmen. Console those who are under sorrow; *It is better to go to the house of mourning than to the house of feasting.* From the one we win the merit of discharging a duty, from the other the stain of a transgression. And again in the one case the reward is yet hoped for, in the other it is received. Sympathise with those who suffer as if ye suffered together with them.

107. Let a woman be obedient not servile to her husband, let her offer herself to be ruled not coerced. Let the husband also direct his wife as her governour, honour her as the companion of his life, share with her as his fellow-heir in grace.

108. Mothers, wean your own children, love them, and pray for them, but pray that their life [1] may be prolonged above this earth, rather than in it, for there is nothing

[1] longaevi super terram.

longlived in this earth, and that which seems permanent is at the best short and fragile. Admonish them rather to take up the Cross of Christ than to love this life. *TO THE CHURCH OF VERCELLÆ*

109. Mary, the mother of the Lord stood by the cross of her Son; it is no other than the holy Evangelist John who teaches me this. Others have told us that in the Lord's passion the earth was shaken, the heaven covered with darkness, the sun withdrew its light, the thief, after a faithful confession, was received into paradise. John has taught what the others have not, how when nailed to the Cross He spoke to His mother, esteeming rather this exhibition of pious offices to His mother than that gift of a heavenly kingdom, which, after triumphing over His pains, He conferred. For if it be pious to grant pardon to the thief, much more pious is it that the Son should shew such solicitous honour to His Mother: *Behold,* He says, *thy son, Behold thy mother.* Christ testified from the Cross, and distributed the offices of piety between the mother and the disciple. The Lord made not only a public but also a private Testament, and John signed this His Testament, a witness worthy of so great a Testator, a good Testament, not of money but of eternal life, written not with ink, but by the Spirit of the living God, Who says, *My tongue is the pen of a ready writer.* *S. John xix. 25. S. Matt. xxvii. 45. S. John xix. 27. Ps. xlv 1.*

110. Nor did Mary fall below what became the Mother of Christ. When the Apostles fled she stood before the Cross, and with pious eyes looked upon the wounds of her Son, for she expected to see not the death of her Offspring, but the salvation of the world. Or perhaps because she who was the Palace[n] of the King had learnt that the redemption of the world would ensue from the death of her Son, she thought that by her own death she might add something to the general good. But Jesus needed no helper for the redemption of all, Who without any helper saved all. Wherefore He says, *I am become like* *Ib. lxxxviii. 4, 5.*

---

[n] The expression 'aula regalis,' applied to the Mother of our Lord, may be illustrated from De Instit Virg ch. xii. § 79. Ipse ergo Rex Israel transivit hanc portam, ipse Dux sedit in ea, quando Verbum caro factum est et habitavit in nobis, quasi Rex sedens in aula regali uteri virginalis. Compare also the expression in S. Ambrose's Hymn on the Nativity, Procedit e thalamo suo, Pudoris aula regia, &c.

LETT. 63. *a man without help, free among the dead.* He received the affection of His Mother, but He sought not aid from others.

111. Imitate her, ye holy mothers, who in her only and beloved Son exhibited such an example of maternal virtue, for your children cannot be dearer to you than hers was, nor did the Virgin seek consolation in the bearing of another son.

112. Masters, command your servants not as your inferiors in rank, but as remembering that they are partakers of the same nature as yourselves. Servants also, serve your masters cheerfully, for every one ought cheerfully to endure that state whereunto he is born; and obey not only the good, but also the froward. For what merit has your service, if ye serve the good diligently; but if ye serve the froward also ye have merit, for neither do the free obtain any reward, if, having transgressed, they are punished by the judges, but herein lies their merit if they suffer wrongfully. Thus if ye, considering Jesus Christ, serve even austere masters with patience, ye will have your reward. For the Lord Himself suffered, the just from the unjust, and with admirable patience nailed our sins to His Cross, that he who shall imitate Him may wash away his sins in His blood.

1 S Pet. ii. 18.

113. In short, turn all of you to the Lord Jesus. Take pleasure in this life so that it be with a good conscience; let the hope of immortality make you patient of death, let your assurance of the resurrection be confirmed by the grace of Christ; let there be truth and simplicity, faith and confidence, abstinence and holiness, industry and sobriety, modest conversation, learning without vanity, sobriety of doctrine, faith not intoxicated by heresy. The grace of our Lord Jesus Christ be with you all, Amen.

LETTER LXIV.[a]

S. AMBROSE replies to Irenæus, who had asked why the manna, which was given to the children of Israel, was not given now, that the Body of Christ, Which is given to Christians, is the true Manna, of which the other was a type, as it was also of Divine Wisdom, which is the food of souls.

AMBROSE TO IRENÆUS, GREETING.

1. You ask me why the Lord God does not now rain manna as He did on our fathers. If you consider, He does rain manna from heaven on those who serve Him, and that day by day. The earthly manna indeed is to this very day found in many places, but it is not now an event so miraculous because *that which is perfect is come.* Now *that which is perfect* is the Bread from heaven, the Body born of the Virgin, as to which the Gospel sufficiently instructs us. O how greatly does this excel what went before it! For they who eat that manna or bread, are dead, *but he that eateth of this bread shall live for ever.* 1 Cor xiii. 10.

S. John vi. 58.

2. But there is also a spiritual manna, the dew that is of spiritual Wisdom, which descends from heaven upon those who sincerely seek for it, and which waters the souls of the righteous, and puts sweetness into their mouths. Wherefore he who comprehends this out-pouring of divine wisdom receives pleasure from it, nor requires any other food, *nor lives by bread alone, but by every word of God.* He who is more curious, will ask what that is which is sweeter than honey. The servant of God answers him, *This is the bread which the Lord hath given you to eat.* And hear further what this bread is, *the word,* he says, *which the Lord hath commanded.* Now this food so commanded by God nourishes the soul of the wise, imparting light and sweetness, brightened by the beams of truth, and communicating to it the soothing sweetness of divers virtues and

S. Matt. iv. 4.

Exod. xvi 15, 16.

---

[a] With this Letter begins what the Benedictines have called a second division of the Letters, containing those which furnish no internal evidence of their date sufficient to justify their being assigned a place in chronological order. They are arranged according to their matter, 1st, those which contain expositions of passages of Holy Scripture, (lxi—lxxv.), 2nd, those which discuss important, and mostly doctrinal subjects, (lxxvi—lxxxiii), 3rd, a few brief letters of ordinary friendly intercourse, (lxxxiv—xci.)

the word of wisdom like that of an honey-comb; for *pleasant words*, it is written in the Proverbs, *are as an honey-comb.*

_{Lett. 64}
_{Prov. xvi 24.}

3. And now hear the reason why it was small; it was because a grain of mustard-seed which is compared to the kingdom of heaven is also small, and because faith, which is as a grain of mustard-seed, can remove mountains and cast them into the sea. Again, *the kingdom of heaven is like leaven, which a woman took and hid in three measures of meal, till the whole was leavened.* Again, Moses ground the head of the golden calf to powder, and cast it into water, and made the people drink of it; for their heart was hardened by the greatness of their perfidy, and he did thus that it might be softened and made refined by faith. Lastly, that woman who grinds meal well and fine shall be taken, but she who grinds ill shall be left.

_{S Luke xiii. 19.}
_{Ib xvii. 6.}
_{Ib. xiii. 21.}
_{Exod. xxxii. 20}
_{S Matt xxiv. 41.}

4 Follow then these examples as regards thy faith, that thou mayest be like that soul which excites in itself the love of Christ, and which, as it ascends aloft, is admired by the host of heaven; that it may rise without impediment, that it may soar above this world with joy and gladness, lifting itself on high like the vine stock and like the smoke, sending forth the fragrance of a holy resurrection, and the sweetness of faith, as it is written, *Who is this that cometh out of the wilderness like the stock of vine burned with smoke, perfumed with myrrh and frankincense, with all powders of ointment?*

_{Cant. iii. 6.}

5. The refined nature of this faith is well expressed by being compared with powder or by the mention of perfume; for we read in Exodus of that prophetic incense which is the prayer of the Saints, as being a subtile perfume and compounded of many things, that it may be set forth in the sight of the Lord, as David also says, *Let my prayer be set forth in Thy sight as the incense.* And so it is in the Greek also, κατευθυνθήτω ἡ προσευχή μου ὡς θυμίαμα ἐνώπιόν σου. And in the Revelation of John we read that *an Angel stood at the Altar, having a golden censer; and there was given unto him much incense, that he should offer it with the prayers of all saints upon the golden altar which was before the throne.* And *the smoke of the incense,* it is said,

_{Exod. xxx. 8.}
_{Ps. cxli. 2.}
_{Rev. viii. 3, 4.}

with the prayers of the Saints, ascended up before God out of the Angel's hand. [TO IRENÆUS]

6. Small too is the navel and the belly of that soul which ascends up to Christ, and therefore it is praised by the words of the spouse saying, *Thy navel is like a round goblet, which wanteth not liquor, thy belly is like an heap of wheat set about with lilies.* [Cant. vii. 2.] For it is rounded and polished with all kinds of learning, and is a spiritual drink not failing in fulness, and in the knowledge of heavenly secrets. The belly of the soul is also like the navel, mystical, and not only strong food whereby the heart is strengthened, but also sweet and flowery food whereby it is delighted, is received therein. And perhaps this is what Moses meant, that by many and pious prayers the sacrilege was to be atoned for.

7. In the book of Kings also, when the Lord revealed Himself to holy Elijah, a small still voice was first heard, and then the Lord revealed Himself to him; thereby to teach us that bodily things are solid and gross, but such as are spiritual tender and so fine as not to be perceptible to the eye. In the same way we read in the book of Wisdom that the Spirit of Wisdom is subtile and lively *for in her is an understanding spirit, holy, one only, manifold, subtile and lively;* [Wisd vii. 22.] and she grinds her words before she speaks, that neither her mode of speech nor her meaning may give offence. Lastly, it shall be said to Babylon herself, when about to be destroyed, *And the sound of a millstone shall be heard no more at all in thee.* [Rev. xviii. 22.]

8. The manna then was fine, and was gathered each day, not reserved for the day following; because the extemporaneous inventions of Wisdom please the most; when made at leisure they excite not the same admiration as when struck out at the moment by the spark of genius. Or it may be that future mysteries are revealed herein: the manna kept till the rising of the sun was unfit to be eaten, in other words, after the coming of Christ, it lost its grace. For when the Sun of Righteousness arose, and the more illustrious Sacraments of the Body and Blood of Christ appeared, lower things were to cease, and the people were to take in their stead what was more perfect.

Farewell; love me, for I also love you.

LETTER LXV.

This letter contains a mystical explanation of the statement in Exodus xxiv. 6. that Moses put half of the blood of the sacrifices into basons and poured half on the altar.

AMBROSE TO SIMPLICIANUS, GREETING.

Exod xxiv. 6.

1. You were perplexed, you tell me, when reading that Moses, after offering sacrifice and the immolation of salutary victims to the Lord, put half of the blood in basons, and sprinkled half on the altar, to know what could be the purport of this. But why need you doubt and inquire of me, when for the sake of the faith, and of acquiring Divine knowledge, you have traversed the whole world, and night and day have devoted the whole time of your life to constant reading? Thus with your keen intellect you have embraced all the objects of the understanding, and are wont to prove as concerns even the books of philosophy, how far they deviate from the truth, many of them being so futile that the words of their writers perished sooner than their life.

2. But since gathering words, like money, is of great profit, and great increase is thereby obtained for the general good of trade, I cannot refrain from mentioning how wonderful is that division of the blood. For part of it seems to signify the moral, and part the mystical discipline of wisdom. That part which is put into basons is moral, that which is sprinkled on the altar is mystical; in that by the Divine gift and a certain inspiration it is instilled into men's minds, that the sentiments they conceive of God may be suitable and full of faith.

3. Moreover, they who have spoken of His majesty, and of heavenly things, whether apostles or holy prophets, have only dared to speak of such things as were shewn them by revelation. Hence Paul has testified in his Epistle that

2 Cor. xii. 4.
Acts vii. 55.

he was *caught up into Paradise, and heard words which it is not lawful for a man to utter;* Stephen also *saw the heavens opened, and Jesus standing on the right hand of*

God, and the Prophet David saw Him sitting on His right hand. And what shall I say of Moses, of whom the Scripture says that *there arose not such a prophet since in Israel, who knew the Lord face to face, in all the signs and the wonders which he did in the land of Egypt.*

TO SIMPLICIANUS
Ps. cx. 1.
Deut. xxxiv. 10, 11.

4. The mystical part therefore is offered to God, Who by the brightness of the Divine Wisdom, Whose Father and Parent He is, quickens the vigour of the soul, and enlightens the mind. But the Wisdom of God is Christ, on Whose breast John lay, that from that secret source of wisdom he might be known to have imbibed Divine mysteries. He himself, conscious of his gift, has recorded this, for he dreaded to claim for himself, and to ascribe to his own genius that which he had received. The Lord also said to the Apostles, opening their mouths, *Receive ye the Holy Ghost*, whereby He declared that He is the same Who said to Moses, *I will open thy mouth, and teach thee what thou shalt say.* Wherefore this wisdom, divine, unspeakable, unadulterated and incorruptible, pours her grace into the minds of her saints, and discloses to them knowledge that they may behold her glory.

S. John xx. 22.
Exod. iv. 12.

5. But that is the discipline of moral wisdom which is poured into basons, and is taken and drank from them. The basons therefore are the organs of the senses. The basons are the two eyes, the ears, the nose, the mouth and other parts suitable to this function; for the eyes are the recipients and ministers of sight, the ears of hearing, the nose of smell, the mouth of taste, and so with the rest. Into these basons that Word in Whom is the Headship of the priestly and prophetic office poured the half of His blood; that He might quicken and animate the irrational parts of our nature, and endow them with reason.

6. Again, having rehearsed and proclaimed the precepts of the Law to the people, and being about to explain the meaning of that mystical ark of the testimony, and of the candlestick, and of the censers, he slew victims, and offered sacrifice, sprinkling half of the blood on the sacred altar, and putting half in basons.

7. A division therefore is made between that mystical or divine and moral wisdom. For the Λόγος is a divider

of souls and of virtues: the Λόγος is the *Word of God, quick and powerful,* which pierces and penetrates even to the dividing asunder of the soul, and which also distinguishes and divides virtues, whose minister, Moses, by the division of the blood, distinguished the kinds of virtue.

8. And forasmuch as nothing is so emphatically declared in the Law as Christ's Advent, or prefigured as His Passion, consider whether this be not the saving victim which God the Word offered by Himself, and sacrificed in His own body. For first both in the Gospel and also in the Law He taught us moral discipline, and manifested it in His own patience and in very act and deed, transfusing into our lives and senses, as if into basons, the very substance and marrow as it were of wisdom, and quickening thereby men's minds to be a seed-plot of virtue, and instructed in piety, and then, drawing near the altar, He poured out the blood of His offering.

9. Should you choose then to understand it thus, the sense is pious; the interpretation also which follows that of Solomon is, if you prefer it, equally concordant, namely, that whereas the prophet Moses put the blood into basons, this is the same blood whereof it is written that *Wisdom hath mingled her wine,* bidding men to forsake foolishness, and seek after understanding. From the bason then we drink wisdom, discipline, understanding, correction, amendment of life, regulation of habits and counsels, the grace of piety, increase of virtue, a fountain of plenty.

10. But by this sprinkling the blood on the Altar you may understand the cleansing of the world, the remission of all sins. For He sprinkles that blood on the Altar as a Victim to atone for the sins of many. For the Victim is a Lamb, but a Lamb not of irrational nature but of divine power, of Which it is said, *Behold the Lamb of God which taketh away the sin of the world.* For not only has He cleansed with His blood the sins of all men, but has also gifted them with divine power. Does not He seem to you to have indeed shed His blood, from Whose side blood and water flowed over the very altar of His Passion?

Farewell; love me as you do, with the affection of parent.

LETTER LXVI.

HERE is a mystical exposition of Aaron's taking the earrings of the women to make the golden calf, and of other details connected with it.

AMBROSE TO ROMULUS.

1. THERE is no doubt that letter-writing was invented that we might hold a sort of converse with the absent, but this becomes more excellent in use and example when frequent and pleasant colloquies pass between a parent and his sons, whereby is really produced a sort of image of actual presence, even though they are separate in body; for by such offices love attains its growth, just as it is augmented by our mutual letters between ourselves. All this I begin to experience much more abundantly in these last addresses of your affection, wherein you have thought fit to ask me with what intent Aaron took the gold from the people when they required gods to be made them, and why the head of a calf was fashioned with that gold, and why Moses was so deeply incensed that he commanded every man to rise upon his neighbour and slay him with the sword. For it is a great thing that the absent should suffer no loss either of kindness or of the liberal communication of mutual knowledge. My sentiments on this point, therefore, as you require it, I will offer for the purpose rather of comparison than of instruction. Exod. xxxii. 2.

2. While Moses was receiving the Law on Mount Sinai the people were with Aaron the Priest. Prone as they were to transgress, we do not find that they committed sacrilege so long as the Law was being delivered, but when the Divine Voice ceased, sin overtook them, so that they required gods to be made them. Aaron, thus constrained, asked for their rings and the women's earrings, which, when given to him, he cast into the fire, and the head of a calf was molten of them.

3. We can neither excuse this great priest, nor dare we condemn him. It was not however unadvisedly that he deprived the Jews of their rings and earrings; for they who

LETT. 66. designed sacrilege could have neither the seal of faith nor ornaments of their ears. The patriarch Jacob too hid the earrings along with the images of the strange gods, when he hid them in Shechem, that no one might come to know of the superstitions of the Gentiles. And he said well, *Break off the golden earrings which are in the ears of your wives;* not as leaving the men their earrings, but in order to shew that they had them not. Fitly also are the earrings taken from the women, that Eve may not again hear the voice of the serpent.

Gen. xxxv. 2.

Exod. xxxii. 2.

4. Because they had listened to sacrilegious counsel, an image of sacrilege was formed by the melting of their earrings; for he who hears amiss is wont to perpetrate sacrilege. Why the head of a calf came forth, the sequel shews, for it was signified thereby, either that in time to come Jeroboam would introduce this kind of sacrilege, and that the people of the Hebrews should worship golden calves; or else that all unbelief bears the semblance of brutal and savage folly.

1 Kings xii. 30.

5. Moses, incensed by this unworthy act, broke the tables, and ground the head of the calf to powder, that he might abolish all traces of their impiety. The first Tables were broken in order to the restoration of the second, whereby, through the preaching of the Gospel, unbelief was broken to pieces, and done away. And thus Moses brought down this Egyptian pride, and repressed this self-exalting arrogance, by the authority of the eternal Law. Wherefore David also says, *The Lord shall break the cedars of Libanus, and shall reduce them to pieces, as a calf of Libanus.*

Ps. xxix. 5, 6

6. The people drank up all their perfidy and pride, that impiety and arrogance might not drink them up. For it is better that every one should prevail over the flesh and its vices, that it may not be said that *prevailing* [a] *death hath swallowed him up,* but rather, *Death is swallowed up in victory; O death, where is thy sting, O grave, where is thy victory?* And of the Lord it is said, *He shall drink of the brook in the way,* for He received the vinegar, that He might drink up the temptations of all men.

Isa. xxv. 8.
1 Cor. xv. 54, 55.
Ps. cx. 7
S John xix 30

7. But in his causing every man to slay his neighbour, the

---

[a] See note c on Letter xliv 10

parents their children, the brother his brother, we find an evident precept that religion is to be preferred to friendship, piety to kindred. For that is true piety which prefers divine things to human, eternal to temporal. Wherefore also Moses himself said to the sons of Levi, *Who is on the Lord's side, let him come to me. And he said unto them, Thus saith the Lord God of Israel, Put every man his sword by his side, and go throughout the camp,* that thus, by the contemplation and love of the Divine Majesty all human ties and affections might be destroyed. It is written that three thousand men were slain, nor need we feel any jealousy of the number being so great, for it is better that by the punishment of a few the body should be exonerated, than that vengeance should be taken on all; nor indeed does any punishment of wrong against God appear too severe.

8. Again, the ministry of the Levites, whose portion is God, was chosen for this work, as being more holy than the others: for they know not how to spare their own who know nothing of their own, for to the holy God is everything. Now he is the true Levite and punisher and avenger, who kills the flesh that he may preserve the spirit, such as he was who says, *I keep under my body, and bring it into subjection.* And who are such close neighbours as the flesh and the soul? What is so akin to us as the passions of the body? These the good Levite slays within himself with that spiritual *sword* which is *the word of God, sharp and powerful.*

9. There is also a sword of the Spirit, which pierces the soul, as was said to Mary, *A sword shall pierce through thy own soul also, that the thoughts of many hearts may be revealed.* Is not the flesh united with the soul by a kind of fraternal bond? Is not discourse also related and akin to our mind? When therefore we check our discourse, that we may not incur the sin of much speaking, we put aside the rights of blood, and loose the bonds of this fraternal connexion. Thus by the force of reason the soul severs from itself its irrational and, as it were, cognate part.

10. And so Moses taught the people to rise against their neighbours, by whom faith was in danger of being

LETT. 76. mocked, and virtue hindered, that whatever in us was straying from virtue, perplexed by error, or entangled in vice might be cut off. By this direction to the people he obtained not only a mitigation of the Divine wrath and a turning away of offence, but even conciliated for them grace.

11. Thus, according to our apprehension, we have explained, since you asked it, our sentiments. And do you, if you have aught preferable, impart it to us, that from you and from ourselves we may learn which to choose and follow.

Farewell: love me as a son, for I also love you.

LETTER LXVII.

S. AMBROSE begins by pointing out that Moses deferred to Aaron in matters connected with the Priesthood, and then goes on to dwell on the rarity and the blessing of true penitence.

AMBROSE TO SIMPLICIANUS, GREETING.

1. THE greatness of each person as regards his own functions is taught us in that Scripture lesson by which your attention has been justly attracted, that Moses, than whom no man saw God more intimately, *neither arose there a prophet since in Israel whom the Lord knew face to face;* he who was constantly with the Lord forty days and nights, when he received the law in the Mount, he, I say, to whom the Lord gave the words which he should speak, is found to have approved the counsel of his brother Aaron more than his own. Was there then any man more prudent and learned than Moses? Nay, of Aaron himself we afterwards read that together with Miriam he transgressed concerning the Ethiopian woman.

Num. xii. 8.
Deut. xxxiv. 10.
Exod xxxiv. 28.
Ib. iv. 12
Num. xii. 1.

2. But I would have you carefully consider this very thing, how Moses excelled in knowledge, Aaron in counsel. Moses was the greatest prophet, who said of Christ, *Like unto me, unto Him shall ye hearken.* And the Lord Himself says of him, *if they hear not Moses and the prophets,*

Deut. xviii. 15.
S. Luke xvi. 31.

neither will they be persuaded, though one rose from the dead. In the matter of prophecy therefore Moses is preferred as a prophet; but where the subject and function and office relates to the Priesthood, Aaron is preferred as being a Priest. Let us now treat the passage itself.

3. A he-goat was slain for sin; offered for an whole burnt-offering. Moses afterwards sought for it, and it was burnt. *And he was angry with Eleazar and Ithamar, the sons of Aaron which were left alive, saying, Wherefore have ye not eaten the sin-offering in the holy place, seeing it is most holy, and God hath given it you to bear the iniquity of the congregation? Ye should indeed have eaten it in the holy place as I commanded.* Now when Aaron saw that Moses was angry he replied to him meekly, *Behold, this day have they offered their sin-offering and their burnt-offering before the Lord, and such things have befallen me, and if I had eaten the sin-offering to-day, should it have been accepted in the sight of the Lord? And when Moses heard that, he was content.* Let us consider what these things mean. [Lev. x. 16—18.]

4. Not to sin is an attribute of God alone: to amend and correct one's error and to do penance for one's sin is the part of a wise man. But this is very difficult in this human life. For what is so rare as to find a man who will convict himself, and condemn his own act? Rare is the confession of sin, rare is penitence, rare among men is the admission of that word. Nature and shame both recoil from it; nature, because all are under sin, and he who wears flesh is subject to transgression. Thus the nature of the flesh, and the allurements of the world are repugnant to innocence and integrity. Shame recoils also, because every man blushes to confess his own fault, thinking more of the present than of the future.

5. Now Moses desired to find a soul free from sin, that it might lay aside the slough of error, and depart, relieved from transgression, without any cause of shame within itself. But such a soul he found not, because an irrational impulse comes quickly on, and a certain flame, whose motions are very swift, feeds upon the soul, and burns up its innocence. For the future is outweighed by the present,

LETT. 67. moderation by violence, worth by numbers, soberness by pleasure, hardness by luxury, sadness by joy, austerity by blandishments, slowness by too great precipitance. And iniquity, which suggests occasions of doing evil, is a thing swift in its nature, for its *feet are swift to shed blood;* but all virtue uses gentle and long delays, judging beforehand and looking narrowly into what is to be undertaken. And thus the good mind scrutinizes its own counsels, and examines beforehand what is becoming and excellent; but in iniquity the act outstrips consideration. Penitence therefore is tardy and abashed, because it is oppressed and drawn back by present shame; having, in itself, regard only to things future, the hope whereof is late, the fruit tardy, and so the desire of them is tardy also.

Ps. xiv. 6.

6. During these strivings of hope and virtue shamelessness runs onward, and by the glare of things present, penitence is excluded, its affections are, as it were, burnt up, and all that has respect to it is lost. The Law seeks and finds it not, for it is scorched by the heat and smoke of iniquity, and the anger, as it were, of the Law is roused. Moses says that the sin-offering ought to have been eaten in the holy place, and rebukes the priests as remiss; Aaron replies that the priestly judgment ought to be cautious; that such a function must not be lightly entrusted to an unsound conscience, lest this error be worse than the first. For by a filthy vessel wine or oil is easily tainted and spoilt.

7. But how could sin be burnt out when the fire was strange fire; and this in the sight of the Lord to Whom even hidden things are known? Can it please the Lord, if a man, while he is yet engaged in sin, and keeps unrighteousness in his heart, professes that he is doing penance? It is the same thing as if one who is sick should feign himself well, he will only become worse; for the pretence of health can avail him nothing; since it is but shadowed forth by words, not sustained by any support of virtue.

8. This strange fire then is lust, this strange fire is every incentive of cupidity, this strange fire is all burning avarice. By this fire man is not cleansed but rather burned

up. For where this strange fire is, if any man offer him- TO
self in the sight of the Lord, the celestial fire consumes SIMPLI-
him as it did Nadab and Abihu who were burned together CIANUS
with those sacrifices which had been offered for sin on the
sacred Altars. He therefore who would cleanse his sin let
him remove from him strange fire. Let him offer himself
to that fire only which burns up the fault not the man.

9. And who this fire is, let us learn from the words, that
Jesus *shall baptize with the Holy Ghost and with fire.* S. Matt.
This is that fire which dried up her issue of blood who had iii. 11.
suffered it for twelve years; that fire, which took away the Ib. ix. 20.
sin of Zacchæus when he said that he would give half of S. Luke
his goods to the poor, and if he had taken any thing from xix. 8.
any man would restore fourfold. This is that fire, which
wiped away the thief's crime, for He is *a consuming fire* Heb. xii.
Who said, *To-day shalt thou be with Me in Paradise.* 29.
Thus He healed those in whom He found a simple and xxiii. 43.
pure confession; no malice, no fraud.

10. Judas moreover could not obtain a remedy, although
he said, *I have sinned, in that I have betrayed the innocent* S. Matt.
blood, for he cherished within his breast strange fire, which xxvii. 4.
urged him on to destroy himself. He was not worthy to
be healed, for he wept not through conversion of his inmost
mind, nor did he diligently do penance; for such is the
love of the Lord Jesus that He would have granted pardon
even to him, had he waited for the mercy of Christ.

11. This fault therefore the priests cannot remove, nor
the sin of him who offers himself in guile, and still har-
bours a desire of transgressing. For they cannot eat of
that which is full of fraud, and has the serpent's scar within; for the food of the priest lies in the remission of sins.
Wherefore Christ the chief of Priests says, *My meat is to* S. John
do the will of My Father which is in heaven. What is the iv. 34.
will of God but this, *In returning and rest shall ye be* Isa. xxx.
saved? In the guileful man therefore there is no food. 15.
Neither again can he taste the sweetness of a feast whose
conscience is not sincere and pure; for the bitterness of
fraud takes away the sweetness of the viands; and an evil
conscience will not permit penitence to refresh and feed
the guilty soul.

Lett 67.

Lev. xvi. 27.

Ib. xvi. 8.

S. Matt. xxiv. 40.

Lev. xxv 6.

12. Such affections therefore, such petitions, such penitence are neither useful nor a pleasure to the priests. And that he-goat offered as an whole burnt offering for sin was deservedly burnt, because strange fire was found in the sacrifice. On that account it was not a pleasing and acceptable sacrifice to God; for that is not accepted which has not been approved among the riches of sincerity and truth.

13. And so elsewhere also you read of two he-goats, one whereon was the lot of the Lord, the other that of the scape-goat, and that that whereon was the lot of the Lord was offered and sacrificed, while the one whereon was the lot of the scape-goat was sent into the wilderness to take away the iniquities of the people, or of any sinner. For as there are *two men in the field, and one of them shall be taken and the other left,* so are there two he-goats, one of which is used for sacrifice, and the other sent into the wilderness. The one is of no use, neither to be eaten nor fed upon by the sons of the priests. For as in matters of food, what is good is eaten, what is useless or bad is thrown away, in the same way we call good works festive, as fit for eating.

14. It will not therefore be pleasing to the Lord if the priest eat of a sacrifice which presents a deceptive offering, not the sincerity of a diligent confession. And therefore that goat is to be sent into the wilderness, where our fathers wandered, where they wandered and could not attain to the land of the resurrection, but the memory of them passed from the land. Hear again what are festive works. *And the sabbath of the land shall be meat for you.* For rest in God, which causes tranquillity of mind, is festive and refreshing. And now let us also rest from discoursing.

Farewell; love me as you do, for I also love you.

LETTER LXVIII.

AN explanation of the text, *Thy heaven shall be brass and thy earth iron.*

AMBROSE TO ROMULUS.

1. BEING yourself in the country I am surprised at your having been led to inquire of me the reason why God should have said, *And thy heaven shall be brass, and thy earth iron.* For the very appearance of the country and its present fertility might teach us how great is the mildness of the air, and how genial is the climate, when God vouchsafes to give plenty, but when sterility, how all things are closed up, how dense the air, so as to seem hardened into the very substance of brass. Elsewhere also you read that in the days of Elijah *the heaven was shut up three years and six months.* [Deut. xxviii. 23.] [1 Kings xvii. 1. S. Luke iv. 25.]

2. By the heaven then being brass is signified its being shut up, and refusing its use to the earth. The earth also is iron, for it witholds its produce, and with hostile rigour excludes from its fructifying soil the seeds thrown upon it, which its wont is to cherish as in the bosom of a tender mother. For when does iron bring forth fruit, when does brass melt into showers?

3. Those impious men therefore He threatens with miserable famine, that they who know not how to shew filial piety to the common Lord and Father of all, may be deprived of the support of His paternal clemency, that the heaven may be to them as brass, and the air condensed into the substance of metal; that the earth may be to them as iron, deprived of its natural productions, and as is usually the case with poverty, a sower of strife. For they who are in want of food commit robberies, that at the expense of others they may relieve their own hunger.

4. If further the offence of the inhabitants be so great that God stirs up and brings war upon them, then their land is truly iron, bristling with crops of spears, and stripped of

LETT. 69.
Exod.
xvi. 4.

its own fruit, fruitful as regards punishment, barren as regards nourishment. But where is abundance? *Behold I will rain bread for you, saith the Lord,*

Farewell; love me, for I also love you.

LETTER LXIX.

In this Letter S. Ambrose answers a question propounded to him as to the ground of the severity of the Mosaic Law against those who disguised their sex.

AMBROSE TO IRENÆUS, GREETING.

1. You have referred to me, as to a father, the inquiry which has been made of you, why the Law was so severe in pronouncing those unclean who used the garments of the other sex, whether they were men or women, for it is written, *The woman shall not wear that which pertaineth unto a man, neither shall a man put on a woman's garment; for all that do so are an abomination unto the Lord.*

Deut.
xxii. 5.

2. Now, if you will consider it well, that which nature herself abhors must be incongruous. For why do you not wish to be thought a man, seeing that you are born such? why do you assume an appearance which is foreign to you? why do you play the woman, or you, O woman, the man? Nature clothes each sex in their proper raiment. Moreover in men and women, habits, complexion, gestures, gait, strength and voice are all different.

3. So also in the rest of the animal creation; the form, the strength, the roar of the lion and lioness, of the bull and heifer are different. Deer also differ as much in form as they do in sex, so that you may distinguish the stag from the hind even at a distance. But in the case of birds the similitude between them and men, as regards covering, is still closer; for in them Nature distinguishes their sex by their very plumage. The peacock is beautiful, but the feathers of its consort are not variegated with equal beauty. Pheasants also have different colours to mark the

difference of the sexes. And so with poultry. How sonorous is the cock's voice, night by night performing his natural office of calling us from sleep by crowing. They do not change their form; why then do we desire to change ours?

4. A Greek custom has indeed prevailed for women to wear men's tunics as being shorter. Be it allowed however that they should imitate the nature of the more worthy sex; but why should men choose to assume the appearance of the inferior? A falsehood is base even in word, much more in dress. So in the heathen temples, where there is a false faith, there also is a false nature. It is there considered holy for men to assume women's garments, and female gestures. And therefore the Law says that every man who puts on a woman's garment is an abomination unto the Lord.

5. I conceive however that it is spoken not so much of garments as of manners, and of our habits and actions, in that one kind of act becomes a man, the other a woman. Wherefore the Apostle also says, as the interpreter of the Law, *Let your women keep silence in the Churches; for it is not permitted unto them to speak, but they are to be under obedience, as also saith the Law. And if they will learn anything, let them ask their husbands at home.* And to Timothy: *Let the woman learn in silence with all subjection; but I suffer not a woman to teach, nor to usurp authority over the man.*

6. But how unseemly is it for a man to do the works of a woman! As for those who curl their hair, like women, let them conceive also, let them bring forth. Yet the one sex wears veils, the other wages war. Let them however be excused who follow their national usages, barbarous though they be, the Persians and Goths and Armenians. Nature is superior to country.

7. And what shall we say of others who think it belongs to luxury to have in their service slaves wearing curls and ornaments of the neck? It is but just that chastity should be lost where the distinction of sexes is not preserved, a point wherein the teaching of nature is unambiguous, according to the Apostle's words; *Is it comely that a woman*

LETT. 70. *pray unto God uncovered? Doth not even nature itself teach you that if a man have long hair it is a shame unto him: but if a woman hath long hair, it is a glory unto her: for her hair is given her for a covering.* Such is the answer which you may make to those who have referred to you.

Farewell; love me as a son, for I love you as a father.

LETTER LXX.

S AMBROSE in this Letter considers a part of the prophecy of Micah as describing the recovery of a fallen soul.

AMBROSE TO HORONTIANUS.

1. THE Prophets indeed announced the gathering together of the Gentiles, and the future establishment of the Church; but as the Church sees not only the continuous progress of strong souls, but likewise the relapse of weak ones, and their subsequent conversion, we are able to gather from the Prophetical books both how the gracious and strong soul advances without stumbling, and also how the weak soul falls, and how she repairs her falls and recovers her steps.

2. Accordingly as in the Song of Songs we read of this continuous progress of blessed souls, so let us now consider, as set forth in the prophet Micah, concerning whom we have begun to speak, the conversion of a fallen soul. For it is not without good reason that the prophet's words, Mic. v. 2. *But thou Bethlehem Ephratah,* excited your attention. For how can that house where Christ was born be the house of wrath? Such is, indeed, what the name of the place signifies, but certain mysterious operations are declared thereby.

3. Let us first consider what Micah signifies in Latin. It means 'Who is from God,' or as we find elsewhere 'who Ib. i. 1. is this man,' the son of the Morasthite, that is, the heir? S. Matt. Now, who is this heir, but the Son of God, Who says, *All xi. 27. things are given unto Me of My Father;* and Who, being

Himself the Heir, would have us His co-heirs. And well may we say 'Who is that man?' not one of the people, but chosen to receive the grace of God, in whom the Holy Spirit speaks, who began to prophesy *in the days of Jotham, Ahaz, and Hezekiah kings of Judah.* By which order is signified the course of the vision, for the progress is from the times of evil kings to that of a good king.

TO HORONTIANUS

Mic. i. 1.

4. Thus as the afflicted soul was first oppressed under evil kings, let us consider what was the progress of her conversion. Being weak she was overthrown, and all her fences were made as a way for the passers-by, or for the inroads of passion; dissolved in luxury and pleasure, she was trodden down and removed from the presence of the Lord. Her *tower was decayed*, that tower which, as we read in the song of Isaiah, was placed in the midst of a choice vineyard. Now this is the case with the tower, when the vine is withered, and her flock wanders; but when the verdure of the vine comes back, or the sheep returns, it grows bright again, for nothing is so decayed as iniquity, or so bright as righteousness.

Ib. iv. 8. Isa. v. 2.

5. To this tower the sheep is recalled, when the soul is recalled from her relapse, and in that sheep that reign of Christ returns, which was in the beginning, for He is *the Beginning and the Ending,* even the beginning of our salvation. Still the soul is first severely rebuked, in that she has grievously transgressed, and she is asked, *Why hast thou learnt evil? was there no king in thee?* that is, thou hadst a king to govern and protect thee, thou oughtest not to have strayed from the path of righteousness, nor to have left the ways of the Lord, Who imparted to thee sense and reason. Where were thy thoughts and counsels, whereby by innate vigour thou mightest have guarded against unrighteousness and warded off transgression? Why have *pangs taken thee, as a woman in travail;* that thou shouldest be in labour of iniquity, and bring forth unrighteousness? For there is no greater grief than for a man to wound his conscience with the sword of sin; nor is there any heavier burden than the weight of sin and the load of transgression. It bows down the soul, it bends it even to the earth, so that it cannot raise itself. Heavy, my son, heavy indeed is the

Rev. i. 8.

Mic. iv. 9.

Ib.

weight of sin. Thus that woman in the Gospel, who was bowed together, and thus bore the semblance of a heavy-laden soul, could be made straight by Christ alone.

6. To such a soul it is said, *Be in pain and labour to bring forth, O daughter of Sion.* For the pains of child-birth work tribulation, and *tribulation patience, and patience experience, and experience hope, and hope maketh not ashamed.* At the same time all that is opposed to virtue is plucked up and cast forth, lest its seeds should remain behind and revive, and put out new buds and fruit.

7. Nor is it without a meaning that horns and hoofs were given to her, that she might bruise all the sheaves of the floor, like the calf of Mount Lebanon. For unless the sheaves were bruised, and the straw winnowed, the corn that is within cannot be found and separated. Wherefore let the soul that would advance in virtue first bruise and thrash out its superfluous passions, that so, when the harvest is come, it may shew forth its fruits. How many are the weeds which choke the good seed! These must first be rooted out, that they may not destroy the fertile crop of the soul.

8. Then the provident guide of the soul has regard to this, that he may circumscribe her pleasures and cut off her desires, that she may not delight herself in them. That father's corrections are profitable, who spares not the rod, that he may render his son's soul obedient to salutary precepts. For he visits with a rod, as we read, *I will visit their offences with the rod.* And so he who smites the soul of the Israelites with a rod on the cheek, by this Divine punishment instructs her in the discipline of patience. But no man need despair who is chastised and corrected, for he who loveth his son chastiseth him. Let no man therefore despair of a remedy.

9. Behold therefore, that house which was to thee 'the house of one seeing wrath,' is become 'the house of bread;' where rage was, there is now piety; where the slaughter of the Innocents, there now the redemption of all mankind, as it is written, *But thou, Bethlehem Ephratah, though thou be little among the thousands of Judah, yet out of thee shall He come forth that is Ruler in Israel.* Bethlehem is the

The meaning of Bethlehem Ephratah.

house of bread; Ephratah the house of one seeing wrath. This is the interpretation of these names. In Bethlehem Christ was born of Mary, but Bethlehem is the same as Ephratah. Thus Christ was born in the house of wrath, and therefore it is no longer a house of wrath, but the house of bread, for it received that *bread which came down from heaven.* But Ephratah is the house of one that was wrath, because while Herod searches there for Christ, he commands the Innocents to be slain, wherefore *In Rama was there a voice heard, Rachel weeping for her children.* TO HORONTIANUS
S. Luke ii. 4.

S. John vi. 50.

S. Matt. ii. 18.

10. But let no man fear any longer; for that rest which David sought after *is heard of at Ephrata,* and *found in the fields of the wood.* A wood, as yet, was the assembly of the Gentiles, but after it believed in Christ it became fruitful, receiving the fruit of the blessed womb. And Rachel died in childbirth, because even then, as the patriarch's wife, she saw the wrath of Herod, which spared not the tenderest age. Or again, because in Ephratah she gave birth to that Benjamin who excelling in beauty came last in the order of the mystery, I mean Paul, who before his birth caused no small grief to his Mother, by persecuting her sons. And she died, and was buried there, that we, dying and being buried together with Christ, may rise again in His Church. Therefore according to another interpretation, Ephratah signifies 'enriched or filled with fruit.' Ps. cxxxii. 6.

S. Luke i. 42.
Gen. xxxv. 19.

11. Now here, that is, in the book of the Prophet, we find the expression, thou art ὀλιγοστός, that is, one of few. But in Matthew we find, *And thou, Bethlehem, in the land of Judah, art not among the few.* In one the expression is house of Ephratah, in the other house of Juda; but this is a difference of words not of meaning. For inwardly Judæa saw this exhibition of wrath, outwardly she suffered it. And she is among the few, because they are few who enter the house of bread by the narrow way. But he is not among the few, that is among those that make progress, who knows not Christ. Nor is she the least, who is the house of blessing, and the receptacle of Divine grace; yet in this she is the least, for any thing which is offered to Christ seems to be offered to her. And he who seeks for the Church seeks for Christ; and He is either honoured or despised in every Mic. v. 2.
S. Matt. ii 6.

little one, wherefore He says Himself, *Inasmuch as ye have done it unto the least of these, ye have done it unto Me.*

LETT 70.
S. Matt. xxx. 40.

12. Now that Bethlehem is the very same place as Ephratah we learn from the passage in Genesis, which says, *And Rachel died, and was buried in the way to Ephrath, which is Bethlehem.* Holy Rachel, being a type of the Church, was buried in the way, that they who go by might say, *The Lord prosper you,* and *they shall come again with joy.*

Gen. xxxv. 19.

Ps cxxix. 8.
Ib. cxxvi. 7.

13. Wherefore every soul which receives that bread which comes down from heaven is the house of bread, that is, the Bread of Christ, being nourished and supported and having its heart strengthened by that heavenly bread which dwells within it. Hence Paul also says, *For we being many are one bread.* Every faithful soul is Bethlehem, as Jerusalem also is said to be, which has the peace and tranquillity of that Jerusalem which is above, in heaven. That is the true Bread which, when broken into pieces, fed all men.

1 Cor. x. 17.

14. The fifth version [a] has the words, 'the house of Bread.' For 'Beth' signifies a house, and 'lehem' signifies bread. From the other versions I imagine that the unbelief of the Jews, who feared to convict themselves, either led the writers to omit it or others to erase it.

15. And that Bethlehem is of the tribe of Judah we learn from that passage in the book of Judges, where the Levite took to him a concubine out of Bethlehem-judah, and his concubine was incensed against him, and returned to her father's house in Bethlehem-judah.

Jud. xix. 2.

¹ a diebus saeculi.
Mic. v. 2.
Ps. xix. 5.
² Saeculum.
Mic. v. 3.

16. Now Christ's *goings forth were from everlasting*¹, because our life² then commenced, when He *went forth to run His course,* and gave to Israel the day of salvation. *Until the time that that she which travaileth hath brought forth.* To that soul to which Christ hath come fruitfulness or bringing forth hath come also; so it was with the Church, who has *brought more than she that had children;*

Is. liv. 1.

[a] Whether the true reading here be 'traditio' as Ben. has, or 'editio' as Rom, the reference must be to the ἐκδόσεις or versions which Origen brought together in his Hexapla, of which the fifth, the sixth, and the seventh, (for there was a seventh,) were only known by their numbers. See Art. by Tregelles on 'Ancient Versions,' in Smith's Dict. of the Bible, vol. iii. p. 1623.

who has brought forth seven, that is, a lawful peaceful and tranquil progeny. Now that soul begins to conceive, and Christ to be formed in her, which welcomes Him on His arrival and is so fed by His plenty that she is in want of nothing, and other souls by seeing her return unto the way of salvation.

17. *And there shall be peace to him*, but it is by temptations that he must be tried; then, when he has shut out or repulsed vain thoughts, when he has subdued all the motions of his rising passions, when distress and persecution and hunger and peril and the sword press hard upon him, will the value of his peace and tranquillity be tested. Then, it is said, *shall be peace;* because in all these things *we are conquerors through Him that loved us*, because we trust in Him that neither death nor the power of temptations shall cast off or separate us from His love. He will send temptations, that the just may be proved. The Lord sends temptations, not that He wishes any man to be beguiled, but because the weak are for the most part vanquished by temptation, whilst the strong are proved by them. [Mic. v. 5. Rom. viii. 37.]

18. Then there shall be to them *dew from the Lord*, and rest; then the soul of the just shall be *as a young lion among the flocks of sheep*. I cannot doubt but that this similitude should, after the manner of the Gospel, be referred to Christ, for He has said, *Then shall the righteous shine forth as the sun in the kingdom of their Father*. For *his chariots shall be broken;* that is to say, the senseless impulses and motions of the body shall be appeased; that condition shall cease wherein *Without are fightings, within are fears*, and over all, that is, within and without, tranquillity shall prevail; nor shall there be any resistance or repugnance to this good will, because the obedience of the flesh, when *the middle wall of partition is broken down*, and both are made one, shall abolish all discord. [Mic. v. 7. Ib. 8. S. Matt. xiii. 43. Mic. v. 10. 2 Cor. vii. 5. Eph. ii. 14.]

19. But if any weak soul, like Israel according to the flesh have stumbled, and, shaken by persecutions, have separated herself in some degree from the love of Christ, she is checked and reproved as faithless, and ungrateful, and unbelieving, as one who, after being freed from the vanities

Lett 70.	of the world, has looked behind her and so relapsed into them again; as one from whom no gifts, no sacrifice of bulls, but only to know what is good and to do justly, has
Mic. vi. 8.	been required. *He hath showed thee, o man, what is good; and what doth the Lord require of thee, but to do justly, and to have mercy, and to walk humbly with thy God?* But since the weaker soul has not kept this commandment,
Ib. vii. 1.	the Lord says to her, *Woe is me, for I am as when they have gathered the summer fruits, as the grape-gleanings of the vintage.* And the prophet, in whom the Lord spoke, says
Ib. 2.	to that soul, *Woe is me, the good man is perished out of the earth.* This is as though the Lord Himself spoke, in compassion for the future punishment of sin, and as weeping over our transgressions.

20. Then the soul, learning that she will gather no fruit from what she has sown; that in the loss of her harvest nothing will remain to strengthen her, that she will press her olives, but will find no oil of gladness, nor will drink the wine of pleasantness; finding also in the works of the flesh all things full of blood, full of circumvention, of fraud and deceit, hollow shows of affection, and pre-concerted guile; nay, those of her own household adverse to her; and therefore that the motions of her companion the body, which are grievous enemies of the soul, must be guarded against; turns to God, and begins to hope in Him, and knowing that the flesh is truly an enemy to her, says to it,

Ib. 8. *Rejoice not against me, O mine enemy, when I fall I shall arise, when I sit in darkness, the Lord shall be a light unto me.*

21. Finding moreover that she is mocked by some power which opposes her following a better path, and domineers

1 Cor. v. 5. over her, so that she has been delivered *for the destruction of the flesh,* to be afflicted with various evils, assigned to her either by the Lord to satisfy for her sins, or by the Evil One who is envious of her conversion, and desires to harass

Mic. vii. 9. and regain her to himself, finding this, she says, *I will bear the indignation of the Lord,* Who either chastens me in my fall, or has given thee power to persecute me, *because I have sinned against Him,* but I will endure *until He plead my cause.* For unless I shall confess, and pay the price of my iniquities, I cannot be justified. But being justified and having paid double for my sins, He shall *execute judgment for me,* laying aside His wrath, since the sentence against me is satisfied. *He will bring me forth to the light, and I shall behold His righteousness* and gaze on His delights. Then she that is mine enemy, that is, the malice of the devil, shall see the light of my reconciliation and *shame shall cover her which saith to me, Where is the Lord thy God?* She shall behold in me His pity and His love.

22. Wherefore let us not listen to him when we are in any of the troubles of this world, be it bodily pain, or the loss of our children, or of other necessaries, let us not listen to his words, *Where is the Lord thy God?* It is under severe pain that his temptations are to be feared, it is then that he seeks to turn the sick soul astray.

23. Wherefore the soul which has not listened to his allurements, seeing afterwards the wonderful works of God, seeing herself in heaven, and the devil creeping upon the earth, will congratulate herself saying, *Who is a God like unto Thee, that pardoneth iniquity and passeth by transgression?* Thou hast not been mindful of Thy indignation, but hast cast all our iniquities into the sea as the lead of Egypt, and hast graciously returned to have pity upon us, both forgiving and hiding our offences, as it is written, *Blessed is he whose unrighteousness is forgiven, and whose sin is covered.* For some sins Thou dost wash away in the blood of Thy Son, others Thou dost remit unto us, that by good works and confession we may cover our errors. The expression therefore *that pardoneth iniquities,* appertains to remission; because He takes them away altogether, so that the things which He remembers not are as though they did not exist. But the words *passeth by transgression,* signify that inasmuch as we confess our failings, and cover them with the fruit of our good works, they are referred to the author of our fault, and the instigator of our sin. For what else does he who confesses his fault do but prove himself to have been beguiled by the craft and malice of that spiritual wickedness which is his adversary?

24. For this therefore this soul gives thanks, that the

Lord both *pardoneth iniquities and passeth by transgressions,* and *casts them into the deep of the sea.* Which may also be referred to Baptism, wherein the Egyptian is drowned, the Hebrew rises again; and whereby by the depths of His wisdom, and the multitude of her good works her former sins are covered, through the riches of the mercy of our God, Who is mindful of the promise which He gave to Abraham, and suffers not that soul which is heir of Abraham to perish.

25. It is by these means that such a soul is recovered. But do you, my son, who from the first flower of boyhood have been an heir of the Church which bore and which sustains you, persevere in your purpose, mindful of the grace of God, and of the gift which you have received by the imposition of my hands, that in this degree [f] also, as in the holy office of deacon, you may shew faith and industry, and expect a recompense from the Lord Jesus.

Farewell; love me as a son, for I also love you.

LETTER LXXI.

S AMBROSE in this letter continues the subject of the last, and, having described in that the steps by which the fallen soul recovers herself, here considers how the faithful soul is taken in charge, taught and conducted to perfection by Christ. and shews that the stages in the progress of such a soul are typified by the journies of Christ

AMBROSE TO HORONTIANUS.

1. IN my last letter I spoke of the soul that has made in its progress certain devious circuits, wavering, as Israel according to the flesh did of old, to and fro. For Israel herself also, when *the fulness of the Gentiles shall be come in,* shall be delivered by the grace of our Lord Jesus Christ: the Gentile soul meanwhile, whose transgression has been lighter, having by her conversion worked her own recovery. In my present letter I will treat of the daughter of the Church; and consider how the Lord Jesus first took her

[f] i e. the priesthood cf. 1 Tim iii 13.

under His care, taught her, and, in His Gospel, led her on to perfection.

TO HORONTIANUS

2. Now it was as she lay in misery and confusion that He first took her under His care,—for how else but miserably can that soul live, which is exiled from Paradise?— and brought her to Bethlehem. The progress then, of this soul is at once signified in that it goes up to the "house of bread[a]," where it can know no death or barrenness of faith. Observe, I am now speaking of souls in general, those souls by which we live and move, not of any soul in particular; for it is not of the individual or species, but of souls in general that I purpose to discourse.

3. Christ went down into Egypt, as Protector and Guide of our soul, from thence He returned into Judæa. He was in the wilderness, in Capernaum; near the borders of Zabulon; by the sea coast; He passed through the corn fields; He was in Bethphage; in Ephraim; in Bethany; then He passed over into the garden, where He gave Himself up; on Calvary, where He suffered.

4. All these are the progresses of our soul, and exercised thereby she receives the graces of a holy life[1]. For the human race, when excluded from Paradise in Adam and Eve, and banished to the village[2], began to roam up and down and to wander about with careless steps: but in His own good time the Lord Jesus *emptied Himself* that He might receive this exile into himself, and re-form her again to her previous state of grace. And thus, when found, she retraced, as the Gospel lesson teaches us, her devious course of error, and was recalled to Paradise.

[1] institutis.
[2] castellum.
Phil. ii. 8.

5. He led her through the cornfields that He might satisfy her hunger, first in the desert, then to Capernaum, making her abode to be not in the city but in the field: next He brought her to the borders of Zabulon, near unto the floods of night, that is, the darker riddles of the prophets; that she might learn thereby to reach to the borders of the Gentiles, that common centre, and not to fear the storms and billows of this world. Why should she, seeing that Christ has ships of Tarshish, mystical ships I mean, which traverse the sea, and bring pious offerings for the

1 Kings x. 22.

[a] Bethlehem.

building of the Temple? In such ships as these Christ sails, and like a good pilot rests in the stern while the sea is calm; when it is disturbed He awakes, and rebukes the winds, that He may anew shew peace on His disciples. Furthermore, by passing over to the Gentiles, He delivers the soul which was bound by the chains of the Law, that she may not pass over and keep company with the heathen.

6. He came to Bethany to the "place of obedience;" therefore was the dead there raised; for when the flesh is subdued to the spirit, human nature no longer lies as if dead in the tomb, but is raised again by the grace of Christ; there also she professes to offer herself to 'suffering'[b] for the Name of God. From the place of obedience, as John tells us, He is led to Ephraim, that is, to the "fecundity of good fruits." Hence He returns to Bethany, that is, to "obedience;" for she who has once tasted the fruit of holy obedience is for the most part ready to preserve it and to be proved thereby.

7. And now, having been proved, she comes to Jerusalem, being made worthy to become the temple of God wherein Christ may dwell. Here it is that the Lord Jesus, sitting upon the foal of an ass, is received with the joy and congratulation of the age of innocence.

8. Afterwards are taught in the garden the words of eternal life; in that place where the Lord permitted Himself to be taken, as John the Evangelist writes, signifying that our soul, or rather human nature, released from the bonds of error, is restored by Christ to that abode from whence in Adam she was cast. Wherefore to the thief who confessed Him it is said, *Verily I say unto thee, To-day shalt thou be with Me in Paradise.* The thief had said, *Lord, remember me when Thou comest into Thy kingdom.* Christ answered not concerning His kingdom, but yet to the purpose, *To-day thou shalt be with Me in Paradise,* that is, What has been lost must first be restored, then the increase bestowed; that thus the progress may be through Paradise to the kingdom, not through the kingdom to Paradise.

---

[b] ענה signifying affliction; ענו one humbled by affliction and so, it was inferred, brought to obedience.

9. For the disciples it is reserved that they may receive an ample reward for their labours; and therefore to the thief He promised a sojourn, but deferred the kingdom. So that to him who is converted under the stroke of death, and confesses the Lord Jesus, to him let an abode in Paradise be vouchsafed, but for him who has undergone long travail, who has fought for Christ, who has won over souls and offered himself for Christ, for his wages let the kingdom of God be prepared; and let him rejoice in the fruition of this reward. To Peter it is said, *I will give unto thee the keys of the kingdom of heaven;* and thus, while the convert from robbery obtains rest, on him who has been proved in the Apostolate authority is bestowed.

TO CONSTANTIUS

S Matt. xvi. 19.

10. This is the Evangelical soul, the soul of the Gentiles, the daughter of the Church, far better than the soul cast out of Judæa; raising herself from her earthly course to the Lord Jesus and to higher things by good counsels and works; received by Christ upon Golgotha. Upon Golgotha was the sepulchre of Adam; that Christ by His Cross might raise him from death. Thus where in Adam was the death of all, there in Christ was the resurrection of all.

1 Cor. xv. 22.

Farewell, my son; love me, for I also love you.

LETTER LXXII.

In this letter S. Ambrose deals with the question of the rite of circumcision, and explains to Constantius why it was established in the Old Testament and yet done away in the New He speaks also of the true and spiritual circumcision which belongs to Christians.

AMBROSE TO CONSTANTIUS.

1. MANY persons have raised an important question why circumcision should be enjoined as profitable by the authority of the Old Testament, and rejected as useless by the teaching of the New; especially since it was Abraham, who *saw the day* of the Lord Jesus *and was glad*, who first received the command to observe the rite of circumcision.

Acts xv. 10. S. John viii 56. Gen. xvii. 10.

Lett. 72. For it is manifest that he directed his mind not to the literal but to the spiritual sense of the Divine Law, and so in the sacrifice of the lamb saw the true passion of the Lord's Body.

2. What then shall we consider to have been the aim of our father Abraham, in first instituting that which his posterity were not to follow? or for what reason are the bodies of infants circumcised, and in their very birth subjected to dangers, and this at the Divine command, so that peril of their life ensues from a mystery of religion. What is the meaning of this? For the ground of the truth is hidden, and either something should have been signified by an intelligibe mystery, or else it should have been indicated by a mystery which was not so full of danger.

3. And why was the sign of the Divine Testament attached to that member which is considered as less comely to sight; or with what purpose did the Creator of our body Himself, in the very beginning of our race, choose that His work should be wounded and stained with blood, and a portion of it cut off, which He, Who has disposed all things in order, deemed proper to form together with the other members, as though it were necessary? For this portion of our bodies is either contrary to nature, and then no man ought to have that which is contrary to nature, or it is according to nature, and that ought not to be cut off which was created according to the perfection of nature; especially since aliens from the portion of the Lord our God are wont to make this a chief subject of ridicule. Again as it is God's purpose, as He has frequently declared, to induce as many persons as possible to the observance of holy religion, how much more would they be invited, were not some deterred either by the danger or reproach of this very circumcision.

4. To return therefore to my first purpose and follow the order I have proposed, it seems good to speak of the nature itself of circumcision. The defence of this ought to be twofold, for so is the accusation, the one brought by the Gentiles, the other by those who are considered as belonging to the people of God, more vigorously on the part of the Gentiles, for they deem men marked with circum-

cision to be worthy even of scorn and disgrace. Yet their own wisest men approve of circumcision, so as to think it right to circumcise those whom they select to know and celebrate their mysteries [a].

5. The Egyptians too, who apply themselves to geometry and observing the courses of the stars, consider a priest who does not bear the mark of circumcision impious. For they believe that neither the wisdom of incantation, nor geometry, nor astronomy can attain their due power without the seal of circumcision. And therefore, in order to render their operations efficacious they choose to solemnize a certain purification of their own by means of the secret rite of circumcision.

6. And we find in ancient history that not only the Egyptians but also some of the Æthiopians Arabs and Phœnicians used circumcision. And in maintaining this custom they think that they are maintaining one still to approved, for being thus initiated by means of the first fruits of their own body and blood, they conceive that by the consecration of this small portion, the snares which demons lay for our kind will be defeated; and that those who attempt to injure the well-being of the whole man, may find their power baffled either by the law or the semblance of sacred circumcision. For I am of opinion that heretofore the Prince of devils has deemed that his arts would lose their baneful efficacy if he were to attempt to injure one whom he found initiated by the seal of sacred circumcision, or one who seemed at least in this respect to obey the Divine law.

7. Now he who diligently considers the functions of our several members will be able to judge that it was for no unmeaning purpose that as regards this little portion of this member the child was not only circumcised but circumcised also on the eighth day; when the mother of the child begins to be in pure blood, having before the eighth day been considered as sitting in unclean blood. Let so

Gen. xvii. 12.

---

[a] Baehr on Herod ii. 37 quotes with apparent approval Wesseling's opinion that in fact, though Herodotus does not expressly state it, among the Egyptians only the priests and those initiated in the mysteries received circumcision. It is to this perhaps that S Ambrose is here alluding. See also the art. on 'Circumcision' in Smith's Dict. of the Bible.

LETT. 72. much have been said in reply to those who are not joined with us in unity of faith; on which account discussion with them, as differing from us, becomes more difficult.

8. But to those who believe in the Lord Jesus Christ we have to offer the following reply, which, when we were disputing against the opinions of Gentiles, we were unwilling to disclose. For if we were *redeemed not with corruptible silver and gold, but with the precious blood of our Lord Jesus Christ,* and purchased from no one but him who had purchased with money, and was owner of, the services of our now sinful race, beyond a doubt he demanded a price for releasing from his service those whom he kept in bondage. But the price of our freedom was the Blood of the Lord Jesus, which of necessity was to be paid to him to whom we were sold by our sins.

1 S. Pet. i. 18, 19.

9. Until, therefore, this price should have been paid for all men which by the shedding of the Lords Blood had to be so paid for the absolution of all, the blood of every man, who, by the Law and solemn custom were to follow the precepts of holy religion, was required. But, since one Lord Christ suffered, seeing that the ransom is now paid for all, there is now no longer any need that the blood of every man one by one should be shed by circumcision, for in the Blood of Christ the circumcision of all has been solemnized, and in His Cross we are all crucified together with Him, and buried in His sepulchre, and *planted together in the likeness of His death, that henceforth we should not serve sin: for he that is dead, is free from sin.*

Rom. vi. 5 sq.

10. But if any one, such as Marcion and Manichæus, deem the judgment of God to be worthy of blame, either because He thought fit to give command concerning the observance of circumcision, or because He published a law directing the effusion of blood; he must needs consider the Lord Jesus also worthy of blame, Who shed not a little but much blood for the redemption of the world, and up to this hour commands us also to shed our blood for the great contest of Religion, saying, *If any man will follow Me, let him deny himself, and take up his cross and follow Me.* But if in the case of a man offering his whole self out of piety, and cleansing himself by the effusion of much blood,

S Matt. xvi. 24.

such an accusation is not just, how can we blame the Law, for exacting a little drop of blood, when we proclaim the command of the Lord Jesus for the shedding of much blood, and the death of the whole body?

11. Nor was the very symbol and semblance of circumcision useless, for the people of God, signed thereby as by a certain bodily seal, was distinguished from the other nations. But the name of Christ being now bestowed upon them they have no need of a bodily sign, for they have obtained the honour of a Divine appellation. But what was there absurd in somewhat of pain or labour seeming to be imposed for piety's sake, to the intent that by such contests devotion might be better tried? It is becoming also that from the very cradle of life the symbol of religion should grow with our growth, and that all of a maturer age should be ashamed to yield either to labour or pain when their tender infancy had conquered both.

12. But now Christians have no need of the light pain of circumcision, for bearing about with them the Lord's Death, they at every act engrave on their foreheads contempt of their own death, as knowing that without the cross of the Lord they can have no salvation. For who would use a needle to fight with when armed with stronger weapons?

13. And now any one may easily perceive how easily the suggestion may be refuted, that more persons might be incited to the observance of holy religion unless they were withheld by the fear of pain or the appearance of labour. For could this terrify an older person, when many infants endured it without danger? Granting however that some Jewish children unable to bear the pain of circumcision and of so keen a stroke may have died, still this did not deter those of a robuster and more advanced age, and one who thus obeyed the celestial precepts it only made more praiseworthy.

14. But if they imagine that this light pain was such an obstacle to confession, what will they say of martyrdom? For if they choose to blame the pain of circumcision, they must blame also the death of martyrs, by whom religion so far from being impaired has received its perfection. But

LETT 72. the pain of circumcision is so much removed from being hurtful to faith, that faith is approved by pain, for greater is the grace of faith if any one for religion's sake despise pain; and such a one has a greater reward than he who was only willing to endure the pain of circumcision that he might glory in the Law, and win praise of men rather than of God.

15. It was fitting therefore that this partial circumcision should take place before His advent Who was to circumcise the whole man, and that the human race should receive a partial preparation for believing in that which is perfect. But if circumcision must take place, in what region of the body ought it rather to fall than on that which seems to some less comely? *And those members of the body, which we think to be less honourable, upon those we bestow more abundant power, and our uncomely parts have abundant comeliness.* For in what member ought men to be rather reminded of his blood than in that which is wont to minister to transgression?

1 Cor. xii. 23.

16. And now is the fitting time to reply to those also who say, If this part of our body is according to nature it ought not to be cut off, but if contrary to nature, then it ought not to have been born together with it. Let these men, being so subtle, themselves answer me, whether the succession of the human race, which arises by generation is according to nature or contrary to nature? If according to nature, it ought never to be interrupted, and then how can we praise the chastity of men, the virginity of maids, the abstinence of widows, the continence of wives? No effort then to promote this succession should be suffered to lie idle. But the Author of nature Himself did not pay this regard to generation, for He gave us, when living in the body, His own example, and exhorted His disciples to chastity, saying, *There be eunuchs, which have made themselves eunuchs for the kingdom of heaven's sake. He that is able to receive it, let him receive it.*

S Matt. xix. 12.

17. Man being made up of body and soul, (for at present it will suffice to speak of these and not to mention the spirit,) he is not naturally the same in both, but what is according to the nature of the body is contrary to the na-

ture of the soul, and what is according to the nature of the soul is contrary to the nature of the body; so that were I to speak that which is according to nature in that which is seen, it will be contrary to nature as regards the unseen, and what is according to nature in the unseen is contrary to nature as regards the seen. It is no incongruity therefore in the man of God, if there should be things contrary to the nature of the body which are according to the nature of the soul.

18. With regard to those who say that more would have believed if circumcision had not been instituted, let them receive this answer, that more would have believed if there had been no martyrdom, but the constancy of a few is to be preferred to the remissness of a larger number. For as many kinds of washings preceded, because that one true Sacrament of Baptism with water and the Spirit, whereby the whole man is redeemed, was to follow, so also the circumcision of many was to precede, because the circumcision of the Lord's Passion, which Jesus suffered as the Lamb of God, that He might *take away the sins of the world,* was to follow. S. John i. 86.

19. My object in writing this has been to shew that it was fitting that circumcision, which is outward, should precede, that now after the Lord's Advent it might seem to be justly excluded. But now that circumcision is necessary which is in secret, *in spirit not in the letter,* seeing that there are two men in one, of whom it is said, *Though our outward man perish* according to the desires of error, *yet the inward man is renewed day by day,* and in another passage, *For I delight in the law of God after the inward man;* that is, our inward man which is made according to the image and likeness of God, our outward is that which is formed of clay. So again in Genesis two creations of man are declared to us, and it is signified that by the second man was truly made.

20. As therefore there are two men, so also is his conversation two-fold; one of the inward the other of the outward man. And indeed many acts of the inward man reach to the outward man, in the same way that the chastity of the inward man passes into bodily chastity. He who

is free from adultery of the heart is free from adultery of the body, but it does not also follow that he who has not sinned in body should not have sinned even in heart, for it is written, *Whosoever looketh on a woman to lust after her hath already committed adultery with her in his heart.* For although he be not yet an adulterer in body, still in affection he is one. So that there is a circumcision of the inward man, for he who is circumcised has put off, like a foreskin, all the allurements of the flesh, that so he may be in the spirit, not in the flesh, and *by the spirit may mortify the deeds of the flesh.*

21. And this is that circumcision which is in secret, as Abraham was first in the uncircumcision and afterwards came to be in the circumcision. Thus our inward man, while it is in the flesh, is as it were in uncircumcision, but when he is now no longer in the flesh but in the spirit, he begins to be in the circumcision not in the uncircumcision. And as he who is circumcised does not put off the whole flesh but his foreskin only, where corruption more frequently lies, so he who is circumcised in secret, puts off that flesh of which it is written, *All flesh is grass, and all the goodliness thereof is as the flower of the field; the grass withereth, the flower fadeth, but the word of our God shall stand for ever;* and there remains the flesh which will see the salvation of God, as it is written, *And all flesh shall see the salvation of God.* What this flesh is cleanse your ears that you may understand.

22. Now that circumcision which is secret ought to be of such a kind as to bear no comparison with that which is outward. He therefore who is a Jew in secret, is he who excels, he who is from Judah, whose *hand is in the neck of his enemies,* who *stooped down and couched as a lion, and as a lion's whelp, whom his brethren praise.* From this Judah the prince departs not, because his word makes princes, such as are not overcome by worldly allurements and ensnared by the pleasures of this world. And since Judah himself was born into this generation, many of those who were born afterwards are preferred, that they may enjoy a pre-eminence of virtue. Let us have therefore the circumcision which is in secret, and the Jew that is in secret,

that is, the spiritual: but he that is *spiritual*, as being a prince, *judgeth all things, yet he himself is judged of no man.* It was fitting therefore, that the circumcision commanded by the prescript of the Law, which was partial, should cease after His coming Who was to circumcise the whole man, and fulfil the circumcision of the Law. And who is this but He Who said *I am not come to destroy the Law, but to fulfil it?*

TO CONSTANTIUS

1 Cor. ii. 15.

S Matt. v. 17.

24. That the fulness of the Gentiles is come in is another reason, if you will attend to it carefully, why the circumcision of the foreskin ought to cease. For it was not upon the Gentiles but upon the seed of Abraham that circumcision was enjoined, for this is the first Divine promise, *And God said unto Abraham, Thou shalt keep My covenant therefore, thou and thy seed after in their generations. This is My covenant, which ye shall keep, between Me and you and thy seed after thee; Every man child among you shall be circumcised, and ye shall circumcise the flesh of your foreskin; and it shall be a token of the covenant betwixt Me and you. And he that is eight days old shall be circumcised among you, every man child in your generations. He that is born in thy house, or bought with money of any stranger, which is not of thy seed, must needs be circumcised, and My covenant shall be in your flesh, for an everlasting covenant. And the uncircumcised man child whose flesh of his foreskin is not circumcised* on the eighth day, *shall be cut off from the people; he hath broken My Covenant.* It is affirmed indeed that the Hebrew text, as Aquila intimates, does not contain the words 'on the eighth day;' but all authority does not rest with Aquila, who being a Jew has passed it by in the letter, and not inserted, 'on the eighth day.'

Gen. xvii. 9. sqq.

25. Meanwhile you have heard that both the eighth day and circumcision were given for a sign; now a sign is an indication of a greater matter, a symbol of a future verity; and a covenant was given to Abraham and his seed, to whom it was said, *In Isaac shall thy seed be.* The circumcision of the Jews therefore, or of one born in his house, or bought with his money was permitted. But we cannot extend this to a foreigner or proselyte, unless they were born in the

Ib. xxi 12.

house of Abraham, or bought with his money, or of his seed. Again, nothing is said of proselytes; when it is wished to speak of them they are expressly mentioned, as it is written: *And the Lord spake unto Moses, saying, Speak unto Aaron, and unto his sons, and unto all the children of Israel, and say unto them . . . Whatsoever man there be of the house of Israel, or of the strangers which sojourn among you, that offereth a burnt-sacrifice.* When therefore they are intended to be included the Law touches them; when the Divine word does not point to them, how can they seem to be bound? Again, it is written, *Speak unto the sons of Aaron,* when the priests are intended; and so as regards the Levites also.

26. Thus it is abundantly manifest that even according to the letter of the Law, although the Law be spiritual, yet that according to the very letter of the Law the Gentiles could not be obliged to observe circumcision, but that circumcision itself was a sign, until *the fulness of the Gentiles should be come in, and so all Israel be saved* by circumcision, not of a small portion of one member, but of the heart. And both the excuse on our parts is sufficient, and the continuance of circumcision among the Jews up to this day is excluded.

27. But as to its being imputed it as a cause of blame, now or in past time, by the Gentiles, I would say, first, it is not competent to them to blame or deride what others who are their fellows do. Suppose however that there were cause for their ridicule, why ought this to move us, when the very cross of the Lord is *a stumbling-block to the Jews, and foolishness to the Greeks, but to us the power of God and the wisdom of God.* And the Lord Himself has said, *Whosoever shall be ashamed*[1] *of Me before men, of him will I also be ashamed before My Father Which is in heaven;* teaching us not to be disturbed by those things which are laughed at by men, if we observe them in the service of religion.

[1] confusus fuerit

LETTER LXXIII.

IRENÆUS having enquired why the Law was ever given, seeing that Paul declares it to be injurious: S. Ambrose replies that it would have been useless, had we kept that natural law which is written on our hearts, and is found even in infants; but that, this being broken, the former became necessary, that it might take away all excuse by its manifestation of that sin which was afterwards removed by the grace of Christ.

AMBROSE TO IRENÆUS.

1. GREATLY, it would seem, have you been moved by the lesson from the Apostle, having heard read to-day, *Because the Law worketh wrath; for where no law is, there is no transgression.* And therefore you have thought fit to ask why the Law was promulgated, if it profited nothing, nay rather, by working wrath and bringing in transgression, was injurious. [Rom. iv. 15.]

2. And indeed, according to the tenor of your question, it is certain that the Law, which was given by Moses, was not necessary. For had men been able to keep the natural Law, which our God and Maker implanted in the breast of each, there would have been no need of the Law, which, *written on tables of stone,* tended rather to entangle and fetter the infirmity of human nature, than to set at large and liberate it. Now that there is *a natural Law written in our hearts* the Apostle also teaches us, when he writes, that for the most part *the Gentiles, which have not the Law, do by nature the things contained in the Law, and, though they have not read the Law, have yet the works of the Law written in their hearts.* [Ib. ii. 14.]

3. This law therefore is not written but innate; not acquired by reading, but flowing as from a natural fountain, it springs up in each breast, and men's minds drink it in. This Law we ought to have kept even from fear of a future judgment, a witness whereof we have in our conscience, which shews itself in those silent thoughts we have towards God, and whereby either our sin is reproved or our innocence justified. And thus that which has ever been

LETT. 73. manifest to the Lord, will be clearly revealed in the day of
Rom. ii. 15. judgment, when those secrets of the heart, which were
thought to be concealed, will be called into account. Now
the discovery of these things, these secrets, I mean, would
do no harm, if the natural Law still remained in the human breast; for it is holy, free from craft or guile, the
companion of justice, free from iniquity.

4. Moreover let us interrogate the age of childhood, let
us consider whether any crime can be found therein, avarice,
ambition, guile, rage, or insolence. It claims nothing for its
own, assumes no honours to itself, never prefers itself to
others, neither wishes or knows how to avenge itself. Its
pure and simple mind cannot even comprehend the meaning of insolence.

Gen. iii. 6. 5. Adam broke this Law, seeking to assume to himself
that which he had not received, that thus he might become
as it were his own maker and creator, and arrogate to himself divine honour. Thus by his disobedience he incurred
guilt, and through arrogance fell into transgression. Had
he not thus violated his allegiance, but been obedient to
the commands of heaven, he would have preserved to his
posterity the prerogative of nature and the innocence which
he possessed at his birth. Wherefore as by disobedience
the authority of the Law of Nature was corrupted and
blotted out, the written law was found necessary; in order
that man, having lost all, might at least regain a part;
attaining by instruction to the knowledge of that which
he had received at his birth, but had subsequently lost.
Moreover, since the cause of his fall was pride, and pride
arose from the dignity of innocence, it was needful that
some law should be passed which should subdue and sub-
Rom. vii. 8. ject him to God. For without the Law he was ignorant
of sin, and thus his guilt was less because he knew it not.
S. John xv. 22. Wherefore also the Lord says, *If I had not come and spoken
to them they had not had sin, but now they have no excuse
for their sin.*

6. The Law then was published, first to take away all
Rom. iii. 19. excuse lest man should say, I knew not sin, because I
received no rule what to avoid. And next that *all the
[1] subditus fiat Vulg world might become guilty* [1] *before God* by the confession of

sin. For it made all subject; in that it was not only given to the Jews but also called the Gentiles; for proselytes from the Gentiles were associated with them. Nor can he seem to be excepted, who after being called was found wanting, for the Law also bound those whom she called. And thus the fault of all worked subjection, subjection humility, humility obedience. And thus as pride had drawn after it transgression, so on the other hand, transgression produced obedience. And thus the written Law, which seemed superfluous, was rendered necessary, redeeming sin by sin.

7. But again, lest anyone should be deterred, and say that an increase of sin was caused by the Law, and that the Law not only did not profit but was even injurious, he has a consolation for his solicitude, because although *by the Law sin abounded, grace did much more abound.* And now let us consider the meaning of this. [Rom. v. 20.]

8. Sin abounded by the Law because *by the Law is the knowledge of sin,* and thus it began to be injurious to me to know that which through infirmity I could not avoid; it is good to foreknow in order to avoid, but if I cannot avoid, to have known was injurious. Thus the effect of the Law was changed to me into its opposite, yet by the very increase of sin it became useful to me, because I was humbled. Wherefore David also said, *It is good for me that I have been humbled.* For by my humiliation I have broken those bonds of that ancient transgression, whereby Adam and Eve had bound the whole line of their posterity. Hence too the Lord came in obedience that He might loose the knot of disobedience and of man's transgression. And so, as by disobedience sin entered, so by obedience sin was remitted. Wherefore the Apostle also says, *For as by one man's disobedience many were made sinners, so by the obedience of one shall many be made righteous.* [Ib vii 7.] [Ps. cxix. 71.] [Rom. v. 19.]

9. Here is one reason the Law on the one hand was superfluous and yet became necessary. It was superflous herein, that it would not have been needed could we have kept the natural Law, but as we kept it not, the law of Moses became needful for us, to the intent that it might teach us obedience and loose that knot of Adam's trans-

gression which has fettered his whole posterity. Guilt indeed was increased by the Law, but pride, the author of this guilt, was overthrown by it, and this was profitable to me, for pride discovered the guilt, and this guilt brought grace.

10. Hear another reason. At first Moses' Law was not needed; it was introduced subsequently, and this appears to intimate that this introduction was in a sense clandestine and not of an ordinary kind, seeing that it succeeded in the place of the natural Law. Had this maintained its place, the written Law would never have entered in; but the natural Law being excluded by transgression and almost blotted out of the human breast, pride reigned, and disobedience spread itself; and then this Law succeeded, that by its written precepts it might cite us before it, and *every mouth be stopped, and all the world become guilty before God.* Now the world becomes guilty before God by the Law, in that all are made amenable to its prescripts, but no man is justified by its works. And since by the Law comes the knowledge of sin, but not the remission of guilt, the Law, which has made all sinners, would seem to have been injurious.

11. But when the Lord Jesus came, He forgave all men that sin which none could escape, and *blotted out the handwriting against us* by the shedding of His own Blood. This then is the Apostle's meaning; sin abounded by the Law, but grace abounded by Jesus; for after that the whole world became guilty, He took away the sin of the whole world, as John bore witness, saying: *Behold the Lamb of God, which taketh away the sin of the world.* Wherefore let no man glory in works, for by his works no man shall be justified, for he that is just hath a free gift, for he is justified by the Bath. It is faith then which delivers by the blood of Christ, for *Blessed is the man to whom sin is remitted, and pardon granted.*

Farewell, my son; love me, for I also love you.

LETTER LXXIV.

IN this letter S. Ambrose explains the meaning of S Paul's expression, that 'the Law was our schoolmaster,' and shews how, while the letter of the precepts fitted the Jews, the spiritual sense which lay under the letter applies to Christians.

AMBROSE TO IRENÆUS.

1. You have heard, my son, the lesson of to-day in the Apostle, that *the Law was our schoolmaster in Christ*, that we might be justified by faith. And by this one text I believe that those questions are resolved, which are wont to perplex many. For there are those who say, 'Since God gave the Law to Moses, what is the reason that there are many things in the Law which now seem abrogated by the Gospel?' And how can the Author of the two Testaments be one and the same, when that which was permitted in the Law, when the Gospel came, was permitted no longer? as for instance there is a circumcision of the body, which was even then only given for a sign, that the verity of spiritual circumcision might be preserved, yet why was it even given as a sign? Why was there such diversity, that then it was esteemed piety to be circumcised, but now it is judged to be impiety? Again it was ordered by the Law that the Sabbath day ought to be a holiday, so that if any one carried a bundle of sticks, he became guilty of death; but now we perceive that the same day is devoted to bearing burthens and to transacting business without any punishment. And there are many precepts of the Law which at the present time would seem to have ceased.

Gal. iii. 24.

Num. xv. 35.

2. Let us consider then what is the cause of this; for it was not without a purpose that the Apostle said, *the Law was our schoolmaster in Christ*[1]. To whom does a schoolmaster belong, to one of riper years or to a youth? Doubtless to a youth or boy, that is, to one of infirm age. For a pædagogus, as the word is rendered in the Latin, is the teacher of a boy; and he cannot apply perfect precepts

[1] in Christo. εἰς χριστόν.

to an imperfect age, because it cannot bear them. Again, the God of the Law says by the Prophet, *I gave them also statutes that were not good,* that is, not perfect. But the same God has preserved more perfect things for the Gospel, as He says, *I am not come to destroy, but to fulfil the Law.*

<small>Lett. 74.
Ezek. xx. 25.

S. Matt. v. 17.</small>

3. What then was the cause of this difference, but human diversity? He knew the Jews to be a stiff-necked people, prone to fall, base, inclined to unbelief, that heard with the ear but understood not, that saw with their eyes but perceived not, fickle with the instability of infancy, and heedless of commands; and therefore He applied the Law, as a Schoolmaster, to the unstable temper and impious mind of the people, and moderating the very precepts of the Law, He chose that one thing should be read, another understood; that thus the foolish man might at least keep what he was reading, and depart not from the prescript of the letter; while the wise should understand the sentiments of the Divine mind, which the letter did not alter; that the unwise man might keep the command of the Law, the prudent might observe the mystery. The Law therefore has the severity of the sword, as the schoolmaster holds the rod, that at any rate by the denunciation of punishment it may keep in awe the weakness of the imperfect people; but the Gospel has indulgence whereby sins are forgiven.

<small>Exod. xxxiv. 9.</small>

4. Rightly therefore does Paul say that *the letter killeth but the spirit giveth life.* For the letter circumcises a small portion of the body; the understanding spirit keeps the circumcision of the whole soul and body; that the superfluous parts being cut off, (for nothing is so superfluous as the vices of avarice, the sins of lust, which nature had not, but sin caused,) chastity might be observed, and frugality loved. The sign therefore is bodily circumcision, but the truth is spiritual circumcision, the one cuts off the member, the other cuts off sin. Nature has created nothing imperfect in man, nor has she commanded it to be taken away as if it were superfluous, but that they who cut off a part of their body might perceive that sins were much more to be cut off, and those members which led to offences were to

<small>2 Cor. iii. 6.</small>

be retrenched, even though they were joined together by a certain unity of body, as it is written, *If thy right hand offend thee, cut it off, and cast it from thee, for it is profitable for thee that one of thy members should perish, and not that thy whole body should be cast into hell.* To the Jews then, as to children, are enjoined not complete precepts but partial ones, and, seeing that they were unable to keep the whole of their bodies clean, they were commanded to keep clean, as it were, one portion of it.

<small>TO IRENÆUS S. Matt. v. 30.</small>

5. They were also commanded to keep the holiday of the Sabbath one day in the week, so as to be subjected to no burthen, and I would that being thus released from earthly works they had escaped, carrying with them to that perpetual sabbath of future ages the burthen of heavy crimes. But as God knew how prone to fall the people were, He enjoined a part upon the weaker by the observance of one day, He reserved the fulness for the stronger: the Synagogue observes the day, the Church immortality. In the Law therefore is a part, in the Gospel is perfection.

<small>Exod. xxxi. 13.</small>

6. The people of the Jews are forbidden to carry sticks, that is, such things as are consumed by fire. He keeps in the shade, who flies from the sun. But to you the Sun of Righteousness suffers not the shade to be an hindrance, but pouring forth the full light of His grace says to you, *Go, and sin no more.* The follower of that eternal Sun says to you, *Now if any man build upon this foundation gold, silver, precious stones, wood, hay, stubble; every man's work shall be made manifest, for the day shall declare it, because it shall be revealed by fire; and the fire shall try every man's work of what sort it is.* Wherefore let us build upon Christ, for Christ is our foundation, that which may not be burnt but purified. Gold is purified by fire, and so is silver.

<small>Num. xv. 33.

S. John viii. 11.

1 Cor. iii. 12, 13.</small>

7. You hear me speak of gold and silver, you think it to be the material substance, you desire to gather it, but you are losing your labour. This gold and silver brings burthen but no fruit. The toil of him who seeks it turns to the profit of his heir. This gold is burned like wood, not preserved; this silver will bring detriment not profit to your life in that day. Another kind of gold and silver is required

of you, that is, a good meaning, a word fitly spoken, of which God says that He gives vessels of gold and silver. These are the gifts of God. *The words of the Lord are pure words; even as the silver which from the earth is tried and purified seven times in the fire.* The grace of your understanding, the beauty of chaste discourse is required of you; the brightness of faith not the tinkling of silver. The one remains, the other perishes; the one has reward, and we carry it away with us, the other, which we leave behind, brings loss.

<small>Ps. xii. 6.</small>

8. If any rich man thinks that the gold and silver which he has hoarded and stored up can avail him for life, let him know that he carries an empty burthen, which the fire of judgment will consume. Leave here your burthens, ye rich men, that your burthen may not add fuel to the fire which is to come. If you will bestow some of these goods, your burthen will be diminished, and what remains will be no burthen. Lay not up wealth, O miser; lest you should become in mere name only a Christian, in work a Jew, perceiving that your burthens are a punishment to you. For it has been said to you, not in the shade but in the sun, *If any man's work abide, he shall receive a reward, if any man's work shall be burned, he shall suffer loss.*

<small>1 Cor. iii. 14, 15.</small>

9. And therefore, as a perfect man, taught in the Law, confirmed in the Gospel, receive the faith of both Testaments. For *Blessed is he that sows beside all waters, that sends forth thither the feet of the ox and the ass,* as we read to-day, that is, who sows upon the people who follow the doctrine of both Testaments; this is that ox of the plough, carrying the yoke of the Law, of which the Law says, *Thou shalt not muzzle the ox, when he treadeth out the corn;* that ox which has the horns of the Divine Scriptures. But the foal of the ass the Lord rides upon, in the Gospel, representing the people of the Gentiles.

<small>Isa. xxxii 20.</small>

<small>Deut. xxv. 4.</small>

<small>S. Luke xix. 33.</small>

10. But I think that since the word of God is rich in meanings, we ought also to understand that the ox has horns full of terror, the bull is fierce, the ass mild, and that this is fitly applied to our present purpose, for happy is he who observes both severity and mildness; that so by the one discipline may be maintained, while by the other innocence

may be cherished; for too great severity is wont by means of terror to tempt to falsehood. God prefers being loved to being feared; for the Lord exacts love, the servant fear, for terror cannot be perpetual in man, for it is written as we read to-day *Behold, in your fear, they whom ye feared, shall fear.*

Farewell, my son; love me, for I too love you.

LETTER LXXV.

THIS letter is a sequel to the preceding, and deals with the context o the passage of S. Paul which that letter discussed. S Ambrose ends by maintaining that the Jews were 'heirs' only of the letter of the Old Testament promises, the Christian being the heir of the Spirit

AMBROSE TO CLEMENTIANUS [a].

1. I AM indeed aware that nothing is more difficult than to treat properly concerning the Apostle's meaning, for even Origen's expositions of the New Testament are far inferior to his expositions of the Old. Yet since in my previous letter you think that I have not explained amiss the reason of the Law being called a Schoolmaster; in what I say to-day too I purpose to unfold to you the actual force of the Apostle's statement.

2. Now the former part of his discourse declares that no man shall be justified by the works of the Law, but by faith, *For as many as are of the works of the Law are under the curse*; but *Christ hath redeemed us from the curse of the Law, being made a curse for us.* The inheritance therefore is not given by the Law but by promise. *Now to Abraham were the promises made, and to his seed which is Christ.* Thus the Law *was added because of transgressions, till the seed should come to whom the promise was made;* and therefore *all are concluded under sin, that the promise*

Gal. iii. 10.
Ib. 13.
Ib. 16.
Ib. 19.

---

[a] Why this letter, which plainly declares itself in the first section to be a sequel of the previous one, is addressed to a different name, it is difficult to say There is a similar difficulty about Letter xxvi, and possibly the same solution may apply here as is suggested by the Ben. Edd. there. See Intiod. to Lett. xxvi.

Lett. 75. Gal. iii. 22. Ib. 25.	*by faith of Jesus Christ might be given to them that believe. But after that faith is come, we are no longer under the Law, that is, under a schoolmaster;* and this because we are *all the sons of God,* and are all in Christ Jesus. Now
Ib. 29.	if we are all in Christ Jesus, then are we *Abraham's seed, and heirs according to the promise.* And this is the conclusion at which the Apostle arrives.

3. Still however he is met with this objection, that even the Jew might say, I also, being under the Law, have an heirship, for the Law is also called the Old Testament, and where is a Testament there also is an inheritance.

Heb. ix. 17.	And although the Apostle himself told the Hebrews that a testament is of no force, until the death of the testator happen, that is to say, a testament is of no strength while the testator liveth, but is established by his death, yet as
Jer. xii. 8.	in Jeremiah the Lord, speaking of the Jews, has said, *Mine heritage is unto Me as a lion,* he would not deny that they were heirs. But there are heirs without possessions, there are heirs also with them; and while the testator lives those whose names are written in the will are called heirs, though without possessions.
Gal iv. 1. Ib. 3.	4. Little children are also heirs, but they *differ in nothing from a servant, in that they are still under tutors and governors. Even so we were in bondage under the elements of the world. But, when the fulness of the time was come,* Christ also came, and now we are no longer servants but sons, if we believe in Christ. Thus He gave them the semblance of an inheritance, but withheld from them the possession of it. Thus they have the name but not the benefit of being heirs, for like children they possess the bare name of heirship without its privileges, and have no right either to command or to use, waiting for the fulness of their age that they may be delivered from their governors.

5. As then young children, so the Jews also, are under a schoolmaster. *The Law is our schoolmaster,* the schoolmaster brings us to our Master; and our One Master is

S. Matt. xxiii. 10.	Christ: *Neither be ye called masters, for one is your Master, even Christ.* The schoolmaster is feared, the Master shews the way of salvation. Thus fear brings us to liberty,

liberty to faith, faith to love; love obtains adoption, adoption the inheritance. Where then faith is there is liberty; for the servant acts from fear, the free-man by faith; the one by the letter, the other by grace; the one in slavery the other by the Spirit; but *where the Spirit of the Lord is, there is liberty.* If then where faith is, there is liberty; where liberty there grace, where grace there inheritance; and he that is a Jew in the letter not in spirit is in bondage, he who hath not faith hath not the liberty of the spirit. Now where there is no liberty there is no grace, where no grace no adoption, where no adoption there no succession. TO CLEMENTIANUS

2 Cor. iii. 17.

6. Thus, the tablets being, as it were, closed, he beholds [b] his inheritance but possesses it not, he has no permission to read it. For how can he say 'Our Father' who denies the true Son of God, Him by Whom our adoptive sonship is obtained for us? How can he rehearse the will who denies the death of the testator? How can he obtain liberty, who denies the Blood whereby he has been redeemed? For this is the price of our liberty, as Peter says, *ye were redeemed with the precious Blood,* not indeed of a lamb, but of Him Who came as a lamb, in meekness and humility, and redeemed the whole world with the one offering of His Body, as He himself says, *I was brought as a lamb to the slaughter.* Wherefore John also says, *Behold the Lamb of God, which taketh away the sin of the world.*

1 S. Pet. i. 18, 19.

Isa. liii. 7.

S John i. 29.

7. Hence the Jew, being heir in the letter not in the spirit is as a child under tutors and governours; but the Christian, who recognizes that fulness of time wherein Christ came, *made of a woman, made under the Law, that He might redeem all who were under the Law;* the Christian, I say, *by unity of faith and knowledge of the Son of God grows up unto a perfect man: unto the measure of the stature of the fulness of Christ.*

Gal. iv. 4.

Eph. iv. 13.

Farewell, my son; love me, for I also love you.

---

[b] The phrase 'cernere hereditatem' is a well-known law-term, meaning literally 'to decide to accept an inheritance,' and then 'to enter upon it.' But as this sense will not agree with the context, it seems necessary to take 'cernere,' as the Benedictine note does, in its common sense of 'to see.'

LETTER LXXVI.

At Irenæus' request S. Ambrose points out the scope of the Epistle to the Ephesians Therein is proposed to us a heavenly inheritance, a seat in heavenly places together with Christ, Who has obtained freedom for us. It sets forth to us charity, whereby we are united to Christ, as the end of faith. He adds that no other Epistle contains the mention of so many blessings, and he briefly recounts these one by one.

AMBROSE TO IRENÆUS, GREETING.

1. You have asked me to set forth to you the scope and substance of the Epistle to the Ephesians, an Epistle which seems somewhat obscure, unless by analyzing it we can gather what those motives are by which the Apostle would persuade us not to despair of the kingdom of God.

2. In the first place then he points out that the hope of reward and the inheritance of those heavenly promises which have been brought within our reach by the Passion and Resurrection of Christ, are wont to be a great encouragement to the good in the pursuit of virtue.

3. To this he has added that not only has a mode of return to Paradise been opened to us by Christ, but that even the honour of sitting in heavenly places has been imparted to this flesh of our body by its fellowship with the Body of Christ; so that you need no longer doubt the possibility of your own ascension, now that you know that your fellowship with the flesh of Christ subsists even in the kingdom of heaven, knowing also that by His Blood reconciliation has been made for all things, both on earth and in heaven, for He descended that He might fill all things: and, further, that by His Apostles, prophets, and priests, the whole world has been established, and the Gentiles gathered in; and that the end of our hope is the love of Him, that we may *grow up into Him in all things;* for He is the Head of all things, and unto Him according to the measure of His working we are all raised and built up by charity into one body.

4. We ought not therefore to despair of the members adhering to their Head; especially since from the begin-

full of the blessings of the Gospel.

ning we have *been predestinated by Jesus Christ to adoption as children of God in Himself.* which predestination He has ratified, instructing us that the prediction made from the first, that *a man shall leave his father and mother, and shall be joined unto his wife, and they two shall be one flesh,* is *a sacrament of Christ and the Church.* If therefore the union of Adam and Eve is *a great sacrament which relates to Christ and the Church,* it is certain that as Eve was bone of the bones of her husband, and flesh of his flesh, so we are members of the Body of Christ, bone of His Bones and flesh of His Flesh. _{TO IRENÆUS Eph. i. 5. Gen ii. 24. Eph v. 31, 32.}

5. No other Epistle has pronounced so many blessings over the people of God as this. For herein the pregnant witness of Divine grace has declared that we are *blessed with all spiritual blessings in heavenly places,* and *predestinated unto the adoption of children,* richly endowed also with grace in the Son of God, *which things have abounded unto the knowledge of the mystery of His eternal will.* Especially now, in the fulness of time, when *all things are reconciled in Christ, both in heaven and on earth,* have we attained an inheritance in Him, to the intent that both what is of the Law and what is of Grace might be fulfilled in us. For even according to the Law we seemed to be elected in that season of youth, by which is signified a holy life, without either the wantonness of childhood or the infirmity of age. We have been taught also how we must vigorously *wage war not only against flesh and blood, but also against spiritual wickedness in high places.* _{Ib. i. 3, 5, 9. Ib 10. Ib. vi. 12.}

6. Wherefore as the possession of lands taken from the enemy fell to their lot, so to us has fallen the lot of grace, that we may become the heritage of God, Who possesses our reins, the seat of chastity and temperance. Do you seek to know this lot? Remember that lot which fell upon Matthias, that he might be chosen into the number of the twelve Apostles. The Prophet David also says, *If ye sleep in the midst of the lots,* because he who is placed in the middle, between the lot of the Old and New Testament, resting upon both, arrives at the peace of the heavenly kingdom. This lot of their paternal inheritance the daughters of Zelophehad sought for, and their petition was _{Acts i. 26 Ps. lxviii. 13. Num. xxvii 1.}

admitted by God's judgment. But they sought for it in the shade, for Zelophehad means 'the shade of the mouth;' they sought it then in dark sayings, they spoke not what was revealed. Hence the supplication for their inheritance by the daughters of Zelophehad was couched in dark sayings, but in our case it stands in the light of the Gospel and in the revelation of grace.

7. Let us therefore be the possession of God, and let Him be our portion, for in Him are the riches of His glory and inheritance. For who is rich but God alone, Who created all things? Especially however is He *rich in mercy*, in that He redeemed all mankind, and, as being the author of nature, changed us, who according to our fleshly nature were the children of wrath, and exposed to trouble, that we might become the children of peace and charity. For who can change nature but He Who created nature? Wherefore He raised the dead, and those that were *quickened in Christ He hath made to sit in heavenly places in the Lord Jesus*.

8. Not that any man has been thought worthy of the privilege of sitting in that seat of God, for to the Son alone hath the Father said, *Sit thou on my right hand*, but because in that Flesh of Christ the flesh of the whole human race has been honoured, because it partakes of the same nature. For as He was subjected in our flesh by His unity therewith, and by the obedience of the body, wherein He was made obedient even unto death, so we, in His Flesh, are *sat down together with Him in heavenly places*. We therefore are not set down by ourselves but in the Person of Christ, Who alone, as the Son of man, sitteth at the right Hand of God; as He said Himself, *Hereafter shall ye see the Son of man sitting on the right hand of God*. To this end has His Grace and Goodness been formed upon us in Christ Jesus, that being dead according to works, redeemed through faith and saved by grace, we might receive the gift of this great deliverance. Our very nature, raised, as it were, in Him, has been made partaker of the Grace of a new creation, that being new created in Christ, we, who had before fallen away through the corruption of our guilty lineage, might walk in good works.

9. For the strife which before existed in the flesh being removed, an universal peace has been made in heaven; that men might be like Angels upon earth, that the Gentiles and Jews might be made one, that both the new and old man might be united, the middle wall of partition, which, as a hostile barrier, had once divided them, being broken down. For the nature of our flesh having stirred up anger discord and dissension, and the law having bound us with the chains of condemnation, Christ Jesus subdued by mortification the wantonness and intemperance of the flesh, and made void *the law of commandment contained in ordinances,* declaring thereby that the decrees of the spiritual Law are not to be interpreted according to the letter; putting an end to the slothful rest of the Sabbath and to the superfluous rite of outward circumcision, and opening to all *access by one Spirit unto the Father.* For how can there be any discord, where there is one calling, one body and one spirit?

10. For what else did the Lord Jesus effect by His descent but our deliverance from captivity into liberty, and the subjection to Himself of that captivity which the bonds of unbelief had fettered, but which is now restrained by the fetters of wisdom, every wise man putting his feet into its bonds? For it is written that when He had descended He ascended also, *that He might fill all things,* and that we might all receive of His fulness.

11. Wherefore *He gave first Apostles* in the Church, filling them with the Holy Spirit, others *prophets,* others *evangelists,* others *pastors and teachers,* that by their exhortations the progress of believers might be accomplished, and the work of the ministry of faith might receive increase. Every one by the growth of virtue is built up unto the measure of the inward life, which *measure,* being that more perfect one of a holy life, that is, *of a perfect man,* taking of the fulness of Christ, has received the fulness of grace.

12. But who is a perfect man, but he who, being delivered from the weakness of a childish mind, from the unstable and slippery ways of youth, and from the unbridled passions of adult age, has attained to the strength of full manhood, and has grown up unto such maturity of charac-

LETT. 76. ter as not to be easily turned aside by the address of a wily disputer, nor cast, as it were, upon the rocks by the turbid violence of foolish doctrine? Who but he that betakes himself to the remedies of error, who follows truth not only in his words but also in his works, and, takes upon him the edifying of himself in love, that he may be united with others in the unity of faith and knowledge, and, as a member, not fall off from his Head, that is, from Christ, Who is the Head of all, *from whom the whole body* of the faithful and prudent *fitted and compacted and joined together by the rational harmony of the Word* (for this is the meaning of συναρμολογούμενον, ἁρμονίᾳ τοῦ Λόγου δεδεμένον [a],) *by that which every joint supplieth, according to the measure of every part, maketh increase of the body unto the edifying itself in love;* that so it may rise as one temple of God in all, and one habitation of the heavenly mansion in the spirit of all.

Eph. iv. 16.

13. Herein I conceive we are to understand that not only holy men but all believers, and all the heavenly and reasonable hosts and powers are united in faith and spirit; that by a certain concord of powers and offices one body, composed of all spirits of a reasonable nature, may adhere to Christ their Head, being so united to the framework of the building, that in no single point of juncture the several members may seem to be severed from each other. For this is the meaning of the Greek ἀφὴν τῆς χορηγίας κατ' ἐνέργειαν ἐν μέτρῳ. And to unite each one to Himself according to the due measure of his merits and faith will not be difficult: for the edifice of love closes and blocks up every crevice through which offences may enter. We ought not then to doubt that in the building up of this temple the company of the heavenly hosts will be united with us; for it is unreasonable to suppose that while the Temple of God can be so built up by human love as that we shall become *an habitation of God in the Spirit,* He should not dwell within the heavenly Host.

14. On this account, that the building may be raised

[a] The words ἁρμονίᾳ τοῦ Λόγου δεδεμένον seem to be a gloss on S. Paul's compound συναρμολογούμενον. They are not part of his text, though S. Ambrose seems here to be quoting them as if they were.

within us more rapidly, the Apostle exhorts us *to open the eyes of our understanding*, to lift them to things above, diligently to follow after the knowledge of God, to unravel the truth, to hide in our hearts the commandments of God, *to put off deceitful lusts* and hidden deeds of shame, to seek to be renewed by the graces of the Sacraments, to moderate anger, to calm all disturbance of spirit before the sun goes down, to beware lest the adversary gain the upper hand of us, that mighty spirit who entered into the heart of Judas, and broke through the gates of his soul, overpowering his resistance, to shut out theft, to eschew falsehood, to rise from the dead, to put on sobriety. He tells us likewise that wives should be subject to their husbands, as the Church is to Christ, and that husbands should offer up their own lives for their wives, *as Christ gave Himself for the Church*. And lastly, that, as good soldiers, we should *put on the armour of God*, and continually fight, not only against *flesh and blood, but also against spiritual wickedness;* that we may neither be corrupted by friends nor vanquished by enemies.

_{TO HORONTIANUS}
_{Eph. i. 18.}
_{Ib. iv. 22.}
_{Ib. 26.}
_{S. John xiii. 27}
_{Eph. v 24.}
_{Ib. 25.}
_{Ib. vi. 13.}
_{Ib. 12.}

This summary account of the Epistle I offer you as the best which I have in my power to give.

Farewell, my son; love me, for I also love you.

LETTER LXXVII.

<small>This letter dwells on the Gospel, as the true Inheritance, and on the contrast between the Jew, who by rejecting Christ made Moses in whom he believed his accuser, and the Christian, who received true liberty in Christ, while the Jew remained a slave.</small>

AMBROSE TO HORONTIANUS.

1. Not without reason have you thought fit to enquire into the nature of the Divine inheritance; and why it should be so highly esteemed that for its sake many should even offer up their lives. But if you will consider that even in human affairs the advantage of inheriting worldly goods gives an additional sanction to the laws of natural

Lett. 77. affection, and that even on this account greater respect is shown to parents, for fear, namely, lest the slighted love of a father may avenge itself by disinheriting or renouncing the rebellious offspring, you will cease to wonder why men so greatly desire a Divine inheritance.

2. Now there is an inheritance offered to all Christians; for Isaiah thus speaks, *There is an heritage for them that believe on the Lord,* and this inheritance is hoped for by the promise, not by the Law. This the history of the Old Testament proves, in the words of Sarah, *Cast out this bond-woman and her son, for the son of the bond-woman shall not be heir with my son, even with Isaac.* The son of Sarah was Isaac, the son of the bond-woman was Ishmael; and these were before the Law, wherefore the promise was older than the Law. We are after Isaac sons by the promise, the Jews are the sons of the bond-woman after the flesh. We have a free mother, which bore not, but afterwards, according to the promise, brought forth and produced a child; they have Agar for their mother, *gendering to bondage.* He is free, to whom grace is promised, he is a slave on whom the yoke of the Law is imposed, wherefore the promise came to us before the Law came to them, and in the course of nature liberty is more ancient than bondage. Liberty therefore comes of the promise, bondage of the Law. But although the promise itself, as we have said, is before the Law, and by the promise comes liberty, and in liberty is love, still love is according to the Law, and love is greater than liberty.

Isa. liv. 17.

Gen. xxi. 10.

Gal iv. 24.

3. Are we not then servants? and is it not written, *praise the Lord, all ye servants,* or how does the Apostle say, *But as the servants of God, doing the will of God from his heart?* But there is also a free and voluntary service, whereof the Apostle says, *He that is called, being free, is Christ's servant.* And this service is from the heart, not of necessity. Wherefore we are the servants of our Creator; but we have a liberty which we have received through the grace of Christ, born of the promise according to faith. Wherefore, being born of the freedwoman, let us, signed in the forehead, offer the sacrifice of liberty as becomes freemen, that we may rejoice and not be confounded, being

Ps. cxxxiv 1.
Eph vi. 6.
1 Cor. vii. 22.

signed in the spirit and not in the flesh. For to us it is rightly said, *Stand fast, and be not entangled again with the yoke of bondage.* He does not say, Be not slaves, but *Be not entangled with the yoke of bondage,* for the yoke of bondage is heavier than the bondage itself.

TO HORONTIANUS

Gal. v 1

4. Isaac also says to his son Esau, when he sought his blessing, *Behold thy dwelling shall be the fatness of the earth, and of the dew of heaven from above; and by thy sword shalt thou live, and shalt serve thy brother. But the time shall come when thou shalt have the dominion and shalt break his yoke from off thy neck.* How then is this to be reconciled, that although he shall break his brother's yoke from off his neck he shall still serve, unless we recognize the difference that there is in servitude? Now in what this difference consists, let the Scripture itself explain to us. Isaac signifies good, and he is good to us, for after him we are born into liberty, and he is a good father to both his sons. His love for them both he proved, in the one case by affection, in the other by blessing, for he commanded his elder son to bring him food, that he might receive his blessing; but while he makes delay and seeks for wild venison from a distance, the younger brother brings him home-food, from the sheep of the flock.

Gen. xxvii. 39, 40.

5. Good food for all is Christ, good food too is faith, sweet food is mercy, pleasant food is faith. These are the meats whereon are fed the people of holy Church. Good food too is the Spirit of God, good food is the remission of sins. But very hard food is the rigour of the Law, and the terror of punishment; and very coarse food is that observance of the letter which is preferred to the grace of pardon. The Jews again are under a curse, we included in a blessing. A ready food too is faith: *The word is nigh thee, in thy mouth and in thy heart* the food of the Law is more tardy. For while waiting for the Law the people fell into transgression.

Gal. iii 10

Deut. xxx. 14.

Rom. x. 8.

6. Thus it was on the son who was diligent and faithful that the father bestowed his blessing, but he reserved one, for he was a good father, for his elder son also, in that he made him servant to his brother. For he did this, not as wishing to subject his family to any unworthy bondage,

LETT 77. but because he who cannot rule and govern himself ought to serve and be subject to one more prudent; that so he may be governed by his counsel, and not fall through his own folly, nor stumble from walking rashly. It is as a blessing then that such a state of service is given. Moreover it is numbered among blessings, together with the gift of the fatness of the earth, and of the dew of heaven from above.

Gen. xxvii. 40.
Ib.
Having said, *By thy sword thou shalt live,* lest he should be harmed by the confidence arising from strength or power, he added, *and thou shalt serve thy brother* that thou mayest thus obtain both the rich fruits of the flesh, and the dew of Divine grace, and mayest follow him who is able to direct and govern thee.

Ib.
7. *But it shall come to pass, when thou shalt have broken his yoke from off thy neck,* that thou shalt have the reward of thy willing servitude, and not undergo the evils of a compulsory bondage. For that kind of bondage is dishonourable which is the result of necessity, that is honourable which is offered by piety. Hence the Apostle says,

1 Cor ix. 17.
For if I do this thing willingly, I have a reward, but if against my will, a dispensation is committed unto me. Better then is it to reap a reward, than to obey a dispensation. Wherefore let us not be restrained by the yoke of bondage, but let us serve in the spirit of charity, for

Gal. v. 13.
Ecclus. i. 14.
Gal. v. 14.
Rom xiii 8
the Apostle says, *By love serve one another.* The fear of the Law becomes the love of the Gospel. Again, *To fear the Lord is the beginning of wisdom,* but the fulness of the Law is charity. And the Law itself says, *For all the Law is fulfilled in one word, even in this, Thou shalt love thy neighbour as thyself.*

8. This therefore is what we asserted, for although bondage is by the Law, liberty is by the Law also, for charity belongs to liberty, fear to bondage. There is therefore both a charity of the Law, and a service of charity, but the Law is the forerunner of charity, the charity of the Gospel is the free giver of a pious service.

Gal. iii 24
9. The Law then is not superfluous; for like a schoolmaster, it attends upon the weak; and by weakness I mean weakness of character not of body, for they are infants who know not how to declare the word of God, who receive

not His works. For if *an unspotted life is old age*, a life full of stains is the time of youth. The Law then, that is, Νόμος, was our schoolmaster, until faith came. *We were kept*, it is said, *under the Law, as being weak, shut up unto the faith which should afterwards be revealed.* But afterwards faith came; he does not say the Gospel, but faith, for that only is faith which is in the Gospel. For although the *righteousness of God is revealed therein* which is *from faith to faith*, still this of the Law is faith indeed when it attains to the fulness thereof. Rightly therefore is this faith spoken of as single and alone; because without it the former is not faith, and in it alone it has its confirmation. Finally, when this faith came, fulness and the adoption of sons came with it, infirmity ceased, infancy was at an end, we grew into a perfect man, we put on Christ. How then can any one be weak or childish, in whom Christ is the power of God? Thus we have arrived at perfection, and have been instructed in its precepts.

TO HORONTIANUS

Wisd. iv. 9.

Gal. iii. 23.

Rom i. 17.

10. You heard read to-day, *Of Mine own Self I can do nothing, as I hear, I judge.* You heard read, *I accuse you not, I judge not.* I accuse you not, *it is Moses that accuseth you, in whom ye trust* You heard read, *If I bear witness of Myself, My witness is not true.* Thus I have learnt what kind of judge, what kind of witness I ought to be. For it is not as being weak that He says, *Of Mine own self I can do nothing*, he rather is weak who so understands it. The Father does nothing without the Son, for between them there is a community of operation and an unity of power; but in this place He speaks as Judge, that we men may learn that, when we judge, we ought to form our sentence equitably and not according to our mere will and power.

S. John v 30.

Ib 45.

Ib. 31.

11. When a criminal is set before him proved guilty and convicted of crime, who does not frame for himself pleas of defence, but prays for pardon, and prostrates himself at the knees of his judge, the judge answers him, Of myself I can do nothing, it is my justice not my power which I exercise in judgment. It is not I but your own deeds that judge you, they accuse, and they condemn you. The Laws are your tribunal, and I as judge do not alter but keep the

Laws. Of myself I originate nothing, but the judicial sentence against you proceeds from yourself. I judge as I hear, not as I will, and my judgment is true because I consult what is agreeable to equity not to my own will.

12. Let us next consider what is the Divine rule of judgment. The Lord of heaven and earth and the Judge of all says, *of Mine own self I can do nothing, as I hear I judge;* and man says to his Lord, *Knowest Thou not that I have power to crucify Thee, and have power to release Thee?* But why is not the Lord able? Because, He says, *My judgment is just, because I seek not Mine own will, but the will of the Father Who hath sent Me,* that is, not the will of man, whom ye see, not the will of man, whom ye only judge as man, not the will of the flesh, (for *the spirit is willing, but the flesh is weak,*) but the Divine will, which is the Origin of law, and the Rule of judgment. So likewise that witness is true, who bears witness not to himself but to another, for it is written, *Let another man praise thee, and not thine own mouth.*

13. In a mystical sense it is well said to the Jews: I judge you not, that is, I, the universal Saviour, I, who am the Remission of sins, judge you not, for ye have not received Me. I judge you not, I freely pardon you. I, who by My Blood redeem sinners, judge you not. I judge you not, for I would not the death but the life of a sinner. I judge you not, for I condemn not but justify those who confess their sins. Moses accuses you, he in whom you trust convicts you. He can accuse you, he cannot judge you, this is reserved to his Creator. He then in whom ye trust accuses you, He in Whom ye would not trust absolves you.

14. O great folly of the Jews! Rightly are they accused of their crimes, for they have chosen one who accuses them, and have rejected a merciful Judge; and therefore they are without absolution, but not without punishment.

15. Well therefore, my son, have you begun by the Law, and been confirmed in the Gospel, *from faith to faith, as it is written, The just shall live by faith.*

Farewell; love me for I also love you.

LETTER LXXVIII.

In this letter S. Ambrose shews, that we, like Abraham, are justified by faith, through which we are sons of the freewoman, that circumcision derived all its efficacy from Christ, and was abolished, after He had undergone it in His own person, by Him. Righteousness is therefore only to be looked for from faith, which if it be perfect, is never destitute of charity.

AMBROSE TO HORONTIANUS.

1. IF *Abraham believed God, and it was accounted unto him for righteousness*, and that which is accounted for righteousness passes from unbelief to faith, then are we justified by faith, not by the works of the Law. Now Abraham himself had two sons, Ishmael and Isaac, one of the bondwoman, the other of the freewoman; and it was told him that he should cast out the bondwoman and the son of the bondwoman, for that the son of the bondwoman should not be his heir. We therefore are children not of the bondwoman but of the free woman, in that liberty wherewith Christ has made us free. Hence it follows that they are specially Abraham's sons, who are so by faith, for the heirs of faith excel heirs by natural birth. The Law is our schoolmaster, faith is free; let us therefore cast away the works of bondage, let us preserve the grace of liberty, let us leave the shade, and follow the Sun, let us desert Jewish rites.

Gal. iii. 6.

Ib. iv. 22.

Ib. iii. 24.

2. The circumcision of one member is of no avail. For the Apostle says, *Behold I Paul say unto you, that if ye be circumcised Christ shall profit you nothing*, not because He cannot, but because He judges those unworthy of His benefits who desert His ways.

Ib. v. 2.

3. And Zipporah of old had circumcised her child, and driven off the danger which hung over him; but then Christ profited while perfection was still deferred. While the people of believers were small, the Lord Jesus came, not as small, but as perfect in all things. He was circumcised first, according to the Law, that He might not

Exod. iv. 25.

break the Law, afterwards by the Cross, that He might fulfil the Law. Thus that which is in part has ceased, because *that which is perfect has come*, for in Christ the Cross has circumcised not one member only, but the superfluous pleasures of the whole body.

4. But perhaps it may still be asked why He Who had come to declare to us perfect circumcision should choose to be circumcised in part. Concerning this however we need not deliberate long. For if He was made sin that He might expiate our sins, if He was made a curse for us that He might annul the curses of the Law, for the same reason He was also circumcised for us, that being about to bestow salvation by the Cross, He might abolish the circumcision of the Law.

5. The Apostle therefore declares that it is from faith that our hope of righteousness in the spirit is to be derived, and that though called to liberty we are not *to use our liberty for an occasion to the flesh. For neither circumcision availeth anything, nor uncircumcision; but faith which worketh by love.* And therefore it is written, *Thou shalt love the Lord thy God.* Now he who loves also believes, and in believing each man begins to love. Abraham believed, and so began to love, and he believed not in part, but entirely. For otherwise he would not have perfect charity, for it is written, *Charity believeth all things.* If it believe not all things, charity does not seem to be perfect. Perfect charity then has all faith.

6. But I would not lightly assert that all faith has immediately perfect charity, for the Apostle says, *Though I have all faith, so that I could remove mountains, and have not charity, I am nothing.* A Christian man has three principal virtues, *faith hope and charity, but the greatest of these is charity.*

7. On the other hand I conceive the Apostle was led to say this by the tenor of his argument, for I cannot see how *he who has all faith, so that he could remove mountains,* can be destitute of charity; nor how such can be the case with that man who *understands all mysteries and all knowledge;* especially as John says, *Whosoever believeth that Jesus is the Christ is born of God,* and the same Apostle

had said before, *Whosoever is born of God doth not commit sin.* Whence we infer that if he who believes that Jesus is the Christ is born of God, and he who is born of God sins not, then he who believes that Jesus is the Christ sins not. But if any man sin, he believes not, and he that believes not loves not, and he that loves not is subject to sin. So then he who sins loves not, *for charity shall cover the multitude of sins.* But if charity exclude the desire of sin, it excludes also fear, charity then is full of perfect faith. _{TO HORONTIANUS} _{1 S John iii 9.} _{1 S Pet. iv. 8.}

8. The Apostles too, who came to be His friends, said, *Increase our faith,* begging the good Physician to strengthen their failing faith. Their faith must indeed still have been weak, when even to Peter it could be said, *O thou of little faith, wherefore didst thou doubt?* Thus faith as the herald of charity preoccupies the mind, and prepares the ways of coming love. Thus where is the perfection of charity there is also all faith. _{S. Luke xvii 5.} _{S Matt. xiv. 31.}

9. For this reason I conceive it is said that *charity believeth all things,* that is, leads faith to believe them all, and that a soul of this kind possesses all faith; and hence wherever is perfect charity there is all faith. Moreover, as it believes all things so also it is said to *hope all things.* And it is on this account the greatest, because it includes the other two. _{1 Cor. xiii. 7.}

10. He that has this charity fears nothing, for charity *casteth out fear;* and fear being thus banished and thrown aside, charity *beareth all things, endureth all things.* He who by charity endures all things, cannot fear martyrdom; and so in another place he speaks as a conqueror at the end of his course, *The world is crucified unto me, and I unto the world.* _{1 S John iv 18.} _{1 Cor xiii. 7.} _{Gal. vi. 14.}

Farewell, my son; love me for I also love you.

LETTER LXXIX.

S. AMBROSE here assures Bellicius, whose recovery from sickness had occurred just at the time when he professed himself a believer in Christ, that both his sickness and recovery were to be ascribed to his so doing, and exhorts him to endeavour to keep Christ near him, and to prepare himself with all diligence for the other Sacraments.

AMBROSE TO BELLICIUS, GREETING.

1. You have sent me word that while you were lying afflicted by a severe sickness you believed in the Lord Jesus, and straightway began to recover. This sickness therefore was unto salvation, bringing greater pain than danger, for you had long deferred your promise. This is the meaning of the text, *I wound, and I heal.* He wounded by sickness, He healed by faith. For He saw that the inward affection of your mind was not without pious desires, but that they were shaken and unsettled by delays, and so He thought fit to admonish you, in a way which while it did not injure your health, excited your devotion.

Deut. xxxii. 39.

2. For how should He do an injury to health Who is wont to say, as we read in the Gospel, *I will come and heal him.* Being invited by your friends to visit your house He doubtless said, *I will come and heal him;* Although you heard Him not, He, as God, spoke to you imperceptibly, and although you saw Him not, still beyond doubt He visited you in spirit.

S Matt. viii. 7.

3. But in truth you have seen Him, for you have believed in Him, you have seen Him, for you have received Him into the dwelling of your mind, you have seen Him in the Spirit, you have seen Him with your inward eyes. Take care then not to let this new Guest depart, long expected, late received, even Him *in Whom we live and move and have our being.* You have tasted the first beginnings of faith, let not the word be hidden in your heart. Herein lies all grace and every gift. For no man judges of the secret recesses of a house by its entrance, since all the

Acts xvii. 28.

fruit is within; nor is it the part of a wise man to look from the window into the house, and it is folly for a man to listen at the door. TO BELLICIUS

4. The mysteries of the more perfect Sacraments are of one kind; for the Scripture says, *Eye hath not seen, nor ear heard, neither hath entered into the heart of man the things which God hath prepared for them that love Him.* Of another kind are the things which the prophets have announced concerning future glory, *unto whom it was revealed, and to whom the saints have preached the Gospel with the Holy Ghost sent down from heaven, which things the Angels desired to look into.* Of another kind again are those mysteries wherein is the redemption of the world, the remission of sins, the distribution of graces, the participation of the Sacraments: when you receive these you will wonder that a gift so transcendent should have been bestowed on man, as to make the manna which we wonder should have been rained down from heaven on the Jews seem to you to have possessed neither so much grace nor so much efficacy towards salvation. For all who received this manna in the wilderness died, save Joshua the son of Nun, and Caleb, whereas he who tastes this Sacrament shall never die.

1 Cor. ii. 9.
1 S. Pet. i. 12.
Exod. xvi. 15, 16.
Numb. xxvii. 12.

May the Lord Jesus send you restoration. Farewell.

LETTER LXXX.

S. AMBROSE here shews that the case of the man who was blind from his birth was the work of Divine power, and censures the question which the disciples asked about him; and dwells on some of the details of the miracle.

AMBROSE TO BELLICIUS.

1. You have heard, my brother, the lesson of the Gospel, wherein it is narrated that as *the Lord Jesus passed by He saw a man which was blind from his birth.* Now if the Lord saw him He did not pass him by, neither ought we to pass him by whom the Lord overlooked not; especially

S. John ix. 1.

LETT. 80. since he was blind from his birth, which is not mentioned without reason.

2. Now there is a blindness in which by the operation of illness the sight of the eyes is obscured, and this by the help of time is mitigated; there is a blindness also which is caused by the entrance of humours, and this, when the defect is removed, is cured by the aid of medicine; and this I say that you may know that it was not by skill but by Divine Power that he who was blind from his birth was healed. For the Lord gave him health as a free gift, not by any medicinal skill, for they whom the Lord Jesus healed were they whom no one could cure.

S John ix 2

Ib. 3

3. But how foolish was the inquiry of the Jews, *Who did sin this man or his parents?* ascribing bodily diseases to the score of sin. Wherefore the Lord said, *Neither hath this man sinned, nor his parents, but that the works of God should be made manifest in him.* That which nature created, the Creator, being the Author of nature, was capable of remedying. He added therefore, *As long as I am in the world I am the light of the world,* that is, all who are blind may see whether they need Me Who am the Light. *Approach ye, and be enlightened, that ye may see.*

Ib. 5

Ps. xxxiv. 5.

4. In the next place why did He Who restored life at command, Who gave health by His word, saying to the dead, *Come forth,* and Lazarus came forth from the grave, saying also to the sick of the palsy, *Arise and take up thy bed,* and the sick of the palsy rose and himself began to carry his bed, whereon, when all his limbs were paralyzed, he had been wont to be carried; why, I say, did He *spit on the ground and make clay, and anoint the eyes of the blind man, and say to him, Go, wash in in the pool of Siloam, which is by interpretation, Sent. He went his way therefore, and washed, and came seeing*—What is the reason of this? Great indeed is the reason, if I mistake not, for he who is taught by Jesus comes to see more clearly.

S John xi 43
S. Mark ii. 11.

S John ix. 6, 7.

5. Observe at the same time both His Divinity and His sanctity; as being Himself Light He touched and so communicated light to others; as being a Priest He fulfilled by the figure of Baptism the mysteries of spiritual grace. He spat, that you might learn that the inner parts

of Christ are light; and clearly indeed does he see who receives cleansing thereby. His spittle cleanses, and so does His discourse, as it is written, *Now ye are clean through the word which I have spoken unto you.* TO BELLICIUS
S. John xv. 3

6. But His making clay and anointing the eyes of the blind was intended to signify to us that the Same Who made man of clay, restored him to health by anointing with clay, and to signify also that this flesh of our clay must receive the light of eternal life by the Sacrament of Baptism. Do you also draw near to Siloam, that is, to Him Who was sent from the Father, as it is written, *My doctrine is not Mine, but His that sent Me.* Let Christ wash you that you may see. Come to Baptism, the time itself is at hand, make haste and come that you may say, *I went, and washed, and I received sight,* that you may also say, *whereas I was blind, now I see,* that you may say, as that man on whom light was poured said, *the night is far spent, the day is at hand.* Gen. ii. 7.
S. John vii. 16.
Ib. ix. 11.
Ib 25.
Rom. xiii 12.

7. The night was blindness. It was night when Judas received the sop from Jesus, and Satan entered into him. To Judas, in whom the Devil was, it was night; to John, who lay on the breast of Christ, it was day. To Peter also it was day, when he saw the light of Christ on the mount. To others it was night, but to Peter it was day. To Peter himself however it was night when he denied Christ. But the cock crowed, and he began to weep, that he might correct his error, for now the day was at hand.
S. John xiii. 27.
S Matt. xvii. 2.
Ib xxvi. 70.

8. The Jews enquired of the blind man, *How were thine eyes opened?* What signal folly! They enquired concerning what they saw; they enquired into the cause, seeing the effect.
S John ix. 10.

9. *Then they reviled him, and said, thou art His disciple.* Their curse is a blessing, for their blessing is a curse. *Thou,* they say, *art His disciple.* They confer a benefit, while they think they are doing an injury.
Ib. 28.

Farewell, my son; love me as you do, for I also love you.

LETTER LXXXI.

IN this letter S. Ambrose seeks to comfort some of his clergy, who were in despondency on account of their labours and difficulties, and sets before their eyes both the reward they may expect, and also the ready aid they will receive from Christ. He then presses upon them passages of Scripture applicable to their case, and exhorts them not to suffer themselves to be separated from Jesus their Saviour.

AMBROSE TO CERTAIN OF THE CLERGY.

1. IT is a fault which frequently besets the human mind, that, if things do not at once fall out according to their wishes, they lightly take offence, and desist from their duty. In other classes of men this is tolerable, but in those who are devoted to the Divine service it is a frequent cause of sorrow.

2. There are certain persons in the clerical function, into whose minds the Enemy, if he cannot otherwise deceive them, thus seeks to creep, that he may instil evil thoughts of the following kind; 'What does it avail me to remain among the clergy, to suffer injuries, to bear toil, as if my own farm could not support me, or, if I have no farm, as if I could not otherwise obtain support?' It is by such thoughts as these that even good dispositions are withdrawn from their duty, as if provision for his own sustenance was the only function of a cleric, and not rather to purchase for himself the Divine assistance after death. Whereas he only shall be rich after death, who on earth has had strength to contend unharmed against the wiles of his numerous adversaries.

3. It is said therefore in Ecclesiastes, *Two are better than one, because they have a good reward for their labour, For if they fall, the one will lift up his fellow.* Where are the two that are better than one, but where Christ is, and he whom Christ defends? For if he who is with the Lord Jesus falls, Jesus raises him up.

Eccles. iv 9.

4. But in what sense is it said, *for their labour?* Is Christ then weary[1]? Yes truly, for He says, *I am weary of crying.* He labours, but it is on us. Moreover after His toil He sat down wearied on the well; but what is the mode of His labours? The Apostle by his own humbler example has taught us in the words, *Who is weak, and I am not weak?* Our Lord Himself has also taught us in the words, *I was sick, and ye visited Me not, naked and ye clothed Me not.* He labours, in order to raise me in my falls.

TO CERTAIN OF THE CLERGY
[1] laborat. Ps. lxix. 3.
S. John iv. 6
2 Cor. xi. 29.
S. Matt. xxv. 43.

5. Hence in Elisha also our Lord is prefigured, for he stretched himself upon the dead child that he might raise him to life, and in this we have a symbol that Christ died with us, that He might rise again for us. Thus Christ placed Himself on the level even of our frailty, that He might raise us again. He did not fall, but of His own will cast Himself down, and in rising raised up His fellow. For He has taken us into fellowship with Himself, being anointed, as it is written, *with the oil of gladness above His fellows.*

2 Kings iv. 34.

Ps. xlv. 8.

6. Well says the Preacher, *If they fall, the One,* not being Himself lifted up, *will lift up his fellow;* for Christ needed not the assistance and aid of another to raise Him, but rose by His own power. Again, *Destroy,* He says, *this temple, and in three days I will raise it up. But this He said of the Temple of His Body.* And it is well that he who has not fallen should not be raised by another, for he who has been so raised must have fallen, and he who has fallen needs assistance that he may be raised. This is taught also by the words of Scripture which follows, *Woe to him that is alone when he falleth, for he hath not another to lift him up.* Again, *if two lie together, then they have heat.* For *we are dead with Christ, and therefore we also live with Him.* And Christ has thus died that He might give us warmth, as He has said, *I am come to send fire upon the earth.*

S. John ii. 19.

Eccles. iv. 10, 11.

Rom. vi. 8.

S. Luke xii 49.

7. I was dead, but because in Baptism I died together with Christ, I received the light of life from Christ. And he who dies in Christ, being warmed by Christ, receives the breath of life and resurrection. The boy was cold,

LETT. 81. Elisha warmed him with his breath, and imparted to him the warmth of life. He slept together with him that being thus buried with him in a figure the warmth of his rest might raise him up. He is cold then who dies not in Christ; he cannot be warmed to whom no burning fire is applied; he who has not Christ with him cannot grow warm by being near another.

8. And that you may understand it to be said as a mystery and not in reference to the bare number that *two are better than one,* he adds a mystical saying, *A threefold cord is not quickly broken.* For that which is threefold and uncompounded cannot be broken. Thus the Trinity, being of an uncompounded nature, cannot be dissolved; for God is, whatever He is, one and simple and uncompounded; and what He is that He continues to be, and is not brought into subjection.

Eccles. iv. 12

9. It is a good thing therefore to adhere closely to that other One, and to put your neck into His chain, and to bow down your shoulder and bear Him, and be not grieved with His bonds; because He went forth from the house of bondmen to assume His kingdom, that *Child who is better than an older and foolish king.* Wherefore they who follow Him are also bound with chains. Paul too is *the prisoner of Jesus Christ.* And Jesus Himself *led captivity captive.* He thought it not enough to destroy that captivity which the devil had imposed, so that he might not again assault those who were wandering at large. But to dwell in subjection to Christ, putting your feet into the fetters of wisdom, and becoming His captive that you may be free from the adversary, this is what He accounted perfect liberty.

Ib. 13.

Eph. iii. 1.
Ps. lxvii. 18.
Eph. iv. 8.

10. Rightly is He called a *Child,* for *unto us a Child is born,* and truly a good Child to Whom it has been said by God the Father, *It is a light thing that Thou shouldst be My Servant;* wise also, as the gospel teaches us, for He *increased in wisdom and stature;* and properly called poor, for, *though He was rich, for our sakes He became poor, that we through His poverty might be rich.* Wherefore in His kingdom He does not despise the poor man, but listens to him and frees him from all straits and troubles.

Is. ix. 6

Ib. xlix 6. puer, Vulg
S. Luke ii 52.
2 Cor. viii. 9.

11. Let us then live in obedience to Him, that that *old and foolish king* may have no power over us. For he, desiring to reign and be supreme after his own will, and not to be under subjection to the Lord Jesus, grows old in sin, and falls into the deformity of folly. For what can be more foolish than for a man to relinquish heavenly and apply himself to earthly things, for him to neglect what is eternal, and to choose the frail and perishing?

12. Let no one then say, *We have no portion in Jacob nor inheritance in Israel.* Let no one say, I am not among the Clergy, for it is written, *Give unto Levi his lots* [1]; and again David says that he who *lieth in the midst among the lots* ascends to heaven with spiritual wings. Say not of your God, *He is grievous to us,* nor of your place, it *is not for our turn,* since Scripture says, *Leave not thy place:* For the adversary would fain deprive thee of it, he would fain drive thee away, for he envies thee thy hopes and thy function.

<small>TO MARCELLUS</small>

<small>1 Kings xii. 16.</small>
<small>Deut. xxxiii. 8. 1 cleros.</small>
<small>Ps. lxviii. 13. Vulg. Wisd. ii. 15. Ib v. 12. Eccles. x. 4.</small>

13. But thou that art in the lot of the Lord, His portion and possession, depart not therefrom, that thou mayest say to Him, *For Thou hast possessed my reins, Thou hast covered me in my mother's womb;* and that He may say to thee, as to a good servant, *Go, and sit down to meat.*

Farewell, my sons: serve the Lord, for the Lord is good.

<small>Ps. cxxxix. 13.</small>
<small>S. Luke xvii. 7.</small>

LETTER LXXXII.

S. AMBROSE tells Marcellus that he has been appointed to decide the case in which he and his brother Lætus and their sister were concerned, and why he undertook rather to act as arbiter than as judge in it. He urges Marcellus to submit willingly to his loss, praising him at the same time for having himself offered so equitable an adjustment of the matter, and tells him why he has nevertheless made some change in the settlement, and ends by shewing how the success gained by the several parties has been without general detriment to the Church.

AMBROSE TO MARCELLUS.

1. THE law suit which you did not indeed institute of your own accord, but took up when begun by others, the

LETT. 82. obligations of piety and a desire of approving your bounty towards the poor leading you thereto, has in the course of its adjudication devolved into my hands. I took cognisance of it by the tenor of the Imperial enactment, and both the authority committed to me by the blessed Apostle and the form and character of your own life and conduct have laid this upon me. Having myself censured the keeping alive amongst you your ancient animosity, I found myself obliged by the parties to hear their cause.

2. I blushed to refuse, I must confess, particularly since the advocates of either party recriminated on each other, asserting that my investigation would make manifest to whose side the suffrages of right and justice would incline. Why need I say more? When the days were almost concluded, and only a few hours remained, in which the Prefect was hearing other business; the advocates in the suit requested that it should be adjourned for a few days, that I might preside as judge. So much zeal was shewn by Christians to prevent the Prefect from interfering with the jurisdiction of the Bishop. They stated moreover that certain matters had been conducted in an unseemly manner, and each party, according to his own inclination, brought forward points as proper to be heard by the Bishop rather than the Prefect.

3. Overcome by these reasons, reminded also of the Apostolical precept, which reproves Christians, saying, *Do not ye judge them that are within?* and again, *If then ye have judgments of things pertaining to this life, set them to judge who are least esteemed in the Church. I speak to your shame. Is it so that there is not a wise man among you, no, not one that shall be able to judge between his brethren? But brother goeth to law with his brother, and that before unbelievers,* I accepted the hearing of the cause, on condition however that I should settle the terms of the compromise. For I saw that, if I decreed in your favour, the other party might not acquiesce; while, if the sentence were given for him, you and your holy sister would abandon your defence. And thus there would have been an unequal rule of decision. Suspicion might also have attached in their eyes to the influence which the

1 Cor. v. 12.
Ib vi. 4—6

sacerdotal relation would exercise over my mind. For when does the defeated party consider the others to have greater equity than himself? And truly, the expenses of this old-standing contest would have been intolerable to both parties, had its termination been without fruit, or without, at least, the solace of munificence.

4. Since, therefore, I perceived that the issue was doubtful, the law disputed, the pleas on both sides numerous, and that petitions to the emperor of an invidious character were being prepared [a] which contained charges of tampering with his decrees, perceiving also that in case of his being victorious he would rigorously sue for double the mesne profits, and for the costs of this protracted suit; while it was unbecoming your office to demand the expenses of the cause, and not competent for you to claim any of those profits which as possessor you had received, I preferred settling the dispute by a compromise to any aggravation of it by a decree. For there were other disputes liable to be raised, and what was still more grievous, although these disputes might be removed, hatreds would remain which are detrimental to feelings of good will.

5. Involved in these difficulties, and feeling that the office of the priest, the sex of the woman and the gravity of her widowed state, and regard for my friend appealed to me with a threefold and weighty claim, I thought that my course of conduct should be to desire no one's defeat, but the success of all. Nor was my intention baffled; you have all overcome, as regards kindred, as regards nature, as regards Scripture which says, *Why do ye not rather take wrong, why do ye not rather suffer yourselves to be defrauded?* 1 Cor. vi. 7.

6. But perhaps you deem yourself aggrieved by the unfavourable issue of the suit, and by your pecuniary losses. Better surely for priests are the losses than the gains of the world; For *it is more blessed to give than to receive.* Acts xx. 35. But perhaps you will say, I ought not to have been exposed to fraud, to have suffered injury, to undergo loss. What then? Would you have inflicted these things? But although you did not do so, he would have complained of

---

[a] It seems necessary to the sense here to insert 'quae' before 'obtexerent.'

suffering them. Consider therefore what the Apostle says, *Why do ye not rather suffer yourselves to be defrauded?* So one may almost say that he who suffers not a wrong, inflicts it, for he who is the stronger ought to be the one to bear it.

7. But why do I treat with you as if this was my concern rather than your own? For in order to compound the quarrel you offered that for the time of her life your sister should possess part of the farm, but that after her death all the property should be ceded to your brother, and that no one shonld sue him either in your name or in that of the Church; but that, if he chose, he should hold it without being called on to dispense any portion to the Church. When I had declared this, and extolled the great grace of munificence which had thus been implanted in your mind, your brother replied that such an arrangement would be pleasing to him if all fear of injury to the property were removed. For how, he asked, could a woman, who was a widow besides, manage a property liable to tribute? How could it profit him, your yielding up to him your right of possession, if he supposed that greater losses would accrue to him from the bad cultivation of the land?

8. The advocates on either side were influenced by these considerations. Wherefore, with the consent of all, it was determined that the honourable [b] Lætus should undertake the farm, and should pay yearly to your sister a certain quantity of corn wine and oil. By this means your holy sister was relieved from anxiety, not deprived of her rights; she relinquished, not the fruits but the labour, not the revenues, but the hazard as it is often called of an uncertain return of them. If violent storms of wind should destroy the harvest, your sister will still retain undiminished the fruits of the seed-time. Lætus will ascribe to himself the unfavourable conditions of the arrangment, and should the pressure of necessity from time to time and of extraordinary imposts become severe, your sister will stand clear both of Lætus' loss and of receiving benefits from you;

---

[b] v. c. here is an abbreviation for vir clarissimus, a title of official rank. see note in p 101

while Lætus will console himself with the proprietorship of the estate.

9. Thus all have gained their point: Lætus, because he obtained the right over the property, which he had not before; your sister, because she will now enjoy the annual profits without dispute or strife; no one, however, will have gained so complete and glorious a victory as yourself, for together with the fulfilment of your bountiful dispositions towards your sister, you have rendered her partner of your fraternal union. For you have conceded, to your brother the property, to your sister the usufruct. But as regards the Church, nothing is lost to her which is gained to piety; for charity is no loss but a gain to Christ, charity also is the fruit of the Holy Spirit. And thus the cause has been concluded according to the Apostolic model. We used to grieve that you were at strife, but your strife has been profitable, because it has led you to put on the form of the Apostolical life and discipline. Your strife was unbecoming the priesthood, but this transaction befits even the Apostolic rule.

10. And fear not that the Church should be placed out of the range of your bounty. She also partakes of your fruits, fruits even more plentiful, for she enjoys the fruit of your teaching, the service of your life, she has that fertility which you have watered by your discipline. Rich in these profits she seeks not temporal things, for she is in possession of what is eternal. But you have added not only Apostolical but also Evangelical fruits, for the Lord has said, *Make to yourselves friends of the Mammon of unrighteousness.* You also have made to yourself friends, and, what is remarkable, from those who were at variance with you. You have made brethren return under the laws of kindred, you have assured then by this charity and this grace that they shall be received into eternal habitations.

11. Thus, under the guidance of Christ, and the directions of two priests, yourself, that is, who gave the first outline, and myself who gave the sentence, the peace which we have made will not fail; for there have been so many concurrent voices in favour of fidelity, that perfidy cannot be without punishment.

12. Lætus will now plough for his sister, whereas before he grudged her the services of others; Lætus will now gather the harvest for his sister, though he could not before endure the gifts of others; he will bear the fruits to the granaries of his sister, and this he shall do gladly[1], in renewed accordance with the proper signification of his name.

13. You meanwhile, being conformed to the image of the Apostle of Christ, and assuming the prophetic authority, shall say unto the Lord, *Thou hast possessed my reins.* This possession better becomes Christ, that He may possess the virtues of His priest, that He may receive those fruits which belong to integrity and continence, and what is more, to charity and tranquillity.

Farewell; love me, for I also love you.

[1] lætus.

Ps. cxxxix. 13.

LETTER LXXXIII.

IN this letter S. Ambrose praises Sisinnius for forgiving his son, who had married without his leave, and compares him with some of the Saints of the Old Testament, and with the father in the parable of the prodigal son.

AMBROSE TO SISINNIUS.

1. YOUR forgiving our son at my request for having married a wife without your knowledge I attribute to your natural affection rather than to your regard for me; for it is better that natural affection should have gained this from you than any one's request. Assuredly it is in the triumph of virtue that the priest's petition has its chief success, for he then obtains most when virtue is powerful, his petition must always coincide with the dictates of natural affection. And nature and your son obtained the more fully their request, in that the consideration of requests is usually a brief matter, whereas the habit of virtue is lasting and natural affection permanent.

2. It was indeed worthily done to recognize yourself to be a father, particularly since your cause for indignation was a just one; for I prefer to admit the fault, so that your fatherly indulgence may gain higher praise; for it was as

a father that you were offended; since you had a claim to exercise the choice of your judgment as to one to whom you were to become a father, and who was to be to you in the place of a daughter. For we obtain children either by nature or adoption; in nature it is a matter of chance; in adoption, of judgment; and we are more liable to blame in the case of our adopted than of our natural offspring; because it is ascribed to nature if our children by birth should happen to be degenerate, but that those who become ours by adoption or other such tie should prove unworthy of it is ascribed to our own mistake. You had therefore cause of displeasure against your son in this his choice of a wife to himself; you have also reason for forgiving him. For you have obtained a daughter for yourself without the danger of making a selection for yourself; if he has married well, he has obtained for you this advantage; if he has been deceived, you will make them better by receiving them into favour, but worse by disowning them.

3. It is with riper judgment that a father chooses a bride for his son, but when she is brought by the son to his father, when she enters her father-in-law's roof as the chosen of her husband, their purpose of obedience is stronger, the son fearing lest his election should be disapproved, the daughter-in-law that her attentions may not be acceptable. While the distinction of the paternal choice elevates the one, the other is humbled by the fear of giving offence and bowed down by modesty. The son will not be able to throw blame on the wife, as if he himself were not answerable for any of those causes of offence which are wont to occur; on the contrary he will strive more diligently to obtain approbation of his judgment in regard of his wife, of his obedience in regard of himself.

4. You have therefore acted the part of a good parent and pardoned readily, but still upon supplication; before this was made, you would have been not pardoning but sanctioning. When this was done, to defer pardon any longer would have been unprofitable to them and very painful to yourself, for your paternal affection could no longer have held out.

Lett. 83.
Gen. xxii 6.

5. Determined by motives of high devotion, Abraham, obeying the oracle of God, offered his son for a whole burnt sacrifice; and, as if destitute of natural affection, drew his sword, that no delay might obscure the brightness of the offering. But when he was commanded to spare his son he willingly sheathed his sword, and he who with this faithful intention was hastening to offer up his only son with still more zealous piety hastened to substitute a ram as a sacrifice.

Ib. xliv. 15.

7. Joseph also, in order to get his younger brother to him, feigned anger against his brethren on the plea that they had concerted an act of fraud. But when Judah, one of his brethren, fell at his feet, while the others wept, he was moved and overcome by fraternal affection and was no longer able to maintain his assumed severity, but sending away all witnesses he told them they were his brethren, and he that very Joseph whom they had sold. He added that he remembered not his own wrong, making brotherly excuses for the malice of their betrayal of him, and referring what was so blameworthy to higher and deeper causes; forasmuch as by the providence of God it must needs so have been, to the end that by passing over into Egypt he might supply his kindred's need of provisions from another country, and in the time of dearth assist in supporting his father and his father's sons.

2 Sam. xiv. 22.

8. And what shall I say of holy David, who at the petition of one woman suffered his mind to be softened, and with paternal compassion received into his house his degenerate son, stained with his brother's blood?

S. Luke xv. 22.

9. So that father in the Gospel, when the younger son had spent all the substance he had received from his father by riotous living, yet when he returned confessing that he had sinned against him, moved by the humility of a single sentence, gave him an affectionate greeting, fell upon his neck, commanded the best robe and a ring and shoes to be brought forth, and having thus honoured him with a kiss, and loaded him with gifts, entertained him with a sumptuous banquet.

10. You have become an imitator of these by that parental affection whereby we approach nearest to the Divine

likeness, and therefore I have exhorted our daughter that, though it be winter, she should undertake the toil of the journey, for that she will pass the winter more commodiously not only in the mansion, but also in the bosom of her father, now that wrath has given place to pardon. Moreover, that you may fully assimilate yourself to the likeness and pattern of the saints, you have accused those who by concocted falsehoods endeavoured to excite your mind against your son.

Farewell; love me, for I also love you.

LETTER LXXXIV.

A BRIEF letter of assent and approval

AMBROSE TO CYNEGIUS.

1. How ingenuous is the modesty with which you have commended yourself, in that you have consulted me concerning a matter which you did not approve, out of deference to your father that you might not injure piety, feeling safe that no reply could be made by me which was unbeseeming holy relationships.

2. But I have willingly taken upon me your burdens, and have reconciled, I hope, the niece to her uncle. Truly I am ignorant with what view he desired that she should become his daughter-in-law, changing his own character of uncle for that of father-in-law. I need not add more, lest this also should be a cause of confusion.

Farewell my son, and love us, for we also love you.

LETTER LXXXV.

S. AMBROSE thanks Siricius for sending him letters by the Presbyter Syrus, whose speedy return he promises.

AMBROSE TO SIRICIUS.

1. I AM always pleased to receive a letter from you, but when you also send to me some of our fellow servants, as

LETT. 86. you have now given our brother and co-presbyter Syrus a letter to me, my joy is doubled. I would however that this pleasure had been more lasting; for as soon as he had arrived he thought he must return, and this diminished my regret and added greatly to my estimation of him.

2. For I love those presbyters and deacons who when they have performed their mission will not allow themselves to remain absent any longer from their duties. For the prophet says, *I have not been weary in following thee.* And who can be weary in following Jesus, when He Himself says, *Come unto Me all ye that labour, and are heavy laden, and I will give you rest.* Let us therefore never cease from following Jesus, which if we do we shall never fail, for He gives strength to them that follow Him. The more nearly you approach to the Source of power the stronger you will be.

<small>Jer. xvii. 16.</small>
<small>S. Matt. xi. 28.</small>

3. Often, while we are thus following Him, the adversaries say to us, *Where is the word of the Lord? let it come now.* But let us not grow weary in following Him, let us not be turned aside by meeting with this crafty question. It was said to the prophet, when he was thrown into prison, when he was cast into the pit of mire, *Where is the word of the Lord? let it come now.* But he followed him so much the more, and therefore attained the prize, and received the crown; for following Jesus he was not weary; for *there is no weariness in Jacob, neither shall sorrow be in Israel.*

<small>Jer. xvii. 15.</small>
<small>Numb. xxiii. 21.</small>

Farewell; love me, for I love one who loves me, and whom I regard as a father.

LETTER LXXXVI.

S. AMBROSE speaks briefly in praise of Priscus

AMBROSE TO SIRICIUS.

1. WHEN Priscus, my friend and co-equal in age, was coming here, you gave him a letter to me, and now that

he is returning I give him the reply which I send both to duty and affection. By this service he has recompensed us both, for he has given me yours, and you mine, and therefore ought to reap the reward of this his service by an increase of favour.

Farewell, my brother; love me, for I love you.

TO SEGATIUS AND DELPHINUS

LETTER LXXXVII.

A LETTER of commendation.

AMBROSE TO BISHOPS SEGATIUS AND DELPHINUS.

1. My son Polybius, on his return from Africa, where he discharged the duties of the proconsulship with credit, passed some days with us, and inspired my heart with singular affection towards him.

2. Then, when he wished to go from hence, he requested me to write to both of you. I promised to do so, and having dictated a letter delivered it to him superscribed with both your names. He asked for another; but I said that I had directed this to both of you according to our custom and usage, forasmuch as your holy minds are gratified not by the number of letters but by the association of names, and that, united as you were in feeling, you would not allow yourselves to be separated in name; farther, that to employ this compendious form of love was a prescribed part of my duty.

3. Why need I say more? He asked for another, and I gave it, but so as neither to deny him what he asked, nor to change my accustomed mode of action. Thus he has a letter to deliver to each of you, for this was all he put forward, his having nothing for one, when he had delivered his letter to the other. And this office of undivided affection I may render to you without any danger of offence, or thought of division; especially since this form of writing is Apostolical, so that either one may write to many as Paul to the Galatians, or two to one, as we read, *Paul a* Philem i. 1.

Lett. 88. *prisoner of Jesus Christ, and Timothy our brother, unto Philemon.*

Health to you; love me and pray for me, for I love you.

LETTER LXXXVIII.

A FRIENDLY letter of commendation of Priscus.

AMBROSE TO ATTICUS.

1. You entrusted my friend Priscus with a letter, which he delivered to me, and I now give mine in turn to Priscus. Continue to love Priscus, as you do, and even more than before; this I advise, because I also value my Priscus highly. For I feel towards him that ancient love, which from our childhood upwards has grown together with our years; but it is long since I saw him before, so that not only in name but from so long an interval of time he came to me as truly Priscus.

Farewell: love me your lover, for I also love you.

LETTER LXXXIX.

A BRIEF acknowledgement of letters.

AMBROSE TO ALYPIUS.

1. Antiochus, a man of consular rank, delivered to me your Excellency's letter; nor did I neglect to reply to it; for I sent you a letter by my own messenger, and another occasion having offered, I sent, if I mistake not, a second. But since the offices of friendship are rather, I think, to be added to than balanced; it became my duty, especially on his return who had laid upon me such a debt of obligation by your letters, to make some return in the way of my own correspondence, that so I might stand clear with both of you, and he with you, bound as he was to bring you back what he had brought from you.

Farewell; love me, who love you.

LETTER XC.

S. AMBROSE dwells on the mutual love of himself and Antonius.

AMBROSE TO ANTONIUS.

1. You never are silent in regard of me, nor ought I ever to complain of being neglected by your silence, knowing that I am not absent from your thoughts. For since you bestow that which is the most precious, how can you withhold that which many others receive, not so much from any habitual affection as from an interchange of civility.

2. And even from my own feelings I can judge in turn of yours, and these lead me to believe that I am never absent from you, nor you from me, so closely are our souls united. Nor do I feel as if we ever required each others' letters, for I daily converse with you as if present in body, turning towards you my eyes, my affections, and all my regards.

3. In such things as these I delight to cope with you; for, to speak openly with one who is inseparable from my heart, your letters make me ashamed. I beg therefore that you will cease to be always returning me thanks, for my services to you have their highest reward, if I may believe I have not been wanting in my duty towards you.

Farewell; love me, for I also love you.

LETTER XCI.

A GRACEFUL letter of affection.

AMBROSE TO HIS BROTHER CANDIDIANUS.

1. GREAT is the beauty of your language, but that of your love is still more apparent, for your letters manifest to me the bright colours of your mind, blessed and most dear brother. The Lord give you His Grace and Blessing,

Ep. 5. for in your letters I recognize your good wishes rather than my good deserts. For what merits of mine can equal such commendations as yours?
Love me, my brother, for I love you.

A.D. 380.

EPISTOLA V.

(See page 19.)

SENTENTIAM abs se in causa Indiciæ latam defendens, Syagrii judicium arguit, quod legitima in eo forma non servata sit. Maximum tragœdiæ auctorem apud se non comparuisse: Syagrium inspectionem virgini contumeliosissimam decrevisse, cum alia, unde judicari virgo debeat, suppetant: inspectionem incertam atque inutilem, aliud enim obstetricum officium esse; non ergo hac ratione causam decidendam; præsertim cum peperisse diceretur Indicia. In quibus inspectio sit toleranda. Syagrium vanam afferre excusationem: Maximum vere accusatorem esse. Postremo accusatione ac testibus rursus vituperatis, refertur Marcellinæ aliarumque pro Indicia testimonium, post quod judicium Ambrosianum subjicitur.

AMBROSIUS SYAGRIO.

PROSPICIENDUM esse ne de nostro obloquantur judicio carissimi nostri Veronenses, propriis texuisti litteris. Non arbitror fore, certe non solent. Aut si obloquantur, de quo obloqui soleant haud dubie liquet: cum exasperati huc veniant, pacifici ad te revertantur; præsertim cum hoc judicium nostrum cum fratribus et consacerdotibus nostris participatum processerit: tu autem sine alicujus fratris consilio hoc judicium tibi solus vindicandum putaris; in quo tamen ante judicium præjudicium feceris, ut puellam Zenonis sanctæ memoriæ judicio probatam, ejusque sanctificatam benedictione, post tot annos, sine auctore criminationis, sine accusatore, sine professore delationis, in periculum reatus deducendam arbitrare : cui invidia esset a vanis, ab hæreticis, ut ipsi volunt, a turpibus personis conflata per scelus, per avaritiam, per intemperantiam, quærentibus proprii libertatem flagitii; ab iis postremo qui domo ejus ejecti atque eliminati forent, quod discolora opera subtexerent, quam prima fronte suæ professionis prætenderant.

SYAGRIO

2. Hujusmodi accusatores, hujusmodi testes in tuo constituebas judicio, qui neque accusare audebant, neque delationis se nexu obligare; atque ita inspectioni adjudicandam constituebas virginem, quam nullus argueret, nullus deferret. Ubi hæc cognitionis solemnitas ? Ubi talis judicandi formula? Si leges publicas interrogamus, accusatorem exigunt : si Ecclesiæ ; *Duobus*, inquit, *et tribus testibus stat omne verbum* · sed illis testibus qui ante hesternum et nudiustertius non fuerint inimici; ne irati nocere cupiant, ne læsi ulcisci sese velint.

S. Matt. xviii. 16.

3. Inoffensus igitur affectus testium quæritur; ita tamen ut accusator prius in medium procedat. Ipsi illi presbyteri Judæorum manus suas prius supra caput imposuerunt Susannæ, et accusationem professi sunt, et pariter addiderunt testimonii auctoritatem, quam imprudenter populus sub errore positus acceperat: sed divino judicio per prophetam retexit et redarguit omnipotens Deus; ut liqueret omnibus eos velle invidiam præseminare adversum innocentis periculum, qui deficerent accusationis argumento, et firmamento probationis, conjicientes videlicet quod si præoccupatis vulgi auribus invidia mentem incesseret, præjudicium examinandæ veritatis inferret. Etenim cum audita præveniunt, aurem obstruunt, animum occupant; ne probatio desideretur, ut rumor pro convicto teneatur crimine.

Hist of Sus. 34 sqq.

4. Nos igitur accusatorem exegimus, et auctorem totius scenæ Maximum perurgendum arbitrati sumus. Verum ille accusationem, quam studio informaverat, verbo detulerat, deseruit professione , et tamen affectu urgebat, arte exsequebatur, sed fugiebat nomine, quod diffideret probationi. Denique sparsis rumoribus, sed etiam epistolis compositis et destinatis, quæsivit acerbare invidiam delationis : sed nequaquam opprimi potuit integritas et circum-

veniri. Nam si habuisset probationes, numquam inspectionem tua sententia flagitavisset.

5. Quid igitur sibi velit, et quo spectet quod obstetricem adhibendam credideris, non possum advertere. Itane ergo liberum erit accusare omnibus, et, cum probatione destiterint, patebit ut genitalium secretorum petant inspectionem, et addicentur semper sacræ virgines ad hujusmodi ludibria, quæ et visu et auditu horrori et pudori sunt? Denique non minima etiam in tuis litteris tentatæ expressionis verecundia est. Quæ ergo sine damno pudoris in alienis auribus resonare non queunt, ea possunt in virgine sine ejus tentari verecundia?

6. Invenisti tibi vile mancipium, procacem vernulam, cur non abutaris pudibundo ministerio, et exponas ejus modestiam; cum præsertim nihil sanctius in virgine sit, quam verecundia? Non enim sacra virgo ut corpore tantummodo integra sit quæritur, et non ut in omnibus ejus inoffensus maneat pudor. Virgo Domini suis est nixa fulcris ad sui probationem, nec alienis dotibus eget; ut se virginem probet: et nec abditorum occultorumque inspectio, sed obvia omnibus modestia adstipulatur integritati. Non placet Deo, quam non suorum gravitas morum probat: non probatur Domino, quæ unius obstetricis indiget testimonio, quod plerumque quæritur pretio. Ea ergo tibi locuples videtur ad fidem, quæ et redimi et falli potest; ut excuset ream, et crimen tegat, aut nesciat, et non possit flagitium deprehendere?

7. Neque vero illud justum arbitror, quod tuis comprehendisti litteris, quia nisi inspecta fuerit, integritas periclitetur, et incerto sui fluctuet. Ergo omnes quæ inspectæ non sunt, periculum subierunt pudoris? Ergo et quæ nupturæ sunt, prius inspiciantur, ut nubant probatiores? Ergo et quæ velandæ sunt, prius subjiciendæ sunt hujusmodi adtrectationi; non enim visitantur, sed adtrectantur: et rectius secundum tuam sententiam inspicitur non probata, quam consecrata.

8. Quid, quod etiam ipsi archiatri dicunt non satis liquido comprehendi inspectionis fidem, et ipsis medicinæ vetustis doctoribus id sententiæ fuisse? Nos quoque usu hoc cognovimus, sæpe inter obstetrices obortam varietatem,

et quæstionem excitatam; ut plus dubitatum sit de ea, quæ SYAGRIO. inspiciendam se præbuerit, quam de ea quæ non fuerit inspecta. Siquidem et proximo id comperimus exemplo: nam quædam conditionis servilis Altini inspecta et refutata, postea Mediolani non meo quidem jussu, sed Nicenti ex tribuno et notario domini vel patroni sui voluntate visitata est a peritissima et locupleti femina hujusmodi artis; et cum simul ista suppeterent, ut neque paupertas obstetricis suspectam faceret fidem, neque indocilitas imperitiam, tamen adhuc manet quæstio.

9. Quid profuit igitur eam inspici, cum damnatio maneat? Nam ut quisque voluerit, aut imperitam medicam, aut redemptam asseret; ita sine effectu ullo injuria inspectionis est. Quid deinde fiet? Quotiescumque emerserit, qui non credat, toties virgo adtrectabitur? Nam si umquam se visitandam abnuerit, secundum adsertionem tuam de crimine confitebitur. Et facilius est ut refutet, quod numquam fecerit, quam quod fecerit. Variabuntur igitur obstetrices, ne suspectæ aliqua repetatur gratiæ. Erit itaque inter plures, quamquam paucarum etiam in magnis urbibus hic usus medendi sit, erit, inquam, vel malevola, vel imperita, quam pudoris claustra prætereant, et per imperitiam integro notam affigat pudori. Vides in quod periculum inducas virginalem professionem, dum obstetricem adhibendam putas; ut jam non solum verecundiæ suæ dispendio, sed etiam obstetricis incerto periclitetur.

10. Nunc consideremus quod obstetricis officium sit. Legimus etiam in veteri Testamento obstetrices, sed non inspectrices; denique ad parturientes ingrediebantur, non ad virgines; ut partus susciperent, non ut pudorem examinarent. Unde et obstetrices dictæ, eo quod obsistant dolori, vel certe pignori, ne laxatis uteri genitalibus claustris, in terram defluat. Secundo et tertio loco in Scripturis invenimus obstetrices adhibitas: sed ubique partui, nusquam inspectioni. Primo ubi Rachel parturit, deinde Gen. ubi Thamar parit, tertio ubi necandos mares Pharao mandat xxxv. 17. Hebræorum obstetricibus; quando responderunt illæ, non Ib. xxxviii. eo more Hebræas feminas parere, quo pariunt Ægyptiæ: 27. sed Hebræas prius parere, quam introeant obstetrices ad Ex. i. 15 sqq. eas. Qui locus ut superiori utilis ad Hebræorum salu-

Ep. 5. tem; ita reliquo confragosus ad obstetricum fidem, quæ didicerunt mentiri pro salute, et fallere pro excusatione.

11. Quid igitur suspecta et dubia captamus; cum majora sint alia examinandæ veritatis documenta et testimonia, in quibus expressiora insignia vel temerati pudoris sint? Quid enim est quod magis publicum sit, quam offensa pudoris, et defloratio virginitatis? Nihil profecto quod magis se prodat, quam castitatis dispendium. Tumescit alvus, et incedentem fœtus sui onera gravant; ut prætermittamus alia, quibus se vel tacita prodit conscientia.

12. At forte sterilitatis obtentu abscondi in aliquibus possit flagitium. Hic vero cum editus partus et expositus, vel necatus, (dum invidiæ magis, quam probationi consulitur,) dissipatus sit per aures universorum, strangulata est libertas calumniarum, si peperit. Nempe Veronæ fuit, visebatur frequenter a virginibus et mulieribus; in honore enim semper erat. Visebatur et a sacerdotibus propter pudicitiæ reverentiam, et gravitatis speculum. Quomodo ergo potuit occulere crimen, quod se vel specie sui proderet? Quomodo texit uterum? Quomodo non refugit adspectum mulierum, oculos salutantium? Quomodo parturiens vocem repressit? Sed hoc non patitur dolor: denique Scriptura hos maximos dicit dolores, qui sunt parturientis. Sic enim inquit, Dies Domini subito venit, et improvisus adest, ut dolor partus, qui intercludit omnia effugia delitescendi.

Gen. iii. 16.

Isa. xiii. 8, 9.

13. Hæc est verior documentorum fides, quam erubescunt et mulieres. Denique Elizabeth occultabat se mensibus quinque; eo quod sterilis conceperat in senectute. His signis et ipsa Mariæ virginitas apud ignaros mysterii probri suspectabatur. Unde et Joseph, cui desponsata erat Virgo, suspectum habebat vitium, dum adhuc nesciret Dominicæ incarnationis sacramentum.

S. Luke i. 24.

S. Matt. i. 18.

14. Quid ergo, negamus inspiciendas virgines? Interim quod nusquam legerim, non adstruo, nec verum arbitror. Sed quia pleraque ad speciem facimus, non ad veritatem; et erroris gratia complura frequenter prætendimus, (sunt enim qui nesciant recte facere, nisi metu pœnæ,) relinquamus hoc illis, quas non verecundia revocat a lapsu, sed solus injuriæ deterret metus: apud quas nulla cura pudoris et castitatis gratia, sed pœnæ timor est. Relinquamus

vernaculis, quibus formido est deprehendi magis, quam SYAGRIO.
peccasse. Absit a virgine sacra, ut obstetricem noverit:
partus putatur, et remedium doloris ducitur, non examen
pudoris. Relinquamus etiam illis, si quæ gravibus appetitæ calumniis, oppressæ testimoniis, strangulatæ argumentis, ad id confugiant, ut se offerant inspectioni, quo vel
corporis probetur custodia; si tamen deprehendi potest,
in quibus nutat pudoris gratia, et disciplina integritatis.
Male tamen se habet causa, ubi potior est carnis quam
mentis prærogativa. Malo morum signaculo, quam corporis claustro virginitatem exprimi.

15. Jam illud præclarum, quod scripsisti insinuatum tibi
a quibusdam quod nequaquam tibi communicarent, si eam
sine visitatione suscipiendam crederes. Ergo judicandi
accepisti formulam. Quales illi, qui volunt præscribere
sacerdotibus quid sequi debeamus? Liberavimus itaque
te a cognitionis gravissimæ necessitate, ne necesse haberes
formulam mandatam exsequi. Quid nobis futurum est,
qui eorum studiis non obtemperavimus?

16. Sed tamen scio illic plerosque esse, qui timeant
Dominum. Nam et hic vidimus dudum, et illic esse comperimus, qui compositam hanc querantur calumniam: quos
aiunt eo offensos favisse Maximo, quod ista virgo non circumeat domos, nec eorum matronas salutet atque ambiat.
Quid igitur fiet, quomodo tanto eam exuemus crimine?
quomodo persuadebimus ut cultus adsumat novos, suos
exuat? Grave flagitium virginem intra secreta domus degere, claudi penetralibus suis! Sic certe lectio docet Mariam
domi repertam, cum ad eam Gabriel Archangelus venisset. S. Luke
Susanna fugiens turbarum inducitur. Denique cum se lava- i. 28.
ret, paradisum claudi jubebat. Quid autem præstantius, Sus. 15
(præsertim in virgine, cujus præcipuum opus verecundia,) sqq.
quam secretum? quid tutius secreto, et ad omnes actus
expeditius? Munia enim pudoris induit, non concursationis. Sed de aliis videro, tuæ nunc mihi respondendum
epistolæ est.

17. Te miror, frater, qui tantopere defendas Maximum
non fuisse accusatorem, sed parentis dolore doluisse invidiam sparsi rumoris; cum ille se inimicum et adversarium
litigatorem, proposito jam jurgio, negare non potuerit ad-

Ep. 5. versus sacram virginem judicia adtentavisse: muroque interjecto, discretas ædes uxoris suæ ac virginis, divisam germanitatis inter sorores societatem; aliaque, quibus doleret quod virgo in agro affinitatis suæ refugisset consortium. Quomodo ergo non accusator, qui affectum accusatoris jamdudum exercuit, qui sermone suo accusationem detulit, aures tuas implevit clamore, et testes auditionis deduxit, cognitionem poposcit?

18. Quamlibet argumentatus, negare non potuisti quod ad Indiciam scripseris, quoniam Maximus seu impulsu aliorum, seu dolore proprio crimen grave detulerit. Sola hæc epistola satis est ad accusationis testimonium; neque enim te ego tuis ad me datis litteris urgendum putavi, sed iis lectis quas ad virginem dederas, adverti diversum esse, quod ad me scripseras: et tamen cum epistolæ tuæ sibi non convenirent, consulendum te, non arguendum putavi. Quid igitur sibi vult illa argumentatio, quia illud detulerit, quod ad me scripseras, delatam videlicet eam in turpi crimine; ita ut editum et obrutum partum dici adserat? Quasi vero istud ad Indiciam, non ad me scripseris. Illa ubi audivit litteris tuis Maximum subduci accusationi, litteras tuas protulit, quibus eum criminis delatorem probavit: ad me datas non legerat, nec quid haberent, sciebat.

19. Ego autem exhorrui a primo calumniam, quia advertebam non crimen intendi, sed injuriam virginis desiderari, cujus inspectio et visitatio postulabatur, non aliquod flagitium deferebatur. Quis enim istud a principio fraude compositum nequaquam sibi congruere et convenire non arbitraretur? Cucurrisse mulieres viles ad monasterium, jactasse partum virginis, et necem pignoris, de monasterio rumorem per populos sparsum, eumque affluxisse in aures novi affinis Maximi, ab ipso interpellatum episcopum, dimissas eas quæ dixisse ferebantur, atque in fugam coactas, ut apud nos patuit: eos qui audisse se dicerent, ad Ecclesiam vocatos prodisse Renatum et Leontium, duos illos iniquitatis viros, quos apposuit Jezabel, redarguit Daniel, subornavit Judæorum populus; ut auctorem vitæ suæ falso appeterent testimonio. Qui tamen cum simul composuissent flagitium, simul ingressi essent viam, et ne quid præteream a juncti Maximo, comitantibus, ut dixit Leontius,

1 Kings xxi 10.
Hist. of Sus. 15 sqq.
S. Matt. xxvi. 59, 60.

iis qui illum rumorem sparserant; tamen ubi in meo SYAGRIO. adstiterunt judicio, cum primo de origine causæ quærerem, diversa et distantia prompsere, non locorum separati, sed mendaciorum divortio.

20. Cum igitur sibi ipsi non convenirent, Mercurium et Leam vilissimæ conditionis et detestabilioris nequitiæ personas amandavissent, aufugisset Theudule, non ignara objiciendi sibi facinoris, quod ante lectum Renati sola cubitavisset, ancilla præsto esset alia, quæ stupro ejusdem Renati se diceret coinquinatam; die ipso, qui dictus erat cognitioni, subtraxerunt se episcoporum conventui; licet etiam pridie subito se profecturos idem Renatus clamaverit.

21. Unde ego judicio præscripsi diem, et tamen nullo accusante, nullis testimoniis perurgentibus, insinuavi sanctæ sorori quod peteres coram ipsa inspici et visitari memoratam virginem. At illa sancte inspectionem quidem recusavit, sed testimonium non declinavit, dicens nihil se in Indicia comprehendisse, nisi quod esset virginalis pudoris et sanctitatis: habitasse eam Romæ in domo nostra, nobis absentibus, nulli eam se vitiorum familiaritati dedisse, optare cum ea sibi a Domino Jesu partem reservari in regno Dei.

22. Paternam quoque filiam nostram interrogavi, quod ab ea numquam soleat discedere, cujus caritas vitæ hujus testimonium est. Itaque etsi quod injurata diceret, fidei sacramento conferendum foret; sub obstestatione tamen professa est alienam criminis quo appetebatur, nec quidquam in ea scire se bonæ vacuum conversationis.

23. Nutricem quoque liberæ conditionis interrogavimus, cui et status haudquaquam degeneri servitio obnoxius libertatem vera fatendi daret, et fides atque ætas ad veritatem adstipularetur, et officium nutricis ad cognitionem secreti. Ea quoque nihil se indecorum vidisse, nihil sibi quasi parenti commissum a virgine aliqua dignum reprehensione.

24. His moti, Indiciam inoffensi virginem muneris pronuntiavimus: Maximum autem et Renatum et Leontium ita involvit sententia, ut Maximo, si errorem emendaret, spes reditus reservaretur; Renatus autem et Leontius excommunicati manerent, nisi forte probata sui pœnitentia,

Ep. 6 et hujus facti diuturna deploratione, dignos se præberent misericordia. Vale, frater, et nos dilige; qula nos te diligimus.

A.D.380.

EPISTOLA VI.

Cum Syagrio quod Indiciam contumeliosæ inspectioni sententia sua addixisset, Ambrosius amice expostulat; eique atrocissimam ultionem, quam Israelitæ ob violatam in levitæ uxore castitatem repetiverunt, ante oculos ponens, totam rei seriem eleganter describit

AMBROSIUS SYAGRIO.

1. Quæ sint in nostro judicio decursa, comperta retines; et ideo nunc quasi animæ portionem convenio meæ, habens apud te pro castitatis contumelia familiarem et dolentem querelam. Itane oportuit inoratam atque inauditam virginitatis causam adjudicari, ut non possit absolvi? Hoc est, nisi sua injuria, nisi ab honesto pudore traducatur ad indecoram sui corporis oblationem, grande videlicet relatura sui testimonium, ut exponatur ludibrio, et procacitatis notetur. Hanc igitur prærogativam detulisti integritati, hujusmodi honorificentiam, qua se lacessiri aut invitari gaudeant, quæ hoc munus recipiendum putant; ut amittant libertatem communis adsertionis, nec se jure tueantur vel sanctæ legis, vel publico, ut non accusatorem exigat, non arcersitorem urgeat: sed impudentiam solam induat, ac sese projiciat ad injuriam?

2. Non ita majores nostri despicabilem habebant castimoniam, cui tantum deferebant reverentiæ, ut bellum adversum temeratores pudicitiæ suscipiendum putarent. Denique tantum fuit ultionis studium; ut omnes tribules de Benjamin tribu extinguerentur, nisi sexcentos qui bello reliqui forent natura editioris loci defendisset; sic enim lectionis divinæ serie expressum tenetur, cujus tenorem recensere congruit.

Judg. xx. 1 sqq.
Ib. 47.

3. Levites vir animo major quam opibus, habitabat in partibus montis Ephræm; ei quippe tribui sortito obti-

Ib xix. 1 sqq.

gerat locus in possessionem terræ datus pro funiculo here- SYAGRIO.
ditatis. Is sibi accepit jugalem de Juda Bethleem. Et
ut se habent prima copularum exordia, ardebat juvenculam
immodica animi cupiditate : simul quia similibus ejus non
fungebatur, exardescebat magis magisque possessione, atque
immane quantum exæstuabat. Unde quia nihil referebatur
ex parte adolescentulæ, vel levitate amoris, vel vi doloris,
quod haud quaquam mercęde pari secum decerneret, cum
eadem expostulabat. Hinc frequens jurgium : quo mulier
offensa, claves remisit, domum revertit.

4. At ille amore victus, qui quod speraret non habebat Judg.
aliud; cum quartum jam mensem fluere cerneret, eo con- xix. 3 sqq
tendit, fretus quod consilio parentum emolliretur animus
adolescentulæ. Occurrit pro foribus socer, generum in-
troduxit, filiam reconciliavit; et ut lætiores dimitteret,
triduo tenuit, quasi repararet nuptias : ac volenti abire,
quartum quoque diem comperendinavit, prætenta humani-
tatis specie, moras innectendo. Pari modo cum etiam
quintum diem vellet adjungere superioribus, et jam novæ
deessent causæ morandi, paterno tamen affectu retinendæ
filiæ desiderium non deforet, promissam profectionis co-
piam distulit in meridiem ut viam cibo curati adorirentur.
Post epulas quoque volens dilationem adtexere, eo quod
jam vesper appropinquaret, generi precibus, ægre licet,
tamen adquievit.

5. Ille iter suum perrexit lætus animi, quod dilectam Ib. 10
sibi recuperavisset. Qui uno comitati servulo, cum jam sqq.
declinaret dies, festino viam celerabant gradu. Mulier ve-
hebatur jumento, viro nullus sensus laboris, qui fructu de-
siderii, simul et vario mulieris ac vernaculi sermone viam
levaret. Denique ubi Hierosolymam appropinquarunt,
quæ triginta stadiis aberat, quam tunc temporis Jebusæi
tenebant; suggessit puer deflectendum in civitatem, quia
sub noctem suspecta essent etiam illa, quæ tutiora sunt,
cavendaque tenebrarum ambigua; maxime quia locorum
incolæ non essent de filiis Israel. Et ideo prævertendum,
ne quid adversa studia gerentes insidiarum inferrent, ob-
scuro noctis dolum quærentibus ad perpetrandum facinus
satis opportuno. Sed domino ejus haudquaquam placuit
sententia, ut inter alienigenas hospitio succederent; cum

Ep. 6. Gaba et Rama non longe abessent civitates Benjamin. Itaque prævalens sententia, posthabuit servuli suggestionem; quasi ex conditione consilium æstimaretur, et non consilio quamvis infima conditio allevaretur. Et jam sol in occasu erat: denique vix occurrit, cum jam urgeretur vespere in civitatem succedere.

Judg. xix 15 sqq.
6. Gabaonitæ incolebant locum, inhospitales, immites, intolerabiles; omnia tamen tolerabiliores, quam si aliquem hospitio recepissent. Denique commodius huic viro levitæ cesserat, si in Gabaa hospitium non reperisset. Verum ne quid deesset offensionis, primo ingressu diversorium non reperit: et cum in publico situs, alienam misericordiam imploraret, offendit advenientem ex agro senem, quem vesper ex opere agresti compulit nocte decedere. Et cum esset ei conspicuus, rogatus quo iret, et unde adventaret, respondit: De Bethleem Juda revertor, contendo ad montem Ephræm, et mulier est mecum: sed ecce huc diverti, et nemo est qui hospitio recipiat, et requiescendi usum ministret. Non quo cibi aut potus sibi, aut pecori pabulorum esset indigentia, sed tecti hospitio prohiberentur: præsto esse illa, nudum tecti hospitium desiderari. Ad ea senior benigne satis et placide: Pax, inquit, tibi: et succede hospes pariter et civis; nam et mihi origo de montis Ephræm partibus, et hic hospitalis habitatio: sed tempore diuturno incolatus sedes fundavit. Itaque receptos domicilio ministerio sui et subsidiis hospitalibus juxta fovit.

Ib. 22.
7. Hortabatur ad lætitiam senior, et frequentioribus provocabat poculis, ut vino aboleret curarum oblivia; cum subito circumsistunt eos Gabaonitæ, juvenes ad omnem projecti libidinem, nihil pensum ac moderatum habentes: quos forma mulieris illexerat, et in omnem amentiam præcipitabat; capti enim ejus decore, et per senectutem hospitis, atque infirmitatem subsidii, accepta spe potiundi, poscunt mulierem, et pulsant januam.

Ib. 23, 24.
8. Itaque egressus senior rogabat eos, ne hospitales mensas turpi flagitio fœdarent, et reverendum jus etiam indomitis barbararum gentium nationibus violandum arbitrarentur: contribulem illum sibi, Israelitem virum legitimi thori subnixum copula non sine indignatione cælestis

arbitri tanta affici contumelia. Quod ubi parum procedere advertit, esse sibi filiam virginem adjecit, illam se offerre majore parentis dolore, sed minore gratiæ hospitalis dispendio : publicum flagitium privato dedecore tolerabilius habere. At illi exagitati æstu furoris, et inflammati incentivo libidinis, eo amplius ardebant formam juvenculæ, quo magis negabatur. Et justitiæ exsortes ridebant verba æquitatis, filiam senis, quia minore invidia sceleris offerebatur, despectui habentes. SYAGRIO.

9. Itaque cum piæ nihil proficerent preces, et seniles frustra hospes manus tenderet, desperato præsidio, rapitur mulier, et per totam noctem injuriæ impletur. At ubi lux finem intemperantiæ dedit, januam hospitalem repetit, non quo viri conspectum exposceret, quem magis declinandum putaret, contumeliæ pudore miserabilis : sed ut affectum viro referret, quæ castitatem amiserat, et contumeliæ suæ funus lamentabili specie ante januam hospitalem exponeret. Egressus itaque levita, cum jacentem invenisset, arbitratus quod verecundia vultum nequaquam adtollere auderet, consolari cœpit : quia non voluntate, sed invita tantæ injuriæ succubuisset : hortari adsurgere, et secum repetere domum. Sed ubi nullum responsum referebatur, quasi quiescentem majore voce e somno excitare. Judg. xix. 25 sqq.

10. Verum ubi mortis supremæ patuit fides, impositas jumento reliquias domum pertulit, et divisos artus mulieris in partes duodecim misit per singulas tribus Israel. Quo commotus universus populus convenit in Massephat, atque ibi querela per levitam cognita, omnes in bellum exarsere, statuentes neminem virorum fas esse in tabernaculum succedere, priusquam de tanti sceleris auctoribus ultio capesseretur. Animis itaque ruebant in prælium ; sed consilium prudentiorum prævertit sententiam, non temere confligendum bello cum civibus, sed prius verbis experiendum de flagitio, et decernendum conditionibus pro delictis : neque justum videri, ut paucorum sceleris pretium ad omnes perveniret, et privata adolescentium peccata statum salutis publicæ labefactarent. Itaque miserunt viros, qui denuntiarent Gabaonitis, ut tanti reos flagitii offerrent : sin autem, cognoscerent non minoris esse criminis tantum facinus defendisse, quam exercuisse. Ib. 28. Ib. 20 sqq.

11. Verum illis superba referentibus, consilia pacis bello mutata. Neque primo aut secundo conflictu cum plurimi a paucis afflictarentur, cedendum Israelitæ adversis præliis æstimarunt; quadringenta enim millia virorum bellantium adversum vigintiquinque millia Benjamin tribus, et septingentos Gabaonitas expertos belli juvenes decertabant. Et cum sinistra sorte duo sibi jam cecidissent prælia; animi tamen promtus haudquaquam deposuit Israel vincendi fiduciam, et ulciscendi præsumtam spem.

12. Sed quia causa numeroque præstantiores, inferiores pugnæ eventu pedem retulerant, divinam offensam rati, jejunio et fletu maximo reconciliationem gratiæ cœlestis affectavere. Itaque orata Domini pace, acriores in bellum revertuntur; ut pote quibus oraculum animos dederat, spem accumulaverat. Et simulato a fronte quod cederetur, ac dispositis per noctem insidiis a tergo urbis, in qua locata erat manus hostium; dum hi cedunt, et illi sectantur, invadendi urbem vacuam facta copia, et mox admoto statimque adulto incendio, flammarum fragor atque æstus furens captæ urbis speciem manifestarunt. Quo et suis fracti animi, et erecti hostium. Nam et Benjamin viri clausos se et circumventos rati, priusquam a tergo invaderentur, dispergere sese, atque in desertum fugere cœperunt; et contra Israel gemino agmine urgere eos, ac palantes persequi.

13. Cæsa itaque virgintiquinque millia, id est, omnes fere de viris Benjamin, præter sexcentos, qui arrepto scrupeæ rupis munimento, partim loci ingenio et subsidio naturæ, partim desperatione victoribus terrori fuere. Nam secundæ res cautionis admonent: in adversis ultio pro victoria habetur. Nec feminarum numerus tanti discriminis exsors fuit: sed omnis tribus Benjamin muliebris sexus cum pueris et puellis, omnique ætate gladio aut igne extinctus; sacramentumque additum, ne quis tribus illius viro filiam suam in uxorem daret, quo reparandi nominis omnis aboleretur successio.

14. Belli finis simul atque iræ factus, et furor in pœnitentiam vertit: armisque positis, in unum convenientes viri Israel fleverunt fletum magnum, 'et celebrarunt jejunium, dolentes unam tribum perisse ex fratribus, atque extinctam

populi sui validam manum: jure quidem pro delicti pretio SYAGRIO. bellatum adversum propugnatores flagitiorum, sed misere in sua populum conversum viscera, et bello civili utrumque afflictum. Lacrymarum effusio movit passionem animi, et affectum perpulit, sævitiæ ratio successit: missique legati ad sexcentos illos Benjamin viros, qui per quatuor menses edito se præruptarum tuebantur rupium, aut deserti indigentia, quæ multitudini obsidentium periculo foret, deploraverunt communem illam ærumnam, quod illi contribules, isti cognatos et socios amisissent; sed tamen non penitus interceptam reparandæ tribus successionem, consulere se in medium quomodo et sacramenti fides sibi constet, et tribus una nequaquam a corpore avulsa intercidat.

15. Altari itaque posito, reconciliationis et pacis oblatum Judg. sacrificium. Et quia Jabis Galaad populus erat pœnæ et xxi. 4 maledicto obnoxius, (obstrinxerat enim se omnis Israel sqq. magno sacramento, ut si quis non ascendisset cum eo ad puniendum flagitium, morte moreretur,) duodecim millia bellatorum directa: ut et viri omnes et mulieres ferro extinguerentur, solas virilis thori exsortes reservarent adolescentulas. Interfectis itaque omnibus Jabis Galaad, solæ virgines quadringentæ exitio ceterorum superfuerunt. Quas accipiens Israel, statuit viros Benjamin belli metum deponere, et in conjugium sibi sumere integras ævi juxta ac pudoris puellas: quibus et causa esset apud viros integra, quod nemo suorum adversum eos bellum susceperat: et caritatis gratia, quia propter eos supremo supplicio ereptæ forent. Hoc igitur modo quadringentis juvenibus quæsita copularum consortia sunt.

16. Sed quia ducenti numero supererant, quibus jugales Ib. 16 deerant, iis quoque sine fraude sacramentorum consultum sqq. accepimus. Die festus in Silo quotannis celebrabatur. Ibi exsultare solitæ virgines, et choreas ducere in honorem religionis: aliæ præire matribus, et totum iter agmine viantum repleri. Dixit unus ex senioribus: Si ducenti illi tribus Benjamin viri intra vineas siti excubias tenderent, donec se omnis feminea turba effunderet, et surgentes ex vineis unusquisque quam occursus dederit, uxorem sibi vindicaret, fraudi id nequaquam futurum; populum etenim favere reparandæ tribus successioni, propter sacramentum

Ep. 6. impertire non posse filiarum suarum societatem: neque tamen contra sacramentum videri, si prohibendum non putaret; quia sacramento neque cogendi, neque prohibendi necessitas imposita videretur: illos sibi sine metu consulere oportere. Sane si puellarum parentes vindictam efflagitarent, partim prece, partim etiam retorquendo in ipsos invitae culpam custodiae, sese revocaturos; quia cum scirent Benjamin viros exsortes esse jugalium, cum filiabus processerint: dignam sane tribum jam non poenam, sed misericordia: satis dure saevitum in eos, et debellatam corporis sui partem: immoderatius exarsisse plebem, ut successionem domesticam extingueret, atque ex suis necaret: placere Deo non perire populo tribum, neque pro una muliere tam acerbe consuli.

Judg. xxi. 23. 17. Probaverunt consilium Israelitae: exsequuti sunt viri Benjamin, et dispositi in vineis loco opportuno et tempore, plenas feminei agminis vias occupaverunt. Praebuit illis festum nuptiarum religionis solemnitas. Avulsae de complexu patrum filiae, tanquam in manum ab ipsis parentibus tradebantur, et velut pactam e gremio matris non abduci, sed prodire arbitrareris. Ita tribus Benjamin pene intercepta atque extincta brevi floruit, documentum exhibens, quod magno exitio sit insolentibus vindicta pudicitiae, et laesae castitatis ultio.

18. Nec hoc solo loco, sed plerisque Scriptura hoc docet.

Gen. xii. 17. Nam et in Genesi legimus exercitum quaestionibus regem Ægypti Pharao, quod Saram adtentavisset; et tamen alienam esse uxorem nesciebat.

19. Est igitur Domino castitatis tuendae voluntas, quanto magis est defensandae integritatis? Unde nulla debet virginibus sacris irrogari injuria; quae enim non nubunt, et

S Luke xx. 36. qui uxores non ducunt, habentur sicut Angeli Dei in caelo. Et ideo coelesti gratiae non inferamus corporalem contumeliam; quoniam potens est Deus, quem nec praevaricatio praetereat, et moveat accepti sib muneris et consecratae virginitatis acerba et gravis contumelia. Vale, frater, et nos dilige: quia nos te diligimus.

INDEX.

A

AARON, called by God to the Priesthood, 373 a pattern for Bishops and Priests, ib. took predecence of Moses as Priest, 404 why he took the rings and ear-rings of the people, 373. the meaning of his rod budding, 18, 270, 376.

Abel, why his offering was accepted, 230

Abraham, ministered to his guests with his own hand, 3 his belief silenced the superstition of his countrymen, 320. the greatness of his faith, 456 and trust in God, 349 his ready obedience, 472 how he saw Christ's day, 423. all Christians his children, 455.

Absolution, follows on confession, 250.

Abstinence, the excellence of it, 366. [see *Temperance*]

Abundantius, Bp of Trent, 33 condemns Palladius, 54 (in p 60. is called Bishop of Brescia)

Acholius, brought up in monastic life, 84 elected Bishop of Thessalonica by the clergy, at the wish of the people, ib Ambrose writes a letter on his death, 80 &c baptised Theodosius, 80 was present at the Council of Constantinople, ib visited Ambrose when sick, 83 designated Anysius as his successor, ib. summoned to Constantinople on the question of Maximus' claim to the see, 77.

Adam, his fall, 304. his greatness before his fall, 305. upheld himself till united to Eve, 317. before his fall was clothed with virtue, after it, was naked, 348. fasting would have saved him from this nakedness, 286. the serpent that tempted him was sensual pleasure, 363 might have retained his original innocence, 434. fell through pride, ib. his folly in hiding himself, 133. said to be buried on Golgotha, 423.

Adoption, the, means Redemption, 231 begun now, perfected hereafter, ib

Æthiopians, practised circumcision, 425

Africanus, his victory over Hannibal appealed to by Ambrose, 102.

Agnes went gladly to her martyrdom, 247.

Ahab poor, Naboth rich, 252

Alani, the, conquered by Valentinian, 179,

Alexander, a presbyter of Milan, 286.

Alexander the great, Calanus' letter to, 216

Alexandria, a church there burnt by the Gentiles and Jews, 263 the Church of, in full communion with Milan, 73

Almachius, Bp. takes part in the Council of Aquileia, 33, 61.

Almon, the river, worship of Cybele connected with, 111.

Alypius, Ambrose replies to a letter of recommendation from, 476

Amantius, Bp. of Nice, takes part in the Council of Aquileia, 33, 60. his condemnation of Palladius, 56

Ambrosia and Ambrosius, daughter and son of Eusebius, 333, 334.

Ambrose, Bp of Milan, alludes to his election as Bishop, 139 to his endeavours to escape from undertaking the office, 379. praised in the Emperor's letter about the Council of Aquileia, 34. celebrated the Holy Communion daily, 132 praises the Clergy who do not desert their duties, 74. devotes all his goods to the poor, 130 pays deference to the Emperors, but will not yield to them in the cause of the Church, 143. pleads illness to Theodosius, 326. visited by Acholius in his sickness, 83 had purposed to be buried under the altar, where the relics of Gervasius and Protasius were placed, 162

Answers a letter from Gratian,

and promises him a treatise on the Holy Spirit, 2 &c induced him not to listen to claims for the restoration of heathen worship, 91

Writes to Valentinian against the same claims, 87 &c prevents a reply to Symmachius' memorial, 101 alludes to this in addressing Eugenius, 341

Relates to his sister the persecutions of Justina, 128 &c. his sermon on the giving up of the Basilica, 131 another sermon against Auxentius, 142 &c introduces the Eastern chanting and singing of hymns, 156 refuses to have his dispute with Auxentius settled in the Consistory before the Emperor, 137 &c

Finds the relics of Gervasius and Protasius, 158. his sermon on the subject, 159 a second sermon on the same subject, 162 mentions the healing of a blind man, and other miracles, 158, 163 writes to the Bishops of Æmilia to settle disputes about the time of keeping the Easter festival, 166.

Alludes to his first embassy to Maximus in behalf of Justina and her son, 178. writes an account of his second embassy to Valentinian, 176 &c warns Valentinian not to trust Maximus, 181.

Writes to Theodosius about the burning of the Synagogue at Callinicum, 257 &c preaches on the subject, 269 &c prevails with Theodosius to withdraw his sentence, 279.

Replies to Siricius' letter against Jovinian in the name of the Council of Milan, 282

Writes to Theodosius after the Massacre at Thessalonica, 324 &c. boldly bids him repent, 327 refuses to admit him to communion till he does, 328

Writes to Theodosius on the death of Valentinian the 2nd, 331

His letter on the dispute between Evagrius and Flavian as to the succession to the see of Antioch, 336

Writes to Eugenius, 341 &c recounts his efforts against the restoration of heathen rights, 342.

Writes to the Church at Vercellae when troubled by disputes, and unable to elect a Bishop, 357 &c.

Ambrose usually writes with his own hand, 312. mentions his Hexaemeron, 287 his work on Paradise, 302 Gives Vigilius an outline of the teaching he should give as Bishop, 114 gives an account of his discussion with an Apollinarian, 306 &c

Ammianus, one of the Bishops of Macedonia, 80.

Anatolius, one of the Bishops of Macedonia, 80

Angels, guard Christ's servants, 146. are grieved to be ministers of vengeance, 227.

Anna, an example of the blessedness of widowhood, 285.

Antioch, schism in the Church of, 71. Synod of Capua deals with it, 336

Anysius, succeeds Acholius as Bishop of Thessalonica, 83 Ambrose writes to him on his appointment, 85.

Apame, concubine of Darius, 238.

Aper, a presbyter, subscribes the letter of the Synod of Milan to Siricius, 287.

Apollinarian heresy, alluded to, 78 an account of Ambrose's dealing with one who maintained it, 306 &c that Christ was perfect God and perfect Man to be maintained against them, 316

Apostles, first-fruits of the Lord, 230, 231 enlightened to interpret Holy Scripture. 188.

Apostles' Creed, mentioned, 284

Aquila, his version mentioned, 431.

Aquileia, Council of, its Acts, 32—61. The occasion of it, 31 its letter to the Bishops of Gaul, 61 letters to the Emperors, 62, 67, 70

Arabians used circumcision, 425.

Ariminum, council of, at first condemned Arius, afterwards was misled, 141. called Christ a creature, 152

Arian heresy refuted at the Council of Aquileia, 32—63. A Church claimed for the Arians at Milan, 128 the troubles arising thence, 129 &c S Ambrose preaches against them, 143 &c refuses to believe the evidence of miracles, 165. called Christ a creature, 141.

Arius, denied to the Son the titles given to the Father, 64. his letter read at the Council of Aquileia, 51 &c.

Ark of the Covenant, interpretation of, 18.

Artemius, a bishop at the Council of Aquileia, 33, 61

Athanasius, his authority appealed to, 76, 79.

INDEX. 495

Attalus, a presbyter, condemned by the Council of Aquileia, 65 signed the Nicene formula, 50.
Auxentius, Arian bishop at Milan, challenges Ambrose to arbitration, 137. Ambrose will meet him in a Synod, 141 preaches against him, 143 &c. Auxentius came from Scythia, 157. formerly called Mercurianus, ib. contemns Christian Baptism, 157
Avarice, perverts men's judgments, 10. [see *Covetous*]

B

BALAAM, his history commented on, 319 &c. his words prophetic of Baptism, 321.
Balance, the, of God's Judgment, 10.
Baptism, is a death to sin, 321 the complete redemption of the whole man, 429 John baptised to repentance, Christ to grace, 157 typified by the Red sea, 115, 420 Faith not sufficient without Baptism, 26 the baptised should be dead to sin, 362. have died with Christ, and live again with Him.
Baptistery, S. Ambrose teaches in, 129.
Barbatianus and Sarmatio, heretics who troubled the church of Vercellae, 360 disparaged strictness of life, 361 worse than Epicurus, 362.
Basilica, those at Milan mentioned, 128, 136, 158 many burnt by Jews in the reign of Julian, 262.
Bassianus, Bp of Lodi, takes part in the Council of Aquileia, 33, 60 his condemnation of Paladius, 55 subscribes the letter of the Council of Milan, to Pope Siricius, 287
Bassus, Bp , 340.
Bauto, an officer of rank under Valentinian, 177, 179, 342.
Beershebah, meaning of, 383.
Bethany, meaning of, 422
Bethlehem, meaning of, 414. mystical interpretation of, 416.
Bishop, the word Sacerdos often used of, 1 instructions for a newly elected, 5, 114 is the pilot of the Church, ib should be filled with Scripture, 6. what he should preach, 7, &c. is a physician of souls, 15 the guardian of his flock, 115. should extirpate prevailing sins, 116. must be husband of one wife only, 375. a pattern of Christian virtues, 377 able to govern himself, ib his unanimous election a proof of the judgment of God, 359 must speak his mind boldly, 257 Bishops the proper judges of questions concerning the Faith, 141 and of Bishops, 138. are judges of emperors not emperors of them, 139 should not readily appeal to the civil sword, 185 must forbid mixed marriages, 115 &c. lovers of peace except in the defence of the Church, 259 their poverty an excuse for non-attendance at distant Councils, 34, 337. their consecration day their birthday, 17. should be chosen for holiness of life, 374
Blindness, spiritual, how healed by Christ, 461.
Body, the, to be chastened, 249. bodily sickness sent for the healing of the soul, 458.
Bononia, 254
Bonosus, letter concerning, probably written by Siricius, certainly not by Ambrose, 339.
Brixillum, 254.

C

CABILLONUM, (Châlons-sub-Saône,) 181.
Caesar, (see *Emperor*)
Cain, a warning to Christians, 8
Calanus, his letter to Alexander the Great, 246.
Calligonus, his threats to Ambrose, 137.
Callinicum, a synagogue there burnt by the Christians, 257 &c.
Camillus, his victory not due to heathen gods, 102
Campania, a pleasant retreat from the troubles of the world, 350
Candidianus, a letter of Ambrose to him.
Capua, synod of, seeks to settle the disputed succession at Antioch, 336 &c deals with the case of Bonosus, 339.
Cassianus, a Bishop, takes part in the Council of Aquileia, 33, 61.
Castalus, an Arian presbyter, seized by the Christians, and rescued by Ambrose' order, 129.
Catechumens, dismissed after the Lessons and Sermon, 129.
Chaldæan astrologers, have no hope in the stars which they watch, 232.
Charity, makes men loved by God, 212.

Chastity, its excellence, 105, 368. (see *Virginity*.)
Children, the three, their freedom, 25
Christians, truly free and wise, 242. in Ambrose's time formed a majority in the Senate, 90. deprived of their common rights by Julian, 89. prospered under persecution, 104. should desire peace, but not fear persecution, 132.
Christ, the true David, 311 almighty, 145. how subject, 229 both Son and Servant, 307. became a servant for us, ib to make us free, 243, 311. perfect God and perfect Man, 309. was made a curse that we might be blessed, 152, 308, 312 came to restore us by Grace, 305 was the true Melchisedeck, 373 His birth of a Virgin maintained against Jovinian, 284 is the Virgin Word, 214. both Priest and Victim, 302. the highest Example, 14. was circumcised to fulfil the law, 78, 3. fasted as a pattern to us, 363 obeyed the law to the full, 23. His healings true miracles, 80, 2. wins men by His goodness, 271 having forgiven, demands of us forgiveness, 272.

Why He wrote on the ground, 184, 188. desires the pardon of all men, 189 his healing of the blind man interpreted mystically, 80.

The praises of Christ the scourge of heretics, 150, His words to His Mother from the cross, 393 His drinking the vinegar, 402 was alone when He redeemed the world, 318 needed no redemption Himself, 23, nor any to help Him to redeem it, 393

Suffered in the flesh, not in the Godhead, 42, 103. died for all men, 272, 373, nailed our sins to His Cross, 394, paid the debt which we owed, 373 was the Rock, 390 the Lamb, 400 the Bridegroom, 214 His Blood the Cup of Redemption, 22 died and rose again by His own power, 463, how the first-fruits from the dead, 230. as Son of Man sits at the right hand of God, and we in Him, 446 sits as Judge, 360. in what sense He does not judge, 454 all Christians are Members of His Body, 273, united to Him as Eve to Adam, 445 the feebler members His feet, 277. is the true chief good of man, 201 His followers in what sense bound, 464 where peace and righteousness are, there is Christ, 359. where Christ is there are all good things, 18 Christ is our Rest, 299. carnal men not in Christ, 256 raises up those that fall, if with Him, 462. to kiss Christ means to confess Him, 274. to be Christ's prisoner better than to be freed by others, 389. how He is the Giant of salvation, 211. the Source of happiness, 202, the Light of the soul, 204 the Fountain of life, 205, the wisdom of God, 399. how He restores the soul, 216.
Chromatius, a presbyter, takes part in the Council of Aquileia, 50, 53, 63
Church, prefigured by the woman who anointed the feet of Jesus, 266, 270 by the poor widow who cast two mites into the treasury, 186 foretold by the prophets, 412 founded not on the Law but on Faith, 152 is a ship in the sea of the world, 5. a rock unshaken by its waves, ib. its members Christ's soldiers, 195 kisses the feet of Christ, 275. is a Virgin espoused to Christ, 370 the only safe resting-place, 371 the true second Tabernacle, 18 looks for immortality, 439 Faith its only possession, 107 its wealth the support of the poor, ib its lands pay tribute to the Emperors, 155. nothing lost to the Church which is gained to piety, 469 what are its true riches, 212. belongs to Christ, not to the Emperor, 156
Cimbri, their spoils used to build heathen temples, 261
Circumcision, why enjoined in the old Test. though abrogated in the new, 423 &c, 437 other questions concerning, 424. practised by the heathen, 425 superseded by Christ's Death, 426 the true Circumcision spiritual, 428, of the heart not of the flesh, 430 not binding on the Gentiles, 431.
Clarus, one of the Bishops of Macedonia, 80,
Claterna, 254.
Clergy, are the Lord's portion, 465. the sole ministers of public worship, 106 their reward future and heavenly, 462. Christ their support, 463. forbidden to contract second marriages by the Council of Nicaea, (but see note,) 379. forbidden to inherit property by wills, 106
Comacine rocks, 335
Comum, the people of, mostly Christians, 19

INDEX. 497

Competentes, (candidates for baptism) S Ambrose taught them the Creed, 129

Confession, justifies sinners, 329 the duty of sinners, 327 urged on Theodosius, ib David a pattern of, 326. necessary for forgiveness, 419

Counsels, different from commandments, 370

Councils, held separately in the East and West, 35. Council of Aquileia 33—61 letters written by S Ambrose in its name, 61, 62, 67, 70. held a second session, 74 not fully informed of the decrees of that of Constantinople, 73 the second council of Constantinople, 79

Constantine, the Emperor, gave to the Bishops the decision in question of faith, 141,

Constantinople, the Bishop's house at, burnt, 262

Constantius, Emperor, ordered the removal of the altar of Victory, 112 gave to the Bishops the decision in question of faith, 141

Constantius, a newly elected Bishop, receives advice from S. Ambrose, 5 etc who commends to his care the see of Imola, (Forum Cornelii,) then vacant, 14

Constantius, Bishop of Sciscia, takes part in the Council of Aquileia, 33, 61. condemns Palladius, 56 signs the Letter to Siricius from the Council of Milan, 287.

Constantius, (or Constantinus,) Bishop of Orange, takes part in the Council of Aquileia, 33, 35, 38 condemns Palladius, 54. was present as representing the Bishops of Gaul, 61.

Conversion, its blessedness urged on Theodosius, 327. no cause of shame, 103. pleasing to God, 268 even at the last, wins paradise, 423 its stages, 423 &c.

Correction, a proof of love, 414

Cross, sign of the, used continually by Christians, and why, 427.

Count of the East, 259, note

Creature, the, how made subject to vanity, 225 &c

Curse, of man, to be desired, if it bring a blessing from God, 392

Cybele, heathen rites in honour of, 111.

Cycle, of nineteen years, for Easter, 166

Cyrus, an instance of reverse of fortune, 113.

D

DALMATIUS, conveys Valentinian's commands to Ambrose, 137

Damasus, Bishop of Rome, writes to S Ambrose, 91.

Daniel, a type of those who refuse allegiance to the Prince of this world, 25 ·

David, his two wives Ahinoam and Abigail, mystically explained, 215. Nathan's expostulation with, applied to Theodosius by Ambrose, 278, his life an example of the change of fortune, 13 guilty before God alone, 243. his humble confession a good example, 327 why he danced before the ark, 347.

Death, the fear of, slavish, 245 not a cause of sorrow since Christ's Atonement, 256

Dead, prayers and offerings to be made for the, 255 not to be mourned for, if in Christ, 256

Debtors, usually set free in Holy Week, 129 mankind debtors, set free by Christ 271.

Decani, who they were, 129, note.

Delphinus, Bp. a letter to, 475.

Demarchus, an Epicurean, (see note.) 365

Demophilus, elected by the Arians Bishop of Constantinople, 70, note

Detraction, evil and danger of, 372

Devil, the, held mankind in slavery through sin, 426. the price of our freedom paid to him, ib. his envy against man, the cause of discord among Christians, 71. allowed to tempt men, that they may be proved, 132. the devil testifies to the miraculous power of the relics of Gervasius and Protasius, 164

Diocese, original meaning of the term. 33, note.

Diocletian, era of, 171, note.

Diogenes, Bishop of Genoa, takes part in the Council of Aquileia, 33, 61. condemns Palladius, 56

Dionysius, Bishop of Milan, driven into exile by Valens, 380. S Ambrose calls himself the successor to his heritage, 149.

Discipline, the contrary of insolence, 193.

Dodona, oaks of, worshipped by heathens, 107.

Domninus, Bishop of Grenoble, takes part in the Council of Aquileia, 33 60.

K k

Drachma, the, in the parable represents Redemption, 20.

E

EAST, civil Diocese of, 259.
Easter, a letter of S. Ambrose as to the time of observance of, 166 &c. Table of, during S. Ambrose's time, ib importance of uniformity in regard of, shewn from Scripture, 168. how to be kept truly, 175.
Eclipses, their causes, 226.
Egyptians, disapproved of the sacrifice of animals, 191 and shepherds, ib. devoted to geometry and astronomy, 425. Egyptian dogs, meaning of, 168. going down unto Egypt means following the vices of the Egyptians, 193 their harvest in the first month of the year 172. their priests were circumcised, 425.
Eight, mystical meaning of, 297, 301.
Eleazar, his history teaches the doctrine of ordination, 377.
Elias, how rich, 252. conquered on earth, triumphed in heaven, 295. strengthened by abstinence, 382. his history mystically interpreted, 383, Acholius compared to, 83
Elisha, how a type of Christ, 363. Acholius compared to, 82. his praying that his servant's eyes may be opened applied, 161.
Enoch, his riches, 252
Emperor, the, should be the first to obey his own laws. 140 should submit himself to God, 343 good emperors love freedom, the bad, slavery, 257. should not forbid obedience to God, 345, is in the Church, not over the Church, 157. the Church benefited by Christian Emperors, 328. who are God's soldiers, 88 and pay honour to God's Altar only, 104. have no power over the things of God, 130. 133. 155. emperors have oftener coveted the Priesthood than Priests sovereignty, 135. what should be rendered to Cæsar, 25.
Ephratah, meaning of, 415
Epicurus, allowed evil consequences from pleasure, 362 better than false teachers among Christians, 364 his followers believed in no future state, ib.
Esdras, Book of, its study recommended, 224
Esther, a pattern of the power of fasting, 368.

Eucherius, consul at the time of the Council of Aquileia, 32.
Eugenius, set up as Emperor by Arbogastes, 341 S. Ambrose writes to him against the restoration of heathen worship, ib.
Eusebius, Bishop of Bologna, takes part in the Council of Aquileia, 33, 35 &c, 60. his condemnation of Palladius, 54. disputes with Secundianus, 57 &c.
Eusebius, one of the Bishops of Macedonia, 80.
Eusebius, Bishop of Vercellæ, his unanimous election, 359. first combined the duties of monk and bishop, 379. was a true confessor, 380. driven into exile by Valens, for refusing to condemn Athanasius, ib.
Eusebius, a layman, friend of S. Ambrose, 333.
Eustathius, one of the Bishops at the Synod of Aquileia, 33, 61
Eustorgius, a confessor, 149.
Entropius, one of the Bishops of Macedonia, 80
Evagrius, his rivalry with Flavian for the see of Antioch, 336 S. Ambrose's opinion thereon, 338.
Evagrius, a presbyter, appears at Aquileia as a deputy, 36, 61.
Eventius, Bishop of Ticinum, takes part in the Council of Aquileia, 60. condemns Palladius, 54 signs the letter from the Council of Milan to Pope Siricius, 287
Exsuperantius, Bishop of Dertona, takes part in the Council of Aquileia, 33, 61. condemns Palladius, 55.

F

FAITH, not to be too readily given, 15. the characteristic of the Gospel, 453. to be willing to face suffering a proof of true faith, 428. prepares the way for love, 457 is strict with itself, 382 justifies, 152 makes free, 443, makes us heirs of the promises, ib. contained in the two Testaments, 298 delivers by the Blood of Christ, 436

Profession of, directed against heresies, 315. a summary of, ib. its greatness, 92

Questions of, to be decided by the Church, not the Emperor, or his council, 144. and discussed in the Church, 142

INDEX.

Famine, one of God's temporal punishments, 409.
Fasting, its efficacy maintained, 286, 363. makes us spiritually fat, 368. instances of victories through it, 363, 367. washes away sin, 363. evil not easily conquered without it, ib. Jovinian's disparagement of fasting condemned, 285. forbidden on the Lord's Day, 170
Faustinus, consoled by S Ambrose on the death of his sister, 254
Faustinus, son, and grandson of Eusebius, 333.
Fear, caused by sin, 241. makes men slaves, ib, 245, 452. yet leads them on to liberty, 442 a means of recovering God's favour, ib. God would be loved rather than feared, 441 Christ's true servants have no fear, 157. inferior to love, 441. the mark of the Law, 452.
Felix and Nabor, a Church dedicated to, at Milan, where the relics were found of SS Gervasius and Protasius, 158.
Felix, Bishop of Comum, S Ambrose writes a friendly letter to, 16. was ordained by S. Ambrose, 19. invited to the dedication of a Church, 17.
Felix, Bishop of Jadera, takes part in the Council of Aquileia, 33, 60. condemns Palladius, 56 signs the letter of the Council of Milan to Pope Siricius, 287.
Felix, an African Bishop, a deputy at the Council of Aquileia, 33 61. condemns Palladius, 55.
Felix, a deacon, bearer of a letter to Theodosius, 357.
First-born, the, represent holy men, 222
Flavian, S. Ambrose writes about the dispute between him and Meletius for the see of Antioch, 336 refuses the decision of the Bishops, 337. the claims of both sides weak, 378.
Flesh, the, united to the soul as a brother, 403. is mortal, soul immortal, 255.
Fool, the, always poor, 193.
Forgiveness, a Christian duty, 385. because we have been forgiven, 272. Jacob, a pattern of 391
Freedom, that of the soul, the true, 240. comes from free-will, 241. exists even in bondage, 243 not good for fools, 237, 248 belongs to the promise, not the law, 450 God's service the highest freedom, 242.

G

GAUL, *the Bishops of*, thanked for sending deputies to the Council of Aquileia, 61.
Geminianus, a Bishop, present at the Council of Milan, 287.
Genialis, a follower of Jovinian, condemned by the Council of Milan, 286
Gentiles, (see *Heathen*)
Germinator, a follower of Jovinian, condemned by the Council of Milan, 286.
Gervasius and Protasius, the finding of their relics, 158 &c.
God, His Name, I am, marks His Eternity, 29. is one and uncompounded, 464 nothing hidden from Him, 318. knows the secrets of the heart, 88. cannot lie, 319 nor do what is contrary to His Nature, ib. to put God before all things, no wrong to any, 90, 267, 341. His worship the substance of our life, 303 to worship and obey Him, true wisdom, 197. will not be worshipped under the form of stones, 103. more to be feared because invisible, 292.
His dwelling place our hearts, 390. He is our Portion, 388, 446. our Rest, 408. alone without sin, 405.
Gospel, the, is the fulfilment of the Law, 187, 298. indulgence the characteristic of the Gospel, severity of the Law, 438. the Law bondage, the Gospel liberty, 242, 450 the law partial, the Gospel perfect, 439. the inheritance of Christians, 449.
Goths, driven from Macedonia by the prayers of Acholius, 82 their admission within the empire by Valens, ib. note supported the Arian cause at Milan, 130. came as heathen into God's inheritance, 134
Grace, forgives sin, 436. gives freedom, 450. God invites by grace, furthers by increase of grace, 271. corrects the redeemed, 190.
Gratian, the Emperor, writes to S. Ambrose 1, cavils not at the manhood of Christ, 1. his humility and faith, 2. S Ambrose promises him a treatise on the Holy Spirit, 4. S. Ambrose announces to him in the name of the Council of Aquileia the results of their deliberation, 62 &c. urges him to support Damasus as Bishop of Rome, 67 &c. gave peace to the Church, 3. put down heathen

K k 2

worship, 89, 114 his example held up to Valentinian, 93. Maximus refuses to restore his remains to his family, 180.
Gregory Nazianzen, his position in the see of Constantinople, 75
Gymnosophists, Indian philosophers, 246.

H

HABBACUC, his miraculous flight, 295.
Hamilcar, an instance of reverse of fortune, 113
Heathen, their worship contrasted with Christian, 101 &c. their endurance, 104. their vestal virgins with Christian virgins, 105 not to be supported by Christian Emperors, 88 &c 342.
Heart, meaning of the expression, 'the hidden man of the heart,' 250.
Heirs, (see *Inheritance*)
Heliodorus, Bishop of Altinum, takes part in the Council of Aquileia, 33, 60 condemns Palladius, 56
Hippocrates, his seven ages of man, 300.
Hope, is looking for the unseen, 232.
Horontianus, a pupil of S Ambrose, 223, ordained by him, 420.
Hosea, his wife of whoredoms mystically interpreted, 187.
Hospitality commended, 392
Humility, its excellence, 11 Joseph a pattern of, ib
Huns, employed against the Juthungi by Valentinian 179
Hyginus, Bishop, cruel treatment of, 181.
Hymns, their powerful effect, 159. introduced by S. Ambrose at Milan during the contest with Justina, ib.

I

IDOLS, (see *Heathen*)
Ignorance, diminishes the guilt of sin, 434.
Illyricum, disturbances in, 79.
Incarnation, (see *Christ*)
Indicia, a Virgin, the case of, 478 &c.
Induction, 172
Infants, weak Christians, 452
Inheritance, the Gospel is the true, 443, 449, &c. what the heritage of God is, 192
Irenæus, several letters addressed to, 191, &c
Isaac, the true first-born of Abraham, 222 foresaw the mysteries of the Church 324.
Isaiah, mystical meaning of his walking naked, 348.
Isis, rites of, 346.
Italy, in S. Ambrose's time free from Arianism, 78.

J

JACOB, a kingly shepherd, 191. his marriage with Leah and Rachel mystically interpreted, 193, &c. a pattern of forgiveness, 391. of industry and perseverance 390. an example in this respect to us, 195 did obeisance not to Esau, but to Christ, Whom he foresaw, ib. his dream a blessing, 86
James, a presbyter of Persia, seeks retirement in Campania, 350.
Januarius, a Bishop, takes part in the Council of Aquileia, 33, 61. condemns Palladius, 56.
Januarius, a follower of Jovinian, condemned, 286
Jason, his history urged as a precedent, 343
Japhet, his reverence for his father mystically applied, 335
Jerusalem, the heavenly, a good mother of souls, 217 (vid errata)
Jews, sinned in the wilderness when God's voice ceased, 401. being stiffnecked required the law as a schoolmaster, 438, 442. a Christian may be in work a Jew, 440. are the sons of the bond-woman, 450 full of slander against Christ and His Church, 264. are under a curse, 451. are in the shade, Christians in the light of the Sun, 455, prefer Moses, who accuses them, to Christ who would pardon, 454. who are spiritually Jews, 430
Jezebel, represents the Synagogue, 383.
Job, his history applied to the persecution about the Basilica, 131, &c, 144 resisted Satan by the help of the Spirit of God, 159.
John, the Baptist, a teacher of abstinence, 368
John, the Evangelist, imbibed Divine mysteries while lying on Jesu's Bosom, 399 signed the Lord's Testament, 393.
Jonah, a lesson from, read in course during the persecution, on which S Ambrose preaches, 136.
Joseph, though a slave truly free, 238,

though naked not disgraced, 349 a pattern of humility, 11 of purity, 12. of the vanity of earthly things, 13 was a type of Christ, 12 neither depressed by adversity nor elated by prosperity, 13.
Josephus, his notion of an earthly paradise, 302.
Jovinian, a monk who had abandoned monastic life, and rushed into extremes of self-indulgence, 280 Siricius writes about him to the Chuch of Milan, ib the reply of the Church of Milan, 282.
Jovinus, a Bishop, takes part in the Council of Aquileia 33, 61
Judas, claimed by Satan as his possession, 389. might have been pardoned had he waited for mercy, 407.
Judge, not to be excluded from communion for inflicting the punishment of death, 182 but should prefer mercy, if possible, 183 the Church leaves them free, 184 even heathen judges were proud of freedom from bloodshed, 183 bishops proper judges of questions of faith, 141 and of bishops 138 (see *Bishop*) condemns himself, when he condemns in another his own crimes, 188.
Julian, cut off his own retreat, 113 his attempt to rebuild the Temple frustrated by fire from heaven, 261. one who threw down an altar martyred in his reign, 263
Julianus Valens, intruded Bishop of Pettau, 65. committed sacrilege by appearing in pagan dress, ib refused to appear at the Council of Aquileia, 16.
Just man, the, is a law to himself, 240. possesses spiritual riches, 192. and ever lendeth them, 251.
Justus, Bishop of Lyons, takes part as deputy of the Bishops of Gaul in the Council of Aquileia, 33, 38 60. condemns Palladius, 54.
Juthungi, a Gothic tribe, ravage Rhaetia, 179.

K

KISS, mystical meaning of, 274
Kings, unhappy condition of, 205.
Korah, his sin to be avoided, 375.

L

LABARUM, the sacred standard, 261.
Laetus, his family dispute. 466 &c.
Laurence, S. his constancy under torture, 247

Law, the Jewish, took the place of the Law of Nature, 433 did not increase, but make known sin, 434. convicts of sin but does not forgive, 436. how a schoolmaster, 437. only partial, while the Gospel is perfect, 439 the law trains for the Gospel, 453,
Law, of Nature, is innate 433 forbids many things which the Law of Moses did not, 353. has moral not arbitrary sanctions, 240.
Laymen, not fit judges of the faith, 139.
Leah, mystically explained, 192.
Letter-writing, its pleasure and profit, 313, 316 401 it brings absent friends together, ib.
Laying on of hands, to exorcise evil spirits, 158, 165
Leontius and Renatus, accusers of Indicia, 484.
Leopardus, one of S Ambrose's Clergy, 286
Levites, the true first-born, because hallowed, 222
Life, its uncertainty common to all, 113
Liguria, mention of, 108.
Limenius, Bishop of Vercellæ, takes part in the Council of Aquileia, 33, 60, condemns Palladius, 55.
Love, the characteristic of the Gospel, 452 brings freedom with it, ib. makes us beloved by God, 242. required by God, 441. excludes offences, 448 increased by intercourse, 316. God's, whether it varies, 213
Lucius, Arian Bishop of Alexandria, his crimes, 277
Luke, S author of the Acts of the Apostles, 368
Lust, compared to a mote 188. often the cause of wars 116

M

MACCABEES, festival of, 263.
Macedonius, Bishop, takes part in the Council of Aquileia, 33, 61
Macedonius, one of the Bishops of Macedonia, 80.
Magnet, the, its lesson, 305.
Man, a combatant whose prize is heaven, 289. made to rule creation, 291, 294 his intelligence kingly, 293. fell from bad to worse till redeemed by Christ, 305.
Manichees, deny that Christ came in the flesh, 286. condemned for fasting on the Lord's Day, 170

Manna, why given to the Israelites and not to Christians, 394 Christ the true Manna, ib 28 it represents the Divine Wisdom, 21, 397.

Marcellina, sister of S Ambrose, his letter to her about the contest with Justina, 128,&c about the discovery of the relics of SS Gervasius and Protasius, 157 &c about the affair of Callinicum, 269 &c.

Marcellus, Bishop, takes part in the Council of Aquileia, 33, 61.

Marcellus, his dispute with his brother and sister settled by S. Ambrose, 465 &c.

Marcus, Bishop of Petavio, 66

Marriage, a good estate, 371 but virginity better, 253. with unbelievers, to be avoided, 116. and within the forbidden degrees, 357 &c should have the Church's blessing, 116, (see *Wife*)

Mary, S remained a Virgin after the birth of her Son, 284, 369 an example to mothers, 393 was the Palace of the King, ib. note.

Martianus, a follower of Jovinian, 286.

Martyrs, buried under the altar, 162 their deaths the perfecting of the Church, 427, love casts out the fear of death, 457 their nobility, 247.

Mass, (missa,) the earliest instance of word S Ambrose's, 129, note.

Maximian, his burial, 332.

Maximus, Bishop of Emona, takes part in the Council of Aquileia, 33, 60 condemns Palladius, 55 signs the letter of the Council of Milan to Pope Siricius, 287.

Maximus, irregularly consecrated Bishop of Constantinople, 75 Ambrose and the Western Bishops deceived about him, ib note.

Maximus, the usurper, revolted against Gratian, 176 S. Ambrose twice goes on an embassy to him from Justina and Valentinian the 2nd, ib. his address to him on the second embassy, 178. warns Valentinian against him, 181. S Ambrose alludes to his first embassy, 135, to Maximus' defeat by Theodosius, 265.

Maximus, the accuser of Indicia, 479 &c.

Mayence,(Moguntiacum,) S.Ambrose meets Count Victor there,178.

Meletius, his connection with the great Schism at Antioch, 71, note. the opinion of the Council of Aquileia upon it, 74

Members, our, how they may be made either instruments of sin or of righteousness, 249.

Memoriales, Recorders, 129.

Merchants, at Milan, fined on account of the disturbances, 129 the fines remitted, 136

Mesopotamia, mystically interpreted, 115

Micah, meaning of the name, 412. of his seven shepherds, 288

Michal, wrongly reproves David, 346.

Miracles, wrought through the relics of the saints. 158, 163 acknowledged by the devil himself, 164

Monastic life, compared with clerical, 382 its happiness, 384

Money, see *Riches*.

Monks, at Callinicum, set fire to a temple, 263.

Morashthite, son of the, meaning of, 412.

Moses, why he ground the golden calf to powder, 396. why he ordered half of the blood of the sacrifices to be poured on the altar, 398 why he broke the tables of the law, 462. saw God face to face, 404, yet deferred to Aaron in regard of priesthood, ib. how a god before Pharaoh, 199. wrote by inspiration, 295.

N

NABAL, mystically explained, 215.

Nabor, (see *Felix*)

Naboth, the lesson of, applied, 149. Naboth truly rich, Ahab poor, 252.

Naphtali, meaning of, 253.

Nature, can only be changed by its Maker, 446 the Creator can remedy the defects of, 460 God the Author of, 31 the law of, superior to national custom, 411

Nectarius, his claim to the see of Constantinople, 75.

Neice, (see *Uncle*.)

Nicæa, Council of, whether it established a cycle for Easter, 166. its doctrine upheld by Theodosius, 141. approved by the Council of Ariminum, ib.

Nineveh, a proof of the power of fasting, 286

Noah, his drunkenness mystically interpreted, 348.

Numerius, one of the Bishops of Macedonia, 80.

Numidius, a delegate of the African Bishops at the Council of Aquileia, 33, 61. condemns Palladius, 55.

INDEX. 503

O

OATH, meaning of, 90.
Obedience, brings remission of sin, 435
Offering, all to be offered to God, 24, 26 not acceptable unless sincere, 408.
Old-age, venerable for good works rather than gray hairs, 86, 103 an unspotted life the true old age, 57.
Origen, his Commentaries on the New Testament inferior to those on the Old, 441.
Original sin, inherited from Adam, 435, 446. a debt incurred by Adam, cancelled by Christ, 271.

P

PALLADIUS AND SECUNDIANUS, condemned by the Council of Aquileia, 31, &c.
Pannonia, 108.
Paradise, man's soul the true, 303. the road into Christ's kingdom, 422.
Partridge, mystical meaning of, 217 &c.
Passover, a type fulfilled in the gospel, 169. the Christian Easter how connected with it, 170 &c the ceremonies of, mystically explained, 22.
Paterna, gives evidence in favour of Indicia, 485
Paternus, consults S. Ambrose as to marriage of uncle and neice, 351 &c.
Paulinus, supported by the Italian Bishops against Meletius and Flavian for the see of Antioch, 71, 74.
Paulinus of Aquitania adopts a life of voluntary poverty, 345
Paul, S., the depth of his writings, 235. difficulty of explaining them, 441. a summary of his Epistle to the Ephesians, 444 &c. his letters an image of his presence, 314. why he wrote with his own hand, 313. condemned and absolved by letter, 314 was severe at first, that he might be gentle afterwards, 270. no teacher of excess, 285.
Paulus, a presbyter of Constantinople, asks for a General Council of East and West, 79.
Pelagia, her martyrdom, 247.
Penitence, difficulty of, 406. no forgiveness without, 407. David a pattern of, 326. urged on Theodosius, 327.

Persecution, applied by Justina in regard to the Basilica at Milan, 128 &c S Ambrose preaches about, 132 &c. persecution continued, 142. S. Ambrose refuses to yield, 148.
Christ persecuted in his servants, 147.
Peter, S , was in darkness when he denied Christ, 461. his vision a proof of the blessedness of retirement, 317. the story of Christ's appearing to him on his way to martyrdom, 147.
Peter, Bishop of Alexandria, 72, 74.
Philaster, Bishop of Brescia, 33, 55. (In p 63 Abundantius is called Bishop of Brescia, and Philaster is omitted)
Philip, one of the Bishops of Macedonia, 80.
Philomarus, the name of a heathen writer quoted by S Ambrose, 362. possibly a mistake for Philodemus, ib. note.
Phineas, his defeat of Balaam's counsel explained, 323.
Phœnicians, practised circumcision, 425.
Photinians, their assemblies forbidden, 66.
Piety, prefers things divine to human, 403.
Plato, his notion of the soul, 224.
Photinus, a follower of Jovinian, condemned, 286.
Polybius, proconsul in Africa, 475.
Pompeius, an instance of reverse of fortune, 113
Portian Basilica, claimed for the Arians, 128.
Prayer, to be used for the dead in Christ, 255 taught and aided by the Holy Spirit, 233 due seasons for, 169. frequent prayer a life of Angels, 384. is a sacrifice, 329. a shield, 391. the prayers of the poor a good defence, 156.
Priest, the title ' Sacerdos ' often used of Bishops, 1. should be clothed with priestly virtues, 377. be different from ordinary men, 196. forsake the ways of the world, 197. be fit for Christ's possession, 470. regard wordly loss as gain, 467. forgiving sins their food, 407. their teaching bitter, but fruit-bearing, 270 are the proper judges in questions of doctrine, 53, 138, 267, 343. bound to reprove sinners, 325. and to be feared by them, 374.
Priscus, an old friend of S. Ambrose, 476.

Proculus, Bishop of Marseilles, deputy of the Bishops of Gaul at Aquileia, 33, 60 condemns Palladius, 56.
Prophets, regard heavenly things, 349, their food to have their message understood, 383
Protasius, see *Gervasius*
Pythagoras, derived his wisdom from the Jewish Scriptures, 196

R

RACHEL, a type of the Church, 416. mystically explained, 192.
Rebecca, her preference of Jacob to Esau mystically explained, 391.
Redemption, equal to all, 22 called adoption, 231. to be of the whole Body of Christ, ib.
Relics, of saints, placed in Churches, 158 work miracles, 160 &c.
Religion, to be preferred to human ties, 403 not to be neglected for fear of ridicule, 432 makes things unseemly in themselves venerable, 346 takes precedence of all things, 92 turns loss to gain, 104
Renatus, see *Leontius*
Repentance, (see *Penitence*)
Rest, the true, in heaven, not here, 299
Rhaetia secunda, its fertility tempted enemies, 108
Rich, the meek rich in God's sight, 251 he who is rich in faith truly rich, 386 the poor in spirit rich, 387. he is not rich who has not more than he needs, 253 the wise man truly rich, 250, 253
Riches, only spiritual lasting, 440 to possess Christ the true riches, 386 should be made to subserve the good of the soul, 8 not in themselves injurious, 387 no defence against death, 10 their best use, to aid the poor, 14 the grasping man poor in the midst of riches, 252 are a burden unless sanctified by charity, 274 are the redemption of a man's soul by almsgiving, 8, 20 are a provision for man's journey, 8 not to be applied to usury, 115 give no claim to deference, 386.
Rome, Church of, called the Head of the whole Roman world, 69 the source of all rights of communion, ib its decision sought along with that of other Churches, 76
Rome, heathen, its plea for its gods, 97 refuted by S Ambrose, 102 often adopted foreign rites, 110.

Rufinus, Prætorian Prefect under Theodosius, 330
Rumoridus, a military Count, attached to Valentinian's Court, 342.

S

SABINIANUS, A DEACON, acts as reader at the Council of Aquileia, 33
Sabinus, *Bishop of Placentia*, takes part in the Council of Aquileia, 33, 47 &c, 60. condemns Palladius, 55.
Sacraments, the greatness of, 459
Sacrifice, not acceptable unless sincere, 408. prayer a, 329. explanation of rules concerning 398, &c the blood on the altar a type of the sacrifice of the Cross, 400.
Saints, God all in all to, 403 ascend upwards to God, 208 work for God even in their rest, 86 fight God's enemies without effort, 82, are the first-fruits of the Gospel, 230
Samson, the lesson of his history set forth, 117, &c.
Sarmatio, see *Barbatianus*.
Satan, means Adversary, 218. how our Lord overcomes his craft, 219.
Scripture, those who add to, or take from, condemned, 47 whether written according to the rules of art, 27, &c a deep well, difficult to draw from, 383 those who drink of it pour forth living water, ib contains mysteries hid under the letter, 189. valuable to us according to our faith, 186 moistens the soul like rain, 200 compared to Paradise, 317
Secundianus, condemned in the Council of Aquileia, 57 &c.
Serpent, the, represents lust, 304
Seven, mystical meaning of, 297, 300.
Severus, a blind man, healed by the relics of Gervasius and Protasius, 158, 163
Severus, one of the Bishops of Macedonia, 80
Shekel and half-shekel, meaning of, 20
Sickness, bodily, sent for the healing of the soul, 458
Simplician, some account of him, 235
Sin, a heavy debt, 271 a heavy burden, 413 its piercing power typified by iron, 238 injures the natural powers, 305 Christians should condemn their own sin, 329 he who punishes sin should be free from sin, 188 must be burnt away by the fire of Jesus, 407. to be confessed in order to be pardoned, 419 its for-

INDEX. 505

giveness signified by the widow's two mites, 196

Sinner, the, is a slave, 245 his name written not in heaven but in the earth, 188

Siricius, Pope, writes to the Church of Milan against Jovinian, 280 the reply, 282.

Sisinnius, forgives his son at S. Ambrose's intercession, 470.

Slavery, all creation seeks deliverance from, 226 he who fears death a slave, 245.

Solon, his ten ages of man, 300.

Sophocles, quoted, 244.

Son of God, co-eternal with the Father, 39. very God, 40 could not die as God, 42 the mighty God, 44 the Judge of all, 45 equal to the Father as touching His Godhead, 47 inferior only in His Incarnation, 48 the contrary opinions condemned in Palladius, 53 &c. no man can say 'Our Father' who denies the Son of God, 443

Christians made sons of God by the Holy Spirit, 228. through the death of Christ, 443.

Spirit, the Holy, teaches how to pray, 233. makes intercession for us, 234. S. Ambrose promises to write a treatise on, 41 true life His work, 228.

Stater, in the fish's mouth, meaning of, 23.

Stephen, supported in his death by the sight of Jesus, 349 saw Jesus standing as his Advocate, 360

Soul, its nature, 224 opinions of philosophers upon, ib. how subject to vanity, 225 does not die, 42 should govern the body, 225 will be rewarded according to its government thereof, ib how Christ is formed in the soul, 417 how it is converted, 412 &c. the stages of its conversion, 421. gazing on Christ, renounces the world, 203 having found Christ, loves Him above all things, 202. and rejoices exceedingly, 214 and becomes His bride, 214 must rise to Him, 203. its food and clothing, 200 how it is restored by Christ, 216. its happiness when restored, 217. is proved by temptations, 417. faithful souls represented by Bethlehem, 416.

Susanna, her case compared with that of Indicia, 479, 483.

Syagrius, Bishop of Verona, his decision about Indicia condemned and reversed by S. Ambrose, 478, &c

Syagrius, Consul in the year of the synod of Aquileia, 32

Symmachus, Prefect of the City, urges on Valentinian the restoration of Altar of Victory, 87. his Memorial, 94, &c. S. Ambrose's reply, 101, &c alludes to it in writing to Eugenius, 341.

Synagogue, the, superseded by the Church, 266 represented by Jezebel, 383 (see Jews)

A, at Callinicum, burnt by the Christians, 257, &c. Theodosius orders it to be restored by the Bishop, ib S. Ambrose writes to remonstrate with Theodosius, ib.

Syricius, see Siricius

Syrus, a presbyter, praised by S Ambrose, 474.

T

Talents, need God's Blessing, 31.

Temple, to be built to Christ in our hearts, 201. how it is to be built, 208, 418

Temptation, comes in different ways, 132, instances of Job, ib. Elijah, 133, John the Baptist, ib is sent that we may conquer it, 327 the weak conquered by it, the strong proved, 417 most to be feared in times of trouble, 419.

Testament, the Old passed away, the New established, 301. the Old represented by the number seven, the New by eight, 297

Timnath, a city of the Philistines, 118.

Thecla, reverenced even by the wild beasts, 369

Therasia, gives up her property to the poor, 345.

Thessalonica, the massacre at, 324.

Theodorus, Bishop of Octodurus, takes part in the Council of Aquileia, 33, 60 condemns Palladius, 56 signs the letter of the Council of Milan, 287.

Theodosius, one of the Bishops of Macedonia, 80.

Theodosius, the Emperor, a blessing sent by God to the Empire, 356. held the Nicene Faith, 141, his piety, 328 hasty, but merciful, 825. restored the orthodox to their churches, 74. restored unity to the Church, 77 his strictness, in regard of the law of marriage, 354

Is appealed to by S Ambrose to end the dissensions at Antioch and

Constantinople, 74. and to call a council, 77.
 Is remonstrated with by S. Ambrose for banishing those who burnt the Synagogue at Callinicum, 257. is reminded of his forgiveness of the people of Antioch, 268.
 Reproved for ordering the massacre at Thessalonica, 324. urged to repentance, 326 &c. is refused the Communion till he has received absolution, 328 &c.
 Addressed by S. Ambrose on the death of Valentinian the 2nd, 331.
 Congratulated on his victory over Eugenius, 354 urged to a merciful use of his victory, 356.
Theophilus, Bishop of Alexandria, the disputed succession at Antioch to be referred to him, 336 &c
Timasius, a general in chief, his fierceness against the monks, 279.
Tigris, one of the rivers of Mesopotamia, mystically interpreted, 115.
Timotheus, his claim to the see of Alexandria, supported by the West, 71.
Timotheus, a Bishop of Macedonia, 80.
Titianus, Prætorian Prefect, his quarrel with Rufinus, 330.
Trinity, the, indissolubly united, 464. knows neither time nor order, 296. hymns sung in praise of, 156.

U

UNCLE, forbidden to marry his neice, 351.
Usury, unbefitting Christians, 115. spiritual usury, 19.
Ursinus or Ursicinus, his history, 68, note. the Bishops at Aquileia request the Emperor to degrade him, 69.

V

VALENS, Julianus, Bp. of Petavio, his history, 65. responsible for the heresy of Attalus, ib. joins with Ursinus in intrigues at Aquileia, 68.
Valence, in Gaul, reached by Ambrose in his embassy to Maximus, 179.
Valentinian the 1st, would not have allowed the restoration of the altar of Victory, had he known of it, 93. ordered that the Bishops should be tried by their own order, 138. refused to be judge of them himself, 139 anecdote of him, ib. note.

Valentinian the 2nd, Ambrose writes to him, urging him not to restore pagan rites, 87 &c addresses to him a reply to Symmachus' Memorial, 101 &c. under Justina's influence claims a Church at Milan for the Arians, 128 &c Ambrose writes to him, declining to have the matter settled by the civil courts, 137 &c. Ambrose sends him a report of his mission to Maximus, 176 &c. alludes to his victory over the Huns and Alans, 179. Ambrose writes to Theodosius on his death, 331 &c. his love for Ambrose at the last, 331. died before he could be baptized, 332. regarded Theodosius as a father, 92. refused a second application for the restoration of pagan rites, 342.
Valentinians, heretics, a temple of theirs burnt by the Christians, 263.
Valerian, Bp. of Aquileia, takes part in the Council held there, 33, 60. his condemnation of Palladius, 54.
Vallio, a general of Valentinian, put to death by Maximus, 181.
Venetia, 108, 358.
Venus, worshipped under various names, 111.
Vercellæ, the Church of, troubled by disputes, 358 S. Ambrose addresses a letter of counsel to it, ib.
Vestal Virgins, contrasted with Christians, 105.
Victor, Count, sent by Maximus to Valentinian the 2nd, 178. his demands refused, ib.
Victory, not a real goddess, 111. the altar of in the senate house, 87. its restoration demanded by Symmachus, 95 &c. resisted by S. Ambrose, 111.
Vigils, kept all night long, 158.
Vigilius, asks S. Ambrose how to fulfil his duties, when newly elected Bishop, 114 &c.
Virgil, quoted, 97, 99, 110, 198, 205.
Virginity, counselled not commanded, 369. a lofty path, 371. its sanctity, 369. the numbers of those who dedicate themselves to it, 104.
Virtue, admits of degrees, 371. considers well before acting, 406. its path upward, 206. admits of no turning, 198.

W

WIDOWHOOD, a good but rough path, 371.

INDEX. 507

Wife, should obey her husband, 392. is his fellow-heir of grace, ib marriage good, virginity better, 283. (see *Marriage*.)

Wisdom, the divine, waters the souls of the righteous, 395. is the food of the soul, 21. Christ the true Wisdom of God, 399. the path of wisdom to be followed, 197. is alone free, 239. is a good sacrifice, 28. Scripture the source of, 236.

Wise man, the, all the world his possession, 9. is steadfast, 236, 243. free, ib. acts from free-will, 241 is guided by God into the truth, 244. becomes His heir, ib. has the true riches, 251.

Word, the, espoused to the Church, His Bride, 214. the dew of the Father, 215. lives or dies in us according to our deserts, 214.

World, the, created by one God, 305. why created in six days, 296. the Gospel the eighth age of the world, 300. An arena of continual strife, 288. its affairs like a dream, 13 gains of this world the loss of souls, 14. the world to be overcome to attain to the Word, 205. the ways of the world to be forsaken by priests, 197. we must go forth from it, 392. we must not give half our service to it, 24.

Works, God to be acknowledged in His, 27.

Wounds, received for Christ bring life, not death, 145.

Y

YOUNG MEN, blamed for their haste to be free, 390. should become old by gravity of conduct, ib.

Z

ZELOPHEHAD, daughters of, meaning of their inheritance, 446.
Zerubbabel, meaning of, 201.

INDEX OF TEXTS.

GENESIS

i. 16	287
26	155, 290, 292
27	219, 318
28	291
ii. 2	296
7	460
24	445
25	348
iii. 1—4	362
2, 3	304
4, 5	218
6	434
7	286, 348
8	317, 318
16	411, 482
18	7
iv. 4	230
7	273
10	8, 165, 219
14	245
v. 24	252
vi. 3	255
viii. 11	276
11, 20	334
ix. 1, 9, 12, 20, 23	334
20	367
21	289
24	335
25	236
26, 27	335
x. 1, 9	335
xii. 17	492
xv. 6	349
xvii. 9	431
10	423
12	425
xviii. 3	392
12	349
xix. 17, 30	206
24	393
xx. 3	349
xxi. 10	450
10, 12	223
12	431
xxii. 6	472
7, 8	28
xxiv. 63	324
xxvii. 4, 20	30
29	237
37	251
39, 40	451
40	452
43	390
xxviii. 1, 2	115
13	86
xxix. 34	222
xxx. 32	195
xxxi. 14	193
15, 16	192
27	194
33	30
xxxii. 24	195
xxxiii. 6	391
xxxiv. 25	116, 195
xxxv. 2	402
17	481
19	415, 416
xxxviii. 27	481
xxxix. 12	348
xli. 48	238
xliv. 15	472
xlvi. 34	191
xlvii. 20, 22	238
xlix. 8, 9	430
12	273

EXODUS

i. 15	481
iii. 5	196, 371
11—14	29
14	204
12	30
iv. 1, 10, 12	29
12	399, 404
v. 2	218
vi. 3	256
vii. 1	199
viii. 26	191
xii. 2	169
3	186
4	22
5—8	173

INDEX OF TEXTS. 509

xii. 8	. . . . .	170
11—14	. . .	174
18	. . . . .	173
29, 31, 33	. .	174
xiii. 2	. . . . .	221
4	. . . . .	169
21	. . . . .	211
xiv 15	. . . . .	219
22	. . . . .	211, 284
29	. . . . .	277, 295
xv 20	. . . . .	285, 369
xvi. 4	. . . . .	277, 410
4, 15	. . .	29
15, 16	. . .	395
15, 16	. . .	28, 459
17, 18	. . .	21
18	. . . . .	308
xvii 6	. . . . .	284, 673
xxi 12	. . . . .	245
5	. . . . .	24
xxii. 29	. . . . .	230
xxiv. 6	. . . . .	398
xxv. 13, 14	. . .	196
22	. . . . .	18
xxix 12, 13	. . .	392
xxx. 8	. . . . .	396
12, 15	. . .	21
xxxi. 13	. . . . .	439
xxxii. 1	. . . . .	218
2	. . . . .	401
6	. . . . .	350, 362
26, 27	. . .	403
xxxiii. 7	. . . . .	392
xxxiv 9	. . . . .	275, 438
26	. . . . .	230
28	. . .	203, 363, 404

LEVITICUS

x 16—18	. . .	405
xii 2	. . . . .	186
xvi 8, 27	. . . . .	408
xvii. 1, 8	. . . .	432
xx 8	. . . . .	188
xxiii. 5	. . . . .	169, 173
xxv 6	. . . . .	408

NUMBERS

iii. 12, 13	. . . .	221
xii.1	. . . . .	404
1, 10	. . . .	376
8	. . . . .	404
xiii. 24	. . . . .	277
xv. 33	. . . . .	439
35	. . . . .	437
xvi. 2	. . . . .	218
3, 32, 48	. . .	374
8—11	. . . .	375
48	. . . . .	18

xvii. 8	. . . . .	270, 373
xviii. 6	. . . . .	403
xx. 11	. . . . .	285
26	. . . . .	376
xxi. 24	. . . . .	277
xxii 12, 19, 25	. .	320
35	. . . . .	321
xxiii. 2	. . . . .	277
8, 10, 11	. . .	321
21	. . . . .	322, 474
xxiv 5—9, 19	. . .	322
xxv. 8	. . . . .	116
11	. . . . .	323
xxvii 1	. . . . .	445
12	. . . . .	459
xxviii. 16	. . . . .	173

DEUTERONOMY

v. 31	. . . . .	371
vi. 4	. . . . .	27
5	. . . . .	456
ix. 4	. . . . .	278
xv. 6	. . . . .	239
8	. . . . .	19
xvi. 1	. . . . .	171
xviii. 10	. . . . .	319
15	. . . . .	404
xix 14	. . . . .	15
xxi. 11	. . . . .	239
12	. . . . .	216
13, 14	. . . .	217
14	. . . . .	240
15, 16	. . . .	221
17	. . . . .	223
xxii. 5	. . . . .	410
xxiv. 14	. . . . .	115
xxv 4	. . . . .	440
xxviii. 11, 12	. . . .	200
23	. . . . .	409
xxx 14	. . . . .	26, 451
xxxii. 2	. . . . .	200
xxxiii. 8, 9	. . . . .	84
16	. . . . .	85
13	. . . . .	290
35	. . . . .	385
39	. . . . .	458
xxxiii. 8	. . . . .	465
23	. . . . .	253
24	. . . . .	276
xxxiv. 10, 11	. . . .	399
10	. . . . .	404

JOSHUA

i. 1	. . . . .	219
ii. 14	. . . . .	392
v 15	. . . . .	196
viii. 23, 29	. . . .	277
x. 26	. . . . .	278

INDEX OF TEXTS.

JUDGES

xi. 36	246
xiii. 8	118
xiv. 14	119
16, 18	120
xv. 16, 18	123
xvi. 20	125
28	126
xix. 1	486
2	416
3, 10	487
15, 22, 23, 24	488
20, 25, 28	489
26, 35	490
xx. 1	486
44	116
47	486
xxi. 2, 3	490
4, 16	491
23	492

1 SAMUEL

viii. 5	218
xxv. 32, 35, 39	215

2 SAMUEL

iii. 28	327
vi. 20	346
21, 22	347
vii 8	264
xii. 7, 13	326
7	278
xiv. 22	472
xviii. 17, 18	208
xxiv. 10	326
12, 14, 17	327

1 KINGS

iv. 33	218
x. 22	421
24	84
xii. 16	465
30	402
xvii. 1	40
3	382
3—6	383
9	252
19	208
3	383
xix. 4	203
6	367
8	382, 383
xx. 23	208
xxi. 3	149
10	484

2 KINGS

i. 14	252
ii. 4	83
11	252, 294
iv. 8, 10, 16	208
34	463
39	368
vi. 6	285
16	146, 161
18	82
vii. 6	82

1 CHRONICLES

xxi. 17	234

2 CHRONICLES

ix. 21	86, 87

EZRA

viii. 21	368

NEHEMIAH

viii. 2	368

ESTHER

iv. 16	368
v. 2	368

JOB

ii. 9, 10	132
v. 17—24, 26	251
vi. 19, 21	197
ix. 25	197
xiii. 19—21	243
xx. 15	253
xxv. 5	244
xxvii. 2	244
xxviii. 14	197, 18, 19, 240
xxix. 15	249
xxxi 33	249, 327
xxxiii. 4	159

PSALMS

iv. 4	377
5	28
6	201
viii 2	150
xi. 2	281
7	186

INDEX OF TEXTS. 511

xii 6	. . . . . 24, 440	lxv. 8, 9 384
7	. . . . . 194, 212	lxviii. 5 178
xiv. 6	. . . . . 249, 406	13 . . . . . 445, 465
3	 305	14 86
xv. 1, 6	 115	18 464
xvi. 2	 205	lxix. 10 286
2	 293	lxxi. 8 274
7	 132	lxxiii. 21 292
xvii 13	 115	lxxvi. 2, 3 134
xviii. 26	 193	lxxviii 2 18
xix 1	. . . 159, 290, 360	lxxix. 1 134
2	. . . . . 160, 162	lxxxi. 6 243
4	 212	lxxxii. 1 360
5	 416	lxxxv. 8 348
xx. 7	 161	13 7
xxii. 29	 200	lxxxvi. 2 310
6, 7	 308	lxxxviii. 4, 5 393
xxiii. 5	 368	lxxxix. 9 292
xxiv. 2	. . . . 5, 350	26, 27 310
xxvi. 4, 5	 372	32 414
5	 385	36, 37 168
xxvii. 4, 13	 200	xciii. 4 5
9	 233	6 326
xxix. 5, 6	 402	xcv. 8 299
xxx. 9	 134	xcvi 5 88
11, 12	 135	xcix. 6 374
xxxi. 5, 8, 11, 16	. . 310	cii 25 290
xxxii. 1	 419	11 253
6	 250	ciii. 5 256
10	 248	civ. 2 206
xxxiii. 16	 388	15 . . . . 22, 214, 383
5	 460	19 226
6	 386	24 296
xxxiv 10	 253	cv. 18 11
xxxvii. 1	. . . . . 372, 385	18, 19 238
26	 251	cix. 4 391
xxxviii. 4, 5	 248	25, 26 307
9	 234	28 392
xxxix. 6	 225	cx. 1 . . . . 347, 399, 446
xl. 1	 232	4 301
xli 1	 63	7 402
xlii 5	 210	cxiii. 5, 6 160
15	 215	7, 8 160
xlv. 1	 393	9 160
2	. . . . . 309, 313	cxiv. 3 284
3	 335	cxvi. 10 274
3	 199	cxviii. 19 198
8	. . . . . 244, 463	22 150
xlvi. 4	. . . . . 5, 383	24 . . . 168, 170, 297
xlvii 1	 346	cxix. 14 253
xlviii 7	 81	46 . . . . 257, 342
1 16	 149	57, 111 . . . 192
20	 372	68, 103 . . . 202
li. 6	 243	71 . . . . . 14, 435
lii. 1	 45	73 290
17	 274	91 310
lv. 7	 81	94 388
lviii. 3	 222	109 204
lxiii. 6	 250	126 . . . . 168, 329
lxiv. 7	 157	131 274
lxv. 4	 200	146 219

512   INDEX OF TEXTS.

cxx. 5	. . . .	351
cxxii 3	. . . . .	8
cxxvi. 7	. . . . .	416
cxxvii. 1	. . . . .	210
cxxviii 5	. . . . .	201
cxxix. 8	. . . . .	416
cxxxii 6	. . . . .	388, 415
cxxxiv 1	. . . .	450
4, 2	. . . . .	372
cxxxix 13	. . . . .	465, 470
cxli. 2	. . . . .	396
3	. . . . .	175
cxlii. 10	. . . . .	201, 233
cxliv 4	. . . . .	225
cxlvii 9	. . . . .	383
cxlviii. 5	. . . .	6, 296

PROVERBS

ii. 13	. . . . .	198
v 15	. . . . .	240
vi 2	. . . . .	8
26	. . . . .	8
27	. . . . .	8
ix. 2	. . . . .	22, 400
5	. . . . .	219
x. 15	. . . . .	388
xi 1	. . . . .	10
xii. 12	. . . . .	253
xiii 8	. . . . .	20, 387
24	. . . . .	248, 414
xiv. 7	. . . . .	249
30	. . . . .	373
xv. 16	. . . . .	8
7	. . . . .	7
17	. . . . .	116
18	. . . . .	377
xvi. 24	. . . . .	6, 396
xvii. 2	. . . . .	239
xviii. 7	. . . . .	249
17	. . . . .	329
xix. 12	. . . .	380
17	. . . . .	156
xxi. 1	. . . . .	104
xxii 1	. . . . .	8, 335
xxiv. 30	. . . . .	249
xxvi. 8, 9	. . . . .	248
xxvii. 2	. . . . .	454
25	. . . . .	200
xxviii. 10	. . . . .	251
xxix. 22	. . . . .	247

ECCLESIASTES

ii 14	. . . . .	217
iii. 1	. . . . .	168, 329
iv. 5	. . . . .	246, 347
9	. . . . .	462
10, 11	. . .	463

iv 12, 13	. .	464
vii 2	. . . .	392
11	. . . . .	304
16	. . . . .	21
x 4	. . . . .	464, 465
8	. . . . .	307
xi 2	. . . . .	187, 297
3	. . . . .	6
xii. 11	. . . . .	6

CANTICLES

i. 1	. . . . .	275
2	. . . . .	274
3	. . . . .	202
ii. 14	. . . . .	215
iii. 4	. . . . .	217
6	. . . . .	396
iv. 3	. . . . .	209
9	. . . . .	205
12	. . . . .	303, 369
v 2	. . . . .	86
vi. 13	. . . . .	212
vii 2	. . . . .	397
8	. . . . .	205
13	. . . . .	256
viii. 6	. . . . .	213

ISAIAH

i. 3	. . . . .	388
6	. . . . .	276
3	. . . . .	168
17	. . . . .	178
v. 2	. . . . .	413
ix 6	. . .	157, 271, 464
xi. 2	. . . . .	296
6, 7	. . . .	430
xiii 8, 9	. . . .	482
xix 20, 21	. . . .	285
xx. 2	. . . . .	349
3	. . . . .	348
4	. . . . .	346, 347
xxv. 8	. . . . .	299, 402
xxx. 15	. . . . .	407
xxxi 1	. . . . .	198
xxxii 20	. . . . .	440
xxxv. 1	. . . . .	212
3	. . . . .	387
xxxviii 8	. . . . .	187
xl 5	. . . . .	308
6	. . . . .	219
31	. . . . .	204
xli 8	. . . . .	310
xlii. 6	. . . . .	311
xliii. 2	. . . . .	8
19	. . . . .	283
xlix. 1—3	. . . . .	310
4	. . . . .	312

INDEX OF TEXTS. 513

xlix. 6	. . . .	311, 464
8	. . . .	169
9	. . . .	272
li 7	. . . .	153
lii. 7	. . . .	199
liii. 2	. . . .	308
7	. . . .	388, 443
liv. 1	. . . .	212, 416
17	. . . .	192, 450
lv. 1	. . . .	239
lviii. 11	. . . .	368
lx. 8	. . . .	87
lxiii. 1	. . . .	219
lxv. 16	. . . .	57
lxvi. 1	. . . .	290
12	. . . .	5

JEREMIAH

i. 11	. . . .	269
iv. 19	. . . .	234
vii 14—17	. .	262
viii 7	. . . .	168
xii. 8	. . . .	442
xvii. 1	. . . .	151
9	. . . .	309
11, 12	. . 217—	219, 312
13	. . . .	188
15, 16	. . . .	474
xx. 9	. . . .	293
19	. . . .	209
xxii. 13, 14,	. . .	209
29, 30	. . .	183
xxiii. 5	. . . .	311
24	. . . .	292
xxxi. 31, 32	. . .	301
xxxiii. 15	. . . .	311

LAMENTATIONS

iii. 25	. . . .	232

EZEKIEL

iii. 17	. . . .	257
18	. . . .	325
20, 21	. . .	258
vi. 11	. . . .	346
xviii. 23	. . . .	454
xx. 25	. . .	438
xxxiv. 23, 24	. . .	311
xliv. 1, 2	. . . .	284

DANIEL

i. 8	. . . .	25, 367
16	. . . .	380
iii. 18	. . . .	25
40	. . . .	367
vi 22	. . . .	363
vii. 9, 10	. . . .	360

ix. 2	. . . .	363
xii 3	. . . .	289
xiv. 30	. . . .	367

HOSEA

i. 2	. . . .	187
ii. 19	. . . .	213
iii. 2	. . . .	187, 293
iv. 6	. . . .	216

JOEL

i 8	. . . .	213, 215
iii. 9	. . . .	207
13	. . . .	206
18	. . . .	207

AMOS

v. 14	. . . .	202

JONAH

iii. 5	. . . .	286
iv 7, 9	. . . .	136

MICAH

i. 1	. . . .	412, 413
iv. 4	. . . .	215
8, 9	. . . .	413
10, 13	. . . .	414
2	. . . .	412-416
v 5	. . . .	298
7, 8, 10	. .	417
vi 3, 4	. . . .	277
8	. . . .	278, 418
vii 1, 2, 8, 9	. .	418
9, 18	. . . .	419

HABAKKUK

ii. 4	. . . .	454
9—12	. . . ·	8
11	. . . .	219
iii. 7	. . . .	351

HAGGAI

i. 2, 4	. . . .	208
4	. . . .	209
8, 10, 14	. . .	210
ii. 6	. . . .	211
7, 8, 23	. . .	212

ZECHARIAH

iii. 3, 8, 12	. . .	311
1	. . . .	149
v. 7	. . . .	11
ix. 10	. . . .	212

INDEX OF TEXTS.

MALACHI

iv. 2 . . . 187, 214, 298

3 ESDRAS

iv 29, 30, 31 . . 238

TOBIT

iv. 21 . . . 116
xii 8, 9 . 363

JUDITH

xiii 16 367

WISDOM

ii 15 . . 465
iv 9 . 87, 103, 453
11 . . . 252
15 . . . 224, 252
vii 22 . . 397
viii. 19 . . . 217
ix. 15 . . 204

ECCLESIASTICUS

i 14 452
xv. 2 . . 214
xviii. 30, 31 368
xix 2 . 368
23, 24 . . 11
xxiii. 18 . 208
xxvii 11 ., 236
xxx 1 . 414

BARUCH

iii. 24, 25 . 81

SUSANNA

15 . . 483, 484
34 . . . 479
43 . . 246

BEL AND THE DRAGON

36 . . . 295

2 MACCABEES

iv. 18 343

S. MATTHEW

i. 18 . . . . 340, 482
23 . . . 284
ii. 6, 18 . . . 415

ii 4 . . . 368
iii. 9 230
11 . . . . 187, 407
15, 23 284
iv. 2, 34 363
4 395
17 202
v 3 253
17 169, 187, 298, 383, 431, 438
27 . . . 183, 128, 430
30 . . 439
37 . . 59
44 . . . 318, 385
44, 45, 48 . . 204
vi 22 20
33 . . 233
vii 3 . . . 188
7 30, 210
14 . 198
15, 16 . 280
17 . 201
viii 2, 3 309
7 458
24 . . . 294
29 163
ix 12 . . . 329
13 . . 329
15 . 214
20 407
x 19, 20 . . . 30, 258
28 . 42
30 . . 22
33 346, 432
39 . 146
xi 12 389
17 . 347
25 . 307
27 . . . 412
28 145, 474
xii 48 . . . 86
xiii. 43 . 236, 417
52 . . . 256
xiv 4 . . 134
26 . . 285
31 . . 457
xv 8 . . . 275
xvi. 18 . . . 290
19 423
24 . . . . . 382, 426
26 . . . 10
xvii. 2 . 461
4 . . . 203
21 . . . . . 286, 363
27 . . . . . 23, 25
xviii. 15, 17 . . . 259
16 . . . 479
19, 20 . . 359
21, 22 . . . 381
23, 35 . . 272
xix 5 283

INDEX OF TEXTS. 515

xix	12	428
	21	24, 318
	26	205
xx.	10	23
	15	201
	23	189
xxii.	12	281, 288
	17, 18	154
	18, 19	24
	21	133
xxiii.	10	442
xxiv	15	275
	35	212, 226
	40	408
	41	396
xxv	21	83
	40	3, 277
	43	463
xxvi	41	234
	59, 60	484
	64	446
	70	461
xxvii	4	407
	23, 25	218
	25	226
	45	393
	46	219
	52	309
xxviii	19	315
	20	328

S MARK

i	24	165
ii.	11	460
iii	17	158
iv	38	294
viii	38	346

S LUKE

i	24	482
	28	483
	34, 37, 38	284
	35	317
	42	415
ii	4	415
	23	221
	28	230
	35	403
	36, 37	284
	37	368
	51	275
	52	464
iii	2, 19	382
	6	430
iv	25	409
	29	318
vi.	45	44
vii.	36—38	270
	43, 47	266

vii.	44	273
	45	274
viii	17	325
ix	23	14
	26	432
x.	2	19
	20	189
	35	186
xi	1	233
xii.	49	463
xiii	11	414
	19, 21	396
	32	168
xiv.	16	288
xv	8, 9	20
	10	278
	17, 19	8
	22	472
xvi	9	469
	13	92
	31	404
xvii	5	457
	6	396
	7	465
	31	206
xviii	42	231
xix	8	407
	17	44
	33	440
	35	145
	40	150
xx	4	157
	36	492
xxi.	2	186
xxii	7—12	167
	42	422
	43	219, 299, 407, 422
	48	275
xxiii	34	308
	44	211
	53	230
xxiv	7	187
	32	206

S JOHN

i.	1	159, 203
	14	310
	16	202
	17	169
	18	57, 159, 293, 310
	26	222, 232, 359
	29	23, 189, 202, 256, 391, 400, 436, 443
	32	277
	36	429
	47	230
ii.	19	170
	19	463
iv.	6	463
	14	207

INDEX OF TEXTS.

iv 26	. . . .	201
34	. . . .	407
v. 10, 30	. .	454
18	. . . .	46
30, 31, 45	.	453
vi. 44	. . . .	48
50	.	415
58	. .	395
vii. 4, 5, 7, 15		188
12	. . . .	44
16	. .	185, 461
37	. . . .	210
38	. .	5, 383
56	. .	. 47
viii. 8, 9	. . . .	183
10	. . . .	189
10, 11		184
11	. . . .	439
12	. . .	206
20	. . .	185
34	. .	217
40	.	48
56		423
ix 1	. . .	459
2, 3, 5—7		460
10, 11	. . .	461
25	. . .	164, 461
28	. . . .	461
29	.	165
x 11		43
xi 33, 34	. .	309
35	. . . .	202
43	. . .	460
50		320
54	. .	422
xii. 1	.	422
5	.	. 278
xiii. 2	. .	. 389
27	.	449, 461
xiv. 9	.	. 155
12	. .	164, 231
21	. .	4
23	.	290
27, 28	.	46
27	. . .	274
30	. . . .	25
xv. 3	. . . .	461
15	. .	243
22	. . .	434
xvi. 15, 16	. .	155
32	. . .	189, 318
xvii. 1	. . . . .	168
3	. . . .	40
11, 14, 18		25
xviii. 8	. .	422
xix. 6	. . .	226
10	. . .	454
25, 27	. . .	393
26, 27, 30		340
30	. . .	402
34	. . . .	400

xx 22	. . . . .	399
xxi 7	. . . .	295
22	. . .	147

ACTS.

i 18	. . . . .	38
26	. . . .	445
ii. 4	. . . . .	27
iii 6	. . . . .	387
6, 13	. .	308
vii 55	. . .	203, 398
56	. . . . .	349, 360
ix. 1	. . . . .	255
5	. . . .	7
x 9	. .	208
10	. . .	317, 363
xv 10	.	. . 423
xvi. 22	. .	289
xvii 18	. . . . .	365
27, 28	.	. . 291
28	. . .	204, 224, 458
xx 24	.	. . 382
35	. . . . .	467

ROMANS.

i 17	. . . . .	453, 454
20	. .	. 37
ii 14	. .	. 433
iii 4	. . . .	319
19	. . . .	434, 436
iv 7	. . . . .	436
11	. . . . .	430
15	. . .	433, 434
v 3, 4, 5	. .	195, 414
19	. .	11, 156, 435
20	.	305, 435, 436
vi 3	. . . .	362
5	. . . .	426
8	. . . .	220, 463
10	. . . .	147
13	. . . . .	249
vii 7	. . .	. 435
8	. . .	. 434
22	. . .	. 429
viii 13, 16, 17	. . .	228
17	. .	295, 362, 386
20	. . . .	288
20—24	. . .	224—232
26	. . . .	233
27	. . . .	234
37	. . .	244, 417
x 2	. .	. 259
4	. . . .	24, 292
8	. . . .	. 451
10	. .	26, 274, 299
15	. . . . .	199
xi 5	. . . .	212
25	. . . .	376, 420
25, 26	. . . .	226

INDEX OF TEXTS.

xi 33	. . . .	253
36	. . . .	205
xii 19	. . .	390
xiii. 4	. . . .	182
7	. . . .	345
8	. . . .	452
10	. .	204
12		461
xiv. 2	. . . .	370

1 CORINTHIANS.

i 1	. . . .	201
8	. . .	37, 48
23, 24	. .	432
25	. . . .	319
27	. . .	220
30	. . . .	359
ii. 9	. . .	232, 459
15	. . . .	351, 431
iii. 2	. . .	7, 207, 384
6, 7	. . .	31
12, 13	. . . .	439
14, 15	. . .	440
18	. . . . ,	220
iv. 3, 4	. .	243
9	. . . .	381
20	. . .	315
21	. . . . .	270
v 3	. . .	313
5	. . .	418
7	. .	173
8	. . .	175
9	. .	361
10, 11, 12	. .	362
12	. . . .	466
vi. 1, 2, 5	. .	153
4—6	. . .	466
7	. .	467, 468
12, 13	. . .	247
vii 4	. . .	368
22	. . .	450
25	. . .	369
26. 32, 34, 35,	.	
37—40		370
34, 38	. . .	283
viii 5, 6	. . . .	305
ix. 1, 17, 19	. . .	242
17	. . . .	452
26	. . . .	289
24, 27	. . . .	243
27	. . .	285, 360, 403
x. 2	. . . .	175
4	. . . . .	290
7	. . . .	362
12	. . . . .	372
17	. . . .	416
23	. . . . .	353
29	. . . . .	248
xi. 1	. . . .	14
3	. . . . .	304

xi 13—15	. . .	411
14	. . . .	216
xii. 7—9	. . . .	22
7, 11	. . . .	233
21	. . . .	279
23	. . . .	428
28	. .	230
xiii 1		322
2, 7, 10, 13	. .	456
4	. . . .	195
7	. . . . .	457
10	. . . .	395
xiv. 15	. . . . .	233
34, 35	. . .	411
xv. 22	. . . . .	423
23	. . . .	230
28	.	14, 227, 229, 308
32	. . . .	280
32—34	. .	364
41	. . . .	160
45, 46, 47	.	295
48, 49	. . . .	213
49	. , .	290
54, 55	. .	299, 402
55	. . . .	308

2 CORINTHIANS

i. 19	. . . .	29, 204
ii. 10	. . . .	270
iii. 3	. . .	153
17	. . . .	443
18	. . . . .	161
iv 6	. .	438
16	. . .	429
18	. . . .	296
v. 4	. . . .	224
8	. . . . .	203
4, 7, 8, 10	.	225
15	. . . . .	301
16	. . .	255, 307
16, 17	. . .	23
17	. . . .	353
17, 19, 20, 21	.	256
17, 21	. . .	308
21	. . . . .	152, 456
vi. 2	. . . .	169
5	. . . . .	285
10	. . . . .	381
15	. . . . .	149
vii 5	. . .	244, 417
viii 9	. . . . .	386, 464
x 10, 11	. .	314
xi. 2	. .	303, 370
14	. . .	149
26	. . . . .	289
27	. . .	368
29	. . . . .	231
xii 2	. . .	86, 203
4	. . . .	234, 398
10	. .	45, 135

INDEX OF TEXTS.

GALATIANS

i	8	281
	15	222
	18	188
ii	4	242
	6	13, 456
	18	338
	19	152
	20	255, 301, 302
iii	6	455
	10	451
	10, 13, 16, 19	441
	11, 13	152
	13	308, 382
	22, 25, 29	442
	23	453
	24	437, 452
iv	1, 3	442
	4	35, 152, 310, 443
	6	228, 231
	8	309
	10, 11	167
	22	455
	24	450
v	1	451
	2	455
	6	256
	13	242
	13, 14	452
vi	11	313
	14	382, 457

EPHESIANS

ii	4, 6	446
	14	359, 417
	14, 15, 18	447
iii	1	464
iv	5	157
	8	464
	10, 11, 13	447
	13	216, 300, 443
	14	236
	15	444
	16	448
	22, 26	449
	32	384
v	3	7
	3, 5	362
	1, 3, 5, 9, 10	445
	14	13
	24, 25	449
	27	369
	31, 32	445
vi	12	144, 289, 381, 445, 449
	13	449
	16	238

PHILIPPIANS

i	23	145
	24	81, 231
ii	6	243
	6, 7	14, 309
	7	23, 307, 310
	7, 8	316
	7, 11	308
	6—8	46
	8	421
	9	387
	16	312
iii	7	156
	8	14
	20	159, 392
iv	7	212, 251
	13	207

COLOSSIANS

i	15	18, 230
	16, 17	210
	18	230
ii	9	316, 368
	13, 14	272
	14	436
	20—22	203
	20	285
iii	11	386
	13	391
iv	3	175

1 THESSALONIANS

iv	4	7

1 TIMOTHY

i	9	240
ii	5	309
iii	2	378
	6	379
	3—7	69
	16	201
v	6	210
	23	367
	24	10
vi	10	10
	16	41

2 TIMOTHY

ii	5	288
	11, 12	411
	19	375
iv	2	258, 270
	7	288
	8	23

TITUS

i	6, 7, 9	378
iii	10	66

INDEX OF TEXTS. 519

PHILEMON

1	389, 475

HEBREWS

i. 3 .	155, 201, 202, 231
5	59
ii. 7 . . .	47
iv. 4	299
12 . . 212, 322,	400, 403
13	318
14	301
v. 1	377
2, 4, 5, 7 . .	373
vi. 13	47
18 . . .	316, 319
vii. 2, 3	373
16, 17 . . .	301
viii. 8, 9 .	301
ix. 4 . .	18
17 . .	442
x. 7	302
xi. 9 . . .	374
26 . . .	346
33, 34, 37, 38 .	380
34	381
xii. 22	222
29 . . .	407
xiii 8	299
12	329

1 S. PETER

i. 12 . . .	203, 459

15, 17—19 . .	386
18, 19	426, 443
ii. 18	394
iii. 3 . . .	253
3, 4 . .	250
iv. 8 . . .	457
v 8 . . .	144

2 S PETER

i. 4	200, 291

1 S. JOHN

ii 18	174, 301
iii. 9	457
iv 18 . . .	457
v. 1 .	456
20 . . .	40

2 S. JOHN

10	69

REVELATION

i. 8 . .	26, 223, 374, 413
ii. 10	288
14, 15 . .	323
iii. 1	227
v. 12	308
viii. 3, 4	396
xviii. 22	397
xxi. 23 . . .	206
xxii 16 .	299

INDEX OF LATIN AND GREEK WORDS.

A

Abdicati, 183.
absconditam pretio humum, 110, note.
acta, 33 note.
aerarii, 155, note.
agnatio, 354.
αἴτιον, 28.
Almo, 111, note
amentata sententia, 16.
amphavit, 308.
apex, 355.
ἀποτέλεσμα, 28.
arca, 89, note.
Astarte, 111, note.
aula regalis, 393, note.
'Αφροδίτη Οὐρανία, 111, note

B

Basilica, 142, note.

C

Castellum, 421.
cernere hereditatem, 443, note.
clarissimus, a title of courtesy, 101, note.
claudebat, from claudeo, to be lame, 84, note.
cleros, 465.
cognatio, 354.
compares, 352.
confundar, conusuas fuerit, 346, 432.
contrarius, 218.
cornici oculum effodere, 219
creaturam, 1.
cubitum, intexti in, 125, note.
curiales, 105, note.

D

Dacia Ripensis, 67, note.
decani, 129, note.
decurions, 105, note.
denarius, 26.
dies saeculi, 416.
diminuit, 308.

dii patrii and indigetes, 97 note.
diœcesis, 33, note.
distinxisti, 258.

E

Enneacaidecateris, 166, note.
ἐνεργούμενοι, 158, note.
ἐντελέχεια, 224
ἐπαρχία, 33, note

F

Fiscus, 89, note.

G

Gigas salutaris, 211, note
gignentia, 110, note.

I

Illustris, a title of courtesy, 101, note, 137, note.
impressio, 379.
incipit=μελλει, 167, note
institutis. 421.

J

Judicium, 219, —io, 219.

L

Laborat, 463.
lætus, 470.
longaevi super terram, 392.
luna, for day of the month, 168, note.

M

Magister equitum et peditum, 279, note.
magister officiorum, 331, note
mensis novorum, 169, note.
missam facere, 129, note.

INDEX OF LATIN AND GREEK WORDS.

Mithras, 111, note.
morsus hominum, 298.
μοσχεύματα, 247.

N

Nevel, 187.
nivei, 6.
nomen and numen, play on, 95.
νοῦς, 306.

P

Pannonia, 108, note.
peculium 98, note.
perdendo, 218.
præfectus prætorio, 33, note, Italiæ, 128, note
præfectus urbi, 94, note.
præpositus cubiculi, 137.
præscriptio, 379.
primitias, 230.
primogenitus, 221, —a, 230.
primitivus, 221.
principes virtutum, 128, note.
propria corporis, 225.
puer, 464. —um, 311.
puleium, 17.

R

Refrigerat, 277.

reprobus, 360, —bum, 361.
Rhoetia Secunda, 108, note.

S

Sacramentum, 275.
sæculum, 416
sobrietatis inebrietas, 368.
sobrii estote, 364.
sola, 368.
sospitatis indicio, 280.
specie, 309.
spectabilis a title of courtesy, 101, note.
spiritum, 274.
statera, 24.
subditus fiat, 434.
superpositus, 65, note.

T

Tractatus concilii Nicæni, 50, note.
tubera, 16.

V

Valeria Ripensis, 108, note.
vela, 129, note.
Venus Cælestis, 111, note.
vibulamina, 247.
vicarius, 33, note.
vivi, 6.

THE END.

www.ingramcontent.com/pod-product-compliance
Lightning Source LLC
Chambersburg PA
CBHW071219290426
44108CB00013B/1225